THE BOY'S WORLD

FOUR GREAT SHIPS

Queen Elizabeth. United States. Anadara (oil-tanker). *Golden Hind.*

THE
BOY'S WORLD

BLACKIE: LONDON AND GLASGOW

BLACKIE & SON LIMITED
16/18 William IV Street, Charing Cross, LONDON, W.C.2
17 Stanhope Street, GLASGOW

BLACKIE & SON (INDIA) LIMITED
103/5 Fort Street, BOMBAY

BLACKIE & SON (CANADA) LIMITED
TORONTO

First Published 1950
New Edition 1960

Printed in Great Britain by Blackie & Son, Ltd., Glasgow

PREFACE

The aim of this book is to supply useful and reliable information on a wide range of subjects interesting to boys. Its contents extend from sports and pastimes, both outdoor and indoor, through the world of Nature to narratives of travel and adventure, due attention also being paid to some of the discoveries of science and engineering. Illustrations and explanatory diagrams have been provided liberally throughout the text.

Contributors are expert in their subjects, and in giving full instructions and descriptions have been careful to avoid any suspicion either of a " text-book " style or of " writing-down ".

The popularity of *The Boy's Companion*, the forerunner of the present volume, encouraged the production of *The Boy's World*. Every effort has been made to ensure that fresh ground is covered, and subjects included here are either new or have been treated from an entirely different angle. It is hoped that among them every boy will find many of his favourite pursuits and special interests.

ACKNOWLEDGMENTS

The Publishers make grateful acknowledgment of permission to use copyright material to the following:

The Oxford University Press for the chapter " The Mohan Man-Eater " from Jim Corbett's *Man-Eaters of Kumaon*.

Wm. Blackwood and Sons, Ltd., for the story " Ingenuity on Disappointment " from Shalimar's *Ships and Men*.

The Royal Geographical Society for the map on page 434.

The Mount Everest Foundation for the photograph of the summit of Mount Everest on which the drawing on page 449 is based.

The Controller of H.M. Stationery Office for three illustrations from *Science at War* reproduced in the article on Radar.

R.K.O. Radio Pictures, Ltd., for the scenes from the Walt Disney full-length, Technicolor features *Pinocchio*, *Bambi* and *Fantasia*.

Halas and Batchelor Cartoon Films, Ltd., for the two illustrations from the C.O.I. film *Charley's March of Time*.

The Scottish Youth Hostels Association for the view of Glencoe Youth Hostel.

The Bristol Aeroplane Company, Ltd., for the diagram on page 183.

CONTENTS

SECTION I.—SPORT

7

COLOUR—BACKGROUNDS—TECHNICAL DEVICES—THE ANIMATION CHART—THE TIME ELEMENT.

SECTION III.—NATURE

SECTION V.—MISCELLANEOUS

COLOUR PLATES

THE SPORTING YEAR

At the dawn of the New Year a sportsman can find much to attract him. The football season has reached its most interesting point when clubs are about to play off the Third Round, which brings the big professional teams into the struggle for the F.A. Cup. He can watch Rugby at Twickenham; or, if he has the money, can visit Switzerland or Austria for the ski-ing and skating, can see the Cresta Run and the Olympia Leap, or can glissade madly down one of the many bobsleigh tracks.

Let us join the throng, say at St. Moritz, at about the end of January. The little town is alive with a babel of tongues—competitors, reporters, officials and mere spectators like ourselves. We climb up one of the silent hills, wreathed in snow, the dark pines showing beneath their load of white; far below is the clear sweep of the rink, with houses clustered about like those on a Christmas card. We watch the skilful skiers winding their way corkscrew-wise through the Slalom, that dangerous line of poles around which each must twist and turn so quickly that it seems inevitable that someone will hit one; and sure enough, one competitor soon does go over, landing in a drift with his head in the snow and his skis in the air. Then there is the glorious thrill of the bobsleigh race, where vehicle and team rush head-first down a narrow chute at breakneck pace. There is a bend ahead of them. They round it successfully and dive onwards still faster to the dangerous final turn, where the banked slope bends like an elbow. They shoot up it; they are over! No, they have righted themselves and raced to the bottom, not the fastest perhaps, but at least all in one piece.

Best of all, we can watch the great ski jump. We see the intrepid athlete poised for the start. He half turns, kicks his way off, and is away down the steep icy slope like an arrow, steering as straight as he can and using every device to increase his speed. He reaches the cliff edge. He is off the ground, rising high above the ice in one

gigantic leap, his body rigid as a statue, crouched forward and with
the skis parallel and directed so as to come down almost flat. After
what seems an interminable time he lands with a bump and with
scarcely a pause rushes away, down past judges and spectators to the
softer snow below, where a smart turn sideways brings him to a halt.
He has successfully leapt more than 150 feet. Would we like to try?
No, we would not. To cool our nerves, we go down to the rink and
watch the figure skating, which seems tame by comparison.

But surely there is something doing on ice at home? We return
to London and what do we find? Rain. We consult our newspaper.

The ice hockey looks good. The Tigers are meeting the Racers, our
favourite team, on our ground. Racers have always been *our* team,
even though there is not an Englishman amongst them; and the
Rink is *our* rink, probably because we live near to it. Although the
great hall is filled to capacity, we manage to get a seat and commence
at once to cheer our own side and to chant their slogan; meanwhile
the visitors from the other side growl or roar like Tigers. We are in
the middle of the straight, almost opposite the penalty box and the
tunnel from which the players will emerge. The rink, surrounded
by a wooden barrier, shines like dull silver, without a scratch upon
it. The sound of potted music strikes our ears. Two pairs of attendants open the barrier and step upon the ice, skating in unison to
either end with a very small goal not unlike a large fire-guard.

There is a pause, some clapping (mainly from supporters of the visitors), and Tigers, arrayed in red, white and blue, enter briskly, skating all over the place and taking shots at goal while they " loosen up ". Their goalkeeper adjusts his various guards and makes passes at the air with his stick, now and again stopping a goal shot with a sound like the crack of a whip. Another pause, and the Racers, in the Home colours of yellow and blue, go through like evolutions.

There is some ironical clapping, a cat-call or two, and a little man with a whistle steps in—the referee, very competent and just, but not more popular than referees in general on such occasions. He blows his whistle and the players sort themselves out, six of each twelve players going into the rest box just beneath us; for only six a side may be on the ice at any one time. The goalkeepers crouch, each of them so heavily protected as to look all fur-clad legs and stick. In front of them are the two defence men, and still farther in the middle the three forwards. The referee drops the puck between the two centres, whose sticks clash, and the puck shoots away to Racers' left wing—the game is on! (This is not an actual game, by the way, but it sufficiently represents the course of events to make it plain to those who are not familiar with ice hockey.)

Up, down and across the rink the players chase the puck, keeping it on the ice with their sticks but frequently overrunning it, so fast do they move. Now one team, now the other, tries a bout of short passing, only to be intercepted; and play switches from one end of the rink to the other so rapidly that it is almost impossible for the men to mark their opposites. Danger! One of the Tigers is approaching the Home goal. The nearest defence man sweeps across the rink and thrusts out his stick, but by a fraction of an inch (or so it seems) the puck avoids it; player and puck sweep right round the back of the goal and out again on the far side. He tries a shot from a bad angle. Bang! right into the middle of the goalie's bat, who clears it upfield without difficulty. Several players have it. There is a scrimmage in mid-field. Somebody (of course by accident) has tripped one of the home players; the whistle goes, and he is penalized, being sent off for two minutes.

Both sides take this opportunity to bring out new men in place of those who retire for a rest, and we notice that, although the night is cool, the players are sweating profusely. To the Racers the penalty

is a great gain, for Tigers no longer have sufficient men to cover
the rink; so the visitors gain time by shooting the puck the full
length of the rink and leaving their opponents to chase it. This
is a good scheme, but it does not always work. The captain of
Racers gets the puck. Working it from side to side as if stirring a
pudding, and dodging one defender after another, he passes clean
through the field. The crowd roars " Shoot!" He has already done
so. The goalie makes a partial clearance in the general direction of
his team-mates, but it is intercepted by a fast winger in blue and
yellow, who sweeps it across to the other winger, who brings it
back again to the advancing captain in mid-field, and the latter

quietly taps it past the goalkeeper into the end of the net. A judge
seated at the rink-side behind the goal immediately switches on a
light, and the crowd stamps, claps, and roars its approval. The
score, one nil, is shown conspicuously on the huge, lantern-like square
structure above the middle of the arena.

So the game goes on for twenty exciting minutes, but the score
remains unchanged. Once the referee has had to leap the barrier
in order to avoid an advancing player. Once a man has been charged
down " with unnecessary force ", and the offender duly booed and
sent off for two minutes; but tempers are not yet hot, nor sticks
raised in wild sweeps, things not unknown in the final period, when
the teams become anxious to avoid defeat at all costs. The players
stream off for a ten minutes' rest; although fit, they have had
enough, for this must be the fastest game on earth.

In the interval we are treated to an exhibition of pirouetting and

caper-cutting by a young lady in white; but not before two lines
of attendants, armed with brooms and sweeping *en echelon*, advance
very amusingly from end to centre of the rink and back, sweeping
the entire surface smooth with scoops and then dexterously directing
the loose snow to the side. There follows a second twenty minutes
of thrills, the game warming up; the score creeps up to three all,
and even the crowd welcomes the break. Again the sweepers perform their rite; and again an artist amuses us, this time a " drunk ",
whose antics betray a highly skilled performer.

Then comes the third and final period. Racers now really mean
business. Their two defence men are brought forward, so as to
give them five forwards, and even the goalie has become a sort of
back. A first raid fails; it is repeated, and this time succeeds. For
the next ten minutes Tigers dash round heroically, trying to make
up the loss; they are all round the Racers' goal, but nothing will
go right for them. The home goalkeeper is all arms, legs and stick,
and holds the fort admirably. One wild shot goes clean over his
head, the puck having to be thrown back by the spectators; but
the way in which all players keep it down is remarkable, as is the
accuracy of their shots from the far end of the rink. While most
of the players are still around the Racers' goal there comes a
shout. Racers' captain has got the puck again and is off like lightning,
furiously pursued across the almost empty rink. He shoots. The
goalie drops on the ice across his goal, but the puck flew high and
strikes the post above him, and on the rebound is knocked straight
into the goal. So, with a home victory of five to three, everyone goes
home happy. Amateur skaters, who are now allowed free on to the
ice, begin to appear, and in a few minutes some hundreds of them
are circling round and round, some quite gracefully, some doubtful,
a few holding on to the barrier what time they are not being helped
to their feet by friends.

Meanwhile, in a quiet street facing the arena another battle has
been going on, between the Tottenham Terrors (one tall, thin, pale-
faced youth and two small, dark boys, all armed with ice hockey
sticks) and the Hornsey Hounds (three similar lads, twelve years
old or thereabouts), the puck being a round piece of some hard,
nondescript material and the goal defined by the railings on one side
and a lamp-post on the other. The game has been furious and the
noise terrific. The pale-faced youth makes a mighty swipe at goal.
Alas, he is no Duke Campbell. There is a tinkle of glass, a sudden

scurrying, a door opens, and an extremely angry woman rushes out. Not a soul is to be seen, not even a hockey stick. "Those boys have broken my window," says the angry lady. After a futile search she retires; whereupon six small figures emerge from the suburban gardens where they have been hiding, and noiselessly beat a retreat. The game is over.

Throughout the winter a crowd of fixtures goes on, and the mere spectator need never be at a loss for a game to watch, be it ice hockey, true hockey, soccer or rugger; and, of course, there is golf and the road. But the only true way in which to enjoy sport is to play it, even if you only kick a ball about on the local common. It can be exacting, if you care to make it so.

Take cross-country running, for example. You undress with a dozen other enthusiasts in a cold and cheerless schoolroom and emerge all too quickly into the keen winter air; but the sun is bright and the fields are only just across the way. Down a lane you start together, split up into twos and threes, turn off at a gate, cross a soggy field, to where a dark copse looms rather forlorn and grim. Over another gate you climb, nearly losing your pants on an undetected nail; you press on through the brittle, rustling, dead brown leaves and twigs, and are pulled up by a ditch with water in it. Some boys leap across, but the far side is slippery, and they nearly tumble back into the water; others plunge down fearlessly (which is the proper course) and splash through the uninviting fluid. So on up the path beyond, past the edge of a lovely wood, out into the glad sunlight and on to grass again. Across the fields you go, towards a line of high road ahead; but a long ploughed field intervenes, and in traversing it you seem to be taking most of the field with you. Splashed with mud from head to foot you gain the road again. There is the school in front. A sharp run in, and you find that the caretaker has provided a hot bath, an urn full of steaming tea, and new cakes. What a grand afternoon it has been, after all! And if you have run well, be sure that somone has spotted you; you may even gain a place in the team for the championships in the spring.

At about this season of the year sixteen other young men are struggling with a get-fit problem which has to be worked in with their studies. These are the Oxford and Cambridge boat-race crews, of whose progress on the Cam and Isis discreet notes appear at intervals in the press. They had commenced training far back in October, when the two Presidents for the year of the O.U.B.C. and

C.U.B.C. had cast critical and expert eyes upon the men sent up to them from the various colleges for the Trial Eights. After much selection, the crews had been formed, coaches had taken them in hand, and strict training was now their daily routine. It is no easy task to pick a university crew. There is always superabundant rowing material, but a member of an eight must be something more than a good oarsman; he must have discipline and must fit into the pattern of the crew, and it is essential that he should have the right temperament. Individualists had better enter for the sculls, for in the ideal crew all its members row, work and think as one. However,

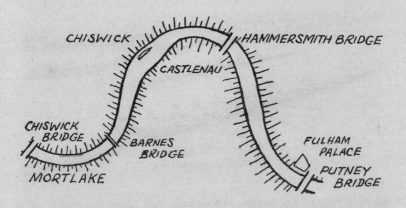

all this has been decided and, as we have said, reports of progress are now coming through. Cambridge are very stylish, but one wonders whether Jones would not be better at bow; Number Four still tends to rock the boat; and so on. As to Oxford—well, they are a very heavy, powerful crew, but somehow do not impress us. Neither crew, of course, is to be compared with those of the early 'twenties, when *we* were rowing.

March comes in. The crews have reached the tideway. Oxford row a full course trial, and to everyone's astonishment break the record; but the wind and tide were with them. Cambridge do a very fast mile. Excitement rises. Strange to say, however, both crews find it difficult to throw off the scratch crews from Leander or London who are assisting them; and Old Blues, shaking their grey heads, explain how different it was in *their* day. The race is to be on a Saturday, in the morning, to suit the flood tide. (It is nearly always rowed on the flood.) Favours appear in shops and at street corners. Cambridge try starts from a stake boat at 37. Oxford, though looking too heavy to do it, actually achieve the impossible and do two minutes at 38. No enthusiast of either side will admit for a moment that the other has a chance.

At last the great day comes, rather cold and windy, with wan bursts of watery sun and nasty little choppy waves on the Thames. Along with almost a million other people we make our way to the river, selecting Hammersmith Bridge because from there we can command

nearly a mile of the course. (Naturally you know the route. It is from Putney to Mortlake, $4\frac{1}{4}$ miles, covered by normal crews in between 20 and 21 minutes. Fairly straight to Hammersmith Bridge, it soon after begins an S-bend at Chiswick, passes Duke's Meadows, and bends back again at Barnes. To Hammersmith is $1\frac{3}{4}$ miles, to Chiswick Eyot $2\frac{3}{4}$ miles, to Barnes Bridge $3\frac{5}{8}$ miles, and from there to the finish at Mortlake Brewery, $\frac{5}{8}$ of a mile.) Until 1949 the boat which was not leading at Barnes Bridge had never won; but, in that year, in one of the most thrilling of all boat races, Cambridge overhauled their rivals at the finish, and just won by a quarter of a length. In 1912, with weather conditions rather worse than to-day's, both crews sank off Chiswick. We ourselves saw the incident from Chiswick Eyot. Cambridge sank first, well out in the stream. Oxford, by the Surrey shore, on finding their boat full of water, got out, emptied it, and paddled away again; but it was declared " No race ", and was re-rowed, when Oxford won.

We talk of this and many other happenings as we wait on the towing path, where the people are four or five feet deep as far as one can see. The bridges are crowded, despite official orders to the contrary; even an electric train finds it necessary to stop for a moment, just when the crews are in sight! There are crowds on barges, on the Eyot, on moored boats, or looking out from windows or hired balconies, even perilously poised on roofs. Although not a penny is at stake, and there are no prizes—no cup, not even a medal—partisanship is extreme; for this is one event about the extreme fairness of which no question can be raised. We are all either Cambridge or Oxford, and we jibe at the other fellows mercilessly.

Favour-sellers, orange vendors, and other gentry of that ilk do a roaring trade in more senses than one. We wait as patiently as we can. We cannot see the early stages, but we know only too well what has happened. The police have stopped all traffic on the river. The judges' launch is flitting restlessly about. Behind it are other launches carrying Old Blues, coaches, and other V.I.P.s, and behind them several river steamers filled with enthusiasts, all straining to get away. There is a shout, " Here they come!" Oxford, as challengers, take out their boat: " Good luck, Oxford!" Cambridge are there too: " Good old Cambridge!" The crews, sixteen stalwart sons of Adam, get in and await orders; the two little coxswains, rulers of their destiny for a brief half-hour, follow them and pick up the ropes. They paddle into midstream and float down to the starting-point. Oxford, who have won the toss, take the sheltered or Surrey side. A long pause, another shout, " They're off!"—and so they are, dead level for a minute or two, when the greater power of the Dark Blues carries them slightly ahead.

Far away at Hammersmith, we can hear the swelling roars of encouragement, cheers and counter-cheers. They have passed Harrods. They shoot the bridge, and at last we discern them; noting with grief (we have been staunch for Cambridge this forty years) that Oxford are just about a length ahead. Both crews have dropped their racing stroke to 28; the water is still choppy, and both boats are shipping a good deal. Hurrah! Cambridge spurt! They don't want Oxford's water and their canvas has overhauled the other. Oxford cannot get across the river, as their cox had intended, but must keep out. Cambridge creep up a little more. As the crews pass out of sight, we cheer our loudest. The crowd breaks up and

we go our several ways; but for us the little spurt of Cambridge—
that was the Boat Race. Half an hour later newsboys are already
running through the streets with the result. We buy a paper. Cambridge have won by half a length. We go home filled with as much
pride and pleasure as if we had done it ourselves.

Another notable event which takes place, occasionally on the
same Saturday as the Boat Race, but usually earlier or later, is
the Head of the River Race. It is rowed over the same course, in
the reverse direction, by crews of various amateur rowing clubs—
twenty or more in all. They start one after the other, and are placed
according to their time, and they have been known to beat the

time of the Varsity crews, although only able to train in the evenings
and at week-ends. A few days before the Boat Race, too, the universities have met on the athletics track. Cup ties are being played
off. The Grand National is run at Aintree. We cannot be everywhere, so let us go north.

The Grand National provides many thrills for those who love
horses, fine riding, and a spice of danger. Like the Boat Race, the
first National was held in 1839. The course is long and testing,
being twice as long as that of the Derby. It has thirty obstacles,
mostly thorn fences 4 feet 10 inches or 5 feet high, of dense twigs
that cannot be brushed through but must be jumped. The course
is a long, narrow triangle, which has to be covered twice, and
although there are large stands it is best viewed from the top of a
car or a bus. It is the one great racing event in which amateur
riders play a conspicuous part and which they have won. The sixth

obstacle, first time round, is the celebrated Becher's Brook, a high fence with a natural ditch six feet wide and four feet deep on the far side. It was named after Captain Becher, a gentleman rider who won the first Liverpool Steeplechase ever held (in 1836).

There are always casualties at Becher's Brook. As the horses come thundering by, one will pull up short and refuse it, catapulting his jockey on to the far side. Another will swerve in mid-air, unseat his rider, and come down sideways on the edge of the brook. For the fallen rider this is a dangerous moment, even if he can disentangle himself from his mount; for the horses following may leap right over upon him without their jockeys being aware of his plight. In one race no fewer than six horses piled on top of one another, and yet none of the riders was seriously hurt. The jockeys usually curl up into as small a bundle as possible, or if thrown clear take shelter right under the fence, in order to avoid the flying hoofs. Another nasty obstacle is Valentine's Brook, and at the turn there is a water jump 12 feet wide, protected in front by a fence only 2 feet high. Horses are very temperamental creatures, and will frequently refuse such low obstacles, although boldly tackling the highest hedge; or when in full chase they may disdain the fence and (not seeing the water beyond at first) land in the middle of the ditch.

We must pass on. Again it is a Saturday morning, this time in mid-April. Throughout the week bursts of hot sunshine have alternated with heavy showers, but to-day the warm sunlight brightens everything, as is fitting; for this is Cup Final day. London is full of blue-and-white and black-and-gold favours, and quite a large part of the population seems to be on its way to Wembley; for a London team is in the final, and this will go down to history as the Spurs' year. (It hasn't happened in reality for a very long time, but North Londoners are still hoping.) The way to the Cup has been long and hard. Starting in January, Arsenal, whose almost impregnable defence and team of five-figure stars made them hot favourites both for the Cup and the League championship, crashed at their very first encounter. The Spurs have shown in-and-out form, as Tottenham Hotspur always do. Twice they have scraped through by a lucky goal, kicked in the very last minutes of the match; and in the semi-final they had to play extra time. The other finalists, the deadly and dashing Wolves, have torn through the Cup fight, on the other hand, with a convincing win every time;

for Wolverhampton Wanderers play the sort of football that ends at
Wembley.

And now, at last, the merits of the two teams are to be tested,
on this brilliant oval of green turf, before some ninety thousand
people. Admission being by ticket only, and all tickets sold out
months ago, one can only admire the sporting spirit of the charabanc-
loads of gentlemen in caps, with huge favours in their coats, who
talk in Midland accents as they prowl about the streets of the
metropolis, or haunt the vicinity of the Stadium car park, or fill
the local bars to overflowing, or wave rattles, or do any of the other
things to which Cup Final crowds are prone. We are certain that
many, nay, most of them, will see nothing of the match; they have
only come to cheer on " t'lads ", to see the sights, to visit Uncle
Ernie or Auntie Bess, and generally to have a good time before they
are packed into their coaches and put to sleep on the journey home.

It is now 2.30, and the great space within the Stadium is almost
full; but we have a press ticket and can pass without difficulty.
We enter the press box and find the air electric with expectation,
people being in the mood to cheer anything or everything, particularly when a stray dog wanders on the field and is chased across
it by a large and rotund constable. The colours of both teams
are there in abundance, but naturally blue and white preponderates.
The crowd contains numerous wags, some of whom burst forth
into whistling and cat-calls. A line of heads stands silhouetted against
the skyline, seemingly as dense up there as down by the barrier;
and we know, though we cannot see them, that thousands more are
prowling round and round outside like hungry tigers, seeking some
off-chance of getting in. If these outsiders cannot see the game
at least they will hear it, and that is better than nothing.

There is a stir in the stands. Everybody gets up as the band
starts to play the National Anthem; for the King has arrived,
escorted by the President of the F.A. Expectation rises. A roar,
and the Wolves run out on to the field, where they have already
earned fame in past years. A fuller-throated roar; the Spurs have
followed them. The teams are lined up. The King, who like his
father is keenly interested in the game—did you know that George
the Fifth frequently took a Saturday afternoon off, just like the
humblest of his subjects, to visit Stamford Bridge when Chelsea
were at home?—the King walks down the centre line, shaking hands
with each team in turn. His Majesty returns to the royal enclosure,

and we now notice before him the aim of every first-class footballer, the F.A. Cup, and the team medals. The photographers have cleared out of the way at last. The referee looks at his whistle as if a trifle surprised to find it in his hand; he blows it, and the game is on.

It is not our purpose to describe the changing fortunes of this imaginary Cup Final, except in outline. Play is fast, but not exciting, and it sways repeatedly from one end of the field to the other. There are cries of qualified encouragement, such as " Come on, Sammy!", " Wake up, Spurs!", " Muffer!", mingled with others of disgust whenever the whistle goes for offside. The Wolves' inside left sees a chance, and takes it. Hundreds of spectators request him,

more volubly than politely, to shoot, and in fact he does so; but the ball, striking the bar, rebounds into play, and the crowd grunts " Ugh!" at the Spurs' narrow escape. A corner is conceded, but Tottenham's goalkeeper, who is in great form, clears the ball, and the game drifts back to midfield again. It is somewhat scrambling football, the stars on both sides being so closely marked that co-ordinated movements are few and far between; and the goal-keeping at both ends is superb.

At half-time, neither side having scored, the crowd takes advantage of the rest to explain how so-and-so should have passed when he was in front of goal, or to laugh at a player whose deliberate clowning provides a little comic relief. The game is resumed. This time the Wolves have decided on swift, wolf-like action. They advance like a pack, all over the opposition. Their outside right, who can move like lightning, has got the ball and is running like the wind, completely outflanking his opposite number. Full back tries to stop him, but an instant earlier he has swung the ball right across the goal mouth to his team's inside left, who, just for a moment, has been unmarked. There is a whirl of leather through the air, a spectacular but fruitless dive by the goalkeeper, the ball is in the net, and ninety thousand voices shout as one, " Goal!"

Nevertheless, one gentleman immediately behind us, possessed of a large check cap and a very hoarse voice, says emphatically, " It was off-side!" The same gentleman, on perceiving that the ball has been returned to the centre, then proceeds to treat us to his opinion of referees in general, and this one in particular. We ignore his protest, for the game has restarted, and Tottenham, stung by their peril, begin at last to play classic football instead of the usual scrambling cup-tie stuff. They weave patterns round the Wolves' defence. It is beautiful to watch—in fact, they do everything but score; which is not an uncommon fault in the Spurs, by the way. Two lovely shots go astray, one just over the bar, the other hitting the post; and with an empty goal! The crowd gasps and is silent at this malignant stroke of fate; but play keeps at the same end. There is a bit of a mix-up on the right wing; then the ball emerges, and the centre half, who has got it out, passes to outside left, he to the centre again, who shoots a clean, clear goal.

One all! The crowd is still cheering when the game restarts, for now Spurs have a new lease of life. A lot of midfield play follows, everyone being very anxious to give nothing away; then comes the accident which changes everything. A Spurs player has dribbled the ball far down the field, only to be badly fouled just outside the penalty area. The whistle goes, and a free kick is awarded. The player, who is hurt, limps to one side, the goal-keeper becomes conscious that he has an immense area to defend, and the silence of doubt and expectation descends upon everyone. The Spurs' crack shot will take the kick; it is not a good angle, and perhaps the excitement of the moment may yet lead to failure. No! He runs up, kicks, the goalie springs, but the ball, passing just beyond his outstretched fingers, drops straight into the net.

Pandemonium breaks out, for the London team is now one up, with only three minutes to go. Keen supporters look at their watches every few seconds, others find the time unconscionably long. There is a furious reaction from the Wolves, but the Spurs are content to put the ball out of play. One minute to go. A last long kick at goal

falls into safe hands. Then comes the final whistle, and Tottenham
Hotspur have won the Cup again after many years of trying, and
the crowd is pouring on to the field, and we are all delighted. May
this happen in reality this season, remarks a Hotspur supporter!

Spring is now at its best and May arrives. The first county
cricket matches have been played before the fate of the football
league championship has been settled; and on many a park playing-
field young men and boys struggle manfully, some in flannels and
some without, against the cold blasts of impending summer; while
on the adjacent bare patch others are still kicking a football about.
Down at Cambridge May Week is on and the bumping races are in
full progress. On the Thames, crews and scullers practise in preparation for Henley. But cricket is the king of summer games,
and as such must now claim our attention. May is followed by
June. Peter May has just made his thousand runs. The weather,
after several unkind shocks, is temporarily settled; and we spectators
rejoice, because a Test Match is on (is it the Australians, or perhaps
the West Indians? Or are they New Zealanders? Well, it doesn't
matter, it's a Test Match!) and we have an engagement at Lord's.

County cricket has been played on Lord's Ground (which, of
course, is the home of the M.C.C., the ruling body in English cricket)
ever since 1814. It was not until 1878 that an Australian eleven
visited this country, and in May of that year they beat the M.C.C.;
but a Test Match was not arranged until the next visit of the Australians in 1880. Lord's is a ground hallowed by tradition and filled
with memories of great cricketers, and it has very fair accommodation
for spectators; but nobody could call it a place of beauty, such as
Canterbury or Worcester. Still less is it like one of those old village
greens where cricket still flourishes in a simpler, happier, and more
carefree sprit—the very essence of cricket being that the game is
everything and the averages nothing. However, we have got through
the turnstiles at Lord's at last, we are up on our favourite perch on
the terrace, and the sun is shining on some twenty-five thousand
spectators.

The bell has gone. Out walk the umpires, very sedately, as if
they had just strayed in by accident and were rather shy at finding
so many people about. They go through the time-honoured course
of looking at the pitch and picking up an imaginary match-stick.
There goes the second bell! The captains appear, to a round of
encouraging claps. They toss. England win, and of course decide

to bat. Out comes the visiting side, not at all overawed by the occasion. The umpires brace themselves for the never-ending game of receiving and returning sweaters, caps, and other belongings of the bowler or the batsman. More claps: England's opening pair are on their way to the wicket, one carefree and debonair, the other dour and grim. They take their stand, the fast bowler takes an extremely long run, and the game begins.

We watch the first few overs with strained attention, which gradually becomes less and less intense; for Test cricket is not as other cricket, except when one side has a demon bowler and the

other is batting on a bad wicket. There is a sort of life-and-death air about the struggle, which reminds us not at all of the cricket that we played when young, and when we slogged twenty in one over and were out to our eleventh ball. After what seems an age the score opens with a single. It is quickly followed by a beautiful drive for four along the carpet; but the fielding is superb, nothing is given away, and an hour's batting yields only forty runs; several hits that should have been boundaries are, in fact, stopped by brilliant anticipation in the outfield and yield only singles. Now the field closes in, short leg being almost on top of the wicket.

Finally, the gay adventurer, tiring of all this, decides to have a go and hits a boundary; but on trying to repeat the stroke he is beautifully caught in the deep field. One for fifty-two. Number Three comes in, and to everyone's dismay is out first ball, beaten by a wicked one, which rose very quickly and scattered his stumps.

Two for fifty-two. The best bat in England is sent in, to stop the rot; now we *shall* see something, we say, and sit up. Instead, he finds the bowler very puzzling, and for a long time scrapes about like a novice. We doze on. Just before lunch, the newcomer, having got his eye in, helps himself to a couple of fours and a six, the best three strokes of the day—such is the " glorious uncertainty " of cricket. The century passed, the players go in to lunch; and we spend the fifty minutes' interval in consuming our sandwiches and talking " shop ". When play is resumed, the wicket is apparently a little easier and the scoring more free. We go home at length, having seen England make 285 for six wickets; and, meanwhile, reporters are writing reams and reams about the day's not very exciting play.

It is all very fine, no doubt. But I would far rather see Surrey set to get 90 in the last hour of a closely fought game and just succeed on the fourth ball of the last over, than any number of Test Matches. Still better, I would rather play myself. Wouldn't you?

For very many years the first Wednesday in June has meant but one thing to sporting-minded Britons all over the world—the Derby. Whether one is working " in the City ", or out on the farm, or mining in Rhodesia, or ranching in Canada, Derby Day, when the best three-year-olds meet on the classic racecourse at Epsom, must never be allowed to pass unremembered.

The first Derby was run as far back as 1780. The prize is a great one, for not only is there a valuable purse (usually about £9000 or £10,000), but the winner acquires a high value for breeding.

The course is grandly situated high up on the Downs above Epsom. For the greater part of the year it is deserted, and hikers may wander over the sward or past the grand-stand, finding no more signs of life there than if they were in a dead world. But by the beginning of Derby Week the little town is filling up, stalls and " all the fun of the fair " have appeared, horses are taking morning gallops (watched by shrewd scouts at long range, armed with pocket-books, pencils, stop-watches and field-glasses). The first day of the meeting is much like any other race meeting; the second, however, which by tradition is Derby Day, is different. From earliest dawn there has been an exodus from London, such as is seen only once in the year—the Rolls and the Bentley, the ancient Ford and the hired motor bus; long, shining coaches in all the colours of the rainbow, cream and scarlet, blue, green, brown, from Manchester, Sheffield, or other far-away places; horse carts

2   (G 487)

and vans, cyclists and motor bikes, the coster and his missus in pearly attire, the top hats, the cloth caps, the bowlers, ladies in silk and girls in cheap cotton: all drawn by the same magnet down the long road through Ewell to Epsom and the Downs. We travel by car, being almost bumper to bumper with other cars for miles; sometimes we stop altogether. Arrived at last, we spend an infinite time in finding a parking place from which we can escape with the least delay when the time comes to go home; no sooner have we done so than a 32-seater draws up right across our line of exit.

Time is early; so we wander round, listening to the antics of gentlemen dressed like jockeys, who for half-a-crown will sell you (in a sealed envelope) the Derby Winner and any other winner you wish. We see the familiar face of the African gentleman who, in a crown of feathers, proclaims in rather thin tones for a king, " I gotanorse!" We watch exponents of the three-pea trick, the three-card trick, and various other tricks designed to extract shillings from the innocent. We rub shoulders with heavy-footed, suspicious-eyed detectives, and with bright-eyed horsey men, in gaiters and pea jackets, with flash ties, pearl pins, and a riding stock. We examine the refreshment stalls, the vendors of lucky charms, the gipsy fortune tellers complete with grime, canary and shawl, the nimble pick-pockets so innocently sidling up at the back of the crowd, and all the other flotsam of Derby Day. Racing is going on, of course. We have not paid much attention to it hitherto; but now we enter the enclosure, just in time to witness the parade.

What magnificent creatures racehorses are! No wonder men—and women—go into raptures over them; no wonder so many have staked all and lost all in some desperate gamble over a horse. Shining and muscular and full of life, with bright eyes, and ears alert, and the poise and grace of their powerful necks, they make a brave show indeed; not the less so because of the multi-coloured silk blouses of their riders and the names they bear. This horse won the Two Thousand Guineas so easily that he became the favourite. Here is the winner of the One Thousand, rumoured not to be a stayer. There is the patron saint of to-day's race, the Earl of Derby himself; and the Aga Khan, and a score of other personalities familiar to racegoers all over the country. We see the Queen's horse, now third favourite; and Sir Gordon Richards, the most famous little man of the turf, who is a trainer now and has hopes to-day, " if the horse is good enough ".

The parade is over. We fancy Swiftsure, we really cannot say why; but we like his proud gait and the rippling muscles on his shoulders. Pushing our way through a solid mass of people, we try to gain the rails on the heath; but by the time we have got sufficiently close to see the course the horses are lining up for the start. It is one minute to three. There is a little delay, because two horses (one of them the favourite too) will persist in facing the opposite way to all the others; but at last they are guided round, the line is fairly straight, up goes the starting gate: they're off! They thunder by, a solid mass of mettlesome horseflesh, legs, jockeys and colour. Before we have had a chance to pick out Swiftsure we are hemmed in by the crowd and can see no more. Nearby, somebody with a loud voice and telescopic eyes is reporting progress, but it seems all wrong to us, for the horses of which so much had been made in the newspapers this morning are nowhere, and some wretched outsider is away in front just behind the leaders.

We move to a better vantage point. They are rounding Tattenham Corner, half a dozen horses in a bunch. Hopeful is on the outside, the favourite nowhere, and the 100 to 1 chance lying right on the rails. Up the hill they come, three horses fighting it out together. Hopeful has fallen back. Where is Swiftsure? Nobody knows, nor does it matter. Adam's Apple, a beautiful grey, is leading; no, he is just behind the sleek chestnut that we admired so much in the paddock. They approach the finishing point. The grey draws level; the jockeys seem to be standing on air as they urge them on with whip and spur. Together they flash past the post, and nobody can say which has won. We wait for a painful five minutes, during which the abject Swiftsure completes the course. Then the numbers go up. The chestnut, the rank outsider, has won in a photo finish. For us, and for millions of people all over the world, the Derby is over.

The photo finish, by the way, is taken by a special type of cine-camera that has now been installed at all the chief race meetings. Behind the lens is a screen with a narrow slot in it; and every fiftieth of a second this slit is illuminated by a flash of light, so as to mark a thin vertical line across the film. As the winners pass in a close finish, the use of this slit enables a line to be drawn just ahead of them, which puts it beyond question which passed the post first.

June, July, August, bring the height of summer and the cream of the sporting events of the year. There are the Lawn Tennis Championships at Wimbledon; the Rifle Shooting Championships at Bisley, where over a thousand marksmen compete for the Queen's Prize and many other trophies; the Open Golf Championship, where an excited and scrambling gallery can watch some of the world's best golfers at play; yachting at Cowes; the British Games at the White City; the A.A.A. Championships; and somewhere on the road the National 50-kilometre Walk, which is held every year as a sound training for the Olympic Games. Where shall we go next? Let us go back into the past, to 1948, and make our way to Wembley, so as to watch a little of the Olympic Games, particularly because it will be many years before they come round to this country again.

The Olympic Games have become so complex and many-sided that no one individual can see them all. Take 1948, for instance. There were 6572 competitors from 59 nations. The events lasted a full fortnight (29th July to 14th August). In the stadium at Wembley one could watch the running, some of the walking, the jumps, and field sports; simultaneously, in the beautiful Empire Pool near by, no fewer than sixteen diving, swimming, and water polo events were being staged. At Harringay Arena large numbers of very tall young men played basketball, which has become exceedingly popular in many countries. Then there were boxing and fencing to be seen at Wembley, rowing and yachting at Henley and Torquay, shooting at Bisley, horsemanship at Aldershot, and football and hockey on various grounds, the finals being played off at Wembley. A million and a quarter people paid for admission, which was by ticket throughout. To which of these many events shall we go? Let us try just one day at the stadium.

We arrive when the Games have been in progress for three or four days. The great car park is nearly full, but we find a home for our own car somewhere. We meet a friend, one of the judges, who, like all the other officials, wears a blue jacket with the Olympic badge on the breast, a neat little grey hat, and grey trousers. On our way in we are stopped repeatedly by autograph hunters, even though we explain that we are not competitors. The crowd is very mixed, young people in the main, but we notice some familiar faces and some very familiar attitudes; particularly a number of lean-looking gentlemen in the fifties, who curl their neatly trimmed moustaches as they think of the day when they ran a mile in 4·20 or cleared the short hurdles in 15 seconds. Working our way through the crowd that seems to circulate for ever round the underground passage beneath the stadium, our friend joins the other great men of the hour; while we make our way up endless steps to our seat high on the periphery of the great ring, at one end of the arena.

It is an unforgettable scene to anyone accustomed to athletic meetings; where (except in such events as the British Games, which have all the publicity of a national newspaper to help them) all that one perceives as a rule is an empty track, a miserable sprinkling of enthusiasts on the otherwise empty benches, a few harried officials, and an inadequate number of competitors. Here, however, the whole vast bowl is full; we have seen fewer people at a Cup Final. Immediately below us the Olympic Flame burns with a fascinating blue, smokeless flame, set in a bowl at this end above the arena. Nearly three weeks ago a Greek runner had ignited a special torch at the foot of Mount Olympus, had run off with it, and a succession of runners had passed it from hand to hand across the whole of Europe to Calais (crossing from Greece to Crete and from Crete to Bari on Greek and British destroyers). From Calais a runner on a British destroyer had brought it to Dover, whence a succession of our own runners had carried it on, the last of whom, John Mark, had run into the stadium with it before the assembled thousands on 29th July and had ignited the flame.

On our right hand is the straight, down which the many heats of the 100 metres are being run off. The whole track is marked out every six inches. An entrance just below us swarms with officials, looking from that height like so many blue-coated flies; and from time to time a competitor emerges from among them, only to be swallowed up again and lost. In our quadrant of the green oval a number of concentric rings have been painted on the grass; they form arcs of a circle, the centre of which is a much smaller ring, some six feet in diameter, just beneath us. Within this little ring men will stand presently in order to throw the discus; and if you think it easy to get that awkwardly shaped disc to fly any considerable distance through the air, just try it for yourself. The outer rings, of course, are to make it easy to mark where the discus falls. At the far end of the arena jumping is in progress.

We decide to watch the sprints *and* the discus, but as is inevitable end up by seeing only a little of each. We watch Mrs. Blankers-Koen beat Miss Manley in the 100 metres; a little later the same redoubtable Dutch sprinter wins the final of the 200 metres. There is a fanfare of trumpets, and the first three com-

petitors—Mrs. Blankers-Koen, Miss A. D. Williamson of Great
Britain, and Miss Patterson, U.S.A. (second and third having finished
almost level), mount the dais, while everybody stands up and the
band plays the Dutch national anthem.

We then watch various athletes, some hefty, some very slight,
hurling the discus. Each man has three chances, and the distance
of each throw is marked; quite a number are disallowed for having
overstepped the circle. The competition is a slow process, but it
grows on one and becomes quite interesting. Farther and farther
afield goes the disc. Then G. Tosi, of Italy, steps out. Mr. Tosi
is by way of being a humorist, a huge man, fat and laughing, who

pokes everyone playfully in the ribs and would no doubt vault
over the rails if the idea entered his head. He picks up the discus
as if it were a cherry stone, steps into the ring, takes one quick turn,
and effortlessly slings the thing right out, seemingly half-way across
the arena. The throw is measured; 169 feet 10½ inches, a world's
record, but what mattered most was the perfect ease and grace
with which he did it. Later, we watch Tosi's compatriot, A. Con-
solino, a much more stylish figure, beat this by more than 3 feet,
but we shall never forget Tosi, his grin, or his throw.

We look again at the running, heats of the 400 and 800 metres.
It has now begun to rain, not hard, but that steady and pitiless
downpour which makes everything seem so hopeless; nevertheless,
we all protect ourselves with mackintoshes and newspapers and
decide to sit it out. They are running the 800 metres now. Among
the men are several American negroes, magnificently built athletes.
The British representative, drawn on the outside, has the awkward

job of seeming to set the pace. It is a fine race, the enormous striding, the perfect start (in the whole day we did not see a single false start), and evenly matched runners lend it a peculiar thrill. In a great finish M. G. Whitfield (U.S.A.) beats Wint of Jamaica by three-tenths of a second, both men breaking the record, while the third man, M. Hansenne (France), equalled it. Incidentally, in the 400 metres it was just the other way round, Wint beating Whitfield easily. The rain continues. We get glimpses of E. Zatopek, a courageous Czech who has already covered himself with glory once, chasing after the speedy Reiff in the 5000 metres; then the rain becomes too much for us and we retire to the covered passage. We pop up again from time to time, for nobody has occupied our seat; but it has been a bad day in the weather sense, and we give it up at last and go home.

So the Games went on, day after day, until the whole long programme was completed—the relay races, the walks, the hurdles and steeplechase, the spectacular pole vault, the hop, step and jump, throwing the hammer, javelin flights, and putting the shot; finally, the dramatic finish of the Marathon, when the gallant Gailly, of Belgium, entered the ring almost at his last gasp, only to be passed in turn by D. Cabrora (Argentine) and T. Richards (Great Britain), the Argentine winning by a mere 15 seconds. Not a good year for Britain; but grand sport.

The year rolls on. Autumn has arrived and football boots are being looked out and softened up. The soccer season, in fact, which every year seems to start a little earlier, opens while cricket is still in full swing. Meanwhile, a number of dirty, oil-stained, and highly adventuresome men, many of whom have broken bones or half-mended ribs, have been trying to avoid breaking their necks round and round the cinder tracks in the eliminating heats for the World's Speedway Championship. Most of them necessarily fall by the way-side, until only sixteen are left.

Some of the survivors are veterans who have been riding for fifteen to twenty years, others are promising newcomers; but they are all genuine motor-cycling enthusiasts, almost every man has at one time or another displayed real pluck, and they are the idols of a crowd which threatens to outnumber even the followers of Association Football. Unlike the professional footballer, however, the rewards of the riders are slight; for unless they are in the very top flight they can make little more than a living out of the game.

This is perhaps the only sport which has caught the national fancy, in which money does not play an overwhelming part, and even here the objectionable practice of " buying " riders has begun; but in the great days of speedway before the war many riders risked their necks nightly for a pound or two, having no retaining fee or even an assurance of a permanent place in the team. No betting is ever allowed on speedway racing. It depends mainly for support on the enthusiasm of hundreds of thousands of young people, mostly keen cyclists themselves, who have worked up sufficient liking for some particular club as to become its supporters.

We revert to the championship. (There is a second championship, the Speedway Riders' Match Race. The holder of this must defend his title once a month against any comer and challengers are never wanting.) The sixteen finalists meet at Wembley, for nowhere else can such a crowd be accommodated, and on several occasions more than 90,000 people have witnessed the racing there. We enter the stadium by ticket only, purchased long beforehand. It is a warm autumn evening, not yet dark; but the lights are on and show up the black ribbon of the track, the four coloured lights above it (red, blue, yellow and white, one for each rider), the white tapes of the starting gate, the motor-driven scraper which levels out the cinders, and the men with hand rakes who perform a like office on a smaller area. Opposite us, in the pits, much noise rises from to time, as supporters recognize their favourite riders. There are flags and rattles, red and white (Wembley), red and blue (Wimbledon), blue and yellow (Harringay), and yellow and black (New Cross), scarves and badges by the thousand, besides many more that we do not recognize.

Over the excellent loud-speaker system the announcer explains what it is all about. There will be twenty heats, and each rider must meet every other rider in turn; therefore, each man will ride five times. For a win he scores three points, for second place two, and for third place one. The winner of most points will be World Speedway Champion. The first heat is announced and the riders come out; we can distinguish them by their colours and particularly their crash helmets, red, blue, white, yellow-and-black. They have special machines, burning special fuel, but all must be of the same capacity. These machines, tuned up like racehorses eager to start, are held in position by each man's attendants just short of the starting gate.

The men are ready. They advance to the tape, the gate goes up, and we hear the engines roar as four machines struggle like one to get on the inside at the first bend. The illusion of speedway racing is greatest when seen from a height, and from where we stand— nobody dreams of sitting down while the race is on—it seems inevitable that all four must crash together—but no! Red has pulled away just in front. White (never mind his name) has come right in from the far side; and when the other two ride a trifle wide he seizes his chance, nips in behind them right on the white line, and is away after Red at a terrific rate. Round they go, at first in procession, Red leading. Lap two. Red still has the advantage and hugs the white line at the track's edge so closely that the man just behind cannot possibly get through; so at the next straight (when they open out their engines again) White tries to ride right round him, but the distance is insufficient, and he is compelled to fall behind again. Lap three. They are still together; nobody looks at the other pair, who have fallen many yards behind. On the straight White tries his rush once more, but again he is just beaten at the bend. As they round the track his front wheel seems almost locked in the rear wheel of the leader. Now at last comes his chance. In turning, Red opens ever so slight a gap, and White, pausing for the merest fraction of a second, hurls his machine into that gap, and away down the straight to the tapes they go neck and neck. The crowd is completely on its feet, shouting itself hoarse. A moment more and both machines have passed the winning post; there could not have been half a wheel between them. We say, " Phew, what a race!" mark up our score card—three points to White, the winner, two points to Red, second, and one point for Yellow, who was a bad third.

The next heat is announced; and so it goes on for twenty heats, some tame processions, others exciting beyond any other kind of sport. Luck plays a not unimportant part too; for if a rider's machine has decided to misbehave itself he may go through the whole evening without scoring a point, be he never so clever. At last it is all over. The beautiful cup is presented to the new champion, who rides round holding it aloft. There are substantial cheques for the leading competitors. The cheering is over, the crowd has departed, and Wembley Stadium, wrapped in autumnal gloom and silence, has gone to rest; and so must we, for our space is ended. Anyhow, we have at least completed our own course; because the next events in our sporting diary are Chelsea versus Manchester City and Wembley Lions versus Brighton Tigers; and that is where we started!

2*

CYCLING

Cycling is one of the few things which gives us something for nothing. And I am not referring to the joys of free-wheeling in the sunshine or to the fitness and strength which comes from healthy exercise in the fresh air. I am talking about an actual free gift, a present, a dividend, which that unique combination of steel, leather and rubber which we call the bicycle offers us as soon as we put a leg across the saddle. For every ounce of energy we spend in making the machine go, the bicycle adds two. Look at it this way: if we were to go for a day's walk, we would do well to cover twenty miles. But we could cover sixty miles in the same time and without being any more tired if we cycled. We would have been " given " forty miles.

What is the secret of this magic? The explanation is that it is easier to wheel a load than to carry it. Ask a Scout whether he would rather transport his camping gear on his back or wheel it on a trek cart! Well, the bicycle is our trek cart and we are the load. Once we mount our machine, our weight is pretty well disposed of. We do not have to carry ourselves about the countryside. The bicycle is ready to be our willing beast of burden.

Some bicycles are more willing than others. Some will move more swiftly and with less effort on our part than others. It all depends on how we look after them.

Fortunately, a bicycle is such a simple thing that it requires very little attention. It is because of this, I am afraid, that its needs are sometimes disregarded altogether.

But before we go on to discuss the care and grooming of the bicycle, let us decide on the kind of mount which will best suit our needs.

There are two main types from which to choose. One is the " safety " bicycle—a name it was given some sixty years ago to distinguish it from the then popular penny-farthing or " ordinary ". The other is sometimes called a " racer ".

Now, some of these so-called " safety " models are not suited to present-day road conditions at all. They were safer, no doubt, than the high-flying " ordinary ". But that is not sufficient for the rider of to-day, whose journeys are to be made midst the busy traffic of a modern road and controlled by so many signals and signs. You must have a bicycle which allows you to stop in traffic without having to dismount. You should be able to sit in the saddle and reach the ground with one foot. If your bicycle is built in such a way that you cannot do this, then yours is certainly not a safe machine.

Some of the " up-turned " handlebar bicycles do have the low-built design and, of course, most of the so-called racers are so built that you can stop without having to leave the saddle.

It is all determined by the height of the bottom bracket (see A in fig 3, page 55). For safety's sake, this should not exceed $10\frac{1}{2}$ inches from the ground. If yours is a juvenile bicycle, with cranks of, say, $5\frac{1}{2}$ inches in length instead of the standard $6\frac{1}{2}$ inches, the distance of the bottom bracket from the ground could be as short as $9\frac{1}{2}$ inches.

Not only is the low-built bicycle safe, it is actually easier to drive. Wind resistance can be the cyclist's toughest opponent, and a low-built machine can help him dodge the elements.

Handlebars.

And this brings us to handlebars. You will see that the sketch favours " droops ". Dropped bars have three main advantages over " upturneds " and no disadvantages. The first benefit is when the wind is doing its worst. We can then crouch low, offering the smallest possible target.

Second—they permit the more natural position. The cyclist's position should be like that of a man rowing a boat. And who ever saw an oarsman with his back kept rigidly vertical?

Third—dropped handlebars permit of the rider having three different ways of holding. This changing of the grip can be very helpful on a longish run. To have to hold on in the same way all the time is tiring, especially on the wrists.

There is an unfortunate prejudice against dropped bars. This is a pity. Few of the objectors have ever tried the sort of position they condemn, and medical evidence disproves complaints that " droops " cause stooped shoulders.

There are all kind of shapes and sizes of handlebars. The pair to suit you should be about the width of your own shoulders and with a drop of some $2\frac{1}{2}$ to 3 inches. Leave the 6-, 7- or 8-inch droops for the fully grown athlete.

Frame Size.

A low-built bicycle with suitable handlebars would be a poor servant if it were too big. Bicycles are made in standard frame-sizes of 18, 20, 22 and 24 inches. While it might be safe enough to buy shoes which are too big for us, on the principle that we would grow to fit them, that would be the worst possible policy by which to select a bicycle. If you measure the inside length of your leg from ground to crutch and from this figure subtract 10 inches, the result will be the size for you. (Example: Leg-length, 29 inches. Deduct 10 inches. Size of machine, 19 inches—and, if you cannot get a 19-inch, take an 18-inch. Better too small than too big. The saddle can always be raised as you grow.) Measure the size of the frame from the centre of the bottom-bracket spindle to the top of the seat tube—under the saddle.

Saddle Height.

But don't anticipate your inches. Don't raise the saddle so high that you have to overstretch. You should be able to " free-wheel " backwards with your heels on the pedals. You should be able to do this without having to wobble. When you come to pedalling the correct way—with the *ball* of the foot on the pedals—you will find that you have left yourself enough " play " to be comfortable.

Now we have a " trek cart " which will carry us comfortably wherever we choose to make it go—though to call a bicycle a cart of any kind is hardly fair. Perhaps it would be better if we spoke of it as our steed, a mount to take us swiftly and silently along the highways and by-ways of our lovely land.

CARE AND REPAIR

But we can be neither swift nor silent on a bicycle which is not in trim. If our chain is rusty, ball-bearings loose or clogged, wheels out of line, we are diddling ourselves out of the free gift that cycling has to offer. And we are not fit company to go cycling with. Our pals will jolly soon tire of having to wait while we attend to " break-downs " which should never have happened. Besides, the boy on the machine which is not road-worthy is a menace to himself and to the safety of others.

Bottom Bracket (A on sketch, p. 55).

Let us then give our bicycle a really good overhaul. Start with the driving parts. Examine the bottom bracket. This is the power house of the bicycle. It is made up of a strong spindle held in position at each end by two steel cups inside each of which is a set of ball-bearings. If the pedals will not spin freely, say, for about a dozen times, without the spindle being loose and shaky, we might well dismantle the whole thing.

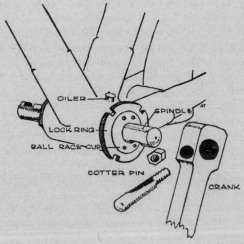

Fig. 1.—The bottom bracket

This is quite a big job. First, we have to knock out the cotter-pins (wedges with nuts screwed on their ends) which fix the cranks to the spindle. If you screw the nuts right off and then hammer the pins out, you will probably find that you have ruined the thread and will not be able to use them again. It is better to unscrew the nut until its head is level with the end of the cotter-pin. Now hit. Once you have moved the pin, even a little, you can take the nut away and drive out the wedge with safety. Remove the cranks, with pedals attached. Fig. 1 will identify the parts for you.

On the side of the frame opposite to the chain-wheel, you will see a big lock-ring. This keeps the cups fixed in place. Screw this off. Next unscrew the ball-cup. Take out the spindle and be sure to have a duster spread ready to catch the ball-bearings as they come spilling out. Clean the spindle, cups, ball-bearings and the inside of the bottom bracket itself with paraffin, and polish with a duster. The balls and the places on the spindle and cups where they run should be shining. If any pitted marks are visible, the offending parts should be replaced.

To reassemble: smear the inside of the cups with light grease and stick in the balls; push the spindle carefully through into the bracket (making sure that the longer end is put in first) until it is seated firmly in the reconditioned ball-race. Now, gently screw up the adjustable ball-cup until it holds the spindle firmly in position. Next, screw on the lock-ring to fix the whole fitting correctly in place. This is a simple job for an experienced hand, but it is as well for a beginner to call in help if things do not go well. The ticklish part is tightening up the lock-ring without moving the ball-race cup so that the spindle will barely turn at all. You will probably have to unscrew the ball-cup and lock-ring once or twice before you get it right.

I have known a number of experts who, once the fitting is nicely set, put a spot of enamel on the junction of the lock-ring and the frame. This prevents its working slack.

Take the chance of the cranks and pedals having been removed to clean them with a paraffin rag before fitting them back on to the spindle. Make sure, when you replace the cotter-pins, that you put them back in their original position. Otherwise your cranks might not be exactly in line.

Your cranks should now spin round, without play, for about twelve times, and, apart from a regular spot of oil, this part of your machine should need no more attention for many thousands of miles.

Now you have served your mechanic's apprenticeship, and should be able to tackle the pedals and hubs with some confidence.

Pedals (B).

To dismantle the pedals, remove the dust-cap on the end; underneath you will see a nut. Unscrew this; then slip off the washer, and the next " nut " to come away is really another cone. When this is screwed off, the ball-bearings will fall out and the whole shell of the pedal can be taken off the spindle. The spindle is different from that of the wheel-hub in that it is tapered. Once again: clean, examine, grease, replace, adjust, tighten, oil.

Front Wheel Hub (C).

If you feel that there is too much " play " in the wheel hub, you can either tighten it or, if you think it may be the worse for wear, make the necessary overhaul.

Unscrew the nuts holding the wheel to the forks. Then, remove the next nut—a lock-nut. Next, slide off the washer. The next " nut " to come off is called a cone. The outside, the part we see, is like a nut, but the other side is really a ball-race. Screw this off, remembering to catch the ball-bearings. Now take out the spindle and catch the spilling balls from the other side of the hub. Clean, examine and replace where necessary.

You will notice that one end of the spindle is slightly different from the other. One of the ball-races is a " fixture ". It screws up tightly on to a certain part of the spindle and is not adjustable. This is the end dealt with first when reassembling. Again, use light grease for sticking the fresh ball-bearings back. Once these have been fitted into the grooves in the hub itself, drop the spindle carefully through the centre of the hub, so that the " fixed " cone is holding the balls on one side of the wheel safely in place. Now carefully screw the other cone home until it is finger-tight on the ball-bearings. Replace the washer, screw up the lock-nut. At this point you will have to make one or two attempts until you have the wheel nicely adjusted and firmly locked. This fitting is also good, except for regular oiling, for thousands of miles of sweet running.

Be careful when replacing it in the forks that you keep the wheel in the centre. Spin it round, just to make sure, before giving the hub-nuts a final tightening.

Rear Wheel Hub (D).

We dealt with the front hub first because it is more straight-forward than the rear. The rear wheel has the added complication of the chain, the cogs or free-wheel and, perhaps, the chain adjusters. To remove, unscrew the hub-nuts; loosen off chain adjusters, if any; lift the chain off chain-wheel, and you should be able to slip out the wheel. The overhauling process is now exactly the same as for the front hub and, again, be careful to keep the wheel " centred " —the chain adjusters will help you here—before final tightening.

Brakes (E).

There is no point in being able to go if you are not able, also, to stop—to stop, that is, as and when you want to. You must have two good brakes. Road accident reports show that boys in their early teens are the most vulnerable of cyclists. They also show that most of the accidents happen when a boy is making a right-hand turn or when his brakes are faulty.

Most brakes on the market are good, but they must be properly fitted and regularly adjusted. Brake-blocks wear out, and screws are fitted to all brakes so that you can tighten them as the blocks get thin. Get your father to check over your brakes and, if you have any doubt about their behaviour, from time to time get him to help you keep them up to standard. You should, if emergency required, be able to lock both wheels immediately.

There are three main types of brakes:

The " pull-up ", which are fitted to most standard upright machines. They are generally good, although they make wheel removal difficult.

The " calliper ", as fitted to the bicycle in the sketch. These can be as good as the pull-up, if properly looked after.

The " hub " brake—not so speedy in action as the best of the rim brakes, but more reliable in wet weather and if the wheel suffers any damage. Lubricate as per makers' instructions.

Steering Column (F).

Now let us take a look at the steering column. This is the part of the bicycle which joins the fork to the frame and allows it to turn. This is done by having a stem fitted to the fork and pushed up inside the head tube of the frame. This fork-stem is then fixed at each end by means of two sets of finely adjusted ball-races.

While there would be nothing wrong in finding a little play, say, in the pedals, there should be none in the steering column. And yet almost half of all the many boys' bicycles I have examined are faulty in this important place.

The accompanying diagram (fig. 2) shows a typical steering column.

To adjust: Slacken lock-nut " a "; tighten adjustable ball-race " b "; tighten lock-nut " a ".

If the bars do not turn smoothly, if there are tight bits and slack places, you probably require to replace ball-bearings or ball-races.

To dismantle, remove handlebars. This is done by unscrewing nut " c " until it has risen about an inch out of the stem. Now hammer this back flat with the bars. As this nut is really the head of a long rod which runs down inside the stem and to which a wedge is fitted, your knock with the hammer will have removed the wedge

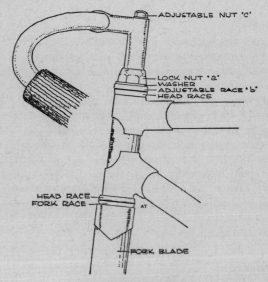

Fig. 2.—The steering column

and will allow you to " work " the handlebars out of the machine.

Now unscrew lock-nut " a "; then adjustable ball-race " b "; and the fork and frame will come apart. Unless you have been prepared, you will now have to go chasing after the scattered ball-bearings.

You know the process now: Clean, examine, replace where needed, grease and reassemble.

Turn the frame upside-down to begin refitting; then stick new ball-bearings into the " bottom " ball-race; fit this into the frame; slide the stem into the steering column until it falls snugly into place. Now carefully turn the frame back to its upright position, slip the top ball-race (complete with its quota of grease and balls) into position. Gently screw the adjustable ball-race on to the stem until it locks the whole assembly in position; on goes the washer (sometimes it is really a lamp-bracket); then the lock-nut and the forks are ready for their important job.

Slide the handlebar stem inside the fork stem, taking care that the wedge is fitted neatly in its slot. When the handlebars are positioned at the most suitable height, tighten nut " c ".

The Chain (G).

The chain should not be slack enough to be liable to come off. This can be a nuisance to the boy who rides a free-wheel, but to a lad on a fixed-wheel it can be dangerous. You will probably find a bit where it is slack and another place where it is taut. Adjust it at the taut point. To lubricate a chain, the simplest way is to brush it occasionally, on the inside, and to trail your oil can along it, again on the inside, as you turn the pedals. The right way is to take the chain off, clean it and let it steep, on its side, in oil or heated grease, so that the lubricant gets inside where it is really wanted.

A new chain fits snugly to the flanges of the chain-wheel. But if you find, when you hold the chain firmly stretched over the chain-wheel, that you can lift a link or two off the flanges, so that you can see a space between the chain and the chain-wheel, then you had better start saving up for a new one.

The Saddle (H).

Now we come to a tender spot. The saddle may not always be kind to you, but make a point of being good to it. It will pay you in the long run—and the longer the run, the more it will pay. Leather is best. Most stock saddles are too narrow for health or comfort, so fit as broad a seat as you feel is suited to you and forget present-day fashions. A new saddle takes some miles to " break in ", but once you get it into shape—your shape—it will prove a real friend. An occasional application of Mars oil, castor oil or dubbin will keep it fit. Don't let it get wet if you can prevent it. If, in time, it sags, you can bring it back to its prime by tightening a nut which you will find under the peak.

PUNCTURES

A puncture is a nuisance but not a calamity. With luck, we can complete the necessary repair in a few minutes. The first job is to find the spot where the air is escaping. As a rule, the familiar hissing sound advertises its location.

It may not be necessary to remove the wheel to get to business.

One side of the outer cover, or, at any rate, the vital part of it near to the leak, must come off. If it is a rear-wheel puncture, remove the side of the cover away from the chain. And, if you need strength for this job, you are probably setting about it the wrong way.

The cover remains on the rim because it has a wire edge which is smaller in circumference than the outer rim of the wheel. How, then, do we manage to " work " the smaller circumference over the bigger one? This can only be done by manœuvring one section of the wire edge well into the bed of the rim. Do this by running your thumbs round the tyre at this section—and the best place to choose is the place opposite to the valve, because the valve-seat prevents the wire from being sufficiently bedded. Now, go to the tyre edge at a point near the valve. Carefully insert a tyre-lever, ease the cover off the rim and clip the lever round a spoke to keep it off. Fit another lever carefully under the cover, a few inches from the first, and take off another stretch of tyre. You will probably not need any more levering to get it all off.

If you cannot now spot the puncture, pump a little air into the tube and listen!

Use sandpaper to clean the tube round the hole—petrol or paraffin serve as well—and smear a little rubber solution over the place to be treated. Give this time to become tacky and then press on the patch. Dust with talc powder and the tube is ready for replacing.

You will notice that the prepared side of the patch in your outfit is covered with linen cloth. This has to come off, of course, before use. The easy way to remove it is to try to tear the patch. The linen will rip but not the rubber, and the tear will present you with a convenient edge with which to remove the material.

Before replacing the repaired tube, make sure that it really is repaired. A tack or a thorn, for instance, has the awkward habit of making a hole in two places in the tube. And run your fingers along the inside of the cover to ensure that offending foreign bodies are not still there.

The really troublesome punctures are the elusive ones. You may know the kind. The tyre will not stay up. The air is seeping out noiselessly. In this case, there is generally nothing for it but to take the whole tube off, inflate it and sink it, a bit at a time, in water. Escaping bubbles will be your guide to the seat of the bother.

If this fails, the trouble may lie in an old patch which is allowing air to escape when it is under pressure. Examine all former repairs. Have a look, too, at the valve seat. A nut here may need tightening.

The really difficult " slow " puncture can be dealt with by squirting a little milk into the tube. When the wheel is spun round, the milk " congeals " in the leak. But this is really only an emergency measure.

To reassemble: pump enough air into the repaired tube to keep it in shape; fit it back inside the cover; make sure that the wire edge is bedded back in its place in the rim and then press the cover, with the fingers, over the rim on the opposite side of the wheel. If you have to use levers to get the cover back again, there may be something wrong. Make sure, first, that the cover is properly bedded in.

Before inflating hard, examine the wheel to ensure that the cover is not nicking the tube. We may not be able to avoid punctures, but we do not need to cause them.

The Cover.

A piece of canvas is supplied in most repair outfits for patching covers which have been cut. To apply, clean both cover and patch and spread on each a liberal coating of solution. Fix patches to inside of cover, avoiding wrinkles. Ensure that canvas overlaps the edges of the cover. In this way the canvas and not the weakened cover will take the strain. Your repair will hold for long enough, although water will rot the canvas in time.

The Valve.

Some deflations are not due to punctures. Sometimes the fault lies in the valve. Before doing any dismantling, make sure the valve is not faulty. To test, wet the finger and apply to valve. It will " bubble " if leaking. It may be that the only puncture to be dealt with is in the little rubber sleeve inside the valve. You will find a replacement in your outfit.

WHEELS

Have you ever noticed that the spokes of a bicycle wheel have one big difference from spokes on, say, a cart wheel? Cart-wheel spokes are radial, they fan straight out from the hub; most bicycles have tangential spoking—the spokes, instead of running straight from the centre to the rim, go off at an angle of about 90 degrees. Each spoke is " pulling against " another spoke. This gives greater strength and rigidity.

If, therefore, your wheels are not as true as they ought to be, if they wobble and are buckled and you have to do something about bringing them into line, you will have to study how the spokes have been set.

The job of trueing a wheel is one for a tradesman. But get-you-home repairs can easily be tackled by anyone who is careful.

If your wheel is twisted and is rubbing on one side of the frame, this can be adjusted by examining the way the spokes are laced, and by then either tightening the ones which will pull that part of the rim away from the place where it is touching, or by going to the spokes on the other side of the wheel and slackening them. This adjustment is made by turning the spoke-nipples with a spoke-key. It is a ticklish job, and do not give a spoke more than half a turn at a time. Tension on the spokes can be judged by plucking them, harp-wise, as you work.

Even where a number of spokes have been snapped and the wheel has buckled, this can be repaired by transferring spokes from other parts of the wheel and refitting them in the weakened place. A standard front wheel has thirty-two spokes and a rear wheel forty. It is surprising how well a wheel can be made to run, in an emergency, after as many as, say, six or even more spokes have been shed.

In all cases, however, where the wheels have been damaged, a cycle-mechanic should be asked to make them true again.

A bicycle reflects the character of its owner. A clean, tidy, well-cared-for machine is one which will go far—as will its owner—and will go with the minimum of bother and inconvenience. Keeping a bicycle in good condition need not be a task. Overhaul it once, give it regular attention and the bicycle will repay in years of trouble-free service. Regular oiling, regular cleaning, the doing of odd jobs as they are needed, is the idea. Little and often is the secret of success.

A B C OF BICYCLE MAINTENANCE

A. *Bottom Bracket*: Lubricate frequently. Heavy oil is best. Should spin freely and without shake. Liable to be affected by water from spray of front wheel. This can cause crackling noise similar to that of broken ball-bearings.

B. *Pedals*: Heavy oil.

C. *Front Hub*: Adjust until free of shake. Weight of valve should be able to swing wheel. Heavy oil. Use duster to prevent oil travelling along spokes to tyres. (Oil is bad for rubber.)

D. *Rear Hub*: As for front hub. Lubricate free-wheel by laying bicycle on its side and spinning wheel to allow thin oil to work its way in. Adjustment of Sturmey-Archer and BSA change-speed gears is by manipulating milled-edge nipple at end of control chain. When gear lever is at normal, end of rod which passes through centre of spindle should be flush with axle-end.

E. *Brakes*: Oil where metal parts rub. Keep brake-shoes close to rim.

F. *Steering Column*: Avoid shake. Thin oil regularly.

G. *Chain*: Allow not more than one inch of up and down " play ". Heavy oil to inside. See that chain-wheel bolts are tight.

H. *Saddle*: Keep dry. Oil if it creaks. Dubbin leather. Saddle top may be tightened by nut under peak.

I. *Valve*: Keep tight. Talc will allow you to slip on rubber replacements.

J. *Mudguards*: Do not allow to be loose.

K. *Reflector*: Keep clean and properly angled.

L. *Rear Light*: Red glass. Essential after lighting-up time.

M. *Head Lamp*: White. Focus to avoid dazzling other road-users. If electric, carry spare bulbs.

N. *Inflator*: An occasional spot of oil will keep leather washer pliable.

   In General: Oil often but sparingly. Keep tyres inflated hard.

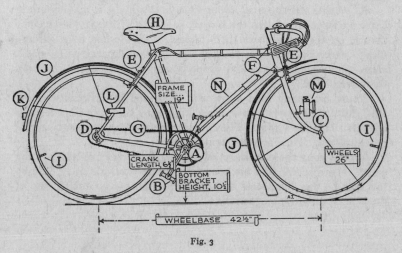

Fig. 3

ROAD MANNERS

The manner in which a bicycle is used, as well as the way in which it is kept, also proclaims the character of its owner. A bicycle is a vehicle. It has to obey the rules of the road just as have all the other vehicles.

Before a driver of a car is allowed to go alone on the public highway, he has to be tested and passed as efficient. How many young cyclists have even studied that booklet, which is one of the most important publications in the English language, the Highway Code? One does not merely become a cyclist by being able to maintain one's balance and make the bicycle go. Before a cyclist goes out on to the road, he should know to keep to the left, how to make the necessary signals, how to make a right-hand turn (teen-agers run into more trouble while making this sometimes difficult manœuvre than in any other way), know the traffic signs, know how to give way to pedestrians, especially at crossing-places. All this most vital information is set out in the Highway Code. If you do not now have a copy, one can be obtained through many Motor Taxation Offices and from local Road Safety Committees or through your Town or County Clerk.

As well as telling us all about signs and signals, it tells us not to carry a passenger (unless the bicycle is specially fitted), not to carry parcels on the handlebars (fit a carrier, a saddle-bag or a basket), not to carry bulky loads, to keep the rear-mudguard white patch clear, the reflector clean and properly angled, and about the need for a rear light.

There are many road-users who disregard the Highway Code, who think they know better, who think they can take liberties and chances. This is a pity. They cause ninety-seven accidents out of one hundred. They are the spoil-sports.

Do not copy them in their silly ways. The real cyclist plays the game. His machine and his behaviour set an example to all. Along this way lie fun, happiness and fitness for those who follow one of the best of all outdoor pastimes.

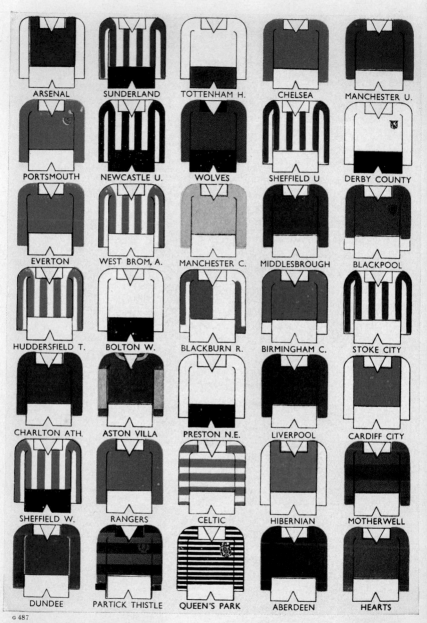

ARSENAL   SUNDERLAND   TOTTENHAM H.   CHELSEA   MANCHESTER U.

PORTSMOUTH   NEWCASTLE U.   WOLVES   SHEFFIELD U   DERBY COUNTY

EVERTON   WEST BROM, A.   MANCHESTER C.   MIDDLESBROUGH   BLACKPOOL

HUDDERSFIELD T.   BOLTON W.   BLACKBURN R.   BIRMINGHAM C.   STOKE CITY

CHARLTON ATH.   ASTON VILLA   PRESTON N.E.   LIVERPOOL   CARDIFF CITY

SHEFFIELD W.   RANGERS   CELTIC   HIBERNIAN   MOTHERWELL

DUNDEE   PARTICK THISTLE   QUEEN'S PARK   ABERDEEN   HEARTS

G 487

COLOURS OF FAMOUS FOOTBALL CLUBS IN ENGLAND
AND SCOTLAND

FAMOUS SOCCER CLUBS

On the plate facing this page you will find the colours worn by some of the most famous clubs in England and Scotland. Because of the size of the plate only a selection of club colours could be included, and you will probably be disappointed if your own favourites are not represented.

Certainly, if space had permitted, such famous clubs as Burnley, Notts County, Bury, East Fife, St. Mirren, and Clyde would have been included. In England, Burnley and Notts County have particularly strong claims, for both were original members of the Football League when it was formed away back in 1888, and both have been once winners and once beaten finalists in the F.A. Cup. In Scotland, too, the East Fife club from Methil, who have had some remarkable performances to their credit in Cup football in the last twenty-odd years, would be well worthy of a place.

It would be easy to add to the list, for Association Football has been played on an organized basis for more than seventy years, and many are the great clubs and great players who have written their names in its history.

Have you ever browsed through one of the football annuals which appear on the market each year and which contain a mass of figures and records and names of the past and present? Or, if you really are interested in the histories of the famous clubs, why not try collecting club handbooks? You can obtain copies by writing to the secretaries of the various clubs at the beginning of or even during the season, and they cost only a few coppers.

Most handbooks give you the records in the League Championship, the Cup, and all the smaller tournaments in which the club has taken part. Many of them include the club's history from its earliest days, and the story of the rise of some of the greatest clubs in the land from very small beginnings is a romance of the triumph of enthusiasm and enterprise over difficulties.

And there's another good reason for learning something of the past history of soccer. You'll be in a better position to argue with

Grandad when he tells you that your favourites of to-day would be no match for the Preston North End " Invincibles " who won both the League Championship and the Cup in 1889, or the great Aston Villa side which performed a similar feat in 1897. Well, if you know your soccer history, you'll be able to tell Grandad that in the year of Preston's " double event " only twelve clubs competed for the First Division Championship, and in Villa's year, only sixteen. Nowadays there are twenty-two clubs.

Undoubtedly, things were a little easier in the olden days, but don't let's dismiss Grandad's claims just because of that. Let's admit, instead, that Cup and Championship in the same season is a remarkable feat, and that the Preston and Villa sides of those days must have been outstanding. And if you glance for a moment at the records on page 64, you'll see that the " double event " has never since been repeated.

If you're a Scot, perhaps your Dad will treat your favourites in the same way. He'll think back for a moment and then tell you that the great Rangers eleven of 1920–27 was far superior to any of the Scottish teams of the present day. Well, maybe it was, but the soccer records show that no matter how often the Rangers of that era succeeded in carrying off the League Championship, not once did they win the Scottish Cup.

Yes, study the record books and you'll have an answer for Dad. More than that, you'll be able to join in the arguments that are so much the joy of the football enthusiast. You'll hear him at it every Saturday afternoon—before the game, during the game, and for a long time after it. You'll hear him in the popular enclosure, in the stands, in the Directors' box. In fact, wherever and whenever soccer enthusiasts gather, the old arguments are raised, and great players and great clubs are discussed and compared.

Are we really justified in making these comparisons between great teams and great players of the present and those of the past? Rules, conditions, styles of play, training methods—all have altered so much down the years that we cannot justifiably say that one team or one player is greater than another. To take only one example— it is very doubtful indeed whether some of the famous forwards of the past would have achieved the fame they did if they had had to contend with the modern " third-back " game. The defending centre half has done much to ruin good forward play, and certainly the centre forward of to-day seldom has the same opportunity for a clear break-through and shot as his counterpart had in the olden days.

One thing, of course, is undisputed. The great player, the real soccer genius in any era—the Matthews, the James, the Cromptons, and the Mortons—will always stand out above their fellows. And so, too, with the great teams. To win the League Championship once is a sign of a consistently high standard of play throughout the season; to win it repeatedly is a sure sign of brilliance. To win the Cup at the same time, or at least to travel far on the road to Wembley or Hampden, is proof that the team that accomplishes it deserves to rank with the greatest teams of all time.

Let's suppose that from the teams listed on our colour plate you had to select the three greatest clubs in English soccer and the three greatest clubs in Scottish soccer. How would you make a choice, and which would you choose? You'd study the records of each, of course, and afterwards you'd probably pick out the following:

ENGLAND

1. *Aston Villa.*

The great Midlands club were one of the original members of the Football League, but their claim to a place among the three greatest clubs in England does not rest there. Nine times they have fought their way to the final of the F.A. Cup, and seven times they have brought the Cup home to Birmingham. Only West Bromwich Albion have competed so often in the final, and only Blackburn Rovers and Newcastle United, each with six Cup wins, can compare with Villa's record.

Six times, too, have Villa been champions of the First Division of the League, and that record is shared only by Sunderland, and surpassed only by the Arsenal who have seven championships to their credit. What a proud record Villa have! And don't let us forget that remarkable season in 1897 when Aston Villa were hailed as both Champions and Cup winners.

In the modern era, they have not been the power they once were in the land, but they still have a great tradition for playing classical football. Forward play has been their speciality, and some of the finest forwards in the game have worn Villa's colours. Perhaps their most outstanding feat was in season 1930–31, when the Villa

sharpshooters shot home 128 goals in the League Championship.
That was yet another record to their credit, for the total has never
been surpassed.

Yes! Aston Villa, say the record books, are the greatest club in
all England.

2. *Arsenal*

If Aston Villa's records belong mostly to the distant past, the
records of the Arsenal are much nearer to the present day. From
the time the Gunners joined the Football League in 1893 until 1925
they did little of note in the soccer world. But in 1925 the late
and great Herbert Chapman took over the managership of the club.
From that year onwards the Arsenal began their climb to the heights
and they stayed on the pinnacle of fame until 1953 when they became champions for the seventh time.

Just look for a moment at the Arsenal's record for that period.
Here it is:

    1926. Runners-up in the League Championship.
    1927. Runners-up in the F.A. Cup.
    1930. F.A. Cup winners.
    1931. League Champions.
    1932. Runners-up in both Cup and League.
    1933. League Champions.
    1934. League Champions.
    1935. League Champions.
    1936. F.A. Cup winners.
    1937. Third in the League Championship.
    1938. League Champions.
    1948. League Champions.
    1950. F.A. Cup winners.
    1953. League Champions.

No club in England in recent times has a record which can compare with that of the Arsenal during that era, and only the feats of
Aston Villa in the past can stand comparison. In the 1930's they
became known as the Bank of England team, so costly were the
players in their ranks. What a really great team they had in those
days! It was the Arsenal who first introduced the " third-back "
game to English soccer, and centre half Roberts was its first exponent. But third-back game or no, what team could have failed to
succeed with a forward line such as Arsenal possessed? Two flying,
goal-scoring wingers in Joe Hulme at outside right and the fair-

haired Cliff Bastin on the left, Lambert at centre, and, scheming behind these three, two of the greatest inside forwards of all time— David Jack and the incomparable Alex James.

The greatest year in the history of the Arsenal was perhaps 1931. In that year, the F.A. Cup was the only trophy for which the club competed that it did not win. Their total of 66 points, too, is the best ever recorded in the First Division.

Seven times League Champions, and thrice F.A. Cup winners. That's the Arsenal record. The fame they gained in the 1930's still clings to them, and everyone still loves to " have a go " at the Arsenal. They are well worthy of their place among the three greatest clubs in the country.

3. *Blackburn Rovers*

You'll be surprised to find the Rovers among the chosen three. Weren't they a Second Division side for ten long post-war years, and didn't they come back to the top grade only in 1958? Yes, that's true; but if you turn to the record books you'll find why they stand above so many others.

With the Rovers, the Cup has always been " the thing ", and they rank with Aston Villa as the most renowned Cup fighters in England. Altogether they have appeared in eight F.A. Cup finals (one less than the Villa), and six times they have been successful.

Blackburn Rovers, too, have one record that Villa can't equal, and one which may never be surpassed. In three successive years— 1884, 1885, and 1886—they were unbeaten in the Cup-ties. In the first two finals, their opponents were the famous Scottish amateur club, Queen's Park, whom they defeated at Kennington Oval by 2–1 and 2–0, and on the third occasion West Bromwich Albion were vanquished by 2–0 at Derby after a drawn game in London.

Rovers' peak years in the Championship were in seasons 1912 and 1914, when they had their only two successes. Not an outstanding performance in League football, but what a Cup record they have!

The Lancashire club has had its ups and downs. Twice in their history they have dropped to the Second Division, but they have come back at last to the top grade. Many years have passed since Rovers last appeared in the honours list (in 1928, to be exact, when they won the F.A. Cup by defeating Huddersfield at Wembley).

But perhaps they are just resting on their laurels. Perhaps they'll find again another Bob Crompton to inspire them to Cup or Championship, for Bob was their greatest player of other days, and one who more than Lancashire folk will tell you was the finest full-back of all time.

SCOTLAND

1. *Glasgow Rangers*

You have learned something of the fine records of the Aston Villa, Arsenal and Blackburn clubs in England, but nothing these clubs have accomplished can compare with the records of this famous Glasgow club in Scotland. Certainly, competition in Scotland is much less intensive than in the south, but that in no way detracts from the magnificence of the performances of the famous " Light Blues ".

In the Scottish League Championship, the Rangers have competed on sixty-one occasions. In thirty of these (almost half) they have been champions, in fourteen they have been runners-up, and only once in their long history have they been as low as sixth. In the Cup, their record is not just so impressive, but it's quite enough to be going on with. Twenty-two times they have been finalists, and thirteen times they have carried off the Cup. In the nine years from 1928 until 1936, Rangers appeared in seven Cup finals, winning six of them, and during that spell had Cup triumphs in three successive years. They repeated their three-cups-in-a-row feat in 1948, 1949 and 1950.

And so it goes on! Record after record they have established. The double event? It's no trouble to the Rangers; they've done it on no fewer than seven occasions. Internationals? They've given more players to Scotland than any other club. But perhaps their finest feats were in 1899, when they won the League without dropping a point, and in 1930, when their first and second elevens won every single competition in which they took part.

The almost complete domination which the Rangers have established in Scotland is undoubtedly bad for the competitive element of the game. But that surely is not the fault of the " Light Blues ". It is for others to rise to Rangers' level, rather than have Rangers fall to theirs.

Rangers introduced the third-back game to Scotland, and they were the first club to model themselves on the Arsenal style—with what success their records will tell you. Fast-raiding wingers, long, accurate, open passing from half-backs to forwards, and a brilliantly organized defence have been the features of their play in the last twenty years.

Scotland is very proud of the Rangers. And rightly so.

2. Glasgow Celtic

Celtic are the only club whose record can stand comparison with that of their great rivals, the Rangers. At one time, in fact, they had an even better record of achievement, but in the last thirty years the Rangers have overhauled and passed them.

In one sphere, at least, Celtic are still supreme. They are the record Scottish Cup holders, having won the trophy seventeen times and been runners-up nine times. In the League, they lag just a little behind the Rangers, having won twenty Championships. Of these, six were won in successive years—a unique record in Scottish football.

Two events of which Celtic enthusiasts are intensely proud occurred in the period just prior to the outbreak of the Second World War. In 1938, they won the Empire Exhibition Tournament in Glasgow against opposition from the best clubs in both England and Scotland. The other event was an individual one. Jimmy McGrory, their International centre forward (and now manager of the club) surpassed the previous best in British first-class football by scoring 550 goals, 410 of which were recorded in League games.

Celtic have a traditional style of football, which differs completely from that of the Rangers. Theirs is an intricate close-passing game— at its best a soccer treat to behold. Celtic have given much to Scottish football, and the records show that they have not gone unrewarded.

3. Queen's Park

You may be surprised to find Queen's Park among the three greatest clubs in Scotland—that is, if you do not know your soccer history. The famous Amateurs are now only a shadow of the once-great team which carried all before it in the early days of Scottish soccer.

The advent of professionalism sounded the death-knell of the

	ENGLAND		SCOTLAND	
Year	Champions	Cup Winners	Champions	Cup Winners
1872		The Wanderers		
1873		The Wanderers		
1874		Oxford University		Queen's Park
1875		Royal Engineers		Queen's Park
1876		The Wanderers		Queen's Park
1877		The Wanderers		Vale of Leven
1878		The Wanderers		Vale of Leven
1879		Old Etonians		Vale of Leven
1880		Clapham Rovers		Queen's Park
1881		Old Carthusians		Queen's Park
1882		Old Etonians		Queen's Park
1883		Blackburn Olympic		Dumbarton
1884		Blackburn Rovers		Queen's Park
1885		Blackburn Rovers		Renton
1886		Blackburn Rovers		Queen's Park
1887		Aston Villa		Hibernian
1888		West Brom. Albion		Renton
1889	Preston North End	Preston North End		Third Lanark
1890	Preston North End	Blackburn Rovers		Queen's Park
1891	Everton	Blackburn Rovers	Rangers and Dumbarton (joint)	Hearts
1892	Sunderland	West Brom. Albion	Dumbarton	Celtic
1893	Sunderland	Wolverhampton Wndrs.	Celtic	Queen's Park
1894	Aston Villa	Notts County	Celtic	Rangers
1895	Sunderland	Aston Villa	Hearts	St. Bernard
1896	Aston Villa	Sheffield Wednesday	Celtic	Hearts
1897	Aston Villa	Aston Villa	Hearts	Rangers
1898	Sheffield United	Nottingham Forest	Celtic	Rangers
1899	Aston Villa	Sheffield United	Rangers	Celtic
1900	Aston Villa	Bury	Rangers	Celtic
1901	Liverpool	Tottenham Hotspur	Rangers	Hearts
1902	Sunderland	Sheffield United	Rangers	Hibernian
1903	Sheffield Wed.	Bury	Hibernian	Rangers
1904	Sheffield Wed.	Manchester City	Third Lanark	Celtic
1905	Newcastle United	Aston Villa	Celtic	Third Lanark
1906	Liverpool	Everton	Celtic	Hearts
1907	Newcastle United	Sheffield Wednesday	Celtic	Celtic
1908	Manchester Un.	Wolverhampton Wndrs.	Celtic	Celtic
1909	Newcastle United	Manchester United	Celtic	Cup withheld
1910	Aston Villa	Newcastle United	Celtic	Dundee
1911	Manchester Un.	Bradford City	Rangers	Celtic
1912	Blackburn Rovers	Barnsley	Rangers	Celtic
1913	Sunderland	Aston Villa	Rangers	Falkirk
1914	Blackburn Rovers	Burnley	Celtic	Celtic
1915	Everton	Sheffield United	Celtic	No competition
1916	No competition	No competition	Celtic	" "
1917	" "	" "	Celtic	" "
1918	" "	" "	Rangers	" "
1919	" "	" "	Celtic	" "
1920	West Brom. Albion	Aston Villa	Rangers	Kilmarnock
1921	Burnley	Tottenham Hotspur	Rangers	Partick Thistle
1922	Liverpool	Huddersfield Town	Celtic	Morton
1923	Liverpool	Bolton Wanderers	Rangers	Celtic
1924	Huddersfield Town	Newcastle United	Rangers	Airdrie
1925	Huddersfield Town	Sheffield United	Rangers	Celtic
1926	Huddersfield Town	Bolton Wanderers	Celtic	St. Mirren
1927	Newcastle United	Cardiff City	Rangers	Celtic
1928	Everton	Blackburn Rovers	Rangers	Rangers
1929	Sheffield Wed.	Bolton Wanderers	Rangers	Kilmarnock
1930	Sheffield Wed.	Arsenal	Rangers	Rangers
1931	Arsenal	West Brom. Albion	Rangers	Celtic
1932	Everton	Newcastle United	Motherwell	Rangers
1933	Arsenal	Everton	Rangers	Celtic
1934	Arsenal	Manchester City	Rangers	Rangers
1935	Arsenal	Sheffield Wednesday	Rangers	Rangers
1936	Sunderland	Arsenal	Celtic	Rangers
1937	Manchester City	Sunderland	Rangers	Celtic
1938	Arsenal	Preston North End	Celtic	East Fife
1939	Everton	Portsmouth	Rangers	Clyde
1940 –46	No competition	No competition	No competition	No competition
1947	Liverpool	Charlton Athletic	Rangers	Aberdeen
1948	Arsenal	Manchester United	Hibernian	Rangers
1949	Portsmouth	Wolverhampton Wndrs.	Rangers	Rangers
1950	Portsmouth	Arsenal	Rangers	Rangers

| | ENGLAND | | SCOTLAND | |
Year	Champions	Cup Winners	Champions	Cup Winners
1951	Tottenham Hotspur	Newcastle United	Hibernian	Celtic
1952	Manchester United	Newcastle United	Hibernian	Motherwell
1953	Arsenal	Blackpool	Rangers	Rangers
1954	Wolverhampton Wndrs.	West Bromwich Albion	Celtic	Celtic
1955	Chelsea	Newcastle United	Aberdeen	Clyde
1956	Manchester United	Manchester City	Rangers	Hearts
1957	Manchester United	Aston Villa	Rangers	Falkirk
1958	Wolverhampton Wndrs.	Bolton Wndrs.	Hearts	Clyde
1959	Wolverhampton Wndrs.	Nottingham Forest	Rangers	St. Mirren

Queen's, at least as far as record-making and record-breaking are concerned. The Amateurs could not be expected to face up to the competition from paid players, for whom soccer was a career and not a pastime. We have to go back, therefore, to the very earliest days to find the really great achievements of the club.

And great achievements they undoubtedly were. For the first eight years of their existence (they were founded in 1867) Queen's Park played without the loss of a single goal! They suffered their first defeat in England after nine years' play, and ten years elapsed before they were defeated in their own country.

Queen's Park have never won the Scottish League, but their Cup record—ten times winners—is inferior only to that of Rangers and Celtic. And they have one splendid distinction in the Cup. In three successive years, from 1874 to 1876, Queen's won the trophy, and they repeated this feat in the years 1880 to 1882.

What does the future hold for the Queen's? Year after year, their players are lured away to professional clubs, and just when they appear to have got together a first-class eleven, their ranks are broken up and they have to start building anew. But enthusiasm is tremendous at Hampden Park—among players and supporters alike—and so far that enthusiasm for the game, as a game, has overcome all obstacles. Queen's will come back to the First Division of the Scottish League; of that there is no doubt. They are the only first-class amateur club in the United Kingdom, and are a distinguished and proud ornament to British soccer.

ICE HOCKEY

Ice hockey is the fastest game on earth and can be appreciated by both sexes, young and old alike. Let us drop in at an ice rink and see what it is all about. The rink we visit may be anywhere from Brighton to Dundee, and we need not specify any particular one, for the game we are about to witness is played along the same lines at all our British rinks, the only difference being, as with any sport, that some teams, of course, play it better than others.

Taking a quick look around the rink, what do we see? If it is a modern rink—and most of them are—we find ourselves in a well-lit arena or stadium which seats 3000 spectators if it is one of the smaller provincial ones, and up to 10,000 if it is one of the big London rinks like Wembley Pool (a swimming pool during the summer months), Harringay, or Earl's Court. The seats rise in tiers from the rink side, row upon row, and a clear view of the ice surface can be had from the farthest seat.

The artificial ice is gleaming white and in perfect condition. This man-made ice is used in Britain in our rinks, as the winter weather is not cold enough to ensure natural ice for long spells, although, in fact, the big rinks in Canada and the U.S.A., where winters are severe enough to guarantee natural ice, prefer artificial ice also. Briefly, the ice is made in the following way. Pipes are laid in the floor of the rink, and then a covering of concrete is run over them and levelled off. The freezing plant is housed in another part of the rink, which resembles a boiler-house, and to it the pipes under the rink floor are connected. Brine and ammonia are forced through them, after the concrete floor has been flooded, and in a short time the water freezes hard, producing that smooth sheet of ice you see down there in front of you.

The size of the ice surface at the rinks may vary in length and breadth by a few feet, but the ideal size for playing ice hockey is 185 by 85 feet. Most rinks are about these dimensions. The ice is enclosed all round by a barrier, which is known as the boards. On both sides, half-way along the rink, a section of the boards has been cut to form a swing gate, which allows the players to go easily on and off the ice during the game. Close by each of these gates is a team bench, on which the players, or those not required on the ice at the moment, sit with their team coach, facing their opponents across the rink. Nearby is the penalty box, to which players are sent for two, five, or ten minutes, depending on the seriousness of their infringement of the rules. The referee, of course, decides the "sentence" to be served. In the penalty box the player usually cools off—so it is commonly known as the " cooler ".

The ice surface has markings on it which may mystify the spectator seeing his first ice-hockey game. I will explain them as briefly as possible for your guidance.

There are two blue lines and one red one, painted into the ice. The blue lines, drawn across the rink at equal distances from the end barriers, divide it into three sections (see fig. 1), known, to a team looking from their own goal towards their opponents', respectively as the defending, neutral and attacking zones. The red line crosses the ice at the centre of the rink, and on it is the centre spot where the puck is "faced" when the game is restarted after a goal has been scored.

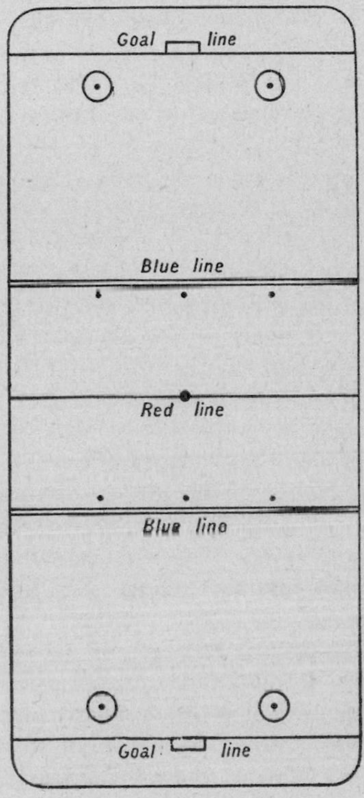

Fig. 1.—Plan of an ice-hockey rink

The four spots near the goals are the face-off spots, which mark the places where the puck may be put for restarting the game if it has been stopped for any other reason than a score.

The two remaining lines are the goal or bye lines, which extend across the rink about 10 feet out from the end boards. On them stand the goals, but in ice hockey, of course, unlike football, play does not stop when the puck goes behind these lines.

The goals, made of iron piping, are fixed into the ice on spikes to keep them in position during play, although sometimes they are " uprooted " when a scramble takes place round the net. They are 6 feet wide and 4 feet high, and look very small if compared with football goals. Nets are fitted to them to snare the puck when it is shot past the goalkeeper, who is, by the way, usually referred to in ice hockey as the goal-tender or net-minder.

So much for the markings.

Out skate the two referees clad in white sweaters. They inspect the nets to make sure that there are no breaks in them. Then the players appear, in their gaily coloured outfits.

The game lasts for an hour, divided into three periods of twenty minutes, plus two ten-minute intervals for cleaning the ice surface, since the flashing skates of the players " shave " it, and cause a good deal of " snow " to gather. This is cleared by the rink staff, who are equipped with ploughs or scrapers. You may see an exhibition of fancy skating between the periods of an ice-hockey game.

Remember, you always see a full sixty minutes of hockey. There is a big electric clock in full view of the spectators, which is set in motion by the timekeeper when play starts, stopped whenever the referee blows his whistle, and restarted when the puck is faced-off again. Thus spectators can tell to the second just how many minutes playing time are left at any juncture of the game.

An ice-hockey team is composed of the following six players: goal-tender, left defenceman, right defenceman, left wing, centre man, and right wing. Not more than six players of a team may be on the ice at any one time. Substitutes are allowed, and this brings the playing strength of a team to eleven or twelve men or more. These substitutes may be put into the game at any time, even while play is going on, although it is customary to wait for a stoppage of play. Then a fresh set of forwards or two defencemen may be put on. This is where the smart team coach can use his men to the best advantage. No substitute is allowed for a player who is in the " cooler ".

The players are all well protected; they wear shoulder pads, padded shorts, knee and shin guards, and they learn to take hard knocks. The goal-tender especially is heavily padded, and he has to be. In addition to the normal padding he wears a chest-protector and enormously thick leg guards. Each player carries a stick made wholly of wood, but most of them reinforce it in places with ordinary electrician's tape. The stick must not exceed 53 inches in length

from the top of the shaft to the heel of the blade; the blade must
not be longer than 14¾ inches (see fig. 2), but the goal-tender's stick
is much wider in the blade than are those of the other players. The
puck is made of solid rubber.

Now the game has started and the speed of it makes one gasp.
It is played on such a confined space that physical contact between
players is frequent. There are legal and illegal body checks. A
player in defence may stop an opponent by " body checking " him,
provided that he uses his shoulder, side or hip. Elbows, knees and

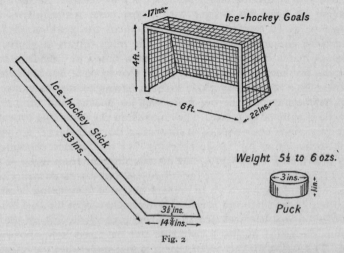

Fig. 2

feet must *not* be used. The puck may be passed from the end
barrier as far forward as the red line at mid-ice without incurring
an offside, but an attacking player must not cross the blue line into
the attacking zone *ahead* of the puck and then receive a pass. He is
offside.

There are many more rules to this great winter game, but if you
grasp these two you will soon learn the rest after you have attended
one or two games.

The speed of the game does result, on occasion, in some players
becoming excited and forgetting that sportsmanship is the main
thing. However, the most enraged player soon cools off, and any
differences of opinion there may be at times during the game are
forgotten when the final whistle blows. This is a fact.

In ice hockey the player who makes a pass to a team mate who scores gets equal credit, the scorer getting one point for the goal, and the assisting player getting one point for the assist. The players who get the most points are usually the ones who are the best known, but as you become familiar with the game you will learn to appreciate the hard-working wingman who skates both ways all evening, and the hard-hitting defenceman who safely blocks many an attack, but is not as spectacular as the goal-scorers are. Every man plays his part, for this is a *team* game.

It is the centre-ice player who is the play-maker. At the right moment he feeds his winger with a fast pass, which allows the winger to go in towards the goal and shoot the puck as hard as he can for the corner of the net. (The puck travels at nearly 90 miles an hour; its flight has actually been timed in Canada at over 88 miles per hour.) Wingmen must be able to skate fast both ways, and to take a pass on the move without having to stop to gather it. The defencemen are the big fellows of ice hockey, and they must be agile in spite of their size. They must stop the oncoming forwards with good clean body checks, or dispossess the puck-carrier by using their sticks, either by " poke checking " or by " sweep checking ". The goal-tender is on skates, but his are different from those of the other players. They are not the tube type, but are made entirely of steel, with little inverted v's to prevent the puck from flying between the blade of the skate and the sole of the hockey-boot into the net.

When a goal has been scored the goal judge (who sits off the ice behind the goals) pushes a switch to put on a red light above the goal. The reason for this arrangement is that sometimes the referee's view is blocked, even though there are two of them in charge of the game. Different leagues have made slight variations in the duties of referees. Some leagues have one referee only, who penalizes players for any infringements of the rules they may have committed, while a linesman (on the ice) has the duty of dealing with any offsides. We in Britain prefer to have two referees with equal powers, who whistle for fouls and offsides when they see them, even if they happen to be on their partner's side of the rink. They patrol, one on each side of the rink, up and down the ice, keeping within ten feet of the boards, and only going into the middle to face-off the puck and start the game. However, here too support is growing for the system of having one referee and two linesmen.

A penalty shot is awarded if a player, going in alone on goal with no opponent between him and the goal-tender, is brought down illegally. In most cases he has been tripped from behind. For the penalty shot the puck is placed on the offending team's blue line at its centre point, and the player taking the penalty is allowed to come up, gather the puck and skate right in on the opposing goal-tender before trying to score.

Remember that players in all zones are allowed to kick the puck with their skates, but they may not score a goal by kicking it into the net. The puck is " dead " when it is out of the referee's sight. He blows his whistle at once when this happens—generally when the puck disappears under one or more players—and a face-off is taken.

I am sure that if there is an ice rink near your home and you go to see a hockey game there, you will become a regular supporter of your local team. Ice hockey has gained its thousands of enthusiastic followers because it really does provide continuous high-speed action and excitement.

KITES AND MODEL AIRCRAFT

While flying, as we know it to-day, has been developed in a bare fifty years, we should find if we looked back in history that many of our ideas are not so new, and were, in fact, tried out in ancient times by that wonderful race, the Chinese. Just as they invented gunpowder hundreds of years ago and used it only to make fireworks for displays at holiday time, so they were amongst the earliest to study flight, and used their knowledge to make the most wonderful kites, again only for displays or as a quiet recreation on windy days. Even to-day in little Chinese villages there are old men who make intricate kites like dragons from a few scraps of paper and bamboo canes, and, as the local kite-makers, are always to the front when there is anything to celebrate.

But there is no need to be a Chinaman to enjoy all the fun of making and flying your own kite. Two forms are in general use for beginners; the simple triangular kite, with its long tail of paper streamers to keep it steady, and the box kite, which is steadier in flight and can be flown with nearly a mile of line after a little practice. While they are quite easy to make, it is perhaps better to buy a ready-made one for a start until the method of flying has been grasped. Even to-day such a kite costs only a shilling or two, and the very cheapest will fly like a bird.

To fly your kite, let out thirty or forty feet of line and run into the wind as hard as you can. This lifts it up in the air; to keep it up it is necessary to keep giving little pulls on the line, so that this is always taut, with the kite being blown away from you. The art is to let out a little more line each time there is a puff of wind, but not so much that the kite begins to fall. The expert can get his kite several hundred feet into the air in a matter of minutes. Never be afraid to ask one of these experts to give you a helping hand. You will find the really good kite-flyer is just as keen to help a beginner to get his kite flying as he is to fly his own.

Of recent years, however, the hobby of kite-flying has rather given place to aeromodelling, or making and flying model aeroplanes. There are something like a million enthusiasts, youngsters, grown-ups, and old men, who spend their spare time building and flying their models, either on their own in the local park, or in contests with others on full-size aerodromes or special flying-fields. Often there are several hundred competitors at a meeting, and crowds of supporters numbering thousands. So it is clear that whoever starts aeromodelling will not want for fellow model-makers.

The popularity of the hobby owes much to the discovery in Central America of a special strong yet light wood called balsa.

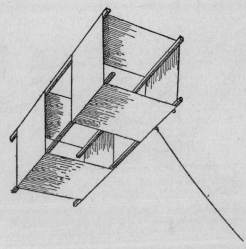

Fig. 1.—A simple form of box kite that will give endless pleasure. The two towing eyes give alternative positions according to strength of wind

This wood is much lighter than cork, can easily be cut with an old razor-blade (or special cutting tool, if preferred), and can be joined firmly with a quick-drying glue, or cement as it is called, that sets rock-firm in a matter of minutes. This wood forms the basic framework for most simple models, and is then covered with special tissue paper, which is treated to strengthen it.

Let us consider the different sorts of model that can be built, starting with the simplest and working up to more complicated and more expensive designs. Models that are already made are often quite expensive, so that the usual thing for a beginner is to buy a constructional set which will contain all the materials he needs

3*   (G 487)

for the model, together with a plan and full instructions on step-by-step building. There is a wide choice of kits (as these are called) from which to choose, at prices from 2s. 6d. upwards.

Most beginners feel they would like a propeller on their first model, so that it can really fly like a full-size aeroplane. Simple propeller-driven models are called rubber duration models, because the propeller is driven by twisted bands of rubber, and they are designed to stay in the air for a long duration of flight. Do not be disappointed because such models bear little resemblance to a full-size aeroplane such as a Spitfire or Vampire fighter; and, above all,

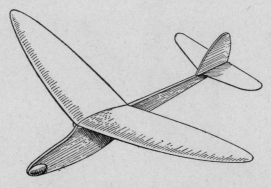

Fig. 2.—The very beginning! A chuck glider of all-wood construction which is the best model of all with which to start aeromodelling

do not be tempted to buy a kit for such a " scale " model. These are for more expert builders and are unlikely to prove successful in a beginner's hands.

Rubber duration models are, however, designed on exactly the same principles that produce the latest full-size machines, but the theory of flying (or aerodynamics) is adjusted to meet their special requirements. These are that the model should be light in weight, have good lifting qualities in its wings, and have a propeller which will take advantage of the peculiar qualities of a rubber motor—which are indeed very different from those of a full-size aeroplane engine. The engine gives the same power all the time; but a rubber motor gives much more power when it is tightly twisted, and then gradually less and less as it unwinds.

Before starting to build that first model there are one or two tools that will be needed. Fortunately, aeromodelling needs fewer tools than almost any other constructional hobby. The bare minimum is an old razor-blade, with one of the edges covered by sticky paper (or, better still, use the single-edged kind), a few pieces of fine sand-paper (the " flour " grade or No. 0), a pair of pointed-nose pliers for wire bending, some ordinary household pins, and a stout smooth plank of wood, or an old pastry-board, to avoid cutting the table—or, even worse, the tablecloth. With these and the contents of a kit you are ready to begin.

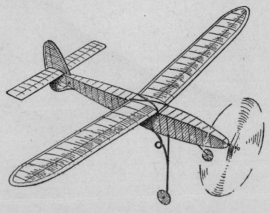

Fig. 3.—An intermediate type of rubber-powered duration model. While very simple in construction, such a model is quite capable of winning contests in all but the most expert company—and sometimes even then!

Let us look inside your box and see what you have bought. First there will be a plan of the model to be built, with every part shown full-size. Instructions may be in a separate leaflet or printed on the plan in brief. There will be one or more tubes of balsa cement for sticking parts together. Materials will consist of several flat sheets of wood with sundry parts printed on them ready to be cut out, and a little bundle of wood strips of varying thickness to make the fuselage or body framework and to put the wings together, wire for the undercarriage, and a thicker piece for the propeller to turn on, several thicker blocks of wood to shape the nose from and to reinforce parts, a pair of wheels, a finished or part-finished propeller, some tissue paper for covering, and a length of rubber strip to make the " motor ". Before starting work be sure to read the instructions and study the plan carefully until you know what each piece is to be used for. There will usually be enough spare wood to allow for one or two mistakes in construction, but do not rely on this too much!

The next few evenings should see substantial progress on the model, but until the time comes for those exciting first flights, let us consider some of the other types of model aircraft.

Fig. 4.—This semi-scale model is driven by its own miniature engine. Wings are about three to four feet in span. Construction could be undertaken by anyone who had built two or three simple models before.

Not so many years ago every beginner expected to go through the process of starting with such a simple model and gradually working up to more ambitious designs, but to-day many aeromodellers are attracted to the hobby when already sufficiently skilful with their hands to start with a fairly complicated design. These "intermediate" beginners may feel the urge to start right away with a machine powered with its own engine, just like the full-size aircraft. This is not beyond them, for there are dozens of such engines on the market which can be started by a novice in a few minutes and will give hours of pleasure.

The tiny engines used for model aircraft vary in size from less than 1 c.c. in capacity to 10 c.c., i.e. they are anything from one-hundredth the power of an autocycle to about one-tenth. They weigh from $1\frac{1}{2}$ oz. to over $\frac{1}{2}$ lb., and will serve as the motive power for models from 18 inches to 7 or 8 feet in wing-span.

Before the war it was necessary to have some quite complicated electrical apparatus as well, which made these baby aero-engines decidedly tricky, but to-day this is not required. They run on a mixture of ether and oil with a little petrol or lighter-fuel added. By swinging the miniature propeller briskly the mixture is compressed in the cylinder head and causes the little explosions that drive the piston up and down. For this reason they are also known as " compression-ignition " engines, which is a better description than " diesel ", but not so easy on the tongue. There are also engines called " glow-plug " engines, which require a battery to start them but do not need it in flight. These are rather more complicated, however, and are not recommended as a first engine.

With one of these diesel engines, then, and again with a simple kit to suit it, the " intermediate " beginner can start right away as a " power " aeromodeller. The kit of parts will be much the same, but the materials stouter and the instructions rather fuller. Here we would give once more the warning not to be led away by too complicated a model. Accept the advice of the shop assistant as to an appropriately simple design.

There will be some who find only a limited appeal in powered models and who would prefer to try their hand at some graceful glider or sailplane. These too are popular amongst the aeromodelling fraternity, and have the advantage, shared with the kite, that upkeep costs—fuel for motors, or new rubber strands—are not required. All that is needed is a finished model and a gentle breeze. In spite of their lack of motive power gliders will give an excellent performance, and can often beat their powered counterparts in the time they will stay in the air. World record for this class of model —held by a Swiss—is nearly an hour and a half!

Those who have been to an air display and seen the pilots looping, flying upside-down, and doing all kinds of stunts, may feel they would like to do the same with a model. This is not beyond them, for there is a special class of model designed to do just that. This is called a control-line model. Here the aircraft is not launched off into the blue, but is held captive by the " pilot " by two thread or wire lines attached to and terminating in a handle which he grasps in his hands. An assistant starts the motor, the model takes off, and then, according to the skill of the flier, it will do nearly everything that a full-size aircraft can be made to do. All this is achieved by the two wires which are connected to a control plate on the machine. This in turn actuates an elevator on the tail-plane, which can be made to turn up or down, producing climbs and dives, and, as experience is gained, loops, inverted flying, figure eights, and all the fun of the " flying circus ". Even without a motor quite

Fig. 5.—A highly efficient sailplane, shown here on its towline just before release. The little streamer on the line enables the launcher to see when the towline has come clear of the hook.

a number of stunts can be done with such an aircraft by " whip-power ". In this case the flier has his model on lines attached to a long pole like a fishing-rod and " whips " it into the air. Many experts look on this whip-flying as ideal training for powered control-line flying later. It is certainly cheaper, and the beginner's initial mistakes do not involve him in new propellers and other replacements.

So great is the control possible with this tethered flying that real jet models have now been flown. The jet engine is like a miniature " buzz-bomb " and works on the same principle. Speeds of over a hundred miles an hour are possible, while the appropriate

no:ses are given off in a very satisfactory way. For this reason it
is certainly not the model to fly near houses where residents would
probably not enjoy the noise so much. All control-line flying should
take place well away from houses where the noise could give offence,
and safety precautions should be taken so that innocent bystanders
do not get hurt. If you want to fly this sort of model it is better to
join a club with its own flying-ground. Do not fly in parks or public
places, and, above all, be sure that you have a third-party insurance
policy just in case of accidents.

Fig. 6.—A beginner's control-line model. Such a design is a good
training model, and while not advanced enough for difficult "stunts ",
would do all but the most complicated after a little practice.

Insurance for model aircraft is very old-established, and for a
few pence a year all the risks of having to pay for damage that
may be done unwittingly can be covered. Even the simple rubber
model *can* go over a wall and break a neighbour's glasshouse—so
take no chances. If you join a club the secretary will handle this
for you; if you fly as a " lone hand " then make a point of finding
out insurance particulars through one of the special magazines
dealing with aeromodelling.

Undoubtedly the peak of present aeromodelling achievement
is the radio-controlled model. Here the model contains, in addition
to its motor—it may even be a big motorless glider—a tiny radio
receiving-set and aerial. On the ground the operator has a trans-
mitting-set that gives signals to the aircraft. As the signals are picked

up by the set in the machine they make or break a circuit, causing a little starfish-shaped wheel to click round. This in turn moves the rudder or elevator, and makes the model respond exactly to the ground directions. A skilled operator can make the machine do exactly as he wishes—turn right or left, climb or dive, and even loop, and finally when the flight is over bring the model in to a perfect three-point landing at his feet. Not many can do all this yet, or even half of it, but this is the aim, and given suitable weather conditions it is within the scope of the apparatus already on the market. Control such as this has great value in full-size aeronautics, and many countries are spending a lot of money developing such models. They are useful in target training already, and may lead to the guided missiles of the future, when wars may well be fought in the air without a single pilot!

We have spoken in general terms of some of the more usual kinds of model aircraft, but really there is no end to the scope of this hobby. When winter comes, and outdoor flying is limited, there are special designs that can be flown in any large hall or gymnasium. These are delicate little feather-light aircraft weighing perhaps one-sixteenth of an ounce, with gossamer wings of microfilm, or " mike " as it is nicknamed. This special covering film, infinitely thin, is made chemically and fastened to a super-light balsa framework. Such models will fly for a quarter of an hour or more. In England they have not achieved any very great following, but in America are extremely popular.

English model-makers have developed a rather more robust model weighing ½ to 1 oz., which is flown tethered to a short pole. Such designs are not so delicate to build, and are within the powers of any average builder. As such, they do much to enliven club nights during the winter months, when contests are arranged on an inter-club basis.

A development of this R.T.P. or round-the-pole flying is to be found in the electrically driven model. Here the current is fed to a motor or motors in the machine along the wires tethering it to the pole, and most realistic flight obtained. Controls may also be fitted in the same way, and the model made to start its engine, taxi, take off, and fly round, all actuated from a miniature cockpit and joystick outside the flying circle. One such model of the Vickers Viking twin-engined airliner did all this as well as retract and let down its undercarriage. During a period of three years it flew a distance of over 3000 miles, wore out fourteen engines and three sets of wheels, took part in exhibitions all over Europe, and starred in a television programme! Another successful electric R.T.P. model was the D.H. Vampire, with an air turbo-jet drive, though this was even harder on its motors than the Viking!

The development of the miniature diesel engine, of course, makes it possible for the more ambitious to build and fly successful scale models of famous aircraft, though as we have warned you, this is not for the novice. In this group, favourites are the old-timer biplanes of World War I, and there is little to beat the appearance of a little Sopwith Pup or an old Bristol Fighter, some three feet in span, lumbering through the air just like its prototype.

There is yet another facet of aeromodelling that still attracts a big following—that of building non-flying " solid " models. These are constructed as replicas of actual aircraft, and the idea is to reproduce in miniature an exact copy of some favourite machine. The most popular size is $\frac{1}{72}$nd scale size, which gives the average modern fighter a wing-span of about six inches. When finished they look most realistic and make a grand decoration for study or den. They can be ranged on the mantelpiece or slung from the ceiling in flying attitudes. As they are small, quite a squadron occupies very little space, and their construction is one of the best possible ways for Observer Corps or Air Reserve identification training. During the war, schools and youth clubs built hundreds of thousands of such models here and in the U.S.A. to help Air Force recognition study, and while not quite so popular to-day it is still a most useful and interesting branch of aeromodelling.

Those of an inventive turn will find in their models a grand outlet for their ideas. It is possible to design one's own models and see for oneself just how good or otherwise they may be. Flying-wing aircraft, or tailless designs, have been favourite unorthodox types, and many of these are flying well, both as gliders and as powered models. So valuable is model research considered that leading aircraft companies have sponsored contests to encourage design, while the Ministry of Civil Aviation has long been helping one group of enthusiasts in their work on low-speed aerodynamic theory.

But the majority of model fliers fly because they like it without any particular thought about it being useful. This is the only hobby that gives indoor handiwork and outdoor exercise according to weather and the time of year, and as such it draws its followers from amongst both stay-at-homes and outdoor types.

Let us now accompany our beginner on to the flying-field to watch his first flights with that kit model. It looks a little rough in places, but bears quite a commendable resemblance to the picture on the box, so that we can hope for some sort of flight from it. The rubber motor has been inserted, and, according to instructions, the builder has lubricated it with rubber lubricant—a mixture of glycerine and soft soap, best bought ready mixed. Oil should never be used for rubber motors! A check is made that the wing and tail-plane are firmly fixed in place with rubber bands, and that both seem free from warps; then the model is held at a point about one-third back from the leading-edge or front of the wings, where it should balance. Then, held by the fuselage, it is thrown forward, rather like a dart, aimed at a point about twenty feet ahead. If all is well it should glide steadily forward, falling gradually all the time. Before doing this our beginner remembered in time to check the wind direction and launch carefully full into the wind.

The first glide was not too bad, but the nose tended to rise, indicating that it was a little tail-heavy. This fault was then corrected by slipping a sliver of thin balsa under the trailing-edge or rear of the wing, where it was held to the fuselage with rubber bands, thus reducing the lift of the wings slightly. Another glide resulted in a steady path and the model was ready for its power test. Had the nose end been the heavier, packing would have been required at the front or leading-edge of the wing.

Winding the rubber motor may be done simply by twisting the propeller in the opposite direction from that in which it will unwind, but the better way is to use a hand-brace with a geared winder, fitted with a small hook in place of the usual drill, which is inserted in a loop at the end of the propeller shaft. This gives more turns more quickly. To get them on the rubber strands evenly it is usual to stretch the motor before winding up to three times its length, or more, which means that a helper is needed to hold the model.

Giving up to a couple of hundred turns for its first flight, the wise beginner inserts another slip of balsa between the top of the nose-block and the fuselage before launching. This takes care of any excess power the model may have and helps to prevent a spectacular crash at the very start. With one hand holding the propeller to stop it unwinding prematurely, he directs the model into the wind, and launches it firmly but positively, rather as it was test-glided, but this time pointing it slightly upwards. The propeller should be released a second or two before this and allowed to revolve freely. If all is well a flight of fifteen to twenty seconds should result. Any undue tendency to turn is corrected with slips of balsa on the opposite side of the nose-block to the turn. When satisfactory flying has been obtained these temporary slips should be cemented permanently in place. A beginner's model well made and properly trimmed— making these first adjustments is called trimming—will fly for as much as five minutes, or even longer if the day is hot and the model is caught in rising up-currents of hot air.

Such a simple model may well be the forerunner of many success-ful rubber-driven machines, and lead to specialization in this branch, considered by some to be the most fascinating of all. There is then no end to what the builder may achieve, for rubber-powered models enjoy the privilege of competing in the best-known international contest of all in aeromodelling, the Wakefield Trophy, competed for annually by teams from all over the world. Each year the com-petition is held in the country whose team last won, so that there is every incentive for the enthusiast to win a place in the team. A special size and weight of model is required for the event, and these Wakefield models are the ultimate end of all rubber modelling. In 1959 the U.S.A. was first, Canada second, and Great Britain third.

Similar international contests exist for both powered models and sailplanes, but none have achieved quite the fame of the Wake-field Trophy, which was started in 1928. Teams have entered from nearly every civilized country—even those as far away as Australia and New Zealand, and including most European countries.

This is yet another of the delightful sides of aeromodelling. It is truly international. English modellers travel to many continental contests, and foreign visitors come over here to take part in ours. Very often the visitors may be ignorant of their hosts' tongue, but a model aeroplane is the common bond, making language a small problem.

Anyone with any interest at all in making things with his hands must feel the urge to build his own model aeroplanes, and then to learn all that he can of this fascinating hobby. To help beginner and expert there are over seven hundred model clubs in the country, organized together for competitions and the general good of the sport, by the Society of Model Aeronautical Engineers, who are affiliated to the Royal Aero Club, the governing body in this country. A line to their Secretary at Londonderry House, Park Lane, London, W.1, will bring full information on your nearest club, while they even have a scheme for " Country Members ", or those unable, because of the location of their homes, to join a club. There are also many school clubs. If you have one already, join it—it is more fun all together. If not, why not make a start and form one?

In addition, there is a whole library of books on aeromodelling subjects, and two monthly magazines devoted exclusively to it. Of these the *Aeromodeller* is published by Model Aeronautical Press. Ltd., 38 Clarendon Road, Watford, Herts., while the S.M.A.E. publish their own journal *Model Aircraft* from 19–20 Noel Street, London, W.1.

SKI-ING

Ski-ing is a method of crossing snow-covered country by means of long wooden planks strapped to the feet. These wooden planks are called Skis (pronounced " Shees "), and are sometimes referred to as " snow skates ".

This method of travelling over snow has been in use for centuries in many countries, but particularly in Norway and Sweden. As a sport it is of comparatively recent origin, only some fifty years having elapsed since men first used it as a means of amusement.

The great advantage which skis have over other forms of snow transit is that they are capable of gliding over the snow, whereas snow-shoes or racquettes have to be lifted at every step. The famous Norwegian explorer Fridtjof Nansen demonstrated their advantages by his crossing of the great snow wastes of Greenland in 1888. Amundsen, another Norwegian explorer, and our own Captain Scott both used skis in the Antarctic.

Now skis have penetrated to the remote snow-clad valleys of Central Europe, and Swiss and Austrian peasants use them as a matter of course in their ordinary occupations for some six months in the year.

The popularity of ski-ing as a sport has increased enormously during the last twenty-five years. In Switzerland, Austria and Bavaria, the Alpine valleys are crowded every week-end during the winter and spring months by enthusiastic ski-runners, and in January and February ski-runners from this country have flocked in their thousands to the popular winter sports resorts in the Alps. Even in this country ski-runners are to be found during the spring months on the snow-covered slopes of the Scottish mountains.

The fascination of the sport is largely due to the immense speed attained without any mechanical assistance; to the smooth passage of the skis over the crisp sparkling snow; and to the beauty of the scenery in which the action takes place. Speeds of thirty to forty miles an hour can be reached under favourable circumstances, and in such cases the sensation produced is that of flying through space with but little contact with mother Earth.

The modern ski is a specially selected straight-grained piece of hickory about 6′ 6″ long, 3″ wide and $\frac{1}{4}$″ thick. The front is pointed like a boat and up-turned so as to ride over the snow and not into it. The running surface is highly polished, and is kept so by the use of wax. The ski is fixed to the boot by bindings of

Standing

various design, which are all hinged at the toe, allowing the heels to rise off the ski, but providing ample lateral control by means of iron toe-pieces. The boots also are specially designed, having rigid strong soles, square toes, and low heels with a groove at the back to take the binding straps and prevent them slipping off. The portion of the binding which goes round the heel is now usually a stout coiled spring about half an inch in diameter which clamps the boot into the toe-pieces, but which in an emergency permits the boot—and the ski-runner—to be shot out of the bindings and so prevent a broken ankle or a twisted knee. Probably the most popular bindings at present are

Knees bent

the " Kandahar ", and the " Alpina " with a " Bilgeri " spring at the back, but there are many others.

In addition to the skis a couple of light sticks are carried, one in each hand. They have a steel spike, and to prevent it sinking too deeply into soft snow a small circular basket ring is fitted about six inches above the spike. These sticks are principally used for climbing uphill, but they also help the balance of the skier when running downhill, and they are occasionally used to assist him in making special turns.

Now it has already been stated that the principal advantage of the ski over the snow-shoe is that it glides forward. The obvious retort by the snow-shoer is—" Surely it also glides backwards "! If this were so, then little progress would be made. The ski, however, does not go back as readily as it goes forward, because the heel of the ski is a square-cut edge which catches the snow, whereas the toe is slightly broader than the rest of the ski and is turned up and tapered to a point so as not to catch the snow. In ascending a steep slope, however, the ski, especially if highly polished, will slip back, and to counteract this two devices are employed. In the first method a special sticky wax is rubbed on to the running surface while climbing, to be scraped off before starting to run down. The other device is to wear skins on the skis. These are long strips of fur which are clipped on to the skis, with the hairs of the fur lying back so that the skis go forward easily but are prevented from slipping back by the hairs catching.

The ski-runner is now ready to start work. He has a pair of hickory skis with bindings attached a little aft of the centre; a good pair of ski boots, roomy enough to take an extra pair of woollen socks; a pair of light ski sticks; and most important of all, a good slope of snow on which to try them out. He steps on to the skis, fits his boots into the toe-irons and clamps the bindings tight. He then stands upright and surveys his prospects. These are not bright, as the first feeling is one of complete helplessness. The skis have swollen to a gigantic size and seem to be made of lead; he cannot turn round, as the skis get on the top of each other; he must turn, however, as his skis are not pointing to the snow slope on which he wishes to practise; he makes another effort and promptly falls sideways. With difficulty he regains the upright position and looks despairingly around. Fortunately, a good Samaritan ski-ing past sees his difficulty and gives him his first ski-ing lesson—how to turn by means of a " kick turn ". This is easy and soon he has mastered it. Now he can move off across the snow. He slides one foot forward cautiously, then the other one, and finds he is moving all right. He helps himself by pushing with his sticks. The slope goes a little downhill, and to his surprise and delight he finds himself gliding smoothly if slowly along. The down slope ceases, and he finds himself going uphill. It gets a little steeper, and suddenly a ski slips back and down he crashes. With the help of his sticks he gets on his feet again. He decides the slope is too steep, so he takes it sideways at a gentle angle. Soon he finds that he is not going in the required direction, so he tries to turn to zigzag back to his old course. Unfortunately, to do so he finds his skis gradually turning to point straight up the hill, and then again a ski slips and down he goes, half smothered in the soft, dry, powdery snow. Then he remembers he should have used the kick-turn, but being a sensible fellow he turns while still lying on the snow, and rises up facing in

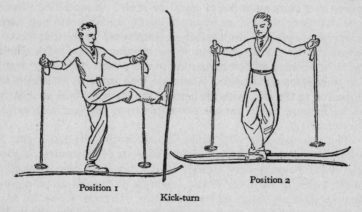

Position 1

Position 2

Kick-turn

the required direction. When next he wants to turn he makes no mistake, and slowly and carefully, supported by his sticks, he does a kick-turn and all is well. Eventually, tired and hot, he reaches the top of the snow slope. While resting, he notices with astonishment a party of skiers coming straight up the slope with apparently little exertion. As they pass he sees that they are all wearing skins, and have come up in five minutes what had taken him half an hour of very hard work.

Having recovered his breath, he gazes down the slope and is surprised to see that it now looks twice as steep as it did from below. However, he has to get back to his hotel somehow, so he tentatively points his skis slightly down and across the slope. Nothing happens, so he turns them slightly more downhill. Suddenly, off they go, and with a wild lurch he recovers his balance and manages to go with them. Then, alas! his right ski runs across the toe of his left ski and over he goes head over heels, skis waving frantically in the air. This is his first real fall, and he finds himself completely mixed up with skis and sticks buried deep, his head downhill with his face well pushed into the snow. A passing skier comes to his assistance, and shows him how gradually to get above his skis with the help of his sticks, place them in the proper position and eventually to start off again. The slope is now very gentle, and to his great delight he glides down on to the level and gradually slows up and stops.

This first attempt has shown the beginner that it is not only necessary to be able to kick-turn on the ascent, but that it is equally necessary to be able to brake or to stop on the descent.

Snow-plough

The method of braking is to " stem ", that is, to form the skis into a V so that they act like a snow-plough. The skier bends his knees, then " knocks " them. This has the effect of turning the skis on to their inside edges, and if the points are brought together and the heels shoved out strongly a perfect snow-plough is formed. This brings the runner to a complete stop if—and it is a big if— the correct position is maintained and the weight of the body is equally distributed over both skis.

It is not proposed to deal here with ski-ing turns and how to execute them, but the brief description above of the " stem " brings out two of the basic principles of ski-ing, namely, " weighting " of the skis and " edging " of the skis.

It is obvious that skis will run downhill in the direction in which they are pointing. If the points of the skis converge, they will run across each other unless restrained as in the stem. If, however, when in the stem position all the weight is transferred to the right ski, this ski controls the direction, whilst the left ski merely skims over the snow. As the right ski is pointing to the left, the skier will turn gradually to the left, the left ski being forced to skid over the surface to the left. This is called a stop stem-turn, and a new motion of the ski—to skid—has been introduced.

A ski lying flat on the snow is not easily pushed sideways; if it is turned slightly over on the right edge, it will move more easily to the left; if turned well over, it will again be difficult to push it sideways or make it " skid ", as the edge in the snow catches and resists the movement. To make a ski skid easily, therefore, it must be turned slightly on one edge, the extent depending on the state of the snow and the speed at which the ski is travelling. If the snow is hard and icy little edging is necessary, as the ski will easily move sideways on ice whilst held flat. This " edging " is done by the ankles and is most important.

In the description of the stop stem-turn above, the left ski is being forced sideways to the left. In order to prevent it catching on the snow, although unweighted, it should be turned slightly on to its right edge, thus raising its left edge and enabling it to ride over any inequalities in the snow.

It will be seen, therefore, that to make the easiest turn in the snow three things have to be kept in mind, namely: the stem position, the weighting of the skis, and the edging of the skis.

Why does one want to turn on skis? The answer is that beginners will usually find the snow slopes are too steep to run down straight; they would go so fast that they would lose control and crash. A steep slope is therefore descended in a series of zigzags just as one ascended, but instead of doing a kick-turn, which means stopping, at each zig the skier does a downhill turn and continues his course on the new zag. Consider what this means. As the runner gets to the end of the first zig going, say, to the left, he must turn round to his right, and for one awful moment he will find himself pointing straight down the steep slope. He has first, however, fallen into the snow-plough position, which decreases his speed. Both skis are on their inside edges. The weight is gradually transferred to the left ski, which then starts to swing round, points downhill, and then swings farther round until it is pointing to the right. The right ski, or inside ski, which started on its inside edge, has gradually been unweighted, then flattened to permit skidding, and finally gradually weighted and turned on to its outside or right edge. At the finish, therefore, both skis are on their right edges and traversing (or crossing) the slope to the right. The ski-runner has completed a downhill stem-turn.

As speed, however, is one of the great joys of ski-running, and the stem-turn is the slowest of all turns, the beginner soon aspires to the fast turns. The most generally used fast turn is the " stem-Christiania ". This, in effect, is started by a slight momentary stem, but at once both skis are skidded round at high speed. The " Christiania " turn is done by a swing of the body, both skis skidding round

The Christiania

without any preliminary stem. In deep soft snow the " telemark " turn is used. It is what is known as a steered turn, like the stem-turn, in which the skis are forced into a certain relative position and held there, causing a steering action to develop which causes the skis to turn in the required direction.

Now it must be made clear that wherever possible the ski-runner runs straight ahead; it is only because he must that he turns. He turns if the slope is too steep to take straight; he turns to avoid obstacles; and he turns to change his general direction. The complete ski-runner must be able to move easily and quickly along the level; to climb steep slopes without undue exertion; and to run downhill at a high speed under complete control. When the ski-runner has achieved all this, he will find himself a master of the most fascinating sport that man's ingenuity has ever devised.

SPEEDWAY RACING

Speedway racing, which is now one of the country's major sports and attracts half a million people to sports stadiums in Britain every week during the season, is no sport for the weakling. It is tough, demanding courage, determination and good sportsmanship, and is a good clean sport in which gambling is strictly prohibited. It is amazing to think that it has been in existence for only some twenty years.

It was started in Australia in 1923 as a novelty at a cattle show. The organizers wanted a " fill-in " item, and Johnnie Hoskins, who became a leading promoter in this country, suggested motor-cycle racing " around the dirt track ". The experiment proved successful, and " dirt-track racing ", as it was then called, became a vogue as an interval attraction at agricultural shows.

That gave Hoskins the idea that this sport could be developed, and he proceeded to get it properly organized. Various promoters in different parts of Australia started organizing meetings, and then it spread to America and Britain.

Tracks began to open up throughout the country, and by the early thirties dirt-track racing was a going concern. Mistakes were made in the early days; certain figures demanded large sums for " appearance money ", and soon the sport began to feel the pinch financially. However, this did not kill it, but it was temporarily crippled. Not until the late thirties did speedway racing become a major sport.

The Speedway Control Board and the Auto Cycle Union—the controlling bodies—tightened up their rules, and although to-day they are still frequently criticized for many of their decisions, they certainly took steps in the right direction at this time.

No promoter could open up a track without the approval of the A.C.U. and the Control Board. A licence was not granted unless the track was suitable and the promoters agreed to carry out specified safety precautions. The promoters were then told that they could not sign a rider unless the Board gave their consent. The idea was that a wealthy track could not " corner the market " for riders. If this rule had not been enforced, League racing would not have been possible. A " super " team against weak opposition would have been farcical. The sport progressed, and to-day the same strict rulings are in existence.

Its mushroom-like growth presented many problems, and the riders decided to form a riders' association. So if a rider has a grouse he can complain to the Association, who in turn will settle difficulties with the promoters and the Control Board.

As the years rolled by and speedway racing became more popular, so many tracks began to open up that it was found necessary to have a National League and several subsidiary leagues. We also have Test matches — between England and Australia — internationals, Cup matches and a World's Championship, the final of which attracts a crowd of 90,000 to Wembley each year.

Hundreds of boys, not content merely to watch their heroes, decided to emulate their daring. They started Cycle Speedway. Improvised tracks were made on any piece of ground they could find. Boys raced on their ordinary bicycles, broadsiding and skidding round corners, and a good time was had by all—except the bicycles. Even the " skid kids ", as they were called originally, started to organize themselves. Leagues were formed, and to-day they are quite a flourishing concern. They are proud, too, of the fact that quite a number have stepped up from their ranks to speedway racing proper. A few have even reached the top rank.

Of course the road to speedway stardom is a hard one. Many fall by the wayside. Knowledgeable promoters declare that they can spot a potential star early on in his career, but that only applies to what may be termed " naturals "—young men who take to the sport as a duck takes to water. In my experience " naturals " are few and far between. Nine times out of ten a star emerges only after years of experience. He gets there the hard way—by trial and error. It is just like a trade—one must serve one's apprenticeship.

After seeing the machines roaring round the track, the uninitiated would probably declare that it is all a question of taking a chance, going full throttle—" grabbing a handful " as the riders call it—and hoping for the best. How wrong this is! Plenty of courage is required, but skilful tactics are what really matter. I have seen a star rider mounted on a very indifferent machine beat a rider whose bicycle was tuned to the last detail. He won through track craft.

Although riders normally take years before they reach championship class, practically every season a young man comes forward out of the blue and surprises everyone, and, of course, it occasionally happens that a rider who has been labelled as " never likely to succeed " suddenly strikes form and shoots to the top.

I am going to devote the remainder of this article to answering some questions typical of those which are so often put to me.

How much money can a rider expect to earn per year at speedway racing?

I should say that a leading First Division man earns about £2000 a year. Of course, the riders have very heavy upkeep expenses. Several hundreds of pounds are spent every season on their speedway machines, and then the fuel—a petrol substitute—is the riders' own responsibility and must be purchased before every meeting. Unless they go abroad—a great many go to Australia in our winter—

riders have a six-months season, from April till October. There is a guaranteed wage of £6 10s. per meeting. Riders are paid so much a start and so much a point. Three points are given for a win, two for a second and one for a third. A rider normally competes in five races per meeting and on an average rides at two meetings per week. He may collect £30 or £40 at an ordinary meeting. Of course, there are special championship meetings where the highest points scorer gets an additional cheque which may range from £40 to £500.

If a rider is injured does he get any compensation?

There is a compulsory insurance scheme to which all riders must subscribe. The amount each man elects to pay dictates how much sick-pay he will obtain. Sums of compensation vary from £10 to £50 per week.

When is one too old for racing?

This depends entirely on the outlook of the rider. Tommy Price won the World's Championship in 1949 when he was thirty-seven years of age and runner-up Jack Parker was over forty. Several of the riders of to-day are bordering on fifty. Few are under twenty and quite a number do not reach their best form until their late twenties.

Is there much skill required in racing?

Most definitely! It would amaze you to know how thoroughly riders work out every move. Many races are won " in the pits ", where the riders decide what tactics they will adopt against particular opponents.

Are there different styles of riding?

Yes. In the early days most popular was the " foot trailer "— a rider who trailed his left leg as he hurtled round the bends. Although that particular style is still the most thrilling to watch, it is a dying art. Riders of to-day feel that " trailing " slows them up and have adopted a " foot forward " style. The " trailer " necessarily covers more ground. He takes a wide sweep at the bends whereas the " foot forward " method allows the rider to hug the white line which surrounds the inside of the track.

Do all the riders use the same type of engine?

Yes—J.A.P. (the proprietary name) engines are used. Riders naturally place great importance on the type of frame. Every season sees the introduction of new ideas and a great deal of money is spent on experiment. Frequently riders go " off form ", and after weeks of results which are anything but profitable it is sometimes discovered that a minor adjustment on the machine makes all the difference between success and failure.

Are there any brakes on a speedway machine?

No, nor is there a gear box. Gear ratios are changed instead. Riders fit different gears according to the track. A mistake in " gear reckoning " can lose a match.

Are all the tracks the same size?

No. They vary considerably, and that is why a rider on his own track has a definite advantage over his opponents. However, First Division stars can master almost any track. The number of tracks changes yearly, but thirty is the average total.

Which track is the most thrilling?

That, of course, is a matter of opinion. My own choice is the Odsal track in Bradford. Peculiarly enough, the track which to me is the least inspiring is the one which stages the World Championships—Wembley.

What countries supply the most famous riders?

England and Australia. An American once won the World's Championship, but most of the competitors are either English or Australian. Test matches between the two countries are held yearly.

What speed is normally reached in a speedway race?

This is rather a difficult question to answer. It depends on the type of track. The shorter the straights, the slower the speed. Forty to fifty miles per hour is the average.

Is the clerk of the course in charge of a meeting?

The real controller is the steward officially appointed by the A.C.U., but the clerk of the course is in charge of the organization and the programme. The steward has the last word on all decisions.

Are women allowed to take part ?

No. There is a definite ban on women racing. In the early days of the sport there were two famous women riders—Eva Asquith and Fay Taylor.

If one decided to become a speedway rider, is the initial outlay considerable?

I should say it is in the region of £150. All riders must provide the regulation riding-suit known as " leathers ", riding-boots, crash-helmets and so on, as well as purchasing a machine which costs from £75 upwards. Another point which must be included in " initial expenditure " is the time-lag between learning and earning.

Keeping a bicycle in trim is a fairly expensive item, and there is no guarantee that any winnings will come the beginner's way, except of course starting money, which may only be £1 a race. Novices seldom get more than one or two races per meeting.

Do all riders go to a training-school before being allowed to ride at a track?

No, but it is useful to have spent some time at a training-school. For years a great weakness in the sport has been the lack of such schools, but now there are several both in England and in Scotland.

Is cycle speedway a great help to young fellows who want eventually to become speedway riders?

I should say that it is. It accustoms them to " taking tumbles " if nothing else, and quite a number of the riders of to-day have taken part in cycle speedway.

How long will speedway racing continue to flourish?

As long as it continues to be a good clean sport with no gambling element.

KINGS OF THE RING AND SOME OTHER CHAMPIONS OF SPORT

Of all the people whose business it is to keep in the public eye, few attract more notice or arouse more frankly expressed likes and dislikes than the champion heavyweight boxer. He may be (and usually is) quite a simple sort of person, more gifted with brawn than brains; but because he is so much stronger and tougher than other men, because his road to fame has been hard, and also because he invariably possesses an excellent press agent, he appeals to the elemental in all of us; and we feel his biceps, and measure his wrist, height and reach, with a gusto worthier of a better object.

Nor does he ever hide his light under a bushel. The famous old-time champion John L. Sullivan used to walk about the town saying, " I am John L. Sullivan, and I can lick any man in the world "; and so he could, until one day a comparative youngster named James J. Corbett thrashed him soundly. Sullivan's spirit was the spirit of them all, even though some of them have merely thought it; without that sublime self-confidence they would never have become champions at all.

I can remember the days when champions fought for very modest sums, for it was not until 1910 that the famous Jeffries-Johnson battle set a new standard and even the loser gained a fortune. Farther back—before my time, of course—the old pugs of the prize-ring battled with each other largely because that was their nature, the purse fifty, twenty, even ten pounds. The champion of England would fight for a hundred pounds if need be. Not infrequently, too, these old exponents of the noble art put up a far better show than many a so-called champion does to-day; and at least they knew how to hurt when they hit.

One of these men, possibly the greatest of them, and himself once world's champion, was old Jem Mace; he had fought both with bare fists and with gloves (the latter being known as a boxing contest, as officially it always is to-day); and he was in the sixties when another Englishman, almost at the close of his career, brought back the title to England from America for the last time, more than

sixty years ago. This was Robert Fitzsimmons, a slender and by
no means awe-inspiring man to look at, a Cornishman, who was
matched against Corbett in 1897. " Fitz ", as everybody knew him,
was little more than a middle-weight, but he was a crafty boxer
and had a tremendous punch. His favourite blow, directed upwards
at the solar plexus, put paid to many an opponent. Corbett was
big, graceful, popular, a beautiful boxer, and he had reigned undisputed for about five years, when the ageing Fitzsimmons climbed
into the ring to meet him. He thought so little of his challenger

that both he and his father staked large sums on the result; but
to the surprise of everybody Fitzsimmons knocked him out (1897).
This was the last time that an Englishman held the coveted title.

Then came Jeffries, whom I at least believed to be the greatest
of them all. James J. Jeffries had a clean sheet. He was never beaten,
and he never looked like being beaten, until he retired; and this is
still a unique record, for both Dempsey and Louis took hidings early
in their careers. If I remember aright, Jeffries was not exceptionally
tall, about 6 ft. 1½ in., but he was tremendously powerful and muscular, so that beside almost all his opponents men called him " The
Big Fellow ". He began in the usual way, as a sparring partner to
the older champions. Then he three times defeated a determined
and plucky little sailor named Sharkey (no connexion with Jack
Sharkey, who was world's champion for a short time some twenty
years ago, and who was really a Lithuanian). In 1899, Jeffries got

his chance of a match against Fitzsimmons. The old champion was
still extremely dangerous, as he could punch his way out of almost
anything; but Jeffries, though outboxed and outfought during
the earlier rounds, wore him down (as he did all his opponents in
turn) and eventually knocked him out.

The new king of the ring was not allowed to rest on his laurels
for long. Corbett challenged him, although at that time thirty-seven
years old; and, in 1900, in one of the greatest fights ever seen, he
battered and boxed Jeffries all over the ring for 21 rounds. (World-
title fights in those days were usually fought to a finish.) But it
made no difference. Jeffries would not yield, and in the 23rd round
Corbett received his quietus. Subsequently the Big Fellow met both
these redoubtable opponents again, when he defeated each of them
much more easily; for he had the essential quality of Dempsey and
Louis, in that he was quick to learn. He retired in 1905, still unbeaten, at the age of thirty-one, and took up alfalfa farming in the
Western States.

Jeffries was followed by the famous Tommy Burns, an Australian,
less than 5 ft. 8 in. tall. Burns was built like an inverted pyramid,
all muscular shoulders and chest; he was a crafty boxer and in-
fighter, extraordinarily quick on his feet. He did not reign long,
for hot on his trail came three equally famous negroes, Sam MacVea,
Sam Langford, and Jack Johnson, of whom Johnson was beyond
question the best.

In those days a widespread prejudice existed against boxing
matches between black and white, and it was nearly two years before
Johnson, after chasing Burns all round the world, at length got him
into the ring in Sydney in 1908. John Arthur Johnson was altogether
a better fighter and boxer than Tommy Burns. He was a strange
type, however, with a lot of negro irresponsibility about him, and
was extraordinarily unpopular, largely because of his behaviour in
the ring. He would jeer at and taunt his opponents even while he
outfought them; also, he married a white wife, and as the colour
bar was so strong this put him almost beyond the pale. A man of
magnificent physique, he was nearly as tall and powerfully built as
Jeffries himself, but slighter in the legs, and he was a superlatively
good boxer, though not always punching his weight. In the first
round against Burns he stepped up to the little Australian and
floored him. Burns fought on, though dazed, and could not be
knocked out, until at last the police intervened and stopped the

fight. " Li'l Arthur ", as Johnson was sarcastically known, had become champion of the world.

Johnson's subsequent indiscretions in no wise removed the prejudice against him; but there was nobody in the world, with one exception, who could stand a chance against the mighty " Jack Johnson " punches of which the champion was capable. I well remember that once he was giving an exhibition in a London music-hall when someone in the circle shouted a rude remark. Johnson had been punching the ball. He looked up, showed his teeth in the famous grin, and with a single blow sent the punch-ball clean off its chain and across the theatre to the offender. He was so tough, too, that he would allow you to hit him on the arm, and if you did it with unprotected fists you merely got sore knuckles! This was the man to whom promoters, despairing of finding anyone younger, at last induced Jeffries to give challenge after five years' absence from the ring.

The old champion, although affecting to regard the new one with contempt, took the match very seriously indeed. He spent almost a year in training; and when at last he climbed into the ring at Reno, Nevada, on Independence Day, 1910, before an enormous crowd, he *looked* like the Jeffries of old, all rugged muscles and hairy chest, in a word, the Big Fellow once more. But Jeffries was thirty-seven, and unlike Corbett or Fitzsimmons at that age, had given up boxing entirely. He had certainly lost some of the most essential points of a champion, continuity of training and judgment of distance in particular, and internally he was not as fit as he looked. Also the day was exceedingly hot (the fight was staged in the open air), and this told on the white man more than on the champion.

The fight itself was disappointing. Johnson was determined to make Jeffries do all the running about and he succeeded. In the early rounds there was too much wrestling; then Jeffries suddenly released a terrific blow, a curious sort of uppercut, but Johnson luckily got his head out of the way, or the fight would have ended there and then. In the eighth round Jeffries landed a tremendous body blow which could be heard all over the arena. It pulled up Johnson short, and two similar blows a little later did him no good. But he was giving two, three, even four blows for one. At the end of the tenth round Johnson was becoming anxious, for Jeffries looked in his corner just as immobile and granite-like as of yore. In the next round, however, the old champion began to weaken, and Johnson, sensing it instantly, started to set about him. But Jeffries would not yield, even though, in the fifteenth round, he was compelled to hang on for dear life and his feet dragged across the ring. Johnson fiercely shook himself free and for the first time in in his life Jim Jeffries went down. Shortly afterwards he was counted out.

This famous fight made fortunes for both men and for the promoter, Tex Rickard, the takings amounting to no less than $270,000, an enormous sum for those days. Jeffries now had plenty of offers to fight again, but he refused them all; his pride in his wonderful record had been smashed and never again did he compete in the ring. As to " Li'l Arthur ", his victory gave rise to acute racial jealousies in the United States; but nothing could be done about it, because there was nobody in the world left to beat him. He held the title until 1915, and might have held it much longer had he not been beaten by sheer exhaustion into throwing in the sponge. It was during his reign that the expression " White Hope " came into use, being applied to any white man who looked to have even a remote chance against him. There was quite a series of these White Hopes, but they all fell before the mighty Jack, except one.

This was Bombardier Billy Wells, a giant Englishman who, from being Army amateur champion in India, had graduated into the British championship, and whose personality was as striking as his luck was bad. Wells stood about 6 ft. 3 in. He was a first-class boxer, very quick, and with a punch like the kick of a mule; most of his fights lasted only a round or two. While still on the upgrade, and undefeated, he was matched against Johnson in London; but— perhaps inadvisedly—some good-natured people protested that he stood no chance, the Home Secretary intervened, and the match was banned. Johnson went back to America and Wells lost his chance for ever.

Wells, by the way, was one of those unfortunate athletes who help others to success at their own expense; but he was a likeable fellow, an all-rounder who played soccer well, and could row and run, so that the public never seemed to tire of him, even though he earned for British boxers the contemptuous title of " horizontal heavyweights ". His great weakness was that his body muscles were not sufficiently robust. He could not assimilate a really heavy body blow, and once this was discovered he was repeatedly knocked out by that means. He was also much too good-natured ever to become a world's champion. For instance, he once fought the young and rising French star Georges Carpentier and had him practically beaten in the first few minutes; then Wells, half out of pity, eased up, and was soon after knocked out himself for his pains.

To return to Jack Johnson, a man was found at last who could stand up to him, in the person of giant Jesse Willard, 6 ft. 6 in. tall and some 18 stone in weight, who towered above the champion and was also strong enough to absorb all the black man's blows. Johnson fought himself to a state of weariness; then he allowed himself to be knocked down, and lay on the canvas looking at the sky until he had been counted out. Along with Corbett and Tunney, he was one of the three finest boxer-fighters of this century.

Willard reigned during most of the first World War, but not for long thereafter. He then accepted a challenge from Jack Dempsey, popularly known as the Manassa Mauler, and one of the greatest fighters of any age.

Dempsey's heart had been in fighting ever since he was a boy. He learned his craft the hard way and had spent many years knocking about the States without attracting any particular notice. After one early beating, however, he went on from success to success until he was considered fit to fight the champion. From the waist up Jack Dempsey was magnificently built, but his ankles and wrists were rather weak, and to strengthen them (he tells us in his fascinating book *Round by Round*) he spent hours on end in monotonous exercises, bending his wrists to and fro. More than any other boxer Dempsey was the exponent of two-handed fighting. He did not stand in the classic English attitude, with the left arm forward, but was on his toes all the time, weaving and bobbing from side to side so as to keep himself out of danger, yet ready on the instant to spring forward, with a punch in either hand that would fell an ox; nevertheless, he did not hit straight as a rule, relying mainly on devastating left or right hooks. Out of the ring he was a quiet fellow, a good sportsman, and good company; in it, he was a savage and ruthless fighter par excellence, never pausing until the bout had ended. To make himself seem more terrifying to his opponents (or perhaps it was only to protect his chin) he generally grew a couple of days' beard before a fight.

In the year before he met Willard he had no fewer than forty contests, winning the lot, usually by an early knockout; for literally nobody could stand toe to toe with the dark-skinned Mauler and

survive for long. Curiously enough, Willard, who had to make a
choice among several challengers, elected to fight Dempsey, as he
seemed the easiest; but his judgment was woefully at fault. Dempsey, on the other hand, thought so little of the giant cowboy that
he promised himself to knock him out in a single round, and he
even backed himself heavily to do so. The fight took place on 4th
July, 1919, at Toledo, Ohio, before the largest audience yet seen
at a boxing match; the takings, $454,000, were a foretaste of the
enormous fortune which Dempsey was to amass through his fists
in the next eight years. From the moment the gong went, the
challenger dashed at Willard like a fury, and in fact he almost did
knock him out in the first round. The bewildered giant never stood
a chance. It was all over in the third round.

Jack Dempsey afterwards fought many famous battles. One,
against a giant " Argentine Bull ", named Firpo, who was almost as
big as Willard, provided a first-class sensation and proved the great
fighting heart of the champion. Firpo was no boxer, but he was
as strong as a bull. After taking a good deal of punishment he suddenly charged at the champion, and by sheer momentum knocked
him clean out of the ring. Dempsey fell on to a typewriter among the
reporters beside the ropes. Strictly, there was time for him to be
counted out, but the excitement was so great that the referee forgot
to count. Dempsey shouted " Push me back, boys ", was shoved
up to the boards again, and soon afterwards put paid to Firpo's
account.

Then there was the famous match against Carpentier, the French
" Prince Charming " of the ring. Carpentier was a very good boxer,
without being in the highest class, but also a plucky and indomitable
fighter. He had gone through every stage from the lightweights
upwards, and he reached the top partly by sheer grit and partly, too,
through the skill of his wily manager, François Descamps. Carpentier
never attained quite the size or weight for a world-beater, being
only about 12½ stone in weight; but he was easily the most attractive
" draw " in the game, and he saw his life's ambition realized when
he was matched at last against Dempsey—" Romance versus a
Sledge-hammer ", it was described at the time.

They met on 2nd July, 1921, at Jersey City, near New York,
before an immense crowd, the takings exceeding $1,600,000. Demp-
sey had a shrewd manager too. They had heard of the Frenchman's
craft and skill, and part of the champion's training was deliberately

to stick his jaw out and invite his sparring partners to wallop it; a
curious piece of prevision, as events turned out. In the first round
Carpentier, whose white body looked quite slight beside the swarthy
skin and huge frame of the champion, sprang at his man like a
tiger; there was no mercy on either side. In this round honours
were even. In the next round, while Dempsey was carrying out his
usual weaving tactics, the Frenchman sized him up with a half
smile, and suddenly released a tremendous punch to the chin. It
just missed the vital spot that would have sent him to sleep; as it
was, Dempsey went grey, wobbled at the knees, and hung on. For
the moment, Carpentier fancied that the coveted crown was to be
his; but Dempsey, like Jim Jeffries, was at his greatest when in
trouble. Carpentier made the mistake of trying to swap punches
with him. He received some terribly punishing body blows, two of
his ribs being broken. In the fourth and final round Dempsey broke
through his guard and knocked him out.

Although repeatedly called on to defend his title, Dempsey
seemed invulnerable against all comers until he should elect to
retire; and in the meantime he made a lot of money by acting in
films, at which he proved to be quite a good performer. But Nemesis
was on his track. A man can remain champion of the world only
by keeping continually up to the mark, otherwise he is apt to get
slower of foot and fist, and to lose his judgment and mastery.
Dempsey had not yet reached this stage, but he was on the way,
when a challenger appeared who could give as good as he took, and
who, like Dempsey himself, did not know what it was to be beaten.

This was Gene Tunney, a magnificently built athlete, fully equal
to the champion in that respect, and a better boxer; in fact, Tunney
was probably the best heavyweight *boxer* since Corbett. Tunney
used his head. He studied the champion, and he practised and
practised again and again, until sure that he could beat him. Then
the first of their two famous fights was arranged, in 1926. Tunney
not only stood up to his man, but beat him, although he could not
knock him out; again the match brought both men a fortune.

Dempsey, however, was not finished with; for, on 22nd September, 1927, he met Tunney for the second time, at Chicago.
Once more the crowd was a record, the takings reaching the extraordinary figure of $2\frac{3}{4}$ million dollars. It was a worthy fight, with
Tunney getting rather the best of it during the early rounds. He had
been warned to avoid the old champion's right hand at all costs,

4*   (G 487)

but in a moment of carelessness he forgot, and Dempsey promptly brought over a powerful hook and down went the champion. The referee commenced to count. Now Dempsey himself had been instrumental in making a rule that when one boxer was down the other should retire to a neutral corner; but in the heat of the battle he omitted to do so, and stood over his man waiting to deliver the coup de grâce should he get up. Tunney lay dazed, while the referee motioned Dempsey aside and started to count again. At the count of nine Tunney regained his feet. Dempsey sprang at him and knocked him all over the ring; but by sheer blind fighting skill he weathered the storm. In the eighth round it was nearly as bad; then Tunney emerged on top, Dempsey fell away, and at the end Tunney won on points. He was known thereafter as the Thirteen Seconds champion, although, of course, it was Dempsey's own fault.

Tunney reigned only for a year, won one other fight, and then retired. His heart, he said, was not in the game. He had seen in boxing an easy way to make a fortune and he had proved his theory. An intellectual among boxers (who as a rule do not shine in that respect), he did not last at the top long enough to show us all that he might have done; yet he undoubtedly has a great place in ring history.

Tunney's retirement brought the usual crowd of contenders for the vacant honour. They included many good boxers, but none of outstanding merit, and several men held the championship in turn for a brief space; such were Jack Sharkey, a hefty Lithuanian; Max Schmeling, a fine boxer and a German; Primo Carnera, the celebrated " man-mountain ", an Italian giant of terrific physique but no great skill; and Max Baer, who spoiled what might have been a great career by his undependable qualities. Finally came James P. Braddock, another good boxer rather than a fighter, who, in 1937, was knocked unconscious by the already famous " Brown Bomber ", Joe Louis. This brings us to the last of our boxing champions.

The wheel had now turned full circle since Jack Johnson's days and a negro was once more heavyweight champion of the world; but the times were different and Louis himself was a very different type from the mercurial Jack, being strictly under control both within the ring and without it. He held the title for twelve years, a longer time than any of his predecessors; this in itself proves his

outstanding merit. But that he was better than Dempsey at his best
—he came nearest to Dempsey, perhaps, in style and fighting tactics
—is doubtful, and he certainly would never have beaten Jeffries or
Corbett in their prime, while Tunney, one feels sure, would have
been a match for him.

But all in all the Brown Bomber was a great champion. He
fought for his title more than a score of times, and usually won
quickly by a knockout; only once until 1947 (when he was ageing
and on the decline) did anyone last the full distance with him, and
that was when he fought Tommy Farr in 1937.

We must spare a word or two for Farr, if only because he was
the first British contender for the crown since Fitzsimmons held it
forty years before. His career must have seemed strange to onlookers, as if he rose like a rocket and fell like the stick. Really,
however, he was ten years in boxing his way to recognition as a
world-contender. When he knocked out the enormously strong
and bear-like German, Walter Neusel, and then easily defeated the
ex-world's champion Max Baer, it was obvious that his chance had
come; nevertheless, good judges in America thought that Farr
stood not the slightest chance against Louis. Farr went over to
New York full of Welsh confidence, got well acclimatized, and
gave the champion the surprise of his life; for he not only lasted
the distance (15 rounds), but in the opinion of many people, including the writer, had the bout been fought to a finish Farr would
have won. In the last two rounds Louis had a very bad time, and he
afterwards admitted—a charming thing about Louis was his frank
self-criticism—" Farr fooled me completely ". Alas, poor Farr! He
might have been given another chance, but the preliminary " testing "
bouts against Braddock and Max Baer went against him; he was
beaten yet again, and then retired. Farr's great weakness was a failure
to punch heavily enough, a common fault among modern boxers.

As to Louis, he went on from success to success, knocking out
his opponents with almost contemptuous ease, until he received
another severe jolt, just ten years after the Farr fight. He was fighting
Joe Walcott, a veteran negro; and Walcott not only knocked the
champion down by way of preliminary, but in a later round did it
again; nevertheless, Louis won on points. The two men met again
in 1948, when Louis won easily; then he hung up his gloves and so
brought to a close one of the finest careers in boxing history.

There have been quite a number of heavyweight world champions since Louis retired, but not one, in my opinion, of the same calibre as the older kings of the ring, except perhaps that redoubtable and rather savage battler, Rocky Marciano.

.   .   .   .

Turning from the hectic atmosphere of the prize-ring to some quieter types of sport, one outstanding performer whose name leaps to everyone's mind is Denis Compton, the Middlesex and England cricketer, and also a great footballer (he was Arsenal's left winger) who, in 1958 retired from first class-cricket after years of pain from a damaged knee.

Compton, one of those rare characters whom success cannot spoil, endeared himself to cricket and football fans everywhere, not only by his brilliant batting, bowling and play on the football field, but also by his unvarying good sportsmanship and cheerfulness. Fortune smiled upon him from the start, but to fortune had to be added much hard work. As a boy, Denis showed a great aptitude for both cricket and football, and was chosen to play for the London Elementary Schools against the Public Schools at Lord's. In that match (1932), the boy not only scored 114 runs but also—an important matter for his future—attracted the attention of Sir Pelham Warner. He was invited to join the ground staff at Lord's; and as a similar opportunity on the ground staff of the famous Arsenal team arose soon afterwards, it was arranged that professional sport should be his career.

Young Compton learned quickly in those two great nurseries of

famous players, but what helped him most was that he possessed
the ideal temperament for big occasions, seeming quite unruffled
or overawed however important the match or critical his team's
position. In his first season for Middlesex he scored more than a
thousand runs. After getting his first England cap against the New
Zealanders (at the Oval) he was rarely out of an England eleven
—a marked contrast to his team-mate and partner Edrich, who
despite some brilliant performances was dropped by the selectors on
a number of occasions. Besides being a first-class batsman, Compton
was a brilliant field and he rated consistently high in the bowling
averages; his famous " Chinaman " (the leg-break ball which
" doesn't "), brought him many a wicket. He was apt at times,
when opening his innings, to scratch around uncertainly for a bit,
but once he had settled down there were few more stylish batsmen in
the country and none so consistently heart-breaking to bowl against.
Denis Compton's best season, perhaps, was in 1947, when he beat
Sir Jack Hobbs's long-standing record of 16 centuries for a season,
and also Tom Hayward's aggregate: Compton made 18 centuries
and scored 3816 runs that year. In the Test Matches he made 753
runs, and with the other " Middlesex Twin ", Edrich, made one
stand of 370 runs, another of 228, and altogether this pair in that
season collected seven double centuries!

Compton also went out with the tourists to South Africa, where
he collected 1781 runs, another record. His pluck was outstanding.
It was particularly shown during a match against the Australians in
1948, when their fast bowler Lindwall was sending up some dangerous
stuff. Compton unluckily played one of these fast rising balls on to
his forehead and was knocked out. He had to have stitches put in
the wound, but returned to the game, at a critical moment for England
and stayed there till the end, scoring 145 not out. In his later years
he also often batted and fielded well, despite the handicap of a
permanently damaged knee.

Denis Compton was equally popular among Arsenal supporters,
and had ten International caps to his credit. He was extremely fast
on the wing and a wizard at heading the ball. He was a fortunate
man to be so outstanding in two great national sports and in two of
the best teams in the country.

At the close of the 1948 season there retired from Test Match
cricket the greatest run-getter in history, the formidable and never-
to-be-forgotten " Don ", who for twenty years had defied some of

the best bowlers in the world; upon his retirement he received the honour of knighthood and became Sir Donald Bradman. What an amazing cricketer the little Australian wizard was! He was worth his place in the team for his captaincy alone, and in the eyes of many people he *was* the team; the usual query being not " How are the Australians doing?" but " Is Bradman out?"

Bradman was largely self-taught, but was a complete master of every stroke in the book. Quick-witted, lynx-eyed, self-possessed, he attained also a wonderful precision of footwork and balance, and one felt sure that even if he stumbled he would hit the ball. He played to rule and his rule was to make as many runs as possible; not for him the tactics of Hobbs and many another famous bat, who after completing their century would gaily throw away their wicket; one century was simply the stepping-stone to the next for Bradman. But for a weakness for attempting wild hooks from impossible angles, which frequently brought about his downfall, there was no particular reason why he should ever have got out.

Of course, he was mainly a good-wicket batsman, as is naturally the case with most New South Wales and Queensland cricketers; but he was also completely master of bad-wicket tactics (though he must have learned them in this country), his defensive strokes and speedy footwork saving many a time in critical situations when others would have failed. Needless to say, he scored ducks; almost every great batsman has quite a collection of them, and I seem to remember that once the immortal Hobbs collected " a pair ". But with Bradman a duck was something to be remembered. Like Compton, he had the ideal temperament for the big occasion. He would stroll casually out to the wicket, his eyes shaded by a big peaked cap, while he accustomed himself to the strong light; and then the leather-chasing began.

In his very first game of importance he scored a century; and before he was twenty-two he had made himself the sensation of the formidable team which visited England in 1930. He made 236 in his first match in England, 131 in his first Test Match, and followed it up with 254 at Lord's. A fortnight later, he made 309 at Leeds in a single day, and went on to score 334. Leeds was a happy ground for Bradman. In his last tour (1948), he made 173 not out there; and in the 1934 Test Match, he and the giant Ponsford added 388 for the fourth wicket. Ponsford, by the way, was a great defensive batsman, whose average rate of scoring was about 25 per hour;

but it was impossible to tempt him into risking his wicket, quite unlike his partner, who had all the great batsman's flair for hitting any ball anywhere if he had a mind to do so. This reminds us of Trevor Bailey to-day, who is just as exasperating at times to watch, and just as valuable to his side in saving the game.

Bradman had been captain of Australia before the war. He also captained the 1948 touring side and proved his title to rank among the best captains on record, his ability to place a field being extraordinary.

He had one weak spot, his " Achilles' heel ". Although he cared nothing for fast bowling, but smote it mercilessly, he both disliked and seemed almost to fear the notorious bumpers or " body-line " bowling of such men as little Larwood, the giant Bowes of Yorkshire, and Voce. In the famous Jardine tour, when Larwood in particular was raising a storm on Australian cricket fields by his body-line tactics, and quite a number of players were hurt, Bradman used to avoid injury by sheer quickness of foot. He would leap to one side and leave his wicket undefended; yet he was so quick that he could still take a swipe at the ball as it passed. These tactics paid, although once or twice the ball dropped on to his undefended wicket. For instance, at Melbourne, against this sort of bowling Bradman made 103 not out, the rest of his team only scoring 90 between them.

Mention of the big partnerships between Bradman and Ponsford recalls the happy fellowship of two other giants of cricket a little before Bradman's day, Herbert Sutcliffe and Jack Hobbs. Their most memorable effort, perhaps, was at the Melbourne Test in 1925. Australia had run up a huge first-innings total, 600, and the wicket was wearing when Hobbs and Sutcliffe started the next day's play and the England innings; they stayed there throughout the day, the score at the close of play being 283 for no wicket. Next day they carried the score to beyond 300, but the rest of the team failed miserably.

England, in those days, very largely relied on this first-wicket pair for their runs, and rarely did they fail them. In 25 Tests they made 15 first-wicket centuries, the finest being at the Oval, in 1926. The wicket was wet, after the Australians had had the advantage of a good day's play; it was feared that the whole England side would be skittled out for fifty. But Hobbs, who was probably the finest bad-wicket player in the world, slowly and skilfully mastered the bowling; and Sutcliffe, who always made all sorts of chancy shots off the edge of his bat with complete imperturbability, was equally impregnable; in the end Hobbs made a century and Sutcliffe went on to reach 161.

To the pleasure of all cricket-lovers, Hobbs was knighted a few years ago, the first professional cricketer apart from Bradman ever to receive this distinction.

One of the finest all-round cricketers of modern times retired just before Bradman's last tour; we refer, of course, to Walter R. Hammond, the massive and unshakable England captain, and for twenty-five years idol of Gloucestershire cricket. Hammond, who was heavily built, was a wonderful batsman to watch. He could clout the ball—" smite it " is perhaps a better expression—all over the field, but his driving to leg was a specially favourite stroke. He did all manner of things with impunity that men of less quick sight dared not attempt; and often scored by a horizontal mowing shot which is against all the rules of good batting! Twice in his career he made 13 centuries in a single season. Hammond was also a very good bowler, and as captain of England he was superlative.

Another great cricketer, who has recently retired, is Sir Leonard Hutton, the idol of Yorkshire and the captain of England in many a hard-fought Test. Hutton's record included 129 centuries and he won his England cap no fewer than 79 times. He had the ideal temperament for international cricket and no one could display better the dour fighting qualities of Yorkshire at the game; but he also belongs to the very small and select band of batsmen who have scored more than 3400 runs in a season (3429 in 1949). In his very first Test Match against Australia in 1938 he scored a century and at the Oval in the same season he notched 364 against the same unhappy opponents, this being the highest single innings ever made in a Test Match. Ten years later, at Johannesburg, Hutton and Washbrook put on 359 runs for the first wicket against South Africa —another record. Hutton received the rare but well-deserved distinction of knighthood in 1958.

One of the greatest personalities in cricket to-day, the Surrey and England captain Peter May, is also one of the world's great batsmen. He has all the strokes and when at his best is delightful to watch. May was born on the last day of 1929, so that he still has many years of good cricket before him.

We have no space for the other stalwarts of cricket lore, the Spofforths, the Tates, Cotters, Veritys, not to mention the remarkable spin bowlers G. R. Lock and J. C. Laker, the Bedser brothers and a score of others; not forgetting that wonderful little old-time bowler Colin Blythe, who was quite unplayable on a wet wicket. Laker has a unique distinction, for it was he who in 1956, during a Test Match against Australia, took 19 wickets for 90 runs, a feat which will probably never be repeated.

By comparison with footballers, cricketers or boxers, the champions of swimming and athletics received only the most scanty and indifferent public notice (except perhaps in Olympic Games years), until the advent of television, coupled with the support of one or two great national newspapers, brought athletics into the glare of publicity. Now, however, the tendency is too much the other way, and a few particularly adept young men and girls are receiving far more publicity than is good for them or for sport, while the many hundreds of good club runners, walkers, jumpers and swimmers, who are the very backbone of the sport, are almost ignored by those to whom " news " is everything. However, in this article we are only concerned with champions.

In the first edition of this book, we concentrated our attention largely upon the mile run, because that distance has long been considered as the hall-mark of running. Since that edition the dream of half a century has been realized and the famous 4-minute mile is now a matter of history. When I first entered athletics, the record for the mile stood at 4 min. 16 sec. It was held by a great little runner, Joe Binks, whom I knew well. To run a mile in 4 minutes then was regarded as impossible; but by a steady improvement in technique and in training methods, the time was shortened bit by bit, until in 1954, fifty-two years after Binks' record, the thing was done at last and Roger Bannister clocked under 4 minutes.

An American, J. P. James, brought the record down to 4 min. 14·4 sec. in 1913 and ten years later that wonderful Finn, P. Nurmi (of whom more below), smashed this by recording 4 min. 10·4 sec. Again ten years elapsed, until in 1933 J. E. Lovelock, a New Zealander and the most formidable rival of our own popular little champion Sydney Wooderson, achieved 4 min. 7·6 sec. In 1937 Wooderson, who for so small a man had a wonderful burst of speed, attained 4 min. 6·4 sec.; but he, like all the generation before him, believed in running the third lap comparatively slowly; one reason for this being that the athlete must have enough power in reserve to fight off any challenge during the vital last lap. Wooderson, however, succeeded in running three-quarters of a mile in 3 minutes, which perhaps started a new train of thought among coaches; meanwhile the two great Swedish runners Andersson and Haegg, between them knocked the bottom out of Wooderson's time and eventually brought the record down to just over 4 min. 1 sec. It was now obvious that before long the 4-minute mile must come. The honour fell to a tall

young medical student of Oxford, Roger Bannister, who in a set attack on the record after a long preparation, made athletics history by running a mile in 3 min. 59·4 sec. (6th May, 1954). Bannister was paced by two other first-class runners, C. Brasher and J. C. Chataway. Brasher led for the first half-mile and was then dropped, Chataway taking up the challenge, until in the last lap Bannister (who then as always ran himself completely out) leaped clean away from him. Bannister's record lasted only a few months, being beaten by a very remarkable runner and beautiful stylist, the Australian J. Landy. At the Empire Games in Vancouver, however, in one of the most thrilling " miles " on record, Bannister had his revenge, and outpaced Landy completely. Chataway, Derek Ibbotson and others, have all since beaten the 4-minute mile; but there has now emerged a young man who looks to be far better than any of them, H. (" Herb ") Elliott, an Australian, who without being in the least distressed, brought the time down to the amazing figure of 3 min. 54·5 sec. (1958). Elliott also in the same year brought the 1500-metre record down to 3·36.

One of the greatest middle-distance runners the world has yet seen was the famous " Flying Finn ", Paavo Nurmi, who ran all manner of distances up to the Marathon like a clock and even used a watch by which to check his progress. On his day, he could beat everyone who ever opposed him; but he was rather phlegmatic by temperament, and if he could only have been shaken out of his customary calm—as did happen once or twice in his long career— would undoubtedly have lowered more world's records than he did.

Like so many of his countrymen, Nurmi was a tall and beautifully built athlete. Even as a boy of eleven he could run a mile in 5½ min.; but he did not take up athletics seriously until 1914, when he was seventeen. He then won a 3000-metre race, covering the equivalent of 2 miles in 10 min. 50 sec. Improving steadily, he next won several 5000-metre (3-mile) races. In 1919, he entered for the Army championship " march " of 20 km., a rather trying event in which each man had to carry his full kit, including rifle, bandolier and pack. Running was permitted and Nurmi elected to run. He finished so far ahead of the other competitors that some doubt was raised as to whether he had really covered the course!

In 1920 he was chosen for the Antwerp Olympic Games, where he was second in the final of the 5000 metres and he won the 10,000 metres in 31 min. 45·8 sec. Next year he lowered the 10,000-metre record to 30 min. 40·2 sec., running to a schedule and with a watch in his hand. He also covered 5000 metres in 14 min. 53·8 sec., although losing a shoe and compelled to run without it for a mile. In the same year he did the mile in 4 min. 13·9 sec. and the 800 metres in 1 min. 58·4 sec. He was still on the upgrade, for, in 1922, he made new world's records for both the 2000 metres and 5000 metres, covering 3 miles in 14 min. 8·4 sec. The feature of all his great runs, too, was that at the end he was not in the least distressed, so that he must have still had a good deal in hand. In 1923 he brought down the figure for the mile to 4 min. 10·4 sec., only 1 second less than W. G. George's memorable effort of 1885.

Then, in 1924, when he was twenty-eight years old, he was chosen again to represent Finland in the Olympic Games, this time at Paris; and despite an injured knee he set up new world's records there for the 1500 metres and 5000 metres. To crown his efforts this year, in a trial run he covered 10,000 metres in 29 min. 58 sec., the fastest ever (though not officially a record). At Paris, too, he won a cross-country event over the same distance in boiling heat, with the temperature at 90 degrees, beating the next man (the famous Willie Ritola, himself a champion) by more than a minute. Finally, in 1931, this amazing runner, although then thirty-four years old, covered 25 miles of the Marathon distance in 2 hr. 22 min.; but his amateur status having by this time been called in question, he was debarred from competing in the Olympic Games. More than almost any other great runner, Nurmi ran to his schedule; the trouble was that his schedules were so fast as necessarily to shake off most of his competitors!

There have been many great runners at various distances since, but nobody, I think of the same calibre as Nurmi, except perhaps the lion-hearted Czech, E. Zatopek, who in 1951 clocked 48 min. 12 sec. for 10 miles and in 1955 when almost a veteran, ran 15 miles in 1 hr. 14 min. 1 sec. These are both world records.

Walkers come less into the limelight than runners, yet it is a harder sport than running, especially over the longer distances, and calls for great stamina, judgment and endurance. Great Britain has always had a majority of the world's best walkers, including such world's champions as T. W. Richardson (100 miles), A. H. G. Pope (10 miles), W. F. Baker (London to Brighton and back, 104 miles), and Lloyd Johnson, several times National Road Walking Champion (20 miles). It was the last-named who, after competing in the 1936 Olympic Games at Berlin, was again chosen for England in 1948. The event was the 50-km. (31½ miles) walk, the day a blazing hot one, and Lloyd Johnson, who is a very tall man with an immense stride, was forty-nine years old; yet he beat the best of our own men and finished third. In D. R. Thompson and T. Misson, England has two of the greatest middle-distance walkers in the world. Thompson in particular has repeatedly knocked the bottom out of the London-Brighton walking record and in 1959 was within an ace of capturing the world's 4-hour record. (Necessarily, official records must be made on the track, because of course no two roads are alike.)

It has been my fortune to know nearly all of these men, some of them well; but the finest walker of them all in my judgment was the late "Tommy" Hammond, of the Stock Exchange and Surrey Walking Clubs. Thomas E. Hammond was a Stock Exchange clerk who rose to be a broker. He was about six feet tall, fair, with attractive blue eyes, and of rather spare build. He served in the Boer War, as a result of which he found himself in ill-health, when it was re-commended that he should take up walking. He did so and competed in the original Stock Exchange London-to-Brighton Walk in 1903.

He walked like a soldier, with his arms at his sides, but finished third, in just over 9½ hr. A few years later he made a new record for that arduous journey of 8hr. 18 min. This has been beaten several times since, but the road is now much easier and the surface altogether better.

In 1907 Hammond walked the double journey to Brighton and back (104 miles) in 18 hr. 13 min., a marvellous performance which stood for twenty years. W. F. Baker beat it by 8 min. in 1926, on a vastly better and easier road; but with every respect to Baker, who was a magnificent walker, this was not equal to Hammond's effort on the rough road and steep gradients of Edwardian days. Like many other walkers, Hammond possessed indomitable pluck. On this particular occasion, he was prostrated at about seventy miles with cramp in the stomach and thereby lost twenty minutes; yet he went on to put up a performance which until Baker's achievement no walker believed would ever be bettered.

In the next year (1908), when the White City was opened and the great stadium there was receiving its baptism, a 24-hour walk was staged on the track. Hammond competed, and although off the track for times which must have totalled up to not far short of an hour, he covered 131 miles in the 24 hours, and he was still doing 5 miles per hour at the finish. Nothing like this has ever been done either before or since; moreover, it was *walked*, there never at any time being a suspicion that Hammond ran—which is more than can be said for some other " records ".

GET YOUR SKATES ON

I am sure that if you are a non-skater, you must often have said to yourself, after seeing someone skating on a frozen pond: " Oh, how I wish that I could skate!" Or perhaps it was a film you saw that made you decide that if you only had the chance, you would like to learn.

The graceful movements of the skating stars of the films afford shining examples of the heights to which the enthusiastic skater may rise. But these stars could not always skate, and most of them found themselves wishing, just as you may be wishing, that they could. And when their chance came along they seized it, so that each day, week, month, and year found them steadily improving until they became the fine performers they are to-day.

So you see that it is not a matter of being born a skater, for even the best have to learn in the same way as everyone else, and if they have become clever skaters, it is because they have shown greater love for the sport than have others, and have practised oftener, and with greater regularity.

Now you may be thinking to yourself: " But I don't want to be a *great* skater. I just want to be able to skate enough to get around the rink, or over the pond, to have fun with the others who can skate."

Well, why not? What others can do you can do, and if you are keen, and can persuade someone to buy you a pair of boots and skates for your birthday or at Christmas, then it need not be long before you are able to skate as well as most of the others.

However, do not be disheartened if you do not succeed in obtaining a pair of boots and skates of your own. Although this is advisable, there is another course which can be taken, for ice-rinks generally run a hiring system, and if the boots and skates which you hire are not in such good condition or are not as well fitting as a pair of your own would be, they are nevertheless satisfactory enough for the beginner.

If you are one of the more fortunate ones, and manage to obtain a pair of boots and skates of your own, then you must see that a good fit is obtained. Otherwise, if they are at all slack, you will soon discover that your attempts are awkward, because you will be inclined to wobble. Usually you will find you are fitted with a boot half a size smaller than the size you normally take for everyday wear.

The skates are bought separately and attached to the boots by screw-nails. This can be done where you buy them, or you may

Be prepared for a few falls

take them to the ice-rink where you intend to skate, and have them fitted by one of the attendants, who are, oftener than not, proficient at this work.

Anyone learning to skate must be prepared for a few falls, and for this reason, it is not advisable to wear your best clothes, as there is invariably a thin layer of water on the ice. I say a few falls, but do not be worried by this, for falling on ice is not quite the same as falling on a concrete pavement. When you fall on ice, you slide, and because you do there is less likelihood of hurting yourself.

You may know something about the training of paratroopers or Commandoes, in which the soldiers, jumping from heights or moving vehicles, are taught to perform somersaults on the ground to lessen the friction, and thus reduce the danger of injury. When you slide on ice after a fall, the friction is similarly reduced, and this results in less chance of hurt.

Whether you are learning to cycle, swim, or do anything else, *confidence* is of necessity the most essential factor, and so it is with skating. You would be better, when you go to the ice-rink, to leave behind your skates than to go without your confidence. So make up your mind that you are going to the rink to skate, not just to *try* to skate, but *to skate*.

There is little that can be written about the details of learning to skate, for as with most other things, it is the effort that counts.

Those of you who have little brothers and sisters may be able to recall the manner in which they first learnt to walk, and how they kept falling after every few steps. One step and then a fall; two steps and then a fall; three steps and then a fall; and so it went on until the time came when they could walk right across the room.

This is the way you must learn to skate. There is no other way. You will fall over and over again, after one step, two steps, three steps—until you can travel right around the rink.

Now, although I have used the word step, I use this only to illustrate the point. You do not step when you skate. You push and glide.

When you push, you do so with the inner side of the blade at an angle, and this is the point which the beginner must observe. The toes must be turned outward, so that the sharp inner edge of one blade will be able to brake against the ice. Then you push, and the other foot will glide forward. It is because they do not know this that so many beginners have difficulty in learning. They think that if they stand as they would before commencing to walk, toes to the front, they need only to push with one foot and the other will travel forward. The very opposite is the result. The foot with which they have pushed has had no way of gripping the ice, and so a fall ensues. But if the foot is turned out at an angle before the push, the entire inner rim of the blade will grip the ice, and presto, you're off. If you keep this in mind, success will come quickly.

Many who have learnt to skate have done so with the assistance of others, using them more or less as a support, while there are those again who have learnt by their own initiative, using the barrier as a support, and moving slowly around the rink, bit by bit.

For my part, I am inclined to favour the second method, if for no other reason than it is more likely to breed confidence, and make the learner feel more independent. And when you fall, you soon discover how quickly and easily with the aid of the barrier you can regain your feet.

What the beginner should bear in mind when he falls is that every other person on the ice around him has had to undergo the same experience that he himself is having. Even that beautiful girl, who is often to be seen in the middle of the rink cutting sweeping figures, will repeatedly come close to falling, as she endeavours to execute new and more complicated movements. And if she is not afraid of falling, then why should you be?

After you have become sufficiently skilful to skate around the rink, there are many courses open to you. Rinks have figure-skating, speed-skating, and ice-hockey clubs which the enthusiast may join.

First, let us compare the types of skates and boots that are used, for each group uses a different type.

Figure-skates, the type with which you should have been supplied when you began, or which you get from the skate-hire service, differ from the other two types mainly in that they curl up at the front, almost on to the toe of the boot. Little teeth have been cut out of this part of the skate, and these are used in the various movements which go to make up the art of figure-skating. At the rear, the blade of the skate juts out about an inch from the heel of the boot.

Speed-skates, on the other hand, are quite different, their most noticeable feature being the length of the blade, which extends well out in front of and behind the boot. Unlike figure-skates, they are not made in one piece, but the blade, because it is much thinner than the blade of the figure-skate, is fitted into a tubular piece of metal. This is for strength. The blade does not curl up at the front, but sticks straight out ahead of the boot, and is connected to the body of the skate by a thin straight strip of metal. There is not much difference in the make-up of the speed-skating boot, except that it is heelless, shorter in the ankle, and the lacing begins nearer to the toe.

The hockey-skate differs from both figure- and speed-skates;

in that the blade is thin and fitted into a metal tube, it resembles the speed-skate, but here the similarity ends. The blade is shorter than are the other two types in order to give the player greater manœuvrability, perhaps the most essential thing in ice-hockey playing, and it projects little at either end of the boot.

It is in the design of the hockey-boot, however, that the greatest difference is to be seen, for it is more like a football-boot than a skating-boot; it has a toe-cap, which appears to be ordinary enough, but which, in actual fact, consists of steel covered over with leather, as it is very necessary that the ice-hockey boot be strong, and give good protection. The stitching is very heavy. A point of interest is that although the boot does not possess a heel, both skate and boot are so designed that the player's heel is raised slightly, so that he can effect the crouch position, in which he must play, with greater ease.

So much for the skates and boots. Next let us consider the different groups in turn.

First comes Figure-skating.

For the boy who is in a position to afford it, there are figure-skating instructors, who, having made a profession of skating and obtained awards for their proficiency, charge a fee for their services.

But here again, there is an alternative—in the figure-skating clubs which I have already mentioned. For a comparatively small annual subscription, the would-be figure-skater can indulge in the privileges which these clubs have acquired. These privileges amount to the use, at certain times, of the rink, and of the section of the ice known as end-ice. Here young figure-skaters may practise their difficult evolutions free from intrusion, and under the guidance of senior members or club-instructors. Then should you become good enough, there is always the chance of skating your way into one of the local competitions. If you can prove your skill in one of these and win an award, then there is no saying where you may end up. Just keep remembering that the best always start at the bottom—no higher!

The movements are many and often complicated, the figure-eight being a favourite. How intricate and beautiful these figures are, you will probably have come to know for yourselves, from glimpses you may have caught of the ice-stars on the films, or, if lucky, at ice-revues.

And now let us turn to Speed-skating.

The fascination of speed must surely appeal to all, and speed-skating, although not quite as popular as figure- and hockey-skating, nevertheless has many enthusiasts. Should you decide that this is to be your choice, again you will have to join one of the clubs, for true speed-skating is not allowed during regular hours at the rink. Arrangements are made with the management by speed-skating clubs, and certain times are allotted for the speed-skaters' practice. Then, of course, a coach will be available to give instruction.

Speed-skaters also have their competitions. Speed leagues have been formed, and picked competitors from the different clubs race against one another. At the end of the season one of the teams, having skated its way to the top of the league, is declared the champion. England and Scotland both have their own leagues, and on occasion representatives of each country meet in an international race.

Lastly, we have Ice-hockey.

Ice-hockey originated in Canada and is played by Americans and Canadians alike, and is now fast taking hold in this country. To-day, the demand is for youth—British youth. The ice-hockey game needs native players, for popular as it is, in order to keep the standard of play at its highest the people who promote ice-hockey are forced to go to the land of its birth for players.

The ice-hockey teams throughout this country are made up, very largely, of Canadians. But the people want to see British players, and so clubs have been formed, and young Britishers are fast being introduced to the game.

You can be an ice-hockey player. If you have mastered the art of ordinary skating, ask to see the ice-hockey coach at your rink, and have him put your name down for one of the " Pee-wee " teams, made up of boys aged between twelve and fifteen. The next step comes when you are called to a special practice session to show what you can do. Should the coach decide that you show promise, then the day will not be far away when you will find yourself out beneath the lights, playing a quick game with other youngsters, before or after one of the senior matches.

Well, there you are—figure-, speed-, and hockey-skating. Take your choice.

To the boy or girl in Canada or in the northern states of the United States, ice-skating is a popular pastime that is to be enjoyed, not only in the ice-rinks, but also on the frozen surfaces of ponds, lakes and rivers—often at night-time by the light of lanterns and fires. In Canada the authorities encourage the boys and girls, to the extent of erecting boards around the playgrounds in the winter months, and having the areas flooded by the fire-department.

But Canada and the United States are not the only countries that indulge enthusiastically in ice-skating, and everyone knows how popular the sport is on the Continent, in Switzerland, and other places.

It is indeed unfortunate for the British ice-skater that his climate is so mild in the winter months. Were this not the case, much money could be saved. But remember that, should you become a regular attender at a rink, you may find it cheaper, in the long run, to make use of a season ticket.

You will enjoy skating at the ice-rink, but when a chance comes to skate over a frozen pond in the crisp winter air, you will enjoy it very much more, for outdoors there is an invigoration to be found that is lacking inside the rink. Certainly you may miss the music of an indoor rink, which has a rhythm designed to help the skater, but that is more than compensated for by the natural surroundings proper to the sport, and the exhilaration of swooping across the ice, warmly clad and glowing with the exercise, and feeling the clear air rushing past your face.

I have always enjoyed ice-skating, and, although I was a little more fortunate, in that I learnt outdoors at an early age on the vast frozen surface of the St. Lawrence river in Canada, there is no reason why you, even with the climate against you, should not learn to enjoy it to the same extent. So get your skates on, and go to it! Good luck!

YOUTH HOSTELLING

The year 1930 was very important for the youth of Britain. In England the Youth Hostels Association was formed, and in Scotland preparatory steps were taken which led to the formation of the Scottish Youth Hostels Association the following year.

Broadly speaking, the aim of both associations is to help all, especially young people of limited means, to a greater knowledge, love, and care of the countryside by providing simple hostel accommodation for them on their travels.

Twenty years have passed, years which have seen steady progress, and now Britain is dotted over with hundreds of hostels for the use of out-of-door enthusiasts.

After you have decided to begin hostelling, the first step is to buy or order a current hostel handbook, price 9d., at a stationer's. It is the type of publication which would give much pleasure to those imaginary people who are constantly being shipwrecked on desert isles, so full is it packed with interesting and varied details, though it might prove cruel to them too in their enforced isolation, for there is something about a hostel handbook which fires the imagination and makes one want to look up railway time-tables right away.

From the handbook you learn the address to which you send your application and annual subscription. The former is according to the district you live in, the latter according to your age.

Scotland.

Juvenile membership (over 5 years and under 16 years), 2s.
Junior membership (over 16 years and under 21 years), 5s.
Senior membership (over 21 years), 10s.
Life membership, £5.

England and Wales.

Juvenile membership (over 5 years and under 16 years), 5s.
Junior membership (over 16 years and under 21 years), 10s.
Senior membership (over 21 years), 15s.
Life membership, £6 6s.

You will notice that although the youth hostel associations are primarily intended for youth, there is no age limit as there is in some Continental countries, Switzerland for example. Here in Britain you may totter around from hostel to hostel until you drop at the age of ninety or more.

In your application for membership you state your name and address and your age, as you are under twenty-one; you enclose a postal order for the amount, and a stamped self-addressed envelope. If you live in Scotland the next step is to have a passport photograph taken. Why? This is intended to prevent the misuse of membership cards, though I have heard the suggestion made that it is to introduce a little mirth into the lives of the wardens who will see it.

Before the card is valid there are several things to do to it. You sign it, paste in the photograph, and take it either to your district office or to a warden to have the photograph vouched for. A list of wardens authorized to perform this rite is given in the handbook.

You are now a member with the many privileges which membership bestows and with the responsibilities too. Your signature on the card commits you to a promise to respect and preserve the amenities of the countryside and to abide by the rules and regulations for the use of youth hostels. When you study the rules you will find that they are not oppressive, being based on common sense and consideration for others, two factors upon which the success of the hostelling movement depends.

One of the most enjoyable features of hostelling is the planning of the route. A hostel map which can be obtained from the Association's office gives the situation of all the hostels, but it is not on a large enough scale for practical use. If you are walking, 1-inch Ordnance Survey maps are best; if cycling, Bartholomew's ½-inch. The daily distances are apt to be fixed by the location of the hostels. Some hostels are placed for climbers, some for walkers, others are at cycling distance from each other. The last can be used on a walking tour if there is transport for part of the way. You can find out what transport there is from the regional guide-books obtainable at district offices.

It is never wise when hostelling to undertake great distances. Twelve to fifteen miles is far enough to walk each day, and should allow you to stop and see over an old castle or abbey, climb to a height for a view, laze in the sun beside a burn, or have a swim in the sea. If you are cycling you will find that forty to fifty miles a day is as much as you will want to do, for it is a poor way of hostelling to press on all day and day after day without pausing to explore byways and places of interest en route.

Hostelling is a convenient word for holidaying by means of sleeping at youth hostels, but is apt to be misleading. Hostels are merely intended as places to wash, make meals, and sleep. The importance of the holiday lies outside the hostel. The hostel is a means to an end, not an end in itself. Its facilities are there for you to use to the full, but the good hosteller does not abuse them by lingering about the place at a time when he should be on the road. The best start is the early start. The morning is the finest part of the day.

You will meet other hostellers on the road, and it is pleasant to have time to stop and talk, exchange experiences, and pick up information from each other on routes. In the hostels in the evenings, when no one can possibly eat any more, there are also opportunities of talking with people of similar interests to yourself. Hostels shelter a great variety of types and also people who are not types but absolutely unique. In conversation with them you will learn a lot, and they will learn from you.

Hostelling is best fun in company with a friend or two, but even if you go alone you will enjoy it. I know people who prefer lone hostelling; they claim they make many local contacts, they mix more with other hostellers, and frequently have company on the road. For your first experience of hostelling, however, the company of a friend of your own is desirable.

You will find that the memory of your first experience will stay with you for a very long time. I can remember mine as if it happened yesterday, and it happened years ago. I was a student and the S.Y.H.A. was in its infancy. Along with two other students, I mapped out a five-day walking tour in the Borders. We felt very adventurous. At the first hostel we were a little nervous, but this feeling rapidly wore off when we discovered that the warden was human and our fellow hostellers friendly. There was a notice " No tipping " above the back door. I remember thinking that it wouldn't have occurred to me to tip the warden, and not until I had to empty some dishwater outside did I realize my mistake! Every detail of that first evening stands out clearly. I can even remember that we had for supper bacon and eggs, home-baked brown bread and fresh butter, tinned fruit and cream, and we rounded this off with a bar of chocolate each. Yes, that was a very long time ago.

In those days hostels were quiet and we never troubled to book in advance. Now it is different. If you are hostelling in July or August, at Easter, Whitsun, or Autumn holiday, or indeed at any week-end, it is safer to book in advance. If you are going to a hostel which provides meals you will require to book them in advance too. Your district office will sell you booking postcards, which you send to the appropriate places. You can order milk and bread when you book, which is an advantage.

When you arrive at a hostel you hand your card to the warden, who keeps it until the moment of your departure; you sign the hostel book and you pay the overnight charge if you have not pre-paid it when booking. This charge in Scotland is 3s. for seniors, 1s. 6d. for juniors, 1s. for juveniles; in England it is 3s. 6d. for juniors and seniors, 1s. 6d. for juveniles. If you are cycling you pay 1d. for your cycle.

The warden may inquire if you have a sleeping-bag. If you haven't, you can hire one from him for the night for 1s. Sleeping-bags are in short supply at present, and it is preferable to have one of your own. If you are able to persuade your mother or sister to make one for you, well and good. If you think you can make it yourself, on you go. Lots of boys make their own sleeping-bags. It is an easy thing to make. First of all you beg a sheet from your mother. You will be doing a lot of begging from her from now on, and this will make a good beginning. She will be relieved when you tell her that the older and thinner the sheet the better. Patches don't matter. Most of us have them already. Cut the sheet down the middle. The under-part should be folded over at one end so that it will, when sewn along the sides, form a pocket to hold a pillow. The upper part is left long so that it can be turned down over the blankets. An ordinary sheet is long enough to let you pare away two long narrow triangular pieces to insert as gussets at each side. This is to prevent tearing when you insert yourself into the sleeping-bag. Finally, you seam the pieces together and sew on tapes at the corners of the top under-part so that the corners of the bag can be tied to the top of the bed.

Some people make a masterly job of sleeping-bags, others pro-duce curious-looking contraptions with half the seams done on the wrong side, gussets of varying sizes, and picturesque patches dotted here and there. The essential is that the sleeping-bag prevents contact with the blankets, three of which, and a pillow, are provided for each bed.

Hostels vary greatly in architecture. Some are specially designed for the purpose. Others may have been castles, mansions, hotels, boarding-houses, mills, schools, churches, boat-houses, recreation halls, villas, crofters' cottages, farm-houses, Nissen huts, forestry bothies; but whatever the style of architecture you can be sure that the interior conforms to a certain pattern. There is a common-room, a kitchen, sleeping quarters for men, sleeping quarters for women, and separate washing accommodation. Doors are plainly marked and you will find your way about with ease. Arrows may even direct you to the particular waste bins for tins, paper, and food scraps.

In the kitchen you will see rows of jugs, tea-pots, frying-pans, and lots of other cooking utensils, all for the use of hostellers. You carry your own cutlery and dishes. This sounds grim, but all you need are a knife, fork and spoon, a mug, and a soup plate. A cutlery set encompassed by a neat clip can be bought for a few shillings, or perhaps your mother will spare you some old cutlery. A mug is easy to acquire. The plate should be a light one, and deep enough to hold soup or porridge. My own plate is an aluminium baking-tin.

You will need a dish towel, and a box of matches. Other essentials are toilet necessaries and personal towel. I always carry a length of stout string if I'm cycling, and a roll of sticking plaster and small pair of scissors whether I am cycling or walking. A small electric torch is a useful thing to have. And of course your maps. If you are walking or climbing it is as well to carry a compass.

These are the bare bones of your equipment. To them you add what you want to take in the way of clothes. The clothes you wear depend on what you yourself find most comfortable. Hostels do not permit nailed boots or shoes to be worn indoors, so if such is your footwear you will need to carry a pair of light shoes. In any case you will want something to put your feet into while your heavy footwear is drying in the evenings. Some hostels have drying-rooms, but they are the exception, and in most hostels you put your shoes to dry in the kitchen after the evening orgy of cooking has expended its force.

5

We shall hope that rain will not dog your footsteps, but the hosteller has to take the possibility into account. A reliable oilskin and sou'wester are an investment.

Changes of underclothing can be posted to strategic positions along with a little extra food. The daily tasks of both postman and warden in rural areas are often heavy, so, if possible, post your parcel to the nearest post office and call for it yourself.

Some hostellers carry an extra shirt and pair of shorts in case of a soaking. I have found that good oilskins give excellent protection, and if the rain is so torrential that they fail to protect, you may be sure that your change of clothes inside your rucksack are in the process of becoming wet too. Never worry about getting wet. Hostels have good fires and you dry quickly before them. Emulate the spirit of the character in an Icelandic novel who said words to the effect that it was just eccentricity to want to be dry! If you are hostelling in winter—and the hardy prefer it to summer!— you will need extra woollies.

A word on rucksacks. The Bergan rucksack is scientifically designed, it is roomy, and its metal framework ensures that the weight goes where it can best be borne. There is, however, a fair weight in it even before it is packed, and many find the frameless rucksack preferable; but if you find you are equal to the weight of the Bergan, then by all means let it be your choice. It is more expensive than the other type, but it will last for ever.

If you are cycling you will need cycle bags. A good roomy single bag is adequate and your oilskins may be strapped to it, but if you are interested in, say, photography or botany and want to carry a little equipment you will find that panniers hold very much more.

Many carry Primus stoves. They shouldn't be necessary, but there are still hostels where cooking facilities are not too good. The Primus is useful also in the open air, and has the added virtue that it does away with the risk of starting fires in dry weather. You already know how dangerous it is to light a fire in woodlands. It is one of those things in the hostelling world that the best people don't do. Leaving gates open is another, leaving litter yet another.

There is always controversy over Primus stoves. People are either violently for or against. Some think the *fors* are inclined to neglect the goddess of the hostel before whom we all should make our bow. There is no doubt that the hostel stove is the centre of hostel life. We cook on it, it dries us if we are wet, it warms us if we are cold, and in the evenings we sit around it and talk or have a sing-song. In return all it wants is a little understanding and a little attention at the right time. It is a mistake, for instance, to go on cooking on a dying fire. You may manage to finish what you are cooking, but the next person will have to mend the fire and perhaps wait quarter of an hour until it burns up again. It is also a selfish policy to remove a lid from a stove and cook on the direct flame. It is quicker, but it spoils the saucepan and it cools the top of the stove for other people's saucepans. By the way, it isn't the warden's job to light the fire in the morning. He may do it for reasons of his own, but generally the first hosteller to rise lights the fire. The wise hosteller looks for sticks the evening before and has them toasted in readiness.

Food is an important item when hostelling. Exercise in the fresh air tickles up the appetite to twice its usual. In England meals are supplied at most hostels, though there are usually cooking facilities for those who wish them. In Scotland only a few hostels provide meals. A list of them is given in the handbook.

You may hitherto have done no cooking, in which case this is a chance to begin. No one will criticize. You won't cook a six-course dinner naturally. It is occasionally done, but unless the hostel is quiet the over-ambitious cook is apt to be unpopular and the warden may intervene. It is enough to have a substantial main course with bread to fill up the corners, and tea or milk.

Rations may be brought with you, posted previously, or bought on an emergency card. The handbook states if each hostel has a store. Stores vary, but generally they stock potatoes, oatmeal, plain biscuits, sandwich spreads, tins of soup. Milk is obtainable at a nearby farm, and in outlying districts you can buy eggs.

At first you may be inclined to stick to very simple cookery, but soon you will want to tackle more elaborate dishes, encouraged by the peculiar concoctions which other people are producing. I have seen hostellers lapping up porridge with sultanas in it, and melted cheese on wheat flakes with green peas sitting on top. Hostel meals are invariably unorthodox. It doesn't matter. Everything tastes good in hostels. The thoughtful hosteller does not take up pot-space on the stove for any longer time than is necessary. It is useful to remember that the stove has an oven. Few hostellers use it unless to bake their socks in overnight, but it can be used for baking potatoes, eggs, milk puddings, thus relieving congestion on the top of the stove.

After the meal is over you clear it away and leave table, sink, stove and floor as clean as you found them. In England, where meals are provided, you and your hostelling companion will be given a hostel duty which may consist of washing all the dishes or cleaning all the cooking-pots or some such job. In Scotland you look after

Glencoe youth hostel

yourself only, but the next morning before you leave you are expected to lend a hand in the sweeping, table-scrubbing, wood-chopping that goes on. The best method is not to wait to be asked by the warden to do a particular job, but to lift a brush and begin.

Once you have done some hostelling in Scotland, England and Wales, you might consider hostelling in Northern Ireland and Eire, which have no language or currency difficulties and which need only a travel identity card obtainable at a labour exchange. Your membership of Y.H.A. or S.Y.H.A. gives you automatic use of youth hostels in many countries as well as in each other.

The Glens of Antrim in Northern Ireland can be explored from hostels, and in Eire there is a hostel in Dublin to begin with and a group nearby in the lovely county of Wicklow.

You may become even more enterprising. What about Norway? At Bergen, the port at which you land, there is a hostel high up on the mountainside. In the interior hostels are spaced not too conveniently for walking, but you can have the help of a bus on the way. When I first came in sight of the hostel at Geilo on the Hardanger Plateau I was struck by its resemblance to our hostel in Glencoe, and then with some amusement it dawned on me that I was reversing the resemblance, for the Glencoe hostel was built on Norwegian lines.

A list of countries which have reciprocity with Y.H.A. and S.Y.H.A. is found in the International Youth Hostel Handbook obtainable at headquarters of the associations. It includes useful information on passports, currency, foreign hostel handbooks, tickets, routes, customs, maps. It is a little book which ought to do much good for the cause of international friendship. Whether it does or does not depends on the members who use it. In a foreign country we hold the reputation of our own country in our hands. It is a responsibility, but it need not weigh heavily on us if we observe the rules of foreign hostels with punctiliousness and exert the same consideration for others as we exert at home.

Good luck and good hostelling!

THE MOHAN MAN-EATER

I

Eighteen miles from our summer home in the Himalayas there is a long ridge running east and west, some 9,000 feet in height. On the upper slopes of the eastern end of this ridge there is a luxuriant growth of oat grass; below this grass the hills fall steeply away in a series of rock cliffs to the Kosi River below.

One day a party of women and girls from the village on the north face of the ridge were cutting the oat grass, when a tiger suddenly appeared in their midst. In the stampede that followed an elderly woman lost her footing, rolled down the steep slope, and disappeared over the cliff. The tiger, evidently alarmed by the screams of the women, vanished as mysteriously as it had appeared, and when the women had reassembled and recovered from their fright, they went down the grassy slope and, looking over the cliff, saw their companion lying on a narrow ledge some distance below them.

The woman said she was badly injured—it was found later that she had broken a leg and fractured several ribs—and that she could not move. Ways and means of a rescue were discussed, and it was finally decided that it was a job for men; and as no one appeared to be willing to remain at the spot, they informed the injured woman that they were going back to the village for help. The woman begged not to be left alone, however, and at her entreaty a girl, sixteen years of age, volunteered to stay with her. So, while the rest of the party set off for the village, the girl made her way down to the right, where a rift in the cliff enabled her to get a foothold on the ledge.

This ledge only extended half-way across the face of the cliff and ended, a few yards from where the woman was lying, in a shallow depression. Fearing that she might fall off the ledge and be killed on the rocks hundreds of feet below, the woman asked the girl to move her to this depression, and this difficult and dangerous feat the girl successfully accomplished. There was only room for one in the depression, so the girl squatted, as only an Indian can squat, on the ledge facing the woman.

The village was four miles away, and once, and once again, the two on the ledge speculated as to the length of time it would take their companions to get back to the village; what men they were likely to find in the village at that time of day; how long it would take to explain what had happened; and finally, how long it would take the rescue party to arrive.

Conversation had been carried on in whispers for fear the tiger might be lurking in the vicinity and hear them, and then, suddenly, the woman gave a gasp, and the girl, seeing the look of horror on her face and the direction in which she was looking, turned her head and over her shoulder saw the tiger, stepping out of the rift in the cliff on to the ledge.

Few of us, I imagine, have escaped that worst of all nightmares in which, while our limbs and vocal cords are paralysed with fear, some terrible beast in monstrous form approaches to destroy us; the nightmare from which, sweating fear in every pore, we waken with a cry of thankfulness to Heaven that it was only a dream. There was no such happy awakening from the nightmare of that unfortunate girl, and little imagination is needed to picture the scene. A rock cliff with a narrow ledge running partly across it and ending in a little depression in which an injured woman is lying; a young girl frozen with terror squatting on the ledge, and a tiger slowly creeping towards her; retreat in every direction cut off, and no help at hand.

Mothi Singh, an old friend of mine, was in the village visiting a sick daughter when the women arrived, and he headed the rescue party. When this party went down the grassy slope and looked over the cliff, they saw the woman lying in a swoon, and on the ledge they saw splashes of blood.

The injured woman was carried back to the village, and when she had been revived and had told her story, Mothi Singh set out on his eighteen-mile walk to me. He was an old man well over sixty, but he scouted the suggestion that he was tired and needed a rest, so we set off together to make investigations. But there was nothing that I could do, for twenty-four hours had elapsed and all that the tiger had left of the brave young girl, who had volunteered to stay with her injured companion, were a few bits of bone and her torn and bloodstained clothes.

This was the first human being killed by the tiger which later received recognition in Government records as " The Mohan Man-Eater ".

After killing the girl, the tiger went down the Kosi valley for the winter, killing on its way—among other people—two men of the Public Works Department, and the daughter-in-law of our Member of the Legislative Council. As summer approached it returned to the scene of its first kill, and for several years thereafter its beat extended up and down the Kosi valley from Kakrighat to Gargia—a distance of roughly forty miles—until it finally took up its quarters on the hill above Mohan, in the vicinity of a village called Kartkanoula.

II

It was on a blistering hot day in May that I, my two servants, and the six Garhwalis I had brought with me from Naini Tal alighted from the 1 p.m. train at Ramnagar and set off on our twenty-five-mile foot journey to Kartkanoula. Our first stage was only seven miles, but it was evening before we arrived at Gargia.

After a very early start next morning we did the twelve miles to Mohan before the sun got hot, and while my men were cooking their food and my servants were preparing my breakfast, the chokidar (watchman) of the bungalow, two Forest Guards, and several men from the Mohan bazaar entertained me with stories of the man-eater, the most recent of which concerned the exploits of a fisherman who had been fishing the Kosi river. One of the Forest Guards claimed to be the proud hero of this exploit, and he described very graphically how he had been out one day with the fisherman and, on turning a bend in the river, they had come face to face with the man-eater; and how the fisherman had thrown away his rod and had grabbed the rifle off his—the Forest Guard's—shoulder; and how they had run for their lives with the tiger close on their heels. " Did you look back?" I asked. " No, sahib," said he, pitying my ignorance. " How could a man who was running for his life from a man-eater look back?"; and how the fisherman, who was leading by a head, in a thick patch of grass had fallen over a sleeping bear, after which there had been great confusion and shouting and every-one, including the bear, had run in different directions and the fisherman had got lost; and how after a long time the fisherman had eventually found his way back to the bungalow and had said a lot to him—the Forest Guard—on the subject of having run away with his rifle and left him empty-handed to deal with a man-eating tiger and an angry bear. The Forest Guard ended up his recital by saying that the fisherman had left Mohan the following day, saying that he had hurt his leg when he fell over the bear, and that anyway there were no fish to be caught in the Kosi River.

By midday we were ready to continue our journey, and, with many warnings from the small crowd that had collected to see us off to keep a sharp look-out for the man-eater while going through the dense forest that lay ahead of us, we set out on our four-thousand-foot climb to Kartkanoula.

Our progress was slow, for my men were carrying heavy loads and the track was excessively steep, and the heat terrific. There had been some trouble in the upper villages a short time previously, necessitating the dispatch from Naini Tal of a small police force, and I had been advised to take everything I needed for myself and my men with me, as owing to the unsettled conditions it would not be possible to get any stores locally. This was the reason for the heavy loads my men were carrying.

After many halts we reached the edge of the cultivated land in the late afternoon, and as there was now no further danger to be apprehended for my men from the man-eater, I left them and set out alone for the Foresters' Hut, which is visible from Mohan, and which had been pointed out to me by the Forest Guards as the best place for my stay while at Kartkanoula.

The hut is on the ridge of the high hill overlooking Mohan, and as I approached it along the level stretch of road running across the face of the hill, in turning a corner in a ravine where there is some dense undergrowth, I came on a woman filling an earthenware pitcher from a little trickle of water flowing down a wooden trough. Apprehending that my approach on rubber-soled shoes would frighten her, I coughed to attract her attention, noticed that she started violently as I did so, and, a few yards beyond her, stopped to light a cigarette. A minute or two later I asked, without turning my head, if it was safe for anyone to be in this lonely spot, and after a little hesitation the woman answered that it was not safe, but that water had to be fetched and as there was no one in the home to accompany her, she had come alone. Was there no man? Yes,

5*   (G 487)

there was a man, but he was in the fields ploughing, and in any case it was the duty of women to fetch water. How long would it take to fill the pitcher? Only a little longer. The woman had got over her fright and shyness, and I was now subjected to a close cross-examination. Was I a policeman? No. Was I a Forest Officer? No. Then who was I? Just a man. Why had I come? To try and help the people of Kartkanoula. In what way? By shooting the man-eater. Where had I heard about the man-eater?—Why had I come alone?—Where were my men?—How many were there?—How long would I stay? And so on.

The pitcher was not declared full until the woman had satisfied her curiosity, and as she walked behind me she pointed to one of several ridges running down the south face of the hill, and pointing out a big tree growing on a grassy slope said that three days previously the man-eater had killed a woman under it; this tree, I noted with interest, was only two or three hundred yards from my objective—the Foresters' Hut. We had now come to a footpath running up the hill, and as she took it the woman said the village from which she had come was just round the shoulder of the hill, and added that she was now quite safe.

Those of you who know the women of India will realize that I had accomplished a lot, especially when it is remembered that there had recently been trouble in this area with the police. So far from alarming the woman and thereby earning the hostility of the entire countryside, I had, by standing by while she filled her pitcher and answering a few questions, gained a friend who would in the shortest time possible acquaint the whole population of the village of my arrival; that I was not an officer of any kind, and that the sole purpose of my visit was to try to rid them of the man-eater.

III

The Foresters' Hut was on a little knoll some twenty yards to the left of the road, and as the door was fastened only with a chain I opened it and walked inside. The room was about ten feet square and quite clean, but had a mouldy disused smell; I learnt later that the hut had not been occupied since the advent of the man-eater in that area eighteen months previously. On either side of the main room there were two narrow slips of rooms, one used as a kitchen, and the other as a fuel store. The hut would make a nice safe shelter for my men, and having opened the back door to let a current of air blow through the room, I went outside and selected a spot between the hut and the road for my 40-lb. tent. There was no furniture of any kind in the hut, so I sat down on a rock near the road to await the arrival of my men.

The ridge at this point was about fifty yards wide, and as the hut was on the south edge of the ridge, and the village on the north face of the hill, the latter was not visible from the former. I had been sitting on the rock for about ten minutes when a head appeared over the crest from the direction of the village, followed by a second and a third. My friend the water-carrier had not been slow in informing the village of my arrival.

When strangers meet in India and wish to glean information from each other on any particular subject, it is customary to refrain from broaching the subject that has brought them together—whether accidentally or of set purpose—until the very last moment, and to fill up the interval by finding out everything concerning each other's domestic and private affairs; as, for instance, whether married and if so the number and sex of children and their ages; if not married, why not; occupation and amount of pay, and so on. Questions that would in any other part of the world earn one a thick ear are in India—and especially in our hills—asked so artlessly and universally that no one who has lived among the people dreams of taking offence at them.

In my conversation with the woman I had answered many of the set questions, and the ones of a domestic nature which it is not permissible for a woman to ask of a man were being put to me when my men arrived. They had filled a kettle at the little spring, and in an incredibly short time dry sticks were collected, a fire lit, the kettle boiled, and tea and biscuits produced. As I opened a tin of condensed milk I heard the men asking my servants why condensed milk was being used instead of fresh milk and receiving the answer that there was no fresh milk; and further that, as it had been apprehended that owing to some previous trouble in this area no fresh milk would be available, a large supply of tinned milk had been brought. The men appeared to be very distressed on hearing this, and after a whispered conversation one of them, who I learnt later was the Headman of Kartkanoula, addressed me and said it was an insult to them to have brought tinned milk, when all the resources of the village were at my disposal. I admitted my mistake, which I said was due to my being a stranger to that locality, and told the Headman that if he had any milk to spare I would gladly purchase a small quantity for my daily requirements, but that beyond the milk, I wanted for nothing.

My loads had now been unstrapped, while more men had arrived from the village, and when I told my servants where I wanted them to pitch my tent there was a horrified exclamation from the assembled villagers. Live in a tent—indeed! Was I ignorant of the fact that there was a man-eating tiger in this area and that it used this road regularly every night? If I doubted their word, let me come and see the claw marks on the doors of the houses where the road ran through the upper end of the village. Moreover, if the tiger did not eat me in the tent it would certainly eat my men in the hut, if I was not there to protect them. This last statement made my men prick up their ears and add their entreaties to the advice of the villagers, so eventually I agreed to stay in the main room, while my two servants occupied the kitchen, and the six Garhwalis the fuel store.

The subject of the man-eater having been introduced, it was now possible for me to pursue it without admitting that it was the one subject I had wished to introduce from the moment the first man had put his head over the ridge. The path leading down to the tree where the tiger had claimed its last victim was pointed out to me, and the time of day, and the circumstances under which the woman had been killed, explained. The road along which the tiger came every night, I was informed, ran eastward to Baital Ghat with a branch down to Mohan, and westward to Chaknakl on the Ramganga River. The road going west, after running through the upper part of the village and through cultivated land for half a mile, turned south along the face of the hill, and on rejoining the ridge on which the hut was, followed the ridge right down to Chaknakl. This portion of the road between Kartkanoula and Chaknakl, some six miles long, was considered to be very dangerous, and had not been used since the advent of the man-eater; I subsequently found that after leaving the cultivated land the road entered dense tree and and scrub jungle, which extended right down to the river.

The main cultivation of Kartkanoula village is on the north face of the hill, and beyond this cultivated land there are several small ridges with deep ravines between. On the nearest of these ridges, and distant about a thousand yards from the Foresters' Hut, there is a big pine tree. Near this tree, some ten days previously, the tiger had killed, partly eaten, and left a woman, and as the three sportsmen who were staying in a Forest Bungalow four miles away were unable to climb the pine tree, the villagers had put up three machans (platforms) in three separate trees, at distances varying from one hundred to one hundred and fifty yards from the kill, and the machans had been occupied by the sportsmen and their servants a little before sunset. There was a young moon at the time, and after it had set the villagers heard a number of shots being fired, and when they questioned the servants next morning the servants said they did not know what had been fired at for they themselves had not seen anything. Two days later a cow had been killed over which the sportsmen had sat, and again, as on the previous occasion, shots had been fired after the moon had set. It is these admittedly sporting but unsuccessful attempts to bag man-eaters that makes them so wary, and the more difficult to shoot the longer they live.

The villagers gave me one very interesting item of news in connexion with the tiger. They said they always knew when it had come into the village by the low moaning sound it made. On questioning them closely I learnt that at times the sound was continuous as the tiger passed between the houses, while at other times the sound stopped for sometimes short and other times long periods.

From this information I concluded (a) that the tiger was suffering from a wound, (b) that the wound was of such a nature that the tiger only felt it when in motion, and that therefore (c) the wound was in one of its legs. I was assured that the tiger had not been wounded by any local shikari, or by any of the sportsmen from Ranikhet who had sat up for it; however, this was of little importance, for the tiger had been a man-eater for years, and the wound that I believed it was suffering from might have been the original cause of its becoming a man-eater. A very interesting point and one that could only be cleared up by examining the tiger—after it was dead.

The men were curious to know why I was so interested in the sound made by the tiger, and when I told them that it indicated the animal had a wound in one of its legs and that the wound had been caused either by a bullet, or by porcupine quills, they disagreed with my reasoning and said that on the occasions they had seen the tiger it appeared to be in sound condition, and further, that the ease with which it killed and carried off its victims was proof that it was not crippled in any way. However, what I told them was remembered and later earned me the reputation of being gifted with second sight.

IV

When passing through Ramnagar I had asked the Tahsildar (the chief revenue officer) to purchase two young male buffaloes for me and to send them to Mohan, where my men would take them over.

I told the villagers I intended tying up one of the buffaloes near the tree where three days previously the woman had been killed and the other on the road to Chaknakl, and they said they could think of no better sites, but that they would talk the matter over among themselves and let me know in the morning if they had any other suggestions to make. Night was now drawing in, and before leaving the Headman promised to send word to all the adjoining villages in the morning to let them know of my arrival, the reason for my coming, and to impress on them the urgency of letting me know without loss of time of any kills or attacks by the tiger in their areas.

The musty smell in the room had much decreased, though it was still noticeable. However, I paid no attention to it, and after a bath and dinner put two stones against the doors—there being no other way of keeping them shut—and being bone-tired after my day's exertions went to bed and to sleep. I am a light sleeper, and two or three hours later I awoke on hearing an animal moving about in the jungle. It came right up to the back door. Getting hold of a rifle and a torch, I moved the stone aside with my foot and heard an animal moving off as I opened the door—it might from the sound it was making have been the tiger, but it might also have been a leopard or a porcupine. However, the jungle was too thick for me to see what it was. Back in the room and with the stone once more in position, I noticed I had developed a sore throat, which I attributed to having sat in the wind after the hot walk up from Mohan; but when my servant pushed the door open and brought in my early morning cup of tea, I found I was suffering from an attack of laryngitis, due possibly to my having slept in a long-disused hut, the roof of which was swarming with bats. My servant informed me that he and his companion had escaped infection, but that the six Garhwalis in the fuel store were all suffering from the same complaint as I was. My stock of medicine consisted of a two-ounce bottle of iodine and a few tabloids of quinine, and on rummaging in my gun-case I found a small paper packet of permanganate, which my sister had provided for me on a previous occasion. The packet was soaked through with gun oil, but the crystals were still soluble, and I put a liberal quantity of the crystals into a tin of hot water, together with some iodine. The resulting gargle was very potent, and while it blackened our teeth it did much to relieve the soreness in our throats.

After an early breakfast I sent four men down to Mohan to bring up the two buffaloes, and myself set off to prospect the ground where the woman had been killed. From the directions I had received overnight I had no difficulty in finding the spot where the tiger had attacked and killed the woman as she was tying the grass she had cut into a bundle. The grass and the rope she was using were lying just as they had been left, as were also two bundles of grass left by her companions when they had run off in fright to the village. The men had told me that the body of the woman had not been found, but from the fact that three perfectly good lengths of rope and the dead woman's sickle had been left in the jungle, I am inclined to think that no attempt had been made to find her.

The woman had been killed at the upper end of a small landslide, and the tiger had taken her down the slide and into a thick patch of undergrowth. Here the tiger had waited, possibly to give the two women time to get out of sight, and had then crossed the ridge visible from the hut, after which it had gone with its kill straight down the hill for a mile or more into dense tree and scrub jungle. The tracks were now four days old, and as there was nothing to be gained by following them farther, I turned back to the hut.

The climb back to the ridge was a very steep one, and when I reached the hut at about midday I found an array of pots and pans of various shapes and sizes on the veranda, all containing milk. In contrast to the famine of the day before there was now abundance, sufficient milk in fact for me to have bathed in. My servants informed me they had protested to no effect and that each man had said, as he deposited his vessel on the veranda, that he would take good care that I used no more condensed milk while I remained in their midst.

I did not expect the men to return from Mohan with the buffaloes before nightfall, so after lunch I set out to have a look at the road to Chaknakl.

From the hut the hill sloped gradually upwards to a height of about five hundred feet, and was roughly triangular in shape. The road, after running through cultivated land for half a mile, turned sharply to the left, went across a steep rocky hill until it regained the ridge, and then turned to the right and followed the ridge down to Chaknakl. The road was level for a short distance after coming out on the ridge, and then went steeply down, the gradient in places being eased by hairpin bends.

I had the whole afternoon before me, and examined about three miles of the road very carefully. When a tiger uses a road regularly it invariably leaves signs of its passage by making scratch marks on the side of the road. These scratch marks, made for the same purpose as similar marks made by domestic cats and all other members of the cat family, are of very great interest to sportsmen, for they provide him with the following very useful information: (1) whether the animal that has made the mark is a male or a female, (2) the direction in which it was travelling, (3) the length of time that has elapsed since it passed, (4) the direction and approximate distance of its headquarters, (5) the nature of its kills, and finally, (6) whether the animal has recently had a meal of human flesh. The value of this easily acquired information to one who is hunting a man-eater on strange ground will be easily understood. Tigers also leave their pug marks on the roads they use and these pug marks can provide one with quite a lot of useful information, as for instance the direction and speed at which the animal was travelling, its sex and age, whether all four limbs are sound, and, if not sound, which particular limb is defective.

The road I was on had through long disuse got overgrown with short stiff grass and was therefore not, except in one or two damp places, a good medium on which to leave pug marks. One of these damp places was within a few yards of where the road came out on the ridge, and just below this spot there was a green and very stagnant pool of water; a regular drinking place for sambur.

I found several scratch marks just round the corner where the road turned to the left after leaving the cultivated ground, the most recent of which was three days old. Two hundred yards from these scratch marks the road, for a third of its width, ran under an overhanging rock. This rock was ten feet high and at the top of it there was a flat piece of ground two or three yards wide, which was only visible from the road when approaching the rock from the village side. On the ridge I found more scratch marks, but I did not find any pug marks until I got to the first hairpin bend. Here, in cutting across the bend, the tiger had left its tracks where it had jumped down on to some soft earth. The tracks, which were a day old, were a little distorted, but even so it was possible to see that they had been made by a big, old, male tiger.

When one is moving in an area in which a man-eating tiger is operating, progress is of necessity very slow, for every obstruction in one's line of walk, be it a bush, a tree, a rock, or an inequality in the ground capable of concealing death, has to be cautiously approached, while at the same time, if a wind is not blowing—and there was no wind that evening—a careful and constant look-out has to be maintained behind and on either side. Further, there was much of interest to be looked at, for it was the month of May, when orchids at this elevation—4,000 to 5,000 feet—are at their best, and I have never seen a greater variety or a greater wealth of bloom than the forests on that hill had to show. The beautiful white butterfly orchid was in greatest profusion, and every second tree of any size appeared to have decked itself out with them.

Safeguarding my neck, looking out for tracks, enjoying nature generally, and listening to all the jungle sounds—a sambur a mile away down the hillside in the direction of Mohan was warning the jungle folk of the presence of a tiger, and a kakar (barking deer) and a langur (*Entellus* monkey) on the road to Chaknakl were warning other jungle folk of the presence of a leopard—time passed quickly, and I found myself back at the overhanging rock as the sun was setting. As I approached this rock I marked it as being quite the most dangerous spot in all the ground I had so far gone over. A tiger lying on the grass-covered bit of ground above the rock would only have to wait until anyone going either up or down the road was under or had passed it to have them at his mercy—a very dangerous spot indeed, and one that needed remembering.

When I got back to the hut I found the two buffaloes had arrived, but it was too late to do anything with them that evening.

My servants had kept a fire going most of the day in the hut, the air of which was now sweet and clean, but even so I was not going to risk sleeping in a closed room again; so I made them cut two thorn bushes and wedged them firmly into the doorways before going to bed. There was no movement in the jungle near the back door that night, and after a sound sleep I woke in the morning with my throat very much better.

I spent most of the morning talking to the village people and listening to the tales they had to tell of the man-eater and the attempts that had been made to shoot it, and after lunch I tied up one buffalo on the small ridge the tiger had crossed when carrying away the woman, and the other at the hairpin bend where I had seen the pug marks.

Next morning I found both buffaloes sleeping peacefully after having eaten most of the big feed of grass I had provided them with. I had tied bells round the necks of both animals, and the absence of any sound from these bells as I approached each buffalo gave me two disappointments for, as I have said, I found both of them asleep. That evening I changed the position of the second buffalo from the hairpin bend to where the road came out on the ridge, close to the pool of stagnant water.

The methods most generally employed in tiger shooting can briefly be described as (a) sitting up, and (b) beating, and young male buffaloes are used as bait in both cases. The procedure followed is to select the area most convenient for a sit-up, or for a beat, and to tie the bait out in the late evening, using a rope which the bait cannot, but which the tiger can, break; and when the bait is taken, either to sit up over the kill on a machan in a tree, or beat the cover into which the kill has been taken.

In the present case neither of these methods was feasible. My throat, though very much better, was still sore and it would not have been possible for me to have sat up for any length of time without coughing, and a beat over that vast area of heavily wooded and broken ground would have been hopeless even if I had been able to muster a thousand men; so I decided to stalk the tiger, and to this end carefully sited my two buffaloes and tied them to stout saplings with four one-inch-thick hemp ropes, and left them out in the jungle for the whole twenty-four hours.

I now stalked the buffaloes in turn each morning, as soon as there was sufficient light to shoot by, and again in the evening; for tigers, be they man-eaters or not, kill as readily in the day as they do at night in areas in which they are not disturbed; and during the day, while I waited for news from outlying villages, nursed my throat, and rested, my six Garhwalis fed and watered the buffaloes.

On the fourth evening when I was returning at sunset after visiting the buffalo on the ridge, as I came round a bend in the road thirty yards from the overhanging rock, I suddenly, and for the first time since my arrival at Kartkanoula, felt I was in danger, and that the danger that threatened me was on the rock in front of me. For five minutes I stood perfectly still with my eyes fixed on the upper edge of the rock, watching for movement. At that short range the flicker of an eyelid would have caught my eyes, but there was not even this small movement; and after going forward ten paces, I again stood watching for several minutes. The fact that I had seen no movement did not in any way reassure me—the man-eater was on the rock, of that I was sure; and the question was, what was I going to do about it? The hill, as I have already told you, was very steep, had great rocks jutting out of it, and was overgrown with long grass and tree and scrub jungle. Bad as the going was, had it been earlier in the day I would have gone back and worked round and above the tiger to try to get a shot at him; but with only half an hour of daylight left, and the best part of a mile still to go, it would have been madness to have left the road. So, slipping up the safety-catch and putting the rifle to my shoulder, I started to pass the rock.

The road here was about eight feet wide, and going to the extreme outer edge I started walking crab-fashion, feeling each step with my feet before putting my weight down to keep from stepping off into space. Progress was slow and difficult, but as I drew level with the overhanging rock and then began to pass it, hope rose high that the tiger would remain where he was until I reached that part of the road from which the flat bit of ground above the rock, on which he was lying, was visible. The tiger, however, having failed to catch me off my guard, was taking no chances, and I had just got clear of the rock when I heard a low muttered growl above me, and a little later first a kakar went off barking to the right, and then two hind sambur started bellowing near the crest of the triangular hill.

The tiger had got away with a sound skin, but, for the matter of that, so had I, so there was no occasion for regrets, and from the place on the hill where the sambur said he was, I felt sure he would hear the bell I had hung round the neck of the buffalo that was tied on the ridge near the stagnant pool.

When I reached the cultivated land I found a group of men waiting for me. They had heard the kakar and sambur and were very disappointed that I had not seen the tiger, but cheered up when I told them I had great hopes for the morrow.

V

During the night a dust-storm came on, followed by heavy rain, and I found to my discomfort that the roof of the hut was very porous. However, I eventually found a spot where it was leaking less than in others, dragged my camp bed to it, and continued my sleep. It was a brilliantly clear morning when I awoke; the rain had washed the heat haze and dust out of the atmosphere, and every leaf and blade of grass was glistening in the newly risen sun.

Hitherto I had visited the nearer buffalo first, but this morning I had an urge to reverse the daily procedure, and after instructing my men to wait until the sun was well up and then go to feed and water the nearer buffalo, I set off with high hopes down the Chaknakl road, having first cleaned and oiled my 450/400 rifle—a very efficient weapon, and a good and faithful friend of many years' standing.

The overhanging rock that I had passed with such trouble the previous evening did not give me a moment's uneasiness now, and after passing it I started looking for tracks, for the rain had softened the surface of the road. I saw nothing, however, until I came to the damp place on the road, which, as I have said, was on the near side of the ridge and close to the pool where the buffalo was tied. Here in the soft earth I found the pug marks of the tiger, made before the storm had come on, and going in the direction of the ridge. Close to this spot there is a rock about three feet high, on the khud (ravine) side of the road. On the previous occasions that I had stalked down the road I had found that by standing on this rock I could look over a hump in the road and see the buffalo where it was tied forty yards away. When I now climbed on to the rock and slowly raised my head, I found that the buffalo had gone. This discovery was as disconcerting as it was inexplicable. To prevent the tiger from carrying the buffalo away to some distant part of the jungle, where the only method of getting a shot would have been by sitting up on the ground or in a tree—a hopeless proceeding with my throat in the condition it was in—I had used four thicknesses of strong one-inch-thick hemp rope, and even so the tiger had got away with the kill.

I was wearing the thinnest of rubber-soled shoes, and very silently I approached the sapling to which the buffalo had been tied and examined the ground. The buffalo had been killed before the storm, but had been carried away after the rain had stopped, without any portion of it having been eaten. Three of the ropes I had twisted together had been gnawed through, and the fourth had been broken. Tigers do not usually gnaw through ropes; however, this one had done so, and had carried off the kill down the hill facing Mohan. My plans had been badly upset, but very fortunately the rain had come to my assistance. The thick carpet of dead leaves which the day before had been as dry as tinder were now wet and pliable, and, provided I made no mistakes, the pains the tiger had been to in getting away with the kill might yet prove his undoing.

When entering a jungle in which rapid shooting might at any moment become necessary, I never feel happy until I have reassured myself that my rifle is loaded. To pull a trigger in an emergency and wake up in the Happy Hunting Grounds—or elsewhere—because one had omitted to load a weapon, would be one of those acts of carelessness for which no excuse could be found; so though I knew I had loaded my rifle before I came to the overhanging rock, I now opened it and extracted the cartridges. I changed one that was discoloured and dented, and after moving the safety-catch up and down several times to make sure it was working smoothly— I have never carried a cocked weapon—I set off to follow the drag.

This word " drag ", when it is used to describe the mark left on the ground by a tiger when it is moving its kill from one place to another, is misleading, for a tiger when taking its kill any distance (I have seen a tiger carry a full-grown cow for four miles) does not drag it, it carries it; and if the kill is too heavy to be carried, it is left. The drag is distinct or faint according to the size of the animal that is being carried, and the manner in which it is being held. For instance, assuming the kill is a sambur and the tiger is holding it by the neck, the hind quarters will trail on the ground, leaving a distinct drag mark. On the other hand, if the sambur is being held by the middle of the back, there may be a faint drag mark, or there may be none at all.

In the present case the tiger was carrying the buffalo by the neck, and the hind quarters trailing on the ground were leaving a drag mark it was easy to follow. For a hundred yards the tiger went diagonally across the face of the hill until he came to a steep clay bank. In attempting to cross this bank he had slipped and relinquished his hold of the kill, which had rolled down the hill for thirty or forty yards until it had fetched up against a tree. On recovering the kill the tiger picked it up by the back, and from now on only one leg occasionally touched the ground, leaving a faint drag mark, which nevertheless, owing to the hillside's being carpeted with bracken, was not very difficult to follow. In his fall the tiger had lost direction, and now appeared to be undecided where to take the kill. First he went a couple of hundred yards to the right, then a hundred yards straight down the hill through a dense patch of ringals (stunted bamboo). After forcing his way with considerable difficulty through the ringals he turned to the left and went diagonally across the hill for a few hundred yards until he came to a great rock, to the right of which he skirted. This rock was flush with the ground on the approach side, and, rising gently for twenty feet, appeared to project out over a hollow or dell of considerable extent. If there was a cave or recess under the projection, it would be a very likely place for the tiger to have taken his kill to, so leaving the drag I stepped on to the rock and moved forward very slowly, examining every yard of ground below and on either side of me, as it came into view. On reaching the end of the projection and looking over I was disappointed to find that the hill came up steeply to meet the rock, and that there was no cave or recess under it as I had expected there would be.

As the point of the rock offered a good view of the dell and of the surrounding jungle—and was comparatively safe from an attack from the man-eater—I sat down; and as I did so, I caught sight of a red and white object in a dense patch of short undergrowth, forty or fifty yards directly below me. When one is looking for a tiger in heavy jungle everything red that catches the eye is immediately taken for the tiger, and here, not only could I see the red of the tiger, but I could also see his stripes. For a long minute I watched the object intently, and then, as the face you are told to look for in a freak picture suddenly resolves itself, I saw that the object I was looking at was the kill, and not the tiger; the red was blood where he had recently been eating, and the stripes were the ribs from which he had torn away the skin. I was thankful for having held my fire for that long minute, for in a somewhat similar case a friend of mine ruined his chance of bagging a very fine tiger by putting two bullets into a kill over which he had intended sitting; fortunately he was a good shot, and the two men whom he had sent out in advance to find the kill and put up a machan over it, and who were, at the time he fired, standing near the kill screened by a bush, escaped injury.

When a tiger that has not been disturbed leaves his kill out in the open, it can be assumed that he is lying up close at hand to guard the kill from vultures and other scavengers, and the fact that I could not see the tiger did not mean that he was not lying somewhere close by in the dense undergrowth.

Tigers are troubled by flies and do not lie long in one position, so I decided to remain where I was and watch for movement; but hardly had I come to this decision, when I felt an irritation in my throat. I had not quite recovered from my attack of laryngitis and the irritation grew rapidly worse until it became imperative for me to cough. The usual methods one employs on these occasions, whether in church or the jungle, such as holding the breath and swallowing hard, gave no relief until it became a case of cough, or burst; and in desperation I tried to relieve my throat by giving the alarm-call of the langur. Sounds are difficult to translate into words and for those of you who are not acquainted with our jungles I would try to describe this alarm-call, which can be heard for half a mile, as *khok*, *khok*, *khok*, repeated again and again at short intervals, and ending up with *khokorror*. All langurs do not call at tigers, but the ones in our hills certainly do, and as this tiger had probably heard the call every day of his life it was the one sound I could make to which he would not pay the slightest attention. My rendering of the call in this emergency did not sound very convincing, but it had the desired effect of removing the irritation from my throat.

For half an hour thereafter I continued to sit on the rock, watching for movement and listening for news from the jungle folk, and when I had satisfied myself that the tiger was not anywhere within my range of vision, I got off the rock, and, moving with the utmost caution, went down to the kill.

VI

I regret I am not able to tell you what weight of flesh a full-grown tiger can consume at a meal, but you will have some idea of his capacity when I tell you he can eat a sambur in two days, and a buffalo in three, leaving possibly a small snack for the fourth day.

The buffalo I had tied up was not full-grown but he was by no means a small animal, and the tiger had eaten approximately half of him. With a meal of that dimension inside of him I felt sure he had not gone far, and as the ground was still wet, and would remain so for another hour or two, I decided to find out in what direction he had gone, and if possible, stalk him.

There were a confusion of tracks near the kill, but by going round in widening circles I found the track the tiger had made when leaving. Soft-footed animals are a little more difficult to track than hard-footed ones, yet after long years of experience tracking needs as little effort as a gun dog exerts when following a scent. As silently and as slowly as a shadow I took up the track, knowing that the tiger would be close at hand. When I had gone a hundred yards I came on a flat bit of ground, twenty feet square, and carpeted with that variety of short soft grass that has highly scented roots; on this grass the tiger had lain, the imprint of his body being clearly visible.

As I was looking at the imprint and guessing at the size of the animal that had made it, I saw some of the blades of grass that had been crushed down spring erect. This indicated that the tiger had been gone only a minute or so.

You will have some idea of the lay-out when I tell you that the tiger had brought the kill down from the north, and on leaving it had gone west, and that the rock on which I had sat, the kill, and the spot where I was now standing formed the points of a triangle, one side of which was forty yards, and the other two sides a hundred yards long.

My first thought on seeing the grass spring erect was that the tiger had seen me and moved off, but this I soon found was not likely, for neither the rock nor the kill was visible from the grass plot, and that he had not seen me and moved after I had taken up his track I was quite certain. Why then had he left his comfortable bed and gone away? The sun shining on the back of my neck provided the answer. It was now nine o'clock of an unpleasantly hot May morning, and a glance at the sun and the tree-tops over which it had come showed that it had been shining on the grass for ten minutes. The tiger had evidently found it too hot, and gone away a few minutes before my arrival to look for a shady spot.

I have told you that the grass plot was twenty feet square. On the far side to that from which I had approached there was a fallen tree, lying north and south. This tree was about four feet in diameter, and as it was lying along the edge of the grass plot in the middle of which I was standing, it was ten feet away from me. The root end of the tree was resting on the hillside, which here went up steeply and was overgrown with brushwood, and the branch end (which had been snapped off when the tree had fallen) was projecting out over the hillside. Beyond the tree the hill appeared to be more or less perpendicular, and running across the face of it was a narrow ledge of rock, which disappeared into dense jungle thirty yards farther on.

If my surmise, that the sun had been the cause of the tiger's changing his position, was correct, there was no more suitable place than the lee of the tree for him to have taken shelter in, and the only way of satisfying myself on this point was to walk up to the tree—and look over. Here a picture seen long years ago in *Punch* flashed into memory. The picture was of a lone sportsman who had gone out to hunt lions and who, on glancing up on to the rock he was passing, looked straight into the grinning face of the most enormous lion in Africa. Underneath the picture was written, " When you go out looking for a lion, be quite sure that you want to see him ". True, there would be this small difference, that whereas my friend in Africa looked up—into the lion's face, I would look down—into the tiger's; otherwise the two cases—assuming that the tiger *was* on the far side of the tree—would be very similar.

Slipping my feet forward an inch at a time on the soft grass, I now started to approach the tree, and had covered about half the distance that separated me from it when I caught sight of a black-and-yellow object about three inches long on the rocky ledge, which I now saw was a well-used game path. For a long minute I stared at this motionless object, until I was convinced that it was the tip of the tiger's tail. If the tail was pointing away from me the head must obviously be towards me, and as the ledge was only some two feet wide, the tiger could only be crouching down and waiting to spring the moment my head appeared over the bole of the tree. The tip of the tail was twenty feet from me, and allowing eight feet for the tiger's length while crouching, his head would be twelve feet away. But I should have to approach much nearer before I should be able to see enough of his body to get in a crippling shot, and a crippling shot it would have to be if I wanted to leave on my feet. And now, for the first time in my life, I regretted my habit of carrying an uncocked rifle. The safety-catch of my 450/400 makes a very distinct click when thrown off, and to make any sound now would either bring the tiger right on top of me, or send him straight down the steep hillside without any possibility of my getting in a shot.

Inch by inch I again started to creep forward, until the whole of the tail, and after it the hind quarters, came into view. When I saw the hind quarters I could have shouted with delight, for they showed that the tiger was not crouching and ready to spring, but was lying down. As there was only room for his body on the two-foot-wide ledge, he had stretched his hind legs out and was resting them on the upper branches of an oak sapling growing up the face of the almost perpendicular hillside. Another foot forward and his belly came into view, and from the regular way in which it was heaving up and down I knew that he was asleep. Less slowly now I moved forward, until his shoulder, and then his whole length, was exposed to my view. The back of his head was resting on the edge of the grass plot, which extended for three or four feet beyond the fallen tree; his eyes were fast shut, and his nose was pointing to heaven.

Aligning the sights of the rifle on his forehead I pressed the trigger and, while maintaining a steady pressure on it, pushed up the safety-catch. I had no idea how this reversal of the usual method of discharging a rifle would work, but it did work; and when the heavy bullet at that short range crashed into his forehead not so much as a quiver went through his body. His tail remained stretched straight out; his hind legs continued to rest on the upper branches of the sapling; and his nose still pointed to heaven. Nor did his position change in the slightest when I sent a second, and quite unnecessary, bullet to follow the first. The only change noticeable was that his stomach had stopped heaving up and down, and that blood was trickling down his forehead from two surprisingly small holes.

I do not know how the close proximity of a tiger reacts on others, but me it always leaves with a breathless feeling—due possibly as much to fear as to excitement—and a desire for a little rest. I sat down on the fallen tree and lit the cigarette I had denied myself from the day my throat had got bad, and allowed my thoughts to wander. Any task well accomplished gives satisfaction, and the one just completed was no exception. The reason for my presence at that spot was the destruction of the man-eater, and from the time I had left the road two hours previously right up to the moment I pushed up the safety-catch, everything—including the langur call—had worked smoothly and without a single fault. In this there was great satisfaction, the kind of satisfaction I imagine an author must feel when he writes *Finis* to the plot that, stage by stage, has unfolded itself just as he desired it to. In my case, however, the finish had not been satisfactory, for I had killed the animal, that was lying five feet from me, in his sleep.

My personal feelings in the matter are I know of little interest to others, but it occurs to me that possibly you also might think it was not cricket, and in that case I should like to put the arguments before you that I used on myself, in the hope that you will find them more satisfactory than I did. These arguments were (*a*) the tiger was a man-eater that was better dead than alive, (*b*) therefore it made no difference whether he was awake or asleep when killed, and (*c*) that had I walked away when I saw his belly heaving up and down I should have been morally responsible for the deaths of all the human beings he killed thereafter. All good and sound arguments, you will admit, for my having acted as I did; but the regret remains that through fear of the consequences to myself, or fear of losing the only chance I might ever get, or possibly a combination of the two, I did not awaken the sleeping animal and give him a sporting chance.

The tiger was dead, and if my trophy was to be saved from falling into the valley below and ruined, it was advisable to get him off the ledge with as little delay as possible. Leaning the rifle, for which I had no further use, against the fallen tree, I climbed up to the road and, once round the corner near the cultivated land, I cupped my hands and sent a cooee echoing over the hills and valleys. I had no occasion to repeat the call, for my men had heard my two shots when returning from attending to the first buffalo and had run back to the hut to collect as many villagers as were within calling distance. Now, on hearing my cooee, the whole crowd came helter-skelter down the road to meet me.

When stout ropes and an axe had been procured I took the crowd back with me, and after I had secured the ropes round the tiger, willing hands half carried and half dragged him off the ledge and over the fallen tree, on to the plot of grass. Here I would have skinned him, but the villagers begged me not to do so, saying that the women and children of Kartkanoula and the adjoining villages would be very disappointed if they were not given an opportunity of seeing the tiger with their own eyes and satisfying themselves that the man-eater, in fear of whom they had lived for so many years, and who had established a reign of terror over the whole district, was really and truly dead.

While a couple of saplings to assist in carrying the tiger back to the hut were being felled, I saw some of the men passing their hands over the tiger's limbs, and knew they were satisfying themselves that their assertion that the tiger had not been suffering from any old, or crippling, wounds was correct. At the hut the tiger was placed in the shade of a wide-spreading tree and the villagers were informed that it was at their disposal up to two o'clock—longer I could not give them, for it was a very hot day and there was fear of the hair slipping and the skin being ruined.

I myself had not looked closely at the tiger, but at 2 p.m., when I laid him on his back to start the skinning, I noticed that most of the hair from the inner side of his left foreleg was missing, and that there were a number of small punctures in the skin, from which yellow fluid was exuding. I did not draw attention to these punctures, and left the skinning of the leg, which was considerably thinner than the right leg, to the last. When the skin had been removed from the rest of the animal, I made a long cut from the chest to the pad of the festering left leg, and as I removed the skin, drew out of the flesh, one after another, porcupine quills which the men standing round eagerly seized as souvenirs; the longest of these quills was about five inches, and their total number was between twenty-five and thirty. The flesh under the skin, from the tiger's chest to the pad of his foot, was soapy, and of a dark yellow colour; cause enough to have made the poor beast moan when he walked, and quite sufficient reason for his having become—and having remained—a man-eater, for porcupine quills do not dissolve no matter how long they are embedded in flesh.

I have extracted, possibly, a couple of hundred porcupine quills from the man-eating tigers I have shot. Many of these quills have been over nine inches in length and as thick as pencils. The majority were embedded in hard muscles, a few were wedged firmly between bones, and all were broken off short under the skin.

Unquestionably the tigers acquired the quills when killing porcupines for food, but the question arises—to which I regret I am unable to give any satisfactory answer—why animals with the intelligence, and the agility, of tigers should have been so careless as to drive the quills deep into themselves, or be so slow in their movements as to permit porcupines—whose only method of defending themselves is by walking backwards—to do so; and further, why the quills should have been broken off short, for porcupine quills are not brittle.

Leopards are just as partial to porcupines as our hill tigers are, but they do not get quills stuck in them, for they kill porcupines—as I have seen—by catching them by the head; and why tigers do not employ the same safe and obvious method of killing as leopards employ, and so avoid injury to themselves, is a mystery to me.

ATOMS AND ENERGY

This article is about some of the latest discoveries of modern science. It concerns many secrets of Nature which have remained hidden from the beginning of time until the last few years. Some scientists have been exploring the depths of space with powerful and still more powerful telescopes. Others have been exploring the world of things so tiny that they cannot be seen even under the most powerful microscope. Here they have found evidence of things so marvellous that it is almost impossible to describe them in words—things so different from the objects which we see every day that a new language has had to be invented in order to be able to discuss them at all. This language—the language of mathematical physics—is hard to translate into ordinary prose, but here an attempt has been made to tell the story of that strange world beyond the microscope. The story is still incomplete, and much patient investigation remains to be made. It has been written here in the hope that some of its readers, now or later on, will join the small but growing number of people who are devoting their lives to the search for truth in the places where it is least known.

Let us imagine that we had the power to make ourselves at any time just as small as we pleased, and decided to make use of this gift to explore the inner recesses of the things we see around us every day. Already when we had shrunk to one-third of our normal size the things around us would begin to look very big: the cat on the hearthrug would begin to resemble a tiger, and we should find it quite difficult to climb up on to the tall dinner table to get out of his way. As we grew smaller, the salt cellar, the water jug, and the knives and plates on the table would grow large as houses; we should notice that the blades of the knives which had hitherto seemed so smooth and sharp were really very rough and blunt, that the tablecloth was made of large coarse fibres like a jungle through which we could, if we wished, wriggle down to the surface of the table beneath. The dust particles in the air which we can just see on a sunny day would seem like large birds floating in the sky beneath the incredibly distant ceiling. We should have entered the world which can be seen through the microscope, full of unfamiliar shapes and objects.

As we grew smaller still, a thousand times smaller than our original size, we should encounter all sorts of strange things: living and half-living creatures like the bacteria and cell-like organisms with which the microscopic world abounds, and photographs of which, taken through powerful microscopes, can be found in books on biology. At last we should penetrate beyond the range of the most powerful microscope into surroundings difficult to imagine and about which little is known, except what can be inferred from difficult clues obtained with the help of the cleverly designed instruments which have been invented by our scientists. At more than a million times smaller than our present size, we should be approaching the world of the molecule and the atom. We should begin to find ourselves in a kind of hailstorm, being continually bombarded by showers of tiny particles, called molecules. The air which surrounds us is really made up of nothing but these molecules, and consists of two main kinds: molecules of oxygen and molecules of nitrogen, together with much smaller numbers of some other kinds, which need not concern us. The molecules fly about in all directions and at all speeds, many of them faster than an express train, so that if we decided to become any smaller we should have to be very careful not to be hit by any of them.

We should notice that not only the air, but everything else was made of molecules of the same kind, many of them like the molecules of nitrogen and oxygen in the air looking rather like dumbbells, and others much larger, with strange elongated shapes. We should see that the water molecules in the water jug, instead of flying about freely like the molecules in the air, were packed rather closely together, but were still moving very quickly up and down, backwards and forwards, always bumping against one another and the side of the jug, some of them escaping through the surface of the water to join the much less crowded molecules in the air beyond. We might observe on close examination that even the glass of the jug was made of molecules, all apparently stuck together, but in continuous agitated motion, and gradually making their way from place to place in the glass. The molecules of salt in the salt crystals in the salt cellar would appear, on the other hand, to be neatly stacked together like a heap of bricks, but still vibrating to and fro in a sort of wave-like formation, and still occasionally breaking free from their positions in the crystal.

If we allowed ourselves to become smaller still, we should see that the molecules themselves were made of smaller units, called atoms. We should find that every molecule of nitrogen in the air consisted of two *atoms* of nitrogen, held together by a mysterious attraction, so that we could pull them apart only with considerable difficulty; and that every molecule of oxygen also consisted of two atoms held together by the same strange attraction. We should find, on the other hand, that a molecule of water was made from three atoms, one atom of oxygen and two atoms of another substance

A molecule of oxygen   A molecule of hydrogen   A molecule of water

called hydrogen. Hydrogen is a gas which is found, mixed with some other *poisonous* gases, in the supply of coal gas used for cooking and heating in our homes; it is very light, and used to be used for filling airships and barrage balloons. Hydrogen burns very readily in the air, and, mixed with oxygen, easily explodes; after the explosion, nothing is left but steam, which is made of small drops of water. The reason for this is that an atom of oxygen would much rather have two atoms of hydrogen attached to it than another atom of oxygen; so that, if a pair of oxygen atoms joined together in an oxygen molecule find the opportunity, they break away from one another, and each rushes to collect for itself a molecule of hydrogen, which consists of two atoms. The speed and confusion produced by the oxygen atoms in their rush to secure pairs of hydrogen atoms appears to us in the form of the heat and light of the explosion; and when the explosion has died away nothing is left but molecules of water, each of which consists of an atom of oxygen with two hydrogen atoms securely attached.

The molecules of salt which we should find stacked so neatly together like bricks in their crystals are made up of an even stranger union: each consists of one atom of sodium and one atom of chlorine. Now it would be hard to find anything apparently more different from salt than sodium and chlorine. Sodium is a rather

soft, silvery metal which rusts so quickly in air that it has to be
kept in oil, and chlorine is a greenish poison gas which was used
in the Great War of 1914–18. When a piece of sodium is placed
in a jar containing chlorine it bursts into flame, and in a very short
time nothing is left but a heap of salt. The sodium atoms are so
eager to find chlorine atoms for themselves that there is a big rush
which appears to us as a flame, and they are all paired off in a few
seconds. The molecules of salt which remain each consist of one
atom of sodium and one atom of chlorine.

So far we have met five different kinds of atom—atoms of
hydrogen, oxygen, nitrogen, chlorine and sodium. There are,
however, many other different kinds, and up to a few years ago it
was believed that there were just 92 different kinds, of which 90
had already been discovered. A list of these atoms can be found
in most books on chemistry; too much space would be needed to
give the complete list here, but a few, selected at random, are shown
in the table below. The atomic number is the number of the atom
on the list, and the chemical symbol is the sign used by chemists
to represent the element or substance made of atoms of that particular kind.

Atomic number	Element	Chemical symbol
1	hydrogen	H
2	helium	He
6	carbon	C
7	nitrogen	N
8	oxygen	O
9	fluorine	F
11	sodium	Na
17	chlorine	Cl
79	gold	Au
80	mercury	Hg
88	radium	Ra
92	uranium	U

Numbers 43 and 85 were missing from the list, but now scientists
have discovered how to make them artificially, and the new elements
have been christened technetium (Tc) and astatine (At) respectively.
A still more interesting discovery, also made in the last few years,
is that there are more than the 92 elements whose existence was

6

previously suspected. Numbers 93–102 have actually been made, and can be added to the list. They are:

Atomic number	Element	Chemical symbol	Atomic number	Element	Chemical symbol
93	neptunium	Np	98	californium	Cf
94	plutonium	Pu	99	einsteinium	E
95	americium	Am	100	fermium	Fm
96	curium	Cm	101	mendelevium	Mv
97	berkelium	Bk	102	nobelium	No

The new elements were christened by the people who first identified them; for example, americium was so called by a group of Americans, and curium was named in honour of the French scientists Pierre and Marie Curie.

The elements 93–102 are not found naturally on the earth, because they do not last very long: they have a tendency to change into other elements which have been known for a long time. To find the reason for this we should have to leave the world of the atoms at which we arrived in imagination by making ourselves smaller and smaller, and make ourselves tinier still. We should then begin to see that the atoms themselves are not made completely of the same stuff, but are built up from still smaller parts. We should find that an atom really consists of a cloud of electricity with a little dot, called the nucleus, at the very centre, rather like a pip at the centre of an orange. The amount of electricity surrounding the nucleus depends on the atomic number: the helium atom has twice as much electricity as the hydrogen atom, the carbon atom six times as much, the nitrogen atom seven times as much, and so on. It is sometimes said that the hydrogen atom has one *electron*, the helium atom two electrons, the carbon atom six electrons, and so on; but the electrons would not appear to us as points, but rather as fuzzy clouds which could merge into one another.

Electrons, the stuff of which electricity is made, behave in some strange ways which are difficult to imagine. In the atom we have found that they form a sort of cloud surrounding the central nucleus. Sometimes they jump right out of their atoms and move away in a form resembling a wave, similar to the waves which are formed on the surface of a pond when we throw in a stone. The waves of two electrons sometimes pass through one another without stopping, and sometimes push one another away and go off afterwards in quite different directions. Unlike the movements of the stars, which can be predicted for hundreds of years ahead, it is, in fact, impossible to say exactly what an electron is going to do; in some ways it *seems* to have a mind of its own. The same is true of all the tiny particles of which things are made; we can see that they may do this, or *this*, or *that*, but we can never tell with any certainty which it will be. It looks just as though the particle has the choice of one of a number of different things, and decides for itself which it shall be. At the same time, it would be ridiculous to suppose that an electron chooses between different things in the same way as we choose what sort of sweets we are going to buy; an electron has no brain, and we have to suppose either that Someone or Something we do not know about makes its decisions for it, or that what happens to it is left to a blind Chance.

Electrons exert quite large forces on one another and on the nuclei which, it will be remembered, lie like pips at the centres of the atoms. This you can verify easily by brushing the end of your fountain-pen briskly along the sleeve of your coat. When you do this, some electrons are removed from your sleeve to the fountain-pen, which will then attract and pick up tiny scraps of newspaper. The action of a magnet in picking up small pieces of iron is rather similar. The electrons in the magnet are whirling round and round in their atoms, always in the same direction, and the forces which they exert on other electrons are responsible for the attraction which is observed. Inventors have found out how to use these forces in making motors entirely run by electricity, and the same sort of thing explains the working of all the electrical inventions which have become familiar in our homes. In the electric light bulb, when the current is switched on, for instance, electrons are forced to run quickly along a narrow wire called the filament under the influence of a strong attraction to one end. As they hurry along the wire, they continually collide with one another and with the atoms in the wire, and create such a disturbance that the wire becomes white-hot and gives out a brilliant light.

In our exploration of the atom we found that it consisted of a cloud of electricity with a tiny nucleus at the very centre. Although this nucleus is so very small, it weighs thousands of times all the electrons put together. To discover what it was made of we should have to become very much smaller even than the infinitesimal size we had already attained. Then it would gradually appear that the nucleus consisted of a number of particles of two different kinds, called protons and neutrons. We should discover that, although they appeared to be stuck together, they were chasing one another round at very great speeds. We should find also that the number of protons was exactly the same as the number of electrons in the cloud of electricity outside, that is, exactly the same as the atomic number. The hydrogen atom has always in its nucleus just one proton, the oxygen atom has eight, and the uranium atom 92.

The number of neutrons in the nucleus, however, is often different even for atoms of the same kind. The ordinary atom of hydrogen has no neutrons at all, but there is another, rarer kind of hydrogen,

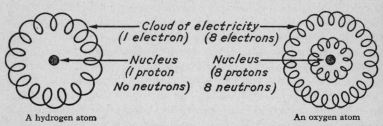

A hydrogen atom   An oxygen atom

called deuterium or heavy hydrogen (because it weighs about twice as much as the ordinary variety), which has one neutron per atom, and still another kind called tritium which has two. There are, in the same way, various kinds of oxygen atoms with 6, 7, 8, 9 and 10 neutrons combined with the eight protons in the nucleus, and there are varieties of uranium with 136, 137, 138, 139, 140, 141, 142, 143, 145, 146 and 147 neutrons per atom. But an atom is usually happiest if it has just a certain number of neutrons to keep its protons company in the nucleus. A hydrogen atom prefers to have none at all, an oxygen atom likes exactly eight, and an uranium atom is most comfortable with 146. Any atom will usually tolerate a few more or less than this preferred number of neutrons, but if the difference becomes at all large, the relations between the particles in the nucleus become extremely strained, and all sorts of troubles are likely to occur. Sooner or later an upheaval takes place, as a result of which one or more unwanted particles generally come flying out of the nucleus, though, in a few extreme instances, the situation is so bad that the whole nucleus explodes, scattering pieces in all directions.

As an example of this kind of upheaval, let us see what happens if a stray neutron enters the nucleus of an oxygen atom already holding 10 neutrons, increasing the total number to 11. This is more than the nucleus can comfortably hold, and in less than a minute something like a violent quarrel seems to occur inside, and an electron comes flying out, rather like a plate out of the window of a house in which there is some disagreement between the occupants. When the disturbance is all over, we find that an amazing thing has happened: the atom of oxygen has changed into one of a substance called fluorine, with 9 protons and 10 neutrons in the nucleus.

The alchemists in olden days tried vainly to turn one element into another, but thanks to the achievements of modern physics we see that this is now possible. It has even been discovered how to turn mercury into gold. There is a kind of mercury whose atoms have 80 protons and 116 neutrons in the nucleus. If another neutron comes along, it upsets the peaceful equilibrium of the atom, and after a day or two there is a minor upheaval, during which an electron disappears from the cloud of electricity surrounding the nucleus, having apparently been brought in to keep the peace. When the upheaval has subsided, it is found that the atom of mercury has changed to one of gold, with 79 protons and 118 neutrons in the nucleus. Unfortunately, although it is possible to make small amounts of gold from mercury in this way, it would cost much more than the gold was worth to manufacture it in large quantities.

One strange thing about processes of this kind is that the weight of the substance finally obtained is not quite the same as the weight of the substances used in making it. For instance, the weight of gold obtained by the process just described is very slightly less than the weight of the mercury, and the weight of the neutrons which combined to make it. The explanation is that when the nucleus of an atom undergoes some change, part of the matter which it contains is often converted into radiant energy. The matter simply disappears, and radiation appears in its place. It is also possible to convert radiation into matter. It is, indeed, very probable that all kinds of particles, and therefore all kinds of matter, could be produced from radiation alone, so that, in a sense, the whole world is made of nothing but radiation.

Now someone may venture to ask: What is radiation? This

is a question which it is impossible to answer immediately. Strictly speaking, we cannot say what anything *is*; we can only say what it *does* and what it *is like*. Radiation carries energy from place to place, and it is like waves. The distance between two successive waves is called the wave-length, and the wave-length of the radiation decides what sort of radiation it is. Radiation with a certain wave-length appears to us as green light. As the wave-length becomes longer, the light changes from green to yellow, from yellow to orange, from orange to red, and finally disappears altogether. But the radiation is still there, and can be felt as heat. As the wave-length becomes longer still, the heat radiation changes slowly to

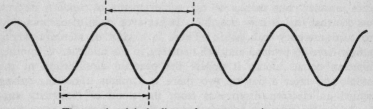

The wave-length is the distance between successive crests or troughs in the wave formation

the kind of radiation which is used at radar (radiolocation) stations for detecting aircraft, then to the kind which is received on the short wave-bands of our radio sets, then on the medium and long wave-bands. By now the wave-length is a mile or more, and passes out of recognition. If, starting from our original green light, we were to make the wave-length shorter and shorter instead of longer and longer, we should find that the green light would change to blue, then to indigo, then to violet, before disappearing from sight. Even then the radiation would exist, and could still be photographed with an ordinary camera; and as the wave-length decreased we should obtain X-rays, which can pass through the human body and other objects, and finally gamma-rays, which are so powerful that they can penetrate and pass through the thickest of metal plates.

In this way we have discovered that radio and radar waves, heat rays, light rays, X-rays and gamma-rays are all different kinds of radiation with different wave-lengths, and that they all carry energy from one place to another. We may ask further, what radiation is made of, whether it is made of particles, in the way matter is made of atoms, and atoms are made of electrons, protons and neutrons. The answer is yes: radiation consists of hosts of particles called photons; but photons are very strange things, even stranger than the electrons which we have already met. We can never discover exactly where a photon is; it is very shy, and, as soon as we try to find it out, it disappears completely. All photons travel with the speed of light, which is 186,000 miles a second (they can travel from the sun to the earth in about eight minutes), and the energy carried by a photon is greater the smaller its wave-length.

Although we have found that energy is carried by photons, we have not yet devoted very much attention to energy itself. It is now known that even a particle which does not move has energy which is greater the greater its mass, or weight; this is called the rest-energy of the particle. But a particle in motion has more energy than when it is at rest, and the additional energy is called kinetic energy, which means energy of motion. The heat energy of matter is just the energy of motion of the molecules which it contains. Of course, we cannot see the molecules moving; they are far too small, and because they are all moving in different directions the substance as a whole does not have to move at all. But, as we have already found out, the molecules in all the things we see around us are moving very quickly backwards and forwards, up and down, and we now find that the hotter the object the more quickly they move.

There is just one other kind of energy, called potential energy. This is energy which is stored up, and can be used when and how we please. The electrical energy which we use in our houses is of this kind, and so is the chemical energy stored in coal and other substances which burn; both kinds can be used for producing heat and light, or for making things move, as in the electric fan and the steam engine. It has been found recently that there is also another kind of potential energy, which may also be used for heating, lighting, and moving things: atomic energy. The atomic bomb is just a device for releasing very quickly the energy stored up in a large number of uranium atoms, so that a great deal of heat and light is produced all in a second or two. To understand how it works, we must remember how much an atom dislikes having the wrong number of neutrons in its nucleus. We saw previously that an oxygen atom does not care to have more than 10 neutrons in its nucleus, and how some sort of quarrel breaks out if an extra one comes along. This upheaval is a very minor occurrence compared with what happens in some other nuclei if an uninvited neutron breaks in.

The uranium atom is never very happy, however many neutrons it has; 92 protons and 136 or more neutrons is really too many for a single nucleus, and trouble is bound to occur somewhere at some time or other. Very often the trouble is settled fairly easily, and only a few light particles are thrown out in the disturbance. There is one particular number of neutrons, however, that the uranium atom cannot tolerate at any price: that is 144. The number 144 seems to be an especially unlucky one for the uranium nucleus; if 143 neutrons are already present and another one should come in, a terrible conflict immediately begins. This culminates in a tremendous convulsion in which the whole nucleus is completely shattered into two or more large pieces, and also quite a number of fragments, which fly off in all directions. The fragments nearly always include several neutrons, and if these should hit the nuclei of other uranium atoms nearby with 143 neutrons already present, the same process is repeated in these atoms as well; and in a very short time the trouble will have spread to all the uranium atoms of this particular kind in the neighbourhood. The result is one gigantic explosion.

The destructive power of such explosions has made the atomic bomb a very fearful weapon in the hands of politicians who have not the welfare of the whole of humanity at heart; and it is very important indeed that it should be prevented from falling into the possession of evil men. Rather fortunately it is not easy to separate the kind of uranium with 143 neutrons per atom from the mixture of several kinds which occurs naturally; and it is still more difficult to arrange for a supply of neutrons to make the release of the atomic energy occur at the right speed and the right time. It is quite certain that the potential energy of the atom can be released at the right speed to provide us with heat and light in the same way as it is now obtained from coal, and so save the miner the difficult and dangerous task of bringing coal up from the mines; so that the power of the atom can be used for the good of humanity instead of for its destruction.

In our exploration of the world of the atom, we have already encountered several different kinds of particles which do not consist of anything smaller: the electron, the proton, the neutron,

The characteristic mushroom-shaped cloud after an atomic
bomb has been exploded

and the photon. It is natural to ask whether this completes the list,
or whether there are still other particles to be encountered. In
truth there seem to be very many more kinds of particles, which
do not occur naturally and were first observed in some mysterious
rays, called cosmic rays, which come from the sky. They often
travel extremely fast, and carry a large amount of energy for their
size. The cosmic rays do not seem to come from the sun or any
particular star, but arrive on the earth from all directions and at
all times of the day. No one has yet succeeded in giving a convincing
explanation of how they are formed. The best theory seems to be
that they are produced by the destruction of atoms of helium,
carbon, nitrogen and oxygen, which are wandering about in the
space between the stars; but how these atoms might be destroyed
we can only guess. It has even been suggested that the rays have
no particular method of formation: that they are being continually
created out there in the heavens, just as all other matter must once
have been created. It is possible that the hidden Maker of the
world has not yet finished His task.

6*   (G 487)

Finally, let us pay a brief visit to quite a different sort of world from the world of the atom—the world of very low temperatures. Here also some surprises await us. We have seen that the heat energy possessed by all substances is the energy of the motion of the molecules which they contain. If the molecules could be brought to rest, a substance would have lost all its heat energy; we should have arrived at the absolute zero of temperature, which is about 273 degrees below the freezing-point of water on the Centigrade scale. This is the coldest anything can possibly be. The air at the North and South Poles is probably never much below 80 degrees below the freezing-point of water; but if the same air is cooled to 192 degrees below freezing, the oxygen in it begins to condense just as steam does when cooled below the boiling-point of water, and at 195 degrees below freezing the air is completely changed to a liquid not much different from water in appearance. This is called liquid air, which to-day is easily made with the help of special apparatus in laboratories and factories. At the still lower temperature of 223 degrees below the freezing-point of water the liquid air itself freezes and becomes solid, like ice. In fact, by the time we reach 261 degrees below freezing, everything, including hydrogen, becomes solid, except helium, which becomes a liquid at 269 degrees below freezing and remains a liquid right down to absolute zero. Of course, absolute zero has never been reached in the laboratory, but scientists have succeeded in reaching temperatures only a few thousandths of a degree from absolute zero.

In this region of intense cold near the bottom of the temperature scale, strange things begin to happen. At temperatures below about 2 degrees absolute, that is, less than 2 degrees from absolute zero, liquid helium suddenly changes its nature. It remains a liquid, but becomes, apparently, very still. This stillness is deceptive, however, for if it is left in an open tube, it disappears, reappearing outside the tube if the temperature there is low enough. This puzzled the investigating scientists very much at first, but soon they found the explanation. The liquid creeps up the walls of the tube and over the top, just like a convict trying to escape from prison. Once over the top, it trickles down to the lowest level it can find. It can never be seen climbing up and down the walls in this way, because it spreads itself out so thinly: the surface of the tube is covered by a layer of liquid never more than a few hundred atoms in thickness; but to make up for this it moves up and down at a speed of nearly a foot per second. It does not matter what the walls of the tube are made of, or how high they are: the liquid escapes just as easily as before, and continues to do so until the level of the liquid outside the tube is the same as inside.

This is quite remarkable, but something still more remarkable happens if the liquid remaining in the tube is heated gently. Then it stops climbing out of the tube and instead begins climbing back. It is just as though the escaping convict finds it too cold outside the prison cell, and if the cell is warmed for him, prefers to go back to prison. As long as the warming goes on, the liquid helium will go on climbing up into the tube until it will not hold any more. Liquid helium below two degrees absolute also possesses a large

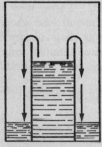

Liquid helium leaving
its tube

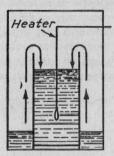

Liquid helium climbing
back into its tube

number of other strange properties, and is called liquid helium "two" to distinguish it from the liquid helium above this temperature, which behaves just like any other liquid.

Another strange thing happens in very many, though by no means all, metals at very low temperatures. For example, at temperatures below 4 degrees absolute (4 degrees from absolute zero) tin suddenly changes its properties. It *appears* to be unchanged, but if we try to pass an electric current through the metal, we find that it has completely lost its resistance. This means that a current flows, however small the potential energy given to the electrons, and that it is possible for an electric current to continue flowing in the metal even when no energy is being supplied at all. It has been found that electrons in a ring of metal can, at these very low temperatures, be persuaded to go on chasing one another round and round the ring for a period of many days without any sign of growing tired. This is the nearest approach to perpetual motion which has ever been found on earth. The metals which have this strange property are called super-conductors. Another interesting thing about a super-conductor is that, if a small magnet is placed above a flat plate made from a super-conducting metal, it does not fall to the surface of the plate as one would expect, but remains for ever hovering just a small distance above the surface, in complete defiance of the law of gravitation.

The explanation for these strange happenings is partly known, and partly still obscure. All scientists agree that they are in some way connected with what is called the quantum theory. Unfortunately, we have now arrived almost at the end of our short journey into the world of science, and there is now no space left to find out exactly what the quantum theory is about. Those who wish to know more and later to help in exploring the still vast tracts of unknown territory are recommended to ask at their library for the latest books on atomic physics,[1] which give detailed information about some things which could be mentioned only very briefly here.

[1] Two useful books, published by Blackie, are called *The Restless Universe* and *Atomic Physics* by Max Born.

MAN'S CONQUEST OF THE AIR

The very perfection of bird flight gives an air of deceptive simplicity, since to climb, sweep, soar and dive, borne only on the unstable air, is almost unbelievably difficult. We must remember, however, that millions of years of slow evolution have given the bird a body and nervous system which is wonderfully adapted to the purposes of flight.

In the short span of sixty years man has striven to acquire something of this matchless skill. Although his aircraft can far exceed the speed of any bird, the joyful evolutions of feathered creation are still, and probably always will be, far beyond his reach. Let us see what are the fundamental obstacles that he has had to overcome to arrive at such mastery of the air as he has achieved.

First there is the still unexplained force of gravity which tends to cause all things to move towards the centre of the earth, a direction usually described as downwards. In flight this force may be overcome either by buoyancy as in a balloon or airship, or by dynamic reaction as in the wings of an aeroplane or the rotors of the helicopter. The balloon, because of its great bulk coupled with low weight, displaces a mass of air weighing more than itself and therefore tends to rise. The airship employs the same principle with the possible addition of a certain degree of dynamic reaction at the will of the pilot.

The difficulty of achieving an adequate degree of control in the three dimensions once the aircraft is in the air was one of the decisive factors which so long delayed the coming of mechanical flight. Many investigators had experimented with man-carrying gliders, but sooner or later, for lack of sufficient control over their frail craft, they came to grief, usually with fatal results.

It was not until 1903 that the Wright brothers, Wilbur and Orville, after years of laborious research and experiment, solved this problem. It had been obvious that to turn to right or left would need the help of a rudder, but how to prevent the plane from being tilted dangerously sideways had eluded all the earlier workers. This problem the Wrights solved by arranging for the tips of the trailing

edges of their flexible wings to be warped downward at the will
of the pilot. This warping device, which they patented, had the
effect of increasing the lift derived from the wing which was deformed.
By continued practice they acquired the skill necessary to use wing
warping in the flight of the first successful man-lifting power-driven
aeroplane.

What is this dynamic reaction to which we have referred? Sir
Isaac Newton stated that if a force is applied to a body it is opposed
by an equal and opposite reaction. If we lean on a table, the table
pushes back with an equal force. If it did not it would move. The
wings of an aeroplane are driven through the air by the thrust
of a jet or airscrew. Now the wings are so shaped and set at

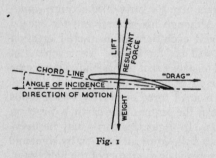

Fig. 1

such an angle to the line of
flight that by reason of
their motion they accelerate
a mass of air in a generally
downward direction. The
resultant reaction provides a
certain degree of upward
thrust or lift which supports
the weight of the aircraft in
flight. If the total lift is
greater than the weight, the
aircraft rises, but if the lift is less than the weight, it will descend.
Thus we see that for uniform level flight lift and weight must equal
one another.

Now that we have stated this general principle let us consider
in more detail the form and behaviour of the wing. Although a
flat surface would have been simpler to construct, study of the
shape of a bird's wings would naturally lead an investigator to
assume that a slightly curved wing section might be more efficient.
Not until many experiments with model wings had been conducted
in a wind tunnel, however, was it realized how great an improvement
in lift resulted from the use of the curved or cambered surface.
Improvement in the construction of wind tunnels and their associated
apparatus led to the discovery of much useful information about
the behaviour of various wing shapes and sections. This research
has enabled designers to produce much more efficient aircraft which
can fly faster without an unreasonable increase in the power required
from the engine.

Fig. 1 shows the cross-section or profile of a cambered wing. First note that the curvature is greatest near the leading edge (the edge facing the direction of flight). The imaginary line which joins the leading edge to the rear or trailing edge, the datum line upon which the form of the camber is based, is known as the chord. In fig. 2, which shows the shape of the wing in plan, the chord is indicated and also the span, which is the length of the wing from tip to tip. The ratio of span to chord is called the *aspect ratio* of the wing. It is generally true to say that the greater the aspect ratio, the more efficient is the wing at low and moderate speeds. You may have noticed the high aspect ratio of the wings of sail-planes. As these aircraft have no engine, highly efficient wings are a necessity.

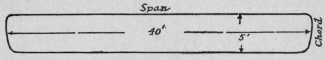

Span

40'

5'

Chord

Fig 2.—Aspect ratio 8

The faster a wing is flown the greater will be its lift, but, unfortunately, a limit is imposed by the greater power required to maintain the higher speed. Part of the dynamic reaction tends to oppose the forward movement of the wing and indeed of the whole aircraft. This opposition is known as drag, and it is the price that must be paid for lift.

How do lift and drag vary with changing speed? If the speed is *doubled* the drag and lift are both increased *fourfold*, for they both increase with the square of the speed. At the same time the power now needed to drive the aircraft at twice the original speed has increased *eightfold*, since the power increases with the cube of the speed. Thus the attainment of high speed is an expensive business, and has been achieved only as the result of intensive research and experiment aimed at increasing the lift of a wing while reducing its drag. The high speeds which have been reached show how successful these labours have been. At the same time engine development has proceeded at such a pace that it has temporarily outstripped the aerodynamic design of the airframe.

Reduction in drag is achieved by choosing such shapes for wings and all other parts of the aircraft exposed to the air flow that they produce as little disturbance as possible to the streamline flow of the air. Skin friction is another form of drag. To keep this low all exposed surfaces must be made extremely smooth.

To return to the problem of control in flight, yawing movement (a turning about the aircraft's vertical axis) is produced by the rudder. Up or down movement is started by the elevators, which are movable horizontal flaps in the tail unit. However, it is wrong to say that the elevator makes the aircraft climb or dive. All it does is to change the plane's attitude with reference to the horizontal surface of the

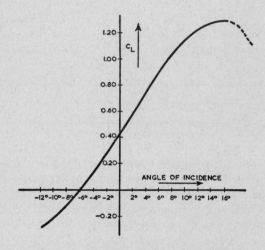

C_L = LIFT CO-EFFICIENT = WEIGHT LIFTED PER UNIT AREA OF WING

Fig. 3

earth. Climbing entails the expenditure of energy from some source or other. In the aeroplane the energy is supplied by the engine, so it is the engine that enables the aircraft to climb. In a glider or sailplane the energy used in climbing is obtained from rising air currents.

There are many different types of wing section, each of which is especially designed for some particular purpose. For high lift one section will be used, for great speed another. For every different section, however, there is one particular angle of attack which will provide the greatest lift, another at which the drag is least, and a third at which the lift-drag ratio is highest. These facts are best shown by a graph. In fig. 3 the vertical distances show the lift

derived from 1 sq. ft. of wing area. The horizontal distances show
the angles of incidence or attack. From this curve we learn that
when the angle of attack is 0° there is still a lift of 0·42 lb. per sq.
ft., and not until the angle is −6° does the lift cease. Also we note
that up to an angle of about 12° the lift steadily increases, but in
the neighbourhood of 15° there is an abrupt change of direction

Flow of air round a wing
in normal flight

Breakdown of air flow after the
stalling angle has been reached

Fig. 4

betokening a sudden drop in the lift. The angle at which this change
occurs is called the stalling angle, and when it has been reached
the wing is said to be stalled. This is a dangerous condition if the
aircraft has not enough height to allow of recovery.

What is the cause of the stall? In fig. 4 it will be seen that in
normal flight the streamlines run smoothly, but if the angle of attack
is too great then this smooth flow breaks down and turbulence is

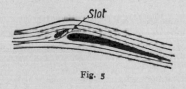

Fig. 5

set up with a consequent loss of lift and increase of drag. So serious
are the results of stalling that special types of aircraft have been
designed to avoid its occurrence, and in one case a special device
known as the Handley-Page slot has been introduced to delay the
arrival of the stall in the normal type of wing. This device has the
effect of sending a stream of air through a portion of the leading
edge of the wing as shown in fig. 5. This causes a re-establishment
of streamline flow near the leading edge of the wing.

Since lift is derived from a downward acceleration of a mass
of air, it would be natural to expect that the lower surface of the wing

would provide the greater part of the lift. However, this is not so, and in fact about two-thirds of the total lift is the result of a reduced pressure existing over the upper surface of the wing. This will be made clear in fig. 6, which shows the air pressure distribution about a wing in normal flight. The length and direction of the lines show the direction and magnitude of the forces arising from this distribution. The reduced pressure over the upper surface is due to the fact that the air is moving faster than the layers above it.

Most of the early aeroplanes were biplanes—that is to say they had two sets of main planes, one more or less directly above the other. The purpose of this design was twofold, to give added wing area and consequent increased lift (a most valuable feature in the days of low speeds), and furthermore to provide a mechanically strong structure without excessive weight. Its chief disadvantage was the high drag caused by the many struts and bracing wires. To reduce drag, monoplanes were designed and built. To make these really strong was at first difficult, and indeed numerous accidents due to structural failure in the air decided the French government to ban their use in France for some years. As time passed the use of new materials such as the light aluminium alloys permitted the construction of a practical cantilever monoplane, so that to-day, except for some training machines, the biplane is obsolete. The gain in aerodynamic efficiency in the new designs has made possible the very high air-speeds which are now common. There have been many different types of monoplanes including those with high wings, mid wings, and low wings. The modern low-wing design is the most popular, but each type has its own advantages.

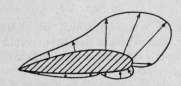

DISTRIBUTION OF AIR PRESSURE OVER
A WING IN FLIGHT.

Fig. 6

POWER PLANTS—JETS

The aeroplane flies because the thrust of the airscrew or jet forces it through the air, thus providing the necessary dynamic reaction. We have noted that the lack of an adequate system of control was an obstacle to the achievement of mechanical flight.

An even greater obstacle was the absence of a suitable type of prime mover combining low weight with sufficient power to drag the aeroplane through the air fast enough for safe flight. As far back as 1894 Sir Hiram Maxim, the inventor of the machine-gun bearing his name, produced a remarkable light compound steam-engine of 180 h.p. Two of these engines actually lifted Maxim's giant aeroplane off the ground for some distance. Two years later, Langley, in America, successfully flew two steam-driven model aeroplanes weighing 26 lb. each. About 1900 the Wrights, finding that there was no engine suitable for their purpose, turned from steam to the internal-combustion engine, and designed and built their own four-cylinder four-stroke petrol engine. This engine, which developed between 11 and 12 h.p., weighed only 2 lb. per h.p., a most meritorious figure for that date. As time went on, lighter and more powerful types of the electrical ignition internal-combustion engine were developed, so that to-day we have piston engines of more than 3500 h.p. with a specific weight of less than a pound per h.p.

The demands of high-speed flight are now requiring far greater powers than are yet available in the piston engine, so that in the search for high power coupled with low weight, men have had to turn their thoughts in other directions. So we have the development of the gas turbine, which has placed an extremely powerful but relatively light power plant at the service of the aircraft designer. Furthermore, the new engine may be used to provide the required thrust either by means of the normal airscrew or jet reaction.

Rockets and Jet Reaction.

Recently the importance of the rocket principle has been brought to public notice by accounts of aeroplanes employing a rocket-assisted take-off. Of their use in the war there is no need to speak. Despite the great publicity that rockets have received, very few people understand how a rocket operates. There is a popular impression that the rocket is driven forward by the blast of hot gases pressing backward on the surrounding air. This is quite wrong, for indeed the rocket will actually work better in a space devoid of all air, provided that the fuels employed have their own oxygen supply in some form or other. Picture two persons on opposite sides of a swing door, the one trying to enter, the other to leave. If both push equally, the door will not move. But let the slightest difference of pressure arise and the door will swing. It is the difference of pressure that causes the motion. Similarly, when the charge is fired within the cylindrical rocket the rapidly expanding gases exert an equal pressure in all directions. Immediately the lower end of the tube bursts open the balance of pressure is destroyed, and the rocket is driven upward by the resulting reaction.

The amount of fuel that the rocket carries is soon burnt and the rocket falls. In the jet-propelled aircraft the problem of the continuous expulsion of the expanding gases has been solved. Thus we have an aeronautical blow-lamp, the reaction of which keeps the aeroplane in flight.

Attempts to apply jet propulsion to aircraft have been made over a number of years, and many have been the methods proposed to provide a continuous stream of expelled gas. There is no reason why the working fluid should not be air, so we find designs to employ the normal piston engine to compress the large masses of air to feed the jet. Such a system is not efficient, and no real progress was made until the arrival of a practical gas turbine. A turbine, as its name implies, is a fast-spinning wheel driven by water, as in the hydro-electric stations, or by steam, as in the large electricity generating stations or marine power plants, or again, by exhaust gases of some form of internal-combustion engine.

Airscrew v. Jet.

The need of far greater powers than were available from the piston engine was not the only obstacle that lay in the way to the achievement of higher airspeeds. It had long been known that the efficiency of the airscrew—its ability to convert the power supplied to it into effective thrust—began to fall off as airspeeds approached 450 m.p.h. Some other form of propulsion was needed that did not suffer from this disability. Jet propulsion satisfied the demand. Its efficiency not only did not decrease with higher speeds, but actually grew greater, and only reached a maximum when the airspeed of the aircraft equalled that of the gases expelled from the jet. On the other hand, however, jet propulsion is extremely inefficient at low speeds, and therefore quite unsuited to aircraft of moderate speed. For such the airscrew must be used to convert the engine power to effective thrust. What was required was a prime mover that could generate great power with relatively light weight, but also be equally suited to either jet or airscrew propulsion.

The Gas Turbine.

During the past three decades the steam turbine has steadily advanced until now it has firmly established itself as a most reliable and highly efficient prime mover, equally serviceable at sea or on land. It might, therefore, be thought that with all the wealth of experience that has been gained over many years in its design and construction the work of the gas turbine designer should be fairly easy. This is not so for a number of reasons. In the steam turbine there is at hand an ample source of steam at constant pressure ready to feed the turbine rotors, whereas in the internal-combustion engine the explosive charge passes through a series of operations at pressures which vary intermittently. To replace these intermittent operations by a system that would provide a steady stream of high-speed high-temperature gases required a great deal of thought and development. Furthermore, the efficiency of the gas turbine depends, as does that of the piston form of the internal-combustion engine, upon the compression ratio and the temperature of combustion. Now there are difficulties in the way of providing high-compression ratios in the gas turbine which cannot be gone into here, but it can be readily understood that the temperature of the burning gases when they pass through the blading of the turbine rotor is extremely high. In modern British aircraft gas turbines the rotor blades have to withstand in normal service conditions temperatures approaching 1500° F. This fact alone will show how difficult are the conditions to be overcome, especially since there is the incentive of higher efficiency to be gained by the use of yet higher temperatures.

At present we may say that increased gas turbine efficiency waits, to a large extent, on the production of new blade materials which are essential if the necessary higher temperatures are to be successfully withstood. In this country, most gas turbine blades are made of special steels manufactured by Messrs. Henry Wiggin & Co., Ltd., and known as the Nimonic Series which can be operated above 1500° F. A world-wide search is being conducted by metallurgists for improved heat-resistant materials for gas turbine blading. That the material should be heat resistant is not enough, for it must also be of such a nature that it is capable of large-scale production and reasonably free from difficulties in handling and fabricating. It would be difficult to prophesy what form the most suitable material will take, but a good deal of experimental work is going on with a view to using ceramics or a combination of metals and ceramics. In the U.S.A. these combinations are known as ceramals.

In the gas turbine steam is replaced by a continuous blast of intensely hot air and burning gases. The air enters at the front end of the unit and is compressed by either a centrifugal or axial compressor. In the axial type there is a series of rotors on one shaft and separated by circular rows of guide vanes, the whole forming a multi-stage compressor. From the compressor the air passes either to a number of " flower pot " combustion chambers equally spaced round a circular frame, or through an annular combustion chamber. In either case atomized fuel under pressure is sprayed through burners into the chambers to be burnt at a very high temperature. In order to keep the temperature of the chambers and turbine rotors within reasonable working limits large masses of secondary air are now admitted and expanded by the heat of combustion. The stream of heated gases then impinges on the rotor blades and passes through the turbine wheel, causing it to revolve at anything up to 16,000 revolutions per minute. The power so generated drives the compressor, which is usually directly coupled to the turbine wheel shaft. So great is the power developed that it is more than is needed to drive the compressor and the excess is used for aircraft propulsion, either by airscrew or jet.

To start the turbine the shaft is spun up by an electric motor. This starts a series of operations. The air rushes through the compressor, heater plugs are warmed up, the atomized fuel is injected and begins to burn. If the unit has a number of combustion chambers there are two heater plugs, and some of the gases ignited by these pass through connecting pipes to the other chambers, lighting the burners in them. The plugs are then automatically switched off, and the turbine rapidly achieves the speed appropriate to the amount of fuel being burnt. It should be noted that, unlike the piston engine, the gas turbine requires no warming-up period, but can be run up to its maximum revolutions in a minute or so.

The control of the turbine is simple from the pilot's point of view, for the speed is governed by a single lever which controls the rate of fuel admission to the burners. There is one very important instrument of the aircraft's control panel. This is the indicator which shows the temperature of the jet pipe. This must be watched in order to ensure that the temperature does not rise above a stated value or serious damage may result.

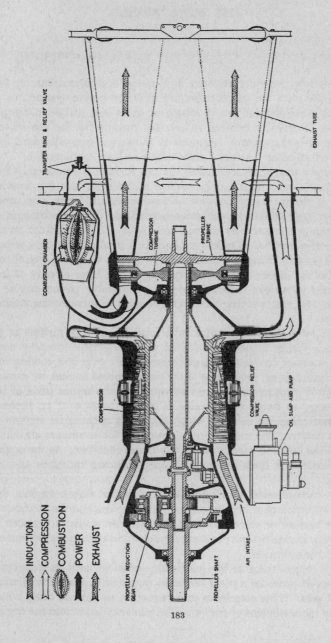

INDUCTION
COMPRESSION
COMBUSTION
POWER
EXHAUST

TRANSFER RING & RELIEF VALVE

COMBUSTION CHAMBER

COMPRESSOR TURBINE

PROPELLER TURBINE

EXHAUST TUBE

COMPRESSOR

COMPRESSOR RELIEF VALVE

OIL SUMP AND PUMP

PROPELLER REDUCTION GEAR

PROPELLER SHAFT

AIR INTAKE

Fig. 7.—Bristol Theseus propeller driving gas turbine

183

GREAT ADVANTAGES OF THE GAS TURBINE

It is not generally realized how many and important are the advantages that the gas turbine has over the piston engine.

The possibility of fire, a source of great loss of life in aircraft fatalities, is greatly reduced in the gas turbine by the use of less volatile fuels than petrol. At present, paraffin is generally used, but diesel oil or other " safety " fuels might well be employed.

Being a purely rotary engine the gas turbine is remarkably free from vibration. This brings several advantages, not the least of which is the increased comfort of passengers and crew who profit by its relative quietness and smooth running. This smoothness of operation is enhanced by the elimination of the intermittent power strokes of a number of cylinders, and their replacement by a steady flow of power. Thus a reduction in structural weight is permitted, and also far higher operational speeds, as we have already stated. The gain in weight-reduction over a comparable piston engine is over 60 per cent, a saving which can be used to increase the aircraft pay-load.

One very important point in favour of the gas turbine is its cooling. Piston engines are cooled to a reasonable working temperature either by leading large masses of air over the cooling fins of the cylinders or, in the case of the liquid-cooled engine, by passing the coolant through the jackets surrounding the upper parts of the cylinders. In both cases cooling is at the expense of an increase in aircraft drag, an increase which absorbs a substantial amount of engine power. The gas turbine is cooled by the secondary air which dilutes the burning gases in the combustion chamber. As the engine is self-cooled it does not require drag-inducing radiators and air scoops.

The complicated lubricating system of the piston engine, due to the multiplicity of highly stressed moving parts and the continuous sliding friction of the pistons on the cylinder walls, is replaced in the rotary engine by one of great simplicity and consequent extremely low oil consumption.

The compactness of the gas turbine coupled with its high operating speed provides a most powerful unit with a wonderfully small frontal area. This also leads to a reduction in aircraft drag, which leads to more efficient operation. The tendency to enclose the engine within the wing to keep drag as low as possible is being achieved by the newer engine, which is especially suited to this course.

An aircraft driven by a pure jet unit, having no airscrew, can be designed with a relatively light and low undercarriage.

CHANGES IN THE MATERIALS OF AIRCRAFT CONSTRUCTION

Wood v. Metal.

It is only natural that during fifty years great changes should have taken place in the types of materials used in aircraft construction. These changes have not been confined to airframes, for equally important changes have taken place both in engines and wings. In the early days of aviation all airframe and wing construction was based upon the use of wood, which had many advantages, including lightness, a plentiful source of supply in many parts of the world, ease of working, simplicity of repair or replacement of damaged members, and comparatively low cost. The wings were of linen fabric stretched over and attached to ribs of wood spaced along the spars. The wooden construction was so shaped as to compel the fabric to assume the correct contour to satisfy the aerodynamic needs of the wing. When fixed in position the fabric was sprayed with a specially prepared varnish or dope, which served the double purpose of tightening the material to a drum-like surface and rendering it fairly water- and weather-proof.

This wood construction, despite its many advantages, was prone to certain troubles when used in very damp or tropical climates. It was then likely to suffer deformation (a very serious fault), and suffer from mould and the attacks of insects. It became obvious that the replacement of wood by metal would be advantageous in many ways, but it was equally obvious that in the event of accident repair would be nothing like so simple as with wood, for which the ordinary carpenter's skill would be sufficient. Repairs to metal work, however, would require the services of highly skilled craftsmen who would generally only be available in the military services.

Eventually, however, it was discovered that the advantages of metal construction outweighed the disadvantages, and in the course of a few years its use became world-wide. To-day the use of wood is confined to gliders, sailplanes, and a small number of training aircraft. Some firms still make use of fireproof plywood for purposes where stresses are low, for the necessity of keeping down weight, despite recent great increases in engine power, is still as urgent as ever.

Stressed Skin

The replacement of the linen fabric wing-covering by metal was not a simple matter. A new technique had to be worked out for the employment of very thin sheets of light metal alloys. When this had been achieved the stressed-skin type of metal wing had arrived. To make a satisfactory job it was necessary to treat the metal to make it weather-proof.

There is, however, another advantage of the stressed-skin wing that is not so obvious. In the case of the old fabric-covered wing the purpose of the fabric was only to provide and maintain the correct aerodynamic shape of the wing. It contributed but little to the strength of the wing structure as a whole. Now, with the use of sheet-metal covering, the wing surface could be designed to add greatly to the wing strength by helping to maintain its shape, and taking its share in carrying the load in flight and the wing weight when the aircraft is on the ground. The system is known as the " stressed skin ", since the thin metal surface itself takes its part in bearing the stresses imposed on the wing.

Equally important is the part played in engine design by the new light alloys and the various types of steel, with the result that when each component is made from the material best suited to it, it is possible to reduce the dimensions of that component and thereby reduce its weight, so contributing to an increased overall efficiency of the aircraft. Thus the modern aircraft is the result of the joint efforts and skill of many workers in different industries. It is an outstanding example of collaboration between science and industry.

MAKING A CARTOON FILM

The cartoon film is not a recent discovery, although most people regard it as such.

The principles of cartoon-film technique were discovered many hundreds of years ago, long before the ordinary live-action film or even the photographic camera were invented. The possibilities of making a static picture move have fascinated both scientists and artists of the past; the scientists were more interested in the problems of light and shadow projection, which eventually led through the magic lantern to the discovery of the modern film projector, while the artists were concerned with the animation of humans, animals and objects. In about 1760 the " Whirling Top " was invented in Paris, a toy which gave a convincing illusion of movement. It became very popular with French children, but it also attracted the attention of scientists, who developed from it the Victorian " Wheel of Life ". This machine was composed of a small wheel inside a larger one. Twelve drawings of a galloping horseman in different positions were fixed on to the smaller wheel, and a square hole cut in the large wheel; by turning a handle attached to the smaller wheel and looking through the square hole the onlooker could then watch what seemed to be a horse actually galloping along. The illusion of movement was achieved in this way because the eye had not time to distinguish one drawing from the other, but could only see all the twelve drawings in a continuous flow. The very same idea is applied to the modern motion picture, only our latest machines can project about 16,000 drawings without stopping instead of twelve—and, of course, thousands of people can watch at the same time.

Cartoon-film making became very complicated with the invention of sound reproduction and colour photography, and other technical discoveries. We can easily see that it would take an artist years to draw a cartoon film single-handed when we realize that he would have to draw between 12,000 and 16,000 pictures, which is the number required for a normal cartoon film ten minutes long. He would also be obliged to trace his drawings on to transparent celluloids and then paint each one, produce between 80 and 100 backgrounds, and finally photograph each transparent celluloid against its background, thus making a composite picture. This would take him another six months, and after that he would still have to join the separate scenes of the film in the right order and synchronize them with the sound track. Thirty years ago, when cartoon drawings were just black outlines, and the stories were shorter and far less complicated, the cartoonist did actually produce films single-handed.

In 1904 Emile Cohl, the inventor of the modern cartoon film, not only thought out the story of his films and made the drawings himself, but also built his own cine-camera and laboratory so that he could do his own photography, developing and printing. At that time it was a one-man affair—now, practically every stage of production is a separate and specialized department. A cartoon-film studio to-day will consist of anything between 40 and 200 artists and technicians. Emile Cohl took twelve weeks to make a three-minute cartoon, using the simplest methods, and he finished that cartoon before starting another. A modern studio of forty artists can produce a ten-minute sound cartoon in six to eight weeks, and can work on four different films at the same time. The new method enables artists to produce cartoons in quantity, but we should remember that so far no machine has been invented to replace the human hand in order to draw individual pictures. Unlike the live-action film, each drawing of a cartoon film must be drawn, painted and photographed by hand. Consequently, the cartoon still retains its characteristic craftsmanship, according to the value of its basic ideas and the skill of the individual artists who turn these ideas into animated pictures, and the process demands an amazing amount of patient effort.

The production of a cartoon film does not start with drawing the pictures straight on to film. First, the story of the film has to be thought of, the story situations have to be worked out, and, if the film is intended to be funny, characters have to be fitted to the situations. While in some good cartoon-film units even the charlady has a fair chance of contributing ideas, it is more usual to have a special Story Department to do this work.

There are roughly three stages in the making of a cartoon: (1) planning; (2) sound composition; and (3) technical execution.

Planning starts with the story department. The function of the artists in this department is to illustrate the ideas of the film with rough pencil sketches, and, after discussion with other members of the unit, to develop these sketches into a more fully worked-out continuity from which, at a later stage, other artists will produce a finished cartoon. About 120 of these rough sketches are made of a size six inches by eight inches; these are displayed in their right order on a board, to be talked over by the story artists, the director, and the key personnel of the unit. After heated argument some of the sequences are rejected, and new ideas proposed; the story is then sent back for improvement. This process goes on until everyone is satisfied. At this point the director of the cartoon takes over; he will be in charge of all the activities which are necessary to turn these sketches into moving pictures.

First, the director will be responsible for timing the action—deciding how quickly or how slowly the figures should move. He will have to see that the characters are sufficiently simplified, because each character will be drawn by different artists several thousand times. His choice of colour will influence the colour supervisor, who will mix the colours for painting the characters, and the artist who will paint the backgrounds; he will also advise the background artist about the design and pictorial composition of the backgrounds. Right at the start, however, the director's main concern is to produce a timed script for the musical director, who will gain enough information from this and from the rough-action sketches to enable him to compose the music for the cartoon. In cartoon films the music is composed before any detailed animation has been drawn, in order that the action may be fitted to the music. It has been found that, once a picture is finished, no orchestra could follow the quick movements of the cartoon figures with the required precision. When the feet of a walking figure touch the ground at half-second intervals the problem of fitting the music would be fairly simple, but it is practically impossible if, for instance, the figure jumps into the air in a quarter of a second and hits a tree in an eighth of a second. To avoid this difficulty, therefore, the music is recorded on a sound track in advance. Listening to this, the expert film editor can then make a very accurate chart of the duration of each bar of the music, and measure out the sound track in film frames; this chart tells the director the precise length of each action. The film runs through the projector at the rate of twenty-four film frames in every second. Each exposure on the film itself is called a frame. If the duration of a music bar is half a second it will take twelve film frames, if a quarter of a second, six film frames, or if the music is really quick—as in a chase—the musical accents may be as close as one-eighth of a second, which is three frames of running time.

If there is dialogue in the cartoon (that is, if the characters or the commentator speak) the process is just the same. The voice of the actor chosen to speak the dialogue is recorded on film, the sound track is analysed by the editor, and each word is measured and noted down again in terms of film frames. The word " Goody ", for example, may take twenty-four film frames, which is exactly one second of running time, and the editor will chart the details of the word thus: G takes three frames, OO seven frames, D four frames, and Y ten frames. Besides this, the main characteristics of the sound track are set down; to the cartoonist it is most important to know whether a double-bass or a flute is playing, for while a double-bass may well accompany the movements of a heavy bear it would be quite unsuitable for a butterfly, which would move more naturally to the sound of a flute. The type of orchestra and the pitch at which it is playing are all registered on the chart which the editor prepares.

With all this detailed information about the sound track at his disposal, the director turns again to the picture material, and writes out precise instructions regarding movements and the behaviour of the characters, which he gives to the Key Animators. Thus the studio is launched on the endless labour of production.

The key animators can now tell on which frame of film a figure's step will fall. Supposing the first step to fall on frame 1, they will know that subsequent steps will fall on frames 13, 25, 37, and so on. It is then possible to proceed to settle finally the position of the figures, doing these steps at the right speed.

At this point the key animator has many problems to think about. How should his figure move? Should his feet step high, like a soldier, or should they drag along the ground, like an old man? Should he look sad or glad? Should he wear a hat or cap, and, if so, should he wear it tilted or straight? Details of this type must all be thought out because it is such details which, if correctly worked out, make the cartoon so enjoyable.

The key animator usually finishes drawings Nos. 1, 13 and 25, &c., himself, and leaves the drawings in between those numbers to other animators to complete. In more complicated movements, as

This is Charley as a blacksmith in the film *Charley's March of Time*. The eight drawings showing him hitting the anvil constitute one-third of a second of running time. He repeats the action several times in the film.

for instance in a fight, where so much happens in one second (only twenty-four drawings in all) the key animator may find it necessary to draw every third position, leaving only two " in betweens " to the other artists.

There may be anything from 48 to 480 drawings in a scene, according to its length. When the scene is ready it is tested for quality. The animation drawings, which are drawn with thin pencil lines on white paper, are photographed frame by frame on to film. When this is projected on a screen the moving lines will show whether the animation is satisfactory. If it is not, the animation is redrawn for a second test. When all concerned are satisfied with the animation the drawings are passed on to the Tracing Department.

Here, other artists trace the animation lines on to thin celluloid sheets, using fine pens and coloured inks. The tracing artists outline the figures very precisely, just as they are drawn, avoiding distortion of forms. Precision is especially required in tracing facial expressions, where the minutest misjudgement of line would make the figure look quite different. To achieve this degree of accuracy, great skill is needed. In this way all the animated drawings are transferred to celluloid sheets. The original drawings, which are no longer needed, can be stored for future reference.

At this point the Painting Department takes over. Up to now they have been busy preparing the various colours for painting the figures. Under the director's guidance the colour supervisor has tried out various colour schemes for all the characters and objects that have been animated and traced. The main purpose is to find colours which underline the types of character represented. For instance, the villain's face will be painted a dark green to look frightening, while the village idiot will be given a red nose to make him look stupid. The colour can also help the mood of the film. When a character becomes envious he can turn green, when he gets very cross he can be red, and when frightened—yellow. The story benefits from the use of colour too. The colour of a tree tells us what season we are in, the colour of the sky shows what time of day it is, besides providing a general atmosphere.

All this, and the number of colours to be used on the objects, are worked out well in advance. The general rule is to use as few colours as possible for the best effect, because the painting of so many figures entails a lot of labour. Usually, seven different colours are used for a figure. These colours are mixed up in bulk, as they

SCENES FROM THE FAVOURITE WALT DISNEY CARTOON FILMS
PINOCCHIO, *BAMBI* AND *FANTASIA*

have to last through the production. Once the colours have been decided upon it is desirable to avoid remixing, owing to the danger of not being able to match up the same tone again.

The painting of the celluloid sheets can now begin. The colourists turn each sheet over, tracing side downwards, and fill in the various parts of the figure according to the colour pattern. The complete figure gradually takes shape. When the colours are dry the celluloid can be turned over right side up again, and as the figure is painted on the back the colours still show up on the front, between the tracing lines. The colour has made the figure the only solid part of the transparent celluloid. The background shows through the transparent, unpainted part of the celluloid, and only the painted figure covers it.

While the animation, tracing, and painting departments have been busy producing thousands of moving figures, other artists have painted approximately one hundred static background pictures for this one cartoon. As all the movement will take place against these backgrounds they play a very important part in the film. They are usually painted in soft water-colours, so that the tones blend well with the painted figures. The artist does not aim at striking colour effects, but rather at creating a unity between the moving forms in the foreground and the stationary forms in the background. As in the case of the characters, the design of furniture or trees is very much simplified, almost symbolic. When watching a cartoon there is no time to look at any particular part of the background while the eye is following the character's action, but taken as a whole the background helps to add atmosphere and pictorial interest to the cartoon.

One by one the painted celluloids are placed over their backgrounds and photographed with a special cine-camera. A normal cine-camera usually runs continuously. A cartoon camera is so constructed that it can take a single frame of film at a time. The camera operator changes the celluloid while the camera is stationary, and then at the push of a button exposes the next film frame. This may sound easy, but modern cartoon-film technique demands more from the cameraman than the changing of simple celluloids. From time to time he has to move the background along an exact amount between each picture. In the finished cartoon this will give the effect of passing scenery, so walking and running movements are achieved with the aid of background movements as well as animation. Actually, the walking figure is drawn in the same position of the film frame,

7 (G 487)

and the background is pulled along behind him. This gives the illusion of a figure walking, and since the same step is used over and over again a lot of animation work is saved.

Another labour-saving device is to separate the stationary parts of a figure from the parts which have to be animated. If, for instance, the walking figure's body is to be kept still, the body is painted on a separate celluloid, which remains still on top of the background for as long as required. On a second layer of celluloid the arms and legs are carefully matched to it, moving in animation. The transparency of the celluloid sheets conceals this labour-saving trick, because the two layers placed together over the background look like one. So the cameraman's attention is fully engaged in carrying out these various manipulations under the camera, and he also has to see that the picture is in focus and exposed for the right length of time.

By adjusting his camera between each exposure he can, when required, " fade out " the picture, in which case it gets gradually darker, or he can " mix in " certain objects, as when a ghost appears. Photographing each frame of a cartoon is a lengthy operation, and even with an assistant it takes the cameraman more than a month to complete the picture.

There may be seventy to eighty separate scenes in a cartoon, some long, some short. Ten to twelve scenes make up a complete sequence. Each sequence represents about one minute of running time. The music is also recorded in separate sequences, so that the editor can match sound and picture tracks together. Even if the final film is to be in colour the picture at this stage is on a separate black-and-white film. This working print of the picture is used by the editor to synchronize the action with the music. For this work he uses a machine which can project picture and sound together or separately, run backwards or forwards, and be stopped at any time. As the editor has analysed the music track at an early stage of production, so that the animators could draw the picture to the music, we shall know quite a lot about it by this time. Nevertheless, he has to exercise the utmost care, especially in the case of characters speaking, when he has to fit every syllable to the right mouth movement.

In most cartoons it is necessary to use two or even three separate sound tracks. The first one will take the music accompanying the film from end to end; the second track will have the speech on it; and we shall probably put sound effects on the third. When each of these sound tracks has been matched exactly to the picture, all tracks are mixed into one single track by an expert sound engineer. This is called the " dubbed " track, which is eventually printed alongside the picture on the film.   Finally, the first colour copy of the cartoon is produced, and the director has a last chance to suggest any adjustments, if the colour balance of the print is unsatisfactory, before the audience sees the film.

The little figures have come a long way since those first rough sketches. They have had to go through several departments, they have been drawn, traced and painted by a number of artists. How is it that they still keep their identity so well, and move so smoothly, without distortions and jerkiness? For all the artist's skill, the pictures would be unsteady unless all drawings and tracings were kept in the same position. This is achieved by the use of the peg bar, which is fitted to every artist's desk and also to the photographic bench. These bars all have one round peg and one square peg, exactly the same distance apart, and every sheet of paper and celluloid which the artists use is punched along the bottom with two holes which fit exactly over the pegs. So all movements are drawn, traced, and painted on the same peg bars, and, since the minutest difference in the position of the sheets would affect precision of movement, this method provides a good universal registration.

Another important production problem is to see that the dozens of instructions which each single scene requires are handed over from artist to artist. This is done on one single paper called the animation chart, which accompanies the animated drawing right through to the cameraman. All essential information about music, or about the animation and celluloids and camera directions, is given on that chart. The chart looks like a single page taken out of an accountant's ledger; it is divided into little frames, each frame representing one film frame. Each set of celluloids is numbered consecutively, and these numbers are written down so that each little frame on the chart tells the cameraman which celluloids to use for every photograph he takes. The chart also tells him when to move the background, and when to adjust his camera for " fades " and " mixes ".

So far, the animated cartoon has mainly been used to amuse people. This may be a good thing, but the cartoon can do other things besides amuse: it can delight the eyes, stimulate the mind and the imagination, and it can also teach people in a new way.

Through the medium of the cartoon, good pictorial composition

These drawings show how the figure of a man on his bicycle evolves into a cradle, through fifteen different stages

and good colour can be developed—an opportunity that is missed in most cartoons at present. The cartoon can also show things which the live-action film cannot do. There is hardly any limit to the imagination of the artist. If he wishes to turn a drop of water into an ocean, or a feather into an elephant, he can do so; he can also make the elephant dance and fly in the air, and he can show the working of its heart-beat, because in cartoon he can penetrate under the surface. The cartoon can also simplify and symbolize forms: a round form like a tennis ball can suggest a face, a square form a house, a form like an ink-blob a town, and so on. A simple dot may represent a person, and a bigger shape may represent many thousands of people. Because of these faculties cartoons can be used for teaching a number of subjects in a new and enjoyable way.

One of the most important things a cartoonist has to realize in developing his skill is the relationship between his own and other arts. He will discover that the elements of design and pictorial composition in cartoon originate in the fine arts, the motion of the characters in the ballet, and commentary and dialogue in the theatre. He will also realize that there is a further element in cartoon—one that matters probably more than all the others, and one that makes the cartoon a new and different art—the *time* element.

When *time* is applied to the movements, to the pictures and the sound, they begin to take dimension in space—they have a beginning and an end. The particles of the film fall into shape, all the different fragments are co-ordinated into unity, and the cartoon begins to live its own individual life.

How is the time element applied? The way any character behaves depends on how its action is timed. Even the simplest walk, for instance, can be very funny when it is speeded up, and when the same walk is timed in a different way it conveys an entirely opposite impression. It is up to the cartoonist to accelerate or decelerate the motion of his figures at will, but at each different speed he will emphasize a different idea. The point where cartoon breaks away from the other arts is in the use of *time*.

When more and more artists have learned about this new art, I expect the cartoons you will see will be of far greater variety and will be even more enjoyable than the present ones. In the meantime, I hope you have followed my description of how a cartoon is produced, and that you will be able to understand and therefore criticize better the next cartoons you see.

MOTORS AND MOTORING

HOW THE MODERN CAR HAS DEVELOPED AND WHY

The motor car is now in its second half-century of development. In the quality of its performance the car of to-day has little in common with the " horseless carriage " of fifty years ago, yet in general it embodies the same components and conforms to the same principles.

How those components have been developed, and how those principles have been applied in different forms make a fascinating study, and some knowledge of these matters adds greatly to the interest of motoring and encourages the proper handling and care of the car itself.

Most of us like to know how things work, and this certainly applies to the motor car which is so much a part of modern everyday life, yet still offers the romance of travel and opportunities of sport, together with utility. All these are made possible by a remarkable piece of mechanism lending itself to the most exact control and skilful handling. We have to remember, too, that this intricate mechanism has to be kept as light as possible to avoid wasting engine power, and hence petrol, on dragging about unnecessary weight, and, moreover, it has to operate exposed to mud, dust, water, heat and cold, with a minimum of attention. It must be as reliable as a locomotive, but without the regular and skilled attention or the smooth and carefully graded track that the railway offers. Yet we expect equal comfort in a saloon car whatever the road surface, and it may be interesting to consider how these difficult problems are being solved.

PETROL ENGINE PRINCIPLES

There have been cars driven by steam engines, and there are many light utility vehicles electrically propelled by motors which draw their power from batteries, the need for charging which, however, limits radius of action. But the petrol engine is almost universally used for the motor car. With few exceptions this engine operates on what is known as the four-stroke cycle, and while many motor-cycle engines are of the two-stroke type, few cars are fitted with such engines.

The term " four-stroke " implies that the piston moves up and down four times within the cylinder to complete each cycle of

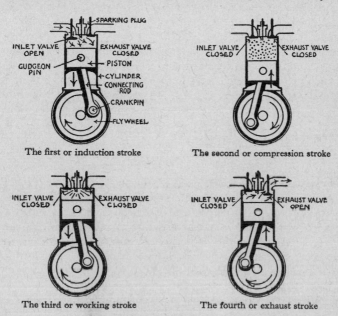

The first or induction stroke

The second or compression stroke

The third or working stroke

The fourth or exhaust stroke

The four-stroke cycle

operations, during which time the engine makes two revolutions. First it moves down to suck in a mixture of petrol and air, through an inlet valve, from the carburettor. The inlet valve closes, and the piston moving up compresses the charge into the small space in the cylinder head. Then the compressed charge is ignited by a spark between the points of the sparking plug, and the pressure of the burning gases drives down the piston. Finally a second valve—the exhaust valve—opens, and the rising piston expels the burnt charge.

These four strokes are described as the inlet, compression, working, and exhaust strokes. Of them, it will be seen, only one provides power, and to keep the engine turning smoothly over the other strokes, a flywheel is used which stores power on the working stroke and gives it out on the other three strokes. With a single-cylinder engine the flywheel must be comparatively heavy, but if the number of cylinders is increased the flywheel can be lightened. Most cars have four-cylinder engines so that there is always one cylinder on its working stroke. Still smoother running is given by six cylinders, for the working strokes then overlap, and even more by eight cylinders which can be set in line, or in two sets of four mounted at an angle to each other.

Four cylinders provide a practical compromise as regards smooth running, simplicity and cost, so that most popular cars are fitted with such engines, which have been greatly improved in their running, particularly at low speeds, by mounting them on rubber, which absorbs vibration before it reaches the car itself.

The Importance of the Valves.

It will be understood that much must depend upon the efficiency of the valves in admitting the gas, and in allowing the burnt gas to be expelled. These inlet and exhaust valves are nearly always of the " poppet " type, that is, shaped like a mushroom with a head which is coned to bed in a corresponding valve seat. They are opened and closed by a cam-shaft, the cams on which push up the valve stems, sometimes directly but generally through push-rods or tappets. Sometimes the valves are contained in a side pocket, when the engine is known as a side-valve type.

More often the valves are fitted upside-down in the cylinder head, and are then operated by push-rods and rockers from a cam-shaft in the crank-case. Where still higher efficiency is required, and cost not too important, two cam-shafts may be used and mounted overhead with drive by chain from the crank-shaft.

Sometimes the inlet valve is overhead and the exhaust valve beneath it, the combustion space in such engines often forming a kind of side pocket. This construction can give very even combustion throughout the working stroke, and is used on some engines famous for their refined performance.

Where power is a first consideration it is usual to set the valves at an angle in the head, into which they open directly to give the gases a straight path in and out. In all cases of course springs return the valves to their seats, and in high-speed engines much care has to be given to the choice of spring, as the ultimate speed of the engine is largely limited by what is known as "valve bounce": the valve ceases to act in rhythm with cam and spring, while at the best the time available for the gas to enter and leave the cylinder gets shorter and shorter.

Many alternative valve systems have been tried, and a cylindrical sleeve between piston and cylinder with holes or ports cut in it to let the gas in and out met with some success. In one case two concentric sleeves moving up and down were used, and in another a single sleeve moved up and down and also to and fro to give the necessary quick opening and closing of the ports. Although discontinued for car engines, the latter type of single-sleeve valve is still used for some aero engines.

Factors of Efficiency.

The petrol engine belongs to the "internal" combustion type as opposed to the steam engine, which depends upon "external" combustion. In the first case the combustion takes place in the actual cylinder of the engine, whereas in the second, combustion or burning takes place in a boiler and the steam generated is the working medium used in the engine.

Combustion implies heat, and it is the aim of the designer to convert as much of the heat in the petrol as possible into energy. At the best he can only utilize a small part, not much more than 25 per cent. The gases are still very hot when the exhaust valve opens, and here the greatest loss in heat occurs, about 40 per cent. Then the cylinders must be kept cool or else they would become overheated. Hence they are surrounded by water jackets, which again carry off much heat which could be better employed. The amount of heat thus lost depends upon the surface exposed to the hot gases. A cylinder head of irregular shape offers much greater surface for a given volume than a spherical one. Hence the use of a hemispherical head, with valves set directly in it at an angle, when greater efficiency is required.

It will be realized that many improvements in engine design can be effected without any visible external changes. These can be appreciated by a comparison of power curves—plotted on squared paper between engine revolutions on the horizontal scale and horsepower on the vertical. At one time such curves climbed gradually to a peak and then declined steeply. To-day they climb steeply, and on a straight line, then flatten out and decline slowly. That

7*   (G 487)

means power increases almost directly with speed and that maximum speed is not far beyond maximum power. This implies good pulling at lower speeds and nearly as good acceleration, say, between 40 and 50 m.p.h. as between 20 and 30 m.p.h.

It may be noted that maximum engine speed and maximum power, as shown on the power curve, do not coincide. Power may commence to fall, but the engine may be capable of running still faster. On top gear this extra speed cannot be taken advantage of, but by

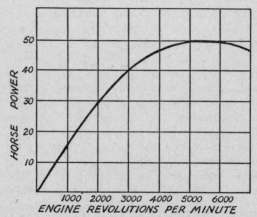

A typical power curve which shows how the highest power and the highest engine speed do not coincide

dropping down to a lower gear less is asked of the engine, and its extra speed will give higher road speed than if the engine is left to pull on its highest gear. This is why extra acceleration can be obtained so often when passing or in an emergency by dropping down into a lower gear.

TAKING THE POWER TO THE ROAD WHEELS

So much for the engine, but the power it develops has yet to be taken to the driving wheels. These are generally the rear wheels, but there are cars which have the front wheels driven, and others, such as the familiar " jeep " and many army vehicles, which drive either through the back wheels only, or if required to negotiate bad ground can have the drive taken to all four wheels which, equipped with heavily ribbed tyres, give a very effective grip.

The first link in the transmission line between engine and driving wheels is the clutch, mounted in the flywheel, and which as its name suggests provides the connexion between the engine and the drive to the road wheels. Once this was a crude affair of a cone faced with leather held in contact with an internal cone in the flywheel by a strong spring. The clutch was held out by a pedal just

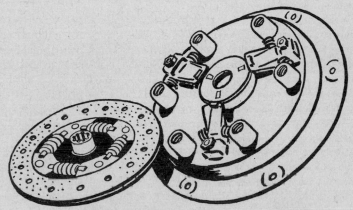

A typical single-plate dry clutch. On the right is the casing and on the left is the plate with ring of friction fabric. The springs give a smoother take-up of the drive. In the centre is a splined boss on which the plate can slide when free.

as to-day, but no longer does the motorist have to throw in resin if the clutch slips or Fuller's earth if it is too fierce.

Now almost every car made in this country has the same type of clutch, and generally the product of the same specialist clutch manufacturers. Instead of a cone, however, the clutch consists for ordinary use of a light steel plate carrying a fabric facing ring on each side. This plate is gripped between the flywheel face and another plate which turns with the flywheel, by springs spaced between the second plate and the casing, which is bolted to the flywheel and encloses the whole clutch. The drive is disengaged by the clutch pedal through levers which draw back the second or pressure plate.

Many refinements have been introduced into this comparatively simple type of clutch so that not only is slip eliminated, but the drive is taken up smoothly and little thrust on the pedal is required to disengage the clutch. Thus the friction fabric has been the subject of much research, so that it may be resistant to both heat and wear, while the plate which carries it is generally slit radially, so that by bending the segments slightly a spring effect is obtained to give a more gradual engagement.

There are variations intended to give the same effect, while to increase the smooth take-up of the drive, the plate may not be rigidly attached to its hub, but drive it through coil springs, giving a cushioning effect.

Yet another variation is to introduce several short levers pivoted within the clutch casing and carrying a roller on their other ends which bear on the pressure plate. As the engine runs faster, centrifugal force tends to throw the rollers, which are also bob-weights, against the plate with increasing pressure. This means that the clutch springs need not be so strong and the clutch pedal needs less pressure, yet the grip of the clutch increases as the power it has to transmit increases.

Such are the details of the ordinary clutch, but there are clutches which rely entirely upon centrifugal force for their engagement. In this case the clutch pedal becomes unnecessary, for when the engine speed drops below a certain figure the clutch disengages itself, and conversely when the driver presses the accelerator the clutch takes up the drive as soon as the engine is running fast enough to give the necessary centrifugal action to the bob-weights.

Another well-known type of clutch is what is known as the fluid flywheel, which was used in ship propulsion before it was applied to cars. This is not easy to describe, but it consists of driving and driven members formed with cups or vanes. Oil is thrown outwards as speed increases, but is guided from one set of cups to the other, so that the driving member acts as a pump and the driven member as a turbine. At low speeds no drive is transmitted, but as speed increases so does the impact of the oil until the two parts revolve together almost as a solid mass. The path followed by the oil is considerably more complex than suggested, but the description will serve to give a simple idea of how the fluid flywheel operates. No clutch pedal is needed as the drive is taken up when the accelerator pedal is depressed. The fluid flywheel does not lend itself to use with an ordinary gear-box, however, as the engine cannot be disconnected without slowing it right down, and hence, as in the case of the automatically operated centrifugal clutch, a special gear-box is really required.

With the fluid flywheel a pre-selector, or self-changing gear-box of what is known as the epicyclic type, is generally used, in which the actual gear required is engaged by friction bands.

Features of the Gear-box.

The next component on the way from engine to road wheels is the gear-box. The ideal form of this would give an infinite number of gears so that the engine could be kept running at its most efficient speed whatever the work it had to do. Unfortunately this favourite problem of inventors still awaits a practical solution. Any methods which do provide something of the kind within limits, introduce other problems, some of them worse.

It can be done electrically or hydraulically. In the first case it means that the engine must drive a dynamo or generator and the dynamo drive a motor or motors. This has been done on cars and is the principle on which the diesel-electric locomotive works, but for ordinary car use, the system is heavy, complicated and costly.

There is a hydraulic system, however, which has been successfully applied and which greatly simplifies the task of driving, for no clutch pedal is required and no gear-lever—except for reverse; just accelerator and brake pedals. This mechanism, known as a hydraulic torque convertor, consists of driving and driven members which also act as a fluid flywheel. The speed of the latter, however, adjusts itself to the work to be done. On hills it runs slower but pulls more strongly, just as do the lower gears of an ordinary gear-box. The only objection is that the lowest gear equivalent is not as low as the usual lowest or first speed of a gear-box, while the engine will not run faster than the speed at which it develops its highest pull or torque.

This is good for the engine and almost eliminates wheel slip on slippery surfaces, but it deprives the driver of the ability to drop into a lower gear and make use of the maximum speed of the engine. Thus the device does not lend itself to use on the sports car, but for cars with large engines and ample power it has many attractions.

Same Principles but Improved in Detail.

The majority of cars still have the same type of gear-box as used in the earliest days and of which a famous French automobile engineer said, " It is brutal but it works ". Since his day many refinements have been introduced. By the use of better materials the gears have been greatly reduced in size, and the whole gear-box made lighter and more compact. More knowledge in cutting and grinding, in the design of the tooth form and in the mounting of the gear shafts has also made for quieter and more efficient gears.

For many years gear-changing was something of an art, and many drivers took an excusable pride in their ability to change quickly and quietly under any conditions. The trouble was that gears had to be engaged which were running at different speeds, and any attempt to change gear while the car was running at all fast entailed unpleasant noises unless something was done to bring the gears more or less to the same speed before attempting to engage or mesh them. Hence what older drivers know as double-clutching. To change up one declutched, moved the gear lever into neutral, let up the accelerator, let the clutch in for a moment, then declutched again, and engaged the next highest gear. To change down the same was done except that the engine was accelerated. In the one case it was necessary to slow down a faster moving gear-wheel, and in the other to speed up a slower one. That procedure, which was a little simpler than it sounds, is nowadays rendered unnecessary by the general use of the " synchromesh " gear-box. In this the actual toothed wheels are permanently meshed, and engagement is by notched rings or dogs, and these embody small friction clutches, so that the dogs to be engaged are first brought to the same speed when the gear lever is moved.

We are all familiar with the free-wheel on the bicycle, and a similar free-wheel is sometimes an addition to the gear-box. It is not often fitted nowadays, but one well-known maker retains it, while another fits it to the lowest or first gear to make the engagement of this gear quite easy, even when the car is travelling at a fair pace, for very few cars provide synchromesh engagement for the lowest gear. The ability to free-wheel on down gradients, or when slowing-up, gives economy in petrol. The objection can be raised that the brakes have to be used more, but actually a driver accustomed to the free-wheel drives accordingly, and there is no noticeable extra brake wear. The free-wheel also makes gear-changing very simple, and changes can be made with its aid without declutching.

Provision is always made for locking the free-wheel when required, and on steep descents or unknown hills it is always advisable to do so, in order that the engine may assist in braking.

There are, of course, many developments in gears and their

operation, particularly in America, but space prevents any description of these, and we must content ourselves with systems commonly employed on British cars.

How the Road Wheels are Driven.

Now we come to the final stages of the drive to the road wheels. The common practice is to mount these on what is known as the " live " axle. This term originated in earlier days when the rear driving wheels were carried on an ordinary solid axle and driven from the gear-box by a chain on each side. Chains were troublesome, and exposed to mud and dust wore rapidly, so that the present shaft drive superseded the side chains.

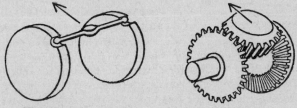

The differential gear, which permits the two driving wheels to turn at different speeds when cornering, &c. The illustration on the left shows the principle, and that on the right how it is applied by means of bevel gears. The arrow shows direction of rotation of the differential and axle as a whole.

In it, each wheel is carried on the end of a half-shaft, the inner ends of which carry " differential " gearing so that one may run faster, and the other slower when a corner is taken. This differential is similar in principle to that used on a pedal tricycle, and its working is best understood from a drawing. Outside the differential there is a large bevel wheel, with a smaller bevel pinion to drive it, the whole and the two half-shafts being enclosed in the axle casing, which you see if you look beneath the car at the back. The bevel drive is necessary to change the direction of the drive, the engine and gear-box being in line with the car, and the axle at right-angles to it. All that now remains is to connect gear-box and axle, and this is done by a shaft, which is hollow for lightness, but of sufficient diameter to resist twisting, and to prevent " whip " at high speeds.

It must be remembered, however, that the gear-box is carried on the frame of the car, but the axle is connected to the frame through springs, and moves up and down as the springs are deflected by road inequalities. So we must fit the shaft with some kind of joint at each end, which will permit it to move through an angle while transmitting the drive. These joints or " universals " in their simplest form consist of two forks, one carried on the gear shaft at the end of the gear-box and the other on the driving shaft. These

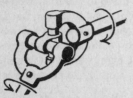

A universal joint of the Hooke type, which allows power to be transmitted through an angle such as between gear-box and rear axle.

are connected at right angles by intersecting pins. Again a drawing explains the idea better than words.

There is still another complication, however. The axle moves up and down under the control of the springs more or less in a straight line, whereas the rear end of the shaft would try to follow a circular path with the length of the shaft as radius. This means that the length of the shaft must be variable, and to provide for this the front end of the shaft is left free to slide within the universal joint on " splines " which take the drive. With engines placed farther forward it is sometimes preferred to divide the driving shaft into two portions, the forward half being carried on the frame.

What has been referred to as the driving shaft is generally termed a " propeller " or " cardan " shaft, and the old name for the type of universal described was a " Hooke's " joint.

BRAKES AND BRAKING

A very important part of the car is its braking system. It must pull up the car in a reasonable distance; it must retain its effectiveness on long descents. It must not require frequent adjustment, and it must give smooth retardation, or deceleration, without too much pressure being required on the brake pedal.

Fortunately the brake can be made to do much of its own work. To understand this it may be simplest to consider the early type of brake which, before friction fabrics were developed, consisted of a band lined with leather, or even wood blocks, which acted on a brake drum. The band was fixed at one end and tightened by a bell-crank lever at the other. It is easy to understand how the drum turning in one direction will tend to resist the tightening of the band. In the other it will tend to carry the band with it and thus further tighten it. This self-wrapping action has its modern equivalent in the "self-servo" action of the modern internal-expanding brake, brought to a high standard of efficiency in the two-leading shoe type. The brake shoes are separated or expanded to come into contact with the drum by mechanical or hydraulic means. In the former a cam may be used or a cone pressed between the ends of the shoes to separate them, this second method requiring very little effort. In the hydraulic system, the brake pedal actuates what is really an oil pump from which pipes lead to cylinders in the brake drums with pistons engaging the brake shoes. Pressure on the brake pedal is then transmitted hydraulically to the brake shoes. Advantages of this system include equal pressure trans-

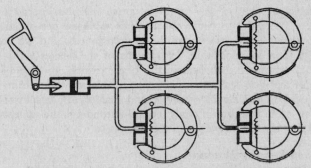

The principle of the hydraulic braking system. The master cylinder, operated by the pedal on the left, applies pressure equally to all four brake cylinders.

mitted to each brake, and the elimination of rods and levers by flexible piping between moving parts, although this can also be simply achieved by the use of wire in a flexible casing.

One system of braking employs hydraulic brakes on front wheels and mechanical braking on rear wheels, which conforms to legal requirements in the simplest manner. The law requires two quite independent braking systems, so that, if all brakes are hydraulically operated, the hand brake at least must be mechanically operated. In what is known as the hydro-mechanical system, the brake pedal simultaneously applies both sets of brakes, but the mechanical brakes on the rear wheels can also be operated alone by the hand-brake lever.

The distance in which a car can be pulled up was greatly reduced when brakes were fitted to front wheels as well as back. It was further reduced when it was realized that it was safe to apply as great a braking effort to the front wheels as to the back or even more. There was a fear of locking the front wheels, which might lead to a front-wheel skid, which is worse than a rear-wheel skid because steering is lost. But when the brakes are applied there is a transfer of weight forward so that the rear-wheel grip on the road is reduced and the front-wheel grip is increased. This effect is greatest when the braking is fiercest, hence the front-wheel brakes can be given at least as much to do as the back. The careful driver uses his brakes as little as possible. He will lift his foot from the accelerator in good time before he comes to a corner or a crossing, for he knows that unnecessary braking not only means brake wear, but also implies waste of petrol.

The latent heat of the petrol is converted into energy by the engine. The need to brake means that we have generated more energy than we can use under the circumstances, and we have to dissipate it in some fashion. By means of the brakes the surplus energy is reconverted to heat in the brake drums, and the need to get rid of that heat leads to other brake problems. The drums must be exposed to the air for cooling, and fashions in coachwork can interfere with braking if they entail shrouding the wheels and obstructing the air-flow around the drums.

Speed and Stopping Distances.

Finally, what are reasonable distances for stopping from various speeds? Certainly greater than generally supposed. Even if the brakes are in perfect condition and adjustment, their ability to stop the car will be limited by the nature of the road surface. The maximum braking which we can employ effectively is that which just fails to lock the wheels. Directly the wheels lock and sliding commences braking is lost and often control as well. Hence the condition of the road and the tyre treads determines the coefficient of friction between road and tyre, which in turn decides what distance we can stop in, even with the best of brakes.

Impossible as it may seem, braking can be more than 100 per cent efficient, although that requires exceptional conditions. About 80 per cent is the general maximum and 70 per cent is quite good. Yet with 70 per cent brake efficiency 43 ft. are required to stop the car from 30 m.p.h. Double the speed to 60 m.p.h. and the stopping distance will not be mere double, but will be four times as much—172 ft. Now suppose the road is wet and slippery, reducing the coefficient of friction and hence the braking efficiency to, say, 30 per cent. Then it will take 100 ft. to stop the car from 30 m.p.h., or 400 ft. from 60 m.p.h.

A driver should always get the feel of his brakes when taking the wheel of a strange car, and should not take those of his own car entirely on trust. If a car has been washed, water may have penetrated to the shoes, and the brakes may not be there when wanted. Driving with the brakes applied lightly will dry out the drums.

The good driver learns unconsciously to limit his speed to that at which he can stop his car within his range of vision. At night it is the range of his headlight beam which should decide his speed.

THE CAR AS A CARRIAGE

We may now consider the car as a carriage. After all, the average motor car is designed not primarily for the pleasure of the driver, but to convey its occupants with speed and comfort.

The first cars were really horseless carriages, for they retained the form of the horse vehicle with larger rear wheels than front, with steering by a front axle pivoted at the centre and shoe brakes acting on the rear tyres. The engine was a horizontal single-cylinder just like a small stationary gas engine with outside flywheel and perhaps with belt drive. The power unit was accommodated beneath the seats, but it was soon realized that the best place for a piece of mechanism requiring frequent attention was in front under a bonnet, where it was easily accessible.

To-day it is still there although it has been pushed farther forward, so that the occupants can all be seated within the wheel-base, that is, between the axles. Formerly the front seats alone were well placed midway between the axles, and the rear passengers were over the rear axle, where they were subject to the maximum movement of the springs.

With higher speeds the contours of the car have changed until we have the " streamlining " of to-day sometimes carried too far, so that entry and exit become difficult and head-room inadequate. Actually streamlining has few advantages at ordinary speeds—unless more attractive appearance—but directly we approach the mile-a-minute mark streamlining appreciably reduces wind resistance, giving more speed for less power and a lower fuel consumption. Wind resistance, it may be kept in mind, does not increase directly with the speed of the car, but with the speed squared. Thus, if we increase the speed of the car from 30 to 60 m.p.h. we do not double the wind resistance, but multiply it four times. Thus it is worth while giving flowing lines to the coachwork, and these in addition give a car which keeps cleaner, and is easier to clean, owing to the

Three stages in the evolution of the motor-car

absence of corners and abrupt changes of contour. Also wind noise is reduced, and it is remarkable how the interior of a car can be quietened if there are no external projections or fittings to catch the wind at speed.

Smoothing out the Bumps.

There remains the problem of adapting our motor carriage to the inequalities of the road. On a perfect surface, springs could be dispensed with, but unfortunately no road approaches the perfect and the wheels have to meet shocks from all angles. To insulate the occupants of the car from these shocks and vibrations is a problem which has been reduced but not completely solved yet. Leaf springs were inherited from the horse vehicle, but the iron or solid-rubber tyre was quickly replaced by the pneumatic type. After all, it is the tyre which meets the obstacle first, and gradually by increased sections and lower pressures it has been made capable of providing better and better protection to both the mechanism of the car and its occupants.

Tyres alone, however, cannot maintain the car on an even keel. To achieve, or rather approach this ideal, we must rely upon some

A typical independent front suspension system of the " wish-bone " and spiral spring type

form of springing. Until recently leaf springs, commonly described as semi-elliptic, although almost flat, were relied upon, but now the designer is turning to other forms such as the spiral spring and the " torsion bar ", while air suspension has been successfully applied, and also rubber.

The new forms of springing have been large introduced with independent front-wheel suspension, which dispenses with a front axle and provides each front wheel with its own spring mounting. This is also provided for the rear wheels on many cars, but independent front suspension is now almost universal. The wheels are generally carried on parallel links more often pivoted laterally and described as " wish-bones " on account of their triangular form. Their design provides some interesting exercises in geometry. If of equal length, the wheel would move up and down in a straight line, but the point of contact with the road would move in and out, which would be bad for the tyre. So the bottom link is made longer, and the wheel tilts as it moves up and down and so keeps the wheel track constant.

Another method of mounting is the "trailing" link, in which the links are parallel to the frame to which it is pivoted forward and the wheel carried at the free rear end. Here the wheel moves up and down in the same plane, but gives a slight variation in wheelbase, but the length of the link is comparatively so small that this variation has no significance.

While a leaf spring set across the frame sometimes serves as one of the links in the transverse system, a coil spring is more usual with wish-bones, but both this and the trailing link lend themselves to "torsion bar" suspension. In one case they are mounted parallel to the frame and in the other across it. The principle involved is that of the "torsion" or twist of a suitable steel bar held at one end. If a twist is applied to the free end, such a bar is capable of acting very effectively as a spring. In this case one of the wish-bones or the trailing link is keyed to the free end of the bar.

There has been a general improvement of steering with the adoption of independent front suspension, but here again geometry is involved, for the two wheels cannot be connected by a single tie-rod as in the case of the axle-mounted wheels, but each must have a tie-rod of the same length brought to a central point to be actuated by the steering wheel and column.

Springs of whatever type have to have their movements restrained or "damped" by shock absorbers, while transverse torsion bars are commonly used at both front and rear to limit the relative up-and-down movement of the wheels on opposite sides of the car, thus serving to prevent the car from rolling or rocking on uneven surfaces.

There are of course innumerable details of car design which are also interesting to consider and compare, but we have surveyed the more-important features of the modern car, the appreciation of which may add to the interest of motoring and may be helpful to those who look forward to the day when they will hold their own driving licence.

RADAR

In 1873, James Clerk Maxwell of Scotland published an epoch-making book, his *Treatise on Electricity and Magnetism*. In this book he proved mathematically that changes in electric and magnetic force must radiate in the form of waves just like light waves and with the same speed of travel (186,000 miles a second), and that this radiation must have many other properties precisely similar to those of light. His theories, however, regarding these electro-magnetic waves lacked experimental proof, and it was not until fifteen years later that Heinrich Rudolf Hertz of Germany produced these waves experimentally and proved conclusively all the predictions that Maxwell had made. These are the waves, often called Hertzian waves, which are employed in radio signalling, and their use for this purpose was first made possible by Guglielmo Marconi of Italy.

These three men then, Maxwell, Hertz and Marconi, are the founders of all forms of radio communication, including, of course, the latest one called radar, but before passing on to that we must consider shortly how it is that energy can be transferred from one place to another by means of wave motion. Perhaps the simplest idea is to consider wave motions in a piece of rope, one end of which is fixed to a support, and the other held in your hand. If you jerk your hand rapidly up and down you can make the rope take on the form of a succession of waves, and by doing so produce friction at the end that is fixed; that is to say, you have transferred energy from one place to another by means of wave motion in the medium (the rope) between the two places.

And there are three other points of interest about this experiment. First, the transfer of energy is not instantaneous; it takes some time to transfer it by this wave motion from one end of the rope to the other. Secondly, as you increase the speed of movement of your hand (the frequency of oscillation), you decrease the distance between the crests of waves, so that the wave-lengths become shorter. In other words, the greater the frequency of the oscillations which produce the waves, the shorter are the wave-lengths. Thirdly, the time taken to transfer energy from one end of the rope to the other is the same whether the waves are long or short. In other words, the speed of travel of all waves in the same medium is the same.

All this is analogous to what happens when energy is transmitted through space from one place to another by radio waves or heat waves or light waves or X-rays, or any other form of electric waves. All these waves are produced by electrical oscillations; they differ in wave-length, but none the less their rate of travel is the same (186,000 miles a second); and the greater the frequency of the oscillations producing the waves the shorter are the wave-lengths radiated.

The frequencies, or rates of oscillation, which produce electro-magnetic waves are almost inconceivably high. Those which produce light waves, i.e. waves that can affect the eye, vary from about 800 billions a second for violet light to 400 billions for red, a combination of all the frequencies between these producing white light, sunlight. The frequencies of oscillations which are used in practice for radio signalling are much too slow to be received by the eye as light— a few thousand millions a second, producing wave-lengths of between, say, 1 centimetre and 20,000 metres (a metre is about $1\frac{1}{10}$ yards).

Radio waves are transmitted by producing very rapidly oscillating electric currents in an aerial wire. The waves radiate out from the aerial into space and produce similar oscillating currents, though of course much weaker, in any other aerials in their path, the greater the distance covered the weaker being the currents in the receiving aerial. As in the case of light waves the radiation takes place in all directions unless arrangements are made to confine it to a certain direction, just as light waves may be transmitted as a beam in a definite direction by using a searchlight.

The medium in which all these electro-magnetic waves travel is not yet fully understood, but it has been given the name of " ether ", which, to fit in with known properties of the waves, must be invisible and intangible and present everywhere.

Since the time of Hertz various methods have been devised for producing and detecting these radio waves, i.e. for producing the oscillatory currents in the sending aerial and for detecting the presence of the far weaker ones in the receiving aerial, but thermionic apparatus, including, of course, the thermionic valve so familiar in broadcast receivers, is now universally used for both purposes. Thermionic apparatus makes use of the emission of minute charges of electricity from a heated body—in the valve's case from the filament.

It was in 1904 that John Ambrose Fleming of England brought out his famous patent for the two-electrode thermionic valve. This device, which he used for improving the reception of radio signals, consisted of an ordinary vacuum-type electric lamp bulb, but with a metal cylinder fixed inside the bulb, surrounding, but not touching, the filament. One terminal of a battery was connected to the filament and the other to the cylinder. When the lamp was lit in the ordinary way an electric current consisting of a flow of electrons (minute charges of negative electricity) passed through the space between the filament and the cylinder in one direction, but not in the other, thus producing a valve-like control of an electric current. This device by itself was no better an arrangement for receiving radio signals than others already in use, but it introduced a completely new idea, the utilization of the flow of electrons in a vacuum, and it changed the whole trend of development in radio communication.

Lee de Forest of the U.S.A. put in a prior patent claim for an idea similar to Fleming's, but it was disallowed in the American courts. But, pressing on with his researches, he eventually inserted a wire mesh or grid between the filament and cylinder with a battery in circuit with it. By this means he could increase the flow of the current as well as controlling its direction. This opened up a new field of advance, including the valve's use as a transmitter. De Forest patented this three-electrode valve, but the validity was disputed. All this gave rise to much bitterness and litigation, but looking back now through those murky mists of controversy we may be justified in concluding that Edison laid the foundations, Fleming gave us the tools, and de Forest finished the job. The thermionic valve is undoubtedly the most important discovery in radio technique since Hertz demonstrated the existence of radio waves. Aptly it has been called " The Aladdin's Lamp of Radio ". Without it there would have been no telephony, no television, and no radar.

Radar was the name first used in the United States for what we here had called radiolocation. It was derived from the initial letters of " Radio-Direction-And-Ranging ", and as it was short and snappy compared with the word radiolocation it became adopted generally.

It is interesting to note that only a few years ago it was discovered that the humble bat uses a most efficient form of radar—one that employs *sound* waves—for his own navigation in blind flying, so the fundamental idea of radar is not quite as new as some of us thought a few years ago. The bat transmits pulses of sound, i.e. very short successions of sound waves. These pulses are supersonic—that is to say, of too high a frequency to affect our hearing equipment, but not too high for the bat's. When they strike material objects, some of the energy is reflected back and the bat hears it as a warning of obstacles in its path. As we shall see, this is exactly what happens in some forms of radar, but with the substitution of radio waves for sound waves.

The idea of echoes—sound waves reflected back from material objects and received by their sender—is so commonplace as to present no difficulty, but light waves, and therefore radio waves (which we have seen are precisely similar), can also be reflected. In fact, if you use a torch to look for something in the dark, you see the object by the waves which it reflects back to you. Of course other people with you can see it too, because the reflected waves are diffused—they do not come back as a beam as the light does from your torch, which uses a mirror to produce one.

Years ago, in studying the travel of radio waves through space, scientists made use of the discovery that short radio waves were reflected back to earth from electrified layers in the upper atmosphere, and it was this aspect of their work which laid the foundations of radar. In their investigations it was necessary to measure the height above the earth of the electrified or " ionized " layers. This was done by transmitting upwards very short pulses of short radio waves which were reflected back to earth by the ionized layer, and then measuring the infinitesimal time taken by the waves to travel up and down again. This time once ascertained, and the rate of travel of radio waves being known, it was simple to calculate the distance travelled. Halving this gave the height of the layer.

But how was the time of travel measured since no mechanical device such as a stop-watch could possibly measure such infinitely short periods of time? It was done by using a cathode-ray tube which, like the valve, is a thermionic device for harnessing the movements of electrons which move at the enormous speed of light and, having negligible inertia, can be started or stopped or have their direction of movement changed practically instantaneously by electrical means. A beam of electrons in the glass tube of a cathode-ray device can be made to produce a glowing spot of light at the end of the tube if this is coated with a special material, which forms what is called a fluorescent screen. If the spot is moving very rapidly it is of course seen as a bright line. It is this spot of light, whose brightness can be varied by electrical means, moving at the speed of light, which produces the image seen on the screen of a television

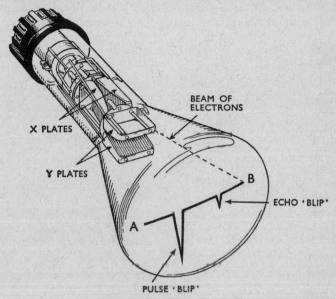

Fig. 1.—A cathode-ray tube, showing the beam of light crossing the screen. The " blips " are caused by the pulse when it sets out and when it returns (as shown in fig. 2). The position of the " echo " on the screen gives the position of the aircraft from which it has been reflected.
Crown Copyright Reserved

receiver, the screen being just the coated end of the cathode-ray tube.

By harnessing the electrons flowing in a cathode-ray tube, i.e. by controlling their movements by electrical means, you have, in fact, a method of obtaining electrically vastly greater speeds of movement and of starting and stopping than is mechanically possible. A cathode-ray tube can be used as a sort of electrical stop-watch for measuring infinitesimal periods of time, or for producing images such as the detailed scenes of television, or the far simpler and

rougher images which appear on a similar screen in one form of
radar, as we shall see later on.

In the kind of radar which developed directly from these experiments in measuring the distance from the ground of ionized layers
in the upper atmosphere, the transmitter and receiver are at the same
place and use the same aerial. The signal is transmitted in the
form of very short-wave pulses with an interval between them of,
say, one thousandth of a second. This interval allows time for

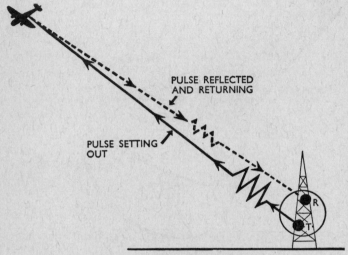

PULSE REFLECTED
AND RETURNING

PULSE SETTING
OUT

Fig. 2.—A pulse setting out from the transmitter *T* and reflected back,
much weakened, from the aeroplane to the receiver *R*.
Crown Copyright Reserved

the waves to be reflected back from the object, in the same way as
light or sound waves are reflected back, and received without inter-
fering with the next pulse to be transmitted. At the receiver a
spot of light on the screen is made to start moving in a horizontal
line from the left of the screen across it towards the right at the
instant that the pulse is transmitted. When the reflected pulse returns
from the object it is shown by a vertical kink or " blip " in the bright
line on the screen. The distance of this kink from its starting-point
at the left-hand edge of the screen along the line of travel of the
bright spot, which has below it a scale marked, say, in thousands
of yards, is thus used to give a measure of the range of the object.

The bearing of the object from the transmitter (the angle between the direction of true north and that of the object) is found by using a very narrow beam of transmitted radiation, and noting the direction of the beam at the moment when the reflected radiation from the object is received most strongly. When the distance and the bearing of the object are known its position can be plotted on a chart, so that by using this radar reflecting apparatus at a single station the position of the object can be ascertained. The elevation can be determined in much the same way.

When radar is used to show the image of objects on the surface of the ground or sea in the form of a map on the screen of the

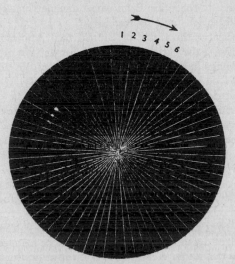

Fig. 3.—The Plan Position Indicator, in which the bright spot moves along the radii 1, 2, 3, 4, 5, 6 and so on in turn. Any reflection (one is shown here in the north-west) shows up as a brighter patch.
Crown Copyright Reserved

cathode-ray tube, the tube is called the P.P.I. (Plan Position Indicator). In this arrangement the bright spot is made to move at very high speed outwards from the centre of the circular screen along the radius to its edge and back again over the same route, then out again to the edge along the line of an adjoining radius, and so on, along each radius in succession round and round the screen. The very small aerials are made to rotate, the transmitting

aerial radiating a narrow beam of radio waves which electrically
" illuminates " (invisibly, of course) a slice of the ground or sea as the
case may be. As the aerials rotate, a large circular area of the surface
below is shown on the screen. The reflections from the ground
produce on the screen a faint overall glow, but such features as
buildings reflect better and stand out as brighter patches. From
the surface of the sea, the radio reflection is practically nil, so that
ships, buoys, &c., show up as brilliant patches on a black background.
Large objects such as towns show up very well from the air, and
in the war it was found possible to distinguish a camouflage village
from a real one by the different appearance produced on a cathode-
ray tube screen by reflection from wood and netting, compared with
that from solid bricks and mortar.

In this country the name of Sir Edward Appleton will always
be connected with the early experiments for determining the heights
of reflecting layers in the atmosphere, and that of Sir Robert Watson-
Watt with the development of radar which grew out of them. Of
course a great deal of work was being done in other countries too,
especially in the United States, on this problem of the travel of radio
waves, but over here the Radio Research Board made a special study
of the subject. The leading position taken up by the Board in all
these investigations resulted in Britain being the first to prepare a
practical scheme for locating aircraft by radar if the need should
ever arise. And the need arose for us first, suddenly and with violence, in 1939. We were the first to be ready with the answer, and
we never lost our lead.

It was in 1934 that the Air Ministry became seriously disturbed
about our lack of defence against possible attacks from enemy aircraft,
and turned to the Radio Research Board for scientific advice. From
this beginning was evolved in due course that wonderful collaboration
between fighting men and scientists which saved the country from
defeat in the autumn of 1940 and led it on to victory.

Let us now turn to a consideration of how the early form of
radar has been developed for practical purposes. In a broadcast
at the end of the war, Sir Robert Watson-Watt said that radar may
be said to date from December, 1931, when the Engineering Department of the British Post Office, in the course of radio experiments
with wave-lengths of about five metres, noted that there appeared
to be some reflection of the waves when aircraft were flying in the
vicinity, an effect which was confirmed the following year by the

Bell Telephone Company in America. The matter was pursued here with great enthusiasm by the Radio Research Board, which produced, for the first time, a technique for locating aircraft by reflected waves operating a cathode-ray tube as already described.

On the strength of these experiments the Board had a lot of very interesting information to give the Air Ministry, and in May, 1935, with the war clouds already gathering, a small party of scientists began installing apparatus at a radio station at Orfordness in Suffolk under the strictest secrecy. They called themselves " The Green Spot Club ", their aim being to obtain " brighter and better green spots ", on cathode-ray tubes. Even their families had no idea of the nature of the work being carried out, and there were intriguing hints about prospecting for oil and searching for rays to stop the engines of motor cars. Before the year was out they had not accomplished much on those lines, but they *had* succeeded in locating the position of aircraft which were flying at a distance of a hundred miles from Orfordness.

So, in 1936, radar, or as they called it, radiolocation, had become a practical technique, not by the work of any one person but by the piecing together of the results of many experimenters over many years. Progress along somewhat similar lines was of course taking place in other countries. In the United States apparatus had been produced for enabling aircraft to find their height above the ground and for locating ships at sea at short distances. In France, the liner *Normandie* was fitted in 1936 with radio equipment by which large ships or icebergs could be located up to ranges of a few miles, and in Germany and Italy there had been progress in developing apparatus for detecting the approach of aircraft. But nowhere was development so advanced as in the " Green Spot Club " on the Suffolk coast.

In 1936, five radar stations, the first in the world, were established on the east coast of England, and in the following year fifteen more were added, covering the whole of the east and south-east coast. These early radar stations were those which helped to win the Battle of Britain, and without them there would have been very little, if indeed any, hope of victory. Our aircraft were at that time far outnumbered, and without our lead in radar the whole course of the war might have been very different. By the end of the war there were some 22,000 people employed at radar stations all over the country.

The stations used in the Battle of Britain for locating the enemy's attacking aircraft used waves of about 10 metres, but it was not possible to pick up low-flying aircraft until development permitted the use of much shorter waves (about 1·5 metres) with beam transmitters and rotating aerials. This apparatus was evolved for use in night fighters. With it a radio beam from the fighter swept round the sky and any aircraft within range disclosed its position by reflecting back waves which were picked up by the fighter. In this way interception of the enemy was first carried out by the ground radar stations, and the fighter directed to within a couple of miles of the enemy bomber, whence it closed up to visual range by means of its own radar equipment.

Ground radar stations were able to distinguish between reflections from our own and from enemy aircraft by equipment called I.F.F. (Identification Friend Foe). This consisted of a small receiver-transmitter which was fitted in our aircraft, and when radio pulses were received from the ground station on this special receiver, the transmitter came into action automatically and signalled back to the ground station a code recognition signal. This I.F.F. apparatus, which was kept most secret, was prevented from falling into enemy hands by being in contact with a charge which exploded if the aircraft crashed.

The first air-borne radar, called A.S.V. (Air to Surface Vessel), using a 1·5 metre wave, came into use just after the outbreak of war, and by 1941 was in general use for the detection of enemy submarines when on the surface. In A.S.V. the waves were radiated in front of the aircraft, and the reflections from the ship or submarine enabled the aircraft to judge when it was flying in the correct direction, and how far it was from the enemy vessel. Large ships could be located by this means up to about ten miles' range, and submarines at shorter distances. Enemy submarines were not slow to counter this arrangement. They fitted receivers which received the strong transmitted pulses from the aircraft before it came close enough to detect the much weaker pulses reflected from the submarine. In this way they gained enough time to submerge before the aircraft knew anything about them, or anyway before it was close enough to take action.

But right throughout the war at sea the use of radar for the detection of submarines was our greatest scientific asset. The enemy was fully aware of this, and as each new device was introduced on our side it was soon discovered and counter-measures were taken. But there was always a lag in time before the counter-measures were installed and working, and it was in fact largely because we were always this lap ahead in the development of radar devices that we were eventually able to smash our greatest menace, the enemy submarine.

In August, 1940, Sir Henry Tizard headed a mission of our radar experts to the United States to disclose all details of what had been accomplished in this country. From that time onwards there was a complete exchange of information about radar between the two countries, and a scientific and operational co-operation was established on a scale never before attained either in peace or in war. The British experts took with them a sample of a new form of thermionic valve called the Magnetron—now the treasured possession of a great radar laboratory in America—which had made possible the use of extremely short waves of centimetre length in radar work.

This new radar technique of using centimetre waves was of supreme importance. It was based on the work, under Professor J. T. Randall, of a team of scientists at Birmingham University, who developed the magnetron valve, which has been called the heart of radar. This new valve was able to transmit radio pulses of extremely short duration in a narrow beam of much greater power than any previously attained. This resulted in the provision, amongst other things, of greatly improved equipment for the tracking down of bombers by our night fighters, and for the mapping device, the P.P.I., mentioned above, by which our bombers found their targets. It came as a great boon too for directing the gun-fire of shore batteries and naval guns. Its efficiency for directing their fire may be judged by the fact that, towards the end of the period of flying-bomb attacks, over 80 per cent of the flying bombs which came into the field of fire of the batteries fitted with radar were shot down. Its first, and most famous, application for naval gun-laying was at the victory of Matapan, and it proved of inestimable value in locating surfaced enemy submarines by providing upon the radar screen a map of the ocean within its range.

What centimetre radar did for us at sea may be judged from this extract of a report by Admiral Doenitz, the head of the German Navy: " At the end of 1943 and the beginning of 1944 one development became very obvious which, long ago, even in peace-time, we had feared, that the enemy might deprive the U-boat of its essential feature—the element of surprise—by means of radiolocation. By these methods he has conquered the U-boat menace. It was not superior strategy or tactics that gave him success in the U-boat war, but superiority in scientific research." It was history repeating itself, as after the first war Admiral Scheer had written: "The English received the news of our movements through their directional wireless which they already had in use, but which was only introduced by us at a much later period. In possessing it, the English had a great advantage in the conduct of the war."

What centimetre radar did for us in the air may be judged from a few words taken from Sir Arthur Harris's *Bomber Offensive*: "At the beginning of the war we had no conceivable means of identifying an average-sized town. Towards the end of 1944 we could hope to hit so small a target as the banks of a canal whenever we wanted to, in any weather."

So far we have considered radar technique over comparatively short distances, but several long-range radar techniques were used in the war, and have been further developed since then. The Gee (Grid) equipment in aircraft, introduced in 1942, provided an aid to navigation, and it was Gee that made possible the thousand-bomber raids. It was so extensively used on " D-day " that it was said by the Services at the time that " G-day " would have been a more appropriate name. Gee is a British system for enabling a ship or aircraft to find its position by receiving short-wave radio pulses from special land stations at known positions. The stations transmit in pairs, and the navigator finds his position by receiving pulses from two pairs and measuring how much longer it takes a pulse to reach him from one station of a pair than from the other. From this he can calculate the difference in his distances from these two stations. With this information he can draw on a chart a curve through all the points whose distances from these two stations differ by that amount. By proceeding similarly with another pair of stations he can plot another curve on the chart. Where the the two curves intersect is his position. In practice, three land stations about 100 miles apart are used, the centre station with one of the others forming one pair, and with the third the second pair. Gee can be used up to a distance of about 300 miles.

Arising out of the development of Gee a system called Loran (Long Range) was produced in the United States. The fundamental principle of working is the same, but longer wave-lengths are used and greater ranges are obtained. Loran shore stations are spaced 300–600 miles apart and are now provided to cover the North Atlantic and most of the Pacific. Working out a position is rather slow so that this system is not suited for high-speed aircraft.

Another system on somewhat similar lines, called Decca, was developed by the British Decca Company. It is not, however, a short-wave pulse system, but employs ordinary commercial waves of about 2000 metres, which is of course an advantage when it comes to arranging for reception in ships and aircraft. It is proving of great value for fairly short-range work such as coastal navigation, pilotage in narrow channels, and so on, but is not at present suitable for ranges over about 250 miles. Decca stations now cover the whole British Isles and a large part of west European waters. There are also four chains in operation in eastern Canada.

A noteworthy British development for air navigation across the North Atlantic is Dectra, a system to provide track and position along a number of air " lanes " which may be 2000 miles in length. It supplements the existing Decca Navigator equipment at ranges above 250 miles. Pairs of stations at Prestwick and Gander send signals which guide the aircraft along its lane and also tell the distance covered. The aircraft position is indicated automatically on a chart to within 5 miles. As it nears its destination Precision Approach Radar guides the aircraft in.

The last of the important long-range systems is called Consol. The ground station radiates dot and dash signals on waves of between 600 and 1500 metres. The position line from a station is found by counting the number of the dot and dash characters during the transmission period of one minute and referring to a special table or chart. The intersection of the lines from two stations gives the position of the ship or aircraft. Consol provides navigational facilities for distances between about 25 and 1000 miles. There are now five Consol beacons placed so that by taking bearings on two of them a mariner may find his position over a wide area of the North Sea and parts of the North Atlantic.

All this radar technique which was developed in the war is proving of the greatest value in peace for the navigation of aircraft and ships; fogs and icebergs have lost their terrors, and conditions in the upper atmosphere which so much affect our weather forecasts are at last giving up their secrets, as are ocean currents and shoals, and the still vast inaccessible areas of the world.

SHIPS GREAT AND SMALL

Out of the sea Britain conjured her greatness and by the sea alone can she hope to retain it. Let us therefore turn our thoughts for a little while to ships and all that they stand for.

There have been endless discussions as to the difference between a ship and a boat. It is a popular belief that a ship has some form of deck to keep out weather and sea, whereas a boat is open to the sky; but the question is not so simple, for a submarine is a boat and so is a motor torpedo boat. Nautical men insist that a ship has sails and three masts, and is square rigged; everything else is a brig, a galleon, a vessel, a steamship, a motor vessel, and so on!

Boats of course came first, but long before their time ancient man had learned to trust himself to floating timber and matted reeds in order to cross unfordable streams; and from standing on a rolling tree-trunk it did not require much imagination to reach the idea of hollowing out a log canoe. Reeds tied together in bundles and built into rafts with pointed ends make excellent primitive boats, such as are employed to this day in the balsas of high, cold Lake Titicaca in the Andes. Ship and boat building is a very conservative business, new ideas being adopted only after much opposition; so we need not be surprised to learn that the Egyptians had reed boats five thousand years ago, while their neighbours in Asia crossed the swift Tigris on inflated skins, just as they do to-day.

The next stage to the dug-out, the inflated skin, and the reed boat or raft, is the canoe, which for ages has been used by primitive people everywhere, especially on swift and shallow streams. The Red Indian in his birch-bark canoe (which he handles with uncanny skill) can glide swiftly and surely down quite wild stretches of rapid and turbulent water, where a bigger and heavier craft would certainly be swamped; and when he hears the roar of a waterfall ahead, he has only to step ashore, cut a path through the undergrowth, and carry his light canoe beyond the obstruction. The ancient British coracles, some of which may still be seen on the rivers in Wales (where there are many rocks and patches of shallow water alternating with deep pools) were canoes. They were oval in shape, built to take one man only. Over the frame of split canes a hide was stretched, and the fisherman used a paddle for propulsion.

To me, the most striking of all canoes, however, is the Eskimo kayak. It is a long, cigar-shaped affair, pointed at both ends, and, like the coracle, intended for a single occupant. The light frame of Arctic willow or birch is tightly encased in skins, which the Eskimo women sew on with their bone needles. In the centre a single round hole is left, into which the Eskimo works himself; his lower half is thus made watertight, and he becomes a part of the craft. He uses a double-bladed paddle, and in his frail kayak can face rollers or breaking waves with indifference; he can even go right out to sea in the teeth of a storm, laughing as the wind hurls spray in his face. But the kayak is a dangerous craft to handle, although the explorer Nansen (who often used one) called it the best one-man vessel in the world; and Eskimos are often drowned while trying to master it. On the other hand, an expert kayaker can roll over and over in the water, letting his head go right down, and come up on the other side; white explorers have sometimes tried this trick, usually to need rescuing just when they were drowning!

The ships of ancient times, though often provided with decks, a mast, a forward-directed spar not unlike a bowsprit, and a large square sail, depended mainly upon oarsmen for propulsion, even in the open sea. It was out of them that galleys developed, so that the type lasted several thousand years. The Egyptian ships are the oldest of which we know very much, it having been the custom to make models and leave them in the royal tombs for the monarch's use in the next world; numerous paintings, too, have survived the centuries. (You can see models of these and many other ships in that boys' paradise, the Science Museum in London, and if you get the chance you should certainly go there.)

Although the Egyptian ships and boats were mostly shallow and spoon-shaped, the larger ones made many long voyages down the Red Sea and far north into the Mediterranean, seas which can be extremely stormy. Even on the Nile there were large barges of 200 tons burden or more; they were used to convey the huge stone obelisks, sphinxes, &c., across the broad river to the royal tombs. The pointed bow and stern of an Egyptian ship rose at a low angle above the water, so that the vessels looked bow-shaped. At prow and stern were high ornaments, the latter being usually a carved lotus flower. The idea of an ornamented prow has persisted throughout the days of sailing ships as the figurehead on the beak.

A typical large ship was about 70 feet long and 17 to 18 feet wide, but only 4 or 5 feet deep. Its shape was maintained and strengthened by stout deck beams, the ends of which passed right through the planking so as to show on the outside. At each end of the vessel was a small deck-house. The steersman stood in the stern, facing the oarsmen, and working a vertical tiller from side to side. Instead of a rudder, there were usually two or more large paddles lashed to each quarter at the gunwale, their upper ends being attached

An ancient Egyptian ship

to the tiller; at a later date one of these steering paddles could be shipped if desired, and the other worked alone. The ship carried fifteen or sixteen oarsmen on either side, while a leader stood in the bow to give them their time. A stout but clumsy mast, made of two spars joined together at the summit, was stepped amidships; it could be lowered when necessary into a cradle aft. On this mast they set a large square sail athwartship; it hung from a very wide yard made of two spars joined in the middle, and had a lower yard of even greater span, but the sail was worked mainly by braces attached to the upper yard. (In Arab dhows and similar sailing ships, this square sail has been replaced by a triangular sail, called a lateen sail, on a long diagonal yard; a great advantage, because it permits the vessel to sail much closer to the wind.)

Long after Egypt had passed her prime, the Greeks, and eventually the Romans, developed their celebrated fighting ships, which, unlike merchantmen, were worked by oars; in Roman days they were called biremes, triremes, and so on, according to the number of banks of oars. These were the first galleys, a type that lasted in the Mediterranean until the Spanish Armada; indeed, even British warships in Nelson's time employed long sweeps during calms, or when it was necessary to turn the ship in harbour. The Greek and Roman galleys did not dispense with sail power altogether; but the Athenians, who were the great naval power of their day, always left their sails ashore when going out to fight, relying upon perfectly trained crews and the extreme mobility of their ships. The Greek triremes were long, low ships with only about 4½ feet freeboard. In the great days of Athens all the oarsmen were protected by bulwarks, and above the crew a shelf or gangway ran down both sides of the ship from stem to stern, so that men could pass without disturbing the rowers. The ships had a definite prow and stern, but the quarter-rudder was still maintained, the stern terminating in a high, graceful gooseneck ornament. The prow of a Greek warship was a terrible menace to an enemy.

In all ships there is a tendency, during storms or in short, choppy seas, for a large part of the hull to be out of the water at any one moment, which throws a great strain on the frame and may even break the ship in half. The Egyptians resisted this hogging tendency, as it is called, by passing strong ropes completely round their ships and hauling them tight. The Greeks and Romans, on the other hand, used stout timbers, called walings, which were built into the structure, and this practice lasted right down to Stuart days, when the larger size of ships necessitated much stronger cross bracing. For many centuries it was a cardinal principle that the walings must not be cut into, lest the strength of the ship should suffer, and it needed a lot of ingenuity to provide gunports in ships of the Middle Ages, without piercing the walings. In the triremes of old, where the bottom walings on either side met forward they were carried out as a heavy spike for several feet, the end being sheathed with a bronze ram's head. The upper line of walings stopped shorter, but was also carried out in two stout spikes. The idea was that in a battle the ship would ram an enemy amidships and drive a great hole into its side; as the assailant continued to advance, the shorter spikes would then push the damaged vessel off its prow and so cause it to sink.

Many attempts have been made to discover just how the two, three, four, five or more banks of oars were arranged. According to one plan, the oarsmen in a trireme formed sets of three above and behind one another, the upper two men sitting on benches a little above and set back from the next below; the foot-rest was cut in the seat of the man in front. The seats were three feet apart. One man had one oar, and all the oars in a single row struck the water in the same line, therefore they had to be of different lengths. The topmost bank of oars was about 14 feet long, the middle bank about 10½ feet, and the lowest only 7½ feet.

The Greeks manned their ships with freemen, the Athenians having 31 men a side in the upper bank and 27 in each of the two lower ones. The steersman had a special seat in the stern, where he worked two steering paddles, one on each quarter, by means of ropes attached to the tiller. Beside him was the captain. Both bow and stern were boarded over, and the custom grew up of placing small shelters there, in which the men stood who were to board the enemy. The Romans improved on this idea. For their oar-power they used slaves. Veritable castles were erected fore and aft, which were manned by soldiers. Near the bow of a Roman galley was hung an unwieldy but very efficient drawbridge, the corvus; when alongside the enemy this was dropped on his deck, gripping it by its curved end, and over the bridge the Romans poured to the slaughter. They also carried catapults for slinging heavy weights at the foe, besides a nasty sickle-like weapon with which they could sweep his rigging and brings down his sails.

Slave-worked galleys haunted the Mediterranean for more than 1500 years. Whenever one sees a model of a galley it is difficult to forget the sighs and groans, the sweat and pain and endless toil of the chained men who, in foul air and semi-darkness, drove such ships through the sea. These were the warships in the heyday of Venetian, Genoese, and Arab power, all these nations employing large, swift galleys for waging war and piracy. By building a support outside the hull for the oars, mediæval shipbuilders overcame a problem which had defeated the ancients, and were enabled to get all their oars in a single line on either side; the oars themselves were immense sweeps 30 feet or more long, very carefully balanced with leaden weights, and each handled by from three to five men.

About the time of Henry VII and Henry VIII, when the English navy first began to take shape, the larger size of ships permitted three masts to be stepped, so that sail power took the place of the oar. The Tudor ships, with their huge fore and after castles or " cage-works ", ill moulded to the lines of the vessel, had a clumsy and top-heavy appearance, but they sat the water well, and though there was many a creak and groan from the straining timbers as they heaved with the sea these ships could outride ordinary gales if well handled. The majority of these vessels were still quite small, varying between 100 and 300 tons burden; but the giants of the English and Spanish fleets, such as the *Ark, Triumph, Elizabeth Jonas,* or the *San Martin, San Juan* or *Santa Catalina,* ran up to 800 or even 1000 tons and carried hundreds of men, besides a wonderfully miscellaneous collection of brass and iron cannon.

All Tudor ships had a large tumble-home, i.e. they sloped inwards very much from the water-line to the decks. Amidships the waist was deep and low. The decks were not continuous, but were broken by steps to suit the construction of the castles inboard. The fore and after castles could be shut off from the waist (where most of the crew lived); and they were commonly provided with a number of small cannon called murderers, pointed at the waist, so as to fire on a boarding enemy and on occasion at the mutinous crew; for life at sea was very colourful just then and mutinies were liable to break out at any time. The captain or the admiral was an absolute tyrant who, although in theory he could be brought to book, acted much as he pleased when at sea and could, if so minded, inflict untold petty miseries upon his unfortunate crew. On the other hand the majority of English seamen, officers and crews alike, were not above a little piracy whenever an opportunity arose; they carried their heads high and kept their cutlasses clean, and a community of risk meant a community of fellowship, so that perhaps life was not so very hard for them after all. Under a man like Drake, who dared all and feared nothing, they were quite invincible.

The admiral and his officers lived aft; the admiral's deck was the quarter-deck, high in the air, and his glazed windows looked out upon the sea astern. The forecastle was the fighting castle, and contained many of the ship's stores. Guns were mounted, some on the upper decks, firing through ports cut into the bulwarks, and others on the deck below, the openings being shut during bad weather by porthole covers.

In a general way the little ships were small editions of the great ones. Those used by the famous explorers were generally small merchantmen, converted for the purpose. Such was the famous

Santa Maria in which Columbus discovered America: a small, 3-masted vessel of about 200 tons, 75 to 80 feet long (no exact details of her construction are known), and about 25 feet beam. She carried a square-rigged foresail, large square mainsail, topsail, spritsail on the bowsprit, and lateen sail on the mizzen-mast; the main sails all bore large emblems of the Cross.

Not very dissimilar, though a century later, was Drake's even more famous *Golden Hind* (originally called the *Pelican*), in which he sailed round the world; she was afterwards preserved in dry

The *Golden Hind*

dock for many years, and you can get a general idea of her appearance from the image on halfpennies. She had a towering superstructure aft, a low waist, and modest forecastle. Drake carried more canvas than Columbus, almost certainly having topgallant sails above his topsails. The *Golden Hind* was a ship of 100 to 120 tons, about 60 feet long, and 20 feet beam, and from keel to waist she was about 16 feet high. She had two main decks, apart from the half-decks in the castles. In the forecastle some of the men slept, and supplies were stored there, but most of the crew slung their hammocks amidships; aft dwelt the officers, and here, too, were the admiral's cabin and his great dining-room where he entertained in state, also the charthouse and the wheel. Over the poop rose the lantern, as you may notice on your coins; by its rolling and uncertain light at night the other two ships of the little squadron followed their leader round the world. By day the *Golden Hind* made a gallant show. Like all the Queen's ships, her masts were surmounted by three gilded crowns. Industrious hands had embroidered or painted emblems on the sails and the long pennants. The decks were holy-stoned white and clean, as only the decks of English naval ships can be (for Drake was a stern leader and would have no slacking or un-tidiness aboard his fleet); while the ship's sides were picked out above in patches of red, blue, green, and other bright colours, the hull bearing alternate stripes of green and white, the royal colours. Of course she carried guns, for the Dagoes had to be challenged wherever they might be found; and you may be sure that the armoury was full, too, and the knives and cutlasses sharp. In this little vessel did Drake and his hard-bitten men traverse the whole of the North and South Atlantic, rounding the storm-swept southern tip of America and sailing up the west coast all the way to California, then right across the Pacific to the Spice Islands, and home round the Cape of Good Hope.

Another famous little ship of those days was the *Mayflower*, which made her memorable voyage with the first American emigrants on board in the year 1620, the *Golden Hind* then being a show-piece at Deptford. Nothing is known of her build, except that she was a small merchantman, of three-masted rig, and probably a pretty strict penance to the pious but freedom-loving landsmen aboard her. She was crowded with about a hundred emigrants, men, women and children, with all their belongings in bales and bundles, who left England so that in the New World they might worship and live as they thought fit. After a voyage of two months they landed near Cape Cod, but then went on to Plymouth, Massachusetts, where the unhappy people were landed, half of them only to perish during the first winter. Out of this obscure voyage of a few dissatisfied men the mighty United States has grown.

As time passed, and the Stuarts succeeded the Tudors, the height of the castles in warships was reduced, the upper works acquired a more regular form, through decks appeared, the very long beak which was characteristic of all galleons was shortened, and the rigging was altered to give a much better spread of sail. These changes resulted in the great three-deckers of the late eighteenth century, of which the most famous ship in Britain's history, H.M.S. *Victory*, was a noble specimen. The " wooden walls of Old England " ranged from sloops and small, fast-sailing frigates (the latter of which served much the same purpose as our modern destroyers, ranging far and wide, scouting for the fleet and generally making themselves a nuisance to the enemy), up to the first-rates, ships of 90 or 100 guns. Frigates had one main gun-deck, and carried 24 to 32 guns. Two-deckers had two gun-decks, mounting from 60 to 74 heavy iron cannon. All had a length-breadth ratio of $3\frac{1}{2}$ or 4 to 1; they had smooth sides, with considerable tumble-home, were built of oak, and were virtually unsinkable and as alike as peas.

Anyone can go over the *Victory* at Portsmouth to-day, where she lies in a dry dock, and see the great ship just as she was at Trafalgar, although it is almost two hundred years since she was built. In this type of warship, not only had the forecastle almost disappeared, but the after superstructure was much reduced, although the square-cornered upper works still overhung the stern. Like other three-deckers, the *Victory* really had five decks; she was built throughout of English oak and on her main deck large parts of the original planking still remain.

Above the immense, cavernous hold, with its smell of bilge water, its ballast of shingle and iron bars, and its racks, floors and floorlets at different levels, its rats, stores, spars, barrels of water and beef, was the lowest or orlop deck. This was well below the water-line, and had a low roof, in places only 5 feet 7 inches high, from which hung lanterns that cast a dim gloom about the vast, mysterious recesses of the ship. Aft on the orlop deck dwelt the midshipmen; close to their quarters was the dreaded cockpit, where the surgeon worked during battle, and where Nelson died. The ship's immense hempen cables were coiled mainly on the orlop, which carried as well vast quantities of all kinds of stores; for 850 men lived on board and had to be provisioned for a four months' stay at sea. Behind the midshipmen's berths the purser, storekeeper in general, had his office and his own little private cabin; and you may be quite sure that whoever went short he never lacked necessaries!

Above the orlop was the main-deck, now known as the lower deck ; it was also the main gun-deck. Through its 28 portholes, 14 a side, as many great 32-pounders thrust their noses. These guns weighed 56 cwts. each and often strained madly on their confining ropes when the ship lurched; sometimes they broke loose and charged blindly across the deck, killing and maiming anyone unfortunate enough to be in their path, before they could be secured again. When the weather was fine the portholes were opened, but during storms they had to be closed; and as two hundred men lived, worked and slept on that one deck alone—it was a completely open space—the atmosphere must often have been pretty thick. On this deck was the main capstan, with twenty long bars, which seamen pushed round to the time set by sea shanties, as they slowly hauled the 8-inch cable and the anchor on board. Aft on the main-deck were the quarters of the chief gunner, the armourer, and their

H.M.S. *Victory*

assistants, and of course the armoury. In the stern were four guns called stern-chasers. Near the roof of the armoury one could see the tiller swinging slowly from side to side; this was controlled by chains from the wheel three decks above, and when the wheel was shot away (as actually happened at Trafalgar) the ship could be steered from the gun-room. Right forward on the gun-deck, just abaft the beautiful but rather ornamental bows, were the huge hawsers, hawse-holes and anchors. They were separated from the rest of the deck by a stout bulkhead, in order to keep green seas from sweeping it clean; and in the confined space between this barrier and the bows a few half-drowned live pigs and sheep were generally to be seen.

Next above the gun-deck was the middle deck. Here also 28

guns were mounted, but of lighter calibre, being 24-pounders. On this deck another 200 men lived, worked and slept. Aft were the officers' cabins and the wardroom, the latter being just above the gunroom. The entrances to the *Victory* were on the middle deck, one on each side; and no one (except when the admiral's step-ladder was hung over the side) could get in otherwise, the smooth sides being quite unclimbable.

The upper gun-deck mounted 30 12-pounders. In the waist it was partly exposed to the sky, but with a broad gangway on either side. On this deck forward, beneath the forecastle, was the sick-bay; aft were the admiral's quarters, including his state cabin and dining saloon. He was separated from the rest of the ship, not only by a sentry but by partitions which (like partitions on most British ships of war) were always removed before an action, so as to reduce the risk of injury from flying splinters. At various periods, according to the caprice of her ruler for the time being, the flagship also had an admiral's stern gallery hanging out over the sea.

Above these apartments was the quarter-deck, which at its after end led to the captain's rooms; for on an admiral's ship there is always a captain, and he, not the admiral, issues all orders to his crew and is responsible for their execution. The roof of his apartment formed the poop, above which hung the *Victory's* great lanterns; these famous lamps now decorate the corners of Trafalgar Square in London. At the break of the poop was the double wheel, by which the *Victory* was steered. Forward was the fo'c'sle, and beneath and in advance of that the beak-head, being a figurehead of King George the Third, a figure of Victory, and many other ornamental beings, all of which stared down glassily at the heaving ocean, except when His Majesty plunged his royal nose therein as she pitched.

The *Victory* had a burden of 2162 tons. To move her enormous mass through the sea, sail power had to be transmitted through three huge masts, the size of which must be seen before one can realize it. Above the mainmast was a topmast, above that a topgallant, and above that the royal. At the summit of each lower mast a horseshoe-shaped platform, from which the shrouds supporting the mast descended to the chains at the ship's sides, was built. It was large enough to hold riflemen; and it was in fact such a sniper on the French ship *Redoutable* who gave Nelson his fatal wound. From the summit of the mainmast to the deck measured 186 feet, the height of a respectable church spire. The fore and mizzen masts were a little smaller. The ship also carried jibs, staysails, studding sails, and so forth, her total number of sails being 38. Her chief sails were enormous things, and had to be provided with many rows of short rope worked into the canvas, so that the crew might take in a reef. Even the maintop sail had an area of 4150 square feet.

Here are one or two types of sailing ships, the names of which sometimes cause confusion.

An East Indiaman, the large vessel which carried goods between Hindustan and Britain, was in Nelson's day much like one of the medium-sized British warships. She carried a good many guns, had trained gunners on board, and was always ready to fight a privateer or even an official foe; but she relied mainly on her superior speed to get away. Such ships were much bulkier about the water-line than warships, since, of course, they had to take so much more cargo.

A schooner is usually a two-masted vessel, having yards only on the foremast, square-rigged, the foresail being set flying; the mainmast carries fore-and-aft sails, i.e. like those on a wherry. In some cases the yard is dispensed with, when the vessel becomes a fore-and-aft schooner. In another variation a mizzen-mast is stepped, having fore-and-aft sails like the main; this is a three-masted schooner. Other vessels having a succession of similar masts, fore-and-aft rigged in this way, are known as four-, five-, six- or even seven-masted schooners.

A brig is a two-masted vessel having yards and square rig on both masts. A brigantine, on the other hand, is rigged forward like a brig but aft like a schooner. A barque is a three-masted vessel having masts and square rig on the fore and main, but fore-and-aft sails on the mizzen. A " ship ", as we said earlier, has three masts, all square-rigged; but almost every kind of vessel is called a ship by someone, so you cannot go far wrong—provided that you avoid calling it a boat in the captain's hearing!

Some of the most beautiful sailing ships ever built were the famous tea clippers of last century, one of which, the *Cutty Sark*, many people have seen afloat, on the Thames or at Plymouth, in our own day. They were not large ships, for their cargo was small and valuable rather than bulky. Being built for speed, and to carry every stitch of canvas possible, they were long, graceful ships, which formed an unforgettable picture on the blue sea, with their white sails all set and billowing out before the breeze. *Cutty Sark* was

212½ feet long but only 36 feet beam (a ratio of 6 to 1, compared with 3½ to 1 in such a ship as the *Victory*). She was 21 feet deep; registered tonnage 963. Her equally famous rival, the *Thermopylæ*, had almost exactly the same dimensions. As it was difficult, and on occasion even hazardous, to set the upper sails in ships carrying such a high and wide spread of canvas, an American clipper in 1853 adopted the device of halving the topsails, topgallant sails and royals, which were set double; and this practice spread to most of the clippers. They even carried a skysail at the mainmast-head, and of course they had several jibs and a multiplicity of special sails, so as to catch every breath of wind which would speed their course. It is not certain where the name of clipper came from, but it was American (the Americans built the first clippers, but eventually withdrew from the fierce British competition); and the word may have meant that they could clip days or hours off the previous fastest time.

The tea clippers were built for the China trade, in order to bring early teas (which had the best flavour and therefore commanded the highest price) from Foochow to London as rapidly as possible. They were composite ships, belonging to the days when iron was still not wholly trusted for ship construction. *Cutty Sark*, for instance, built in 1869, had an iron framework covered with wooden planking, yet her keel, stem and sternpost were wooden. The wooden skin had one advantage, as it enabled her to be sheathed with copper; this increased her sailing qualities by reducing the multitude of marine growths that always fasten on the bottoms of steel or wooden ships, especially in tropical seas. Her lower masts were made of rolled iron, but the upper ones were spars.

There was a famous race in 1866, when three tea ships, the *Ariel*, *Taeping* and *Serica*, left Foochow together for London, the *Ariel* having a few minutes' start. Ninety-nine days later, although they had not seen each other during the long voyage round the Cape, all three appeared in the English Channel. The *Ariel* passed the Downs, Dungeness, about ten minutes before the *Taeping*, the *Serica* being only a few hours behind. This was by no means the fastest performance for that voyage, however. In 1869, the *Sir Lancelot*, a British ship, covered the same course in 88 days, her best day's record being 354 knots for the 24 hours. The opening of the Suez Canal, and the general introduction of steamships, marked the end of the clippers; but a number of them long served in the Australian wool trade, during which *Cutty Sark* and *Thermo-pylæ* engaged in some famous duels.

Despite all the changes of the last seventy-five years large sailing ships continued to be employed until quite recently; but they were much larger than the clippers, since they needed to carry so much more cargo in order to yield a profit. These ships were built of mild-steel plates and sections, thereby greatly reducing their weight. Many of them were of 3000 tons or more; and the Germans, who specialized in this trade, built several five-masted ships during the present century, which ran to 5000 tons or more. Although relying mainly on sail power, they also carried auxiliary engines. The fifth mast, by the way, was called a jigger. One great ship, the *R. C. Rickmers*, had a gross tonnage of 5548. She was 441 feet long, 53 feet 7 inches beam, and 30 feet 5 inches deep; she could carry 8000 tons of cargo and could spread 50,000 square feet of canvas. On her first voyage, in 1906, she kept up a speed of 13 knots for long periods. Similar big ships have sailed from Portland to Iquique, Chile, in 62 days, and from Newcastle, N.S.W., to Valparaiso in 29 days. During the four years 1925–29 the *Herzogin Cecilie*, a ship that many of your fathers may have seen, averaged 100 days for the voyage from Australia to the English Channel. *Cutty Sark* once made the same passage in 71 days.

Although steamships of one kind or another have been in service since about 1801, it was many years before they supplanted sailing ships for long voyages, and then only gradually. Right up to the Crimean War the Admiralty used wooden ships that employed both sails and steam. The earliest steamships all had paddle wheels, but, about 1840, screw propulsion began to come into use; this too had a long struggle before it was adopted, and of course we still use paddle steamers from London to Ramsgate, among other routes.

The most famous of all paddle steamers was undoubtedly the *Great Eastern*, a source of loss and disappointment to her owners, but by far the largest and, in some respects, the most remarkable ship of her period. She was unique in that her designer, I. K. Brunel, the celebrated engineer, provided her with screw propulsion as well. From keel to water-line she had a double hull, with a space between of 2·8 feet; the deck was double, and she was also divided into watertight sections every 60 feet by transverse bulkheads up to the second deck, besides having watertight compartments in bows and stern. The ship was built of ¾-inch steel plates, riveted to a steel frame. Two great tunnels ran through the ship, near the water-line; this proved very serviceable when, at a later date, she became a cable-laying vessel. The *Great Eastern's* gross tonnage was 18,914. She was 692 feet long and 82½ feet wide (but 120 feet if measured across the paddle boxes), and she was 58 feet deep. She could carry 10,000 tons of coal, 6000 tons of general cargo, 800 first-class passengers, 2000 second-class, and 1200 steerage. Many of her cabins were large rooms, ornately gilded and luxuriously furnished. She had five funnels and six masts, being rigged with fore-and-aft sails. Her 20 anchors, with their cables, weighed 253 tons.

The *Great Eastern*

The *Great Eastern* was built on the Thames at Millwall, where large shipyards existed for many years. She was launched sideways, but the slope gave way under the great weight on the cradles (12,000 tons), and she had to be launched inch by inch, a job which took three months. In June, 1860, she made her first Atlantic crossing, averaging 14 knots; but she proved so costly to run that, after a few years, she was taken off this service, part of her cabin accommodation was broken down, workshops and cable-laying plant were installed down the middle of the ship, and she was then employed in laying submarine cables, both across the Atlantic and from Bombay to Aden, &c. Eventually she ended up in the scrap yard (1888). No larger ship was built till the close of the century.

Meanwhile, keen international competition had begun for the valuable transatlantic passenger trade, and in this the Cunard and White Star Lines, which possessed immense resources and eventually combined, played an important part. Larger, faster, and better-equipped ships were built. The famous Parsons steam turbine was invented, which revolutionized the engining of steamships, and in the present century heavy-oil internal-combustion or Diesel engines have had nearly as great an effect. The *Oceanic*, built at Belfast in 1899 for the White Star Line, was the first liner to exceed the *Great Eastern* in length, though not in tonnage. She was 704 feet long, rated at 17,040 tons gross, and could steam 24,000 miles at 12 knots without refuelling, with a maximum speed of 20 knots. She was followed by many famous liners, both in this country and abroad: the *Celtic*, *Carmania*, *Baltic*, *Caronia* (there is now a new *Caronia*, the largest post-war ship in the world, a magnificent liner of 34,600 tons), *Kaiser Wilhelm II*, *Nieuw Amsterdam*, *Mauretania*, *Lusitania* (the sinking of which by a German submarine in 1915 largely contributed to bring the United States into the war), and the huge *Titanic*, whose 43,000 tons was wrecked on an iceberg during her first voyage, with terrible loss of life.

The possession of the Blue Riband of the Atlantic for making the fastest double crossing became a much-coveted honour; but the competition ceased when the *Mauretania* took the water in 1907, and for more than twenty years that famous liner (known even to-day to lovers of ships as " the grand old lady of the Atlantic ") had no rival. In 1873 the Atlantic crossing took nearly 8 days, but successive improvements enabled the *Mauretania* to reduce this to 4½ days. In the middle 'twenties the Germans made a determined effort to re-capture the honour. They built two magnificent ships, the *Europa* and *Bremen*, and at her first attempt the *Bremen* beat the old time westward by nearly 9 hours. But the *Mauretania* was not yet finished with. Although she had now steamed nearly two million miles, and was still using her original Scottish boilers and direct-drive turbines, she made what was described as a " routine crossing " in 1929, knocked several hours off her own times in both directions, and got within 3¼ hours of the *Bremen's* record. To the regret of all ship-lovers she was then taken out of service and broken up. The present splendid *Mauretania* is her successor.

After a fleeting challenge by the Italians, the French next secured the Blue Riband, by building that ill-fated giant, the *Normandie*,

1000 feet long and 80,000 tons. She had turbo-electric-driven quadruple screws, and made her first crossing (May, 1935) to Ambrose Light, New York, in 4 days 3 hours 2 minutes, at an average speed of almost exactly 30 knots; the return voyage took 23 minutes longer, but the distance was greater, and she averaged 30·35 knots.

Meanwhile, the Cunard-White Star people had not been slumbering, and a new giant was fitting out at John Brown & Co.'s famous shipyard at Clydebank. This was the *Queen Mary*, which had been launched by H.M. Queen Mary on 26th September, 1934. She and her near-twin, the *Queen Elizabeth*, are the two largest and most magnificent liners afloat. At her first crossing, just a year after the *Normandie*, the *Queen Mary* failed by several hours to equal that ship's record, but she subsequently beat it easily. On 8th August, 1938, she reached New York in 3 days 21 hours 48 minutes, her average speed being 30·99 knots. On the return journey she passed Bishop's Rock, near Land's End, in 3 days 20 hours 42 minutes, the fastest crossing ever made by a liner until in 1952 the Americans built the *United States*. Much smaller than the *Queens*, this fine liner of about 51,500 tons at once regained the Blue Riband, with an outward voyage of 3 days 10 hr. 40 min., and a return time of 1½ hours longer.

Everyone knows the general appearance of the two *Queens*, their enormous superstructure, stepped-back upper decks, the three huge funnels of the *Queen Mary* and the two of her consort. The *Queen Elizabeth* is a shade the larger and four years younger. But what manner of ships are they? Let us look at the older *Queen* a little more closely.

She measures 1019½ feet overall, is 118 feet wide, and 92 feet 6 inches high to the promenade deck, or 124 feet to the top of the upper lounge. Her gross tonnage is 80,773 and she weighed 35,500 tons at launching. She has provision for 2130 passengers and 1100 crew; but, during the war, when serving as a transport, carried many thousands more. The *Queen Mary* has 12 decks, an uppermost or sports deck, sun deck, promenade deck, main deck, and below that are decks A to H. Decks A, B, C, D and E extend throughout the vessel; those below are broken by the spaces required for the five boiler-rooms and the engine-rooms. The promenade deck and those above it are stepped back successively towards the stern. Besides the great main bridge forward, there is a second bridge aft, overlooking the stern.

She is, of course, built of steel and has endless tunnels, passages, watertight doors and bulkheads. Nearly 10 million steel rivets were used in her construction, in addition to a great deal of welding. A thousand tons of Burma teak, which is very resistant to weather conditions, went into her decks, ladders and hand-rails. Her rudder weighs 110 tons, and with the stern frame and shaft brackets 600 tons. It includes the largest steel casting ever made (except, of course, the *Queen Elizabeth*'s). When the ship was launched most elaborate precautions were taken, and she was held back by 18

The *Queen Mary*

groups of chain drags weighing 2350 tons; nevertheless she travelled nearly a quarter of a mile in two minutes before being brought to rest. Her four anchors each weigh 16 tons. The cable for them is of huge chains, each link being $24\frac{1}{2}$ inches by $14\frac{3}{4}$ inches and $4\frac{1}{8}$ inches thick; the weight of the cable is 150 tons. This, and all the other heavy operating machinery, is controlled by electric motors.

The *Queen Mary* carries 24 steel motor lifeboats, mostly 36 feet long, with a total capacity of 3266 persons. The ship has 66 automatically controlled watertight doors. The precautions against fire necessitate 47 separate fire-control stations and $3\frac{1}{2}$ miles of fire hoses.

The propelling machinery, boilers and boiler plant occupy ten immense watertight compartments, five of which are boiler-rooms. She has four screws, each driven by an independent set of Parsons single-reduction geared turbines. The bronze propellers weigh 30½ tons each, yet they are so beautifully balanced that they can be turned by the pressure of a finger. To provide fresh air in the machinery spaces fans and plant deliver 400,000 cubic feet of air per minute.

The ship carries 7 electric turbo-generators, 578 electric motors of all kinds, and 29,000 electric lights. Her luxurious cabin accommodation, with its lounges, swimming-baths, gymnasia, shops and conveniences of every kind, is too well known to need description.

Huge though they are, the *Queens* must yet obey the will of a single man, who, by merely putting over the helm, can turn the ship in whatever direction he pleases. To attain such control over a vessel one-fifth of a mile long, which never weighs less than 50,000 tons, calls for a wonderful combination of science and mechanics. The navigating officer steers or cons the ship from the bridge, immediately beneath which is the great wheel-house. The wheel-house has glass windows, two of which are fitted with revolving glass screens (the Kent clear-vision screen), so as to give a view even in foul weather. Two steering-wheels stand side by side, but either alone will control the ship. The steersman gets his orders by audible telephone. Before him is a compass on a binnacle, the accuracy of which is ensured by a master compass hidden away in the ship. She also has a gyro-compass, which remains steady in any weather, besides a gyro-pilot, the indicator of which shows infallibly if the ship goes off her course. Miles of telegraph wire transmit orders from the bridge to the engine-rooms. The rudder, three hundred yards away in the stern, obeys almost instantly, despite its enormous weight and the resistance of the sea. This rudder is nearly square, measuring about 20 feet each way; its square stock is held by powerful cross-arms called the crossheads, and the turning of the rudder depends upon the pressure which is placed on the crossheads, a pressure which is applied by hydraulic power and electrically driven pumps. To operate the whole vast system one need only depress a switch; and the mechanism is so sensitive that the rudder stock will turn if the hand-wheel in the wheel-house far away be moved only the distance between two spokes.

Ships, ships, ships—there is no end of the varieties of them: mighty battleships, the extraordinary aircraft carriers, swift destroyers, fussy little tugs and launches, cargo ships of every kind, tankers, grain ships, dredgers, ice-breakers, lightships, train ferries, whaling ships, and many more.

One remarkable ship of our day is the S.S. *Southern Venturer*, the largest of the world's floating whale factory ships. She is a very curious-looking vessel, built rather like a tanker. She has twin funnels placed side by side towards the stern, above the propelling machinery. She is very strong, with no awkward angles, for she has to reckon upon occasional buffets from ice-floes in the Antarctic, an ocean that spares no ship, whatever its size, and is always looking out for weak points in their armour. The stern of the *Southern Venturer* is square and has an enormous square hole in it; up the inside runs a ramp for hauling the huge whales on board to the flensing deck. The whales are stripped of their blubber on board. It is boiled there, and is stored in nine great oil chambers, with a total capacity of 19,150 tons of oil. She also carries plant for extracting liver oil from whales and for dehydrating the meat. The *Southern Venturer* is 550 feet long, 74 feet 3½ inches wide, 57 feet deep and has a displacement of about 32,300 tons. She acts as parent ship to the small whalers which roam the Antarctic far and wide, and which actually catch the whales.

We have mentioned tankers, a class of ship which the world's incessant demand for oil has recently brought to great perfection. There now several scores of tankers afloat, all larger than most liners; the greatest, the *Universe Apollo*, 69,100 tons gross and 104,520 tons deadweight, is the largest ship afloat apart from the two *Queens*. These great ships have the funnel and the propelling machinery far aft; some have twin screws but the tendency is to employ a single shaft when possible; mostly the ships are powered by geared turbines. A medium-sized oil tanker carries up to 3 dozen cargo oil tanks in a double or triple row; they are served by turbo-driven pumps capable of handling 1000 tons of oil per hour, or more. They also have miles of piping for heating coils, besides much special apparatus.

Finally we must mention the nuclear-powered submarine *Nautilus*, the U.S. nuclear-powered ship *Savannah* (the first ship of this kind ever built), and a nuclear-propelled merchantman which Britain is contemplating as an experiment. The design and construction of these unique vessels are partly experimental and partly a matter of prestige; for no one can foresee yet by what date they can be built purely on economic grounds.

THE SOLAR SYSTEM AND BEYOND
THE SOLAR SYSTEM

The Sun is the most important to us of the heavenly bodies. We depend upon it for our light and heat, and ultimately for life itself. The ancients recognized its importance, and worshipped it as a god; and one of the charges against Socrates was that he denied the divinity of the Sun. The Sphinx, near the pyramid at Ghizeh in Egypt, was the largest and most famous monument dedicated to the Sun. Some of you will have seen Cleopatra's Needle on the Victoria Embankment in London. This came from the ancient temple of Heliopolis, partially buried in the sands of the Egyptian desert. It was dedicated to the worship of the Sun, and the daughter of its high priest was married to Joseph (*Genesis*, xli, 45). Joseph must often have read the inscriptions on the Needle when he visited his father-in-law at the temple. The Needle was removed to Alexandria in 14 B.C., and was in A.D. 1877 taken to its present position in London, after having been lost in transit for a while at the bottom of the sea in the Bay of Biscay.

Now we know much more about the Sun. It has a temperature of 6000 degrees F. at the surface, and is very much hotter inside. It is 860,000 miles in diameter, and is therefore more than a million times the size of the Earth; and it is distant about 93 million miles from us.

Sometimes spots form on the surface of the Sun. These are due to electric storms of great violence which occasionally affect the Earth, disturbing radio and telephone communications, and producing brilliant displays of the Aurora Borealis. These sunspots come to a maximum every eleven years, and so too do the extent and brilliance of the Aurora.

Next to the Sun, the Moon is the most important to us of the heavenly bodies. It lights us at night, and with the Sun causes the tides of the sea. The Sun is responsible for high tide and low tide, and the Moon for the difference between neap and spring tides. The Sun shines by its own light, but the Moon only reflects the sunlight. Consequently, when the Sun and Moon are in opposite parts of the sky, there is full moon; when they are nearly in the same part, the Moon is new. Spring tides (when the high tide is higher and the low tide is lower than usual) occur at full and new moon; neap tides at the first and third quarters (half moon).

Sometimes the Moon comes between the Earth and the Sun, partially or wholly hiding the Sun, causing a partial or total " solar eclipse ". Or the Earth may come between the Sun and Moon; a shadow of the Earth is cast on the Moon, and a partial or total " lunar eclipse " occurs. In 1959 there were three eclipses, two of the Sun and one of the Moon.

The times of eclipses can now be foretold correct to the nearest minute. Even in ancient times they were predicted with moderate accuracy, and records are frequent. It is related that about 2000 B.C. two Chinese astronomers Hsi and Ho were executed for failing to predict or observe a certain eclipse. In Assyrian records the eclipse of the Sun on 15th June in 763 B.C. is noted thus: " Insurrection in the city of Assur. In the month Sivan the Sun was eclipsed "; and, in different language, the same eclipse is recorded in the Bible (*Amos*, viii, 9). The historian Herodotus records an eclipse of the Sun foretold by Thales, which occurred on 28th May, 585 B.C., during a battle between the Lydians and Medes. The eclipse frightened the combatants, who forthwith ceased fighting. A Viennese work, *Canon der Finsternisse*, by T. R. Oppolzer, gives a list, with maps, of all solar and lunar eclipses which have occurred or will occur from 1207 B.C. to A.D. 2161.

What would the Moon be like if we could land on it? It has no air, and no water. So no life, as we understand it, could exist there. It has a cloudless day a fortnight long, when the Sun shines with a terrible glare, and the heat would be unendurable for any animal or plant we know. There is no twilight, but night descends suddenly, and for a fortnight there is a pitiless cold, the thermometer sinking to over a hundred degrees below zero Fahrenheit.

The Moon is remarkable for the large number of craters on its surface, of all sizes up to 100 miles in diameter. The ring of a crater may be as much as 20,000 feet high; and there may be a peak in the centre of the crater. They are probably extinct volcanoes, which were extremely active long ago, when the Moon was very much hotter than it is now. If you look at the Moon through a telescope of quite low power (preferably at or near first or third quarter) you can quite easily see these craters, and if you examine the line dividing the dark part of the Moon from the light part you will see the Sun rising and illuminating fresh peaks or setting and darkening them, if you stay long enough at the instrument and keep the Moon in the field of view. From the lengths of the shadows of the mountains in the Moon, it has been possible to calculate their heights.

The Sun and Moon have given their names to two of our days of the week, Sunday and Monday. The Moon has often been supposed to exert an evil influence upon the human mind; thus we talk of a person " mooning about ", or being " moonstruck "; or he may be a " lunatic ", i.e. " possessed by the Moon " (Latin, *luna*).

The Sun is surrounded by a number of stars called planets (fig. 1) which move round it in nearly circular orbits or paths. These stars are called *planets*, i.e. wanderers, because they move about against the background of the fixed stars outside the Solar System. Nearest to the Sun is the planet Mercury. It is the hottest of all the planets. It revolves round the Sun in 88 days, and its distance from the Sun varies from 30 to 40 million miles. Owing to its nearness to the Sun it is extremely difficult to see, and the famous astronomer Copernicus never saw it at all. When it is visible, it appears near sunrise or sunset close to the Sun as a small object of a leaden white colour.

The next planet is Venus, whose year or time of revolution round the Sun is 225 days. It is by far the most brilliant of all the stars, and at its brightest can easily be seen in broad daylight. Occasionally this planet crosses the face of the Sun, and is seen as a black spot on its surface. This event, known as a " transit of Venus ", last occurred in 1882; another transit will not come until 2004.

The next planet is our Earth, which, as everyone knows, travels round the Sun in 365¼ days. Formerly, it was not looked upon as a planet. It was supposed that the Earth was the fixed centre of the universe, and the Sun and Moon, together with Mercury, Venus, Mars, Jupiter and Saturn were regarded as the seven planets moving round the Earth.

Mars is particularly interesting. It can easily be distinguished from other planets by its red colour. It not only comes nearest to us of all the planets except Venus (sometimes coming as near as 35 million miles), but it is most like our own Earth, and is the only planet which has very probable signs of life. Mars has a day slightly longer than our own, 24 hours 37 minutes 22·67 seconds, to be exact. This is known to be correct to one-fiftieth of a second, as the result of 300 years' observation of the planet. But its year is nearly twice as long as ours. The atmosphere is very thin, but gravity is weak, and a man on Mars would weigh half as much as on Earth.

The Earth has one Moon; but Mars is favoured with two, and the story of their discovery is remarkable. Many of you will have read *Gulliver's Travels*, written by Dean Swift in 1726. In this most interesting story the astronomers of Laputa claimed to have discovered two satellites or moons to Mars, one of which revolved round the planet in 10 hours, the other in 21½ hours. This would have been deemed impossible by any astronomer of the time; but the strange thing is that it very closely fitted the real facts. For, in 1877, Professor Hall, of Washington, discovered two satellites, the outer revolving round the planet in 30 hours, the inner in 7½ hours. So an observer on Mars would see its inner moon rising and setting three times a day.

On the very first day of last century a new planet was discovered. It had long been known that a large gap existed between Mars and Jupiter, which should have been occupied by another

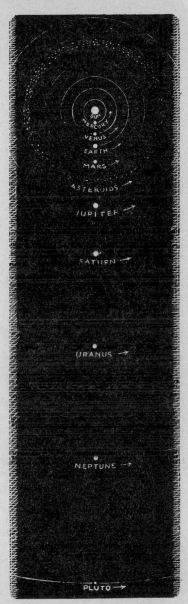

Fig. 1.—The Sun and the planets
(showing distances to scale)

planet; and search for it was continually made, but for a long time without success. At last, on 1st January, 1801, the Italian astronomer Piazzi discovered a small planet in this region, which he named Ceres. But it was not of the expected size, being only 480 miles in diameter, instead of thousands of miles, as are the other planets. This puzzled the astronomical world. But soon afterwards three more were discovered, and named Juno, Pallas and Vesta. These four together, however, were not large enough to satisfy expectations. It was a number of years before more were discovered and now more than 2000 have been definitely found. These bodies, known as Minor Planets or Asteroids, all (with a few exceptions) revolve in orbits between those of Mars and Jupiter more or less as shown in fig. 1. They vary in size. Some are just great masses of rock; others have surfaces a few hundred square miles in area; the largest, Ceres, as we have seen, has a diameter of 480 miles. It is probable that about 40,000 minor planets are within the range of our telescopes, the great majority of which have not yet been observed.

What is the origin of these bodies? This is a highly controversial subject; but it now seems probable either that they are the fragments of an exploded planet, or that they are a planet " spoiled in the making ".

The planet Jupiter comes next. It is by far the largest in the Solar System, and is the brightest except Venus. It is distant about 480 million miles from the Sun, and takes about 12 years to go round its orbit; its day is only ten hours long. This giant planet is only a little heavier than an equal volume of water. It is covered by a very complicated system of clouds and it has been suggested that it may have a poisonous atmosphere, consisting of ammonia and marsh gas, stretching up to a height of 6000 miles. The temperature all over the planet is far colder than our Arctic regions. So it is unfit for any life as we know it.

The influence of the planet Jupiter once robbed us of a magnificent display of shooting stars or meteors called the " Leonids ", which used to come once every 33 years and appeared last in 1866. They were expected again in 1899, and some people stayed up all night on the anticipated date, but they never appeared. It seems that some time before 1899 the meteors travelled too near Jupiter, and were diverted from their usual course by the attraction of this heavy mass. So now these meteoric displays are lost to us for ever.

If you look at the top of a medical prescription, you will see a mark of this form ♃. This is the astrological sign for Jupiter, and dates back to the time when medicine was influenced by astrology; and surgical operations were performed and treatment given when the planets were in certain positions. Another relic of this superstition is the word " jovial ". This means " born under the joyous influence of Jove ", i.e. Jupiter, and therefore " merry " or " joyful ".

Jupiter is attended in his journey round the Sun by no less than twelve satellites. Until the invention of the telescope in 1610, it was supposed that the Earth was the only planet to have a moon. But with this new instrument, Galileo discovered four moons to Jupiter. This startled the scientists and theologians of the day, but the discovery was confirmed by others. These four satellites can be seen with a pair of field-glasses, and one of them occasionally with the naked eye. Others were found later, and the last was discovered photographically by Dr. S. Nicholson with the 100-inch telescope (i.e. a telescope having an aperture of diameter 100 inches) at Mount Wilson in California.

Saturn was an old Italian god. It is related that he was dethroned by Jupiter, and fled to Italy. Here he reigned as a beneficent king, and mankind enjoyed perpetual prosperity. This was always remembered as the " Golden Age ". Finally he disappeared, but his memory was preserved in the festival of the " Saturnalia ". During this time no war was declared and no punishment inflicted. Gifts were exchanged, and master and servant banqueted at the same table. One day of the week, Saturday, was named after him; so too was the planet we are just going to describe.

The planet Saturn is one of the most beautiful objects that can be seen through the telescope, especially when its rings are visible. It is accompanied by nine moons. It was the most remote of the planets known to the ancients. Like Jupiter's, its atmosphere consists largely of marsh gas and ammonia; and the surface of the planet is as cold as that of Jupiter.

The rings consist of a large number of small bodies, each moving in its own orbit round the planet. Once every 15 years the rings disappear from our sight, when they are presented edge-wise toward the Earth. It is probable that in the remote past a satellite came too near to Saturn and was disrupted by the gravitational force of the planet. The fragments thus produced came to form the rings we now see.

The planet Saturn was supposed by astrologers to have an evil influence on mankind. This idea has been perpetuated by our word " saturnine ", indicating a heavy and gloomy disposition.

On 13th March, 1781, Sir William Herschel observed with his reflecting telescope (which he had made himself) a small object, which was not a fixed star, in the constellation of Gemini. At first he thought it was a comet, and reported it as such to the Royal Society, but further observations showed that it was a true planet. Herschel named the new planet " Georgium Sidus ", in honour of King George III; other European astronomers called it " Herschel "; but these names were finally abandoned in favour of " Uranus ", the father of Saturn in Greek mythology.

Uranus takes about 84 years to revolve about the Sun, and its day is less than eleven hours long. It has five satellites. Like Jupiter and Saturn, Uranus is extremely cold. It is about 200 times as far from the Sun as we are. It is just visible to the naked eye.

Neptune was the first planet to be discovered before it was actually seen. When Uranus had been moving for some time after its discovery, it was found that it was not accurately following its expected path round the Sun. This suggested that there was another planet beyond, whose attraction was causing Uranus to depart from its regular course. Two mathematicians, J. C. Adams of Cambridge, and Leverrier of Paris, independently set to work to calculate the position of a planet which would cause this divergence. The calculations were long and laborious, but ultimately the position was found. The astronomers were told to direct their telescopes to this place, and there they found the suspected planet. It was named after Neptune, a brother of Jupiter and ruler of the sea.

The planet Pluto, which attracts Neptune and Uranus away from their regular paths, was discovered in a similar manner. This planet has an average distance from the Sun of more than 3000 million miles, and it takes 248 years to go round the Sun. Pluto, in Greek mythology, was the god of the underworld.

Before leaving the Solar System, we must describe those occasional visitors, Comets and Shooting Stars, which used to terrify our ancestors. In ancient times comets were regarded as portents of evil. A comet which appeared in A.D. 66 was looked upon by the Jews as a warning of disaster to Jerusalem. Similarly, with the comet of 1066, when William invaded England. Some of you will have seen pictures of the Bayeux Tapestry, which shows this comet with the legend " Isti Mirantur Stellam " (they marvelled at the star);

and the consternation on the faces of the English observing it. (You can see a picture of it in the *Encyclopædia Britannica*, 14th Edition, article " Bayeux Tapestry ", and in the *King Penguin* book on the same subject.)

It was Edmund Halley (who succeeded Flamsteed, the first Astronomer Royal) who showed that comets were just as much ordinary members of the solar system as the planets and their satellites. He proved that some comets return at regular intervals, and foretold that the comet he observed in 1682 would return in 1757. When this forecast was fulfilled after his death, it was agreed to call the comet " Halley's Comet ". This returns once in every 66 years (nearly); its last appearance was in 1910 when King Edward VII died. The comet of A.D. 66 and of A.D. 1066 were earlier appearances of the same body. It will next return about 1976.

Comets are composed of a *nucleus*, usually an immense number of small stony particles; a *coma*, a foggy-looking gaseous disc surrounding the nucleus; and a long, bright tail which is extremely tenuous or thin, and is always directed away from the Sun. So rarefied are the gases composing this tail, that when, on 19th May, 1910, the Earth passed through the tail (19 million miles long) of Halley's comet, scarcely any effect was noticed.

Everyone has seen a *shooting star*, or *meteor* as it should be called. For these objects are not stars, but small portions of matter coming from space into the Earth's atmosphere. They are moving very quickly, and the friction with the air makes them so hot that they are usually burnt up and disappear before they reach the Earth. Occasionally, however, a large meteor falls to the Earth, being only scorched on the outside. It is then called a *meteorite*. Specimens of these can be seen in many museums. Peary, the North Pole explorer, brought three large meteorites from Greenland. They are now in the Natural History Museum, New York; the largest weighs 36 tons. On 30th June, 1908, one of the largest meteorites known fell in Siberia, devastating an area of three thousand square miles. The scorching effects of the hot air from the meteorite were felt 10 miles off and trees blown down at a distance of 30 miles.

Where do meteors come from? They are the debris of former comets. This has been observed in the case of Biela's comet, which revolved round the Sun in about 7 years. In 1845 it split into two parts. When it returned in 1852 these two portions had moved a million miles apart. After that the comet disappeared, but in 1872, when its return was expected, a brilliant shower of meteors occurred on 27th November. These meteors were obviously portions of the comet.

BEYOND THE SOLAR SYSTEM

When we leave the Solar System, we pass over an immense gulf before we come to the *nearest* of the fixed stars, which is called " Proxima Centauri ". The light of the Sun, which is 93 million miles off, takes about 7½ minutes to reach us; but the light of this star only arrives after 4 years. Thus the *nearest* fixed star is about 200,000 million miles off.

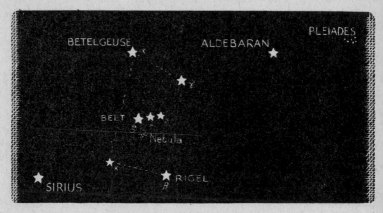

Fig. 2.—Orion with neighbouring stars

The fixed stars have been grouped into *Constellations*, most of which were known to and named by the ancients. Perhaps the most remarkable of these is Orion (fig. 2), named after a mighty hunter in Greek mythology. Orion is mentioned several times in the Bible, twice in the book of Job, and once in Amos. If on a clear winter's night you look towards the south, you will see a quadrilateral of four brilliant stars, which represent the hunter. The one on the top left, Betelgeuse, is easily distinguished by its brilliancy and its yellowish-red colour. In the opposite corner is the star Rigel. The three stars δ, ε, ζ in the middle of the quadrilateral are the

" Belt of Orion ". The constellation was also known to the poet Homer, who refers to it in the Odyssey, and to the Eskimos, who look upon the stars forming the constellation as seal-hunters who have lost their way home.

To the left of the constellation, and slightly below it, can be seen (fig. 2) the brightest fixed star in the sky, Sirius, known to the Romans as the " Dog-star ", and associated with the hot " Dog-days " of July and early August. Above Orion, to the right, is the brilliant red star Aldebaran.

Fig. 3.—The Great Bear with Cassiopeia and the Twins

Another very important constellation is that known as Ursa Major or the Great Bear (fig. 3). This can be seen in the north all through the year, for in northern latitudes it never sinks below the horizon. At 11.0 p.m. in April it can be seen directly overhead; in September it is low down in the north; in July in the west; and at Christmas in the east. It consists principally of the seven stars marked α, β, γ, δ, ϵ, ζ, η, in the diagram. If a line joining β and α be produced, it will pass on very close to the Pole Star, which is the brightest star in that neighbourhood, and easily detected. This is the only star which does not (except very slightly) share the general motion of the fixed stars round the sky. It is, in fact, almost exactly at the Pole; and anyone facing that star is looking towards the north. So the Pole Star is very useful in finding our direction on a clear night in the country. On the other side of the Pole, about as far from it as is the Great Bear, is the constellation of Cassiopeia, in shape like a capital W. Thus, if you have found Cassiopeia and the Great Bear in the sky, the Pole Star is midway between them.

Now look up at the stars named δ and β in the Great Bear (fig. 3). Join them in imagination by a straight line in the direction δβ and this will lead you to the two brilliant stars Castor and Pollux, which are midway between Orion and the Great Bear. The Constellation of Gemini (the Twins) contains these two stars and is named after them. In ancient times the twins Castor and Pollux were regarded as the friends of sailors. The ship which carried St. Paul from Melita (Malta) to Syracuse was named after them (*Acts*, xxviii, 11).

One very interesting cluster of stars in the northern hemisphere is the group known as the Pleiades (fig. 2). They are easily identified, and can be seen high up in the south-west about midnight at Christmas time. They are all close to each other, and are said to be seven in number, but only a very keen eye can see more than six. With a telescope, however, even of low power, hundreds can be seen. This cluster was well known to the ancients; it is mentioned by the Latin poet Ovid, and also in the Bible (*Job*, ix, 9).

If you look up at the sky on a clear frosty night in winter, you will see the Milky Way, or Galaxy. This consists of an immense zone of apparently minute stars, girdling the northern and southern hemispheres, so that the Sun, and indeed the whole Solar System, is in the middle of the Milky Way. These stars are really suns comparable in size with our own Sun, and look so small because of their stupendous distances away.

Among the constellations of the southern hemisphere, the chief is the Southern Cross, which consists mainly of four bright stars, forming a cross. It is perhaps the most beautiful constellation in the sky, and greets the traveller from north to south almost as a wonderful surprise one night in the course of his journey south.

Lastly, we come to the Nebulæ. There are many small patches of light in the sky, which cannot be entirely resolved into individual stars. These are known as Nebulæ (Latin *nebula*, a cloud), and consist mainly of extremely rarefied gases. Some of these are within the Galaxy; these are called *galactic* nebulæ. But by far the greatest number are situated far beyond the Galaxy, and are known as *extra-galactic* nebulæ. We will describe two nebulæ in detail.

If you look up to the constellation of Orion on a very clear night, you will see a faintly hazy patch just below the Belt (fig. 2). This is the " Great Nebula in Orion ". It is within the circle of the Milky Way, and is one of the nearest of the nebulæ. Yet it is so distant that its light, travelling at eleven million miles a minute, takes 600 years to reach us. It is greenish in colour, and its gas is thinner than the most perfect vacuum we can produce on Earth.

One of the nearest of the extra-galactic nebulæ is the " Great Nebula in Andromeda ". This is about the size of our Galaxy, and its light takes nearly a million years to reach us. It is spiral in form, consists of myriads of stars, and can just be seen with the naked eye. The number of extra-galactic nebulæ which can be detected with the 100-inch telescope at Mount Wilson is about two million.

We have been dealing with stupendous distances. To state them in miles would convey no adequate impression; so, in order to have a reasonable scale, we make use of the speed of light. Let us review what we have discovered. Light, as we have seen, travels at eleven million miles a minute. So the light of the Moon, distant a quarter of a million miles, reaches us in just over one second; that of the Sun in about seven minutes; that of the *nearest* fixed star in about 4 years. The light of most nebulæ takes millions of years; that of the most distant yet observed takes 500 million years. When we look up at some of the stars and nebulæ, we see not what is happening *now*, but what took place when the large reptiles ruled the Earth, and man had not yet appeared.

A large 200-inch telescope was erected in 1948 at Mount Palomar, in California, which penetrates twice as far as the previous largest, the 100-inch one at Mount Wilson. A reproduction of one of the first photographs taken by this instrument of the nebula Messier 81 in the constellation of the Great Bear shows considerably more detail than earlier photographs.

RAILWAYS AND TRAINS

If there is anyone so lacking in imagination that he cannot respond to the achievements of the railway-builders, the bridges, viaducts, tunnels in the marvellous steel network that covers the earth; or if he cannot take pleasure in the skills and inventions that move the trains—*if* there is such a fellow, then he should be sent on the grimmest railway journey that can be found. It is said that there is a particularly dreary line in Manchuria. He might be consigned on the longest through train journey in the world—nearly 6000 miles—on the Trans-Siberian Railway from Moscow to Vladivostok. He would be nine whole days and nights in the same train, long enough, no doubt, to get thoroughly tired of it, except that Russian railways are so peculiar that they might excite this dullard's interest. For one thing, they have the largest loading-gauge in the world, so they are able to build locomotives more than sixteen feet high.

Some say that the most dreadful railway journey in the world is that on the Transcontinental Railway of Australia, where it crosses the waterless Nullarbor Plain. The line goes dead straight; there's not a curve, not a single tree nor a drop of water in 328 miles.

But in contrast, of course, there are plenty of railways where the track is never straight and never level, where, indeed, it goes up or down and round and round in hair-raising loops and spirals. Among the many thrilling mountain railways, those of Switzerland are particularly interesting and important. They are also very spectacular. They are important because they connect the main lines of France, Germany, Austria and Italy, and spectacular because to carry the through traffic between these countries they have to surmount the great barrier of the Alps. Immense engineering works—wonderful steel bridges and dizzy viaducts over the gorges, innumerable tunnels, straight and spiral—take the railways up and through and over the Alps. The Simplon tunnel, $12\frac{1}{2}$ miles long, is the longest in the world; two other main-line tunnels, St. Gothard and Lötschberg, are both more than 9 miles long. And there are extraordinary corkscrew tunnels — spirals inside mountains — by which the trains gain height. The lines are always making loops and twists. They plunge into a mountain-side and return to day-light almost over the point where the tunnel began, but a hundred feet or so higher up. On the St. Gothard railway there is a difference in level of nearly a mile. In getting over that difference the train goes through eighty tunnels and over more than three hundred bridges between Lucerne and the Italian frontier.

The Swiss railways, like those of other mountainous countries, are all electric. In such countries there is ample water-power for generating the current, and electric traction is not only cheaper but more suitable—for several reasons. With steam trains it would be very difficult to keep the long tunnels free from smoke and poisonous gases. Electricity can be generated in large quantities and carried at high pressure over long distances with very little loss. Electric trains have the advantage of great economy—they take from the conductors just as much current as they need from mile to mile of the journey, and no more.

The Beginnings.

The first *public* railway on which trains were hauled by *loco-motives* was that between Stockton and Darlington, opened in 1825. We need to be very emphatic with the words public and locomotive, to avoid giving the impression that the Stockton and Darlington was the first railway ever—which it wasn't. Between 1801 and 1825 no fewer than twenty-nine " iron railways ", varying in length from a mile or two to thirty miles, were either opened or being built in various parts of Britain. Most of them joined collieries or ironworks with canals or rivers, but one of them, the Surrey Iron Railway, was the first really *public* railway. It was authorized by Parliament in 1801 to provide a connexion, nine miles long, be-tween Croydon in Surrey and the Thames at Wandsworth. The rails or " plates " were flanged, and anyone who paid the tolls might haul his merchandise over them. At that time, tolls had to be paid on the roads, too, but the railway made haulage easier.

Horses, mules, donkeys—even oxen—but no locomotives were on the railways then. The " iron horse " snorted and clanked its way upon the scene very slowly and at heavy cost in disappointment. In 1804 the first steam locomotive to run on rails (they were *flanged* rails) was built by Richard Trevithick for the Pen-y-darran tramway in South Wales. It weighed about five tons and could haul a load of fifteen tons at five miles an hour. But it was not a success; it was too heavy for the tramway, which was always breaking. In the same year (1804), Trevithick built another locomotive, this time for the Wylam Colliery, near Gateshead. This engine had flanged *wheels* and was the first to run on narrow rails. But here again the rails came to grief and the locomotive could not be used.

For twenty years before the opening of the Stockton and Darlington Railway, steam locomotives appeared here and there, and —mostly—disappeared very soon. Very fearsome things they were. They had no springs and the short cast-iron rails made a very imperfect track. The engines and their trains of twelve or fifteen little wagons jolted and rocked in a very alarming way, though the speed was only that of a brisk walker's. They made a terrible noise, they belched live coals from red-hot chimneys and they were much less satisfactory than the horses they supplanted.

Why, then, did the colliery-owners bother to go on experimenting with these dangerous, extravagant, troublesome travelling engines? Why not stick to horses? The answer is that events were happening at the beginning of the nineteenth century that brought many changes in the ways of doing things. One such event was the war with France, which called for horses in ever increasing numbers. More and more horses were sent to " the war ", until there were not enough left to do the work at home.

In spite of all their shortcomings, the first locomotives were truly remarkable achievements in craftsmanship. Everything had to be made by hand, and it is hard for us to realize what that meant in days when there were no machine tools. Then, every casting— cylinders and wheels, for instance—had to be worked up to the finished dimensions by hand, the wrought-iron boiler plates were bent and shaped by hand, the rivet holes drilled by hand; every forging in the moving parts, every nut and bolt and screw, could be fashioned only by skill and toil—and the incentive of a good idea. But the good idea was not fully vindicated for nearly five years *after* the Stockton and Darlington Railway had been opened—not until George Stephenson's " Rocket " won the prize at the trials held to decide whether or not locomotives should be used on the Liverpool and Manchester Railway, opened in 1830.

The Steam Locomotive.

For most of us probably (and certainly for the writer, who has travelled many hundreds of miles on the footplate), the romance of the railway is most completely summed up by the steam locomotive, which of all machines is the most dramatic, the most suggestive of power and speed. It is sad, therefore, to have to say that appearances are somewhat deceitful and that, in fact, the steam locomotive is not a highly efficient kind of engine; it does not make the best possible use of the heat units in the fuel it burns. It is fast being replaced by diesel power and electricity. Yet it still has some advantages. It is relatively cheap to build, it is extremely reliable and it has a very long life at small cost in maintenance. And it is safe to say that steam locomotives will continue to puff for many years to come.

When the railways of Britain were built, between 1830 and 1845, the builders failed to leave enough room for engines and trains to grow. Our tunnels are too small, bridges too low, retaining walls and other structures too near the rails. Thus it is that British locomotives have become marvels of compactness; a hundred and fifty tons of high-pressure steam-raising plant and beautifully balanced machinery are crowded into a very small space.

Every steam locomotive is a direct descendent of the " Rocket "; all work on the same principle—the pistons pushed backwards and forwards in the cylinders, and the impulses transmitted to the wheels through connecting-rods and cranks. And the boiler is still the " Rocket's " boiler—in principle. The success of the " Rocket " was chiefly due to George Stephenson's use of the multitubular boiler and the exhaust blast, neither of which, strictly speaking, was his own invention. There were fifteen fire tubes in the boiler of the " Rocket "; there may be 2000 or more in a modern locomotive, narrow tubes of thin metal through which the intensely hot gases from the firebox pass via the barrel of the boiler to the smoke-box and in so doing convert the water surrounding them into steam.

So long as the engine is in motion the furnace is maintained at white heat by the exhaust steam from the cylinders, which issues through a cone-shaped blast pipe situated in the smokebox, just under the chimney. This gush of steam—one puff to every stroke of a piston—creates a partial vacuum in smokebox and boiler tubes, drawing in air for the fire through dampers under the grate. When the engine is standing, a jet of live steam, called the blower, is used to urge the fire.

In one type of steam locomotive, used in parts of Russia, and in other countries where water is very precious, there is no exhaust blast. Instead of wasting it in the atmosphere, the exhaust steam is changed again to water in a condensing-plant carried on the tender. In such engines a fan is used to keep the fire going.

Steam is a gas, an invisible gas; the white plume from the locomotive (or the kettle) is not steam but steam condensate. The work that steam can do in any steam engine depends on its power to expand, and its power to expand depends on the temperature. It must be very hot indeed to get the best results. Therefore, after entering the regulator which controls the supply to the cylinders, it is made to pass through an arrangement of narrow tubes exposed to the furnace gases. From this " superheater " it goes to the cylinders at a temperature of about 700° F.

This brings us—perhaps a little unexpectedly—to the subject of streamlining. Moving gases, like everything else that moves, are retarded by friction, and it is obviously important to reduce the friction as much as possible. One of the most remarkable locomotives ever built was designed by a very brilliant French locomotive engineer, André Chapelon. It was a " Pacific " type engine, in which Chapelon took great pains to provide the easiest possible path for the steam, both in and out of the cylinders. It developed a record horse-power for its size and the principle was soon followed in other countries. The wonderful engine " Mallard ", which in 1938 (on what was at that time the London and North Eastern Railway) attained the world speed record for steam trains—126 miles per hour—is a good example of this internal streamlining. " Mallard " has very large, gently curving steam pipes and double blast pipes. The outward and visible streamlining that looks so impressive is in fact less important than the internal. The streamlined casings of locomotives make inspection more difficult—and more expensive—and they have been discarded by British Railways.

The locomotive boiler is a masterpiece of constructional skill. Of the many interesting and ingenious adjuncts and fittings that keep it under observation and control perhaps the most remarkable is the injector. The injector is the beautiful device by which a jet of steam keeps the boiler supplied with water. Reduced to the simplest terms, the injector consists of two hollow cones, one inside the other. The outer cone connects with the water supply, the inner one with steam from the boiler. The steam comes through the tapered nozzle of the cone with very high velocity, and as it comes in contact with the water some of it condenses, forming a partial vacuum which sucks in the water. The impact of the jet of steam on the incoming stream of water gives to the latter a forwards speed of hundreds of miles an hour. This momentum carries the water past

A Chapelon locomotive of the French National Railways at speed

the boiler valve and into the boiler against a *higher* pressure of steam than that which actually works the injector. The explanation of what seems a paradox lies in the terrific speed of the steam in passing through a hollow cone. (See the diagram on page 266).

It may be as well to mention that the boiler is never seen—except in the works. What we see is only the painted outer casing which, as well as hiding the boiler, covers a layer of insulating material to keep the heat in.

Turn now to the engine. In the boiler the heat energy of the fuel has been changed into pressure, and the next step is to change the pressure into mechanical motion. Valves control the supply of steam to the cylinders so as to give impulses, first to one side of the pistons and then to the other side. Each cylinder has a " valve-chest " —a box, or a second small cylinder—in which the valves are housed.

The simplest valve is the slide valve. In this, the valve-chest is a compartment with a flat face, near the centre of which are two ports, in line, these ports being the openings of the steam passages to the two ends of the cylinder. The slide valve itself can be imagined as a

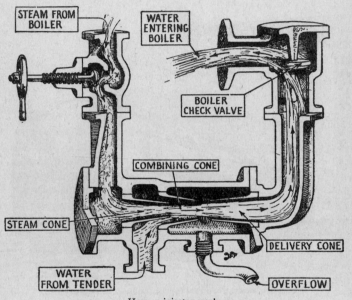

How an injector works

box without a lid, moving upside down to and fro over the flat face of the valve-chest, and of such a size that its ends completely cover both the ports. The outside of this upside-down box is exposed to live steam from the steam pipe, but the inside of the box is a space connecting only with the exhaust pipe.

Now, if the valve is moved—forwards or backwards—the ports will be uncovered; one of them is open to the live steam, which rushes into the cylinder and pushes the piston; and the other is open, not to live steam, but to the spent steam on the opposite side of the piston. This spent steam escapes under the valve into the exhaust pipe. And as the valve slides to and fro the ports are successively opened and shut, live steam pushing against one side of the piston while on the opposite side the spent steam is free to escape. *Partly* spent steam, one should have said, because there is a great deal of expansive force left in the steam even after it has pushed the piston. To get the most out of the steam it is often used again in another cylinder of larger diameter, where it gives up the last of its power. This is the principle of compound engines.

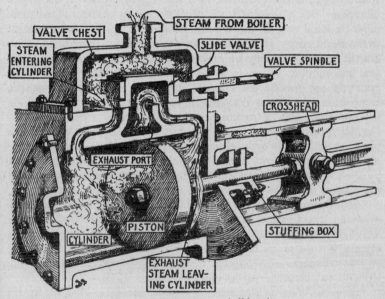

The cylinder with piston and slide valve

Tens of thousands of locomotives are worked by slide valves. But with steam at very high pressure (the Merchant Navy class engines on the Southern Section of British Railways work at 280 pounds pressure to the square inch) the slide valve is pressed against the seating so tightly that great friction must be overcome to move it. So in very powerful locomotives another type of valve is often used which has less resistance to the steam. This is the piston valve, which works on just the same principle, covering and uncovering the cylinder ports alternately, but is quite different in arrangement.

The place of the box-like slide valve is taken by two small pistons on the valve-rod, moving in a little cylinder attached to the main cylinder. Another and entirely different kind of valve is occasionally used, the poppet valve, which has much in common with the valve mechanism of internal-combustion engines.

Whatever the type, the valves get their motion from the driving-axle, which receives the push and pull of the pistons through connecting-rods and cranks. A very simple mechanical arrangement would suffice to move the valves if the engine always moved in one direction. But it is sometimes necessary to go backwards, so there must be some way of altering the position of the valves in relation to the steam ports. If, when you look at an engine, there is no valve-gear to be seen, you may be pretty sure that the gear is the Stephenson link motion, which is always placed inside the frames. The gear you see outside the frames, connected to the driving-wheel, is most likely to be the Walschaerts valve-gear. Both types work on the one principle: a rocking motion is given to a curved slotted bar called the expansion link. The end of the valve-rod is fixed to a block on which this expansion link is free to slide. The reversing-rod is connected to one end of the link, to raise or lower it, and so, by altering the relative positions of the block and the link, alters also the relative positions of valves and ports.

The reversing-gear has a very important use besides actually reversing the direction of travel. You may have wondered why the link should be called an *expansion* link. Well, the link itself doesn't expand, but the steam does, and the link controls the entry of steam in the cylinders. It controls what is known as the cut-off—the moment at which the valves close the steam ports.

To grasp the true importance of this, remember that the steam locomotive has no differential gears as a motor car has—no means of varying the ratio of speed of engine and wheels; its reserve of power is in the immense expansive force of steam. In ordinary running this great reserve of expansive power is not needed. It is not necessary to keep the steam on for the full stroke of the piston (it would, in fact, be harmful to do so, for the piston would be driven too forcibly), so the steam port is closed well before the stroke is finished. The position of the piston at the moment when the port is closed— the cut-off—depends on the work to be done To start a train, an immense effort is needed to overcome the inertia of hundreds of tons dead weight, so the regulator is opened wide to admit plenty of steam and the gear is adjusted to keep the ports open for as much as two-thirds of the stroke, or even three-quarters. But when the train is well under way and running easily at speed, the regulator is partly closed and the gear " notched up " to cut off the steam when the pistons have travelled no more than a fifth or sixth of the stroke. Saving steam is the same as saving coal—and water.

And water is a very expensive thing. There are very few regions where it is free from minerals (chiefly calcium and magnesium) that cause trouble by forming scale in boilers. To remove these impurities the water is treated in " softening " plants, and as the process is expensive care is taken not to waste the softened water. The tenders of the largest British express engines hold from 9–10 tons of coal and from 4000–5000 gallons of water. That quantity of coal suffices, but the water is not enough for the longest runs. However, water can be taken in, while the train is travelling at high speed, from water troughs between the rails. The troughs are about a quarter of a mile long and are placed where the track is straight and level. When the train is over the trough the fireman lowers a hinged pick-up scoop, and the water rushes up this into the tender.

There are many differences in the kind of work locomotives have to do, from shunting in the sidings to hauling crack expresses, and therefore there are many different types. Locomotives are classified —all over the world—according to the wheel arrangement. Thus, an engine with a leading 4-wheel bogie, 6 coupled wheels and a pair of trailing wheels is everywhere of the 4—6—2 or " Pacific " class, however much one may differ from another in detail.

The purpose of coupling the wheels is to give a better grip on the rails. In the very early days of railways the idea prevailed that smooth wheels would slip on smooth rails, and inventors complicated their locomotives by providing cog-wheels that engaged with studs at the side of the rail. " Racks " of that kind are used on very steep mountain railways, but smooth wheels will grip smooth rails unless the gradient is steeper than 1 in 12. The power of adhesion—the grip—depends on the weight carried on the driving-axle, but by coupling other wheels with those on the driving-axle, so that they turn in unison, the weight distributed on all so coupled is made available for adhesion.

The limit to the number of wheels that can be coupled is decided by the curves in the track—a " decapod " (o—10—o) would be off the rails on a curve that was only of sufficient radius to take a " Pacific ".

One way of getting over this difficulty is by coupling two distinct sets of driving-wheels, each set being free to move independently. Locomotives of this kind are called articulated. They are really two separate engines on swivelled trucks supplied by a single boiler. Some articulated locomotives have as many as thirty-two wheels, arranged 4—8—4 + 4—8—4, and with so many the weight on any one axle is much reduced. Articulated locomotives are employed where heavy trains have to go on tracks with light rails and sharp curves.

By articulation—putting joints in the middle, as it were—locomotives can be built to enormous size, weight and power. Those of the " Big Boy " class of the Union Pacific Railroad of America weigh 534 tons. They have 24 wheels, 4—8 + 8—4, a 4-wheel leading bogie, then two sets of 8 coupled driving-wheels, then a trailing 4-wheel bogie. The tender has 14 wheels.

All steam locomotives have a common disability—they cannot manage without a daily rest. After the day's work they must retire to the engine sheds, where the boilers are washed out, the tubes swept, smokeboxes and ashpans emptied, and all the intricate moving parts examined and cleaned. And when that has been done and everything put in order and finally inspected, to make doubly sure that all is well, it is the duty of the driver before he takes an engine out again to test every gauge and valve and cock, every cotter and nut and tightening-bolt.

Diesel Locomotives

Internal-combustion engines need less frequent " servicing ". Just as a farm tractor continues to work without rest so long as it is supplied with fuel, so does the diesel locomotive. This instant readiness is particularly useful where continuous shunting goes on, as in the marshalling-yards, where trains are made up, day and night. But because the power transmission to the wheels is through clutch and gearbox, diesel locomotives of this type are necessarily small. The limitation is not in the engine but in the clutch, which cannot gently take up a strain much more than twice as heavy as is called for in the biggest motor bus. By doing away with the clutch and turning the driving-wheels electrically, the power of the diesel engine can equal that of steam.

A diesel-electric locomotive is really a travelling electric generating station. It costs about twice as much to build as a steam locomotive of equal power, but it makes more economical use of its fuel—crude oil. The engines and generators are mounted on the longitudinal axis of the locomotive, with the cooling-plant and auxiliary machinery on each side of alleyways for the engineers. The traction motors are geared to the driving-wheels as in ordinary electric locomotives. Locomotives of this type compete in hauling the heaviest trains—and the fastest.

Speed always depends on load; heavy trains are slower than light ones. Before the outbreak of the second world war, diesel-electric trains in regular service both in Europe and America ran at higher speeds than any steam trains. The record was held by a train that covered the 157·8 miles between Berlin and Hanover in 114 minutes—an average speed of 83·1 miles per hour. Other diesel-electric trains had scheduled speeds almost as high. At that time the fastest regular steam train belonged to Belgium. It ran between Brussels and Bruges, 57·7 miles, at an average speed of 75·3 miles per hour. But the diesel-electric " flyers " were very light trains, consisting only of two or three coaches, carrying about a hundred passengers, and the routes for them had been realigned and relaid at great cost, particularly in Germany.

The system has now reached its highest development in America, where 6000 horse-power diesel-electric locomotives weighing more than 400 tons haul heavy trains for distances of a thousand miles and more at average speeds of well over 60 miles per hour, including stops. One train, an experimental one, consisting of six cars and a 4000 horse-power diesel-electric locomotive, made an astonishing non-stop run between Chicago and Denver, more than a thousand miles, in a little over twelve hours—an average speed of 83 miles per hour.

Another kind of diesel locomotive, called a diesel-hydraulic, has a gearbox like the diesel-mechanical type, but instead of a clutch, a clever device known as a torque-converter completes the power transmission. This is somewhat similar in construction to a fluid flywheel (which is only a form of clutch) but the converter, as its name implies, does more than just connect the drive and is able to convert or employ the power developed at any engine speed to the best advantage for hauling in each of the gear ratios. Locomotives of this kind are also used for fast expresses and heavy trains, and are usually lighter than a diesel-electric locomotive of similar horse-power. There are many locomotives of this kind in Germany. Diesel-mechanical (those which have a clutch and gearbox), diesel-electric, and diesel-hydraulic locomotives are all used on British Railways.

Main-line diesel and electric locomotives are classified throughout the world by the number of driving and carrying axles of each locomotive, or of each bogie truck. The number of driving axles is indicated by a letter—A for one, B for two, and so on. The number of carrying axles is shown by figures. So a locomotive with a carrying axle, four driving axles and a carrying axle is shown as 1—D—1. If this same locomotive were mounted on two bogie trucks, each of one carrying axle and two driving axles, it would then be shown as 1B—B1. A small " o " after the letters shows that each driving axle is driven by a separate electric motor. If the locomotive arrangement used as an example had separate motors on each axle it would be described as 1Bo—Bo1. If the — (minus) sign is replaced by a + (plus) sign it indicates that the bogies of the locomotives are articulated, or linked together, so that the locomotive frame or chassis, does not transmit any pulling power. On the Continent and elsewhere, diesel shunting locomotives are described in the same way as a steam engine, o—4—o or o—6—o. Some of the arrangements to be seen on British Railways are shown on page 273.

Railways in Britain To-day

Because Britain is a " coal " country the diesel principle has been slow to make headway. But under the British Railways £1500 million modernization programme, which began in 1955, electric and diesel power is now replacing the steam engine, for both passenger and freight trains. About 1460 route miles of our railways are to be electrified, including lines in the suburban areas around London and Glasgow, and the main lines in Kent; from London to Birmingham, Liverpool and Manchester; London to York; and London to East Anglia. Diesel locomotives and the little green diesel trains with " bus " type engines under the floor, are already widespread because they can be brought into use as quickly as they can be built. Electrification demands a lot of preparatory engineering work—the erection of overhead electric lines, and the raising of bridges over the railway to allow sufficient height between trains and the undersides of the bridges.

Our famous named expresses will again be as fast as any in the world, but much has still to be done to make that possible. Our main lines are not only very crowded, but complicated by hills, curves and junctions. There are surprisingly few stretches of main line, such as those on parts of the line between London and York, and between Swindon and Paddington, where trains can go at top

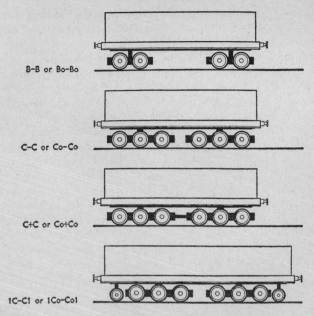

B–B or Bo–Bo

C–C or Co–Co

C+C or Co+Co

1C–C1 or 1Co–Co1

speed. Though on such stretches the speed may be over a hundred miles per hour, the average speed on long journeys comes tumbling down through " slacks " enforced by curves, bridges, junctions, track repairs and other things. But in 1937 the " Coronation Scot " ran from Crewe to Euston, 158 miles, in 119 minutes, an average speed of 80 miles per hour. The run, an experimental one, was with a train of six coaches only, but it set up a world record for the distance for a steam train. And " Mallard's " record, 126 miles per hour, remains unbeaten.

To adapt our railways for the highest speeds attainable will mean realigning them—straightening curves and their approaches, building fly-over bridges at busy junctions—at places where the gain in speed will justify the enormous cost. Elsewhere, to speed the trains, engineers are concentrating on better permanent way, and better means of controlling traffic. A new type of standard rail is being used, flat-footed, and heavier and longer than the bull-headed type. These rails are 60 feet long and weigh 109 lbs. to the yard. They are too heavy to be laid by hand, so a new method of mechanical laying has come into use. Lengths of track—rails, sole plates and sleepers complete—are preassembled and taken to the site where they are to be laid, on long, low bogie trucks. When the lengths have been placed in position by special track-laying cranes, ballasting machines go over them and pack the ballast between the sleepers to a truer level than can be done by hand. The longer the rails the fewer the joints in them, and, therefore, the less of the *clickety-clack* of the wheels in going over them. By welding rail joints and so making longer continuous lengths, the track is made still smoother for the travellers. Some rails in Britain are over three miles in length.

Given the best possible permanent way, comfort on the railway depends on the coaching-stock. Railwaymen always speak of " coaches ", never of " carriages " because that is what they have been called ever since railways began. The word is an interesting survival from the Stockton and Darlington Railway, where, to begin with, the passengers travelled in ordinary road coaches (some of which were bought second-hand) adapted to run on the rails. Every increase in comfort means more work for the engine; more dead-weight to be hauled for each passenger carried. Coach-building has become a most complicated trade; the things that most make for comfort cannot be seen. British rolling-stock is necessarily small because of the loading-gauge; coaches seldom exceed 60 ft. in length or 35 tons in weight. A train of sixteen coaches, weighing with engine and tender about 700 tons, is an exceptionally heavy one. Express passenger trains of over 1000 tons are everyday affairs on the Continent, still more so in America, where freight trains of 5000 tons go gaily along at sixty miles an hour.

One of the advantages of electric traction is the very rapid acceleration of electric motors. The trains gain speed more quickly and consequently more trains can be run in a given time. At the " rush " periods on some of the London tube railways there are more than forty trains an hour, a rate of traffic that could not be maintained without a completely dependable signalling system. On most electric railways the signals are entirely automatic, that is, they are worked by the trains. Instead of semaphore arms, colour-light signals are used which are clearly visible on the brightest day and on the dullest. When a train enters a section of line, the wheels short-circuit an electric current in the rails, keeping the signal behind at danger. When the track-circuited section has been cleared the red signal in the rear changes to amber—caution—showing that the train has entered the next section. Not until there is an un-occupied section separating two trains can a signal change to green

—all clear. Colour-light signals which show four aspects—red, double-amber, amber and green—are widely employed on main lines and will eventually replace all the semaphore arm signals.

The apparatus of signalling is very intricate, but the principle is simple. It is based on the " absolute block ". The method of communication between the signalmen, and the mechanism for working the signals and points, make it impossible—if the rules are obeyed—for two trains to be in the same section at the same time. Beneath the floor of every signal-box is the locking frame, in which the levers for signals and points are interlocked, to make certain that they agree.

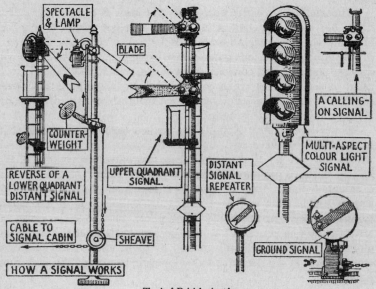

SPECTACLE & LAMP

BLADE

COUNTER-WEIGHT

REVERSE OF A LOWER QUADRANT DISTANT SIGNAL

UPPER QUADRANT SIGNAL.

DISTANT SIGNAL REPEATER

A CALLING-ON SIGNAL

MULTI-ASPECT COLOUR LIGHT SIGNAL

CABLE TO SIGNAL CABIN

SHEAVE

GROUND SIGNAL

HOW A SIGNAL WORKS

Typical British signals

In modernized signal-boxes there is no need for physical exertion. The heavy manual levers are replaced by electric switches which control electric or electro-pneumatic motors for actually operating the signals and points. Everything is automatic that can be—the trains even send automatic messages to the signal-boxes, showing their exact positions on large illuminated diagrams of the track. That is not to say that signalmen are no longer required. They are —more skilled and more highly trained than ever before.

WEATHER FORECASTING

Throughout the ages anyone who could foretell the weather has always held a high place, especially when his prophecies happened to come true. For the professional forecaster of to-day, however, times have changed, and he is just a civil servant doing a job. What is that job? And how does he go about it? Let us sketch the problem first.

The shell of air which surrounds the earth is at least 200 miles thick, but more than half of all the air in it lies within four miles of sea-level. We imagine the atmosphere as a countless multitude of tiny bubbles of various gases, which expand and tend to rise when they are warmed, and contract when chilled; thus, there are more of them in a given area when cold than when hot, and as the composition of dry air does not vary much from place to place, cold air is heavy and warm air is light.

At sea-level the air globules are packed together so closely that 15 lb. weight of air presses upon every square inch of our bodies; we do not feel it, of course, because we ourselves contain much air, the outward pressure of which is just the same. As one ascends a mountain the bubbles become freer and freer, until at 20,000 ft. the air weighs only half as much, while at 40,000 ft. it has fallen to one-quarter. In the higher atmosphere, far above the range of aircraft, there is almost a vacuum, so few and scattered are the air globules, yet there are still enough of them to heat the meteoric stones which strike the earth's envelope and to make them flash into light.

As one ascends above the earth the air becomes steadily colder, losing about 1° Fahrenheit for every 300 ft., and it continues to do so until, at about 7 miles above sea-level in our latitude, the temperature has fallen to −65° or thereabouts, i.e. 100° below freezing-point. It then remains stationary over a considerable height, and in the upper atmosphere begins to rise again. The point where it ceases to fall is called the tropopause. It is the boundary between the stratosphere above and the troposphere below; nearly all the facts of importance to weather forecasters are found in the lower zone.

The next point to notice is the importance of clouds. Clouds are made of fog, countless points of water vapour, which has ascended to such a height that the cooling has chilled it and made it visible. There is a vast amount of other, invisible, water vapour in the atmosphere. It is sucked up by the thirsty, dry, warm winds from lakes and rivers, and from the immense expanses of the ocean; but it is very unevenly distributed, and as it weighs only about five-eighths as much as dry air it disturbs the balance between the globules and so causes currents of air to flow.

You will, of course, be aware that in a fluid the pressure tends to become the same in all directions. Air varies so much in pressure, thanks to its varying heat and cold, dryness and moisture, that it is always in motion; and its larger and more general motions cause the winds. We can perceive this very readily at the seaside on a fine day, when a little way inland from the coast huge billowy cumulus clouds begin to form in the blue sky. Such clouds are due to warm, moist air, which has been drawn in from the sea and heated above the land, rising and condensing into cloud. As the heated air rises it draws cooler air in below to take its place. Such a current is called a convection current and is one of the most important features of atmospheric circulation. If the clouds accumulate or drift together, further condensation among the higher, colder droplets will make them sufficiently heavy to fall through the cloud; in doing so they grow by picking up more droplets and eventually reach the ground as rain.

Why does the air lose its warmth so steadily on ascending above the earth? The reason is simple. It is heated mainly from below. You might think, naturally enough, that the sun's direct heat should warm it, in which case the upper parts would be the hottest; but sunlight is a radiation of very short waves, which pass through the air without much effect (except that about half the total sunlight is dispersed by particles of water vapour in the high atmosphere, thus giving us our blue sky; if it were not for that, the sky would be black).

The waves of sunlight are absorbed readily by the ocean, however, which gives some of the heat back, rather slowly, to the overlying air in the form of long waves that can affect it. Over the land, solar radiation is absorbed very greedily, as you may test for yourself by touching rocks or exposed metals on a hot day; but the land cannot hold the heat as long as the sea, and radiates much of it back each evening. Thus another circulation arises, both daily and seasonal, towards the land by day and towards the sea by night, while the Continental centres have light, hot air above them in the summer, and cold, heavy air in the winter.

There is much more to it than this, of course; but we have said enough to show that the atmosphere contains regions of high pressure and others of low pressure, between which the air must flow in its ceaseless efforts to establish a balance. If the high- and low-pressure areas are near to one another, the gradient or slope of the air-flow is obviously steep, and one must expect storms; if they are far apart, then nothing worse than steady winds will happen. The whole business is complicated by the nature of the ground over which the winds flow. If it be mountainous, and they are wet sea winds, they will be forced to disgorge most of their moisture; this occurs, for instance, in the Welsh and Western Scottish mountains. The dried wind, passing on, leaves the eastern parts of our island much less affected.

For British weather experts, the most significant thing about atmospheric pressure regions is the existence of a more or less permanent low-pressure area near Iceland. Towards this depression the south-west winds that have crossed the Atlantic make their way, but never succeed in filling it up. There are also, of course, countless minor depressions, often followed by smaller or secondary depressions, wandering about in the ocean of the air; and there must, therefore, be likewise a good number of high-pressure areas connected with them.

The air tends to flow gently out of a high-pressure area (or anticyclone, as it is called), in all directions. On the other hand, it flows into a low-pressure area, usually in the form of a spiral, which in our part of the world runs anti-clockwise. If the low-pressure area is moving, you may have a cyclonic storm, with still air at the centre and violent winds surrounding it. Spirals, by the way, arise because of the earth's rotation; for a point on the Equator must move faster than one farther north, and as the air above the Equator travels north (or south) it has a greater speed than the earth beneath, and so becomes a permanent wind. That is the reason why Britain's predominant wind comes from the south-west.

All such facts as these, and many more, the weather forecaster must take into account, and to help him he uses many most ingenious instruments; but he is dealing with fine measurements, and as no instrument is perfect he is compelled to make numerous corrections to the recorded results before they can be used in his estimates.

First and foremost, he must ascertain what change, if any, there has been in the *pressure*, for that is the key to all atmospheric movements. Then he wants to know the temperature, the moisture or humidity, and the strength of the wind; whether clouds are about, and if so, are they rain clouds; and so on. We will refer to the instruments in a moment. The results, to be of more than mere local value, must be spread over a wide region. This is done by having a network of observers at fixed stations, whose information is telegraphed to a central meteorological station by means of a pre-arranged code of signals; and the central station digests and summarizes the data, then draws its conclusions from them and broadcasts the results. The British Isles are served by about forty local stations, besides others on the Continent; and in addition the forecasters receive a great deal of information from aircraft and from ships at sea. Except in time of war, a large natural region like Western Europe is regarded as one unit for weather forecasting purposes, the observations being organized by international agreement; but during war it is, of course, vital to conceal details of the local weather as much as possible, lest valuable information be given to hostile aircraft.

So much for the general system. Now as to the instruments.

The first of these is the barometer.

The principle of the barometer is to balance the weight of the air against that of a column of mercury. The mercury is contained in an inverted glass tube having the upper end closed and the lower end open; the lower end being sunk into a trough of mercury that is freely exposed to the air pressure. As the mercury does not fill the tube, any variation in pressure on the trough causes the column to rise or sink, and this movement can be measured by a scale and a small magnifying glass. The standard is taken at sea-level, when the height of the mercury is either 760 mm. (30 in.) or 1000 millibars, equal to 29·53 in.; the temperature 12° Celsius. As the earth is not a perfect sphere, its gravity pull varies from one latitude to another; the standard is taken as latitude 45°, which is that of Bordeaux and Venice. Observations made at any other temperature, height or latitude must therefore be corrected suitably, and this is provided for by tables. The standard British instrument, the Kew barometer, has a double scale reading both in inches and millibars, and a thermometer is also attached to it.

A very convenient type of barometer, mainly used by travellers and in aircraft, is the aneroid, so called because it contains no air. It is essentially a small air-tight metal box that is capable of contracting or expanding slightly in response to pressure changes. It is very sensitive at low levels, but is apt to err at high altitudes. The barograph, which is essentially an aneroid, uses a pen to trace a line on a drum of paper and so give a continuous reading, showing the variations in the pressure.

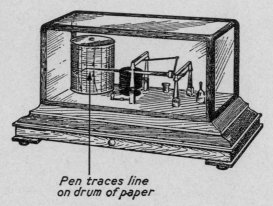

Pen traces line on drum of paper

The barograph

Temperature, of course, is measured by thermometers, which you may perhaps think too simple to need description; but, although we lack the space to describe them here, thermometers are curious things, full of traps for the unwary, and are worthy of close study. In addition to the ordinary direct reading of the upward or downward movements of a column of mercury or spirits of wine against a graduated scale, some thermometers have a small metal pin inserted in the tube, which moves up the scale until it records the maximum temperature between readings; then, when the fluid sinks, this pin is left behind. Similarly, there are thermometers which record both the maximum and minimum temperatures in a given period.

Thermometers are not very sensitive instruments, and take an appreciable time to acquire the true temperature of the air outside;

they are also liable to many errors on account of radiation both from without inwards and from the glass outwards. As far as possible, the meteorologist's instruments are protected from the sun and wind, by being enclosed in louvred boxes four feet above the ground. When, as is usually the case, ground observations are also needed, a thermometer is supported on the ground, with its bulb just touching the blades of grass.

We have seen that humidity is a factor which the forecaster must take note of. He does this by means of a hygrometer, which comprises two thermometers side by side. One is an ordinary dry-bulb

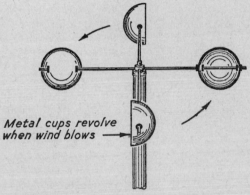

Metal cups revolve when wind blows ——

Cup anemometer

thermometer. The other has a single layer of muslin over its bulb, which is kept moist by a wick made of cotton strands, the end of the wick lying in a container of water. Now when the air can hold no more moisture it is said to be saturated and both instruments will read alike; but when the air is drying the moisture in the muslin evaporates and this causes it to chill the bulb, so that the reading of the wet-bulb instrument falls. By means of tables this difference registers the relative humidity of the atmosphere.

To measure the force of the wind, always a needful item, a cup anemometer is used. This is quite simple, comprising merely three or four metal cups on horizontal arms, which are attached to a vertical at a fixed height above the ground, just like a weather vane; as they revolve, a revolution counter keeps a record of the movements, which can then be translated into miles per hour. This, however, is only the mean force of the wind and does not show sudden gusts or lulls, unless the former are extremely violent.

By tradition, and for good practical reasons, seamen and airmen are trained to measure wind force by the Beaufort scale, a rough-and-ready means of measuring wind speeds, but very sound when used by a trained observer. The Beaufort scale ranges from o to 12, o being a dead calm and " 12 on the Beaufort scale " a hurricane of anything over 75 miles per hour. A full gale, such as will send the tiles hurtling down from roofs into the street, is about Scale 9, a gentle breeze Scale 2.

The forecaster also has to watch the clouds. He soon learns to estimate how much of the sky is cloud-covered, and by means of a simple measuring-rod with a horizontal arm, called a nephoscope, he can guess at the approximate speed of a cloud. To ascertain its height (or rather, the height of its base, for the thickness of the cloud can only be measured by passing through it), several methods are used. An aircraft may go up, or a pilot balloon; or it may be measured simultaneously by two observers a known distance apart and its height fixed by trigonometry; or (and this is one of the easiest methods) two searchlights may be focused on it and the angle ascertained. The clouds themselves are classified into a whole series of types, according to their shape, height, and general appearance; and they form a useful adjunct to a forecast, and in some cases a sound pointer to rain or fine weather, but they must be considered in conjunction with the pressure variations, if any, and other instrumental facts.

Another thing to be noted by all observers is the visibility. This is usually done by reference to some standard object under various conditions, which, of course, gives a scale with which subsequent observations may be compared.

For observations of the upper air, reliance is placed mainly upon aircraft, which fly as a routine duty daily from Mildenhall, for instance, carrying instruments on the struts and levelling out at various fixed altitudes. Pilot balloons and radio beams are also employed on the same service.

Having assembled all his data, the observer must transmit them as rapidly as possible, in the agreed international code, to his central station. There others are waiting to record the data on a chart as they come in; and with great speed a map is made which shows the high-pressure and low-pressure areas, the distance between them, and all the other essential facts. Comparison with the last chart shows certain changes, such as the advance of a low-pressure area, or its filling up and disappearance; and on these facts the tendency for the next twenty-four hours is deduced.

If the gradient between high- and low-pressure areas is steepening rapidly, and the low-pressure " front " is approaching our country, that is a sign of deteriorating weather. If wide areas have even air pressure, and the low-pressure regions are insignificant or distant, that is a sign of stability and fine conditions. Of course, the temperature changes during the period must be considered, and the likelihood or otherwise of their continuance must be guessed at. Clear weather or fog, rain or thunder, hail-storms or snow, may likewise be deduced from the existing conditions coupled with what has recently gone before.

All this is done by the weather forecasters as a matter of routine and in the space of a few hours. Their report then goes out and they prepare for the next one. And if, as frequently happens in Britain, the forecast is wrong, do not attribute it to the meteorologist's lack of skill, but rather to his bad luck; for being on the edge of a continent and in a comparatively northern latitude, our island is peculiarly subject to rapid, unexpected changes; and no forecaster can take account of all these, unless he is provided with constant new facts from a multitude of local stations—which, of course, would be too costly a business altogether.

LIFE ON OTHER WORLDS: SPACE TRAVEL

LIFE ON OTHER WORLDS

For centuries the question of life on other worlds has occupied the mind of man. Now it does so more than ever; for he has, with the aid of telescopes, much more knowledge than the observer in the past. If we look up at the sky on a clear frosty night in winter, we see thousands of stars, which we know to be suns, possibly in some cases attended by planets. With the telescope, millions more can be seen. As we watch this magnificent sight, we are filled with awe, and feel that we are in the presence of a majestic design, serving some mysterious purpose. Surely, this vast multitude of worlds contains somewhere some specimens of life, and even of intelligent life? Let us see what evidence there is for this, and whether we can find any traces of life, past or present, in those portions of the universe nearest to us.

The first place in which we should look for signs of life is naturally our nearest neighbour the Moon, which is only a quarter of a million miles off. But here there is no air, and no water; and therefore no seas, no rivers, and no clouds. No sign whatever of anything which suggests life can be seen even with the most powerful telescope, which brings the Moon to within a distance of forty miles. It is true that some astronomers claim to have seen light green patches appearing on certain parts of the Moon, indicating perhaps a low form of growth such as lichens or mosses growing on bare rock. But these observations have not been supported by other observers. Even if they had, there is the difficulty of any life surviving either the scorching day a fortnight long, with the temperature in some places rising above 200 degrees F.; or the still more deadly cold of the equally long night. Mr. H. G. Wells, in his clever romance *The First Men in the Moon*, portrayed a world in which a thin atmosphere remained on the surface, most of the air and water having sunk into the hollow interior of the Moon. Here lived a community of beings more intelligent than those on Earth; they had renounced war, and lived in peace. But even this rarefied atmosphere cannot be admitted, for it is quite certain that the Moon is completely without air or water.

We next come to the planet Mars. Here the quest is more hopeful, for not only are the conditions on Mars more like those on the Earth than is the case with any other planet, but it occasionally comes nearer to us than any other heavenly body except Venus and the Moon. In July and August, 1939, we had an excellent opportunity of observing Mars, for it was then at its closest approach to the Earth, being only 35 million miles off, with its day surface opposite our night surface, so that our astronomers could easily examine the planet's markings. The skies were clear. Night after night the planet rose with undimmed splendour, outshining all other stars except the planet Venus. Many large telescopes were directed to it. Dr. Slipher, director of the observatory at Flagstaff, Arizona, U.S.A., went to Bloemfontein in South Africa, and there took 7000 photographs of the planet.

The question of life, even of intelligent life, on Mars centres round certain markings on its surface which are called " canals ". And here it will be necessary to give a detailed account of the observations which have been made so far. Early in the eighteenth century two white patches were noticed at the poles of Mars. These were seen to increase or melt with the seasons. They are, in fact, polar snow-caps. In 1877, and again in 1879, the Italian astronomer Schiaparelli reported the discovery of a great number of fine lines or " canals " crossing the planet in all directions; and, in 1881, he announced that some of these canals became double. These discoveries were later confirmed by Flammarion and other astronomers; and by the twentieth century more than five hundred canals had been observed, joining small dark areas called " oases ". It is to be noticed that both canals and oases grow larger or smaller according to the season of the year.

In 1894, Professor Lowell founded the observatory at Flagstaff, Arizona, U.S.A., in clear steady air at an altitude of 7250 feet above sea-level for the special purpose of observing the surface of Mars. He found that the canals really existed, and that they doubled from time to time. The canals were thousands of miles in length, and passed along the shortest course between one " oasis " and another. This indicated that they might have been constructed by some intelligent agency. Lowell concluded that the planet was covered by a system of waterways conveying water from the melting polar snows to the drier parts of the planet. In summer the polar snows partially melt, and water flows along the canals. Vegetation appears and the canals and oases become darker. The dark lines we see are broad strips of vegetation on both sides of the waterways; the canals themselves are too narrow to be seen.

Part of the planet is covered with grey or greenish patches, which were at first supposed to be seas and were so called. But the change of colour of these patches to a brown hue at regular seasons suggests that we see here the growth and decay of some kind of vegetation. The rest of the planet (except the snow-caps) is orange in colour. It probably consists of extensive deserts of red sand, swept by frequent sand-storms.

It should be remembered that Mars is a smaller planet than the Earth, and therefore must have cooled sooner. Life would have started there earlier than here, and presumably have reached a higher stage of progress, resulting perhaps in a more intelligent organization of the natural resources of the planet. As time passed, the planet would get drier; water would become extremely scarce and would have to be fetched through some distance from the polar snows. We are already doing something like this on Earth, where water is obtained for our larger cities from a distant water supply. Thus Manchester is supplied from Thirlmere and Haweswater in the Lake District; Liverpool from Lake Vyrnwy in Wales, and so on. A single design for the water supply of the planet suggests a world-wide community peacefully co-operating under one rule. A common enemy, the fear of thirst, has caused the inhabitants of Mars to combine.

Such were Lowell's arguments. Later investigations show that some of his conclusions were correct, but not all. It is now generally agreed, partly as the result of Dr. Slipher's 7000 photographs, that the canals actually exist, and that the dark lines do really represent vegetation in its various stages of growth and decay. There is not sufficient evidence to show that intelligent life or even animal life is present on Mars; but it may very well have existed in the past. Mars is a dying world. It has lost most of its atmosphere and of its moisture. The air being thin, radiation takes place rapidly. The temperature is highest at noon; at sunset it falls rapidly, and in the middle of the night it is more than a hundred degrees below zero Fahrenheit. The climate of Mars is like that on the top of a very high mountain on a clear day. Such vegetation as does exist on Mars will find life more and more difficult as the planet loses more of its atmosphere and moisture, and gets colder; this vegetable life is doomed to extinction after some millions of years, when the planet has finally lost its heat.

The next planet on which we might expect to find signs of life is Venus. It is very like the Earth in size, in mass and in its density. So here we might reasonably hope to find conditions somewhat like those on the Earth. The path of Venus round the Sun lies inside the path of the Earth. It comes nearer to us than any other planet, and is sometimes only 26 million miles off. Being so near the Sun, it can only be seen near sunrise or sunset; in the former case it was known to the ancients as the " Morning Star " or " Phosphorus "; in the latter case as the " Evening Star " or " Hesperus ". It has a dense atmosphere, rich in carbon dioxide, but with very little or no oxygen; and it must be extremely hot. It is, in fact, very much like the Earth in the earlier stages of its existence. In the remote past, the Earth was much hotter than now, and its atmosphere had an abundance of carbon dioxide. As the Earth cooled and vegetable life appeared, the green plants absorbed carbon dioxide from the air, retained the carbon for their growth and returned the oxygen to the atmosphere. We may, therefore, expect the same process in Venus. As it cools, conditions will become more and more suitable for life; vegetation may appear and may possibly develop into higher forms of life, and even into intelligent life. Of the three planets we have discussed, Venus is in its infancy, the Earth in maturity, and Mars is in its old age with life almost spent.

The other planets can be briefly considered. Mercury is far too hot over most of its surface, and contains no oxygen or water-vapour. The asteroids are too small to have retained any atmosphere. The larger planets are far too cold, and for the most part their atmospheres contain poisonous gases. Life, therefore, as we know it is impossible on these.

May there not be life outside the Solar System? There are vast numbers of stars in the universe, each of which is a sun in itself. May not some of these suns be surrounded by planets, some of which are the abode of life? These are questions which are often and naturally asked. They cannot be answered by direct observation, for the fixed stars are too far off; but the possibility or even probability of life in these distant regions can be estimated. We have seen that our Milky Way, which contains the Solar System, and very many of the stars we see, is an " island universe " in itself. And we know that when we go far beyond the Milky Way, we come to other " island universes " similar to our own and containing hosts of stars. These from their cloudy appearance we call " nebulæ ". It is calculated that there are about 100 million such universes. In each universe are many millions of stars, i.e. suns. Even if the chance is a million to one against any particular star being surrounded by planets, this would still give us many millions of planetary systems. And the probability is that among those millions of planets we should find some which are sufficiently like our Earth to be the homes of life; some in the past, some in the present, some in the future.

TRAVELLING THROUGH SPACE

The idea that human beings might be shot off the Earth in some kind of container so far that they could travel through space has long been a favourite among fiction writers. It is fiction still, but the great improvement in giant rockets since the last World War has brought it very much nearer.

In order to escape from the Earth, or even to get into the highest part of the atmosphere several hundred miles up, a projectile must have a very great speed; but as the friction of the dense air near the surface would rapidly heat up the projectile until it was white-hot, the speed must be built up gradually. The Russian Sputniks and the American Explorers, Vanguards and Pioneers have all been constructed accordingly; that is to say, they are multiple-stage rockets like giant pencils fifty feet or more in height, which are discharged vertically from a special platform; in the nose of the pencil is the comparatively small projectile proper, the satellite. We have all seen pictures of the launching of such a rocket and have heard the hiss and terrifying roar as it hurtled up straight into the sky, perhaps to pass through the clouds and be lost from view for good, except to the radio telescopes which are picking up its course, or perhaps to explode prematurely a moment later. At a predetermined height of anything from 40 to 80 miles or so, where the air is comparatively rare, the second stage is fired, the tail falls off, and the front part continues to ascend with all the acceleration given to it by the explosion; meanwhile It has begun to turn in a curve in response to an automatic control. When it is perhaps 150 miles up the third stage is fired and again the tail falls off. Continuing to curve, the rocket is almost in orbit round the Earth when the small head is released and speeds on round and round the globe, at anything up to 17,000 or 18,000 miles per hour. Rare though the air is up there, it is still sufficient to slow down the satellite steadily, until at last, after weeks or months it descends again and either breaks up or falls back to the ground.

Before looking at the possibilities of space travel more closely, let us consider what has actually happened to some of the numerous satellites which have been launched so far.

The famous Sputnik I was launched by the Russians on 4th October, 1957. (" Sputnik ", by the way, means literally " fellow traveller ", which is a reasonable equivalent of " satellite "!) It was a three-stage rocket, weighing somewhere about 100 tons, in the head of which was the satellite, an aluminium sphere 23 inches in diameter. The sphere contained two radio transmitters, aerials, and self-recording instruments so designed that the changes in them could be transmitted by impulses to the ground: altogether the Sputnik weighed 184 lb. at ground level. When at a height of between 100 and 400 miles, Sputnik I was set free; travelling at a rate of about 5 miles per second, it encircled the Earth some hundreds of times. The batteries failed, and the instruments ceased to transmit, after a fortnight; but the satellite continued round and round the globe for 92 days, gradually slowing down and falling, until at last it fell rapidly and disintegrated. This first attempt at high-altitude navigation was followed almost continuously by the great modern radio telescope at Jodrell Bank in Cheshire.

In the meantime Sputnik II had been launched. It comprised two spheres joined together like a dumb-bell, and in one sphere was a Samoyede dog, much to the indignation of many people. Sputnik II had an erratic orbit, reaching 900 miles above the Earth and travelling at the immense speed of 18,000 miles per hour. It lasted for more than 5 months before falling; but the batteries failed after only a week, the instruments ceased, and the dog apparently lived for only 8 days. Sputnik III, launched in May, 1958, was a great technical triumph, for it got into outer space although the satellite proper weighed almost a ton; it was expected to stay up there for about a year. The Russians scored a great success with their lunar missiles or Luniks. Lunik I went right past the Moon into space. Lunik II was reported to have struck the Moon about 34 hours after launching. Lunik III is making regular journeys in a great ellipse from some 30,000 miles from the Earth to the Moon and back, its instruments sending down valuable information to the Earth.

The American satellites have had a more chequered history, but most of them have been intended to reach great heights and some to encircle the moon. The Americans also sent a couple of small monkeys up about 70 miles in a single-stage rocket; this fell nearly where it was intended and the animals were recovered alive and apparently unharmed by their terrifying experience.

With all these events in mind, let us now return to our would-be traveller into space and try to guess what would really happen to him. That he could be taken up there is obvious; but the cost in money and labour would be gigantic. It would involve many millions of pounds and endless ingenuity and prior experiments. There is a shell of very rare air between 100 and 400 miles above the Earth, which requires much more examination than it has been found possible to give as yet; for in this shell there are zones (or so-called "layers"), which reflect radio waves. There is also what we may call the impact zone between the cosmic particles and the Earth's denser atmosphere, and this too requires investigation. A man or men encircling the Earth at such a height, in a closed chamber, would be able to exercise a much closer control of the self-recording instruments beside him, than people far below on the surface can do from the wirelessed records which these instruments have sent out hitherto. On the other hand, many claims in respect to the value of other work aloft have been grossly exaggerated. For instance, you may read that this uppermost air shell affects our weather; this, I believe, is a complete mistake, for all the Earth's wind circulation, the high and low pressure regions, the fronts and depressions of which we hear nightly on the TV, arise from the lower parts of the atmosphere.

However, if we neglect all these reasons for and against space travel, and imagine that a satellite will actually be set in orbit somewhere between 150 and 400 miles up, and that it will contain human beings, what is this satellite to be like? Whatever the outer shape, whether it be a shuttle, a ball, or a giant dart, it must contain a regular interior chamber with adequate space for the occupants to move around in; and this would of course contain all the instruments and a radio transmitter, besides chemicals to keep the air pure. As the satellite would ascend vertically and would then curve over, and might twist spirally or perform all sorts of unexpected evolutions, the chamber inside would probably have to be set in gimbals and gyroscopically balanced; otherwise the occupants would be violently ill even if not rendered senseless. As the observer would need to look around him and at the Earth far below, some sort of window would be necessary; and this, simple though it seems, is a great practical difficulty, because it is almost impossible to keep the window opening completely air-tight. The naturalist Beebe found this out when making his famous descent of half a mile into the ocean, in the first Bathysphere; for despite all precautions the window leaked.

Another danger up aloft is the uncertainty of how far the minute particles which permeate the so-called " empty space " might penetrate even a dense alloy or other material. A third danger is the heating-up of the interior through radiation from the heat collected by the satellite when it was exposed to the full glare of the sun; and conversely of course, the intense cold which would ensue immediately the sun withdrew. These contractions and expansions would also make it difficult to keep the windows airtight.

The Russians and Americans have proved that there is no insuperable difficulty about setting such a satellite in orbit round the Earth; but how to get it back again at a given spot is as yet unsolved. The path of a simple high-altitude rocket can be predicted with reasonable accuracy, even though the course must be affected by unknown factors such as minute differences in the power of the explosive charge, the effect of winds, and other forces which affect all missiles; but to plan the path of a manned satellite is a different matter. In order to avoid overheating by the friction of the air, the satellite must be brought back within the atmosphere gradually, and the latest suggestion as to how this can best be done is by giving the satellite an external shape rather like a giant paper dart. It is hoped by this means and the aid of counter-rocket charges which would diminish the speed of descent, to land the satellite on Earth again undamaged; but how far the point of landing can be controlled, either from the satellite itself or by radio from the ground, remains uncertain. One thing is obvious, however; no man should be subjected to such hazards until unmanned satellites have made many similar journeys.

A far more difficult proposal is the sending of human beings to the Moon; this has been much discussed since the Russian rocket, Lunik II, hit the orb in September, 1959. To begin with, the route is not a straight line, but a curve the course of which can only be determined after much calculation. Moreover, this curve only leads to the Moon as an object out in space; but we must remember that the visible area of the full Moon is really very large. It is the size of all North America and has upon it high mountain chains, individual peaks large and small, deep craters by the hundred, and cracks and clefts of all sizes. The occupants of the space-ship, therefore, must be able to guide themselves to a safe landing place, i.e. they must see the Moon ahead all the way down. This involves (a) a window in the nose of the space-ship; and (b) some navigational device

Ordinarily, navigators depend upon pressure for their results—wind in a ship's sails, water against the rudder, air against the aircraft's fins, etc.; but out in space there is nothing upon which such pressure can be exerted. Rockets can be made to change course by exploding minor charges from within them; but how far this could be controlled so as to permit of a safe landing on the Moon is a pretty problem.

Assuming, however, that the lucky explorers did make such a landing, how could they possibly take off again? Their space-ship must be turned round and so fixed that it would stand vertical, without the aid of all the supporting frame which was essential to their correct discharge from the Earth on the outward journey; and in addition, they would have to be shot up at a high speed from the explosion of more charges from within, and then boosted by further charges so as to carry them out of the Moon's influence— even though the force of gravity there is only one-sixth of that exerted by the Earth. Once back in the Earth's outer atmosphere, the whole business of finding and maintaining their position would have to be gone through again; with, in addition, the serious risk of overheating through striking unexpectedly a layer of denser gas such as was actually encountered by one of the recent satellites. These and many other considerations make it highly problematical when, if ever, a safe journey to the Moon and back, which would include a landing, can be undertaken.

As to journeys to Mars, such projects will not stand the slightest detailed examination. To take one aspect alone, we are told that at its nearest, Mars is " only " 35 millions of miles from the Earth. At the highest speed of which we can think at present as practicable, say 25,000 miles per hour, it would take at least two months to cover that distance, and if the true route is as involved as those of the Luniks to the Moon it would require 5 months for the Martian journey, plus another 5 months coming back. The state of mind of one or two men, shut up in a tiny chamber for all that time, living on canned food, breathing chemically treated air, and rushing through empty space, can better be imagined than described!

CATCHING WILD ANIMALS ALIVE

Most people when visiting zoos probably wonder how all the strange animals and birds to be seen in these fascinating places were brought there alive. As will be easily grasped by one and all, the stocking and restocking of big zoos is certainly no easy matter. Once a zoo is well stocked, however, many baby animals will be born there year by year; and these usually charming little creatures not only add to the size and value of the various collections, but bring much additional pleasure and knowledge to visitors and students alike.

What a joy it is to watch young lion, tiger, and leopard cubs. Most zoo visitors take the greatest delight in watching these big wild kittens tumbling over one another and playing with their long-suffering parents' fine tails and furry ears. Indeed, baby creatures of all kinds are usually the most popular exhibits in any zoo.

They are popular also with the authorities in charge; but these yearly births are seldom sufficient to keep any good zoo well stocked. Many wild animals never breed at all in captivity; and when such creatures eventually die of old age, or from other causes, they have to be replaced either by newly captured animals, by exchanges with other zoos, and by occasional welcome gifts.

It sometimes happens that valuable wild animals are sent as gifts from the rulers of distant countries to the Sovereign or to other members of the Royal Family, who in their turn present them to the zoo, where they can be properly cared for by scientists; and usually these are particularly fine examples of their kind and greatly appreciated.

Also, gifts of animals and birds are received from British and other officials in far-off lands, or from casual visitors to and from such places; and strange animal mascots belonging to the various Services are occasionally deposited in zoos for months, or even years, at a time. Very often, too, exchanges of animals take place between various zoos at home and abroad, and, in this way, many new varieties are secured.

All this is very helpful; but it is not, of course, entirely sufficient in itself for restocking purposes. It is also necessary to receive occasional consignments of newly captured wild animals and birds from their actual native haunts, not only to add to the exhibits, but also to improve the old stock. For this reason, directors of the more important zoos instruct well-known big-game hunters and wild-animal collectors to hunt and bring back alive for them certain creatures they are anxious to possess. Many zoos send out special hunters and collectors of their own to collect for them alone.

These wild animal collectors, in their turn, themselves employ native assistants in the various countries they visit—mostly in tropical parts of the world, or amongst mighty mountain ranges, and also in the Arctic and Antarctic regions. Most of the native assistants are likewise experienced animal hunters, or, at least, know the haunts of the various creatures required. Others are accustomed to dealing with different kinds of captured animals.

An expedition of this kind may consist of a large number of native assistants, from twenty to forty, or even up to several hundreds; others may consist only of a few picked individuals. Everything depends, of course, on the animals to be caught and on the kind of country through which the journey is to be made. Some hunter-collectors are occasionally invited to take part in hunting parties, which may be accompanied by many native soldiers and a great number of trained State elephants. Though, in the latter case, the main object is a pleasure hunt, the zoo collector himself may thus have an excellent opportunity of securing some living specimens, or at least, of learning of their whereabouts for a private expedition of his own later on.

Sometimes it may take many months, or even a year or two, to find out ways and means of securing the specimens he is seeking for the various zoos he supplies, and it is always to his great advantage to make important friends wherever he goes.

Big-game hunting is always a perilous occupation, and when the animal collector is out to secure living specimens to bring back to his own home country, it is more perilous still. These bold hunters who go out into the wildest parts of the world to collect and bring back alive all kinds of strange and dangerous creatures need to be men of the greatest courage and utmost resourcefulness. It is one thing to sit comfortably on a State elephant in India, to ride accompanied by many attendants and soldiers, into the jungle, and to shoot dead a charging rhinoceros or a savage tiger as it springs, but it is quite another thing to capture these same snarling or rampageous maddened beasts and bring them back alive from their natural haunts, where poisonous snakes and other dangerous creatures likewise abound. But it is a life of thrilling adventure, and most wild animal collectors and hunters would not willingly exchange it for any other occupation.

In the earlier days of zoos, it is probable that a good deal of cruelty was used by natives in the capture of living wild animals, and many splendid beasts were wantonly destroyed in the process of securing a few specimens only; but present-day collectors are much better equipped with scientific means and methods, and they will not permit their native assistants to use the old bad methods while in their service. Most famous collectors have only one desire regarding the creatures they have to do with—that they shall have been captured by the most humane means possible and that they shall be undamaged perfect specimens in healthy condition and with their tempers as little impaired as can reasonably be expected. Naturally, human safety in this perilous occupation comes first, but needless cruelty is always sternly forbidden. Most successful collectors know much about wild-animal life (many of them are eminent zoologists, scientific as well as practical) in addition to having a good working knowledge of animal psychology, and they choose their assistants with the utmost care.

And now, let us consider some of the means employed for the actual capture alive of certain well-known wild animals. We begin with the biggest, elephants.

There are several ways of catching wild elephants. The most successful and the safest is by means of the keddah—also known as the corral, or the stockade enclosure. This method is the most popular one used in the forest wilds of India and Burma. The first thing the animal collector does is to visit the various native villages in and round about the vast forests where wild elephants are known to abound; here he arranges with the headmen, or chiefs, for young native hunters—often several hundreds, but sometimes considerably fewer—to take part in a grand "round-up". Having done this, he gets the more skilled workers to build a large keddah as near as possible to a spot which he has learned a good herd is known to be using as a feeding-ground, taking care, however, that it shall be at a sufficient distance to prevent the elephants from hearing, seeing, or scenting what is going on.

The keddah builders, therefore, work as quietly as possible; and they do their job thoroughly, driving huge tree-trunks and strong stakes into the ground all around a large enclosure, and binding them together securely, but leaving a wide opening at one side with a strong gate that can be held up until all the captives are safely inside, and then dropped suddenly and fastened firmly to prevent escapes. A smaller keddah is also built alongside with an opening leading to the large one, so that captives can be driven into this

Elephants being driven into the keddah

smaller compartment, one at a time, to receive their first preliminary training separately.

When the keddah is ready, a group of several hundred natives rush out at great speed and try to surround the elephant herd before it has time to scent them and get away, and these beaters, or drivers, carry with them any old kettles or pans they can lay hands on, which they beat like drums to make a tremendous noise, at the same time shouting and screaming for all they are worth. This din scares the elephants, so that they dash hither and thither, and by degrees they are driven by the yelling natives nearer and nearer to the keddah, the opening of which is kept clear, with the strong gate held up by other workers ready to be dropped into place as soon as all the " catch " has been rounded up and driven inside.

10*

When the wild elephants have been safely driven into the enclosure, they are carefully inspected from a position of vantage by the collector, who selects the particular beasts he considers best for his purpose. Those chosen are then driven, one by one, into the smaller keddah and roped securely to the walls, in readiness for their training. The remainder of the elephants rounded up but not required are released and allowed to return to their forest haunts.

The selected animals are well fed, watered, and cared for, and once they have got used to the human beings around them they usually soon become more tractable and their preliminary training can proceed. The training is sometimes done by roping and hobbling the animals to tame elephants, from whom they quickly learn to obey the orders of the mahout, or driver, riding on the tame beast's neck. After this, an experienced mahout can usually finish the newcomer's training by himself, since elephants—more particularly the Indian variety—are very intelligent and teachable creatures.

When only one wild elephant is required, this is sometimes caught by means of a pitfall, a huge deep hole being dug at a spot likely to be passed by a wanderer from the herd, and covered over with branches and leaves. But this method is not often permitted by a good collector, as the elephant may crash too heavily and damage itself severely. A most exciting method of capturing elephants separately is for the hunter to chase his would-be " catch " on the back of a trained elephant, and, when within a likely range, to lasso it with a strong rope; then, with the aid of the tame beast and numerous assistants, he drags it into a small keddah. Yet another method is to send out several tame female elephants as decoys who, with mahouts on their necks, surround a fine-looking young male and, making friends with him, gradually entice him to follow them many miles until he is tired out—when the native hunters are able to capture him the more readily.

The keddah system is usually regarded as being the most popular and the safest way of catching wild elephants in India, and, when properly carried out in as humane a manner as possible, is probably the least harmful to man and beast alike.

A method of capturing African elephants—seldom so tractable as the Indian variety—now used in the Belgian Congo is for the hunters (mostly experienced mahouts) to set forth, accompanied by others on horseback armed with rifles and ropes, chains and shackles. Having discovered a herd, the mounted hunters and rope-carriers come up to within ten yards or so of it, when the rifles are fired into the air. The noise of the firing startles and stampedes the elephants; and in the confusion which follows, many young ones become separated from their mothers, and several half-grown specimens are also unable to get away with the main herd, so that most of these are captured by lassos and their limbs roped. The larger captives are fastened securely to strong trees, until a couple of training elephants, known as monitors, are brought up from a nearby camp. Each young elephant is secured firmly to a monitor on either side of it and is marched to the camp, where the young captive usually soon becomes docile and obeys the bidding of these stern teachers, who will stand no nonsense and use their trunks very effectively for chastising as well as teaching purposes. The baby elephants left behind by the stampeding herd are easily caught by hand, roped, and led to the training camp without much trouble.

To continue with large and tall beasts, giraffes are usually caught when quite young, as adult members of a herd can more easily get away from their would-be captors because of their great speed in running. The young ones, however, when a hunt is on, are not able to keep up with the wildly galloping herd, and, tiring more quickly, they can usually be caught readily by means of a lasso wielded by hunters on horseback. Because of its slender legs and extremely long stiff neck, great care has to be taken not to scare a young animal into a wild stampede lest it should fall and break its delicate bones. Once secured, however, a young giraffe, being a gentle and docile creature, is no further trouble to its captors— except in the matter of transport. Enormous crates are required for " boxing " even a half-grown giraffe.

Sometimes full-grown giraffes are lassoed, but these much taller captive animals can usually be disposed of only to zoos in their native land or in countries adjoining, where they do not need to be passed under railway bridges or to cross an ocean, and where they can be transported by motor lorries. Giraffes intended for European zoos, therefore, are generally quite young ones only.

Adult rhinoceroses are almost impossible to capture alive. A rhinoceros hunt is an even more dangerous business than a tiger shoot, for a charging adult rhino is one of the most savage creatures in the world to tackle. Even when a rhino has been surrounded by hunting elephants ridden by experienced mahouts, there is little hope of lassoing it alive, and if caught in a pit-trap, the ferocious creature is almost impossible to keep in captivity afterwards, since it usually retains an ever-increasing hatred for its human captors or attendants.

The animal collector, therefore, puts all his energies into the capture of young rhinos, from babies to half-grown calves, for these, though always capricious in temper, gradually become accustomed to their native caretakers, so that by the time they approach the adult stage, they are thoroughly used to human beings and to a quiet safe life in captivity, having forgotten the thrills and dangers of their early jungle lives.

Frank Buck, the famous American collector, in his book *Bring 'em Back Alive*, describes how a young rhinoceros was captured for him in the State of Nepal—almost the last place where the nearly extinct one-horned Indian rhino is now to be met with. When the several hundreds of hunters engaged in this enterprise had managed to surround a cow rhino with a calf running at her side, they first of all, unfortunately, found it necessary to shoot the mother beast, just as she was about to charge them in her mad fury at being cornered. Then they quickly made a circle around the scared calf, holding up a strong sort of rope fencing to make a temporary enclosure, the latter measuring nearly an acre in extent, and to serve as a netted mobile wall which could be held taut every time the hefty infant—which already had a surprising strength and was afterwards found to weigh quite a ton—plunged and charged frantically into it, thus preventing the captive from damaging itself as it tried vainly to escape.

Meanwhile, a much stronger, small keddah enclosure of logs and tree-trunks was quickly being built on the outside of the temporary rope fencing, with a high bank of stones and earth piled up behind it, and when it was ready, the rope fencing was removed, and the captive remained in this strong pen for several weeks. Here it was left to calm down. It was well fed daily on a mixture of fresh goat's milk, sugar, and boiled rice, and fresh leaves were put down for it every day. It soon settled down to its new life and became quiet and tractable with its human attendants, and even indulged in playful romps in its keddah enclosure. As soon as it was considered sufficiently quiet, it was put into a strong wooden box or crate and thus began its travels.

Sometimes, during a rhinoceros hunt, a baby rhino may be abandoned by its mother, who may become so scared by the noise and presence of human beings that she loses control and thinks only of her own safety. Occasionally, when the hunt is over, the cow may return to the same spot to seek for her abandoned infant, in which case she is usually allowed to take it away; but if she does not return, the latter is then easily secured by the still watching hunters. Young rhinos, too, are sometimes caught by means of a pitfall.

A full-grown hippopotamus, though not normally a savage creature when left to its own devices, is extremely difficult to capture alive, and, even when caught, will probably not live long on reaching its destination, being usually already too old satisfactorily to change its ways. A baby hippo, however, is gentle and tractable from the first, and, if transported early in its life, will live happily and contentedly in its new home for many years after reaching the adult stage. What is more, hippos, caught young, will mate in captivity; and many of these roly-poly babies have been born in zoos in Europe and America.

So the animal collector usually turns his attention solely to securing baby, or very young, specimens, when commissioned to bring back alive a hippo to a zoo. But, despite the natural gentleness and helplessness of these baby animals, they are not always easy to secure. To begin with, in the warm African rivers where these creatures abound, a baby hippo always travels about on its mother's neck; and adult hippos, on catching the scent of an approaching human being—and their sense of smell is very acute—immediately sink below the water to elude their only too likely enemy by walking away from him at quite a brisk pace along the bottom of the river, where they can remain for some considerable time before coming up again to take in a fresh supply of air, because of the flap of skin inside their nostrils, which they can close at will. Also, if the hunters are in a native boat, the great lumbering creatures think nothing of coming beneath it and rising up suddenly, upsetting it and tossing out the occupants, who may quite possibly then fall victims to lurking crocodiles. So powerful are the enormous jaws of an adult hippo that they can bite through a canoe with the utmost ease. So, although it is a vegetarian and perfectly harmless when left alone, it can be a very dangerous creature when angered.

Sometimes native hunters will boldly enter a river—at a point where no crocodiles are visible—and succeed in seizing a young half-grown hippo. Binding it with ropes, they drag it to the bank, where it can be bound more securely and transported to some collector's temporary quarters. Also, a baby hippo, as it rests or sleeps on its mother's neck, is sometimes lassoed from the bank, or even snatched away from beside its parent while the latter is indulging in a nap on the river's muddy edge. There is no frantic charging by the whole hippo herd, as in the case of a group of rhinos, and a captive baby hippo soon becomes the pet of its captor, who will patiently feed it with milk from a bottle until it is able to feed itself from the various kinds of rice and corn porridge provided for it later on. It soon takes readily to sugar-canes and bamboos. A baby hippo, too, is easily boxed for transport, but a half-grown specimen gives considerably more trouble because of its more powerful jaws, which break up anything that looks like a crate.

Full-grown apes—gorillas, orangs, chimpanzees—and the larger monkeys, are seldom caught alive, and they are certainly the most difficult of all animals to capture, owing to their greater intelligence. It is not easy to outwit an ape or a monkey, though it has been done successfully many times. The fine group of Abyssinian sacred baboons, which have been a popular feature on Monkey Hill at the London Zoo for many years, were captured alive by means of a clever trick. The collector boldly set up a hut in the midst of their rocky home in the heart of Abyssinia, and to this he attached an open sliding door, which could be closed instantly by means of a long string. Having strewn a trail of maize—a dainty he knew these apes to be fond of—from the forest to the inside of the hut, he took up the string attached to the door of the hut and hid himself nearby. After waiting patiently, he saw the baboons come crowding up, led by the biggest male of all. Having strolled up and devoured most of the long trail of bait, and seeing still more of the delicious food inside the hut, the leader, driving back his followers, very gingerly entered the trap—and down fell the sliding door! A travelling box, well strewn with more maize, was next brought up with its own sliding door lifted, and placed against the hut door, which was again drawn up, and, after another long wait, the watcher outside was rewarded by his captive making a sudden dash into the box to feast once more upon the titbits within. The door was dropped and the box, after being securely fastened, was ready for transport. After this, the well-pleased hunter found it a simple matter to catch and box up in the same way over one hundred of these often very savage creatures, many of them full-grown males, and also mothers with babies. The baboons were rather snappy and rampageous on their way to this country, but once they were let loose on Monkey Hill at the Regent's Park Gardens, they soon settled down contentedly. Other young apes and various kinds of monkeys are usually captured in very much the same way, few of them being able to resist some titbit they happen to be particularly fond of.

Most people think that a full-grown tiger must be, perhaps, the most thrilling of all creatures to catch alive. But, though an awe-inspiring incident could—and does, on occasion—actually take place, it is a very rare occurrence. Quite apart from the difficulty and danger involved, full-grown tigers are seldom sought by the animal collector for zoos, because, at that age, they are not likely ever to become sufficiently tame to be dealt with as public exhibits. It is much more satisfactory to secure very young, or half-grown specimens, and baby tigers, for many months after birth, can readily be handled by their keepers, and are often almost as docile and quite as playful as domestic kittens.

When, however, an adult live tiger is required by a collector, it is usually secured by means of a pitfall. It is, however, by no means easy to get the great beast out of the pit undamaged and without harm to the hunters, who must exercise extreme caution or they may be badly mauled during the process. Usually, a strong box-cage, with a sliding door fixed at one side and containing a recently killed small animal or jungle fowl, is lowered by ropes or chains into the pit and left there until the captive, attracted by the bait, slinks inside to devour it. Instantly the sliding door is dropped, and the cage is hauled up to the surface.

Another way is to raise the furious beast to the top of the pit by means of a number of ropes cleverly dropped over head and limbs, and to hold it there until the box-cage—with the sliding door open and uppermost—has been lowered to the bottom of the pit, and then to let the striped fury drop back into the bottom of the cage. Before he has time to right himself, the slide door is pushed into place from above by means of a stout stick or hooked implement, and the box is then ready for hoisting up again with the captive safely secured.

Yet another method is to drop the box at the opened sliding door and exactly over the tiger below, but this means that some intrepid hunter must also climb down into the pit at the same moment in order to slide the door under the angry beast before it can push the box away in its frantic squirmings. This plan is almost too ticklish and dangerous to attempt—though Frank Buck once boldly did it in the case of a man-eating tiger he captured alive in Johore, as he relates in his fascinating book already mentioned.

Sometimes a tiger is caught in a big strong square net laid flat on the ground, with its four sides threaded with ropes attached to a strong-growing giant bamboo or other flexible tree bent over in an arch and firmly secured in that position to form a mighty catapult. The net is covered with leaves and twigs as camouflage and baited in the middle with a dead sheep or other animal. When the great beast appears and, eager for the titbit, unwarily jumps upon it, the thongs holding the bent-over bamboo or tree are instantly cut by hidden watching assistants, so that the arch springs back in true catapult fashion and the ropes threaded around the net are thus drawn together, making a closed bag with the tiger inside. The net and its savage prize are then lowered into a travelling box, from which the net is afterwards withdrawn. Lions are sometimes caught by similar methods.

Full-grown polar bears are often caught alive from canoes, several of which are firmly fastened together, and from these the King of the Arctic is lassoed. As soon as he feels the rope around him, he swims away as fast as he can, dragging the canoes after him. He is allowed to do this without interference until he becomes thoroughly exhausted, and then the performance is continued in reverse, the canoes being paddled quickly back to the main vessel whence they started, with the tired-out bear now being dragged behind. So exhausted is he by this time that it is a comparatively simple matter to bind him with strong ropes and bundle him into a cage, which is then hauled on board the ship, ready for the return journey—probably in company with a walrus or some seals, also caught by means of lassos.

Brown and black bears, owing to their fondness for honey and other sweet stuff, can usually be easily tempted to come to close quarters, and are eventually captured without great difficulty. Grizzlies, however, are a much more dangerous proposition, since they may attack a human being on sight. It is seldom that an adult grizzly is captured alive, but cubs can sometimes be tempted with sweet stuff and brought away, if the mother bear is otherwise engaged—which is not often the case. Grizzlies, however, are hardly ever seen now, outside the great Animal Reserves of Canada, and are fast becoming extinct. When seen in zoos, they grow to an immense size and often live for many years, learning many of the amusing tricks for which the smaller bears are so famous.

The larger antelopes and deer are usually chased on horseback and lassoed, and once they have recovered from their preliminary fright, they do not, as a rule, offer much resistance. Members of the wild cattle tribe are caught in the same way, though young examples are usually selected. The capture alive of wild goats, however—in particular, the magnificent markhor, the Rocky Mountain goat, and even the much smaller ibex and chamois—is attended with great risk, owing to the mountainous heights which these sure-footed creatures haunt; the bold hunters who seek them need to be good mountaineers themselves.

Reptiles, such as crocodiles and alligators, are very ugly customers in more senses than one, and usually provide a hard and dangerous task for the natives who catch them. The latter, however, step boldly into the warm sluggish river where one of these reptiles is lying with merely his curtained eyes and snout tip showing above the water, the remainder of his hideous body being hidden below. Swiftly they fling a lasso first around his neck and then around his limbs and body; if they are lucky, they get this preliminary proceeding done before the monster begins to thrash about with his heavy armoured tail. Then comes the ticklish job of dragging the creature on to the bank of the river; he resists furiously, and the captors must be very spry to avoid injury from the lashing tail and wide-open mouth with its fearsome teeth. Eventually, they manage to bind the strong biting jaws and hold down the flail-like tail until, at last, they can shove and push him into a travelling crate.

The larger members of the snake tribe, such as boa-constrictors and pythons, owing to their tremendous constricting powers, would likewise be very awkward customers to deal with if capture were attempted at a time when they were ready to feed. As, however, these great serpents—sometimes twenty to thirty feet in length—eat only at long intervals and then make huge meals—often a whole deer, or wild pig—after which they lie almost torpid for hours and even days at a time, a python is usually tackled just after one of these big feeds. Then a dozen or more men can seize it at one and the same time and box it up fairly easily, for the well-gorged reptile is too torpid to struggle much or bring its full powers of constriction into play, especially as it is held firmly in a more or less straight line by its captors, who proceed to "pay it out", foot by foot, into a strong box like a coil of rope. If its travels take a fairly long time, it will be necessary to feed the captive again just before the end of its journey. Then it can be dealt with on arrival in very much the same way and deposited in its future home at some zoo before the effects of its meal wear off.

Poisonous snakes are usually captured by means of forked sticks or long metal forks which pin them to the ground at intervals, or by a kind of special lasso-like apparatus which can be used at close-quarters; but such dangerous serpents as cobras and king-cobras or hamadryads are mainly secured by collectors from Indian snake-charmers, who have their own strange methods of dealing with the reptiles they exhibit as star performers. Probably these "charmers" use a certain amount of hypnotism while they play their queer musical instruments to induce their dangerous captives to "dance" or wave about in the graceful but rather alarming contortions for which they are so famous. Some remove their captives' poison-sacs before training them to perform, but others leave them in and declare that they rely for their safety upon their own powers and upon the various amulets or charms—such as the famous "snake-stone"—they wear. Often a performing cobra has been seized by its owner's bare hands alone, which grasped it firmly behind the head, so that the reptile could not operate its poison fangs, and skilfully stuffed into a basket or, with the aid of a couple of assistants, laid out flat and bound to a strong tree branch. If the latter method has been employed, the helpless and temporarily harmless snake can be carried with ease and transferred to a basket or box later on. Many collectors buy their dangerous snakes secured in this manner.

Occasionally it happens that a usually gentle, harmless wild creature can give considerable trouble—not so much during actual capture as at a later period, perhaps when travelling or on delivery to a collector or at a zoo. Mr. Frank Buck relates a remarkable story of a great struggle he once had with a tapir—usually an amiable and docile creature. To capture the more harmless beasts, a very simple sort of trap will suffice, such as an enclosure fenced in with a strong wall of logs, about five feet high, with an open gate at one side which can be swung back and closed instantly the required animal has walked, all unwarily, through the opening.

Many collectors regard birds as being often more difficult to secure than savage jungle beasts—though, of course, the dangers involved in capturing feathered folk are not so much from attacks by the specimens themselves as from the risks to be expected when attempting to capture denizens of the tree-tops, cliff-ledges, mountain precipices, and jungle depths.

Giant birds, such as the ostrich, emu, and cassowary, are comparatively easy to capture, as they are usually hunted down on horseback and lassoed, or even stalked on foot and lassoed while the herd or " mob " is resting. Though it is said that an ostrich can run as fast as a race-horse, it can usually be tracked down readily

Tapir

enough because of its curious habit of running in circles. Nevertheless, a " cornered " ostrich can be a very dangerous proposition, as these big birds are great kickers and their long, tremendously strong middle claws are terrible weapons. Ostriches and emus are sometimes caught for collectors by natives who, having first killed an adult bird, skin off its plumy coat and, dressing themselves up in it, with the head still attached, move about among the " mob ", pretending to be one of them; often they are able to secure and bind a live specimen before their trick is discovered and the herd dashes away. Once an ostrich or other big running bird has actually been caught, it is usually fairly easy to deal with it—for these birds are not noted for their brains. If a bag is tied firmly over its head, it is willing enough to be led away to an enclosure or compound, as it becomes entirely helpless when unable to see where it is going.

Many big birds are also caught by means of an ancient device known as a " bolas ", which consists of a long strong rope or leather thong with a rounded stone or metal circlet firmly secured to it at each end. The bolas is not retained in the hand as in the case of the lasso, but is thrown at the bird's legs, in which, by means of its weighted ends, it becomes entangled, so that the victim is brought to the ground and easily captured. The bolas, or bola, is also used for capturing wild animals of the cattle and antelope tribes, and for zebras, wild horses and asses, and others, but the lasso is often preferred as being less likely to cause damage to the hunted creature.

For the smaller birds—such as birds of paradise, sun-birds, humming-birds, &c.—bird lime is used to a great extent; but the spreading of this substance on branches in their tree-top haunts, and their careful boxing or " bagging " or quick seizure by hand, is likewise a very ticklish job. Many birds are also caught by means of nets, either the butterfly kind or large loose nets that can be flung, or by bags left open with strings that can be drawn after the victim has entered to pick up some tempting bait laid inside.

Collectors and native bird-catchers need an immense amount of patience to secure the rare specimens they seek; days and weeks are often spent in preliminary watching to locate exactly the home or district of the hoped-for captive, and in the consequent waiting with baited cage or net for it to " oblige " its eager captor. The taking of nests with eggs or young birds in them is a favourite method of securing certain specimens which may afterwards be brought up by hand, provided suitable food can be secured for them —not always a simple task. Birds that live together in large colonies, such as gannets, penguins, and other sea-birds, can usually be secured fairly easily, because of their vast numbers.

Having secured the commissioned specimens, the collector of wild animals has still many problems before him—keeping them well-fed upon their own natural food or providing substitutes they will take to readily; getting them used to their human attendants before long journeys are attempted; arranging the quickest and most suitable methods of transportation to their various destinations; keeping them in good health and spirits during the journeys; and delivering them to their final purchaser on landing. In the earlier days of zoos, many valuable creatures died on the journeys from their native lands, and many mistakes were made regarding their diet and general well-being. Nowadays, however, with the greater scientific knowledge of collectors and zoo authorities alike, our swift and wonderful methods of transportation, the more generous and practical ideas regarding modern up-to-date zoo architecture and commissariat problems, and the care taken of animals in our up-to-date zoo sanatoriums by highly skilled veterinary surgeons, not only are remarkably few creatures lost in transit and in their gradual acclimatization in countries so different from their own, but

Lien Ho, the giant panda, eating bamboo shoots

they live far longer in their new homes than the earlier zoo exhibits did—in fact, it is known that many animals exhibited in zoos live longer and enjoy better health than their relatives in their far-off native lands.

Many of the more valuable animals are now transported by air—the trying journey thus occupying a few days or less, instead of weeks or even months. When animals are transported by sea—which is still occasionally the case—the greater speed of modern ocean-going vessels makes journeys very much quicker than they were even a few years ago; and the methods of accommodating these wild passengers on board and of feeding and caring for them during the journeys have all been improved in accordance with modern humane and hygienic ideas.

Sometimes highly experienced keepers are sent over to the country of embarkation to take charge of certain valuable creatures; and in certain cases, native attendants with specialized knowledge of some particular beast may accompany and remain with it for some months in its strange home, to help it to settle down and get used to its new keepers. The ever-popular, most amusing young giant panda, " Lien Ho ", which lived for over four years in the Regent's Park Gardens, travelled by air all the way from Cheng-tu in western China, where it was captured, in company with Mr. Ma Teh, a young Chinese student, who never left his valuable charge during the whole journey. A one-year scholarship to the London University, with all living expenses paid and return fare by air, was offered to Mr. Ma Teh for undertaking to accompany Lien Ho to England; and he visited the panda many times after he had seen it safely installed in the zoo.

Not only, then, are our modern zoos well planned and scientifically laid out and equipped with well-trained, animal-loving attendants, all in charge of practical zoological scientists of the highest order, but it is now possible to keep them well stocked with interesting creatures from all parts of the world, secured by the most humane means possible and transported thither with the utmost speed to ensure their least discomfort. During the process their human collectors and travelling attendants may have suffered many headaches—to say nothing of narrow personal escapes (for escapes on board ship, or even in the air, are not unknown)—but the wearers themselves of fur, feather, scaly armour, or tough skin coats, once safely boxed, have no further troubles to endure, but may look forward to a good time of comfort, plenty, and admiring interest for the remainder of their days.

GETTING TO KNOW THE BIRDS

What do we mean by *getting to know* the birds? We mean becoming familiar with them, being able to name them by their appearance or song, and knowing something of their interesting habits. It is not easy to name every bird we see or hear, and learning their life-stories requires many years of patient watching, but the undertaking is a fascinating one which will add a new and never-ending interest to our country walks. Indeed the difficulty we encounter when bird-watching is one of its greatest charms. Watching, from only a few feet away, a shy bird approaching its nest; knowing the little points of difference in the appearance of birds which look alike; being able to tell one song from another, and how songs and call-notes change with the passing seasons; these are only three of the difficult but interesting problems we have to solve in getting to know the birds. If we are afraid of difficulties we shall never be very successful in overcoming them; but if we enjoy problems which call for all our skill and patience we shall succeed in the end, and while solving them we can be sure of many happy days in the most delightful corners of our woods and meadows and hillsides and streams . . . and in the cheerful companionship of the birds. Let us discover what are the chief difficulties we shall encounter in getting to know the birds, and then we shall find ways to overcome them.

The first difficulty is, of course, the very great number of different kinds of birds which we have in this country . . . but who would want to make things easier by lessening them! There are few countries in the world which have such a wealth of bird life for their size as we possess in this lucky little island of ours.

The second difficulty is that so many of our birds look very much alike. We all know the Song-thrush of our gardens, but how many of us could tell it from the Redwing and Fieldfare, cousins of the Song-thrush which come to winter with us from Scandinavian countries across the North Sea? And what about the different members of the Crow family, and those puzzling little brown birds,

the Warblers? It is birds like these, very similar to one another
in appearance, which add to our difficulty of naming, or, as we say,
identifying, the birds. These are the two main problems we have
to solve in becoming familiar with the birds. Let's see how we
should tackle them.

The Thrush Family: Song-thrush, Redwing, Fieldfare, Missel-thrush

The Ways by which Birds are Named.

There are four different ways by which we can identify or name
the birds we see. As it is very important that we remember them
we shall put them down in this way:

1. Naming by Appearance.
2. Naming by Call or Song.
3. Naming by Actions.
4. Naming by Haunts, or Place Seen.

One of these four ways may be all we shall require when naming
a bird. Appearance, for example, would be all we needed to name
the Robin correctly, just as call or song would allow us to name
the Cuckoo without fear of mistake. Very often, however, we shall
find that one of these " aids " is *not* sufficient, and in such cases we
shall have to use *more* than one. Suppose we heard a bird singing,
and that the song reminded us of the Skylark's music. If we were

not quite certain of the Skylark's song we would be left in doubt
as to the name of the bird, but if the song were coming from high
up in the summer sky our doubts would vanish and we could say
with confidence that it really was a Skylark we heard. In this case
call or song was not sufficient by itself to allow us to name the
bird, but haunts came to our aid and enabled us to identify the
bird we heard singing. As we practise using these four aids we
shall find that we can often name a bird by appearance alone, or by
call or song alone, or by actions alone, but it is seldom we will be
able to do this with haunts. The last of our four aids is helpful
only when used along with one or more of the other three.

Now, if we have been thinking carefully about these aids and
how to use them, we must have noticed that before getting any help
from them it is necessary that we *already know* something about
the birds. We couldn't name the Robin by its appearance unless
we *already knew* that it had a red breast. Nor could we name the
Cuckoo by its call unless we *already knew* that it called " Cuckoo ".
Nor could we name the Skylark by the place where it was singing
unless we *already knew* that this little bird loved to sing high in
the sky. Before we can use our aids we must already know something about the birds—something about their Appearance, Call or
Song, Actions and Haunts—so our next task will be to discover
how we can gain this knowledge.

There are two ways in which this can be done. The first, and
perhaps the ideal way, is to have an expert companion who is able
to tell us what we want to know about the birds. Such a friend will
be able to name the birds we see or hear during our walks together,
and draw our attention to the little points about their appearance
and song which enabled him to identify them. He will also be
able to tell us many interesting things about the birds' habits—
how the Kestrel hovers while searching the ground beneath for food;
how the Dipper dances on the spray-soaked stones of the stream;
how the Lapwings and other plovers bend curiously at the knees
when picking up food from the field—and it is by noticing just such
little actions as these that we get to know the birds.

Such companions are, however, rare. We are usually left to
learn about the birds by ourselves, and it is then that we must turn
to our second source of help—books. Books play such an important
part when we are getting to know the birds that we must not pass
on without saying something about them.

Books about Birds.

Very many books have been written about the birds of our own countryside. Some of them are excellent, some are good, and some are, well, not so good. For *our* purpose, which is to *learn* about the birds and not just *read* about them for pleasure, we should be sure to get the very best books we can afford to buy. Unfortunately, the best are rather expensive, but this need not prevent our reading them or referring to their coloured pictures, for we can always borrow such books from our local library. It is essential that the books we use when identifying birds should have reliable, coloured plates of the species we want to name, and all the best books have these, together with notes about habits, nests and eggs, song and call, haunts, and other details. Here are a few of the bird books which the writer can recommend. The first two may be too expensive for us actually to own, at least for some time, but we can borrow them from a library; the others are books costing only a few shillings each, but all are first-rate volumes for our purpose.

> *The Handbook of British Birds.* (In five volumes.) Published by H. F. and G. Witherby, Ltd. This splendid book contains all we know to-day about the birds of the British Isles. Though written and read by expert bird-watchers it is a book we can easily read for ourselves, for all the information it contains is clearly and simply explained. The many plates, too, have been carefully coloured, showing pictures of every species, adult birds and young birds, male and female, winter plumage and summer plumage.

> *The Birds of the British Isles and their Eggs.* (In three volumes.) By T. A. Coward, M.B.O.U. Published by Frederick Warne & Co., Ltd. Though published in three volumes we need refer only to the first two, the third dealing with rare birds which we are unlikely to see. This book was the writer's main guide to bird life for many years, and is still one of the best bird books we have. The coloured pictures are by famous bird artists, and there are also excellent coloured plates of the eggs.

> *The Observer's Book of British Birds.* (In one volume.) Published by Frederick Warne & Co., Ltd. This is really a

small edition of the last two volumes, with shorter notes about the birds, and the same, but reduced, pictures. It is a very handy little volume, which, while it does not mention quite so many birds, will answer our purpose with most of the birds we see during walks.

How to Know British Birds. (In one volume.) By N. H. Joy. Published by H. F. and G. Witherby, Ltd. This is a book specially written and illustrated to help us when identifying the birds. The pictures draw our attention to the points to look for, and at the end of the book there are valuable notes on Descriptions, Songs, Nests and Haunts.

Bird books should not be carried with us during walks. They are what we call " reference books "—books to be studied carefully at home, till we become familiar with the picture of every bird shown in the illustrations, and acquainted with its habits, haunts, time of year when it is to be seen, and so on. The only book we should actually carry with us is a small note-book in which to jot down descriptions of the birds we see during rambles; then, when we return home, our " field-notes " can be compared with the descriptions given in the reference book and the names of the birds we have seen discovered. But the Nature note-book is so important to the bird-watcher that we will have a special talk about it later on. Just now we have another important subject to talk about, and that is how to approach the birds so as to see them at really close quarters.

How to Approach Birds.

Before we can hope to name a bird by its appearance we must first of all see it, and for this purpose the closer we can get the better. But how often we fail to get a close view of a perching bird through not knowing the correct way in which to approach. We see a strange bird perched on the laneside hedge a few yards ahead, and, walking slowly and quietly, keeping our eyes fixed in its direction, we move forward step by step. Then, when we are reaching a position from which a clear and close view can be had, the bird opens its wings and flies seven or eight yards farther down the hedge. Good, we think, it hasn't flown away altogether; and once again we begin our stealthy approach. And again, just as we are reaching the desired spot, off goes the bird to another spray some distance away. So it goes on, careful stalking on our part followed by a retreat on the part of the bird till, arrived at the end of the hedge, away the bird goes across a wide field or pond or river and we come to a disappointed halt. Obviously something is wrong with this manner of approaching birds, but what is it? Just this. The perching bird knows that we can see it, and is watching us as we approach along the hedge. So long as we do not show any special interest in the bird it remains on its perch, but when we begin to walk stealthily towards it, staring at it all the while, it decides that things are " becoming too hot " and retreats a safe distance down the hedge.

How, then, should we approach perching birds? As they will be watching us all the time, waiting to see whether we are going to notice them, the plan is to pretend that we have not noticed them at all, or, if we have, that we are entirely uninterested in them. So, having spotted a bird, we must be careful never to look straight at it. We should walk casually along, looking up at the clouds or down at our feet, perhaps humming or whistling softly to ourselves, pretending to be interested in everything around us—except the bird. Approached in this way most birds will remain contentedly on their perch, allowing us to pass within five or six feet; and, as we *do* pass, we can examine the bird from the corner of our eyes. It is remarkable how clearly we *can* examine things in this way, without looking directly at them. Then, if we wish to see more of the bird, we need only continue on our way a short distance, turn casually, and again pass the bird. Birds can be passed and repassed in this way many times, and it is even possible to take out our note-book and make notes or a rough sketch as we walk up and down in front of the unsuspecting percher.

The writer has found this method of approach successful in nine cases out of ten, but it can be used only when birds are perching in the open; that is, when they are perched in full view of the passer-by, know that they can be seen, and are relying on their wings to carry them off should danger threaten. A very different plan must be used when birds are hidden, screened by branches, reeds, bracken or tall grasses.

Watching Hidden Birds.

Suppose we are walking along the bank of a stream, and, on turning a bend, we see a Water-hen or Coot paddle in among the reeds fringing the opposite bank. It is no use walking carelessly up and down waiting for the bird to appear again, no matter how innocently we seem to be examining the clouds above or the sheep and cows around us. In this case the bird is relying on being hidden, and, watching from its reed shelter, will never reappear while we are in sight. What must we do in a case like this? We must creep into hiding ourselves, and then begins a game of I-Spy between us and the bird. There is almost always some form of cover on a river bank, or at the edge of a pond. It may be reeds or bushes, or ferns, or tall grasses, and once we are comfortably curled up in our hide-out there must be no waving sprays or other movement to betray our presence to the watching bird. We must remain perfectly motionless and quiet, for we are pretending that we are not there at all, and then begins a competition in patience between us and the bird. If we lose patience first, then the bird has won. Watching us rise from our hiding-place it waits till we have gone, and then paddles out to continue its interrupted meal. But if *the bird* is the first to lose patience then *we* have won the game, and our reward is seeing the bird come out of hiding, and watching it for perhaps the next half-hour, and from only a few feet away. This is where patience is required in bird-watching—not when actually *watching* the birds, but when waiting for them to appear. Hidden behind our screen of reeds or bracken we may have to wait for half an hour, or even longer, but that is only if we are out by ourselves. If we are accompanied by a companion we can puzzle the hiding bird and make it show itself in very much less time. Let's see how it is possible to do this.

Birds Can Count.

Yes, it's quite true—birds *can* count. They are not very good at arithmetic, for we can puzzle them by forcing them to count above two. Let's pretend that we have just seen a Water-hen disappear into reeds at a river bank, and that we have hidden to wait for its reappearance. Here is what happens. The hiding bird peeps out from its cover, and says something like this to itself: " One human was walking along that bank over there. No human has yet walked away. Nothing from one leaves one—the human must still be there!" And because it knows we are still there the bird will wait and wait, and will appear again only if we tire it out at the game of patience, in half an hour or so. But suppose we have a companion when we see the bird paddle in among the reeds; and suppose we ask our companion to walk on while we slip into hiding. Then the watching bird says: " Two humans were walking over there. One is now moving off again. One from two leaves one!" But it isn't quite so certain about this answer, and because of this it will paddle into view again in fifteen minutes or even less. Now suppose we have *two* companions, and that both of them walk away while we hide. Then we have entirely puzzled the bird. We have set it a sum that is too difficult for its knowledge of arithmetic. Watching our friends walking away it says to itself: " Three humans came along here—or was it only two? No, there's two walking off again. Now what does two from three leave?" And then it makes the mistake, and says: " Two from three leaves nothing—they've all gone away!" And out it comes just as soon as our friends have disappeared round the first bend of the river bank.

This method of puzzling the birds is used by bird photographers when photographing from a little tent or " hide " set up alongside the nest. They go to the hide with two companions, and as they slip inside their companions walk off, puzzling the watching owners of the nest. If the photographer has only one companion he gets him to take off his coat or jacket, and, holding out an arm, the companion dangles the garment from his wrist as he moves away. The bird then thinks that two people are going off! What the bird photographers do to induce birds to return quickly to the nest, we, as bird-watchers, can also do to tempt from its reed hiding-place the timid creature we would see at close quarters.

Naming the Birds by Groups.

We have now discovered the four ways by which birds can be recognized and named—Appearance, Call or Song, Actions and Haunts. We have also learned something about the best books to consult if we are not lucky enough to have a friend who can help us. And now we know how to get really close to the birds, so as to see all those little details by which one species differs from another. But we still have one big difficulty to overcome—the great number of different kinds of birds to be found during even a short walk. It is now time for us to tackle this problem.

No matter how anxious we are, and no matter how carefully we approach and observe them, we shall not be able to name *every* bird we see during walks—at least, to begin with. So we must not be disappointed if, just at first, we see many birds which we cannot identify among the pictures and descriptions in our books. Remember what we discovered earlier—that a great many of our birds look very much alike. Through time we shall be able to name them all, and to name them when we have little more than glimpsed

The bird will think it sees two people walking away

them flying past or slipping through the undergrowth. When we first set out, however, let us work to a plan, and take the birds in groups, becoming familiar first with one group and then with another. Tackled in this way, the biggest difficulty in getting to know the birds will disappear without our realizing that it ever existed. Let us understand fully, then, what we mean by this " grouping " of the birds.

When we set out on our first bird-watching walk we should make up our minds that we are going to pay special attention to the naming of birds which belong to one group—say those which appear to be black-and-white. If we are able to name any others good and well, but we won't worry about them if we cannot; we are out on this special walk to name the black-and-whites. In this way we shall get to know such birds as:

Lapwing   Oyster-catcher
Magpie   Dipper
Pied Wagtail   Pied Flycatcher

Black-and-white birds: Oyster-catcher, Wagtail and Lapwing

We must understand, of course, that these birds only *appear* to be black-and-white because we are seeing them from a distance. If we had them in our hand we would find in many cases that their plumage contained other colours, but for the sake of our simple grouping we can call them black-and-white, or pied.

Having become familiar with these birds, we can then turn our attention to birds which show a patch of bright colour in their plumage, and this time our list of names will be longer, including:

Chaffinch   Bullfinch
Greenfinch   Goldfinch
Great Tit   Yellow Bunting
Coal Tit   Linnet
Blue Tit   House Martin
Goldcrest   Grey Wagtail

This list does not contain *all* the birds which show a bright patch of colour, but it contains those which are to be seen more or less all over the country. Other, more local, birds we shall discover in our own different districts.

Our next group might contain those birds which, for their size, have long bills, or long legs, and here we would add to our growing list the names of:

Heron   Curlew
Woodcock   Snipe
Redshank   Sandpiper

and, once again,   Oyster-catcher.

Some birds with long legs or long bills: Snipe, Redshank,
Curlew and Heron

We shall be able to add other groups of our own: birds which frequent streams and ponds; birds which are seen in the evening; birds which are found around farms; and so the list of birds we can name at sight grows gradually larger and larger. We are, as we say, " narrowing down the field ", till at last we are left with the most puzzling birds of all, the birds which look alike—the Warblers, the Crows, the Larks and Pipits, and a few others. But by this time we shall have learned how to observe, how to spot those little points of colour and shape by which one bird differs from another, and this knowledge and experience will be of the greatest value in helping us to name the more difficult species.

Now let us, as lawyers say, " sum up " what we have learned about naming the birds. First, we must get hold of a good bird book with reliable pictures, and we must study these until we are familiar with the appearance of all the birds we are likely to see during a walk. It is an excellent plan to ask a friend to test us in this, by showing us the pictures with the names of the birds covered up, and seeing how many we can name quickly and correctly. Second, we must set out among the fields and woods armed with note-book and pencil, and note down details of all the unknown

The Crow Family: Raven, Rook, Jackdaw and Crow

birds we see—their colouring, shape, size, call, and any other particulars which we think would be helpful. We can't make *too many* notes. Third, on returning home we get out the bird book and compare our notes with its pictures and descriptions. If we have observed carefully we should have little difficulty in discovering the names of the birds we have seen.

In many cases we shall be able, right away, to name the bird we see in the field from our memory of its picture in the book; in other cases we shall have to rely on our written notes; but whether named on sight or after long and careful observing and comparing we shall find the identifying of the birds a fascinating and exciting game.

Bird-watching offers us a whole lifetime of healthy, interesting days among the fields and woods, on moorlands and hillsides, by the seashore, and beside streams and ponds and lakes, for the birds are to be found everywhere. Even if we live in the city we shall find many different kinds of birds in its parks and botanic gardens. And this delightful hobby need cost us nothing at all. We can borrow from a library the few books we need, and the rest depends on ourselves—on our eyes and ears and enthusiasm. There are, however, two things which will help us greatly: one is the note-book we have already mentioned, and the other is a pair of binoculars or field-glasses. The last are expensive things to buy, but most of us will know someone who owns a field-glass and who would be willing to lend it to us for our bird-watching walks. It is not essential, but a good glass is a very great aid to close observing of our shyer birds. The note-book, however, is of such importance to the naturalist that we must describe it, and its purpose, in greater detail.

About Note-books and Note-keeping.

If we are to become serious observers of the birds we must make notes about them, and for this purpose we should carry with us on all our rambles a little note-book and a pencil. Stained with mosses and grasses, and scratched by rocks and branches, the little book will become a dear companion; and, when its pages are filled, a reminder of happy days and interesting discoveries. It will be always there to refresh our memories about details observed long ago when we wish to compare them with more recent discoveries. Did we see the Chiffchaff earlier this year than last? On what day last year, or the year before, did we first hear the Cuckoo? How many eggs were there in the Long-tailed Tit's nest we found last summer? How many times did we hear the Corncrake last year? Such are the questions to which our old note-book will give reliable answers—answers which would have been merest guess-work had we relied on memory alone. It may do even more. We may read in some paper or book that a certain bird has never been seen in such-and-such a locality, or never been known to do such-and-such a thing. Careful notes taken on the spot may prove that we have made a discovery; and what satisfaction to know that we have added a little bit to the knowledge of the countryside and its birds!

Writing about the importance of note-keeping, Mr. T. A. Coward has told in those excellent little volumes we've already mentioned, *The Birds of the British Isles and their Eggs*,[1] how as a small boy he was lifted up to look into a sand-hole at a long-billed, brilliantly plumaged bird. " Possibly because I was familiar with pictures of birds," he writes, " my infantile brain registered a vision of a Bee-eater on its nest. Not until many years later I learnt that the bird had never been proved to nest in England, and that it nested in a hole. It may have been a Kingfisher, yet I knew the picture of that bird well. I can never satisfy myself now." We can almost hear a sigh in that last sentence. Coward was one of our most careful naturalists, and we can understand how keenly he must have felt the loss of that observation of his boyhood. In Nature Study it is the note-book, and the camera, which alone can prevent occasion for the sad words, " It *might* have been ".

Now what type of note-book should we carry? It doesn't really matter, but the book should be a slim one which will tuck comfortably away in our pocket, there to lie until it is needed. The writer's own choice is a thin loose-leaf book, with limp leather covers, from which pages can be removed without damaging the binding. New pages can also be added as required, and it is possible to interleave ruled pages with unruled ones on which rough sketches can be made. It is a good plan, too, to mark inches, down to sixteenths, along the edge of one cover. This handy rule can be used for measuring the width of nests, length of eggs, and so on.

The ideal pencil is a propelling one, containing a rubber, but it should have a strong clip for fixing to the pocket. It's so easy to lose a pencil while struggling through bushes or heather, or crawling along a hedgerow ditch!

The note-book is for field-work only—for notes taken down on the spot. These should be copied out on our return home, either into a larger book with an alphabetical index, or, better still, on to separate cards which can then be filed away in what business offices call " card-index " style. In this way we can have one card for each bird, and further cards can be added if we make more observations about some birds than others. Suitable cards can be bought very cheaply at any shop which supplies office stationery equipment.

As to what should go down in our note-book, the answer is anything and everything which arouses our interest. Descriptions of birds for identification—their appearance, habits, calls, nests and

[1] Wayside & Woodland Series—Warne.

eggs, haunts; the dates of the arrival and departure of our migrants; birds which are common and rare in different districts; notes on the quality and length of bird-song; nesting materials and time taken in building. All these are worthy of a place in our note-books. With *every entry*, too, there should be a note stating the date, time of day (it's best to use the twenty-four hour system for this), locality and weather conditions at the time our observation was made. Without these particulars really valuable discoveries may prove worthless later on, for it is very often in the future, perhaps many years afterwards, that the true value of our notes will be appreciated.

So with this parting advice on note-keeping, let us set out among waysides and woodlands to learn more about the birds from the birds themselves. With *them* for company we will never know loneliness or lack of interest, for, at every exploration into their haunts, the birds will

" . . . sing a more wonderful song,
Or tell a more marvellous tale ".

BUTTERFLIES AND MOTHS

How can one tell a butterfly from a moth and vice versa? This is not an easy question to answer in a straightforward manner, because, while both these kinds of insects are very similar in many ways, their differences are less apparent at first sight. You may say that butterflies are active during the daytime, whereas moths seldom come abroad until after dark. Well, this is certainly true in the majority of instances, but by no means in all. The showy burnet moths, for example, may often be seen sunning themselves on the blooms of thistle and scabious, and flying rapidly from one flower-head to another. These burnets also serve to contradict the claim advanced by many people that butterflies are always gaily coloured while moths are invariably drab and unattractive. In their scarlet and dark-green livery they are no less resplendent than the peacocks and tortoiseshells when seen in the full sunlight, and several of the tiger moths are even more gorgeous. On the other hand, the " brown butterflies "—as their popular name indicates— are nearly all dull-coloured, and so are the little skippers.

The bodies of moths are usually stouter than those of butterflies, and the hind-body or abdomen is joined to the thorax (the part immediately behind the head) by a less obvious " waist ". Moreover, when moths are at rest they usually hold their wings horizontally, or " flat ", in relation to the leaf or other object on which they may be sitting. Frequently also the fore-wings are moved backwards so that they completely cover the hind-wings. But when a butterfly settles it folds its wings vertically—that is, in an upright position— over its back; all except the skippers, which rest with their fore-wings held up and their hind-wings flat, or nearly so.

Probably the best way to distinguish between a butterfly and a moth is to look closely at the insect's antennæ or " feelers ", if you can get a sight of them. In both cases these organs are made up of numerous joints. But if they are uniformly slender as to the main shaft and have a knobbed tip—something like a long-handled club in miniature—we may take it for granted that we are dealing with a butterfly. For the antennæ of moths, although they vary enormously in structure, are almost always pointed at their free end. Yet here again an exception must be made where the skippers are concerned, since, although their antennæ end in a club-like swelling, the extreme tip of all carries a small, pointed hook—as may be seen with the aid of a pocket lens or magnifying-glass.

Butterflies and moths together make up a kind of tribe or " order " of insect life called Lepidoptera by scientific naturalists—a double-barrelled word, derived from the Greek, which may be translated " scaly-winged ". It refers to the fact that insects of this sort have their wings clothed with minute, stalked scales. These, when viewed under the microscope, are seen to be arranged in overlapping rows, something like tiles on the roof of a house. The way in which these scales are grouped together and the fact that they are differently tinted account for the particular colour-scheme of the wing—gay or sombre, as the case may be.

Like most other insects, butterflies and moths have in general two pairs of wings and three pairs of legs, all springing from the thorax or middle segment of the body. The head, as we have seen, carries two antennæ or feelers, and there are also two prominent eyes, which are called " compound ", because the surface of each consists of a very large number of separate lenses, enabling the insect to see in many directions all at once without altering its position—though how far and how clearly it can see we do not know. Instead of biting-jaws, such as those of beetles, wasps, ants, &c., a butterfly or moth has a trunk or proboscis which in many instances is sufficiently long and slender to reach the bottom of a flower's tube, where the sweet juice called nectar is stored. When an insect feeds in this way it often carries pollen on its head from the stamens of one flower to the pistil of another, and so helps the plants to set their seed. The proboscis when not in use is coiled up like a watch-spring beneath the head, where it is often almost hidden by two brush-like outgrowths called " palpi ", which are used, perhaps, chiefly to sweep dust and pollen from the surface of the eyes.

The way in which insects, including butterflies and moths, breathe is particularly interesting. Unlike beasts and birds, they have no lungs, but take in air through small holes, called " spiracles " —of which there are usually ten pairs—along the sides of the body. After entering through the spiracles the air circulates through a system of minute tubes termed " tracheæ ", which form a network among the insect's living tissues, so supplying the various organs with the oxygen that they need. If you look carefully at a large moth when it is at rest you may be able to detect some of the spiracles along its sides, and you will probably notice the alternate expansion and contraction of its hind-body which accompany the act of breathing. An insect's heart is a long, tubular structure extending along the back, almost from head to tail; but the colourless or pale-green blood, instead of being pumped through veins and arteries, circulates freely in the spaces of the body between the various organs, to which it carries nourishment derived from the food which is eaten.

Another point worth noting is that the soft parts of an insect are not held together and supported by an inner framework of wonderfully jointed bones. On the contrary, insects may be said to wear their skeletons outside, like old-time suits of armour. Indeed, this " exoskeleton ", as it is called, does protect its owner from injury, and at the same time supports the body and provides points of attachment needed for the muscles to set the legs and wings in motion and keep air circulating in the breathing tubes. In the case of beetles and many other insects this exoskeleton is thick, rigid, and often smoothly polished, but with butterflies and moths it is comparatively thin and flexible and clothed with coloured scales like the wings.

You see, therefore, that the body of a butterfly or a moth is constructed quite differently from yours or mine, although broadly speaking it performs the same kinds of services for its owner—such as seeing, feeling, feeding, digesting, breathing, and moving about. But as a butterfly or a moth " grows up " its body undergoes some very remarkable changes which together are termed its " transformation " or " metamorphosis ". This series of form-changes (which is what is meant by these rather alarming words) begins with the laying of an egg by the mother insect, usually on or close to the kind of food that will be needed by the offspring for its nourishment when it hatches. Butterfly parents always lay their eggs on the leaves of plants, and it is marvellous to see how unerringly they search out the right kind of plant. Tortoiseshells and peacocks, for example, lay their eggs on stinging nettles, while the brimstone or sulphur butterfly searches the woodlands until it finds a buckthorn bush—this being the only " food-plant " that its caterpillars fancy.

When the egg hatches a tiny caterpillar is produced which spends most of its time eating—its first meal often consisting of the egg-shell out of which it has just emerged. Eventually, after a certain number of days during which it grows rapidly and casts its skin several times, it reaches the limit of its development as a caterpillar, and changes to a pupa or chrysalis, from which, in due course, the actual butterfly or moth comes forth as if by magic. This extra-

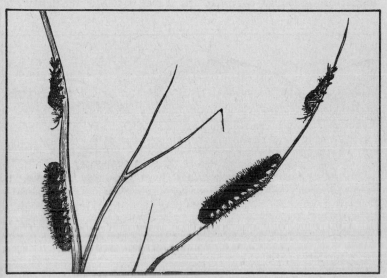

Caterpillars which have just cast their skins
(old skins above)

ordinary life-history—so totally different from that of a cat, a rabbit, or a human being—has become so familiar, because we have so often been told about it, that we are all too apt to overlook its mystery and wonder. All readers of these pages who have not yet seen with their own eyes how a caterpillar becomes first a chrysalis and then a butterfly should take the earliest opportunity that offers to study these strange and fascinating happenings. " Seeing's believing "— as the old proverb testifies; and to see things happening with one's own eyes is a better and more lasting way of learning than to read about them in books.

11*   (G 487)

Rearing caterpillars is really a fascinating hobby. You might make a start in May by collecting a few of those of the small tortoiseshell, clusters of which may often be found on clumps of stinging nettle by the roadside; or, if you are content to begin with a kind which in many seasons is all too common, visit the nearest cabbage plot rather later in the summer, and you are almost sure to find the yellow eggs or young caterpillars of the small and large white butterflies. These are quite easily told apart, because the former are green all over like the leaves, whereas the latter are

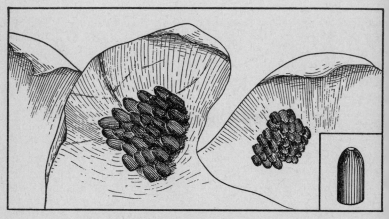

Egg clusters of Large White Butterfly on underside of cabbage leaf

yellowish-green marked with a great many dark—almost black—spots and dots. By the way, butterflies—and most moths too—nearly always lay their eggs on the underside of the selected leaf, sometimes close together in groups, sometimes singly. Most of these eggs are large enough to be seen quite clearly with the naked eye; some indeed—laid by the larger moths—are about the size and shape of small glass beads; but they vary a great deal in appearance.

Caterpillars should be handled as little as possible, for they are easily injured or crushed to death. They are best carried home in tin boxes: empty cocoa tins, thoroughly cleaned inside and aired, serve quite well; so take one or two of them in your pocket, when you go collecting. From these temporary containers your captives should be transferred as soon as possible to a roomy breeding-cage, and kept plentifully supplied with their proper food until such time as they " turn up ", i.e. change to chrysalides or pupæ. Breeding cages may be bought from dealers in natural-history apparatus; or they may be made fairly easily from light wooden boxes. One side at least should consist of perforated zinc, since the occupants will thrive best when they have plenty of fresh air. Another side may be of glass, to allow of easy observation; while a false bottom, with holes in it through which the stems of the food-plant may be pushed into a vessel of water placed beneath, is a great convenience, as in this way the leaves will be maintained in a fresh condition for several days, and one need make less frequent excursions in search of supplies. Caterpillars cannot be expected to thrive on food that has been allowed to become dry or withered. As regards the choice of food, wherever possible your captives should be given the kind of leaves which they were eating when you collected them—or those of the plant on which the eggs were laid. Some caterpillars, as we have seen, eat leaves of only one sort, and will starve to death rather than sample any others. Those of the brimstone butterfly, for example, must have buckthorn—in some districts a rather uncommon shrub. Others greedily devour almost any foliage that is available—apple, oak, blackthorn, hawthorn and plum being especial favourites.

Caterpillars, as you know, are very different-looking creatures from the butterflies or moths into which they eventually develop. They have long, rather worm-like bodies composed of some twelve similar segments behind the head, no wings, and more legs than the customary three pairs of the ordinary adult insect. These legs, however, call for some explanation. The so-called " true legs " are the three pairs which spring from the first three segments of the body, and they alone are inherited by the full-grown butterfly or moth. All the rest, of which there are normally five pairs, are called " false-legs ", " pro-legs " or " claspers " by naturalists. They are temporary structures—mere muscular outgrowths, so to speak— which enable their owner to grip firmly the twigs and leaves of its food-plant; but when the caterpillar moults for the last time they are discarded with the old skin and are seen no more. In one large family of moths, of which there are some 270 British species, most of the caterpillars have only two pairs of pro-legs or claspers, these being situated at the hinder end of the body. An example is the caterpillar of the well-known magpie moth. Watch it in motion

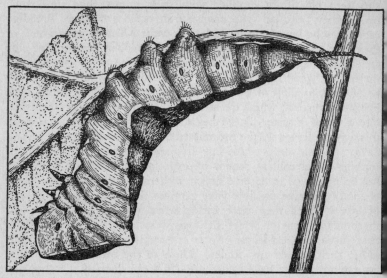

Puss-moth caterpillar (hanging back downwards) showing spiracles, true legs and pro-legs (about twice life size)

and you will see that it first grasps a twig or leaf with its six " true " legs, then brings its four pro-legs forward until they nearly touch the front part of its body, thus throwing itself into a sort of arch or loop at each " step " which is taken. Hence, these particular caterpillars go by the name of " loopers ". Some of their kind are also called " stick insects " because, when they are not feeding, they have the habit of holding on to the food-plant by their pro-legs and stretching themselves out stiff and straight, so that they look like a shoot or twig. That this habit is life-saving or protective seems clear, since a hungry bird on the look-out for a meal would very likely fail to recognize the caterpillar as something good to eat.

When a caterpillar has eaten all the food necessary for its development it makes its preparations for changing into a pupa or chrysalis. At this time it becomes restless, and you will notice that it wanders about the breeding-cage as if in search of something that it has lost. The caterpillars of many moths burrow into the soil and pupate below ground in a little cell or chamber which they make by wriggling their bodies in the soft earth. This is what happens to the big hawk-moth caterpillars; so if you have been feeding any of these you must provide them with a box or tray of moist soil. Other caterpillars, like those of the beautiful emperor moth (whose chief food-plants are willow, blackthorn and ling), spin a silken cocoon round themselves before changing to the pupa—usually fixing it to a convenient stem or leaf. This, as you probably know, is what the silkworm does; and it is from its cocoon that is unwound the delicate thread from which yarns and fabrics of many different kinds are manufactured. Before the days of artificial silk, the raw

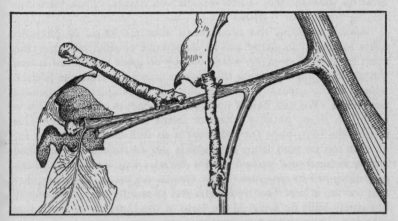

" Stick " caterpillars in characteristic resting attitude

material from which all such things were made came solely from the cocoons spun by silkworms.

Unlike the caterpillars of moths, those of most butterflies do not burrow in the ground or spin cocoons when they are ready to pupate, but usually hang themselves up, often head downwards, first spinning a little pad of silk which they grasp with their hindermost pair of pro-legs. After it has been suspended thus for some hours, the caterpillar's skin splits behind the head, and by muscular movements is gradually worked backwards, revealing the pupa or chrysalis—at this stage white and soft—beneath. Then, by a series of deft movements not easy to follow with the eye, the newly formed chrysalis manages to fix its tail-end (which is provided with a number of minute hooks) to the pad spun by the caterpillar, at the same time jerking away the latter's discarded skin.

What is the difference between a pupa and a chrysalis? Well, " pupa " is a word taken from the Latin and signifies a " doll " or a " mummy ". It can therefore quite properly be used to describe any insect in the resting or quiescent stage of its existence, when it has finished its feeding as a larva, i.e. a caterpillar or a grub, and is preparing to complete its transformation into a perfect insect. On the other hand, " chrysalis ", strictly speaking, can only be used to describe certain kinds of pupæ which (like those of the tortoise-shells and fritillaries among butterflies) have brilliant metal-like areas on their surfaces, since it is derived from a Greek word signifying " gold " or " gilded ".

After discarding the caterpillar's skin the pupa or chrysalis alters somewhat in shape and its outer husk or shell hardens; but apart from these changes, which occupy no more than a few hours, the whole period separating the larva or caterpillar from the perfect, winged insect appears outwardly like one of completely suspended animation. We can detect no movement, no change; no food is eaten; in short, nothing whatever seems to be happening. This is why the term pupa (or mummy) is so well chosen, because for all that can be seen from the outside the creature might be dead and embalmed and packed up for burial. But inside marvellous operations are in progress. The various organs of the caterpillar that was are at first dissolved into a sort of creamy fluid, then slowly but surely built up again in the form of the butterfly or moth that is to be. Thus, when the husk of the pupa or chrysalis eventually breaks open and the insect emerges it is complete and perfect in every respect—save only for the wings, which need time to expand and harden.

On their first appearance the wings are small, pad-like outgrowths from the thorax or middle segment of the body; but almost at once blood begins to flow into them, and they expand rapidly, attaining their full size and normal shape in the course of ten or fifteen minutes. After this the butterfly or moth remains hanging from its chrysalis skin, or from the point of vantage to which it has climbed, for an hour or more, until the wings have hardened sufficiently for flight. Then it soars away into the air—an exquisite being, differing in a thousand ways from the worm-like caterpillar from which it originated. When a butterfly or moth —or for that matter any other kind of insect—reaches its adult or perfect state its transformation is complete. Thereafter it does not increase in size or alter in appearance. This fact has prompted the statement that " insects never grow ", which is quite true in so far as butterflies and moths as such are concerned, but fails to take into account the lengthy period of increase and development which marks the early stages of their life-histories. You might just as well say that an adult human being never grows if you choose to ignore his or her childhood and youth!

This brings us to the question, How long do butterflies and moths live? The answer depends upon the particular kind or species which we have in mind, because while some run through two, or even three, generations in the course of twelve months, others accomplish no more than one in the same period. Also, different species hibernate—i.e. spend the winter—in different stages of development. Several examples will illustrate these points. The first eggs of the small garden white butterfly are laid in April and May by parents that have passed the winter as pupæ. These eggs hatch in about a fortnight; the caterpillars feed for some three weeks, then change to pupæ, from which butterflies emerge in July, and lay eggs from which a second brood of caterpillars hatch; and these, in their turn, change in the late summer or autumn to the pupæ, which eventually give rise to the butterflies that we see during the following spring. Thus, it is clear that the lifetime of the second brood is considerably longer than that of the first, for the reason that the latter's pupæ are forced by the inclemencies of winter to remain dormant for seven months or more; whereas in the case of the first brood the corresponding stage lasts several weeks only.

Now compare with the above the life-history of the beautiful peacock butterfly. The perfect insects emerge from their chrysalides in August, and may be seen visiting flowers or sometimes imbibing the juice of over-ripe or rotting fruit in orchards until the late autumn. But the advent of the first frosts drive them into their winter hiding-places—among the rafters of barns and outhouses or in the hollows of trees. Now and then we find them in the attics of our dwelling-houses, or in cupboards. Occasionally, during an exceptionally mild spell, one may be seen flying in the sunshine in midwinter; but normally they stay asleep until late April or early May, when the males and females pair and the eggs are laid from which the next generation of caterpillars hatch out. Only the one brood occurs annually, and as the perfect butterflies may survive for a month or more after their task of egg-laying has been performed, the complete life-spell of the insect must often exceed a year. One of our native butterflies—the alert and dapper small copper—is, by comparison, short-lived, since if the weather is favourable as many as three broods may complete their transformation in twelve months; which means that three relays of the perfect insects appear successively, in April, in June, and again in the early autumn. The longest-lived scaly-winged insects are certain moths whose caterpillars pass their time boring in the trunks and branches of trees, feeding on the particles of wood which they gnaw away. The caterpillar of the big goat moth, for example, does this for two years or more before it is ready to spin its cocoon and change to a pupa.

All told, the different kinds or species of scaly-winged insect which have been found in Britain must number well over 2000. The majority of these are moths, some large like the great death's-head hawk-moth, others tiny like those whose caterpillars devour our furs and clothing. The number of British butterflies is usually given as sixty-eight; but of these the resplendent large copper, once quite common in the Fen districts of eastern England, became extinct about a hundred years ago. Of the remaining sixty-seven many are common and widely distributed, several are found only in restricted areas, a few are more or less abundant in certain places and during certain seasons—thereafter dying out almost completely for a longer or shorter spell of years—while four are merely occasional visitors from countries overseas. One of these four, the Monarch, as it is known in its American home, is probably the most adventurous butterfly in the world, having since 1870 or thereabouts extended its range from the Western to the Eastern Hemisphere by way of the Pacific Islands, making its first appearances in England during 1876, in which year three specimens were captured in Sussex, one at Poole in Dorset, and one at Neath in South Wales. Since this date it has turned up at intervals in such widely separated counties as Kent, Cornwall and Pembrokeshire, but has not yet occurred as far north as Scotland. When seen it is easy to identify. Its English name of " Black-veined Brown " describes fairly accurately its scheme of colouring, while its wing-expanse of fully 4½ inches secures for it the title of " the largest British butterfly ".

Most of our British butterflies have been " classified " by scientific naturalists into five groups called " families ". Using our common popular names, these are the tortoiseshells and peacocks,

BRITISH BUTTERFLIES

Painted Lady

Purple Emperor

Peacock

Common Blue

Small Copper

Marbled White

Swallow Tail

Orange Tip

Brimstone

Dark Green Fritillary

Red Admiral

the browns and ringlets, the hairstreaks and blues, the whites and yellows, and the skippers. Besides these there are two other families, represented by hundreds of species in the warmer regions of the globe, but by only one each in Britain, these being the handsome swallow-tail, seen most frequently in East Anglia, and the little Duke of Burgundy fritillary—which is not really a fritillary, though it looks like a small edition of its namesakes.

The family of the tortoiseshells and peacocks includes also the famous Purple Emperor, Painted Lady, Red and White Admirals, and Comma, as well as all the fritillaries large and small, and the handsome Camberwell Beauty—the last named being an occasional visitor from overseas which in some years appears in unexpected places and has always been regarded as a great rarity highly prized by collectors, who in the past have willingly paid pounds for authentic British-caught specimens when butterflies exactly similar in all other respects could be bought from Continental dealers for a few pence. The comma butterfly, whose colouring and appearance suggests a dingy and dilapidated small tortoiseshell, is nevertheless easily identified by the sickle-shaped white mark—resembling a " comma " as printed, or the letter " C "—in the middle of each hind-wing on the underside. Formerly common, this insect seemed gradually to grow scarcer during the last century, and eventually was seldom seen outside the counties flanking the English and Welsh borders. But of recent years it has been spreading steadily westward and southward again, and bids fair in the long run to re-establish itself in all its ancient haunts. The principal food-plants of its caterpillars are hop, stinging nettle, and red currant.

The family of the browns and ringlets gets its name from the prevailing colour of its members—brown in almost every conceivable shade—and from the fact that many of them, though not all, have dark, white-centred " eye-spots " on their wings, more especially on the underside. Well-known examples are the meadow brown, speckled wood, wall and grayling, all of which feed on grasses in the caterpillar stage of their existence. The mountain ringlet is a true alpine butterfly, which has been captured on grassy slopes as much as 3000 feet above sea-level. Its near relation, the so-called Scots Argus, ranges from York to Inverness, and has a special liking for rough, moorland country, but does not venture higher than 800 feet. Mention should also be made of the marbled white, which looks as if it should be classed with the family of " Whites ", but is actually an authentic

" Brown ". It occurs throughout England as far north as Durham, but is local, and seems to like best dry, broken ground, such as chalk or limestone hillsides, though it is sometimes found in less arid localities.

The hairstreaks and the blues, together with the small copper already referred to, make up a family of some sixteen members, several very rare or very local. The largest of the blues, for example, is seldom seen nowadays outside the south-western peninsula of England, and there only in one or two favoured areas on or near the coast. On the other hand, the common blue, as its name suggests, occurs almost everywhere in Great Britain as far north as the Orkneys, as well as in Ireland. The purple and the green hairstreaks, or " Theclas " as they used to be called, whose caterpillars feed respectively on oak and on bramble, broom, &c., are the most likely of their kind to be seen, the former in woodland glades, the latter on waste land or by the roadside where its food-plants grow. The females of the blue butterflies, by the way, are usually far less attractively coloured than the males, much of the wing area being brown.

The whites, as a family, number nine, including, besides the familiar examples seen everywhere during the summer months, the clouded yellows, the brimstone, the orange-tip, and the rare black-veined white; also the dainty little wood-white. The last named frequents coppices and spinneys where its food-plants (vetches and cow-wheats) grow; but it is by no means generally distributed, and does not occur at all farther north than Cumberland.

All eight members of the skipper family are thick-set, with a characteristic and rapid mode of flight. Several of them are plain tawny or brownish in colour, but the silver-spotted skipper is easy to recognize by its whitish, almost silvery markings, especially on the under surface of the hind-wings. The grizzled skipper (black, dappled with variously shaped white spots) and the dingy skipper (brown with numerous darker and lighter lines and spots) are both common throughout England and southern Scotland, the latter also occurring in south and west Ireland. Finally, the chequered skipper, whose wings are orange-spotted on an almost black ground, is a scarce butterfly, confined to a few restricted areas, mostly in the Midlands. The caterpillars of all these little butterflies may be found feeding on grasses or low-growing plants, such as the bird's-foot trefoil.

The families of British moths are too numerous to describe separately here. Mention has already been made of the hawk-moths —of which we have seventeen species, some common, others rare— and of the loopers or carpets, most of which rest with their wings spread out flat. This latter family is a large one, with its 270 odd species, but that of the owl-moths is even larger, comprising more than 300 British members. The majority are dull-coloured and fly at night, resting by day upon tree-trunks or fences, with which the tints of the fore-wings (which are folded over and so conceal the hind-wings) harmonize wonderfully, so that they are often very difficult to detect. This " protective resemblance ", as it is called, is especially remarkable when, as in the case of the red-underwings, the hind-wings are showily coloured. A fairly good type of the owl-moths in general is the well-known cabbage moth whose caterpillars are almost, if not quite, as much of a nuisance in our gardens as those of the white butterflies. This caterpillar has ten pro-legs, and burrows into the soil before changing to the pupa. But other caterpillars in this family have fewer legs and behave differently. That of the beautiful burnished-brass moth, for example, has what may be called a " semi-looper " gait, its pro-legs being reduced to three pairs; and when full grown it spins a cocoon of white silk among the leaves of its food-plant—the stinging nettle.

Only one more family of moths can be mentioned here, that comprising the puss, kittens, prominents and their relations. Many of their caterpillars have a most unusual appearance, a good example being that of the puss-moth, an excellent subject for the breeding-cage, which may be found throughout the British Islands, wherever its food-plants, willow and poplar, flourish. The coloration of this caterpillar when full-grown—purple-brown above and yellow-green below, with a white dividing line—is very striking; so, too, is the pair of whip-like tails at the tapering hinder end of its body. Tickle it gently with a grass-stem when it is quietly feeding or enjoying forty winks, and it will turn its head quickly and make an ugly face at you! If you don't believe this—why, you had better try the experiment and see for yourself!

MUSHROOMS AND TOADSTOOLS

Have you ever had the thrill of searching for mushrooms in a meadow at five o'clock in the morning when the dew is still wet on the grass and the whole countryside hardly awake? The thrill comes, I suppose, partly from the fact that five o'clock in the morning is rather an unusual hour for most of us to be up and partly because there is an element of the treasure hunt about searching for the white satiny buttons and umbrellas amongst the meadow grasses.

When the word " fungus " (or " fungi " in the plural) is mentioned, most people think of mushrooms and toadstools, but there are dozens of other kinds. Yeast, which is used for making bread rise, is a fungus, and so is the mould on cheese or the mildew on football boots left uncared for between seasons. The black spots on sycamore leaves in early autumn or the red " rust " on groundsel or willow in summer, the " smut " which attacks corn, or the minute plant which aids the ripening of tobacco, all are fungi.

Fungi are colourless plants in the sense that they do not possess chlorophyll, the green colouring matter of leaves and flowering plants. Lack of this means that they cannot be independent plants manufacturing their own food from simple substances with the help of sunlight. They have to get their food second-hand, and so must live on a living host or on the remains of an animal or plant or their products.

Autumn is the best time to hunt for the larger fungi, though some can be found all through the year and a few at an earlier season only. There are many interesting ones in the fields and woods in early autumn, and once bracken and dry grass begin to die down they are easier to see. They grow in all sorts of places, often in profusion. In a wood against the background of dead leaves and under the shade of tree-trunks their colours show up vividly. Although technically colourless plants through not possessing chlorophyll, many fungi are brightly coloured, golden yellow, blue or red or pink. Incidentally, they are of great service in helping to destroy dead bodies of animals and plants and restoring certain chemicals to the soil in the process.

In a meadow there may be Puff-balls, interesting fungi which when mature or accidentally crushed, burst and shed a brownish powder like a puff of smoke. Actually this brown powder consists of millions of minute specks of life called spores, each spore being capable of growing into another fungus plant if conditions are favourable. Some Puff-balls contain as many as seven billion spores, but, of course, very few of them actually grow into new plants. Otherwise the countryside would be just one mass of Puff-balls.

On the edge of the meadow or just outside a wood you may come across a curious toadstool in the grass, the Parasol Mushroom, which has a white top checked with brown and tapering to a point like the " nub " of an umbrella, while its stalk looks like the handle; and it has a frill just like a sunshade's. Underneath the umbrella part there are white " ribs " called gills, where the spores are made. In the Puff-ball the spores are in a bag, but in the Parasol Mushroom they are produced at the edge of a gill and shed into the gill-spaces and distributed when they open.

There is a third way of releasing the spores from a toadstool-type of fungus—from pores. This is exemplified by a fungus which grows on the edge of a wood just under the shade of the overhanging trees, called Edible Boletus. It is easy to recognize because it looks almost exactly like a brown penny bun lying in the grass, for its stalk is stout and short, and the rounded part of the fungus touches the ground. From underneath, this fungus looks like a green sponge, the holes of the sponge being the pores from which the spores are released when they are mature. As the name implies, this fungus is edible, but it is unwise to gather fungi to eat unless you are absolutely certain that the type *is* edible, and if in doubt always leave them alone.

Many people think there is only one fungus you can eat—the mushroom—but actually there are dozens of varieties which are edible. The common edible mushroom is found in meadows grazed by cattle, occurring in the patches of dark-green grass so often found there. There are usually two crops, one in June and a second in August and September if the weather is favourable. The mushroom first appears as a " button " amongst the grass. The rounded part visible is the pure white glistening satiny cap or pileus. If pulled up at this stage the cap and stem together have the appearance of a peg-top. The part of the mushroom appearing above ground is the fruiting body, the rest of the plant being underground. As growth continues the cap becomes flat. Running from the top of the short white stem to the outer margin of the cap are the plate-like gills. In the " button " these are white, but at the stage when the mushroom is usually picked they are a delicate pink. As the purplish spores ripen and are discharged the gills take on a dark-brown and finally black appearance.

The pellicle or skin of the mushroom cap projects slightly beyond the margin and serves to protect the gills during development. A partial veil connects the edges of the cap with the stalk, and is torn apart when the cap expands and flattens, leaving around the stem a frill or ring.

There is one fungus, the lovely Scarlet Flycap or Scarlet Agaric, which is deadly poisonous. It grows in the birch woods, and may be found near the foot of the trees in autumn. The Flycap is so called because people used to make an insect poison from it. It is a tall handsome fungus with a white stalk and a red cap spotted with white. This is the fungus of our Nursery books, on which elves and pixies love to sit. It is certainly very attractive to look at, but that is as much as you should do. By all means look at fungi, possibly gather them, though it is extremely difficult to preserve them as specimens, but do not eat them. As a matter of fact it is more interesting to know *where* to find different fungi than to attempt to gather and preserve them.

A good place to search for larger kinds is on an old tree-stump. Often a stump will bear several different varieties and the stumps of different trees will bear different ones. For example, old beech stumps often bear groups of the Beech Tuft fungus, which grow up in groups and are a silvery white all over, smooth and glistening like a mature beech trunk. Another kind grows on beech stumps, and on ash too, the Wood Oyster, so called because it looks like a collection of oyster shells. Its top is flat and greyish-brown with white wavy lines running round it, but from underneath it looks more like a handleless umbrella blown inside out with all the ribs showing. These ribs or gills are white and contrast with the greyness of the upper surface. Groups of Wood Oyster fungus look like a lot of funnels or inverted triangles growing out of one another.

Look on elder wood, either dead or alive, to find a queer fungus, called the Jew's Ear fungus, because an old legend states that Judas Iscariot hanged himself on an elder tree, and the lobed and crinkled shape of the fungus and its texture is very like that of a brown fleshy human ear sticking out of the bark. It has a dusting of a grey powder which adds to the effect.

Another interesting fungus found in meadows is the Ink-cap fungus. The stem is often eight or nine inches high and the cap four inches across. Underneath the cap are the gills from which the thousands of black spores are produced. The edge of the cap is very ragged. A peculiar feature is that the cap and gills undergo self-digestion, with the result that the cap begins to change into a

| Mushroom | Fairy Ring Champignon | Scarlet Flycap |

runny black inky-looking liquid. This happens first at the edges, which roll back as the process advances, and so the black spores are shed without hindrance.

The Fairy Ring Champignon, a common fungus of pasture land, sometimes causes the appearance of a " fairy ring " on a lawn. It is buff-coloured, with a flattened cap, which, however, has a central prominence rather like a Chinese coolie's hat. Fairy rings—those green rings often seen in meadows—are the result of a cycle of events. The body of a fungus of the toadstool type is underground; the parts above ground are merely to produce the spores. Fungi tend to spread in circles growing from the centre of dissemination. As a fungus grows, it utilizes certain " food " materials in the soil and produces its own waste products, which kill the grass, leaving a brown area. At its margin the fungus releases certain chemicals, which are changed into nitrates which stimulate the growth of the grass, making it both luxuriant and green. This causes the deep-green fairy ring which really represents the margin of the advancing fungus. Often there is a brownish ring just inside the green ring because so much fungus material is present that drainage is temporarily interfered with and the grass killed. Later, as the dead fungus-remains near the centre of the circle decay, the grass in that area becomes stimulated.

Another fungus, found in meadows though a related form lives on the edge of a wood, is Blue Leg or Blewits. It is edible and has a greyish or lilac-tinged cap which is smooth and shining. The somewhat wavy margin of the cap overhangs the gills, which are themselves very well-marked and rather like the pages of a book. This fungus has rather a pleasant smell—unlike so many of the others which may smell of garlic, rotten fish or camphor. In the Midlands Blewits are gathered and sold in the markets as a breakfast delicacy.

Sometimes on a tree-trunk you will find what appear to be small shelves of a hard rubbery substance. These are bracket fungi. They look just like brackets or small corner shelves sticking out from the trunk. One of them is a Polyporus fungus, often to be found on an old dead birch tree. Its spore cavities are long narrow tubes closely crowded together so that the open ends all occupy the fertile surface of the fruiting body which is the under-surface of the bracket fungus. One of the Polyporus family is the Beefsteak fungus, an edible form growing on old oak trunks.

In the Middle Ages people were afraid of toads and held them to be bewitched because they were found in damp dark places—the very places where so many fungi grow. Hence the association of some of the larger fungi with toads.

Remember, though, that these large fruiting bodies which we call by the general name of mushrooms and toadstools are only one general type of a huge family of colourless plants which have considerable economic importance. One fungus makes it possible for linen threads to be prepared from flax, another assists the making of leather, and one causes the souring of milk so that milk cheese can be made. On the other hand, also remember that one is responsible for dry rot in timber, causing thousands of pounds worth of damage each year, and another may completely destroy a cabbage crop.

MYSTERY LIVES OF SALMON AND EELS

Just as the lion is said to be the King of Beasts, so the salmon has always been regarded as the King of Fish—not only because of its beauty of form, colour and grace, but also because it so often reveals a brave determination in following its destined way of life and a haughty disdain for all obstacles in its path, qualities which seem to many of us to be those of the noblest human beings. It has also been called a royal fish because of the excellence of its delicate pink flesh which, in ancient times, was reserved for the tables of the highest in the land.

How different is this graceful fish in its glittering silver and royal-blue coat from that wriggling, snaky-looking creature, the eel, with its dull greenish-brown, slimy, almost finless body, squirming like an " out-size " worm when touched, and almost entirely devoid of beauty!

Yet these two water creatures, the beautiful salmon and the ugly squirming eel, are bracketed together as the most wonderful and mysterious of British water folk—wonderful because of the complicated lives they live, and mysterious because scientists and naturalists have never yet been able to solve the reasons why they both do the things they do.

To those of us who have seen the salmon only in its adult form, it is wonderful to think that it began life in a tiny jelly-like egg. This egg is deposited with thousands of other similar ones—often as many as from 16,000 to 17,000, should the mother salmon weigh as much as 18 to 20 pounds—in the shallow gravelly bed of a river, perhaps in Scotland (though salmon are found in many parts of the world and are particularly plentiful in Canadian rivers); and this event usually takes place in the middle of the winter. Here the eggs lie in a deep hollow made by the mother fish to form a safe nursery-bed for them; and for extra safety, she partly covers them over with pebbly gravel. She never even looks at them again, since, very soon afterwards, she leaves the district and makes her way to the sea with her mate.

A good many of these minute eggs float away down the stream, and are eagerly snapped up by the fry of other fishes. As they are slightly gummy, however, many thousands remain " put "; and there they stay for about three to four months, slowly developing in the icy-cold water. Then, when the right time comes, the baby salmon issue forth from their jelly-egg nurseries; and so minute are they that they can scarcely be seen by the naked eye. Nor are they the least bit like any kind of fish, though they now have a definite head and something that presently begins to look like an almost transparent body and tail; but these are attached to a bag bigger than themselves, which is filled with a kind of yolk-food, upon which they immediately begin to feed. They cannot be said to feed in the usual sense of the word; but the contents of these fishy " nose-bags " are gradually absorbed into their tiny bodies, thus providing them with all the nourishment they require, so that they become less transparent and more solid-looking from day to day. They are now known as " alevins ".

At the end of a month or so, the yolk-bags have entirely vanished and the alevins have actually become tiny fishlets nearly an inch long. They are now described as " samlets ", or " salmon fry ", and are able to feed themselves upon the minute larvæ of tiny insects. Many of them, in their turn, are snapped up by bigger fishes, who find them very tasty titbits. However, there are still many thousands of them left who have been lucky enough to escape being swallowed; and these go on growing until, in the early autumn, they may be about three inches long. They grow very slowly indeed; and it is not until their first winter has passed that they reach a length of four to six inches. By that time, however, they are quite sturdy little fishes, and have the true graceful salmon shape, showing a regular pattern of dark " finger-marks " on either side of the top part of their bodies.

The young fry in their second year are now known as " parr ". They still provide very tempting food for larger fishes, who chase them ruthlessly; but those who escape and pass safely through another winter, when seen again in the following spring, are about eight to ten inches long and are spoken of as " smolts ". These young fish, with glittering silvery scales, are strong, lively, and already beautiful.

It is at this period of its young life that a very strange thing happens to the salmon-smolt. For some mysterious reason or other, it is no longer satisfied to remain in its pleasant home river, along with all the other river fish it has always known; instead, it develops a great desire to travel—to get down to the sea, though it has no knowledge of such a big watery world. This strange desire which so suddenly seizes it is a real mystery which has not yet been solved.

In company with many thousands of other salmon-smolts, it

Two alevins and a parr   Head of a cock salmon
(life size)   (The hand shows actual size)

begins to make its long journey down to the sea. The travellers meet with many dangers on the way, and thousands of them fall victims to bigger fishes, to herons and other large river-dwelling birds, and, later on, as they reach the estuaries, to gulls. Finally, on entering the sea proper, they meet with real monsters for the first time. Those who manage to escape from all dangers remain in the deeper waters for a varying number of months, during which time they continue to grow, and are later known as " grilse ". Then they may be regarded as half grown. The time taken for a young salmon to reach this stage, however, varies very much indeed, as do the various other stages mentioned above, some members of the family developing much quicker than others—again for some unknown mysterious reason.

Another strange thing is the fact that all salmon return to their home rivers to lay their eggs—or to spawn, as this proceeding is more correctly called. By some equally strange and mysterious instinct, they must realize, or sense, that their eggs will not develop into living fish in salt water, and that they must go back to their river birthplaces to lay their precious eggs in fresh water.

Sometimes they set forth in the grilse stage; sometimes they wait until they have attained to their last stage as fully-matured salmon. In either case, the journey of the salmon from the sea to the river spawning-grounds is one of the great wonders of Nature. They come up from the sea in their thousands, mostly full-grown beautiful salmon, all now clad in their kingly attire of silver and royal blue, and enter the river mouths filled with one idea—to reach their spawning-grounds with the least possible delay. Nothing must stand in their way; and no obstacle is regarded by them as too great for them to overcome. Up, up, and ever onward they go, a seething mass of silver and blue, swarming over one another, and leaping upwards, high over the rocks, with the utmost ease. They take the most tremendous leaps over the rapids and falls they encounter, often springing out of the water a distance of ten to fifteen feet or more, and continuing to swim along at an astonishing speed of about thirty miles an hour. Sometimes they come in such swarming multitudes that great numbers are pushed out on to the banks, where they often fall victims to otters and other fish-eating creatures.

On this most amazing journey from the sea to the rivers, the salmon never stop once to feed; and one of the greatest mysteries about them is the fact that they are able, at this particular period in their lives, to exist for so long without food. When salmon are fished for at this time, no trace of fresh food is ever found in their stomachs.

When they finally reach their breeding-ground, the females choose their nursery sites and proceed to lay their millions of tiny eggs, the males duly fertilizing these. Afterwards, the whole tribe returns again to the sea, there to remain until the next breeding season comes round in a year's time. Some salmon visit the breeding-grounds once only during their lives; others visit them two or even three times, and then spend the remainder of their existence in the sea. A curious point about the male salmon is that at the actual spawning time he develops a great hook in his lower jaw; and when the breeding-season is over, the jaw returns to its usual shape. Also at this time, after making the journey from the sea in bright colours, he now takes on a dull and rather ugly reddish colour. The female likewise changes in appearance while actually laying her eggs, looking blackish and lumpy. On returning once more to the sea, however, both sexes quickly regain their pristine beauty and regal looks.

The life-story of the Common European Eel is equally remarkable. Eels reverse the order of the salmon's curious wanderings, since they begin life in the middle of the ocean, then work their way across the top of the sea to the various rivers, lakes, ponds, and even ditches, where they spend from three to eight years growing and feeding, wandering from place to place; then they go all the way back to mid-ocean once more, where, after spawning, they die. Unlike the salmon, they never lay their eggs anywhere else than in the sea, sensing that their offspring will not develop except in salt water—yet they have this mysterious urge to spend the main part of their lives in fresh water, where they often encounter considerable trouble and inconvenience.

Nothing is yet known about the eggs of the Common Eel, nor even whether it actually lays eggs, though this is, of course, presumed to be the case. Nobody has ever seen them. Here, then, is the first mystery about this queer creature.

What is more, the very first stage in which they have ever been seen does not give the impression that such strange objects could ever become the snaky fishes we know as eels. They seem to be merely minute, leaf-like, flat, transparent creatures, looking at first glance as though made of the finest glass. These tiny objects, however, go through no less than eight stages of growth, emerging from each stage looking less transparent and leaf-like, and they develop cylinder-shaped narrow bodies which become rounder as they grow. After about three years of slow growth have passed, all their transparent leaf-like parts have been gradually absorbed into their now worm-like bodies, and they are practically little eels, about three inches long—in which stage they are known as " Glass Eels " or " Elvers ". They already have tremendous appetites, and eat all the small fry that come their way; and these big appetites they keep for the whole of their lives, eels being among the most voracious of fish.

Long before this time, however, when they were but a few months old, the tiny leaf-like creatures had already experienced that strange mysterious urge to make their way to the fresh waters where they are destined to spend their lives; and, helpless though they appeared to be, they began their long journey from the bottom depths of the Atlantic Ocean to the rivers of Europe. Gradually they rose nearly to the surface of the water and allowed themselves to be swept along by the strong currents; and by the time they reached the estuaries, three full years had elapsed, they had covered round about 3000 miles, and had slowly developed into their early elver stage, from which they gradually grew into true elvers.

The young eels by this time have their curiously snake-like forms, and are of a dull olive-green colour; and they also have the sharply pointed snake-like head and slightly flattened ribbon-like tails of the adult eel, although still merely a few inches long. By the time they are ready to begin their amazing journeys up the rivers—fairly soon after arriving in the estuaries—they have also become equipped for taking short spells on land. Their gills are now capable of storing up water or moisture in an inner chamber developed for the purpose, so that, if necessary, they can remain out of water for some considerable time.

In vast hordes the now well-developed and ever-growing elvers make their journeys up the rivers, streams, and canals, overcoming all obstacles in their path. Though they do not leap like the salmon, they can wriggle their sinuous bodies up high rocks and boulders; and at times, if stone or brickwork impedes their progress, they leave the water and travel overland until they reach another and more convenient waterway. They devour large numbers of frogs and larvæ, worms, snails, crayfish, and other river molluscs to satisfy their ever-increasing appetites. As they grow longer and more active, they devour any small fish that comes in their way; soon they become as much the terror of the streams and rivers as are the savage pike—though they themselves try to avoid the latter if they possibly can.

Having made their way up the rivers for many miles, they often go overland from choice and settle themselves in lakes, ponds, and even muddy ditches for a change; and here they remain until the supply of food round about gives out, or their chosen home pond or ditch happens to dry up. It is then no trouble for them to return to the river and continue their travels by water.

During the winter, the young eels usually bury themselves deeply into the mud at the bottom of ponds, lakes and ditches, where they rest safely in a half-dormant state; but in the spring they issue forth once more, all as hungry as hunters.

As the years go on, the eels increase in size slowly, and they practically never cease to grow. The older they are, the longer and thicker they become. The female eel is always about twice the size of the male, and by far the more energetic and adventurous of the two. The largest male eel seldom measures more than three feet in length, whereas the female may attain to a growth of any-

Infant eels and elver (life size)   Grown eel chasing a frog

thing from five to seven feet long, or more, and to a good thickness in proportion.

Male eels seldom journey farther than the estuaries of rivers, preferring to remain where food is always plentiful without needing to work too hard to find it. Therefore, it is usually the more adventurous female who is found forging ahead up the pleasant higher river reaches between interesting banks with overhanging drooping tree branches. Here are the thrilling haunts of water-voles and kingfishers, whose burrows the lady eel can explore in her earlier and more slender years, her pointed, dart-shaped snout being exactly right for such " snooping " tactics. The reason she is able to slither into bank-side burrows with such ease is that her skin is always slimy, there being numerous slime glands or pockets connected with it.

Unlike other fish, too, it has no outward scales, the latter being extremely minute and cunningly embedded in the skin. Hence the expression " as slippery as an eel ".

The eel's overground travels generally take place at night or in the early dawn hours, when there is likely to be some slight moisture about, even during a drought—though land journeys are also sometimes made in the day-time by these extraordinary creatures; and it is owing to this semi-amphibious quality that eels are so frequently found in mountain-top lakes, in reservoirs, and moorland ponds and streamlets.

Finding a pond during these amazing land journeys, eels will eagerly snatch a duckling from it at dawn. They have even been known to visit a hen-run and take a chick or an egg or two from it—finding it easy enough to squeeze their slimy elastic bodies through coarse wire-netting or to burrow under any muddy patches.

After spending several years—the time varies from six to ten or more years—in idle wanderings and constant feeding, eels suddenly seem to pull themselves up sharply and to feel an impelling urge to return to the sea and produce a family. First of all they dress for this most important occasion. They have already changed their garb twice—the first time being when they completed their development from their transparent baby clothes into the olive-green skin covering their new form as tiny elvers; the second change of colour occurring on their reaching fully developed eel status, when their slimy skins became of a deep olive-brown tint.

On first feeling the urge to return to the sea and mate, the eels indulge in a wonderful transformation. All their dull browny-green tints vanish as they develop a dazzling coat of a bright silvery metallic sheen; and for the first time in their lives they are almost beautiful—at least, as regards their colouring, though they likewise seem to be more graceful still in their movements. At this time, too, they are more often to be seen practically " standing-up " in the water in a vertical position, resting their entire weight upon their flattened tail-tips, like long highly polished silvery candles, and swinging backwards and forwards in quite an elegant manner.

Being thus arrayed smartly in their " wedding garments ", the eels now set forth upon their return journey to the middle of the ocean—thousands upon thousands of them hurrying, scurrying and slithering over one another in their sudden eagerness to reach their birthplace once more; and on reaching the estuaries, they are joined by their waiting mates. Many members of this vast wedding party never reach the ocean depths at all, since their dazzling bridal attire renders them an easy mark for birds and larger fishes. Nevertheless, though thousands may perish on the way, many luckier thousands manage to reach the ocean breeding-grounds; and here it is presumed that the females deposit their eggs. All kinds of " old wives' tales " have been told to account for the actual beginnings of eels. They were said to be formed from the mud and dew; to issue forth from the bodies of dead eels; to have glided from hollow straws; to have developed from horses' dropped hairs; to have issued forth from other fishes' gills, or from water-beetles; and, in ancient times, country folk actually believed these absurd tales. So far, however, the strange transparent leaf-like larvæ described above is the earliest form of the eel yet definitely known to science—though the mystery is being still pursued by eager research workers.

Unlike the salmon, eels never again visit the rivers in which they have lived for so many years; and soon after their return to the sea, having mated and laid their eggs, they seem to lose all interest in living any longer, and so just tamely die.

There are, by the way, two varieties of the Common Eel: the European—which has been described—and the American. Both begin life in mid-ocean, but on their journey to fresh water, when they reach the neighbourhood of Bermuda, a sudden separation takes place. The European variety continues onwards towards the east, and the Americans make their way to the west, both seeming to know instinctively in which direction to go—another wonderful mystery! They both develop in very much the same way, and live similar lives. It has been discovered, however, that the American eels develop much more quickly than do their European cousins, which perhaps seems only proper and to be expected of inhabitants of the waters around this newer, go-ahead country!

There are several other species of eels which spend all their lives in the ocean and are sea-folk only; but, though some of these creatures are very wonderful, surely they cannot be any *more* wonderful or mysterious in their ways than our well-known friends the Common Eel and the Kingly Salmon!

STORIES IN STONE

A CHAT ABOUT FOSSILS

Most fossils are plant and animal remains, dating back from a few thousand years up to many, many millions of years ago. The rocks of England are full of them, the rocks of Scotland less so; they are also abundant in Wales (but only in certain places), and others occur all over the world. As different types of creatures lived at different periods, and those belonging to the same period in different countries are often more or less similar to one another, they enable geologists to date the order in which the rocks were laid down.

This is important to coal-miners and oil prospectors, to whom the characteristic fossils indicate the presence or otherwise of the rocks they are seeking. Fossils also have a tremendous value in the eyes of naturalists, because they carry back the story of living things to a date so remote that the untrained man cannot appreciate it; merely saying that it was many hundreds of millions of years ago means nothing to him.

Let us go to one of the fossil cemeteries of our land, say to the long line of great triangular cliffs in Dorset, grey in the west and yellow in the east, which runs from Lyme Regis to Bridport Harbour. If we step on the rocks east of Lyme, at low tide, we shall see a platform on which are dozens of coiled flat spirals like shell-fish, but twelve or more inches across; and on the rocks we may find smaller ones, which have a shelly coating that comes away in our fingers. Some of these rocks are black and in paper-thin layers, like a stone book. We gently break them apart and find on the leaves impressions of other spiral shells crushed flat. At another place, we may notice similar objects, but much smaller, only a quarter of an inch or so across; they glisten like gold, being coated with iron pyrites. Looking up, we see the ledges of the high Church Cliffs above us; and on gripping the underside of a ledge to steady ourselves, we feel it rough; we break a piece off, and lo! it is covered with unmistakable blackish-grey shells, not unlike some ancient oysters. They *are* ancient oysters. What does all this mean? How did these things, if they were once alive, become stone? And how are they now found, buried under a thickness of hundreds of feet of rocks?

It means just what it appears to mean, incredible though that may seem. The large, coiled flat spiral objects are molluscs of a kind, but not ordinary ones. They are called ammonites. They were distantly related to the pearly nautilus, which now swims in warm eastern seas, and still more distantly related to cuttlefish. At the mouth of the shell were the animal's tentacles, which, of course, perished when the creature died.

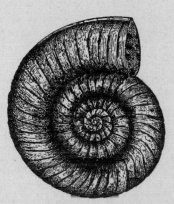

An Ammonite

The shell itself lay buried in grey-black ooze. Subsequently fresh layers of mud covered it; and as the sea-floor sank beneath them they in turn were covered by other layers. Thus every ledge that we can see on that great cliff was in turn part of the sea-bed; for on every ledge can be found some traces of marine life.

The whole assemblage of similar rocks comprises a geological formation; it is to geology what a great king's reign or a brief dynasty is to history, in that it acts as a time-marker, and, of course, it has a particular name. The rocks of Lyme Regis are called the Lias; they were laid down on the sea-floor perhaps 40 or 60 million years ago, and are one of the most important fossil graveyards in the world. The ammonites, which lived in the sea for millions of years, have a special interest, because one finds the same species in places far apart; and as each species has, on the whole, only a very short vertical range, they serve admirably to date that particular rock in different countries.

Now, as to the oysters. You can find them on the underside of these cliffs in hundreds; they are known as Gryphæa and were oysters of an ancient pattern which lived on the same sea-bed.

But there are far more interesting things to be found here, by those who will look diligently for them; and in that connexion, you might like to recall that it was a child of eleven, named

Mary Anning, who found the first fossil sea dragon at Lyme Regis.

If one takes a walk along the cliff, or at its foot, towards Charmouth and Golden Cap, one may find much larger ammonites, even up to two feet across, on which are the shelly remains of other animals; thus, when the creature had died, other life floating about in the sea settled down on the empty shell and grew there. Hence, the bottom of the old sea must have been fairly quiet and calm. Many marine animals live on others to-day: look at a lobster shell, which generally houses seaweeds, small marine worms, tunicates, and other growths—until the lobster, by moulting, gets rid of the lot!

In our search we shall find quite a number of more ordinary shells, ancestors of types still dwelling in the sea to-day; but in addition there are some things, obviously not natural rocks, which are very puzzling at first sight. Many of these resemble fat pencils, pointed at one end, black, and with radiating lines at the other. These are the hard skeletons which once supported the soft body of an ancient squid-like creature, called a belemnite. The modern squid, as you may know, has an ink-bag, and when attacked ejects the fluid into the water, so that it may escape behind the murky cloud. The ancient belemnite did the same, for its ink-bags have sometimes been found fossil, and their ink was capable of being written with.

There are other objects, not unlike these, but shorter and fatter, just like teeth in fact. Teeth they are. They belonged to a terrible monster which dwelt in the Lias sea. It was called Ichthyosaurus, or Fish-lizard ("saurus" simply means "lizard"). Ichthyosaurus was the lord of the ocean in those times. It had a long, stoutish body, four immensely strong limbs which worked like paddles, and the usual long, slender tail and neck of the ancient "dragons". It dwelt well out in the sea. Its snout was prolonged into a terrible sword, stronger by far than a modern swordfish's; and with this weapon it could probably kill any opponent. As its conical teeth, as big as our fingers, prove beyond doubt, it was a flesh-eater. From time to time complete skeletons of Ichthyosaurus are found in the Lias rocks, but scattered bones are more common. Sometimes, when the monster had died, and its flesh had decomposed, and the skeleton was slowly sinking in the mud, ammonites would descend upon it, there to be buried in turn; and you may see many of them, in such a skeleton now, on the wall of the Natural History Museum, South Kensington.

If one searches certain ledges on the high cliff of Golden Cap east of Charmouth, one may find remains of lobster-like shell-fish, and numerous petrified bodies of unmistakable starfish, among many other things. All these creatures lived and died in the Lias sea. As the rocks of that sea stretch right across England in an almost straight line to Whitby, one may find some of them—usually ammonites—in the heart of the land. This seems to call for a little explanation, for everyone except the trained geologist is puzzled by the occurrence of marine fossils that are buried in hard rocks in the centre of the country.

If we sink a bore-hole, or descend a pit in the earth, the temperature rises, at such a rate that somewhere about 50 to 100 miles down all the rocks known to man must be in a molten state. The solid crust of the earth everywhere rests on this liquid base. The pressure from within outwards balances that from above inwards, on the whole, but not quite. At most places where large rivers pour into the sea it is certain that the delta lands are sinking, and it is the fact of their sinking which in some instances has determined the course that the river takes to its mouth. Now, every river carries down an enormous volume of mud and sand, and this is laid down year after year, bed above bed, the floor sinking just about as much as the thickness of new matter laid on it, so that, on the whole, the depth of water is fairly constant. This may continue for many thousands of years; then the upward pressure begins to make itself felt and a reversal of the process takes place; this, of course, brings the delta above sea-level, when immediately the natural agents of destruction (winds, waves and rivers, frost, and so forth) begin to carve into the flattish, newly-exposed land.

But if the rise should continue (as has often occurred) for scores of thousands of years, while the rivers are all the time eating into the land and the waves trying to cut cliffs along its edges, then necessarily there develops a hilly land, just as you will find in many parts of the world to-day. All the plant and animal remains that were buried formerly in the old delta are now high and dry, and exposed to the eye in river cuts or quarries, or upon the seashore.

That, in a nutshell, is what has been happening to many parts of the earth for ages, and not solely in deltas, either. The movement, though very slow, has been measured in the Baltic, on the Atlantic coast of America, and in the Mediterranean Sea, among other places. It may amount to several inches in a century, which, slow though it may seem by human standards, is quite fast by those of Nature.

Let us keep along the Channel coast to the fine sandy cliffs of Bournemouth. We shall find there many fossils of a quite different kind; they are largely protected now, but similar ones may be gathered in the white pipe-clays of Alum Bay nearly opposite, in the Isle of Wight. These are the impressions of plants—beautiful leaves of many tropical species, including large fan palms and many other species indicating a climate more like that of India than our own.

A little farther along, on the shores of the Solent, are literally multitudes of snail-like shells, trumpet shells, elongated auger-like shells, bivalves of many kinds, all or nearly all white and bleached, and all belonging to warm-water estuarine species now extinct, but often belonging to families found in such places to-day. These,

Tiny shells (Foraminifera) from a piece of chalk (much magnified)

though still millions of years old, are very much younger than the ammonites of the Lias Clay. They are called Eocene (" Dawn of the Recent ") because in that age creatures lived which first foreshadowed modern types. When we hold the fragile things in our hands, and note on the volute shells the beautiful markings and undamaged spikes and points, it seems incredible that they could have existed long before the Alps or Himalaya rose from the sea; yet such is the case. It is proven by the fact that certain large foraminifera (some species of which form part of the scum that you may notice at the line of high tide on sandy beaches), which are younger than these shells, have got themselves entombed in rocks that now stand 11,000 feet up in the Pyrenees and 19,000 feet up in the Himalaya.

Let us now go back to the other side of Bournemouth, to where the Old Harry rocks stand sentinel before Swanage Bay; or, if you like, cross to the Isle of Wight and wander round bold Culver Cliff near Sandown. These points, of course, are chalk, and the Chalk, one of the great natural time-markers of geology, forms long lines of bold hills in southern and S.E. England, the North and South Downs, Chiltern Hills, and the Lincolnshire and Yorkshire Wolds.

The Chalk, too, is full of fossils, but being themselves white or lemon-coloured, they need some looking for. If we take a little chalk from a quarry ledge or a weathered part of the cliff, shake it repeatedly in a bottle and gently break up the lumps, washing off the limy grains which form the larger part of it, the residue may show us something interesting. Put this residue beneath a microscope, and, sure enough, there are some shell-like bodies, besides spines of sea-urchins and occasional fragments of shell. The shell-like bodies belong to foraminifera, organisms which for the most part do not exceed one-tenth of an inch in diameter. They are very primitive indeed, little more highly organized than the slimy Amœba; but they have learned to build themselves some extraordinarily beautiful and complicated shelly homes, and it is the latter which are preserved fossil in countless multitudes.

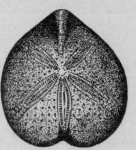

Sea-egg or Echinoderm
(from the chalk)

Here is another curious thing. The commonest Chalk species is called Globigerina; it can only be distinguished by experts from the modern Globigerina which lives, also in countless multitudes, in the clear blue water of warm and tropical seas over much of the world. This can only mean that much of the Chalk was formed by the slow descent through that ancient ocean of an incessant rain of dead Globigerinæ and other surface-loving foraminifera; and, as the Chalk is many hundreds of feet thick, that will give you some idea of the enormous time involved.

Here is another instance. At many a place in the Chalk one may find an egg-shaped or potato-shaped body in a hard, lemony rind, which sparkles when rubbed, like crystalline limestone. Clean such an object and you will find it to have a five-starred radiate pattern on its two or three inches of length; while at one end may be a hole, and underneath is an overhanging letter-box-like opening. This object is a sea-egg, sea-urchin or echinoderm. It was an ancestor of the common sea-urchins which live off our coasts (and elsewhere) to-day. The little pimples on its surface, to which it owes its name (echinoderm means " urchin-skinned ", and an " urchin " in that sense is a pimple), are the joints on which the creature's defensive spines once rested. If we are lucky, we may find a few spines in the Chalk alongside the body; but this is not too common. The five-starred pattern, with its characteristic holes, leads to the animal's mouth. It was through these holes that the creature moved little limblets, or rather processes, which caused tiny currents of water to drive down to its mouth, thus conveying thither the even smaller objects upon which the sea-urchin lived.

But here is something much more marvellous. Covering the edge of the food-groove, and also on the spine-joint, are unmistakable spirals of minute worms, just like those one sees on a lobster's claw; but, in this case, the spine must have fallen off, and the animal been dead, before they took up their abode there. They in turn died and one of them is covered by a bit of limy seaweed-like growth, which turns out (under our magnifying-glass) to be an exquisitely beautiful little chain-like thing, just like the furry growths seen on seaweeds to-day. It is known as a bryozoan or moss animal; and in each of its little cups a polypite once lived, thrusting out a circlet of tentacles into the water. Thus the sea-egg lived and died on the sea-bottom; and then the Spirorbis or Serpula (the worm) took up its home on the empty shell; and then it in turn was covered by the moss animal; and then the slow rain of organisms from above, together with the quiet drifting of mud along the bottom, covered the whole and preserved them for ever.

The Chalk, by the way, is intermediate between the Lias rocks and the Eocene sandy beds of Bournemouth.

We have seen now that fossils can be preserved in many ways. They may be simply buried by the mud, sand or ooze, in a sea, a lake, or a river, and so sealed up, as it were, for future generations to discover; or they may, like the leaves, be pressed down on the mud so as to leave impressions only of themselves, the plant matter decaying completely; or they may be transformed into metal images of themselves, as with the iron-pyrites specimens mentioned at Lyme Regis. Sometimes the shell is preserved unaltered; but in old rocks, as a rule, it has undergone a change, the shell being dissolved particle by particle and simultaneously replaced by some other (usually harder or siliceous) matter. The animal parts inside are in most cases quite destroyed; but by the markings on the inside of bivalve shells a great deal can be deduced about the mollusc itself.

The most remarkable instance of replacement by silica is in pieces of fossil wood, which are so like the original that the genera can be made out by grinding fine microscopic sections; and yet the whole thing is nothing but stone. Such are the trees of the famous Petrified Forest of Arizona, where whole trunks have been preserved, from a date prior to the Lias sea. A large piece of one of these trees, several feet high and also across, is to be seen at South Kensington; its interior is a mass of beautiful colours, like a mosaic; but it still retains the organic structure. In other fossil trees only the outer coat remains identifiable, the inside being a core of sandstone; such are the large trunks, twenty to forty feet long, which are often uncovered by coal-miners, and much dreaded by them, because in falling they tend to bring down the roof of the mine.

It has often happened in the past that animals have become bogged, and, after struggling vainly to get out of the mud, have slipped farther into it, to die and be covered there. Such was certainly the fate of many Mammoths, cousins of the elephant, but larger, with huge and frequently incurving tusks, which wandered about the grass lands during much of the Great Ice Age. The Mammoth was covered with long, coarse, dark-brown hair. It seems to have ventured upon treacherous, perhaps half-frozen ground in search of food, especially in Siberia; then it got bogged and perished, afterwards being sealed up in the frozen subsoil. More than one has been disinterred since, in which the flesh was so well preserved that dogs ate it. Another curious collection of Mammoth remains was found, many years ago, in Hungary, where a primitive race of men dwelt about 12,000 to 14,000 years ago. These men hunted the Mammoth, and at one spot left the bones and teeth of more than 500 individuals, a real elephant cemetery!

A very curious fossil bed, also relatively modern by geological reckoning, has been found at Rancho La Brea, in California, where a deposit of soft and very treacherous tar-like sand occurs; it has yielded an extraordinary richness of animal remains of many kinds, the creatures clearly having wandered upon the yielding surface unsuspectingly and been entombed there.

Even the old Dinosaurs were often bogged, and the places where their bones occur to-day are still soft, clayey mudstones, so much cut up by rain and weather that they are known as badlands. They occur particularly in Alberta and Mongolia, two of the chief sources of dinosaur remains; but the monsters themselves were world-wide in range, some of the biggest even inhabiting our own Oxfordshire plain between Lias and Chalk times.

12*

"Dinosaur" means "terrible lizard". It is a true description of many of the monstrous dragons, which were anything from twenty to forty feet long, besides being ferocious flesh-eaters, as their strong conical teeth prove. Such dinosaurs as Tyrannosaurus, Atlantosaurus, and Ceratosaurus, while possessing the usual very long tails of the tribe, had their hind legs much stronger and stouter than the fore limbs; in fact, the thigh bone of some species was as big as a man. The fore limbs, on the other hand, were slender and adapted to clutching, for they terminated in very strong, savage-looking curved

Thunder lizards browsing in a tropical creek

claws; and it is pretty certain that the animal could raise its huge bulk upon its hind legs and tail and from that firm tripod could drop with its full weight on whatever prey it could seize—usually, no doubt, one of the even larger but relatively inoffensive plant-eating dinosaurs.

The giant plant-eating reptiles ranged up to sixty feet in length, exceptionally even more. Their necks were usually very long; they terminated in a small head, having a brain no bigger than a hen's egg. The huge creature, clad in horny skin (impressions of which have been found occasionally), and walking on all four feet, was very unbalanced sideways; but it probably lived in the water, frequenting marshlands and browsing on the succulent reeds there. It was no match for the flesh-eaters, to which it probably afforded many a meal. The giant of this type was known as Brontosaurus, or thunder lizard, so-called because an American is said to have remarked, on learning the creature's huge dimensions, " Is it, by thunder!"

To protect themselves as they degenerated into mere huge help-lessness, some of the plant-eating dinosaurs acquired a very strange kind of defence. Along the back they developed rows of large, thin bony plates, each up to two or three square feet in area, which must have made it difficult for another animal to spring on them; the neck was shortened, while the tail acquired some formidable pointed spikes, with which no doubt the aggrieved monster could lash out at its assailants. This type was known as Stegosaurus. It was the acme of hideousness.

Not all the dinosaurs were large. Some early ones were little bigger than a hen and several did not exceed the size of an ostrich. The early bird-like types have left striking memorials of their existence in the shape of footprints in the mud; these have been found, for instance, in the red sandstone rocks of Cheshire and in similar rocks in the United States.

Dinosaurs laid eggs, in clusters, apparently quite unprotected except for the rude hollows in which they were buried. By a wonder-ful freak of fate, some of these eggs have been preserved through all the millions of years since they were laid. A large number were discovered, about twenty years ago, by some American scientists in the Mongolian desert, looking for all the world like so many clusters of potatoes. Such a strange preservation is most excep-tional, however; for it commonly happens that where the bones of the old dragons lie near the surface, and are exposed to the action of moisture, they are very soft, making it necessary to paint them with some kind of glue before they can be touched; and scientists have often spent days in slowly digging the remains out of the sand around them.

One strange creature of Lias and Chalk times has left its remains in slabs of very fine-grained slaty rock, originally a fine mud. This was the Pterosaurus or flying lizard. Its structure was singularly bird-like. It had a keel or breast-bone like a bird's. Its tail was sometimes short, sometimes long. It always had a long pointed beak, toothless in some species, but with separated teeth in others. The fourth finger of each forefoot or " hand " was enormously extended, somewhat like a bat's, to act as support to a huge membrane which extended over the whole animal's back and by means of which it could glide or fly; its hind feet, on the other hand, were minute. Despite its great size—some species were from twenty to twenty-eight feet across the extended wings—the flying lizard was extremely light, all its bones being of paper thickness and pneumatic, i.e. filled with air. Probably it hung up on the reeds during the day and flew by night, for its eyes were extraordinarily large; yet it was a nasty, horrible thing, and with its spear-like snout could inflict a terrible wound on the fish, &c., which probably formed its food.

Flying lizards

Remains of these flying lizards have been found in the Dorset Lias, and others in Yorkshire, among many other places.

These animals were buried in the softest of lake muds, which disturbed their natural arrangement very little. Far more wonderful than this is the preservation for several hundreds of millions of years of soft-bodied creatures such as jelly-fish and marine worms, which left almost perfect impressions in the mud of an ancient (Cambrian) marine cut-off, known to scientists as the Wapta Pool.

A famous geologist named Walcott was searching the rocks near Field, in the British Columbia mountains, when he discovered a large fallen block of shale full of remains of trilobites and other early arthropods. (A trilobite has some points of similarity to a large wood-louse, but is biologically very different.) The block was traced to its source; and after working there for several seasons the Americans discovered a vast number of fossil remains of the time—seaweeds, trilobites, shrimp-like creatures, marine worms, jelly-fish, some of the latter so beautifully preserved that even the outlines of the internal parts could be seen. The Cambrian rocks, in which these things were found, are almost the oldest rocks that bear any fossils; they are named from Wales, where they abound, especially near Haverford-west and from Harlech to Bala. By diligent search there, you, too, might find fossils, but you will soon discover that it is far easier to look for them among the soft limestones and sandstones, the shale and sands of the eastern and southern coasts.

Although the upper part of the sea, at least, abounds in fish,

Ancient fishes from the Old Red Sandstone

fossil remains of fishes are none too common. A great series was found many years ago, however, in Scotland, in what is known as the Old Red Sandstone. This is a real romance of fossil history. The man concerned was a humble but acute Scottish mason, his name Hugh Miller. He was largely self-taught, but was resolute and inquiring; and he discovered that, by breaking open the nodules of sandstone which abounded in parts of the Cromarty Firth, he was adding to science a whole series of new and most curious fishes (or rather, ancestors of fishes, for though in general fish-like they were highly clumsy, and even grotesque). The Old Red Sandstone fishes had the whole front part of the body encased in an armour of bony plates, and many of these were ornamented with scrawls and patterns, like the scutcheons on a knight's armour. The plates were jointed, and overlapping fish scales were rare if not unknown. Hugh Miller worked out the skeletal arrangement of a good many of these strange creatures, and he embodied his results in one of the most fascinating scientific books ever written, *The Old Red Sandstone*.

The Old Red Sandstone occasionally yields another kind of imprint, fossil rain-marks. The rocks, which are enormously thick in Midland Valley of Scotland and in South Wales, are mainly red, a certain sign that they were laid down in a dry, desert climate; and their nature and remains prove this. Large areas of the earth at that time must have been arid deserts, the lakes in which were apt to dry up; but when an occasional shower fell, its imprints were sometimes preserved on the soft, muddy shores by the waves quietly rolling a layer of muddy grains over the marks.

Coal is of fossil origin, and so is petrol. One may frequently pick out of the household coal what looks like a ribbed piece of bark, with little oval scale-marks upon it. It is, in fact, a ribbed piece of the bark of a great Coal Age or Carboniferous tree, called Lepidodendron, which predominated in the marshy forests of that date. This tree was sometimes seventy feet high or more. Its lower part, at least, was covered with long, narrow leaflets or scales, and when these broke off they left scars, the scars on the coal in your cellar.

Not all coal was made of such stuff; indeed, the bulk of coal is made up of the stems and branches of ferns (now quite indistinguishable), together with immense numbers of their spores, the latter occasionally being visible beneath a microscope when properly prepared. Literally for ages this decayed and decaying vegetable matter accumulated in delta lands not unlike the great Sundarbund of the Ganges; and at times the sea broke in and covered them, only for fresh plants to grow there in the delta, and form new masses of black mud. Subsequently the dead plants were buried deeper and deeper, their moisture was nearly all pressed out, and they acquired the characteristic texture of coal.

Now the fossils in the coal itself are only to be discerned, if at all, by the technique used by a skilled scientist; but anyone can search the slag heaps at a colliery, where the washings and screenings that formed clay or shale partings between the coal seams have been thrown; and there, in abundance, one may find beautiful impressions of Carboniferous ferns and other fern-like plants. Here is another thing. By searching the rocks we may sometimes discover remains of marine shells in the sandstone layers between the coal; thus, our assertion above about the sea coming in and drowning the delta is not a mere imaginative guess, but is *proven*!

There are no fossils in natural petroleum, of course; but it is derived from fossils, though the exact mode of its formation is still not certain. At several times in the earth's long history large areas have abounded in diatoms, tiny plants each of which yields an oily residue; and the remains of fishes and certain weeds may also have yielded oil. Thus innumerable minute globules of oil became trapped in the rocks, and when the increasing pressure from above had transformed it into the nature of petroleum, it either saturated the rock in which it occurred or was forced to migrate into a coarser-grained or more porous rock where it could form underground pools. The former case is shown by the Oil Shales of Scotland, which have to be distilled before they will yield oil; the latter is the more valuable source of so many oil wells in the Americas, Persia, Burma, and other places.

I suppose that the most fascinating fossils, to the majority of people, are the remains of fossil men; but these are so rare that you are hardly likely to find any; and yet one never knows! The Piltdown Skull, one of the most famous of all human relics, was found by some workmen who were digging a trench in a Sussex field, and who, not realizing its importance, broke it with their tools; but science soon stepped in and recovered most of the pieces.[1] You can see the reconstructed result at South Kensington.

I propose to close this chat with a reference to ancient human beings and their surroundings, for some at least of the objects that our ancestors used, and of the bones of animals which were contemporary with them, may readily be found by anyone.

A long time ago by human reckoning, but very recently in the geological sense—perhaps three-quarters to one million years ago—the earth's climates were slightly milder than at present; this is known mainly through finds of fossil plants, which are excellent and sensitive temperature indicators. Possibly there was little ice, if any, in Antarctica and Greenland. These days were called Pliocene; they have left no fossils in England, except in Cornwall and parts of East Anglia.

Then the temperature grew cooler. There was much snow, and as more fell than could be melted in the summer, it consolidated to form ice-fields; and when the ice-fields were thick enough they

---

[1] The ape-like jaw which made this fossil very puzzling was only discovered after a later search. Recent tests imply that the jaw is comparatively modern, but there is no doubt of the great age of the original skull.

overflowed in all directions, like an over-full bowl of clotted cream. The great centres of ice accumulation were numerous. Three of them ringed round Hudson Bay, others filled the mountainous backbone of western America, yet another formed over the Baltic, its edge eventually overtopping the Norwegian mountains and flowing down into the Atlantic; other ice-caps covered the Alps and Himalaya, Greenland and Antarctica. The Scandinavian ice filled the North Sea as far down as Norfolk, even crossing the British coast in places; and, as snow almost always falls more heavily upon the rim of an ice-cap then on the cap itself, there were large local ice-sheets in Britain too, the glaciers of which streamed out in all directions, the southern ones reaching the line of the Thames.

Ancient stone implements

Naturally vegetation died, and the animals of the time—which included many warmth-loving creatures, such as the hippopotamus and the rhinoceros—fled to warmer climes; they could do this because at that time England was joined to the Continent across the Straits of Dover. Later, small animals beyond the ice edge tried to weather the severe climate, but sometimes they failed; remains of lemmings, for instance, have been found coiled up under the formerly frozen downwash from ledges in Sussex, when the ice lay north of the Thames. Men had not yet been evolved, but apes and ape-like creatures lived farther south, in France, Germany and Italy.

Then a strange thing happened. The ice melted away. It probably took many thousands of years for this to happen, and it is doubtful whether the ice-caps disappeared completely; but the melting freed large parts of the earth, and for a time conditions were much warmer than they are now. Then cold supervened once more, to be followed after a most severe spell by another mild stage. There were four of these glacial stages, separated by three warm ones. Altogether the series probably lasted half a million years. At each cold spell the plants died and the animals fled; at each warm one both kinds of life regained part of their old homes.

In the last interglacial spell there is abundant evidence of man-like creatures, but true men date only from the last cold spell, remains of our oldest known ancestors having been found in caves. Much earlier traces of creatures with many human characters are known, especially in the shape of flint and other stone implements which could only have been fashioned by intelligent animals, but "human" bones and skulls, usually very fragmentary, are excessively rare.

The first cousin of modern man was the famous Neanderthal type, so-called because the original one was discovered in a cave at Neanderthal, in Western Germany. Many remains of him have since been found, including one almost complete skeleton; and he is the oldest quasi-human creature of which we have any exact knowledge. He was heavily built, about five feet six inches high, with a brutish projecting jaw, and heavy ridges above the eyes. He had very powerful hands and arms, and he could not stand quite upright, probably shuffling along. The Neanderthaler's brain was very large, but not highly intelligent. As the cold of the last icy stage came on, he took refuge under overhanging cliffs and in caves, where his remains are usually found. He cut and shaped characteristic, rudely made tools in stone. What happened to him during the long cold stage, many thousands of years in duration, is not known, but at its close, when the weather began to ameliorate, a new and definitely human type had emerged, with negroid characteristics, but decidedly above Neanderthal man in the scale.

All the vast variety of human types to-day go back to these ancestors. Geologists have means of dating that period pretty closely; it was somewhere about twenty thousand years ago. A succession of different races of men occupied most of the earth. They also developed a series of quite different types of stone implements, besides such things as bone needles and carvings on reindeer horns, elephants' tusks, &c. Their implements are unmistakable, although the use to which they were put may not at first sight be apparent to you; they *look* like tools—piercing tools, flint knives, axes, and so on, and some of them are of most exquisite workmanship, being shaped by pressure. You may find such things buried among the gravel in a river's bank—thousands have been found on the Thames, for instance; or in the gravel beds of quarries. Later, men learned to polish their stone tools, when, of course, their artificial character became still more obvious.

For a long time many men lived, with their wives and children, in caves, probably in the most primitive and coarse way, hunting each other and the wild animals which still abounded; there is also good reason to believe that they were not above cannibalism, and they certainly had ideas of magic. Their hearths, ornaments, tools, and the bones from their feasts are often found in caves; Kent's Cavern at Torquay is, perhaps, the best-known in England, but there are many others. These caves, moreover, were at one time or another the homes of the wild animals themselves, including the cave bear, the cave lion, and the hyena; and man probably had to fight for the right to such poor shelter as the cave afforded, on many an exciting occasion. The caves were formed by the solution of limestone by percolating water; as you know, the lime drops in the shape of beautiful stalactites from the roof, while the growing deposit on the floor forms stalagmites. The overflow spreads across the cave earth like a firm stony cap, securely entombing anything that may be there. It is by breaking through this limestone crust and excavating the cave earth that so much has been learned about our savage ancestors.

Here is a final point about fossils. Peat bogs cover large parts of the higher, wetter parts of Britain, especially on the Welsh and Scottish hillsides. This peat sometimes contains twigs of birch and willow so little changed that they are still firm and springy; but, like coal, a lot of it is also indistinguishable plant debris, mingled with multitudes of spores from trees that have decayed away. These spores have been studied by botanists; and they show—what was already known from other evidence—that the climate has been changing slowly but continuously almost down to historic times. Thus, after the warm spell which succeeded the last great ice-cap, and when birch and pine trees grew at much higher altitudes in the Highlands and on the Northumbrian and Yorkshire moors than they do to-day, it became colder once more; then warm again, then cold again, and has continued so, without much noticeable change, to the present.

All of which inspires us to remark, that if you feel that you possess the talents of a Sherlock Holmes, and fancy your ability first to accumulate facts and then to draw conclusions from them, you can do worse than to take up fossil hunting.

INSECT COMMUNITIES

No doubt you have read or been told of the wonderful things that go on in a bees' hive, or perhaps you have actually watched bees at work through the glass side of one of those " observation hives " which nowadays form part of the teaching equipment at certain schools. If so, you know that in the spring of the year the population of the hive consists of a single " queen " and large numbers of " workers ". The latter, as their name suggests, are responsible for all the activities of the hive, outside as well as inside. They form, in short, a community or co-operative society, labouring to ensure the prosperity and safety of the hive as a whole. The strange thing is that they are governed and kept in order not by a code of laws and a police force, but solely by what we call " instinct "—though what instinct really is nobody has so far been clever enough to explain. Even the so-called queen exercises no authority or control. Her chief duty is to lay her eggs in the waxen cradles or " cells " made by the workers—one egg in each; and when they hatch they produce white, legless grubs—for bees, like most other insects, undergo a marvellous transformation or metamorphosis as they grow up. In about five days the grub—being fed by its nurses, the workers—changes to a pupa; and then—after a resting period of thirteen days more, creeps out of its skin as a perfect bee, with legs, wings, and a long " tongue " all complete. The young worker bee is at first weak and inexperienced, as might be expected; but in about twenty-four hours' time she is strong enough to commence work in the hive as a nurse, cleaning and feeding the grubs which are still in their cells. Ten or twelve days later she leaves the hive for her first flight in the air and sunlight, and soon learns how to gather nectar and pollen from the flowers— the two substances on which bees live and rear their grubs.

During the winter the bees remain in their hive, clustered together for warmth, and feeding on honey stored before the close of the previous summer—or, when this stock is exhausted, on sugary liquid provided by their owner, the bee-master. All this time there is little work to do. But with the return of spring, and

as soon as flowers begin to open, some of the workers creep out
of the hive and fly off to visit snowdrops, crocuses, and other early
blooms, as well as the catkins of certain shrubs and trees, such as
the hazel and the " pussy " willow, which yield an abundance of
pollen—the rich and nourishing substance urgently needed at this
season when brood-rearing commences.   Throughout the busy
summer days the workers toil unceasingly from dawn to dusk,
literally wearing themselves out, so that they seldom live longer
than two months. But all this time the queen is laying eggs at the

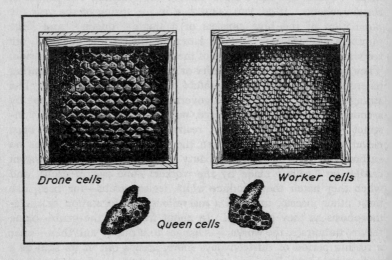

Drone cells

Worker cells

Queen cells

rate of 1500 or more every twenty-four hours; so that there is
never any lack of young and vigorous workers to replace those
which are dead and done with.

As the season advances, from three to four hundred drones, or
male bees, are reared in special cells—larger than those used for
rearing workers or for storing honey. Drones take some twenty-four
days from the laying of the eggs to reach the adult state. As their
name suggests, they do no kind of work, although they enjoy the
shelter of the hive and are fed from the common store. You may
call them, if you like, the princes of the bees' community, for perhaps
some day one of them may be needed to mate with a bee-princess,
or young queen, some of which are also reared about this time in

large, thimble-shaped—or " royal "—cells, made by the workers. The food fed to the grubs which are destined to becomes princesses, or perhaps reigning queens, is extra nourishing, so that they develop rapidly, and reach maturity in from fifteen to seventeen days.

When the increase of the worker population of a particular hive threatens to become greater than the space will accommodate, preparations are made for " swarming ". At this time the old reigning queen becomes greatly excited, and the ordinary routine of the

An exceptionally shapely swarm of bees hanging from a branch

community comes temporarily to a standstill, while many of the workers flock to the storage cells and gorge themselves with honey—just as if they knew (as perhaps they do, by instinct) that an exhausting adventure lies ahead of them. Then scouts are sent out to explore the neighbourhood; and soon a whole host of workers, headed by the queen, issues from the hive in a dense cloud. This is what is known as the " swarm ". The bees which compose it never return to their old quarters, but—led by the queen—eventually found a new community or bee-city. After flying round and round for a time they usually gather in a cluster on the branch of a tree or some such convenient resting-place. The alert bee-keeper will now " take the swarm "—i.e. accommodate it with a new hive;

and you may, perhaps, have watched from a distance while this was being done. But if for any reason the bees are left to their own devices, they will sooner or later make a fresh home for themselves, in the hollow trunk of a tree, among the rafters of a shed or out-house, or in some similar situation. The workers begin at once to construct combs, in some of the cells of which the queen lays eggs, while others are used for storing honey; and in this way the new community is founded.

Meanwhile, back in the old hive, the workers which have not taken part in the swarming liberate one of the young princesses, which up to this time have been held prisoners in their cells. Her

Queen   Drone   Worker

The three members of a hive-bee community

first act is to tear open the other royal cells and to kill with her sting all her sister princesses. This seems to us savage and ferocious in the extreme, but the unwritten laws of the hive enact that one queen and one queen only shall be allowed to reign; not even a queen dowager or a queen mother is permitted. About a week later the sole remaining princess—or, as she must now be called— the queen elect, leaves the hive for what is called her " nuptial flight ", followed by a bevy of drones, with one of which she pairs— high up in the sunlit air. She then returns to the hive, there to settle down to her task of egg-laying, which continues without a break— except during the winter, or if she herself heads a swarm—until she dies. As for the drones—which have no stings, and so cannot protect themselves—they are now treated with scant courtesy, and those which attempt to return to the hive are often set upon and killed by the worker door-keepers. In any event, they are all turned out of the hive at the end of the summer and allowed to perish from hunger and cold.

Hive bees are very careful to keep their habitation clean and well ventilated. Refuse of all kinds, as well as the dead bodies of their comrades and grubs, are carried out and deposited at some distance, while in warm weather they practise a very remarkable system of fanning with their wings, so that air is drawn in through the door of the hive on one side and expelled at the other, after having circulated through all the passages between the combs. Each separate bee works its wings for a short time only—about a minute— after which another takes its place and starts fanning, to be followed by a third, and so on, until a sufficiency of air has been circulated through the hive for the time being. This task is very necessary, since bees dislike draughts, and carefully stop up any cracks or openings in the walls of their hive—except the one small entrance door—with a kind of waterproof cement, called propolis, which is really a resinous substance collected principally from the bud-scales of certain trees and plants.

As is well known, bees make their comb of wax, which they produce from their own bodies. When supplies are needed a number of workers first gorge themselves with honey, then hang together in a dense festoon until wax issues in the form of tiny, semi-transparent scales between the plates of the abdomen or hind-body on the underside. These scales—in all eight are produced simultaneously by each bee—are chewed up with the insects' saliva and moulded into the eight-sided cells of which the comb consists. As wax is made by the bees at the expense of honey, bee-keepers long ago hit upon the device of supplying their stocks with what is known as " comb foundation ", i.e. sheets of pure beeswax, obtained from old combs melted down and freed from impurities, and then stamped by machinery in the exact form and size of the real cell bases. In this way the bees are saved the trouble and labour of wax-making to start with.

The comb is suspended from the upper part of the frame or hive, though when complete it may often be strengthened by attachments at the sides and the bottom. The separate cells are eight-sided, and are arranged in two series back to back in such a way that the base of one cell is formed by the union of the bases of three opposite cells. If you examine a piece of dry and empty comb you will see that this is so; and you will also notice that each cell has a slight upward tilt, which prevents the honey from spilling out while the cell is being filled and before it has been " capped " like a pot of newly made jam.

In ordinary conversation we say that bees visit flowers to gather honey. But this is really less than half the truth. What bees get from the flowers is a sweetish juice, properly called " nectar "; and if you had to eat this spread on your bread you would probably find it unpalatable. But the bee sucks this nectar into its crop, whence it is later emptied out into a cell when the insect returns to the hive; and while the nectar is in the crop it is mixed with certain secretions from the bee's digestive glands. This changes its sweetness from what the chemists term cane-sugar into " glucose " or grape-sugar, and in this way the nectar produced by the flowers is changed by the bees into the honey which is extracted from their comb. Honey nowadays is classed with jams and marmalades as a pleasant addition to our diet. But there was a time, three centuries or more ago, when it was the only sweetening substance in general use, since sugar, as we know it to-day, was unobtainable.

Ants have long been thought to exchange information by stroking or tapping one another's antennæ, and it seems probable that bees often do the same. But a close observer of their habits (Professor K. von Frisch of Austria) has recently discovered that in certain circumstances these insects communicate by means of a kind of dance language. When a worker bee returns home after finding a specially bountiful supply of nectar or pollen, she makes known her good fortune to other inmates of the hive by dancing a jig upon the comb. Near-by workers are attracted, show signs of excitement, and soon afterwards set out in search of the food whose existence has thus been made known to them. Two distinct types of dance have been noticed and called respectively the " round dance " and the " waggle dance ". If the location of the find is not more than fifty yards or so distant, the round dance is performed by the home-comer as a signal that the other bees should disperse and search around the hive for food having the same odour as that adhering to the dancer's body. The waggle dance, which takes the form of a very broad figure-of-eight, and during which the bee waggles her hind-body from side to side in a peculiar way, signifies that the food must be sought at a greater distance. Moreover, it indicates to the other bees not only the direction in which they must fly to find it, but also tells them how far they must go. All this sounds rather like a fairy tale, but its truth is vouched for by eminent scientists whose conclusions were reached after long-continued observation and many carefully planned experiments.

Our native wild bees in Britain—of which there are many different kinds—are for the most part " solitary ", i.e. the males and females pair and conduct their nesting arrangements without the aid of any " workers ". The bumble- or humble-bees, however, form true social communities, though of a much simpler type than those of the hive bee. Some make their homes in holes in the ground or under the flooring of a shed or outhouse; or, again, a nesting-box set up in the garden for the benefit of the birds may be appropriated. Others are content to build their cells on the bare earth, under a covering of moss, dead leaves, and so forth. The mother or queen of the big black-and-yellow banded humble-bee with a tawny tail—one of our commonest species—often takes possession of a ready-made cavity, such as the deserted burrow of a field mouse. Here she constructs a roughly made container— hardly regular enough in design to be termed a cell—using a waxy substance, and coating the inner side liberally with honey-saturated pollen. In this she lays four or five eggs, and roofs them in, leaving the grubs when they hatch to fend for themselves, though bringing them further supplies of food from time to time. Her next care is to make two or three tubs, as we may call them, also of a coarse kind of wax, filling them with pollen and honey as a reserve to be drawn upon in rainy weather when supplies cannot be gathered direct from the flowers. After this she fashions more containers and lays more eggs in them, so that in a short time—as the grubs pupate and change to perfect insects—she is surrounded by a little family of young bees, all her offspring, and all able and ready to take part in her labours—some of these " workers " eventually laying eggs on their own account, and so helping to swell the population of the nest.

In a humble-bee community the workers vary considerably in size and strength. The larger and stronger individuals go out to collect food and building materials, while the smaller ones usually remain at home, where they act as nurses to the grubs and keep the nest clean. As autumn approaches a few males or drones are produced, as well as a somewhat larger number of princesses— these latter, after pairing, being destined to survive the winter and found new colonies in the early summer of the following year. For humble-bees do not swarm, nor do their communities last for more than a single season. At the first onset of the cold weather work in the nests comes to a standstill, and the inmates perish—all except the young princesses just mentioned; and these seek out snug and dry crevices, where they can sleep soundly until they are warned by that mysterious something called " instinct " that the time has come to bestir themselves.

A humble-bee community is never very numerous. Even in the case of the larger kinds, the population of the nest is unlikely to exceed 400 at the height of its prosperity at the summer's end; while that of the smaller kinds which make their homes above ground, rarely numbers more than a score or so, all told. Some of these latter are known popularly as " carder bees ", because they thatch their habitations with the worked-up fibres of grass or moss. Such nests are often approached through an arched passage or tunnel of the same materials, and are usually cunningly hidden amongst herbage. But carder bees readily adapt themselves to circumstances, and have been known to make their abodes in such places as straw-filled packing-cases or deserted birds' nests. An instance is on record in which a queen humble-bee of this sort invaded a wren's nest and eventually succeeded in driving out the rightful owner, and heaping up her own brood cells and honey-pots among the eggs! Another little humble-bee community flourished for a time in the mud-walled home of a pair of house-martins.

Besides the hive bee and the humble-bees we have in Britain two other kinds of social or communal insects, namely, the wasps and the ants. Of the former there are seven different species—including the hornet, which is really an extra large wasp, but with brown-and-yellow livery instead of the black-and-yellow which characterizes its smaller relations. Social wasps have been called " the first paper-makers " because they use for nest-building a material which resembles a coarse sort of brown paper. This they make for themselves by rasping wood-fibres from a fence or tree-trunk, and working these into a plastic paste with their saliva. Only a tiny pellet is made by each wasp at one time, but when hundreds, or even thousands, work together much can be accomplished between dawn and dusk.

In the beginning, however, everything depends upon the activities of the queen wasps which pass the winter in hiding—for wasp colonies, like those of the humble-bees, last only for a single season. British wasps, according to their kind, build their nests in different situations—three in underground chambers, three among the

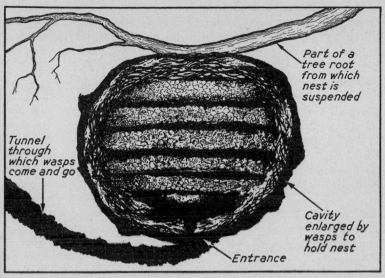

Part of a tree root from which nest is suspended

Tunnel through which wasps come and go

Cavity enlarged by wasps to hold nest

Entrance

An underground wasps' nest in cross-section, with the outer covering removed
to disclose the hanging " combs " of cells in which the young are reared

branches of some tree or shrub, while the hornet usually favours a hollow tree-trunk or a site among the rafters of a barn or cottage. In all cases the nest hangs from a support and is built from above downwards. Hence the queen wasp, fresh from her winter sleep, uses her first pellets of paper-like material to construct a sort of stalk attached to the root, branch or beam which she selects for her topsy-turvy foundation; then, on the free end of the stalk, she fixes a few cells, in each of which an egg is laid. A little later more paper is used to form an umbrella-like canopy above the cells, and this is subsequently enlarged into a globular covering. So at the end of a week or so the queen's unaided labours result in a pretty little ball-shaped nursery, about the size of a small apple, grey, brown or light fawn in colour, and with a small opening, or door, beneath.

A wasps' nest, although it is constantly added to and so grows steadily in size from day to day, never appears unfinished. Its outer covering is always round and shapely, for as the work of comb-making proceeds it is continually cut away from within and replaced by fresh layers added on the outside. Thus, the interior is kept snug and warm and dry even when the nest is suspended in a gorse bush or from the low branch of a pine tree, where it is exposed to all weathers. In the case of those nests which are built in holes under the ground the workers have to devote much of their time to enlarging the cavity, which is often quite small when the queen first takes possession of it. Fragments of soil and very small stones are carried out bodily through the tunnel leading to the open air, while those which are too heavy for the insects to lift are under-mined and allowed to fall to the floor of the cavern.

Social wasps, although they are greedy for sweet juices, feed their grubs largely on insect fare, and so—in the earlier part of the season, at all events—must be good friends to the gardener and fruit-grower, for they destroy enormous numbers of the tiny " pests " which infest our orchards and crops. But in the late summer and early autumn they are often guilty of much damage to ripe fruit of all kinds.

A prosperous wasp colony at the end of the season consists of thousands of workers, all the direct offspring of the original queen. At this time some extra large cells are added to the lower combs, and in these some scores or hundreds of males (or drones) and princesses are reared. But with the advent of the first frosts this hard-working and prosperous community is doomed. Starvation ravages it; for the wasps have stored no rations within their paper walls, and can no longer gather supplies from outside. Thus they die of cold and hunger, the enfeebled workers often dragging the half-grown grubs from their cells and casting them abroad to share the common fate. Of all the vast concourse only the adult princesses survive, destined to found new colonies in the year to come. After mating with a drone, each seeks a hiding-place in which to pass the winter wrapped in deepest slumber.

We now come to the ants, whose community life is even more remarkable than that of the bees and wasps, although they are less notable as architects, and have no special building materials com-parable to wax or paper. Some kinds, of which the little yellow meadow ant is an example, make underground nests, with the soil excavated from the galleries and chambers piled up above like a domed roof. But in Britain the largest nests are those made by the red wood-ant, or horse-ant as it is sometimes called. Above these nests the ants pile up such oddments as pine needles, small twigs, and other dry vegetable refuse, which in the course of years become mounds several feet in height. Such nests usually contain several egg-laying females or " queens " and many thousands of workers—all wingless. The workers vary a good deal in size, and as with humble-bees the larger and stronger engage in foraging expeditions and collect food and building materials, while the smaller act as nurses, and seldom leave the shelter of the nest. The workers never have any wings; but during the summer broods of winged

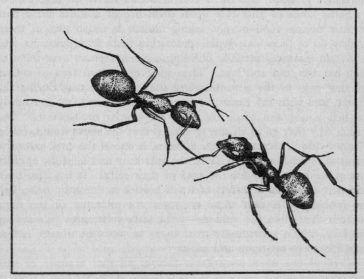

Ants " talking "—exchanging information by stroking or tapping one another's antennæ

princes and princesses are reared. On a day during a spell of fine, warm weather these fly away from their old home and pair, and, although most of them are quickly destroyed by birds and other insect-eating creatures, a few of the princesses—now to be called " queens "—succeed in founding fresh communities. They discard their wings as soon as suitable quarters have been found.

Ants devote the greatest care to the rearing of their young. The queens of the nest are fed and tended by relays of workers, some of which also collect and carry off the eggs as they are laid. But these are not put separately into cells. On the contrary, they are constantly moved from one part of the nest to another as the temperature varies, so that they may have the most favourable conditions for their development. Then, when the grubs hatch, they are fed by the workers at regular intervals, cleaned, arranged in groups according to their age, and often carried from one chamber to another lest they should be exposed to too much warmth or cold. Just before changing to pupæ, the grubs of certain ants spin oval cocoons, and these are commonly sold as " ants' eggs " for feeding pheasants, goldfish, and other creatures that thrive on insect food.

Some kinds of ants rely upon plant-lice or aphides for a part of their normal food-supply, taking almost as much care of them as they do of their own grubs, protecting them from enemies, and in certain instances actually building earthen shelters over them to keep out the cold and wet. They have even been seen to collect aphides' eggs in the autumn, store them in their nest during the winter, and with the return of warm weather carry out the newly hatched young and place them on the proper food-plants. The reason why they go to all this trouble is that the sweet liquid, called " honey-dew ", secreted by the aphides, is one of the ants' favourite forms of nourishment. In short, the ants keep and tend the aphides just as we keep cows for the sake of their milk! It has also been said that ants keep a variety of small beetles as domestic pets; but the probability is that these creatures are tolerated in the nests because they—like the aphides—yield tasty substances relished by the ants, which accordingly treat them as welcome guests, not as intruders to be set upon and killed.

Perhaps the most remarkable fact of all that a study of ants and their ways has brought to light is the slave-keeping habits of some of the larger species, which actually raid the nests of their smaller and less warlike relatives and carry off as many grubs and pupæ as they can lay hold of. With these they hurry back to their own nest, where they carefully tend them so that when the adult workers emerge they can make use of them as slaves. This happens in the case of one of our native wood-ants. Strange to say, the slaves seem perfectly happy, serve their captors faithfully, and make no attempt to escape.

Some of the smaller ants which live in subterranean nests, and seldom roam far afield, may be kept as " pets " in specially pre-pared houses, or " cages ", made of two sheets of glass placed one above the other, but kept from actual contact by narrow slips of glass cemented round the edges. An ants' nest having been found and opened up, the top glass of this contrivance is removed and a number of the insects, together with a small quantity of soil, are hurried into the shallow trough formed by the lower sheet with its surround of cemented slips. A queen ant—she is much larger than any of her subjects—must also be included; and then the top glass is put on and clamped into place by means of metal clips. At first confusion reigns in the " cage ", but after a few hours the ants will be found to settle down in their new quarters and to make themselves at home. They excavate chambers and passages in the soil—a large one for the queen and her attendants, with many smaller ones as store-rooms and nurseries. They collect all the grubs and pupæ that they can find, sort these according to age, and begin at once to groom and caress them. In short, they take up the thread of their interrupted activities as if nothing out of the ordinary had happened. But, because the space between the upper and lower sheets of glass is only just sufficient to allow an ant to walk about in comfort, all the apartments and passages which they construct are necessarily floored and roofed with glass. Hence, the doings of the ants are plainly visible from the outside, and by means of a tripod magnifying-glass their every action can be watched.

Ants cannot tolerate light in their dwellings, but by keeping them carefully covered when not actually under observation their comfort in this respect is assured. Indeed, a community of these insects housed between two sheets of glass in the manner which has just been described will continue in health and prosperity for an indefinite number of years. A narrow opening must be left at one point between two of the slips used to keep the upper and lower sheets of glass apart, and this is normally kept closed with a plug of cotton-wool. But once a month, from April to September inclusive, this door is opened and about a teaspoonful of water poured in. A little honey should also be inserted, after which the cotton-wool is replaced. This is all the attention that the ants require, and in winter even this small ration of food and moisture is not needed, since cold weather puts a temporary check upon their activities.

For ants which habitually roam abroad in search of food another kind of residence must be provided. A suitable one may be contrived from a half-plate photographic printing frame, into which a glass cage similar to that described above is fitted, a small portion of the wooden frame being cut away at one end so that the insects may come and go freely. The whole construction stands upon four legs in a pan of water, which prevents the ants from escaping; but they are able to wander all over the printing-frame, on the top of which food may be placed for them. A little inclined plane should be provided so that they can go down to the water to drink. If a view of the interior of the nest is desired, half of the frame's cover may be raised, allowing the ants and their workings to be plainly seen.

One other group of communal insects remains to be mentioned, viz. the so-called " white ants ", which in fact are not even dis-

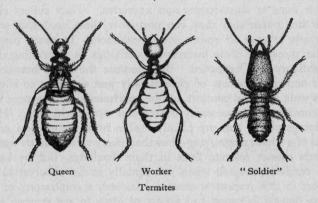

Queen   Worker   " Soldier"

Termites

tantly related to the true ants, and are much more fittingly referred to by their scientific name, " termites ". None are found in Britain; but in the warmer regions of the earth they are numerous, ranking among the most formidable foes with which mankind has to deal. Only iron and other hard metals resist their onslaughts, and wherever they go they leave a trail of devastation behind them. Furniture, clothing, books, flour and other foodstuffs are quickly devoured, while woodwork is rapidly reduced to a heap of powder and chips. The tale is told of an officer in the Indian Army who once left an ordinary cricket bat lying on the ground overnight. The next morning when he returned to claim his property it crumbled to dust in his hands, although to all outward appearance it seemed solid and uninjured. This incident illustrates the manner of the termites' attack. Physically a feeble folk, much relished as food by a host of insectivorous beasts and birds, they take no undue risks, but approach the object of their desire through tunnels and covered ways; so that it is not an uncommon occurrence to find doors and window-frames crumbling without warning. For when termites obtain access to a building they eat away all the interior of the wood-work, always leaving a thin outer shell intact, and never once exposing themselves to view.

The reason why termites have been misnamed "ants" is that both in appearance and habits they are remarkably ant-like—a resemblance which we may suppose to be due to their similar mode of life. The members of a "termitarium", i.e. a community of termites, vary in number from a few hundreds, in the case of some species, to many millions in others. They are always divided into a number of grades, or castes, which can be clearly distinguished by their form and size. In general these castes fall into two classes, namely, the propagators—males and females, which in their youthful state are winged—and the workers. But the latter usually include a number of individuals easily distinguished by the superior size of their heads and jaws, and these have been termed "soldiers", though the extent to which they live up to this name is open to question.

At a certain season of the year large numbers of males and females or princes and princesses are reared, and on a suitable day these issue forth into the open, where most of them fall victims to birds, reptiles, &c. But a few escape this fate and go off in pairs to found new colonies. It is a curious fact that after reaching the ground they tear off their own wings. Normally, a termitarium contains a single royal pair. The male or king, having discarded his wings, is not an imposing personage, being not very dissimilar to one of his subjects, the workers. But before her reign is far advanced the queen becomes the most astonishing of all insects. Her abdomen swells until it may weigh 1500 or 2000 times as much as the rest of her body, while she may produce as many as sixty eggs per minute! In a word, she becomes a vast egg-laying machine, helpless and inert, housed in a specially large cell, together with the king, at the very heart of the termitarium.

Termites employ earth and wood for building, and always chew up and swallow these materials before making use of them—a habit which ensures thorough grinding and mixing with the saliva, as well as the extraction of any nourishment which they may contain. Indeed, termites are frugal to a fault. Not only do they subject their very "bricks and mortar" to a digestive process; they actually

13 (G 487)

eat over and over again the same food until (so we must suppose) it has no further nutritive value. Moreover, these insects maintain a spotless cleanliness in their abodes by the simple process of eating all refuse matter. The explanation of all this seems to be that the termites' chief food being wood, which is not very nourishing, they live perpetually on the verge of starvation, with no margin for waste.

The habitations or nests of termites vary greatly in size and appearance. Some of the species dwell within the decayed stumps and branches of trees, and their greatest architectural achievements consist of a few partitions erected across the natural hollows of the wood. Others rear structures so enormous that they resemble man-made landmarks. The conical dwellings of the African " warlike " termite may in time reach a height of ten feet or more, with a circumference of thirty feet, while the towers erected by certain Australian species sometimes measure twenty-three feet from the ground level to the summit.

SOME ODDITIES OF THE OCEAN

Not so long ago our only means of learning about under-sea life was by sending down divers, clad in elaborate diving-dresses too heavy and clumsy to enable them to move easily, or to remain long below the waves. Now, a diving-helmet has been invented which enables an explorer to prowl about on the sea-bottom, while air and oxygen are pumped into his helmet from above by means of a hose-pipe or metal tube.

More recently still, a wonderful device known as the *Bathysphere* has been invented. This consists of a large sphere enclosing a globe-shaped room with thick but clear windows made of fused or melted quartz, through which scientists can gaze forth in comfort as their strange vessel is gradually lowered into the watery depths. The Bathysphere is provided with a constant supply of fresh air, and searchlights are installed to illuminate the inky darkness around, enabling photographs and cinematograph films to be taken, or paintings to be made. Other wonderful devices of this kind are now being invented and developed; and with their use our knowledge of life in the ocean depths is constantly increasing.

In this short article, it will be possible to describe only a few of the curious and astounding creatures to be met with in the oceans of the world; and, for convenience, we shall divide these few chosen fishy folk into Big and Little Sea Oddities, and begin with the larger ones.

It is taken for granted that most readers know something about those huge ocean monsters, the Whales and Sharks; here we shall deal only with the strangest of these giants.

The Killer Whale and the Narwhal are almost the smallest members of the Whale family; but they are as strange as any of their relatives. The most aggressive of all the Whale tribe is the Killer or Grampus, whose jaws are filled with large and terrible teeth and which will attack any other creature on sight. It is a cannibal too, and, though measuring but thirty feet in length, thinks nothing of attacking the monster " baleen " whales (baleen is the whalebone of commerce—a horny substance that hangs from the roofs of their mouths in long narrow strands and serves as a sieve through which sand and unwanted substances are sifted), and biting great chunks out of their sides. It is a real glutton, chasing and devouring any other sea beast it meets, and it will even hurl itself on to the edges of the pack-ice of the Antarctic regions and snap up penguins by the dozen when larger prey is not sufficiently plentiful.

The queerest-looking of all the members of this particular family of sea-mammals is the Narwhal, the male of which has a tusk in the upper jaw which develops into a spirally twisted dagger-like weapon

A 100-foot long blue whale attacked by a herd of 30-foot long killer whales

about eight or nine feet long, sticking out straight ahead in a most alarming manner, rather like the single horn of the fabled Unicorn. Its main purpose seems to be for fighting duels with other males of its kind, and it provides a very fine ivory.

Of the Shark family the oddest is the Hammer-head. Its head is drawn out into a wide horizontal shape and resembles the head of a monster hammer—with the glaring eyes placed at either end and the great ugly mouth appearing just below on the under-side. In all other ways it is like any other kind of shark, though it is regarded as being even more savage than the rest.

The Skates and Rays belong to the Shark family, and all of them are odd-looking in addition to being savage and dangerous. All are flat and have wide bodies expanded into a disc-like form.

Some take on a squarish shape, rather like a square set corner-wise, having the head at one corner and the tail at the opposite corner, while the two side pieces or corners flap about almost like wings. The head and body are really all in one piece with the rest of the body, for there is no neck at all. One side of the flat body is blackish, and the other side—which lies next the sand as the creature rests on the sea-bottom—is white. The ugly face appears on the white side, as though pressed thereon. When a ray rises

Hammer-head shark chasing a young turtle

up from the ocean floor and goes undulating up into the water above, this weird white face gives it a most ghostly appearance.

The largest ray is a monster often measuring eighteen to twenty feet across and weighing 1250 lb. or more; so fearsome and savage is this creature that it is often spoken of as the Devil Fish. It is found in the Atlantic Ocean around the coast of Florida, and along the Pacific coast of America.

Another of these alarming creatures is known as the Whip-ray, or Sting-ray, so called because its tail takes the form of a long whip-lash. This terrible whip-tail ends either in a poisoned sting, or jagged edges like those of a saw; it is equally deadly in either case. The Sting-ray will follow a shoal of herring or mackerel, or similar fish, and lash its tail around them to force them into a smaller compass. Then it plunges into the closely packed mass to eat its fill. So strong is its lashing tail that it has been known to slash a huge fish in two. This fearsome creature sometimes measures nearly fifteen feet when found in tropical waters, but those seen round about our own coasts are usually under two to three feet across.

Yet another of these most unpleasant fishes is known as the Electric Ray or Torpedo Fish, which is capable of giving its victim so severe an electric shock as to numb it completely before devouring it.

The four-cornered oblong egg-cases of the Rays and Skates, usually from three to five inches long, are often met with on our own sea-shores. They are sometimes spoken of as " Mermaids' Purses " or " Pixies' Pockets ".

The Sword-fish and the Saw-fish are both big creatures and extremely fierce. The Sword-fish often reaches a length of fifteen feet, and although not especially ugly in its general appearance, it is provided with a warlike weapon which makes it a very unpleasant customer to encounter. Its snout ends in an elongated narrow-pointed bone, as sharp and dangerous as a sword, which is often a yard or more long, about three inches thick at the base, and tapering off to a fine dagger-like tip. So strong is the Sword-fish's bayonet that it is able to transfix a huge tunny-fish, or even a shark, as easily as a kingfisher can harpoon a small minnow with its sharp beak. This fish is bad-tempered and easily angered; it will even dash furiously at a ship or a boat and can drive its sword through a boat's woodwork.

The Saw-fish is still larger and better armed. Not only has it a sword drawn out into a long bony weapon, but this has deeply toothed edges on either side of it like the teeth of a double-edged saw. This dangerous creature measures anything from eighteen up to twenty-four feet in length; quite a quarter of the length is taken up by the double-edged saw which, in some of the larger specimens, is not far from a foot in width. With this unique and terrible weapon the Saw-fish hacks its way through schools of por-poises and shoals of smaller fishes, such as mackerel; it will even saw off enormous chunks of blubber from the tough sides of a whale. With one blow of its powerful weapon, the Saw-fish has been known to cut a man in half.

Another ghastly sea ogre, which is likewise an oddity, is the famous Octopus. Although boneless, it is extremely strong and tough. The body is like a wobbly bladder-shaped bag, joined by a short neck or waist to a nightmarish head, also somewhat bag-like, which is encircled by a fringe of eight long squirming snaky arms or feelers, each of which has a double row of suckers on the underside. These enable it to cling tightly and relentlessly to any object with which it comes in contact.

The Octopus propels itself through the water in a very curious manner, with its eight arms or tentacles held close together in cylinder form. By taking in and expelling water over its gills through a siphon-tube apparatus, it not only gets all the air it needs for

Common octopus
Above—Swimming backwards by " jet-propulsion "
Below—Capturing a young edible crab

breathing, but is also enabled to shoot itself backwards, body first, with its fringe of long snaky arms streaming out behind the head. Through its siphon-like body, too, it is able to shower forth an inky fluid, which provides it with a sort of " black-out " screen, behind which it can escape from an enemy. At the top of its soft, brownish head, just below the fringe of tentacle arms, appear two large glaring eyes mounted upon long movable stalks, which can be shot forth suddenly in a very alarming manner. These add considerably to its gruesome looks.

These horrible creatures vary considerably in size, some being quite small and having tentacles little more than a couple of feet or so in length. In tropical seas, however, they grow to an immense size, the largest of all being found in Australian waters. Here the tentacles of a giant Octopus have been known to measure as much as forty feet in length, with a thickness equal to that of a man's thigh, which, at times, grows to a vast size—especially in tropical waters. while each tentacle resembles an " outsize " python or anaconda.

The Squid, or Cuttle-fish, is another octopus-like creature It has ten arms or tentacles, and discharges an even denser inky fluid known as " sepia "—a pigment used by artists.

Globe or porcupine fish—defending itself and scaring off a marbled eel

Let us now turn to some of the equally curious smaller oddities to be met with both in ocean depths and sea-shallows.

One of the most unbelievable of all is the Globe-fish—also known as the Giant Ball-fish, the Porcupine-fish, or the Sea-hedgehog. It is mainly found in East Indian waters, and at times it can be a most hideous object. It is usually about a foot and a half in length, broad and squat in appearance, with a huge square head practically in one piece with its body. It has a short rounded tail and is rather sparsely finned. The pectoral or shoulder fins are wide and waving; the tail fins are posed one on the top and one underneath the " waist " or base of the tail. There is a thick wide mouth extending across the whole front of the head; and, for its size, it has enormous eyes.

The colouring of the Globe-fish is greyish and black, and the thick skin is covered with strong spines, usually about two inches long. Usually, these spines lie closely to the skin. It has, however, the curious power of blowing itself out into a perfect globe, this swelling causing the spines on its stretched skin to stand out stiffly like a hedgehog's or a porcupine's. When it takes on this spiky ball shape, it instantly turns upside-down and floats on its back, becoming completely helpless and at the mercy of the waves and currents, which toss it hither and thither. Nevertheless, its swollen prickly appearance serves to scare off most of its foes quickly enough —with the exception of the shark. The latter is too savage and ever ravenous to be deprived of anything in the way of an extra titbit, and so does not hesitate to swallow the huge prickly ball at a single gulp. But he very soon wishes he had done nothing of the kind, for the Globe-fish sets to work to eat its way through the shark's side, making such a fearful wound therein with its sharp teeth, horny snout, and sharp spines that the big sea ogre often dies soon afterwards. But the victorious Globe-fish issues forth still very much alive, and rolls away none the worse for his alarming experience.

In the wonderful Aquarium at the London Zoo there was to be seen during its early years a unique lantern hanging in the entrance to the Tropical Hall. This was really the distended body of a fine Globe-fish, which had been dried, and from which most of the inside had been removed to make room for an electric bulb. When the light was switched on, it illuminated its strange lamp-shade with a weird and ghostly gleam.

Among the many rainbow-tinted and fantastic-looking little fishes to be found in the warm waters around Madeira, there are a number with strange habits. Among them are the Puffer-fish, which, like the Globe-fish just described, are fond of puffing and blowing themselves out until they look like tiny balloons. They are quite small, from three to four inches long, and at a first glance they seem to be ordinary enough, although they look rather fat and top-heavy.

These Puffer-fish are olive-green in colour, plentifully besprinkled with brownish spots on the top, their under-parts being much lighter and having no " polka dots " on them, and their fins are extremely small. Nevertheless, their defence tactics are very similar to those of the larger Globe-fish. As soon as the Puffer catches sight of an enemy fish approaching, it immediately blows itself out into a perfect ball-shape, the elastic skin being stretched

13*   (G 487)

to its utmost extent, as though it might burst at any moment. It looks just like a tiny toy balloon. Sometimes, however, the swelling process seems to be confined to the much lighter under-parts only, and it then looks like a duck's egg with a fish's head at one end and a finned tail at the other.

When some of these little Puffer-fish were kept in a tank in the London Zoo Aquarium, they behaved in a very curious and inelegant manner. As soon as a visitor drew near to their tank, they would rise to the surface and squirt water at the intruder; and though this tiny fountain could not, of course, reach the watcher, their action was certainly startling. This trick they would continue to perform as long as the amused visitor remained, only diving down now and again to take in a fresh supply of water.

Another strange little fish which hails from the waters around Bermuda is the Surgeon-fish, which is actually able to draw a sword upon its foes or prey. It is about ten inches long, and of a rather curious shape, having a barrel-like body, slightly pointed at each end. There is a long dorsal frill-like fin on the top, running down the entire length, and a smaller fin, also like a frill, along the underside. It is whitish-brown in colour, with darker stripes and streaks. The reason for its somewhat surprising name is the fact that when attacking another fish it suddenly shoots forth a sort of spear or spike, rather like a doctor's lancet, which penetrates the unlucky victim's skin, producing a neat wound. This remarkable weapon is then withdrawn again into the " Surgeon's " body, where it is completely hidden.

An even more curious fishlet from neighbouring waters is the Dentist-fish—a rather lovely creature about three to four inches long, which looks as if it had four eyes instead of two. The reason for this is that on its glistening silvery body it has a bold black velvety spot set on either side of the tail base; and as it also has jet-black eyes of exactly the same size, it appears to be provided with a pair of big black orbs at either end of its body. This glittering little creature is said to act as a sort of dentist to the larger fishes into whose mouths it glides to pick out the tiny parasites that so frequently infest the teeth and jaws of certain sea giants.

There are many thousands of other fishy oddities to be met with in the seas. Fortunately for our delight and further information large numbers of them are now to be seen in Aquariums.

AFGHANISTAN

Most people know very little about Afghanistan: perhaps only that it is a country in Central Asia, that it is mountainous, and that the Afghans are a fighting race. Some know also that the usual route into Afghanistan is through a pass that is famous in history—the Khyber Pass. But this remote country is not so well known to most of us as are many other countries even farther away. This is a pity, for Afghanistan is a very interesting country situated in a most important position.

This short account of Afghanistan was written by one who had only recently returned from there and who was able to travel widely within its borders.

The Country.

If you look at the map on page 397 you will see that Afghanistan is about the size of France and that it lies between Russia on the north and Pakistan on the south, and also between Persia on the west and China on the east. This position is obviously very important, something like that of Switzerland in Europe. Indeed, Afghanistan is often called the Switzerland of Asia.

If you wished to enter Afghanistan overland you could do so from Russia by crossing a wide and swift river called the Oxus or by travelling through desert country farther west. If you were in Persia you could take one of the several poor roads leading to Herat. Most people, however, enter Afghanistan from Pakistan, either going to Quetta and making for Kandahar in the south, or, more commonly, going to Peshawar and, passing through the Khyber Pass, making for Kabul, the capital. The Khyber Pass, which is controlled by Pakistan, has a very good road through it, which winds up and down around hairpin bends. On large rocks by the roadside are cut the crests of many famous regiments, British and Indian, reminding the traveller of the fighting which took place here in the old days of the Indian Empire. If you were coming from China you would have a very difficult journey over high mountains passes, through a region called the Pamirs and known as the roof of the world. This journey was made by the great Italian traveller Marco Polo in about the year 1300.

Imagine yourself with a camel caravan making a journey into and through Afghanistan. You would move only at a fast walking-pace and the journey would take you many days. You would carry water in goatskins on the camels' backs, and for food you would eat bread, mutton or goat meat, and fruit. If you found shelter for the night you might be able to obtain a dish of rice with meat, and get hot tea to drink. You would not expect to ride your camels if they were loaded with merchandise, for the camel cannot carry very heavy loads. You might be able to ride on a donkey or on a horse, but most camel-drivers have to walk with their beasts. You would make your way slowly up and down rough roads under a broiling sun, and through passes and gorges in the mountains in which the wind would whistle coldly. The writer was travelling through such a pass in northern Afghanistan after a long and lonely journey and was feeling cold and hungry. On rounding a bend in the road he saw a most welcome sight—a tea-shop! Not at all like a tea-shop in Britain; only a mud hut with a raised floor and an open front, where squatted a Mongol awaiting custom. At his side was a water-boiler, using dried dung as fuel, and an array of small coloured teapots in a rack. He could have served few people other than occasional camel-drivers—certainly very few folk travelling in motor cars; but he seemed to be content with his poor living and accustomed to solitude.

Afghanistan is a land of great mountains, fertile valleys, desert areas and swift rivers. The mountains are mostly bare and are often of strange shapes and colours. In the bright sunshine the scenery is strangely beautiful: a blue sky; mountains which are pink, rose-red and brown; and valleys in which grow young crops of a vivid green. But in other parts of the country the mountains are grey and the valleys narrow and dry. A traveller passing through them and finding himself out of the sun feels ill at ease and wishes to hasten on.

The main mountain range, the Hindu Kush, rises to heights of more than 15,000 feet and upon its peaks there is everlasting snow. Over great areas of this high ground the foot of man has never trodden. The writer travelled by aeroplane from Kabul to Meshed in Persia, over the mountains of Afghanistan. Although the day was

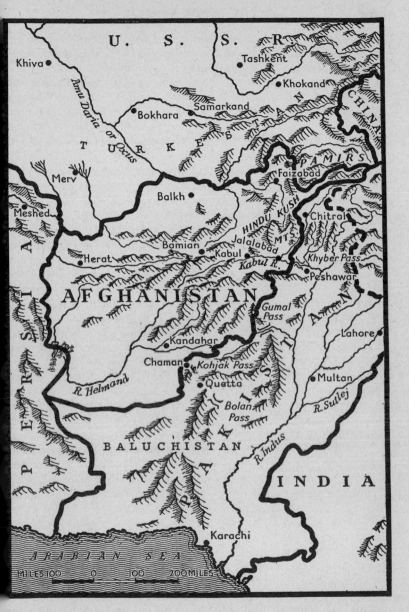

one of brilliant sunshine, the sight of the fearful country below made him anxious to get beyond the mountains and over the desert, where a landing would always be possible.

Afghanistan is so mountainous that only about one quarter of the land can be used for growing crops. But this land is very fertile, if it can be supplied with water; then it will blossom like the rose. The desert areas in Afghanistan are unpleasant places. In the deserts of the south dwell the scorpion and the tarantula spider, and they are best avoided. When a wind blows and lifts up the sand, the road or pathway is blotted from view and progress is as difficult as it is in a London fog. In the north the camel caravans on the route to Persia pass through a desert area. Travellers making this journey come upon the skeletons of camels who have died on the way.

There are no railways in Afghanistan and only a few airfields. Transport has to be by road, and the roads are not very good.

In our country we picture rivers having their origin in springs and being fed by rain-water draining through the soil and collecting where the land is low. It is not at all like this in Afghanistan because, for the greater part of the year, there is no rain at all. The rivers there are fed by the melting of the snow on the mountains, and for this reason more water flows in the rivers during the summer than during the winter.

There is another difference between our rivers and those of Afghanistan. Ours all flow to the sea, but many of Afghanistan's flow to the desert and end there. They either form lakes, or continue as many streams spreading out like the fingers of the hand, evaporating in the dry air all the time.

Some of the rivers are wide and swift and carry great volumes of water. One such river flows past a town in the north-east of Afghanistan called Faizabad, a very old town. Afghans from Faizabad sometimes ride down the river for sport, using air-bags made from goatskins. The skins are sewn up and blown into by the mouth as we would blow up an air balloon, until they contain a good deal of air; then the mouthpiece is tied up. They are ridden as we should ride a horse, and the mounted men travel down the river on them at a great speed. The riders get ashore by the skilful use of eddies and by swimming. The whole effort is not without danger because of hidden and jagged rocks, and the riders offer up prayers before they begin their journey.

It is strange that the rivers on the south side of the Hindu Kush contain no fish, whereas those flowing from the north side have plenty.

Afghanistan is a part of the high plateau of Central Asia, and it is far from the sea. The result is that it enjoys bright sunshine from cloudless skies for month after month. It is hotter in the summer and colder in the winter than in this country. A little rain falls in the spring, but for the most part the climate is very dry. Snow falls in the winter, and in many parts of the country the winter cold is intense.

The traveller from a country such as Great Britain, with its moist air, finds the extremely dry air of Afghanistan rather trying. It makes his lips very dry and his throat a little parched. But the dry air helps him to endure the high summer temperatures, the rapid evaporation of moisture from the skin having a cooling effect.

Much of the country is high above sea-level. For example the capital, Kabul, is 6000 feet higher than London. This means that the air is less dense, or is rarer, and that a given volume of air in Kabul contains less oxygen than the same volume of air in London. So to do the same amount of work a man must take in more air by breathing rapidly; if he does not, he must do less work. Most people prefer to do less work if they can, or to work more slowly. Another effect of high altitudes is to lower the temperature at which water boils. In Kabul water boils at about 94° C., not 100° as in London; in some other towns in Afghanistan it will boil at 90° C. This means, for example, that an egg requires longer to cook in Afghanistan than it would here.

A traveller often feels the effect of high altitudes when journeying by air. To offset the effect of breathing rarer air, it is best to sit still and to breathe deeply. Otherwise more oxygen is required and it can now usually be supplied. If we travel at great heights, as we shall do in the future, more oxygen must be provided.

It is frequently quite cold at night in Afghanistan, even when it is hot in the day. Indeed, a wide daily variation of temperature is all too common and is very trying to those who have to live in the open.

A Little of Afghanistan's History.

There is a story that the Afghans came from Palestine in the time of Nebuchadnezzar, but this seems unlikely. They are, as we are, a mixture of races.

If you read the story of Alexander the Great—and you should, because it is a wonderful tale—you will see that he marched his army from Greece to India by way of what is now Afghanistan. That was more than 2000 years ago. He founded several towns in this part of Asia and left Greek settlers in them. Then from the north came people from Turkestan, from the west came Persians, and from the south came inhabitants of Northern India. They were not all mixed together at first, because they dwelt as tribes in various districts. But in the course of time they did mix.

Many of these people worshipped a god called Buddha, and in one beautiful valley in Afghanistan, at a place called Bamian, they carved great images of Buddha in the near-by cliffs.

This was before the time of Jesus, and the teachings of Jesus never reached Afghanistan. Instead the teaching of the prophet Mohammed was taken there, much later, and all Afghanistan accepted this religion. We now say that Afghanistan is an Islamic country, following the beliefs of Islam.

It is a strange thing that, during the 500 years between Jesus and Mohammed, no one had taken the Christian gospel to Afghanistan. And since then no one has been able to preach it there, for the Afghans have never allowed Christian missionaries to remain in their country.

Many of those who carried the teaching of Islam and who moved eastward into Afghanistan came from what is now Turkey, and, in the northern part of the country, people of this race are called Uzbegs. So by this time there was a mixture of peoples in Afghanistan, all worshipping God in the way taught by Mohammed. They built wonderful mosques in several of their cities and they were turning more and more to education.

Then occurred one of the most dreadful events in history, one which is hardly mentioned in schools here, but which the Mohammedan world will remember for all time. This was the invasion of Genghis Khan, which took place not long after the signing of Magna Charta, when Henry III was King of England and Alexander II was King of Scotland.

Genghis Khan came from far northern Asia and he had built up an empire by means of warrior horsemen. He invaded China first and then turned westwards. His men lived simply and hard. They drank the milk of mares taken along with them. They needed no baggage train and were able to travel swiftly and far. They fell upon the Islamic cities of central Asia and utterly destroyed them. Not only were the people killed but their buildings were left in ruins. One great town so destroyed was Balkh, in northern Afghanistan. Its walls still stand and they enclose a great square, within which was once the city. The writer has climbed these walls, built of mud, very thick and high, and still standing after the suns and the snows of 700 years. Nothing is seen within them but rank weeds and grass; all is deserted and still. Nothing seems to breathe. No one has since wanted to live there and it is unlikely that anyone will. Such is the mark of Genghis Khan, repeated often in Asia, and never to be forgotten by Islam. Some of the inhabitants in northern Afghanistan are Mongols and are descendants of the warriors of Genghis Khan. They are called Hazaras.

Great Britain became interested in Afghanistan when Russia began to move south towards the river Oxus. British troops were then in India and we watched the approach of Russia with anxiety, because Afghanistan is the key to the defence of India. When the Afghans accepted Russian help, a British army entered Afghanistan and occupied Kabul. That was in 1839. A mixed British and Indian garrison was left at Kabul, but its position became impossible when the Afghans rose in revolt. The army left Kabul in the depth of winter on its long and terrible march to India. Although the Afghans had agreed to this march, they attacked in the mountain passes and the defiles, and destroyed the army. Only one man escaped, a Dr. Brydon, and a famous picture exists showing his return on horseback, wounded and exhausted. British women with the army, and some officers, were taken prisoner and kept at Bamian, a town which has been mentioned earlier. Another British army invaded Afghanistan to rescue the prisoners and to punish the Afghans. Later, yet another Afghan war broke out after Russia had sent agents to Kabul. Afghanistan is free and independent and has been at peace for a long while; everyone will wish that it should remain so.

The People.

Writers have often described the people of Afghanistan as fierce and cruel. They have been fierce and cruel, and doubtless they could be so again. But if they are left to develop their country in peace, and if they are helped to do so by the more fortunate nations, they should show their finer qualities, for they are a manly people.

The people in the north are fair-skinned, although their faces and hands are much tanned. Some of those in the south, however, are less fair and may even be called dusky. They have about the same stature as people in these islands and are spare and muscular. They are very good horsemen.

The true Afghan costume is a loose pair of white trousers, a white shirt worn outside the trousers, a kind of waistcoat of sheep-skin, and, in the winter, a long quilted coat. A coloured turban is worn on the head, over a skull-cap, and a pair of shoes is worn with-out socks. This costume is still general throughout the country, but only among the peasants and workers. The upper classes wear European clothes, and this practice is spreading downwards; few wear European hats, however. Most of them wear a round brimless hat made from lambskin. The priests of the country, called mullahs, wear dark clothes with white turbans.

Afghan women are closely veiled from head to foot. The portion of the head-dress over the face is usually white and is pierced by a number of small holes through which the wearer can see. But very little can be seen through these holes and any Western girl would be unhappy if she were asked to wear one of the Afghan hoods. When Afghan women work in the fields, they only partly cover their faces, but they hasten to cover as much as they can on the approach of a stranger. The veil has one advantage: it protects the wearer from the ever-present dust in Afghanistan. Afghan women are skilled at needlework of all kinds and, of course, they make very good rugs.

The boys and girls of Afghanistan have to work hard tending the flocks and helping in the fields. The fields in Afghanistan are not fenced in, and the children have to watch the beasts and bring them within the village wall at night. Children also watch the asses as they walk in a circle to work the endless chain of buckets bringing water from a well to flow into the irrigation channels. They also tend the oxen as they tread the corn. We read about this method in the Bible. Patient oxen walk round and round in a small circle and tread upon the corn, often dragging a heavy sled after them. The peasants throw the corn in the path of the oxen. Finally, men with shovels toss the corn high in the air in a breeze; the wind blows the chaff to one side and the heavier corn falls almost directly down. This operation can be witnessed all over Afghanistan after the har-vest. As the oxen tread the corn they push their heads down and eat what they require, and remind us of the saying in the Bible, " Thou shalt not muzzle the ox when he treadeth the corn ".

The children play few games; they have no interesting books and papers to read, such as children have in this country. As a result, they tell stories to each other. One typical story is of a boy who sent everyone to a place near the mosque, saying that they were giving nuts away there. Presently he also began to run to the mosque.

Donkeys (near Kábul) operating an endless chain of buckets which lift water for irrigation

A friend asked why he was running too, and he said, " Well, they *may* be giving nuts away there."

The Afghans are strict Mohammedans and they neither eat pork nor drink wine. Their food consists mainly of bread and fruit, together with rice, mutton, chicken and goat meat. The cow is not bred for its meat nor its milk, both of which are very poor in the Afghanistan climate. Afghans drink water and tea.

Their bread is wholemeal, made in large flat loaves, and it tastes good. Meat and the rice are usually taken together for a meal. Fruit is abundant in most parts of the country, the commoner fruits being the grape, peach and melon. Oranges and lemons grow in the south.

At one time the country had several fairly large forests, but these have now almost all been cut down for fuel. As the country has very little coal, the fuel situation is quite desperate. This has its effect upon the food which the people eat and the houses in which they live. One favourite dish consists of small pieces of meat on a skewer grilled over a small charcoal fire; this wastes nothing and requires little fuel. If you cannot get fuel, it is no good building a large house with windows. So we find, in the north of Afghanistan, where wood

Typical mud houses, found mainly in northern Afghanistan

is very scarce, that the houses are just small chambers, built of baked mud, with no windows and having a small hole in the roof. This "beehive" type of house has been used by the dwellers in central Asia for hundreds of years. The troops of Alexander the Great had to use them when they were wintering in the country, and they complained about the cold which they had to experience within them.

Imagine, then, that you are living in a small town or village in Afghanistan, that it is winter, and that your parents are working people. Your home may be a single room with only a door. It will probably have rugs on the earth floor and a few cushions, but little or no furniture. You will have a small charcoal fire and this will have to be used for cooking and for warmth. At night this fire will be put under a small table, over which will be placed a carpet, hanging to the floor, and you, and the other members of your family, will lie on the floor in your clothes and sleep with your feet under the hanging carpet and near the fire for warmth. It will be a sad life and you will long for the coming of the spring.

The conditions of life for poor people in most parts of Afghanistan are hard and only the strongest survive. It is because of this and because the people live so much in the open air, that the Afghans are so fine a race physically.

Afghans are most hospitable and helpful to the stranger. If a meal has to be prepared for visitors, far, far more food will be placed before them than they can possibly eat. This is simply good manners. If a traveller gets into difficulties, as always happens, help is given by the passer-by willingly and with no thought of reward. The writer recalls many such occasions. At one time the motor car in which he was travelling ran out of cooling-water when climbing a high pass; the men of a camel caravan which overtook the car provided water willingly, and without payment, from their precious supply carried in goatskins on the backs of the camels. On another occasion a number of Afghans passing at night lifted the car out of deep sand, where it was stuck, and helped to get it going.

The Afghan takes a very calm view of life. Whatever befalls him, he believes that this is the will of God, and that it is no use worrying. When the spring of the motor car breaks and it is necessary to wait—well, that is unfortunate, but it makes a good occasion to sit on the sand and eat melons. If, when overtaking a caravan, you scatter the animals or unseat a horseman, you are not the object of anger; usually you receive smiles, for is not this all in the day's work? Afghans like to sit and talk for hours, eating fruit or smoking tobacco. Probably they love talking because they have few books to read, even if they are able to read. There are a few newspapers, and there is the Koran, the holy book; but there are no magazines or story books, and, indeed, very little paper for such purposes. Paper is made mainly from wood, of which Afghanistan has little, and all paper used in the country has to be brought by road over long distances at great cost. This is why the Afghans can neither write very much nor read very much, and why the telling of stories has remained so popular.

The Mohammedan religion requires prayer five times daily:

before sunrise, several times as the sun sets in the evening, and after dark. Most Afghans pray publicly at these times. The driver of your car will stop at the appointed time, walk off the road, and, facing the setting sun, pray upon his knees, bending his body until his forehead touches the ground. This will be done with no intention of showing-off, and without much thought of time. Indeed, time in Afghanistan is not a thing to worry about. There are no trains to catch, very few clocks, no great need to do a thing to-day, for, after all, there is to-morrow.

The Afghans are very modest in their habits and think that it is bad manners to show one's body in public, for example, when bathing in the river. They prefer to wear plenty of clothes when entering the water. The women, of course, never show even their faces in public. In many parts of Afghanistan water is scarce and it is not easy to wash regularly or properly; and if water is there, soap is often not to be had.

It is worth thinking for a moment what you would do and how you would live if you were placed in a dry country where water was so scarce that it should not be wasted, where soap was not available, where there was no paper to use and no books to read, and where fuel was very, very scarce. It is likely that you would live the kind of life that the Afghans live, using their methods and adopting their habits. You would perhaps not be happy at first; but after a while you would see that many of the things you thought so very important here were not so important after all.

Schools in Afghanistan.

You may wonder what the schools are like in Afghanistan and what is taught in them. Well, there are not enough of them to take all the boys in the country. Very few girls can attend school. Schools usually have brick floors, because wood is difficult to obtain. They have no windows, because glass is scarce and dear, for it may have had to be brought from Russia. The desks and forms are of wood, but they are stronger and rougher than those in our schools. During the summer the classes are often taken in the open air, in the shade, preferably in the shade of a tree—for, although wood is so scarce, large trees are often to be seen in the school grounds. You may see a class sitting cross-legged on the ground upon a large carpet, the blackboard propped against a tree, and the pupils and the teacher working together on a problem in arithmetic. The pupils often do all their work upon the blackboard, and they become very expert in this.

The classes meet only in the mornings, usually for five hours, and the boys go home in the afternoon to help on the land. All schools close in the winter because they cannot be heated. Afghan schoolboys have to learn three languages, Persian, Pushtu and Arabic. Persian and Pushtu are both spoken in the country and they are almost as different as are French and English. Arabic is learnt because the Koran has to be read in Arabic. All three languages use the same alphabet, the Arabic. The words are written from right to left, and school books are read from what would be to us back to front. The learning of three languages is hard enough, in any case, but the Uzbeg boys have a still harder task, because their mother tongue is not one of these three but an entirely different language.

Much of the writing in school is done not with a nib but with a wooden splint with a broader end than a nib. This is entirely suitable for the Arabic script and the effect is a bold and firm letter form. This must be a very old way of writing in ink; indeed the method may be to some extent the cause of the Arabic forms, in the same way as the brush has moulded Chinese forms.

Afghan boys have physical education in much the same way as do boys in this country. They do various exercises to develop the body, and use gymnastic gear when they can, invariably in the open air.

Afghan Games and Amusements.

Young people in Afghanistan play very few games. They are too much occupied in tending cattle and crops. They sometimes play a school game called " wally " ball, in which a ball as large as a football is knocked by hand over a net separating two teams. The losing side is the one with the most dropped balls. In Herat, which is near the Persian frontier, the writer watched a football game between two school teams. The game was played just as it is played here, and it was fast and vigorous. Several boys, however, had to play without boots, but bare feet did not spoil their game in the least. Their feet must have been very hard. The boys who watched the match did not cheer or shout for one side or the other, as boys would do in this country.

Afghans are very fond of playing chess and they become expert in it. Some of their chess moves differ from those that we use.

Onlookers often give advice freely and this is always taken in good part. The game often becomes the centre of much argument, which holds up progress, and, of course, makes it difficult for a player to spring a surprise upon his opponent.

Horse-riding ranks high in Afghan pastimes. At holiday time, arrangements are made for what we call " tent-pegging ". In this the horseman spears a small piece of wood on the ground, towards which he rides at a gallop.

Afghans love a circus as much as we do. In one which the writer saw, again at Herat, held after dark, the people sat on the ground in rows around a central shallow bowl. Here a large timber framework carried the gymnasts' equipment: the tight-rope, the horizontal bar and the rings. They performed by the light of oil-lamps and to the sound of music in which the same few notes were played again and again. A small boy took a gymnast's part with great skill. He had thick black hair and he was lifted by it by one of the men, who held the hair between his teeth. The boy was lifted high in the air and was made to turn and to swing. He did not seem to be in any pain because of this. Other men held a net beneath him in case his hair came out or was pulled from between the man's teeth. Of course, there was a clown, who was very clever in his seemingly foolish actions. He had his face slapped hard countless times in the course of the evening. In the last act a man sprang from a springboard through a flaming hoop taken higher and higher, and turned somersaults before reaching the ground. The men of this particular circus team were all Uzbegs and were very fine types.

Afghan music is not very tuneful to our ears. Usually three men will perform. One plays a guitar, and sings; another plays a drum, often two, using the ball of the hand to strike the skin; and the third jingles two metal pieces together. The singer tells a story of war or of love, and it is usually long. The Afghans also play the bagpipes very well and in the Scottish fashion. It would be of interest to know which nation played the bagpipes first! There is another link with Scotland, in the Kabul museum. On the wall are two golf clubs and several balls, not very much like those we now use, but showing that the Afghans at one time played a rather similar game.

The cinema is making its appearance in Afghanistan, but at present there are only one or two and their influence is small. It will be some time before the Afghans can make a habit of going to the pictures.

The Bazaar.

If you went shopping in Afghanistan you would go to the bazaar and buy your goods for the best terms you could agree upon. The goods would not carry prices, as they do in the shops here, and the price would really be what you and the vendor could agree is reasonable.

Most of the bazaars consist of long lines of open-fronted shops on each side of a narrow roadway, which is covered by a kind of thatched roof. The floors of the shops are raised above the ground, and the shops are about as large as one of our average-sized rooms at home. The walls are lined with goods for sale and the shop-keeper sits or reclines gravely on the floor waiting for custom. Here are shops selling tea, tobacco, trinkets and jewellery, cloths for turbans, harness and shoes, sheepskin coats, cloth for trousers and dresses, fruit and nuts, and a thousand other things. Often the tradesman will ply his trade before your eyes: the metal-worker, the tailor, the shoemaker. The cook will bake skewered mutton over a small charcoal fire and the baker will bake the large flat loaves in a mud oven. Sometimes the tradesmen work under great difficulties. The writer watched a blacksmith heat a piece of iron in a very small charcoal fire and use an anvil which was little larger than one of our domestic irons. A small boy sat behind the fire and blew it by using two large cloth air-bags which he pushed one at a time with his hands. The heat from the fire was not enough to heat the iron properly and the blacksmith had great difficulty in shaping it.

Shafts of brilliant sunshine from without pass through holes in the rough thatched roof and light the movement and colour within the bazaar. Donkeys and camels, loaded with merchandise, thread their way through the crowded thoroughfare and pass with an air of boredom. Veiled women come to shop or to sell, and appear to be humble and neglected. Water-carriers pass through, splashing water upon the roadway to lay the dust.

You will always find numbers of men in the bazaar drinking tea and chatting. They sit or recline on a raised floor outside the tea-shop and seem to be very content to let the time pass by in quiet talk and laughter.

Trade and Wealth.

Afghanistan is largely a country of farms and orchards, and it exports fruit and wool. But its principal export is neither of these:

it is the skin of a particular kind of lamb, bred in the northern and western parts of the country. The skins of these lambs have close tight curls and in colour are usually grey, brown, or black. They are not very large, and more than thirty are required to make a lady's coat, so that the cost of it is high. The skins are dried on the hot desert sands and are guarded by men and dogs. This export trade depends upon fashion and the desires of women in other countries. It is not therefore completely reliable.

Afghanistan also has large quantities of marble, and it is an interesting sight to see the great blocks being sawn up and afterwards polished. Amongst the rarer stones found there is lapis lazuli, from which ultramarine is obtained, that lovely colour which artists delight to use for skies and seascapes.

But perhaps Afghanistan's greatest wealth lies in its vast deposits of the ores of more common metals. These deposits have not yet been fully explored and some of them are difficult to reach or to work. Before they can be used, much power will be required, but this can be obtained from the rivers of Afghanistan.

When a great river flows, it presents to the engineer a splendid source of power. He usually blocks a gorge through which the river is flowing and causes the level of the river to rise. Then letting the water flow through a passage he directs it to a turbine, which is really only a water-wheel. The turbine turns an alternator, a machine for making electricity, and thus we get electrical energy from water energy. The engineer also uses his trapped water to irrigate the land. These two things are what Afghanistan badly needs: electricity for lighting, heating and power; and water to bring the parched land into production. If Afghanistan can obtain these two, the country will develop and become much more wealthy. In this great work much help is needed from countries like Great Britain.

The Nomads.

The winters in high Central Asia are very cold and life there is hard. Many of the pastoral people move south in the winter to find a warmer clime and better grazing for their flocks and herds. They return north again in the spring. The movement of one of these tribes is a most interesting event. All the worldly goods of the people are transported, usually on the backs of camels and donkeys, and the caravan may stretch half a mile or more.

One such caravan which the writer met was very long and was

winding its way along a mountain road in a lonely part of Afghanistan. In the front were many animals running loose: calves, sheep, goats and young donkeys. Then came the stately camels, carrying tents, bedding, water, cooking-utensils and even live chickens—which seemed to be quite at home perching on their swaying supports. The women often rode horses or camels, and they were veiled. Small children walked or rode; on their hats and clothes were sewn medallions of many kinds. Most of the men walked at

Camels in Afghanistan

intervals at the heads of the camels, but others, including the headman of the tribe, rode on good-looking horses. Many black oxen plodded along stolidly amongst the camels. The young camels, very graceful and attractive beasts, kept close by the sides of their mothers.

Such a long caravan on the march in the dry climate of Afghanistan raises clouds of dust which cover everyone and everything. Fortunately the dust is easily shaken off, but it is really unpleasant. We know how trying was the discomfort of the soldiers of Alexander the Great as they tramped along the dusty tracks of Central Asia, mile after mile, day after day. Similarly our own troops were greatly troubled by dust on their long marches. Lord Roberts, talking of his campaigns in Afghanistan, mentions not only the dust and heat of the day, but the coldness of the night, for the range of temperature is very great. He mentions the action of the Highlanders who gave their greatcoats to the plucky Gurkhas at night because they admired their courage and fighting qualities.

The busy scene when a large caravan halts for the night can be well imagined. All is seemingly confusion—but it is not so. Everyone, even the children, has his or her own task. The animals are freed to graze, usually by a river, watchers being posted to prevent undue straying. The black tents go up, bedding is spread, small cooking fires are lit and the simple evening meal is prepared. As darkness falls all that can be seen are the bright points of light where the fires burn, all that can be heard are the coughing of the camels and the barking of the dogs.

The so-called Afghan hound is rarely seen in Afghanistan. The dogs which are usually met with in the country, and particularly in the nomad camps, are large mastiffs who show great courage. They will race towards an approaching car and often hurl themselves at it, frequently injuring themselves. They would probably be less fierce towards familiar things such as a horseman or foot traveller, but if there were any doubt about the attitude of the dogs, the traveller would be wise to wait for a man of the tribe to come to him, for the dogs have the fierceness of lions.

The children of the nomads have a strange life. They have no school to attend and they are required to take their share of all the labours of the camp. When a stranger appears they rush towards him with excited cries.

Afghanistan's Future.

In order to feed and to clothe its people, who are growing in numbers, and to give them warmth in winter, Afghanistan needs to harness the power of its rivers. The abundant waters, fed by the melting snows on the high mountains, can be used to make the arid land fertile; they can also provide electrical energy, which will supply electric light, heat and power, for factories and homes.

The abundance provided by nature can be used for the benefit of mankind, but only if mankind is well enough educated to control the natural forces. Everyone knows how the immense energy of the Falls of Niagara has been used to place power in the hands of hundreds of thousands of people in the United States of America and in Canada. When the engineer in a factory starts his motors, when the metal-worker operates great furnaces, when cities are lit, when the housewife switches on a fire or a light, all this is possible there because the energy of the Niagara Falls has been harnessed by man.

So it will be one day in Afghanistan, with its fast-flowing rivers. When they are more fully used than at present the Afghans will be able to water much more land and make it productive; they will be able to have more factories and to make many things which they now have to buy elsewhere; they will not have to rely upon charcoal or dried dung for heat when cooking; they will not have to suffer the winter cold because fuel is so scarce; and they will not have to put up with oil-lamps.

In the future, people will want to visit Afghanistan for holidays as they now visit Switzerland. They will be certain of sunshine and will enjoy fine scenery. They will also find themselves amongst a people with many fine qualities, among which hospitality is one of the chief.

EXPLORATION BY AIR: FLYING ACROSS THE POLE

The story of exploration is never ended. The great explorers of the last century—men like Stanley and Livingstone, Shackleton and Scott, Nansen and Peary, Sven Hedin, Doughty and Joseph Thomson, opened up, by their courage and pertinacity in facing many real and some imaginary dangers, lands and whole regions of the world where nobody had ever ventured before; but they left a multitude of details to be filled in, and even to-day some parts of the earth are almost unknown. Naturally the worst obstacles occur in the most savage places—the polar regions, where ice crushes ships and blizzards overwhelm sledge parties; the vast deserts of Asia, Africa and Arabia, where lack of water and the fanatical jealousy of native tribes were equally effective difficulties; and the dense forests of the Congo and the Amazon, where a gang of men needed a whole day to cut a couple of miles through the jungle, while blood-sucking flies and malarial mosquitoes infected the unhappy traveller with dangerous or even fatal fevers.

The advent of the aeroplane made it possible to overcome many of these dangers; for, although of course man could not discover the minute details of plant and animal life, or how the savage tribes lived, or what went on upon the vast, frozen ice-caps of Greenland and Antarctica, without getting down there and examining such things on the spot, he could at least by the aid of a plane and an aerial camera lay out the broad outlines of a country quite easily in as many hours as his predecessors had required months. Much of this aerial surveying has been simple routine work, no more exciting to the aviator than a train journey to the ordinary man; but much of it has also called for great courage and capacity, has led men into some very tight corners, and has produced some splendid episodes of travel. In this chapter we propose to glance at a few of the more outstanding flights, mainly in the Arctic regions.

Exploration of the Arctic by air began a few years before the Wright brothers designed their first successful aeroplane. In 1895 the North Pole seemed immeasurably remote, for no traveller had ever got to within hundreds of miles of it. The heroic Norwegian giant, Fridtjof Nansen, had sailed into the frozen ocean two years before, in his famous ship *Fram*, but nothing further had been heard of him. He was, in fact, with his one companion Johansen making a life-and-death struggle across the floes and water channels north of Franz Josef Land to some spot where they might winter safely, at the very moment when S. A. Andrée, a Swedish balloonist, put forward a well-conceived and highly adventurous proposal to sail over the Pole in a balloon. Andrée really intended to sail; for his balloon, besides having a trailing rope by which it was hoped to keep near the ice in the event of contrary winds, was also to carry a sail with which to take advantage of favourable ones. Foolish though this scheme may seem in the light of what we know now, it received international support, the necessary money was found, and in 1896 Andrée took his balloon to Dane's Island, north of Spitsbergen, built a house there for it, and inflated the gasbag. But the winds were against him and the adventure was put off till next year. Then at last he went up with two companions, Fraenkel and Strindberg. After one false start they floated away to the north and were last seen moving off at about 22 miles per hour—not much by to-day's standards of aircraft speeds, but immense to men who had learned that eight or ten miles' sledging over the ice was a good performance. Nothing further has ever been heard of them. They probably drifted to some spot from which it was found impossible to return, and perished miserably of exhaustion and hunger in a vain endeavour to regain the land.

Then came the aeroplane. For some years after its invention, it was in far too experimental a stage to be used for exploration; indeed aircraft afforded all the thrills that any man could desire, merely to fly them; and when, after many pioneers had been killed or maimed by flying accidents, Louis Bleriot flew across the English Channel, 21 miles, in 31 minutes it was hailed as a triumph of human achievement. The early aviator was a true " flying man ", not merely a skilled motor driver as to-day. He took his life in his hands whenever he went up and pitted his skill against all the unknown dangers of the new art, bumpy air, cross currents, imperfect balance, defective engines, inadequate wing support, poor landing-grounds, and shaky landing-gear (if indeed he had any).

The needs of the first World War greatly increased the safety and efficiency of aeroplanes. When, not long after its close, Alcock and Brown made their memorable first crossing of the Atlantic, Sir Frederick Sykes and his able team of pioneers were already laying down the first Empire air routes to the Cape and Australia; the aeroplane as a means of exploration had begun to come into its own. Thousands of photographs of enemy country were taken from planes during the war, and it was soon realized that these afforded a ready means of reconnaissance mapping; with specially trained pilots using improved instruments aircraft could be made to yield most valuable results. Thus, flights over the Turkish lines in Mesopotamia disclosed that what on the ground had seemed mere shapeless mounds of rubbish were really the orderly lines of some ancient city, with wide streets where chariots could pass, all now buried under the dust of ages. The airman, viewing the earth from 6000 feet up, saw it as a map. He saw rivers winding through densely forested country, where those below could discern nothing but trees and had to feel their way forward through the never-ending gloom. He saw the limits of the forest, the best ways past patches of sand dunes, the route to a water-hole or a town, in a manner that was impossible to the traveller below. Fairly rapidly a whole new technique of mapping from the air grew up, assisted by the invention of expensive machines which enabled the photographs to be reduced to contour maps of surprising accuracy. Cameras were now properly housed in the aircraft and were automatically controlled; and, after a long time, by flying on a radio beam, and using navigation instruments which disclosed the slightest deviation from a straight line or change in the height above the ground, the comparative perfection of modern aerial map-making was evolved.

In the last resort, of course, everything depends on the aerial camera. It is a special instrument, loaded with film. It can take photographs at constant speed, and is mounted in the floor of the aircraft, as a rule forward or astern. One may take long strips of vertical photographs, which show the ground just as in a map, but with no relief; or oblique ones, which can be used to sketch in buildings, hills, mountains, although the outer parts of the field are distorted; or stereoscopic ones, also used for making contour maps. By this aid areas of difficult country far larger than the United Kingdom have been quickly surveyed and reduced to excellent maps, in such places as Northern Canada, where there are countless lakes, waterfalls, winding rivers, and patches of forest and swamp almost insuperable obstacles to the ground traveller; moreover, there is little risk beyond that of a forced landing, and even this is not too serious as a rule, because the airman is in touch by radio with his base and can speedily summon relief. It was not always so easy.

One of the first to use aircraft for exploratory work in the Arctic was Roald Amundsen, the famous Norwegian, who beat Captain Scott to the South Pole. Amundsen was a singular man, a real hero, of boundless courage and great endurance, but crafty. He always prepared for his many journeys in the most thorough way and literally overlooked nothing, but he was greedy of fame, secretive and impatient. He knew the Arctic as few men know it. At the beginning of the century, in a tiny ship of only 47 tons, he had made the first North-West Passage ever recorded, besides the first visit to the North Magnetic Pole (in Boothia, northern Canada) for seventy years. He had then, largely through the help of his old friend Nansen, hired the famous *Fram* for a North-East Passage, intending to follow Nansen's route along the Siberian coast to Bering Strait, then push into the ice and drift across the Pole. They sailed in 1910; but when everyone at home, including the subscribers, thought him well into the Arctic, he suddenly turned up at Madeira and announced that he was bound for the South Pole instead. It was but a year since Peary, sledging across the ice from North Greenland, had conquered the North Pole after twenty years of toil and sufferings. Captain Scott's second expedition was on the way to tackle the Antarctic; and Amundsen clearly thought that unless he acted quickly he would lose the South Pole too. So, without a prior word to anybody, he turned the *Fram* south, and as we all know, by sheer ability, courage and faith conquered greater difficulties than almost any man has had to face, and by an entirely new route reached the South Pole in December, 1911.

He was bound in honour, however, to complete the project upon which he had set out. More funds were raised; but first the *Fram* failed to get through the Panama Canal on her way to Bering Strait, because of a landslide; and then the war broke out and the expedition was postponed until near its end. In 1918 Amundsen at last put to sea, this time in a new ship, the *Maud*. Repeating the experience of Nansen and others, he worked the ship along the shore channels off the bleak and barren tundra of Siberia, and after being frozen in off Cape Chelyuskin for one winter successfully emerged at Bering Strait, the first man ever completely to circumnavigate the Arctic Ocean.

It remained to finish the project by putting the ship's head into the ice again and drift across the Pole, frozen in among the floes. There are strong currents in this sea and a first attempt to get into the pack failed, so they returned to Alaska. The years were passing, and by this time Amundsen, who above everything was a man of action, yearned for something more vital than the dreary routine duties of work on the little steamer. Nansen, much in the same mood, had left the *Fram* on his wonderful sledge journey across the icy ocean; Amundsen now proposed a similar course, but by air. He had in fact a small aircraft on the *Maud*, but she was not intended for such work and was left with the ship. While the leader remained at Nome, Captain Wisting took the *Maud* back towards Siberia, but failed to get far enough north, and after a long struggle near the New Siberian Islands was drifted towards the shore again. His aeroplane was damaged in attempting to take-off on a flight, and in July, 1923, it was wrecked. The *Maud* eventually emerged into open water again.

Meanwhile Amundsen had moved to Point Barrow, the northern-most tip of Alaska, where there is a small mission station for the few Eskimos and others in that dreariest of all Arctic spots. He had a Curtiss seaplane, in which he planned to fly with two companions direct across the Beaufort Sea to the Pole and straight down to Spitsbergen. This at that date was literally a jump into the unknown. Ice from the Beaufort Sea drifts ashore at Barrow, but strong currents run both east and west and nobody had been out very far upon it. It was, in fact, the largest unknown patch of the Arctic and was completely unexplored. To come down there would probably be fatal. This did not deter the intrepid Amundsen. After the North-East Passage his reputation was again high, and the Norwegian Government even sent aeroplanes to Spitsbergen to welcome him home. But the Curtiss broke its under-carriage, everything went wrong, and Amundsen, who was no foolhardy adventurer, wisely called the whole thing off. He tried to raise more money. Nothing fails like failure, however, and these repeated setbacks caused him nothing but humiliation. Amundsen never accepted defeat, however black the outlook. After a long time he interested Mr. Lincoln Ellsworth, an adventurous young American, who agreed to put up most of the money for a new flight to the Pole, on condition that he himself was taken. He was not a pilot, but Amundsen agreed to his terms. Thus began another story of heroism and endurance, worthy to rank with the best in travel lore.

To meet the more modest circumstances which now ruled, they decided to fly from Spitsbergen to the Pole and back, employing two aircraft and six men in all. The machines were Dornier Wal flying-boats, each powered by two 360 h.p. Rolls-Royce engines; these were placed tandem in the centre-line of the plane, one propeller pushing and the other pulling. The men formed a remarkable

Dornier Wal flying-boat N.25, used in Amundsen's 1925 expedition

team. Amundsen himself had unique experience of both Arctic and Antarctic conditions. His friend Lieutenant Dietrichsen, a first-rate man, piloted one machine (N.24); the other, N.25, was under Captain Riiser-Larsen, who in subsequent years made scores of flights over the hitherto unknown coasts of Antarctica, largely on behalf of the Norwegian whaling fleet. Lincoln Ellsworth, too, later made the famous aerial crossing of the Antarctic continent, which we shall mention later. Omdal and Feucht, the two mechanics, were also first rate.

Transporting the bulky aircraft on two small steamers across the wild Norwegian Sea to Spitsbergen was a tricky business, and unloading them at the dreary little haven at King's Bay, on the west coast, was even trickier; but they were got ashore unharmed and were assembled, and the engines tuned, by experts from the works.

Amundsen had decided to have no trial flights, for a trial might result in accident and an accident now would completely sink his credit. It was to be all or nothing. De-icing was not then well understood, but the engines were protected against cold, and the petrol and oil pipes were bound round with linen tapes to prevent breakage through vibration. The Dornier had a great bird-like hull, sufficient to cover a single runway; so they dispensed with floats in order to save having to cut two more runways whenever the machine came down. Each machine was overloaded by more than half a ton.

In fine weather, 21st May, 1925, they took off, first getting the heavy planes down on to fjord ice in the bay, a ticklish business. They headed for the land, i.e. up the fjord, took the air just in time and after circling the bay made for Cape Mitre and the Pole. They had only just left the land when they ran into the thick fog which seems constantly to haunt that corner of Spitsbergen. They flew through and above it for over one hundred miles, Amundsen steering by the sun and using a special " sun-compass ". This gave their direction, but without observing the ground or sea ice below it was impossible to say how far the wind was drifting them off their course; and they were in fact blown quite a lot off course by a strong N.E. wind. It was now discovered that their sextant was the wrong type, but Amundsen relied on his magnetic compasses, and they sped north uneventfully hour after hour.

Down below was the ocean, two to three miles deep, covered with floating ice and marked by water cracks from time to time— probably not a nice surface on which to make a forced landing. Then Amundsen was told that half the petrol in N.25 had been used. A patch of open water lay ahead, sparkling in the sun; it was a good place to come down and Amundsen decided to do so, as he was not certain of his position. Both planes accordingly circled and descended, but by a curious accident the engines of both backfired. Riiser-Larsen in N.25, carrying the leader, had almost to crash-land; he came down on newly formed ice in a small lead, with heavy floes on each side and ice blocks thrust up from the surface. One wing brushed against a hummocky ice ridge, fortunately without oversetting the plane, and she came to rest at the very edge of the floe. Her crew tumbled out and ruefully surveyed their position. It was extremely unsafe, for these leads between the floes open and shut continually, and the plane was in fact slightly nipped soon afterwards. Meanwhile, N.24 had disappeared altogether. It had come down safely in the water, close to a big seal. Dietrichsen recognized the danger of the floes closing, and the crew, after much difficulty and some damage, got the heavy plane on to a floe. Several hours later they joined the others.

Amundsen was now really on his mettle. An observation had shown that they were still about 130 miles short of the Pole and far to the west of their true course. One plane was damaged by its ascent of an ice-floe, the other was in danger of destruction because it could not be got up on one! There were six men to provide for, ill supplied with food or stores for a long stay, and far too distant from any land to seek safety by a march across the slushy ice in midsummer. To crown all, it was doubtful if sufficient petrol remained to carry both planes back to Spitsbergen, even if they could take off—which seemed unlikely. And finally, they were very short of trenching or digging tools.

First, the rations must be cut, a severe privation in the keen hungry air of the Arctic. It was reduced to half a pound per man per day. " We may," said the leader, " be here only a few hours, but we must provide against contingencies." They were, in fact, on the floes nearly a month—twenty-five days packed with hardships, with unending toil, with constant soakings in the sea, with the weakening grip of hunger upon them, and virtually no hope except in their own stout hearts and the example of their leader. With an axe, an ice-anchor, and a long knife fastened to a ski stave they started to get N.25 out of the lead, and built a slipway and an ice bridge about 300 feet long over small, rotten floes to where good firm ice could be found. The danger was that by its weight the machine might sink so deeply that the next nip would destroy it. It took five days' frightful toil to make this approach, and then the 3-ton machine, driven by its engines, mounted to the floe and the first obstacle seemed overcome. Examination of Dietrichsen's plane (N.24) decided Amundsen to abandon it and to rely upon taking all six men back to Spitsbergen in his own; so everything that they might need had to be taken out and conveyed across the half-frozen leads to the other floe.

All this time, of course, the floes, which are cakes of ice varying in area from several acres to a few square yards, were drifting with the Polar sea, crushing together and forcing up water and ice blocks into pressure ridges, opening again and disclosing the clear blue ocean, the cold surface of which often froze again into thin or " pancake " ice. The great difficulty now was to find a line long enough and smooth enough from which N.25 could take-off. One lead opened on 29th June; it froze to a depth of 7 inches, and they ventured the machine upon its ideal surface; but alas, the plane broke through, so they all had to set to work to dig it out once more, and while they were so engaged it was nipped by the pressure of opposing floes. Amundsen exhorted, sweated, swore; his team, with bitterly cold fingers and aching limbs, at last got the plane out and on to a floe again. Here there was a clear field at last. They made a track 900 feet long, but no sooner was it finished than the floe opened and ruined it. On 5th June yet another floe was seen, about half a mile away, which looked as if it would resist anything. They therefore cut a passage for the plane through a pressure ridge 12 feet high, built a causeway of ice blocks across the water, and drove the N.25 over this quaking road on to the new floe. On 8th June they tried a take-off, with all six men on board; but the surface was soft snow and the machine refused to budge, so they had to start all over again, tramping down a hard surface backwards and forwards, until the runway was 1800 feet long and 36 feet wide. This took three whole days, and then it thawed again and the whole thing had to be repeated.

At last, on 15th June, dangerously overloaded, and with certain death before them if they should make a forced landing, they got into the air, but before the engine was running at full speed they had cleared the floe, jumped a lane 6 feet wide, and bumped on another floe beyond it. After eight hours' steady flight they sighted the Seven Islands, just north of Spitsbergen. The rudder controls now refused to work, which made the aircraft almost unmanageable; but with great skill Riiser-Larsen brought her down in the open sea and then taxied to the beach. Soon afterwards they were seen by a sealing ship, which took them back to King's Bay.

The really serious risks which early aviators ran over the ocean was shown by the experience of Mr. George Binney, leader of the

Oxford University Arctic Expedition of 1924. The party, which also used King's Bay as a base, had as part of its programme flights over the lesser-known parts of mountainous Spitsbergen and above North-East Land which adjoins it. They used a modified Avro seaplane, driven by a 170-h.p. Lynx engine. On one of these flights, when Binney and the pilot only were in the plane, a piston broke about 15 miles out from King's Bay, the engine stopped, and they came down in the sea. The accident was not observed. The wind was getting up, night was approaching, and the current was drifting the plane away. One man sat on each float, with his feet in the icy water, and with paddles made from ice-axes, to which pieces of a sledge box lid had been tied with string, they tried to guide the machine landwards. Three hours' work produced no result. The waves were now breaking over them and they were numb with cold. In an effort to stop their motion they made a sea anchor from a length of rope, the engine tools, and a fire extinguisher, they themselves getting so cold in the process that they had to enter the cabin, lie there in a sleeping-bag, and drink a little brandy to revive their circulation. It was now night, waves seven feet high were breaking over the plane, it was becoming waterlogged, and clearly the end was in sight. The wind was rapidly drifting them away from the land again. They poured oil on the water to lessen the sea's violence, and they put on their life-jackets, expecting every moment that the plane would sink beneath them. Then, at last, " at the last minute of the eleventh hour ", as Mr. Binney so aptly expressed it, they were observed. Two young Norwegian brothers named Devold saw the black object tossing about in the water; and having with a telescope verified that it was not a whale, they enlisted the aid of a young fisherman and the three went out in a 16-foot open launch to investigate. The wind was now whistling a pretty sharp tune; waves broke over the boat and repeatedly extinguished its spluttering engine; once even the tiller was swept away. But they reached the plane and at considerable risk of upset got its two half-frozen occupants on board, thus undoubtedly saving their lives.

We return to Amundsen. Undeterred by his many failures—spurred on, rather, by the sharp goad of defeat—he was soon at work again, planning a new attempt to reach the North Pole. Aircraft had failed him; perhaps an airship would be luckier. Eleven months later he was back at King's Bay, Spitsbergen. Ellsworth,

Riiser-Larsen, Dietrichsen were all there (for, like Shackleton, the brave Norseman had that quality in him which made his friends willing to follow him to the world's end, whatever the odds). They had acquired a small Italian semi-rigid airship, the *Norge*, commanded by Colonel Nobile, and a crew of thirteen. They were to fly straight across the Pole and the Beaufort Sea to Alaska. This, of course, was the old plan, but in new dress; however, Amundsen was cheated of the prize after all by a mere matter of three days. This introduces a new character to our story, Commander (now Rear-Admiral) Richard E. Byrd, of the U.S. Navy.

Like Amundsen, who was 54 years old, Byrd had passed the age when youth accepts all risks gladly. He was a mature man of 37, a trained aviator, and had already made his mark in helping to build up his country's air arm. In the previous year, he had accompanied an expedition to Smith Sound, West Greenland, that savage, remote, ice-filled passage which is full of the ghosts of explorers and seamen who have died there in the fight for the Pole. There Byrd made some long flights which gave him a taste for Arctic travel that he never lost afterwards.

In May, 1926, Byrd appeared off King's Bay aboard the S.S. *Chantier*, which also carried his two aircraft and his companion in the proposed adventure, Lieutenant Floyd Bennett. He intended to fly straight to the Pole and back, using a Fokker monoplane. Amundsen was expected at any moment with the *Norge*. One of his little ships, the *Hobby*, was even then lying in the bay; and a Norwegian gunboat was coaling at the little quay in readiness for his arrival, and naturally would not give way to let Byrd in. It was therefore necessary to unload the plane without proper tackle. The ship was anchored, four boats being tied together to make a pontoon, and on this contraption the smaller plane was safely floated ashore. It had now begun to snow and ice was forming in the bay; but the wing of the Fokker, 63 feet wide, was hoisted on deck, when the wind got up and stopped the operation altogether. Next morning the wing was transferred to the raft, but the bay was now choked with ice. The Norwegians on the *Hobby* came to the rescue and cut a circle round the ship; then, with boathooks and picks, a channel was opened through which the pontoon was hauled ashore. We mention these details, which are taken from Byrd's own graphic story to the press at the time, just to show you how easily difficulties arise and how essential it is to master them.

The plane was quickly assembled, but the thought that Amundsen would soon be up made the aviators hurry matters so much that they only succeeded in delaying their own start. They cleared a runway, decided on a trial take-off, and promptly damaged one of the plane's skis and the landing-gear. This was put right and the runway lengthened; then, in the first trial flight, Bennett ran the *Josephine Ford* straight into a snow-bank and again smashed the landing-gear. Byrd now began to realize a little of what the Norwegians had been through in the preceding summer. All the available labour was recruited, and they spent many arduous hours in packing down the bumps and hardening the snow. Next afternoon they started in earnest, but once more the plane refused to take-off and buried its nose in a drift; so a further stretch had to be added to the runway, in which Norwegians and Italians sportingly assisted, for the *Norge* had just arrived. Finally, at 12.30 a.m. on 9th May, Byrd and Floyd Bennett took the air. Soon they were 1000 feet up, despite their heavy load, and the frozen peaks of Spitsbergen were slipping behind them. A few minutes later they crossed Dane's Island, where until recently the bleached ruins of poor Andrée's balloon-shed could still be seen. Then, passing above the edge of the ice pack, they headed due north.

At first Bennett piloted the plane, while Byrd steered, but from time to time they changed places. Byrd steered by a sun compass, which unluckily for him was outside the machine on a trapdoor; and when he looked at it he had to stick his head out into the windstream and promptly got his nose frozen, but withdrew it again just in time. As we have said earlier, steering north by the sun is all right, provided that you can keep one eye on the ground so as to detect the amount which the wind drifts you off course. When Byrd tried to make this observation he had to open the trapdoor in the bottom of the plane and touch the drift indicator; this, of course, froze his fingers, which then had to be nursed back to life again. As, on the average, he calculated the speed and drift every three or four minutes, making corrections when necessary on the sun compass, he had both a busy and uncomfortable time; otherwise, the flight was without incident. They had wonderful views of the illimitable ice-field below, seamed by a thousand water cracks and with the lighter shadows of pressure ridges criss-crossing everywhere. The plane was making about 90 miles an hour, and although she was using too much petrol there was still enough for the journey

14*

Fokker monoplane, the type of machine used by Byrd on his flight to the
North Pole, May, 1926

home. Because of having so constantly to stare at the sunlit snow with unprotected eyes, Byrd now began to suffer that agonizing pain snow-blindness in his right eye; fortunately the other one was not affected. After flying another hour they found a leak, apparently from one of the motors, a serious matter; but they decided to " keep on for the Pole and decide what to do after reaching it "; which was undoubtedly the proper course, because if anything went wrong they were lost men anyhow; they were only an hour's run from the Pole and were completely cut off from any hope of succour. The offending motor was stopped, but they still made 60 miles per hour on the other two. Compare this with Nansen's progress on the ice below, when by really superhuman efforts he could not achieve more than two or three miles per day!

The Pole was reached at 9.04 a.m., after 8½ hours' flying; they circled it and photographed the ice. Of course, there was nothing special to see; it was just ocean, covered with floating ice, and, except for the fact that from this point all directions were south, it might have been any other part of the Arctic. But it was a triumph for Byrd, who was only the second man ever to reach the Pole, the other being Peary in 1909. The airmen now found to their relief that the leak was not in the motor after all, but came from a spare oil tank. A course was laid straight for Spitsbergen, in bright sun-shine and clear sky. So simple did the flight become that once when at the controls the hum of the engine caused Byrd to doze; he woke with a start to find the plane's nose dipping seawards and had to pull her up sharply. As the wind was now behind them the *Josephine Ford* made about 100 m.p.h. At 2.30 p.m., i.e. after only 5½ hours, land was seen ahead; it was still about a hundred miles away, but at that speed they soon came out over the blue sea and the mountains of Spitsbergen once more; then round to King's Bay, where they saw the ship and the runway far below. Bennett made a perfect landing; and the two men clambered out to receive the congratulations of their friends. Byrd, however, heard not a word. He had forgotten to put on his ear-stoppers during the flight and was temporarily deaf.

With the true chivalry which is part of his character, Byrd sought out his rival, went over the details of the flight with him, and gave him his sextant, sun compass and chart. Only two days later, at nine o'clock in the morning, Amundsen sailed; he had lost the Pole, but plenty remained yet, and this time all went well. The airship followed practically the same course as Byrd, its speed ranging from 60 to 90 miles an hour, at a height of about 2000 feet. After a voyage of twelve hours, nearly all of it in bright sunshine, they reached and circled the Pole at one o'clock on the morning of 12th May, 1926. Thus did Amundsen achieve the ambition of a life-time. It was the second time in three days that the North Pole

Amundsen's airship, the *Norge*

had been attained; wags even asked about the chances of an excursion service thither!

So far the flight had been uneventful, but beyond the Pole lay the unknown hazards of the Beaufort Sea; mountainous islands, even, might rise there, as occurred north of Canada, but in fact they found nothing. They ran into fog, and on rising to get out of it were still baffled by thick clouds which hid the sun. It began to snow, and although the snow in these regions is usually dry and powdery, moisture settled on the metal rigging and weighed down the ship. Pieces of ice dropped off repeatedly in the line of the propellers, which then shot them forward like a stream of bullets into the airship. The gasbags had been strengthened against this very contingency, but the fabric covering them and the keel was punctured repeatedly, and the crew had to cover the holes with patches. The *Norge* was steered for some hours by magnetic compass alone, nothing being seen below; this was a dangerous business so near to the Magnetic Pole (where the compass is practically useless), and Amundsen was glad when at last they got a sight of the sun and could direct the ship's nose towards Point Barrow. Thirty-four hours after leaving the Pole land was seen far ahead for the first time, but it was wrapped in mist; they knew that high mountains lay a short distance inland in Alaska, and they turned more to the west towards Bering Strait. It grew colder, foggier and damper, and ice began to weigh down the airship once more. She was buffeted by a strong wind, but in the baffling mist nobody knew where they were.

When at last they saw open water they had crossed Alaska completely and were passing out into the Pacific, largely forced thither by the squalls. Amundsen was anxious to land, even if it were only on one of the drifting floes in the ocean beneath, for the airship was tossing about wildly in the bumpy air. Then they picked up the Nome aerial, which was transmitting to another station, and they got its bearing; but they could not make the little town and came down at a small post some distance away, called Teller.

With the voyage of the *Norge* it seemed that Amundsen's life of adventure was over, but fate still had one heroic deed for him to perform. Despite the experience of that little airship, which had proved (as many people believed) the unsuitability of lighter-than-air machines for such work, the Italians were now seized with a desire to send a more ambitious expedition, partly scientific and partly for the glory of Fascist Italy, to the Polar regions. The new airship was the *Italia*, and Nobile, now a general, had command of her; she was well equipped and carried a body of distinguished scientists on board. In calm weather, with clear skies, such a craft could undoubtedly do much useful work; but in the uncertain weather conditions of the misty north, with furious gales likely to arise at any time, her great expanse of surface must render any airship most difficult to manage. That is what happened to the *Italia*. She had only sailed a little way north of Spitsbergen, when her wireless messages ceased; and as many days elapsed and nothing further was heard, Europe was shocked at the thought that a terrible disaster must have happened. This was towards the end of May and beginning of June, 1928. Afterwards it became known that the ship had been carried down to the floes by a squall, had struck the ice violently, breaking off one gondola and hurling out its occupants, and had then drifted on some distance and crashed. Many of her people escaped, including General Nobile. They were rescued, at great peril to themselves, by airmen of several nationalities and by the Russian ice-breaker *Krassin*. Before this happened, however, Amundsen had met his end. He agreed to go on a search flight in the region he knew so well, accompanied by his old comrade Dietrichsen and piloted by the French captain Guilbaud. They took off from Tromsoe on the 18th June, heading for Spitsbergen in a Latham seaplane, and were never heard of again. They undoubtedly crashed in the sea, for some weeks later one of the floats of the plane drifted ashore on the Lofoten Islands. So ended a wonderful, colourful career.

From Byrd's successful Polar flight in 1926 to the Russian flight of October, 1945, the North Pole was reached no fewer than sixteen times by air. On eleven occasions this was by Soviet airmen, as was only to be expected; for the Russians, forced by the German invasion of their country to develop navigation along the Siberian shore, built a whole fleet of ice-breakers for freeing cargo ships, and employed aircraft as spotters to pick out the best routes for them. Thus they acquired invaluable Arctic flying experience. Twice they flew right across the Pole from Moscow to the United States; a third expedition with the same object passed the Pole and was never heard of again. The 1945 flight was so commonplace that the crew described it as " routine ". It was made by M. Titlov, with four companions, in a Douglas type land plane, and was done as part of an ordinary reconnaissance north of Cape Chelyuskin. They covered more than 4000 kilometres in fifteen hours, an incredible advance over the days of Nansen and Nordenskjöld, when the *Vega* and the *Fram*, frozen into the ice off that iron-bound promontory, spent a whole season in getting round it!

The most striking Russian adventure in the Arctic, so far, however, has been Ivan Papanin's famous expedition of 1937. On 21st May in that year he and his three companions were deliberately taken far north by air, were landed on the ice, with abundant tents, food, fuel and scientific instruments, and left there to drift wherever it might take them. They had wireless equipment, with which they kept in regular touch with Moscow. They worked through the winter, just as the crews of the *Fram* and *Maud* had done, taking soundings, recording temperatures, and having all the small adventures from packing of ice-floes and the opening of water cracks with which earlier travellers have made us familiar. They drifted across the Polar sea for nine months towards Spitsbergen, now this way, now that; and as the spring came on, and they got free, their floe steadily dwindled until it was only a few yards across. Then the ice-breaker *Taimyr*, which had been summoned by radio to their relief, picked them up; and so terminated their drift of twelve hundred miles over the ocean.

In this article we have been concerned only with North Polar flying. You will be aware, of course, that Byrd and Ellsworth also did some remarkable pioneer flying in the far south. Byrd, in fact, showed all the qualities of a great explorer. In 1928-9 he took a large American expedition to the Ross Sea, including several air-craft. A winter home was set up at the Bay of Whales, close by Amundsen's old base. Sledge parties laid depots on the Barrier ice and planes dropped others at the foot of the great Antarctic mountains 400 miles inland.

In the spring (29th November, 1929) four men, including Byrd, took off in a Ford plane for the South Pole, more than 800 miles away. They were heavily loaded, carrying a sledge, sleeping-bags, food sacks, stoves, tents, to the tune of nearly seven tons. When they reached the mountains they found, as Amundsen had done, that they were 15,000 feet high, and that the best way up even for an aircraft was to follow a glacier. They did so, feeling closely con-fined between the savage, ice-clad rocky walls. The plane rose and rose till the altimeter registered 9600 feet; that was its ceiling, but still the glacier rose ahead. Byrd heaved overboard a precious sack of food—125 lb. The plane rose a little, but still not enough; so overboard went another 125 lb. of food, cocoa, pemmican, and other stand-bys of the Antarctic traveller crashing down to the ice below. Then at last they topped the pass. A wide expanse of utter desolation, more than 10,000 feet high and stretching for many hundreds of miles in every direction, lay beneath them; the Antarctic ice-cap, the place on which Shackleton and his friends, tightening their belts and hauling their heavy sledges like true heroes, had marched on and on until sheer necessity compelled them to turn back when only 97 miles from the Pole. This was the place, too, where Amundsen's dogs, freed at last from the interminable toil

up the glacier, had leapt forward joyfully to the south; and it was
the same ice that Captain Scott, Wilson, Bowers, Oates and Evans
had trod, only to find their efforts vain, and the prize another's.
Over it the Ford now shot with contemptuous ease, making ninety
miles per hour. After reaching the Pole, Byrd and his men were
safely back at their base, Little America, in a mere nine hours. Scott
had been dead only seventeen years. Can any story of progress
be more wonderful than this?

Ellsworth too earned his niche in the Temple of Fame. He
decided to cross Antarctica by air from Graham Land to Little
America, and despite repeated heart-breaking setbacks year after
year actually did so in November, 1935. It was a flight packed with
thrills, the story of which we must tell some other time. He and
his companion lost their way; they came down in the middle of
the icy plateau and could not get off again; and when they did get
off their petrol gave out just before they reached Little America,
which, incidentally, they could not find for a long time as it was
buried under the snow!

The valuable part which aircraft play in modern exploration could
not be shown more clearly than in the Trans-Antarctic expedition of
Dr. Fuchs and Sir Edmund Hillary in 1957-58. As we all know,
the aim was for Fuchs and a land party to complete the journey in
which Sir Ernest Shackleton had failed gloriously exactly forty years
before, by crossing the South Pole from the Weddell Sea to Scott's
old base at Ross Island; meanwhile Hillary would ascend the vast
mountain range which fronts the Ross Barrier ice and would lay
depots along the high ice plateau towards the Pole, for the Fuchs
party to pick up as their own supplies gave out. Thanks to good
organisation, motor tractor transport, perseverance against mechanical
breakdowns, and the usual measure of good luck, the expedition was
a triumph; but it owed much to the four small aircraft—two Austers
and two Handley-Pages—which were, in a sense, its eyes and nose;
for from them a way through the ice-pack was picked out, supplies
for depots were dumped well ahead of the land party, valuable
surveys were made of the ice-clad mountains, and Hillary was
enabled to journey to the Pole itself. Still more remarkable, a party
of American scientists had spent an entire year at the South Pole,
being provisioned by air from their base on the Ross Sea side and
supplied with everything they needed. What a contrast to the old
heroic figures of Scott and Shackleton, with their brave, unfaltering

comrades, who manhauled their sledges out and back for over 1600 miles, entirely on their own resources; or even of the gallant Amundsen, who did the same thing, but with dogs!

We have not said much so far about the British, but the Arctic is in fact haunted by the spirit of many a gallant British seaman, some of whom sought to gain the Pole, but most of whom were in search of the North-West Passage. One of the most spectacular British achievements in this region has occurred since the war—to be precise, in May, 1945—when the R.A.F. Lancaster plane *Aries* crossed the Pole. *Aries* had a very important mission, and her captain, Wing-Commander D. C. McKinley, D.F.C., two definite objects. He was to try out in northern regions, where the lines of longitude converge on the Pole, a new system of finding one's position, known as the Greenwich Grid. In addition to this navigation problem, he also had to ascertain what had become of the North Magnetic Pole, or rather, where it had gone; for the Magnetic Pole wanders over a large area, and as all ordinary compass observations are based upon it, you can see how essential a duty this was. He also wished to learn how far magnetic instruments, when carried above the earth in a moving aeroplane, could be relied upon to give scientists information about the earth's magnetism.

The machine was an ordinary service Lancaster, modified. Its armament was removed, the nose and tail streamlined, and the fuel tanks enlarged so as to give her a range of 5000 miles. Suitable clothing, food and other supplies had to be taken to provide against a possible forced landing. She was only partly protected against icing-up, and they could not arrange the usual precautions of warm air and electrically heated clothes for the crew; if anyone felt cold he could go forward into the cockpit, where the sun shining through the glass roof would warm him—if, of course, the sun was shining. The crew numbered eleven. They were specially trained, having had to live in an ice chamber and eat dehydrated food for two whole days before their departure. McKinley and his second pilot flew the aircraft, and in the intervals acted as engineers, photographers and meteorologists. The first navigator was responsible for all external observations, the second navigator handled the radar and plotted the ship's course. The research officer did the magnetic work. There were also two wireless operators, a medical officer, and a maintenance crew of three; these last had to keep the machine in full flying trim, and scarcely got a moment's sleep during the cruise.

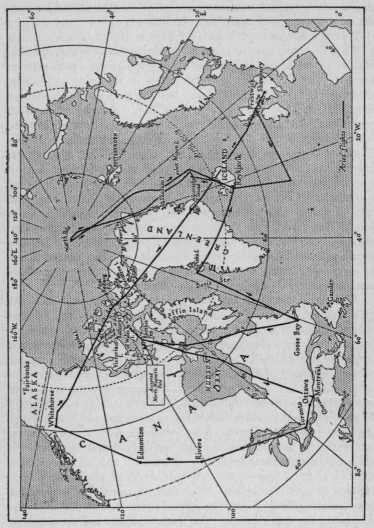

Route of the *Aries*

To make the necessary observations, it was essential that the sun and moon should be in certain relative positions. This meant that only about five days in all, in mid-May, were available for everything.

They left England on 10th May, 1945, for Iceland, heavily loaded. Six days later they rose above Reykjavik, still heavily loaded and in half a gale, being bound for the North Pole. Soon after rounding Iceland's Cape Horn they ran into fog and could not get out of it; all round them dim light shone through the ice crystals, ice began to form on the wings, and their speed became dangerously low; nevertheless, they went on, but after nine hours returned to Reykjavik. Two hours later *Aries* had been refuelled and they started again, keeping this time more to the east, so as to avoid the fog over Spitsbergen. They swung across to Peary Land, the northernmost part of Greenland, and then straight north to the Pole; once the ship became heavily iced, but passed out of it again into fine weather.

Flying at 14,000 feet, they had the magnificent coast of northeast Greenland visible for a vast distance, and once they passed a large black-and-white goose, flying at about 12,000 feet. The ocean beneath was covered with glittering floes, separated by the dark streaks of the water lanes. Every few minutes the navigator had to check their position; the pilot's job, on the other hand, was relatively easy. Shortly before 2.0 a.m. on 17th May they circled the Pole, and the doctor threw a bottle of beer and the Union flag (the name " Union Jack " is of course properly applied to the Union flag only when flown at the bow of a ship) overboard in honour of the occasion. Another seven hours and they were back at Reykjavik, without a hitch of any kind.

They had now but two days left in which to reach the North Magnetic Pole. After only three hours' sleep they started once more, at 3.0 a.m. on 18th May. The position of the Pole was not certain. It had last been fixed by Amundsen more than forty years before, when it was in Boothia Peninsula, northern Canada; the Astronomer Royal, however, had predicted that it would probably now be 200 or 300 miles N.N.W. of its old position. They, therefore, steered for the Peninsula first, intending to cruise northwards afterwards until the compass needle dipped 90 degrees, which would mark the position of the Pole itself. Almost at once they ran into cloud, through which they crossed the east coast of Greenland, with its tooth-like fringe of mountains up to 11,000 feet high, and behind that the ice-cap, which was not much lower; so that necessarily they flew high. They never saw the coast, except as dots on their radar screen. Then the weather cleared, and they crossed the ice-cap to Disko Island on the west coast in two hours. This was not far from the route taken by Nansen in his memorable first crossing of Greenland in 1888, when he sledge-sailed and skied across in as many months as the *Aries* took hours.

Just before reaching the west coast an electric generator failed, which, of course, threw the full load on the other one. It was decided instantly to go south to Goose Bay, Labrador, for repairs, a mere matter of 1200 miles; they did so, and reached it at five o'clock in the afternoon! There remained now just thirty-five hours in which the sun and moon would afford suitable fixing-points for their observations over the Pole, but it was sufficient. Another early start, a few storms, Hudson Bay, and then Boothia Peninsula loomed up below. The magnetic compasses were now wandering aimlessly round the circle, so they steered by astro-compass. Over the old position of the Pole the angle of dip was now only 87 degrees; the Astronomer Royal had been right. They followed the dipping needle N.N.W. until, after about 250 miles, it registered $89\frac{1}{2}$ degrees. They then turned and flew direct to Montreal down the east coast of Hudson Bay, a place where little ships push in and out among the sea ice and the many islands, usually with exceeding difficulty. Dorval Airfield was hidden by fog, but they landed safely by radar. Another overhaul, a much-needed rest, and they left on the return journey; not, as one might imagine, by the ordinary Atlantic crossing, but west and north, past Toronto, to Edmonton in Alberta, then up the Yukon to Whitehorse (almost on the Pacific Ocean), then back again straight across the new position of the North Magnetic Pole, so as to close their series of observations. Flying without halt or trouble they continued right across the Arctic, over Greenland, and touched down again at Shawbury, their starting-point, at 12.45 p.m. on 26th May.

This was the first non-stop flight between the Pacific Coast of Canada and N.W. Europe. In the 110 hours spent in the air more than 30,000 magnetic observations had been made and many other data which it would take months to sift. Truly, the crew of *Aries* had kept the flag flying.

CLIMBING MOUNT EVEREST AND THE MATTERHORN—TWO GREAT FEATS OF MOUNTAINEERING

Organized mountain climbing began nearly a century ago, and within four or five years most of the great Alpine summits had been reached, largely by Englishmen who had had to master their arduous craft by tough experience. The Swiss guides of that date were simply adventurous peasants who loved the hills and acquired skill through ascending such as overlooked their native villages. The peaks, especially such as were usually wrapped in mist and storms, were often regarded by the peasants as the homes of evil spirits, a reputation which clung especially to the Matterhorn; for climbers, guides and tourists went there, looked, shuddered, and retreated from its appalling precipices. It is indeed almost a unique mountain. Although not exceptionally high (about 14,800 feet) it conveys an impression of utter inaccessibility, even though it has now been ascended many hundreds of times. Its almost vertical brown, red and grey cliffs rise like a giant tower for more than a mile above the white glaciers at their feet. When a stone tumbles off its crumbling ridges (a daily occurrence) it may make a clear jump of 2000 feet, smash on a ledge, and then jump down a further 2000 feet before it strikes the earth. Despite this, in the year 1861, two men at least thought that the Matterhorn could be climbed. One, Jean Antoine Carrel, was a bold but self-willed stonemason from Val Tournanche, an Italian village near the southern base of the mountain. He had already explored its lower slopes, and he was, besides, one of the finest rock climbers in Europe. The other man, Edward Whymper, was an English artist, twenty-one years old, who, up to the previous year, had never even been on a mountain. He too was bold and fearless, with a profound belief in his own ability to overcome any obstacle. Whymper had to learn his mountain craft the hard way and narrowly escaped disaster on several occasions, but it never seemed to shake his nerve.

From some angles the Matterhorn looks like a huge finger

sticking up, with its top joint bent so as to make the precipices actually overhang. It is a gigantic rock pyramid, the sides of which end in sharp, cliffy ridges. These ridges are the natural routes up the mountain, being less exposed to the showers of stones that are always falling from above; moreover, the precipitous sides of the

The Matterhorn from the north

peak, where scalable at all, are usually glazed with ice, a single slip on which would instantly send the mountaineer sliding down to destruction. Seen from a distance, the ridges form simple lines, but at close quarters they are frightfully rough, being interrupted by buttresses like the towers of a castle, or seamed by smooth-sided gullies where no foothold can be obtained, or supporting perilously loose blocks of rock that a single touch may bring down on the climber's head. As seen from Zermatt on the north and from Breuil on the south two ridges alone offered a climber the slightest chance. That on the Zermatt side, the north-east ridge, led up to a vertical and even overhanging cliff near the summit, which everyone, including Whymper, regarded as impracticable. The approach from Breuil, though awe-inspiring enough, seemed to the bold Carrel and his various employers to offer better chances. This south-west ridge, as our drawing shows, started at a notch, the Col du Lion (so-called because the little peak beyond it resembled a lion's head), and ascended very steeply to a narrow, flattish ridge, to which it was joined by the Shoulder. Beyond the Shoulder only a small final pyramid, it seemed, needed climbing.

Whymper first visited the mountain in 1861. He engaged Carrel, but always some obstacle prevented them from getting anywhere near the summit.

Whymper realized from the start that it would be impossible to climb the peak and descend again in a single day; camps would be essential. At first he set up a tent on the Col, but this is a mere ledge, with a frightful precipice on both sides, and a tearing wind that threatened to blow the tent away. Then he and Carrel built a small platform under a huge buttress above the Chimney, known as the Great Tower; and here he erected a new tent of his own design, the famous Whymper tent that has been so greatly used since by explorers everywhere. In their mountain eyrie they once had to weather a terrific storm, when the sky was dark as night, the roll of the thunder following almost instantly on the vivid lightning flashes, while the very air sizzled with electricity and mighty echoes rolled back weirdly from a neighbouring peak; but in Whymper's tent they could laugh at it.

On one of his annual visits Whymper, defying all the laws of good mountaineering, nearly lost his life. He had gone up to the base of the Great Tower alone, to see if the tent was safe; and, the day being fine, had lingered there, sleeping that night calmly on the edge of the precipice. Next morning he climbed the rocks above until he found himself spread-eagled, and could only get free by leaping sideways like a monkey. He had foolishly left his ice-axe in the tent, as it had been an encumbrance on the way up; and after descending safely to the Col du Lion, was upon the aforementioned glassy slope, when he had to cross a gully that sloped down like a funnel, which ended in a sheer drop of 800 feet to the glacier. Here he slipped, and in an instant was tumbling down in great bounds, each larger than the last, his head and body striking the rocks on either side, until a final leap of 50 feet hurled him, bleeding and scarcely conscious, on to some rocks, where he instinctively clawed and checked his descent. He climbed back to safety, stopped the bleeding from a deep gash in his head with a pad of snow, and then fainted. Eventually he got down to Breuil again.

Numerous other attempts on the Matterhorn having failed, Whymper, in 1865, decided to attempt the north-east face from Zermatt, but soon came to grief. He then sought out Carrel once more, arranging with him to try the north-east angle. Carrel, however, had deceived him, having in fact promised his services to a more important patron, a high Italian government official; and Whymper learned when too late that the guide, with several other Italians, had already set out from Breuil by the usual route, intending to fix ropes and ladders up the mountain for the patron's benefit. Whymper knew that such a task must take at least a week, but he could get no other guides, and he was almost despairing of success when an unexpected chance presented itself. He found at Zermatt two parties of Englishmen, both of whom had designs on the Matterhorn. One was composed of Lord Francis Douglas, a young but skilled mountaineer, his experienced guide Peter Taugwalder and two of the guide's sons. The other party comprised the Rev. Charles Hudson, who was considered to be the best amateur climber of his day, Michael Croz, a great Swiss guide, and Mr. Hadow, a young man of limited mountaineering experience, but who had just made a notable descent from Mont Blanc. They agreed to join forces, and so, on 13th July, 1865, they all left Zermatt on the fateful climb. The party, perhaps, was too large for a first ascent; four men would have been ample.

They soon discovered that the appearance of the peak from this side was deceptive. Its lower slopes proved " so easy ", says Whymper, " that we could run about ". The cliff formed a gigantic flight of steps, the many rocky ledges being inclined inwards, and where they were filled with snow or rubbish these could be kicked out and a firm foothold obtained. The tent was pitched at 11,000 feet, and the youngest Taugwalder now returned. Next morning they started before daylight, climbed without much difficulty a further 3000 feet, and by ten o'clock were higher than the previous best. They kept just under the ridge, which was unsound and crumbling to pieces. Now came a place where the cliff was steep and badly glazed. Here only one man moved at a time, Croz leading; when he was secure the next man passed, and so on, over a vertical distance of 400 feet. This obstacle passed, nothing remained but an easy climb over soft snow to the summit. They had been wondering whether the Carrels would get there first, and in their anxiety Whymper and Croz actually ran to the top. No one had yet set foot upon it. The summit was a fairly level ridge about 100 yards long, with two small peaks on the Italian and Swiss sides. Looking down to the south, Whymper discerned the Italians far below. Croz's blouse was hoisted on a tent-pole for a flag, and they also hurled down rocks to attract attention; but the superstitious Italians, who knew nothing of Whymper's latest venture, mistook them for the demons of the Matterhorn, became panic-stricken, and fled all the way back to Breuil again.

Now came the really dangerous business, the descent. Whymper had suggested that at the bad place a fixed rope should be placed, to prevent slips, but by the time they reached it this idea had been forgotten. Croz led, followed by Hadow; they were roped to Hudson, Douglas and old Taugwalder. Whymper and young Taugwalder, who had lingered behind, formed a roped pair; but, just before reaching the dangerous spot, Douglas requested that they join the others, for greater security; and this was done. As before, only one man moved at a time, and Croz even took pains to place Hadow's feet where he wanted them. He had been so engaged, and was standing up, not having his axe in his hand, when Hadow slipped and knocked him over. Croz shouted a warning. The rope was taut between Hadow and the two men behind him. Whymper was up above, round a corner and out of sight. On hearing the cry, old Peter Taugwalder hurled himself on the rocks and hung on tight; Whymper and young Taugwalder did the same. The others were slipping in a line towards the precipice. Taugwalder succeeded in holding on, but the rope did not. It broke between him and Douglas; and the four unfortunates, thus released from control, went over the edge, bounding from precipice to precipice down the whole face of the mountain to the Matterhorn glacier nearly a mile below.

For the next two hours Whymper never expected to survive the day. The Taugwalders, crying and paralysed with fear, would not stir, and until the elder one moved so as to shorten the rope Whymper could not move either. Both exclaimed: " We are lost! We are lost!" Eventually the elder guide fixed the rope to a rock, and by cutting off lengths from time to time, and using them as fixed supports, the dangerous place was passed, but night came before they were off the Matterhorn. As they hurried down, two vast crosses appeared in the mist opposite to the dying sun, a not uncommon happening, but awful indeed at that moment.

A day or two later three of the bodies were recovered, lying just as they had fallen, but of Lord Francis Douglas there was no trace.

So ended the five years' siege of the Matterhorn in mingled triumph and disaster.

The attack on Mount Everest was quite another matter. Not only is the great mountain more than twice as high as the Matterhorn, but it is far off the beaten path and until 1921 nobody had ever seen it at close quarters, so that the first reconnaissance party took more than a month to find the mountain.

Everest rises in a gigantic three-sided pyramid more than six miles across at its base. Its vast western ridge was quite unapproachable. The South-Eastern ridge ran in a graceful curve down to the many-toothed peak of Lhotse and can only be approached from Nepal, which at that time was closed to Europeans. This left only the third or North-Eastern ridge, which seemed from below to offer no serious climbing difficulties if only one could get up to it. This ridge runs up from some 25,000 feet to about 28,300 feet above the sea, with a sheer drop on the southern side and a slope as steep as a house roof on the other; at the upper end it was interrupted by two small but decided steps or cliffs, above which rose the final summit. Upon this side of the mountain most of the many efforts prior to 1951 were concentrated. The direct approach was by a roundabout march of many days through Tibet to the Rongbuk Monastery, which lies close to the foot of the Rongbuk glacier. This monastery was filled with cheerful but indescribably dirty lamas, whose abbot claimed to be the guardian of the mountain; one of his ancestors in fact was said to have flown to the top on a sunbeam!

The first serious assault on Everest was in 1922. It was led by Colonel Norton, and included many famous mountaineers. A camp was established at the head of the glacier 23,000 ft. above the sea, which was almost as high as anyone had ever climbed before. Just beyond the little tents a great ice-cliff arose to a high pass between the N.E. Ridge of the mountain and a lesser peak; such passes are called Cols and this one acquired unenviable fame as the Everest North

Col. A camp with supplies of food and fuel for hot meals must be established on the North Col before any further ascent could be attempted; nobody otherwise could possibly reach the summit and return within a single day. It is only from a point like the North Col that the real difficulties of the ascent—the tremendous height, the rare air, and the furious west wind which incessantly strives to blow tents, climbers and everything clean away—become apparent. At great heights the air is very rare and at the top of Mt. Everest any exertion requires a great effort, for at every few yards the climber must stop to rest and gasp for breath. In 1921 oxygen equipment for mountaineering was still in its infancy; but Norton's party carried oxygen cylinders which weighed 5 or 6 lb. each. There were two hotly opposed schools of thought in the expedition, those who believed in using this oxygen and those who held that the ascent could be made without it. All were agreed, however, that successive camps must be made, comprising tents, sleeping bags and food and fuel, up to the highest possible point, so that the party making the final climb would at least start fresh.

Up the ice-cliff below the North Col steps were cut and ladders fixed, so as to establish a camp (Camp IV) on a convenient shelf a little way below the Col, where there would be some protection from the savage and almost Arctic west wind.

From Camp IV the first assault party set out. Their names deserve to be remembered: Norton, Mallory, Somervell, Morshead, all mountaineers of great experience and determination. As soon as they showed their heads above the Col the wind (which always blows through such gaps with the force of a battering ram) drove them on to a steep and treacherous snow slope sheltered by the ridge itself, and from here they managed to get up on to the N.E. face of the mountain. At 25,000 feet another camp was pitched on the sloping mountain side, such that the upper occupants of the two small tents spent the night in rolling down upon the lower ones and the lower ones in being rolled upon. Another trouble was the difficulty of fixing the tents firmly enough to stop the wind from hurling them and their human occupants down the precipice to the glacier more than a mile below. At this height, too, even the simplest jobs took a ridiculously long time; and although the four climbers rose early it was 8.30 in the morning before they could get away. After a short while Morshead, who up till then had been the strongest and most active, broke down and returned to the tents, while Norton had acquired hugely frostbitten ears and Mallory three frozen fingers. This side of Mount Everest is formed of great rocky slabs inclined outwards like the tiles of a house-roof and just as slippery; as they were also partly glazed with frost and drift snow the slightest slip might be fatal, hence the men were roped together for safety. It took them six hours to reach the N.E. shoulder of the mountain and they were then still only 27,000 feet up, with the summit more than a mile away. As the temperature up there at night might be 40 or 50 degrees below freezing point, there was nothing for it but to descend to Camp IV again. While on the snow slope above the North Col, all four being roped together, three men suddenly slipped. The fourth, Somervell, who was leading, instantly thrust his ice-axe down to its head in the snow and hung on; fortunately the rope held, or they must have perished. Darkness came on. The wind had now dropped and the air was so still that it was possible to light a candle and by its feeble rays to continue the descent. At one place they had to jump down fifteen feet on to snow and across a gaping crack; it might have been 1500 feet in the gloom, but it had to be done. Eventually they reached the shelter of Camp IV, exhausted.

A second attempt to climb the mountain also failed; then a third was made, which ended in a terrible disaster, Mallory, Somervell and one other climber, with 14 picked Sherpa porters being overwhelmed on the ice cliff by a snow avalanche from the Col. The Europeans, who knew that in such a crisis the best thing to do was to flail one's arms around so as to keep the snow from packing too high, emerged at the bottom scarcely harmed; but seven of the porters fell into a crevasse and lost their lives. So ended the first assault on Mt. Everest.

Another major expedition was launched in 1924. It comprised most of the last party, but did not get much nearer to success. The same route was followed as before and they succeeded in placing their high camps nearer to the summit; but the weather was very un- favourable; and the party also suffered much from the harsh dry cough which is so common in the dust-laden valleys of Tibet; yet the great slopes of the mountain seemed mockingly easy and lured them on. It snowed repeatedly, thus increasing the danger of a sudden slip. This thought was in everyone's mind when four porters out of a party of twelve took fright, refused to cross a snow bridge for fear of slipping sideways into the chasm below, and remained huddled together all night in danger of freezing to death. As soon as it was light enough next morning, Colonel Norton, with

Mallory and Somervell, climbed the ice cliff at considerable risk to themselves. They were roped together. Somervell led, cutting steps and continually stopping to lean his head on his arm and cough. The others paid out the rope, the remote end of which had been made fast. As he approached the dangerous point he came to the rope's end, the four marooned Sherpas being still several yards away at the top of an icy slope which they dared not descend. He tried cracking jokes with them. Two men then ventured on the slope and were caught by the collar and hauled to safety; the other two slipped but pulled up miraculously on the very edge of the abyss. Somervell now drove his ice-axe into the snow, untied himself, and with the extra rope thus made available he stepped out until his outstretched arm could just reach the unhappy men. Each in turn was grasped and literally hauled back to safety.

From the higher camps two attempts on the summit were made. There seemed to be no serious climbing problems, but the sheer lassitude due to moving about at 28,000 feet proved too much for both parties. The first, comprising Norton and Somervell, after working along the roof-like face of the mountain for some distance, was compelled to give up and descend. The second party, comprising Mallory and Irvine, together with the geologist Odell, managed to camp close to the ridge. Next day, while Odell stayed to examine the rocks the others set out and were last seen by him to be climbing steadily; one stood at the top of a cliff and the other was ascending it. They disappeared from view and were never seen again, although Odell searched for a long time, scanning the endless red and yellow slabs for any sign of his lost comrades. Either they had been overtaken by darkness higher up and frozen to death, or (which seemed more likely) had slipped and slid helplessly over the abyss to the glacier far below.

After this disaster Everest was abandoned for nine years. In 1933 a party of new men made a third attempt; they included two of the world's best-known mountaineers, Frank Smythe and Eric Shipton, and like their predecessors they relied partly on the use of oxygen cylinders and partly without. They got very little farther than before and in the final effort Smythe found himself spreadeagled on the steep rocks with no proper foothold and only a quaking hand-hold to keep him from glissading down into eternity. This expedition however recovered an ice-axe which was lying on the N.E. face of the mountain and had belonged either to Mallory or to Irvine.

Several other expeditions had a look at Everest, Shipton in particular being indefatigable in trying to find new ways to approach it. In 1951 the mocking pyramid beckoned man again and another reconnaissance was made by a party led by Shipton, this time from the southern side, where the chief difficulty was to get on to the mountain at all. The party included Edmund Hillary, a New Zealander, and it had to march right across the formerly forbidden State of Nepal, up and down gigantic hills until the end of the great Khumbu Glacier was reached, which has its head beneath the very summit of the peak. As seen from below, there curves down from the summit a long S.E. Ridge to a small icefield, the South Col, which is the counterpart of the North Col on the N.E. Ridge; beyond this gap rose the tremendous many-peaked mass of Lhotse, a mountain 28,000 feet high. From the upper part of Lhotse a great sheet of ice dropped many thousand feet into a hollow between Lhotse itself, the southern face of Everest and the lower but still very high mountain opposite, which was called Nuptse. This deep hollow had been named the Western Cwm; it was full of ice, which tumbled over several steps down to the head of the Khumbu Glacier, where it ended in a frightful ice-fall, a place impracticable to any but the most practised mountaineers; for here the glacier dropped more than 2000 feet in a chaos of great blocks and chasms, with countless smaller cracks, to the smoother part of the Khumbu Glacier beneath. Moreover, the ice was in constant motion, groaning and cracking and changing its pattern even in a few hours, so that the explorer could never be certain of following the route taken by those in front of him; and yet it was essential for at least 15 to 20 men to get up into the Western Cwm with tents, food, fuel, oxygen and all the other paraphernalia, before anyone could think of setting foot on Everest itself. Shipton and his comrades, however, thought that it could be done, and the British therefore set about preparing for an all-out attack on the peak in 1953. Meanwhile, in 1952 a party of Swiss experts tried the same route. They surmounted the ice-fall and they even got above the icy slopes of Lhotse and on to the Everest Ridge itself, in two attempts during May and September, but they had very bad weather and were beaten in the end. Their highest point was reached by the guide Lambert, accompanied by the celebrated Sherpa climber Tensing. This pair spent an unforgettable night in a small tent on the S.E. Ridge, having surmounted all the difficulties lower down only to find themselves exhausted and almost blown down the precipice, which here drops 10,000 feet sheer to the Western Cwm below. Above them it was now seen that Everest had two summits, the lower or South Peak being above their heads, while the higher one was some hundreds of yards farther on and separated by unknown ground. They were compelled to leave the problem in this unsatisfactory state.

In 1953 the British made the eleventh attempt to climb Everest. The party, led by Colonel Hunt (now Brigadier Sir John Hunt), was organized down to the last detail, almost as completely as if it were an Arctic expedition, and to this its success was probably due. Endless supplies of all necessaries had to be relayed somehow up to the head of the Western Cwm and smaller supplies of tents, fuel, oxygen and food must be taken thence up the very dangerous face of Lhotse to the South Col. They took medical supplies, the warmest possible clothing, spare boots, even goggles, for it had been found that on Everest the climbers not infrequently became snowblind, an extremely painful experience. There were ten picked men, all from the Commonwealth and all Alpine experts, and they included Hillary and others who had taken part in recent reconnaissances. It was hoped to acclimatize them to the great altitude by advancing more or less leisurely from the capital of Nepal, far-famed Khatmandu, up and down endless forested ridges and across frail rope bridges far above madly rushing streams, until they approached the eternal snows. A whole army of Sherpa porters carried the supplies and a select band of the best were taken on and participated in the actual climbing. Tensing took charge of all these men. Hunt himself not only organized the transport of the goods, but also had to write reports and watch over everybody, to inspire the others and (like them) to carry loads of anything up to 50 lb., in order to keep the expedition moving. Their heaviest burden (but one which all now recognized was essential) was the oxygen equipment, the loaded cylinders weighing some 30 lb. apiece.

At the Khumbu Ice-fall there was great trouble and incessant peril. Such places can sometimes be passed by a perilous climb along the mountainside but here the danger from avalanches forbade such an act of madness. A way was pioneered, with the aid of metal ladders, across the cracks and round the huge shattered blocks, but as we have said it had to be repeatedly remade when the ice moved. Everyone was roped and when a man went spinning headlong into an abyss, as happened to a number of them, he was pulled up breathless at the end of the rope and hauled back to safety. So at last the advance party and its supports got up to the head of the Western Cwm, where its little tents were established at Camp V, 22,000 feet above the sea and right under the face of Lhotse. As they faced that mountain Everest was on their left. A very steep gully led up almost to the South Col, and this was the way that the Swiss had taken; but it was considered to be unsafe for the porters, so steps had to be cut and ladders carried up the icy front of Lhotse, for several thousand feet, before a traverse could be made sideways to the left, in order to reach the Col. This involved an ascent of 4000 feet over ice and snow cliffs where any slip would probably be fatal. Half-way up a temporary camp (Camp VI) was made and above that another (Camp VII), the latter being hidden from below and somewhat sheltered from the wind. At this spot all progress ceased for a time, but the difficulties were overcome and at last the climbers stood on the wind-swept South Col, where they established Camp VIII. They now had to face a steep gully or couloir (a sort of natural channel down which ice, snow and rocks tumbled from above), which would carry them another 1200 feet up to a point on the S.E. Ridge of Everest. In this glassy gully steps had to be cut, which the next snow shower (for it snowed repeatedly) would obliterate; and at the worst places only one man moved at a time, the others being prepared instantly to check a slip.

The final attack comprised two parties each of two men. The first and major attempt was made by Charles Evans and T. Bourdillon, the latter of whom had had the arduous task throughout the expedition of handling all the oxygen equipment. If they should fail, then a second pair, Edmund Hillary and the Sherpa Tensing, would make another attempt. To support each party, Hunt himself and others would carry up tents and supplies to a final camp.

The first party started under promising conditions. Their supporters, Hunt and one of the best Sherpas, started off earlier, both carrying heavy burdens. Evans and Bourdillon, who were more lightly laden, soon overtook them and went on climbing easily. On the glassy slope above the Col, and in the gully, where the angle was more than 45 degrees, the greatest care was necessary, but all overcame this danger. Hunt and his companion were now feeling the great altitude acutely. They passed the highest camping point reached by the Swiss, but then, being almost exhausted, left the tent on the mountain and began to return, from a height of about 27,500 feet. They were very feeble, but got down the gully; then they met Hillary and Tensing ascending, were helped to the South Col, and both collapsed. Meanwhile Evans and Bourdillon, helped by the life-giving oxygen, were approaching the top of the South Peak of Everest over a fragile hard crust with deep snow beneath and only crumbling rocks for a hold. As the oxygen was used up the rate of ascent became slower and slower; then, quite suddenly, they found themselves on the lower summit, 28,700 feet above the sea; this

The summit of Mount Everest from the south-west

much surpassed anything that had ever been done before. The main peak was but little more than 400 feet higher, but the way to it was shrouded in cloud and was in fact both difficult and extremely dangerous. It ran along a narrow knife-edged ridge, with a sheer plunge on the left straight down for 10,000 feet; while on the other side the frozen snow hung over a second precipice in giant cornices like breaking waves and upon this it would have been madness to venture. There was not enough oxygen left to ensure a safe return, they were very tired, and they wisely decided to retreat. It took them two hours to descend 1500 feet to the wreck of the Swiss tent, both men slipping repeatedly. They then had to face the gully. At one place Bourdillon had just reached the end of the rope and fixed the axe in the snow when Evans shot past him like a flash and both men slipped rapidly down in the groove. At this crisis Bourdillon managed to turn over on his stomach, using the pick end of the axe as a brake; and between them they at last pulled up; but it was a near thing. Down on the South Col they found Hillary and Tensing with the other pair and the support party. These last ascended and managed to fix the final camp (Camp X) at 27,900 feet, a remarkable achievement. Up to this point Hillary and his comrade ascended without difficulty. On the sloping mountainside they built themselves a little platform, just large enough to take the tent; it rested on two shelves both of which sloped downwards. Tensing took the lower one and calmly went to sleep on the edge of the abyss; while Hillary, with his back against the tent wall to steady it against the incessant gusts of wind, spent a restless night with his feet stretched out below. At 6.30 a.m. next day they started off, Hillary first having to thaw out his frozen boots over the Primus stove before he could get them on. They passed a very dangerous place, where a snow cover lay on glassy ice, but by 9.30 a.m. had reached the South Peak. The outlook ahead was not promising, but Hillary thought that if they could keep just off the knife-edge and avoid the cornices at all costs, it might be practicable to continue. This they did, proceeding with the greatest caution, one anchored fast while the other advanced to the rope's end. Nearly two miles vertically below them they could see the two tiny tents of Camp IV, a thrilling and unforgettable experience. The weather remained perfect, but they had not conquered Everest yet; for now they were confronted by a rocky cliff some 40 feet high, up which no easy foothold could be seen. Between the rock and the great overhanging cornice, however, there was a tiny gully or groove; and here Hillary chanced everything, turning round, driving his heels into the snow and ascending the gully backwards; he then hauled up Tensing. Once the top of this cliff had been gained, they plodded over what seemed to be never-ending billow after billow of snow, until they suddenly found the ground falling away in front of them. After 21 years of stern effort, the world's highest point had been reached at last! Tensing hoisted the flags which he had carried wrapped round his ice-axe. The two brave mountaineers then photographed each other and took views all round; and then, weary but triumphant, and still moving with the greatest caution, safely regained the South Col after a long and anxious descent. The epic of Mount Everest was ended.

COLLECTING—THAT MAGPIE HABIT

Match-box labels—priceless jade—train numbers—china poodles —postage stamps—ships' funnel-markings: happy is the Collector, whatever form his hobby may take. For him life is never dull. There is always his collection to arrange, to brood over, to admire. There is always the missing Post Office Mauritius or Red Anchor Chelsea figure which *may* turn up round the next corner. There are always the other " chosen " to gossip and swop with. And there is that genuine interest in and love of the subject itself, of which the collection is merely the visible form.

Collecting can be either of quantity or quality, and generally begins by being more of the first and ends up by being more of the second. As the collector gets more violently bitten by his craze, his original impulses towards " a lot for the money ", towards colour and a crammed album, slow down, for reasons of space if nothing else.

Besides, for the true collector, only the best is eventually satisfying—the best, that is, not in money-value, but according to those involved and highly personal rules which collectors have to make for themselves. If you collect tram tickets, then is a bus ticket eligible? Or must you begin a collection of bus tickets as well? What of the trolley-bus? Or—in a more expensive field—can you afford to be led off after a bargain of a red herring in Meissen porcelain when you really go in for English china?

Collectors have many a hard tussle with their consciences, but the more firmly you control your bargaining instinct and keep to your chosen field, the greater will be your inner flush of pride as you regard your smaller, but far choicer, collection. For, after all, none of us, however enthusiastic, can collect everything.

Then there is the problem of the fake. Do you remember the conversation in that detective classic *Gaudy Night* by Dorothy L. Sayers? Lord Peter Wimsey has just bought an antique chess-set as a present for Harriet Vane, who has fallen in love with it. Harriet asks him if he would have bought it if he had discovered that just one pawn had been faked. Not at any price, he emphasizes, and she agrees that it would have been so tedious always to explain that it was not quite perfect.

Every collector knows these mental fidgets. That rare stamp that looks so imposing to the casual admirer—some inner power forces the constant admission " Yes, but it's torn ", or even, " Yes, but I'm afraid it's not genuine ", until the stamp, instead of being the pride of the collection, becomes a constant, shaming reminder of a bargain that was not a bargain. That brings us to another good rule. If anything is really laughably cheap, try to find out why. Maybe the seller is not just such a silly ass as he appears at first sight.

Collecting takes so many forms that it would take a work the size of the London telephone directory merely to catalogue its forms. There are collections of Old Masters and of beer mats, of ebony elephants and of rubbings of church brasses. There are collections—quite valuable ones—of old " comics " as well as of folio Shakespeares—of autographs and of horse-brasses—of theatre bills and of birds' eggs. There could even be a collection of lists of what other people collect.

Stamp Collecting.

Probably the most universal of all forms of collection is that of postage stamps. Everyone has collected stamps at some time, even if only a few foreign stamps roughly torn from their envelopes.

The story of Rowland Hill's pre-paid penny post and the world's first issue of adhesive stamps in 1840 in this country is too well known to be repeated here. Rapidly imitated by parts of Switzerland, and by Brazil, by Trinidad, Mauritius and the United States, the postage stamp spread like a forest fire. Nowadays there are about 200 territories issuing their own stamps, but the number of states which have gone out of existence is the stamp collectors' living reminder of the impermanence of the most seemingly permanent things. Grandfather's or even Father's ready-printed album would be quite unusable by a present-day collector, so many are the countries which have disappeared.

Your collecting differs from Grandfather's in other ways too. For one thing, you are much more fastidious. A stamp was a stamp to Grandfather, whatever its condition. Many of the odd types of stamps to be found in his album are not postage stamps at all, but revenue stamps or railway parcel stamps. Even " Postage Dues " are little collected now—usually they are rather dull, and besides, there are so many, many thousands of real postage stamps from which to choose.

So your collection is probably cleaner, less torn, more methodically arranged and far more specialized and selective than Grandfather's. But the general collection is still the best for the beginner. " Let specialization come later ", says one of the world's greatest stamp authorities. " A beginner will learn far more of the background by starting out with a general collection."

In this way you will also find out what you really want to collect. Many collectors take on only one or two countries. In every land, its own stamps are the most popular, and so here United Kingdom and Empire stamps are the most widely collected. The stamps of King George VI are tremendously popular, and a first-time-ever catalogue of these stamps alone, issued recently by one of the leading stamp dealers, went to 90,000 copies.

Penny Black, 1840

Collectors of U.K. George VI stamps would seem to have an easy task. But there are actually a considerable number of variations in paper, perforation, colour or design that test the skill of the true collector. Most of these variations are very small—such things as an extra pearl in an ear-ring in the twopence halfpenny Silver Wedding issue of 1948, a white blob on a rose thorn in some of the shilling stamps, an acute accent on the first E in " Revenue " in a Coronation stamp.

For those for whom such sleuthing is too finicky, there is " thematic " collecting, the ugly word that covers the collecting of all stamps whose designs follow a particular theme, animals or architecture, bridges or industries, native races or general habits, or railway trains, which is one of the most popular.

A tendency, which is deplored by the dealers themselves, is an increased commercialism in stamp collecting. Business men " put away " their money in stamp collections, hoping for the values to increase—which they have done very considerably. Though there are changing fashions in stamps as in everything else, early British issues and early United States are among " the gilt-edged securities " of the stamp world.

Amateurs, however—and good luck to them—usually overvalue

the stamps in their collections. We all tend to think that ours is one of those rare variations quoted in the catalogue, and wild are the hopes over the stamp not listed at all. Still—who knows? A rare Post Office Mauritius turned up recently—and it had been buried in an old collection.

Match-box Labels.

The phillumenist is also an extremely active collector. What! you don't know what a phillumenist is? Well, neither does the *Shorter Oxford Dictionary*, but it is the name by which the devotees of Match-box Label Collecting identify themselves. Here is a hobby with much of the fascination of stamp collecting and not quite so much of the expense. As for scope—the largest collection in the world is owned by a German living in the Russian zone of Berlin, and it consists of 90,000 different labels! In this country there are at least two collections of over 40,000 labels.

Match-boxes had labels at least a decade before the first postage stamp was issued. It was in 1830 that John Walker issued the first label in this country, and a year earlier America had printed what is believed to be the first match-box label. This is the famous Troy Trotting Horse, of which an example, on loan at the Schoolboys' Exhibition in London in 1950, was insured for £100.

In match-box labels, specialization is generally either by country of origin or by subject. Animals, birds, flowers and forms of trans-port are usual types for collection, while considerable collections can be made up of match-boxes containing numbers in their names, such as " Three Crowns ", " Three Rings ", " Three Birds ".

A large dog carrying an oriental clown, piebald horses in a futuristic landscape, a many-handed, elephant-headed Indian god, sharks, and scorpions are among the colourful designs carried by match-boxes. But some of the most valuable labels from a collector's point of view are the rare early labels with little decoration at all.

Especially in the Far East, where many cannot read, pictures are used to convey propaganda. There is a series of Japanese wartime match-boxes labels which I should dearly love to own. " Churchill and Roosevelt in prison garb and chains, looking downcast ", and

" Japanese soldier with fixed bayonet with Churchill and Roosevelt, who are showing fear, at his mercy ", are among its imaginative designs.

The match-box collectors have their own magazine—*The Phillumenist*—their own match-box label catalogue, and their own shops, where enthusiasts pick over boxes and books of labels. Descriptions of the labels are not standardized, as with stamps, so that it is only at first-hand that an ardent collector may be sure which, for example, of the several hundred Japanese labels depicting dragons are new to him.

Cigarette Cards.

Cigarette cards have almost disappeared from current packets, but cigarette card collecting goes merrily on. Known to its initiates as " cartophily ", it embraces among its collectors the elderly as well as the young. In a " Hobby " shop, I saw one white-haired old gentleman eagerly acquiring John Player and Sons' 1912 series of 25 " Ships' Figureheads " for five shillings. A few moments later the dealer was disappointing two schoolgirls in their search for Lambert and Butler's series of 25 " Pirates and Highwaymen ".

The cigarette card is not merely an attractive lure to the smoker, it fulfils the useful role of stiffening the packet, and is still known to the trade as a " stiffener ". About 60 years ago, some genius in the States had the idea of making this stiffener into an attractive card, and the cigarette card was born.

The first British card was almost certainly the famous Ogden " Guinea Gold " series of photographs, which were issued between 1899 and 1904. About the highest price paid for *one* card—not a series—was for one of this set —£10 for No. 1081, a picture of old-time actress Nina Randolph. But this is the rarest card, of which only three or four copies are known to survive, in the whole series of 1148 cards.

A complete set in " mint " or new condition of Player's unnumbered series of 50 " Wild Animals of the World " might fetch about £10. But these are the big prices, and a very few shillings will purchase a complete set of cards, with all the interesting information on the back, ranging from " Motor Car Bonnets—1925 ", through " Paintings on Silk ", " Feathered Friends ", " Stonehenge ",

" Famous Scots ", " Cookery Lessons ", " Conan Doyle Char-
acters ", " Cage-bird Life ", " Curious Signs ", " Howlers ",
" Boxing Lessons ", " Cathedrals ", " Silverware ", " Kings and
Queens of England ", " Do you Know?", and " The World's
Most Beautiful Girls " to " A.R.P.". In all, there are nearly 3000
known *series* of cigarette cards.

At one time, so great was the craze for card-collecting, that
transfers and even tiny gramophone records were produced on cards.
Free gifts of every kind—I still use a series of excellent maps
" swopped in " for cards by my father—tempted the smoker. Such
extravagances are not to be regretted, and it will be a brighter day
when the simple and gay cigarette card reappears.

The collection of postcards was a tremendous craze in Victorian
and Edwardian days, and if now not so popular, it still has its addicts
after such series as " Old Halls ", " Clyde Watering Places ",
" Picturesque Hats " and " Large Birds ". The most enthusiastic
collectors are those who go in for bus and tram postcards, especially
from horse-drawn days, and reproductions of railway engines. But
I was told that, surprisingly enough, aircraft are not so popular as
they were.

Railways.

As for trains, the vast army of railway enthusiasts collect postcards, old railway bills, the rather charming and somewhat scarce
railway prints, luggage labels, platform tickets, railway maps, books
about railways, and everything else bearing even remotely on their
favourite subject.

That brings us to another type of collection—not the object
itself, but a record of it. When you last made a long railway journey
you probably noticed numbers of boys and others old enough to
be their fathers or even grandfathers gathered at the end of the
longest platform of the station. They would be watching the arrivals
and departures of the trains, often consulting reference books and
making notes of engine numbers. Yes, the engine-spotters. What
boy has not felt the fascination of the steam locomotive? Generally
other interests supersede the original enthusiasm, but with some
people it remains—and when they get together, they can reminisce
for hours about the old Great Northern Atlantics, the Great Western
Dukes, the old Webb compounds, and about the relative products
of Crewe and Derby and Swindon, and of the feats of main-line

expresses hauling heavy trains up the gradients of the Pennines and the West Country.

A cross-country journey—perhaps by football excursion—over a strange bit of line is a first-class thrill for the railway enthusiast. But even the most home-bound railway " spotter ", who cannot make long trips by train, gets plenty of interest simply by watching the comings and goings of engines at some busy terminus or junction.

He will tell you that every engine works to a roster. For example, a Great Western " King " will haul an express from London to Plymouth and probably return that same evening with an express back to Bristol or London. A mixed traffic engine will take a fast goods overnight from Camden in London to Liverpool, will haul various local passenger trains in the Liverpool area during the following day, and return that night on another goods train back to London. Furthermore, the engine-spotter will tell you that every engine belongs to its own shed, which is usually indicated by a code number on the front of the smoke-box, and that you may expect to find certain sheds working certain turns.

The excitement comes when a stranger, or " foreigner ", suddenly appears. This may be a brand-new engine in its gleaming livery, straight out of Doncaster or Derby, or it may be some engine that has strayed outside of its usual working, which would normally keep it inside its particular area.

The Flying Scot

For the railway enthusiast, the highlights of the year are such occasions as Cup Finals and August Bank Holidays, for it is then that the unusual is most likely to turn up, as when a supposedly obsolete engine from some remote shed suddenly appears hauling a main-line train. What joy such a sight brings to the railway enthusiast!

Early in 1949, when British Railways experimented with the capacities of their new acquisitions, there were many sensations, as for instance when an L.N.E.R. " Pacific ", which normally works between King's Cross and Edinburgh, pulled into Plymouth North Road, and when a Southern Railway locomotive began working Scottish expresses. That was a purely experimental phase, but there are regular workings which would have been unheard of before nationalization, such as an ex-L.N.E.R. engine working into New Street, Birmingham, on a through train for Cleethorpes.

15*   (G 487)

Through workings, both in passenger and goods trains, have since increased greatly.

Steam engines are being replaced rapidly by modern diesel and electric locomotives and trains under the British Railways modernization programme which began in 1955. This is because every diesel or electric locomotive can do the work of two or more steam engines. But although steam is passing and will have disappeared completely in a few years time, the fascination of railways remains. Engine spotters are as keen as ever and are just as anxious to catch the numbers of the new locomotives as those of the old steam engines. These modern, sleeker forms of railway motive power have an appeal of their own and the future is far from bleak for railway enthusiasts of all ages.

Ships.

The markings on ships' funnels and house-flags are my own particular form of collecting. As with the engine-spotter, I must have seen them myself, but I allow myself to correct any detail wrongly observed by reason of distance, smoke or obliterating grime. House-flags are far older than funnels, but are not flown at sea, whereas the funnel markings are a permanent guide to identification. Thus my collection contains a far greater number of funnels than of house-flags. But perhaps the most prized of the lot is a house-flag without a funnel—the plain black letters " G.E." of Gustaf Erikson, the Åland owner of the last of the sailing ships.

Napier, the famous Clyde engineer, is commonly given credit for the first coloured funnel. He gave to the ships he engined the distinguishing mark of a black-topped red funnel, and the giant Cunarders (with the addition of black plate-lines) bear it to this day. The rampant lion on a red ground of the Cunard house-flag owes its origin to the coastal Burns-Laird Line (their Lion is on a blue ground) in recognition of financial aid given by Burns to Samuel Cunard.

The origin of the Blue Funnel Line's name dates back to its first ship. She was bought after the death of her former owner, and in those days—and even occasionally now—it was the custom to paint a blue " mourning band " round the hull of a ship whose owner had died. The economical Holts painted the ship's funnel with left-over blue paint found on board.

The funnels of British steamship lines tend to be conservative.

P. & O. are black; Anchor Line and the Union-Castle have red with a black smoke-top; the Orient Line and the Canadian Pacific steamships are buff-funnelled. But there is always something new. Recently the General Steam, which with its bird-named vessels claims to be the oldest existing steamship company, added its house-flag emblem of a globe to its previously plain black funnels. A recent new British funnel is based on the 1939–45 medal ribbon—equal parts dark blue, red and light blue. Other instances of blue-topped funnels are rare, though there are the red, white and blue funnels of the Salvesen whaling fleet, and the blue-topped buff funnels of the American Matson liners.

Canadian Pacific funnels (yellow with red and white checks)

National colours are often repeated in ships' funnels. Sweden makes much play with blue and gold, often intertwined in elaborate monograms. The Norwegians—there are still so many one- and two-ship lines from this seafaring land that Norwegians top almost any funnel collection wherever made—often use red, white and blue designs, generally shown on a white-banded black funnel. The Germans used to go in for most complicated arrangements of stripes, flags and initials: the black-buff-black-white-red-white-black-buff-banded funnel of the German East Africa line earned it the nickname of " The Pyjama Line ".

Pictorial funnels include a whale displayed by one whaling line; the sun and moon funnel of a German firm and the blue snake of another; the imposing eagle of the Eagle Oil and Shipping tanker line; the clever black diamond of the Cory colliers; the Prince of Wales' feathers of the Furness Withy Prince Line; the gory red hand of Ulster on the funnels of the Belfast-owned Heyn ships; Soutar's wheatsheaf; and a complicated stag on the funnels of Joseph Robinson's ships. The shamrock is surprisingly displayed, not only by an Irish, but also by a Finnish line. Similarly it is a Norwegian company which makes use of the Greek Olympic rings.

When a big line swallows a little one, generally the lesser funnel marking disappears, but often the house-flag is allowed to continue, flown underneath the flag of the new owner. In this way, though the white diamonds on black of the Bucknall line have gone, the Bucknall houseflag, as with the City, Hall, and Westcott and Laur-

ance house-flags have been allowed to persist within the great Eller-
man combine.

Beachcombing.

Let us finish with a form of collecting as original, as personal
and as exciting as any there is—finds from the Thames at low water.
I met one of the collectors, Mr. Ivor Noel-Hume, the enthusiast
who is also in charge of all the finds brought to light in the City of
London's rebuilding, in the mediæval Guildhall. In one corner of
his office a bright-faced youth was " playing jigsaws " with some
broken pottery. Suddenly he called us over. He had fitted the top
on to a large smashed pitcher. Another moment and the handle
was added and the pitcher was almost complete.

" How old is that?" I asked.

" Roman."

During the day that youth works in a library. Another of Mr.
Hume's keen helpers is in a grocer's shop. None is a trained archæo-
logist, though their knowledge leaps with their enthusiasm.

But his collecting from the bed of the Thames, Mr. Hume does
alone. He produced a small cardboard box which contained the
spoils of the last two week-ends' " beachcombing ". There were
perhaps a hundred small objects.

" These two are eighteenth-century pewter hypodermics—you
can see them in Hogarth prints—this is rather a charming button,
probably Tudor, with two hands clasped, two hearts and a crown—
and this is an early seventeenth-century cuff-link—oh that, it's a
' cartwheel' penny of George III—and that's an Elizabethan
shilling—now this is a ' plug ' farthing. See this little copper
plug right through the middle to prevent forgery." (Forgery of a
farthing!) " They were made in the reigns of Charles II or James
II or William and Mary."

Mr. Hume " hunts " the Southwark shore of the Thames
foreshore between Southwark Bridge and London Bridge. His
first find was a clay pipe—there are hundreds of them down there
—and recently the first dated pipe was found, marked " S A 1683 ".
Then his eye got in, and now every low-tide hour yields its treasures.
He never disturbs the surface, just searches the shingle. " It's not
so dirty as you'd think, either."

Treasures in the Hume collection, and in the Green collection,
which has been made by Mr. Robin Green and his helpers are

extraordinarily varied. There is a four-inch piece of the cheekpiece of a Roman helmet, and brand-new Roman coins from Billingsgate, believed to have been thrown to the water god from the Roman bridge. The beachcombers have found many Saxon beads the size of shoe-buttons, bright in many colours—navy, royal, saxe and baby blues, rose-hip red and maize yellow. Attractive pilgrim signs are common; the reason is believed to be that returning pilgrims from Canterbury celebrated in London, and then flung cap and pilgrim signs over London Bridge.

From the houses on old London Bridge probably fell these children's toys—a Tudor toy dachshund, a fifteenth-century pipe-clay lion, similar to those seen in church brasses of the period, a 1600 toy arquebus two inches long, miniature pewter dishes. The seventeenth century yields most finds, and it is speculated that householders, fleeing from the Fire of London to the meadows on the south bank, often lost their belongings in the river. Pepys notes overcrowded barges capsizing near London Bridge. There were floods, too, in his day.

A Roman coin

Other finds which prick out the history of London are the tokens —a stylized cock gleaming brassily for " The Cock of Maiden Lane"; the seal of " Wm, King, Pinmaker, Tooley Street "; and the " Town Peice, Bath ". Heraldic cloth seals tell the tale of mediæval and Tudor trade. Then there are such " odd " finds as the " underground " button, showing Charles II's head, which was worn by Royalists during the Commonwealth, there are wig-curlers and a seventeenth-century watch dial, bits of Roman pavement, jews' harps, an eighteenth-century pipeclay whistle, an Edward I York penny, a Charles I half groat, and a tiny crystal button containing a lock of some once-loved-one's hair.

The rich trove of the Thames cannot be unique. Much must await the diligent searcher of such rivers as the Avon below Bristol, the Nidd at York, the Ver at St. Albans and the Dee at Chester.

DOGS

Introduction.

That great naturalist Charles Darwin has said: " It seems highly probable that the domestic dogs of the world have descended from two good species of wolves (*Canis lupus* and *Canis latrans*), and from two or three other doubtful species of wolves, namely the European, Indian, and South African forms; from at least one or two South American canine species, and from several races or species of the jackal and perhaps from one or more extinct species."

This is a fairly comprehensive statement, and the eminent man was evidently taking no risks! His theory, however, received unqualified support until early in this century; but more recently there has been a tendency for some naturalists to conclude that the dog is descended from a single species, the common wolf, which was the ancestor of the various species mentioned by Darwin, and is known to have existed in countries in which evidence of domestication of the dog is first found.

There is no doubt that the dog is very closely allied to the wolf in physical features and structural anatomy, including the number and arrangement of the teeth; also the two will interbreed freely, which is usually regarded as an indication of close relationship.

In his researches into the origin of species Darwin collected a large number of fancy pigeons of widely differing varieties and colours which he allowed to breed together indiscriminately for a few years, with the result that they all reverted to a uniform type which was that of their original ancestor, the blue rock dove, which is found in large numbers in suitable places on the west coast of Scotland. It is highly probable that if the same experiment were carried out with dogs that a type would evolve which would bear a close resemblance to the ancestral dog. This, experts agree, would closely approximate in type and appearance to the " wild dog " of Australia, which is known as the Dingo.

There are some ninety varieties of British and foreign domesticated dogs recognized by the Kennel Club of this country, and if to this number be added the breeds which are established in other

countries it would probably not be far wrong to say that throughout
the world some hundreds of different varieties have been produced
from the common ancestral animal, whatever it may have been.

The Kennel Club, which is the authority and legislator on canine
affairs in Britain, divides the ninety breeds into two main groups:
"sporting breeds", including gundogs and terriers, and "non-
sporting breeds", which also includes toy dogs; but a study of the
attributes of the breeds based on their capacities, appearance and
descent suggests that they fall fairly naturally into a number of
reasonably well-defined groups, most of which are particularly fitted

The Dingo

to some special purpose, or set of purposes; and an attempt has
been made here to segregate these groups and specify the most
important varieties in each. Of course there are quite a few breeds
which could be included in more than one group; these might be
regarded as forming connecting links, and have in fact in some cases
been produced by crosses between individuals of two or more
groups.

In all, eight groups have been classified, and before considering
these in greater detail it might be useful to form some idea as to
the range of size and weight in domestic dogs. The height is measured
to the "withers", which is the top of the shoulder blades just
where the neck joins the back; it may vary from 34 in. in a Great
Dane or Irish Wolfhound to 6 in. in the case of a small toy dog.
Weights vary from about 180 lb. to 4 lb.

Owing to difference in formation, "height" and "weight" do not necessarily follow each other; thus a heavily built bulldog 16 in. high may weigh fully 50 lb., whereas a lightly made whippet 18 in. high may only scale 18 lb.

The Eskimo Group (or Spitz Group).

Dogs belonging to this group are found mainly in the cold northern areas of the world, and are very wolf-like in appearance, with thick double coats and prick (or erect) ears. The only way in which they are unlike the wolf is that they carry their bushy tails curled over the back, a trait which does not occur to any appreciable extent in any of the known ancestral forms.

A leading member of the group is the Eskimo or Husky of North America, which is used for drawing sledges, hunting, and sometimes for sheep herding. A difference between the American and Siberian dogs is that the former, like the wolf, do not bark, whereas the latter do. As barking is regarded as being a result of domestication, it suggests that this breed is nearer to the " Wild " than other members of the group. They are powerfully built, and may be from 20 to 24 in. high, and weigh up to 60 lb.; colour may be almost anything.

Another member is the Samoyed, which is white in colour and closely resembles the Eskimo in appearance except that it may be rather smaller. Its native habitat is the northern coast of Siberia, where it is used for pulling sledges and herding reindeer. It is now seen frequently at dog shows.

The Chow, which comes originally from northern China, also belongs to the group. In its native country it fulfils much the same purposes as its predecessors, although in the distant past dogs of the Chow type were largely bred for human consumption. It is rather shorter in the head than other breeds of the group, with a thick blunt muzzle. In colour it can be black, tan, blue or white, and a peculiarity is that the roof of the mouth and tongue are almost black.

The Norwegian Elkhound is a very typical member of this group, and is now bred and exhibited in Britain. It is a very handsome animal with all the characteristic features of the tribe. Its colour is blackish grey suffused with lighter shades of grey, and it is about the same size as the Husky.

Other varieties attached to the group are the Finnish Spitz, the

Keeshond, the Schipperke, and the Pomeranian. When the last-named was first imported from northern Germany shortly before the end of last century it was a medium-sized dog of about 25 lb. weight, conforming closely to the group type; it made a strong appeal to breeders in this country and America, and has by selective breeding been reduced in weight to as little as 4 lb. It is found in all colours and is one of the most popular " toy " dogs. The Eskimo group merges almost imperceptibly into:

The Sheepdog Group.

This group contains a number of breeds primarily developed for herding sheep and cattle, although many of them are now regarded mainly as exhibition varieties.

The Alsatian, or German Sheepdog, is a large animal 22 to 26 in. high, and 60 to 65 lb. in weight. The head is of medium length, with a pointed nose and prick ears; the coat is flat and of a rather coarse texture; it is often blackish grey in colour, suffused with a lighter shade which may predominate on the legs, chest and head. In its native country it was originally used for guarding and herding sheep, but its activities have been greatly extended in the last thirty years, and it is now extensively trained as a police dog, for use with the army, and as a guide dog for the blind. Alsatians were imported into this country from Germany in considerable numbers after the 1914–18 war, and their rise to popularity was rapid.

The Collie, either rough or smooth coated, is a native of Scotland, and the modern show dog is in the main identical with the animal bred for centuries as a sheepdog both in the Highlands and Lowlands. Since it has been developed for exhibition purposes it has become more refined and stabilized in type. It is a large dog, 22 to 24 in. high and weighing about 50 lb. The coat, which is a special feature, is long, profuse and flat, bushy on the chest, legs and tail; usually tan or black and tan, with white on neck, chest and legs. The same colouring applies to the smooth-coated variety, but the hair is short and lies close to the skin. In both, the head is very long and pointed.

The Bearded Collie, or Beardie, is another old Scottish variety, formerly much valued for his all-round ability as a herding dog; it has a rough shaggy coat, and the head is shorter and wider than that of the preceding variety.

The Old English Sheepdog is probably a close relation to the

Beardie, to which it bears a strong resemblance except that the coat is very profuse and long. It is mainly a show dog nowadays.

The Shetland Collie definitely originated in the islands of that name, and bears the same relation to his larger brothers as the Shetland pony does to the horse; weight about 15 lb. In appearance it should be a small replica of the rough-coated collie, except that the head is not proportionately so long.

By far the most important member of the group is the Border Collie (or working collie), that wonderful dog which is seen at sheep-dog trials displaying almost human intelligence. Comparatively little attention has been given to stabilization of type, which is so important in dogs bred for the show bench, but nevertheless it is extremely interesting to note, that as the result of breeding for brains, herding instinct, and physical stamina only, a particular type of dog has evolved which is fairly uniform in appearance. It is 18 to 20 in. high, is very often black with white chest and paws, and is extremely lithe and active.

The first trials took place in Wales in 1873, and several years later spread to England and Scotland. International trials were inaugurated subsequently at which the best dogs from each country compete.

Although doubtless a number of breeds have been used in the production of this dog, there is little doubt that the working dogs formerly found in southern Scotland and northern England have played a major part, as the name suggests.

The forebears of the Welsh Corgi, which probably bore a close resemblance to the modern dog, had been natives of the Principality for up to 1000 years, and were developed mainly as cattle-herding dogs. They " fetch and drive " the cattle and ponies by running around and nipping at their heels, skilfully avoiding the kicks which often result. It is a short-legged breed standing some 12 in. high, and weighing from 20 to 25 lb. The coat is of medium length, and may be tan, sable, or black and tan, usually with white on chest and paws; the head is foxy in appearance and the ears are prick.

The Coursing Group.

Most of these are tall, and strongly but lightly built, as they depend upon speed for catching their quarry. In the past they were known as " gaze hounds ", because, unlike the hound group proper, they rely more upon sight than scent when hunting. Ancestral types are of great antiquity, and it is known from Egyptian sculpture and monuments that dogs of this description existed several thousand years B.C. From that time through the ages until the wild animals they hunted became extinct, dogs of this group were extensively used for the capture of wild boar, wolves, deer, and even bears. Nowadays their chief occupation (in this country at least) is catching hares—both natural and artificial.

The leading member of the group is undoubtedly the Greyhound, which is the breed used for coursing in Britain. The Waterloo Cup is to coursing what the Derby is to horse-racing, and is competed for every year by the best and swiftest dogs. The greyhound stands from 25 to 27 in. high, and weighs from 60 to 70 lb.; he has a deep chest giving ample room for lungs and heart, upon which his great speed makes heavy demands, and the muscular development of the thighs indicates their tremendous propelling power. Apart from these two features he is lightly built. The comparatively long neck adds to the height of the eyes above the ground and increases the range of vision. Colour may be brindle, black, blue, fawn or pied.

The Irish Wolfhound is one of the oldest breeds known to the British Isles; it is a very large, powerful and shaggy-coated animal, rather more heavily built than the greyhound, and was used in Ireland for hunting wolves until they became extinct there early in the eighteenth century. Its height of 34 to 36 in., and weight of 120 to 140 lb., makes it perhaps the tallest dog in existence.

The Deerhound is probably the result of crosses between the two foregoing breeds, but favours the greyhound in appearance except for his longish coat, which is often a dark blue-grey colour.

One of Russia's most ancient breeds is the Borzoi, or Russian Wolfhound, which is still used quite extensively for coursing wolves in its native country, where this is a great national sport. In the days of the Czars it was a royal dog, and bred almost exclusively by Grand Ducal families. The Borzoi first appeared in this country about 1870. It resembles the coursing dogs already mentioned in general type, but the head is very long, lean, and " Roman-nosed ", and the chest is exceptionally deep. The coat is long, silky and waved, and is mainly white in colour, but with black or tan markings. Height 30 in., weight 100 lb.

The Saluki, or Gazelle Hound, is a native of Arabia and Persia, where it is used for coursing game. It differs from the greyhound in having large pendulous ears, and some long hair on the ears and tail. It is a comparative newcomer to the show bench here. Height about 25 in.

The Whippet in appearance is exactly a greyhound in miniature. It is used for coursing rabbits and " racing to the rag ", which is a very popular sport in Scotland and the north of England. The handlers or owners are stationed at the finishing point, where they wave their " rags " and shout encouragement to their competing dogs, which are held in leash at the starting point, and liberated at a pistol shot. These dogs are from 15 to 18 in. high, and have been bred from greyhounds by selection.

The Mastiff Group.

There is reasonable evidence to show that large dogs of this type were introduced to Britain about 600 years B.C. Britain became a Roman province in 50 A.D. when Claudius defeated Caractacus, and at that time there were " Pugnaces " or " Broad-mouthed dogs of Britain " which were used for fighting in war; these were the ancestors of the Mastiff group. The great dogs appealed strongly to the Romans, who sent numbers of them to Rome to take part in the sports of the Amphitheatre.

During the next 400 years or so it is fairly clear that these dogs became generally distributed throughout southern Europe, and may well have been largely responsible for the St. Bernard dogs of Switzerland, which are of similar type and size. In the fifteenth, sixteenth, and part of the seventeenth centuries ancestors of the mastiff were called " alaunts ", and took a prominent place in the sports of bull and bear baiting which reached their zenith between 1550 and 1650. Towards the end of the seventeenth century baiting declined as a fashionable sport with the aristocracy, though it still remained popular among other classes with whom, however, the cost of maintaining such large dogs was a serious consideration. This led to alterations in the methods of baiting which favoured the use of smaller and more active dogs, and by the middle of the eighteenth century, by selective breeding, this type had been produced and was called the bulldog. It weighed some 50 to 60 lb., but was not nearly so low and solidly built as the modern show dog. By crossing this early type of bulldog with other breeds several varieties have been established.

The group leader is, of course, the Mastiff, which is a large and heavily built dog, weighing around 170 lb., and standing about 30 in. high, with a large, wide, but short head, pendulous lips, and drooping ears of medium size; the colour may be either fawn or brindle, and the face is usually black.

The modern Bulldog, which has been produced by selective breeding from the mastiff, is a smallish but very heavily built animal, as will be realized from the fact that although it is not more than 15 to 17 in. high it weighs 50 or 60 lb. The head is massive and very short, with the nose receding from the lower jaw in order that the dog might be able to breathe freely whilst hanging on to the nose of the bull, which was the usual method of attack. They may be of practically any known canine coloration.

When bull baiting was prohibited by Act of Parliament in 1835 the bulldog's specific occupation was gone, but a substitute sport was found in dog fighting. It was found, however, that the bulldog, though lacking nothing in courage and tenacity, was not sufficiently agile where quickness of movement is of primary importance, so, in order to introduce this quality, he was crossed with the Old English Terrier, a lighter and more active animal. This produced the " bull and terrier " or Staffordshire Bull Terrier, which was the breed used for organized dog fighting until (and after) it also was prohibited by law. The Staffordshire of to-day is not unlike the bulldog of 1800 in appearance except that it is more lightly built, and the nose does not recede from the lower jaw; the neck and chest are sturdy and muscular, and the jaw is immensely powerful with great biting power. Height about 16 in., weight from 35 to 40 lb. The predominating colours are brindle, tan or pied.

Another member of the group is the Bull Mastiff, which is a cross between the two breeds, but strongly favours the latter; it was developed largely as a companion for gamekeepers, and other protective work.

The Great Dane, or German Boarhound, may be considered as a connecting link between the coursing group and the mastiff group, and is believed to originate from a cross between the mastiff and greyhound. This magnificent dog was developed in Germany, where it is extremely popular as a hunting dog and a guard to person and property, and no German castle was considered complete without at least one of these great dogs as guardians. In build it is about midway between its progenitors, sturdier than a greyhound but not so solid as a mastiff; in height it is taller than either, being

32 to 34 in. high, and weighing from 120 to 140 lb. Fawns and brindles are the colours most usually seen, and the coat is short, dense, and sleek-looking.

Other breeds belonging to the group are the Boston Terrier, which comes from America, the French Bulldog, and the Boxer, which was developed in Germany and is now very popular in this country.

The Gundog Group.

Into this group fall the various breeds which are used by shooters of game for work with the gun; this includes " finding " and " flushing " of live game, and " retrieving " it when shot. The group is marked by its low-set pendulous ears, full upper lips, and long muzzle. It works largely by its powers of scenting, which are very highly developed.

Pointers and Setters are used for indicating the proximity of unseen game, which they do by standing rigidly with their noses pointing in the direction of the quarry as soon as they get its scent; for this reason it is desirable to work them against the wind.

The Retriever's job is to find and bring in game which has fallen to the gun, often some distance away, which may or may not have been killed; in either case the dog depends very largely on scent for the successful accomplishment of its work.

The Spaniels, of which there are some half-dozen varieties, can also retrieve, but are used extensively for " flushing ", which consists in driving game (both fur and feather) out from its cover, or place of concealment, in order that the gunners may have a chance of shooting at it. The spaniel is, in fact, a sort of general handyman.

The Pointer, which originated in Spain, is a large smooth-coated dog about 25 in. high, weighing 60 lb. or so; the colour is mainly white, often with tan or liver markings. No doubt this gay colouring is most easily seen when the dog is working among heather and coarse vegetation.

Setters are very similar in shape and general appearance except that they are rough coated. There are three main varieties: the English is a white dog with blue-grey ticks, spots and splashes, and is now mainly a show animal, the Irish is mahogany red, and the Gordon is black and tan; the two latter are becoming increasingly popular as workers.

The Retriever family are large dogs about the same size as

Setters; most of them appear to owe their origin to dogs that came to this country as a result of the trade in timber with Labrador and Newfoundland, and the curly-coated variety was probably produced by crosses with the Irish Water Spaniel. The Labrador Retriever has during the past fifty years gained a very high reputation as a worker both on land and in water, and as a winner of show bench honours; it is, in fact, one of the few breeds where the same individual can score both as a worker and a show dog without sacrificing anything in either capacity. The coat is shortish, dense, and usually black in colour, although there are yellow ones, called Goldens. The head is of medium length, and the ears, which are not very large, droop closely against the head. In build they are sturdy, weighing about 65 lb.

The Springer Spaniel is smaller than the setter, being about 19 in. high. The coat is long and rather shaggy, and the ears long and drooping; usual colours black and white, and liver and white.

Cocker Spaniels are smaller than springers but resemble them closely; they are roughly 16 in. high, and weigh 25 to 30 lb. They were originally used for flushing woodcock, hence the name of " cocking " or " cockers ". This variety is still used for work, but is also a very popular dog on the show bench. It is by far the most popular dog in Great Britain, and the Kennel Club registrations for 1948 numbered over 21,000, the next in order of popularity being the Alsatian with about 10,000 registrations; no other breed had more than 6000. They are found in all colours and combinations of colour.

Other members of the group are the long-backed black Field Spaniel, the heavy and large Clumber Spaniel, with its white body and tan-marked St. Bernard-like head, and the shaggy, curly-coated Irish Water Spaniel, which is liver coloured, and whose ancestors were in Ireland before the Christian era. The Pekinese and King Charles Spaniels also belong to the group (see *Toy Dogs*).

The Hound Group.

With these are included those breeds which hunt mainly by scent. They must not be confused with dogs of the gundog group which do not hunt to kill, and they differ from the coursing dogs in that they rely on scent rather than sight. Hounds are usually worked in packs which may contain up to forty dogs. Most of the modern varieties are descendants and variants from the Talbot

Breeds of dogs (showing the various groups)

Hound, which was introduced to this country by William the Conqueror. The ears are pendulous and the coat is usually short.

The Bloodhound probably approximates most closely to the ancestral Talbot hound in appearance, and is the largest of hounds. In early days it was used for hunting deer, but before long its highly developed scenting powers were made use of in tracking men, and from the Middle Ages it was increasingly employed for this purpose; bloodhounds are still kept by some police authorities to aid them in tracking criminals. It weighs about 100 lb., and is around 26 in. high. The coat is short, and often greyish black with a variable amount of tan on the legs and underside; the skull is domed, sometimes rising to quite a sharp peak, the ears are very long, and the face and lips heavily wrinkled; the animal is heavily built, with well-developed bone and muscle.

Harriers and Beagles are small dogs used for hunting the hare—the human followers being unmounted. The former are larger than the latter, but both are smooth-coated and are white with black and tan, or tan, markings.

Probably the best-known member of the group is the Foxhound, which has been bred for speed and staying power, both necessary when hunting the fast and tireless fox. This hound stands fairly high, 22 to 24 in., and is substantially built, with strong bone and ample chest capacity. In its present form the breed is of comparatively recent production, its ancestors probably being the Talbot hound, the Greyhound, and the old Welsh hound; it is typical of the group in respect of head and ear formation. It is a very handsome animal with its sleek short coat, and gay colouring of white, black and tan.

An interesting member of the family is the German Dachshund, which is the smallest of the hounds, and was used for " going to ground " after foxes, badgers, &c. (" Dachs " is the German word for badger.) It is probable that some terrier cross was used to produce the reduction in size, and to inculcate the tendency to penetrate into the holes in the ground in which its quarry was to be found—which is really a terrier characteristic. The breed has become very popular in this country as a show dog, and is registered at the Kennel Club in large numbers. It has a hound-like head, with the large drooping ears which are typical of the group. It is very long in body, with short bent legs; weight 15 to 20 lb., but height only 12 in. or so. Colours, black and tan, liver and tan, or tan.

Other breeds attached to the group are the Dalmatian—the white dog with the black spots—and the Otterhound.

The Terrier Group.

The Terriers can hardly be referred to as a group as they differ so greatly in appearance and conformation. Originally a " terrier " was any dog sufficiently small and game to pursue foxes into their " earths ", and badgers into their " setts "; but the group name now includes many varieties of small dogs that are—or should be—good at killing vermin.

It would perhaps be permissible to divide them into two types, the short-legged and the long-legged. The former originate almost entirely in Scotland, and are nearly always rough-haired, the common ancestor being a short-legged, rough-coated, foxy-headed little dog which existed in Scotland for centuries. The long-legged types have been developed more in England and Wales and are sometimes smooth-coated.

As a whole the group are alert and agile. By selection from the original Scottish ancestor a number of varieties have been evolved.

The modern Scottish Terrier is short-legged and carries a rough coat usually dark brindle or black in colour. The head is long in proportion to the size of the dog, and the ears are carried erect, or prick. Weight 20 lb.

The Cairn Terrier, which probably most closely resembles the common ancestor, is a smaller and more lightly built animal, shorter in the back than the Scottie, and with a short fox-like head. It takes its name from its ability to penetrate into cairns or heaps of stones. It is found in a number of colours ranging from " wheaten " to dark brindle. Weight 12 to 15 lb.

A very closely related variety is the West Highland White Terrier, which is white as the name suggests. Not so very long ago Cairns and Whites turned up in the same litter!

The Skye Terrier is another short-legged dog with a very long back, owning an extremely long flat coat of a blue-grey colour which extends to the head and ears; it is the heaviest of the Scottish group and may be from 20 to 25 lb., although the height rarely exceeds 12 in.

The Dandie Dinmont Terrier of the Border counties was probably the result of crossing the ancestral type with other small dogs, very possibly the Border Terrier, which was a little tan or grizzle dog descended from a hardy race of working terriers found in the Lake District in the north of England, of which the present-day Lakeland Terrier is certainly a direct descendant. The Dandie is very short-legged, with a long rather sinuous body, large head and drooping ears; the coat—which may be either " pepper " or " mustard " in colour—is rough or linty in texture, and is encouraged to grow on top of the head, where it forms a " topknot " of whitish silky hair. He weighs 20 lb., although the height is about 10 to 11 in.

By crossing the Dandie with some of the north of England longer-legged types, very likely the whippet, a dog called the Bedlington Terrier was bred, which takes its name from the village of that name in Northumberland, and is a lightly built rather whippet-like dog with a bluish-grey or brownish-grey coat of a shortish curly texture, rather like that of a young lamb. It is used for coursing rabbits, stands about 16 in. high, and weighs some 24 lb.

Another terrier to be developed in the north of England is the Airedale Terrier, which is the largest member of the group and is sufficiently powerful to be used as a guard dog and also for police and army work. The Airedale was created about the middle of last century by crossing the Welsh terrier with the otterhound, and is rough-coated with a black back and tan legs, feet and head; it is about 20 in. high, and weighs from 40 to 50 lb.

The Fox Terrier is one of the best-known members of this group, and may be either smooth- or wire-coated. Its original duty was to run with packs of hounds to " bolt " foxes that had " gone to ground " (i.e. escaped by going underground). The breed in its modern form began to evolve about the middle of the nineteenth century, and was built up from such breeds as the white English terrier, the old English terrier, the black-and-tan terrier (all now extinct), and the bull terrier; quite a mixed bag. The dog is now a very smart and trim little animal with a long narrow head, a fairly sturdy body, and well-boned legs and feet; the ears are small and carried at half prick, which means that the base of the ear points in an upward direction, but the top half folds over forwards and lies along the side of the skull. The colour is mainly white with black and/or tan markings. Height 15 in., weight 16 to 20 lb.

The Welsh Terrier assumed its present form in Wales about a hundred years ago, and doubtless owes its origin to selective breeding among the various small terrier-like dogs which had existed there for a very long period. It is rather like a wire-haired fox terrier in appearance except that its head is shorter and more strongly built; the back is black, or greyish black, with tan legs and head.

The Bull Terrier was produced about 1850 by crossing the Staffordshire bull terrier with the white English terrier. The head is long and appears " Roman-nosed " in profile; this terrier has erect ears, a small dark eye, and a sturdily built body; the colour may be white, brindle, tan, black or pied. It differs from the Staffordshire principally in shape of head and in weight, which is around 50 lb.

The Irish family of terriers all spring from two or three original types which have existed in Ireland for a very long time, and consist of the Irish, Kerry Blue, and Soft-coated Wheaten terriers. The first is an active wiry-coated tan dog, with a long head and small semi-erect ears; 18 in. at shoulder, weight 26 lb. or so. The Kerry Blue is rather more sturdily built, and although the same height weighs some 34 lb. It carries a profuse soft coat of a smoke-blue colour, which for show purposes is clipped to give a short curly effect, except on the forelock, beard and legs, where it is allowed to grow to full length. The Wheaten is intermediate in weight between the two, and the long shaggy wheaten-coloured coat is allowed to grow as nature intended; otherwise it is very similar in build, though the head is somewhat shorter and stouter.

The Sealyham Terrier is a variety which was " made " about 1850 by crossing various types of fox-terrier-like dogs, and is the only short-legged terrier that did not originate in Scotland; it is compactly built, with a fairly long head and half-prick ears. The coat tends to be profuse, and is trimmed in much the same way as the Kerry; the colour is white with a few small patches of tan; the height is about 10 in. and the weight 20 lb.

Toy Dogs.

This group really consists of a number of " dwarfs " which, strictly speaking, belong to the other groups; for instance, the Eskimo group contributes the Pomeranian, which has all the characteristics of the group in miniature—long, flat coat, foxy head, and curly tail. By selective breeding its weight has been reduced to 4 lb. or so.

The coursing group supplies the Italian Greyhound, which is just a tiny greyhound weighing 7 lb.

The spaniel section of the gundog group is responsible for several varieties of toys, including the Pekinese, which is the most popular toy dog; its country of origin is China, from where it was introduced to this country less than a hundred years ago. It is a long-coated, short-legged dog with a wide short head, a very snub nose, and drooping ears; weight about 10 lb. It occurs in all colours from white to black.

The King Charles Spaniel, which takes its name from Charles II, is typical of the toy spaniels which had a vogue of great popularity in the seventeenth century. In appearance, it is typical of the group except for size and the formation of the head, in which the nose is extremely short and retroussé. The long silky coat, large pendulous ears and shape of body are all reminiscent of its larger prototype; they weigh 8 lb. or so.

The smallest dog in existence is the Chihuahua (she-wa-wa), which is a tiny animal of the spaniel group which comes from Mexico and is descended from the Aztec sacred dog. In the fourteenth century it was an article of food. The skull is round and apple-shaped, with a short pointed muzzle, and its ears stand out from the head rather like a butterfly's wings. The smaller individuals, which are most highly prized, weigh from 3 to 4 lb.

The Pug is the contribution which the mastiff group makes to toydom. It appears probable that it originated in China, and came to this country about 200 years ago. It is sturdily built and smooth-coated, either fawn or black in colour; the nose is short, like a bulldog's, and the face covered with crinkles and wrinkles; its ears are small, the eyes round and prominent, and the tail tightly curled. Weight about 15 lb.

The terrier group has produced several toy dogs. The Brussels Griffon is a small Belgian dog which is derived from various small terriers found in Belgium. This little animal has a short head, large prominent eyes, and semi-erect ears; it may be either smooth-or rough-coated; in the latter case the hair is stiff and wiry, except on the nose and chin, where the whiskers are long and profuse, giving a most griffon-like expression. The colour is usually a mixture of black and tan, and the weight 5 to 6 lb.

The Black-and-tan miniature terrier is rather exceptional in that it has survived, although its progenitor—the normal Black-and-tan— is now practically extinct. This slim and elegant little toy, of 7 to 9 lb., began to be shown about the middle of the nineteenth century, and some years later gained notoriety as a rat killer. The coat is smooth, glossy and black, except for tan markings on the muzzle, throat and feet.

SIMPLE HINTS ON FIRST AID

Have you ever thought what those two words First Aid mean? First Aid is help and assistance given to injured people or those taken suddenly ill, *before the arrival of a doctor*.

Unfortunately, accidents of one sort or another, from a cut finger to a serious injury, happen only too often, in the home, on the highways, at sports, during work-times, and at play, so that a knowledge of what to do, properly applied, may save a life or prevent the loss of a limb. A knowledge of the simple treatment of an injured person is therefore of great value to the individual, to the community, and the country.

If you make yourself proficient in First Aid, you will add much to your usefulness, especially as things learnt while you are young are likely to be remembered throughout your life.

The trained First Aider can follow simple rules used by a doctor and in hospitals, but it is important to remember that the First Aider, however efficient he or she may be, can never replace a doctor or nurse. While waiting for skilled assistance after an accident, the First-aid boy or girl should know what to do, and equally important, what not to do. You will make matters worse if you do the wrong thing, but bear in mind that a simple injury may be prevented from becoming serious if attended to at once.

In the case of a serious accident, it is your duty to get a doctor and tell the police at once. If you do not know where to get a doctor, inquire at the nearest house or shop. The quickest way to reach him might be by telephone and you should know how to use a public one. Whether you go for the doctor, ring him up, or send a written message, describe very clearly and exactly where and when the accident happened. Be ready to answer any questions the doctor may ask as to the condition of the patient, or as to what has been done for him.

Never try to move an injured person and do not try to get him to stand up. Should he be lying in a strange position or if his limbs are distorted, he may have broken a bone, and it is important that a broken limb should not be touched until the doctor comes. If there is bleeding, efforts must be made to stop it at once. Make the patient as comfortable as possible, place his head gently on a pillow, by rolling up a coat or rug, and cover him up well. Whether the injury is slight or serious, there will be shock, and the treatment for this is warmth and rest.

To be a good First Aider, you should be observant and notice all signs and symptoms. Signs are those which can be seen and symptoms what can be felt and described by the patient. You must learn to be resourceful and make the best of things at hand. Gentleness and cheerfulness are essential; be sympathetic, but remember

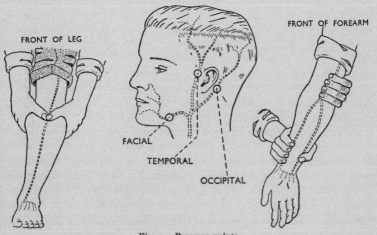

FRONT OF LEG

FRONT OF FOREARM

FACIAL

TEMPORAL

OCCIPITAL

Fig. 1.—Pressure points

that a happy expression will inspire confidence and help the patient to forget. Always keep cool and do not fuss. Never crowd round an injured person; you will only hinder other people giving skilled attention. If you cannot assist, then your wisest plan is to keep right away and advise others to do the same.

To stop bleeding you must know where to find the " pressure points " and be able to feel for the heart beats or " pulse ", which can usually be felt easily at the wrist. The heart beats 70–80 times a minute. The pressure points are places where an " artery " or blood vessel passes near a bone, and can be pressed hard enough to stop the blood flowing towards the wound. There are pressure points on the leg and arm and three on the head (see fig. 1).

If there is no " foreign body " in the wound, apply pressure to the wound itself, by covering your finger with a clean dressing or pad. But if there should be a foreign body, such as grit or glass, then cover only lightly with a dressing and apply pressure to the proper arterial point, which is done by means of a pad and bandage. Extreme pressure with a tourniquet should never be attempted by an inexperienced person.

Suppose you were asked to render First Aid to someone with a cut in the palm of the hand. You would raise the arm, which would help to minimize the flow of blood to the hand. Place a clean pad of lint or linen over the wound and close the fingers tightly over it, apply a bandage and tie very firmly. Support the arm in a sling, still keeping it slightly raised.

You have all heard about " germs " too small to be seen by the naked eye, but to be found everywhere, especially in dust and dirt. If they enter a wound, they grow and produce poison, making the wound " septic ". If the poison passes into the blood stream, it causes blood poisoning and fever. It is, therefore, necessary to keep the germs away by having everything perfectly clean.

To treat wounds such as *minor cuts and grazes*, first wash your hands thoroughly; then, with soap and water, wash gently round the wound, always working away from it, at the same time being careful not to disturb any blood clots, as if you do, you may restart the bleeding. Take a piece of clean lint or a packet of dressing, touching the edges only, and with clean scissors cut the dressing twice the size of the wound and fold it in two, place it gently over the wound, covering with cotton wool, and then bandage. Never touch the wound with your finger, and if there should be a foreign body in it, apply a clean dressing very lightly and take the patient to a doctor or hospital.

Blisters. A very common place for a blister is on the heel, probably developed during a long walk or due to uncomfortable shoes. A simple blister caused in this way should be pricked, which will give relief, and this is how to do it. Holding a clean needle, strike a match and pass the needle through the flame, and do not wipe off the soot or touch it afterwards. Wipe the blister with cotton wool and a little methylated spirit, then pass the needle through the skin at two points. Press the fluid out with a clean dressing, then secure a small dressing over the blister until it heals. Remember, never remove the blistered skin.

Foreign bodies in the eye, such as pieces of grit or a fly, can sometimes quite easily be removed by allowing the eye to water freely, as tears will help to wash away the offender. Make the patient blow his nose to help the tears to wash the foreign body into the lower lid. Wash your hands and gently turn down the lower lid and, if the particle can be seen, remove it with the corner of a soft handkerchief. Put a drop of castor oil inside the lower lid to soothe the pain. If the particle has not been removed, apply the castor oil and cover lightly with a pad and bandage and take the patient to a doctor.

Foreign bodies in the nose and ear are very common with children, who often push peas, beads, and small objects up their noses or into their ears. In either case, do not try to poke the object out. Tell the patient to blow the nose violently, and if this does not dislodge the object, take him to a doctor at once.

If the foreign body is in the ear, try turning the patient's head on one side and the object may drop out, but if this is unsuccessful, take him to a doctor. Never attempt to touch the ear yourself as you may do very serious damage.

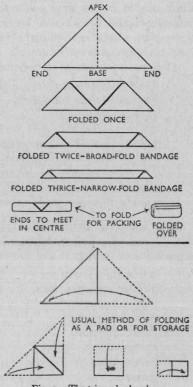

Fig. 2.—The triangular bandage

Scaled leg may easily result from a kettle boiling over or a pot being upset. Make the patient sit down and support the injured part. Next, very gently remove the shoe and stocking, lifting the stocking away from the leg as much as possible. Soak strips of lint or linen in warm water and baking-soda (two teaspoonsful to a pint of water). Wring the strips out and apply to the scald as quickly as possible. After this, add a layer of cotton wool and bandage very lightly. Make the patient warm and comfortable and send for a doctor.

The triangular bandage is the most useful for First Aid, because it is easily made or improvised; it can be used in many different ways, such as dressings, pads, for keeping dressings in position, slings, and it can be very easily removed. When not in use, the bandage should be washed, ironed, folded and stored (fig. 2). Remember, a bandage should always be tied in a " reef knot ", which does not slip and is easily untied.

Here are a few points to remember when rendering First Aid:

> Do the important things first, without fuss or panic.
> Do not attempt too much.
> Stop any bleeding.
> Guard against and treat for shock.
> Do not remove clothes unnecessarily.
> Do not apply wet dressings; they make wounds sodden and therefore may spread infection.
> Send for a doctor and notify the police.
> Do not allow people to crowd around.

The following articles would be useful to have in a First-aid Box at home, or to take with you when you are going for long cycling expeditions or outings in the country:

> 2 triangular bandages.
> 2 roller bandages, 2-in.
> 1 packet adhesive wound dressings.
> Adhesive plaster.
> Packet of gauze.
> Packet of lint.
> Safety-pins.
> Scissors.
> Common salt.
> Soap.
> Castor oil.

YOUR LIBRARIES

Those of us who like reading—and that probably means you, or you would never have got as far as this—usually discover that our shelves at home, and the money in our pockets, are not enough to keep us supplied with books. So we turn to libraries—to a subscription library, or to the children's section of a public library, eventually to the shelves of the general library, and maybe—if some hobby or study is beginning to bite us badly—to the more unusual books stocked by the special libraries.

But I feel sure I am speaking the truth when I say that nearly all of us have a pretty vague idea of what goes on in the library. Generally we run our eyes along the " open access " bookshelves until we strike a title or an author that pleases us, take a quick glance inside to see the type is decently broken up into digestible fragments, and we are satisfied for another week.

I have been learning that there are far greater possibilities to a library than that. Do you know that there are *forty million* books available through even a small branch library? How on earth are they all sorted out? What are they about? Who reads them? How does it all work?

Well, suppose we have *written* a book—and a very fine book it is, of course, which should be on the shelves of every library. How does it get there?

First of all, it must be selected for the library. Perhaps the chief librarian " spotted " it through a book review—he reads them all—or through one of the " Book Indexes " and " Book Lists " which catalogue current literature. These books about books, or bibliographies, are the librarians' tools.

Before the war, many of the books bought for libraries were second-hand, but now our book probably arrives direct from the bookseller (special library discount).

Then it has to be " accessioned ". That means that, like a new recruit, it has to have its details entered in the library records, so that its life-history can be recorded. Down go particulars of subject, author and title, of publisher and edition, of the price or donor.

And space is left for its retirement date when, battered or neglected, it will be withdrawn from the library altogether.

After this our book is " processed ", or prepared for the shelves. The pocket for the issue card is pasted inside the cover. The library number is stamped on its spine. That number brings us to one of the most fascinating aspects of library work—classification. This is the miracle of librarianship—the sorting out of that torrent of books which pours incessantly from the publishers' presses of this and all other countries. Remember, too, there is also a stream of periodicals, maps, prints, lantern slides, gramophone records, microfilms, and goodness knows what else as well. Just take one or two of the books about you, and try to classify them. Try this simple one, *Model Aircraft*. Will you classify it under Models or under Aircraft? And what about the section on air currents? Shouldn't that go under meteorology?

Many librarians in many countries have hammered away at this problem, and it is significant that in this country an American system—the decimal system originated by Melvin Dewey in 1876, and afterwards enormously extended—is the one most generally used in our libraries, while our special libraries often employ the Brussels " U.D.C." modification of the Dewey system. Others employ an Englishman's (Brown's) subject classification, or a system invented by an Indian. But probably our book will be classified according to Dewey—which means we can walk into most of the libraries in the country, and find it under the same number in the catalogue.

All libraries nowadays have card or sheaf catalogues, arranged by Subject and Author, in which, by cross-references, every book in the library which refers to a particular subject can be found, even if it is catalogued under quite a different main subject. What a lot I have missed until recently by being put off by those perplexing numbers you see on the back of a library book. Yet a librarian will be only too glad to explain them to you—and what worlds of new and exciting reading they open up! Perhaps the library also runs to an Index of Titles.

Now let us imagine that our book has reached those shelves, and it only remains to find it readers—perhaps through a jacket display or a lecture, or perhaps it is asked for by other readers attracted by the subject or by a review, perhaps chanced upon by a browser. When a score or so have borrowed it, its original glory is tarnished, and it has to go off for binding in the extra-hard-wearing (and sometimes rather dull) livery of the library. Then it is good for perhaps another hundred borrowings.

So much for our book. Now for the libraries themselves.

Though all of them work on much the same system, they vary between vast affairs like the reading-room of the British Museum, or the Bodleian at Oxford, to rooms in parish halls, where the books are laid out on tables. Some districts are very well served by libraries, others—and they are not all remote either—are poorly off. It is largely a matter of the keenness and prosperity—or the reverse—of the local authorities, because there is no Government department in charge of libraries. Manchester has a highly organized and efficient library system, and the libraries of Derby County are an example of what can be done with a county. We won't quote bad examples.

One of the reasons for all this unevenness is the haphazard British way in which the library system has grown up. Until 1919 only one penny in the pound of the local rates was allowed to be spent on libraries in England and Wales. Northern Ireland was only freed of a rating restriction in 1947, and poor old Scotland was held to threepence in the pound of the rates for her burgh libraries until 1955! If it were not for the benevolence of the Carnegie Trust, which paid for many early library buildings, we should all be much worse off.

But the attitude to libraries is changing all the time. Librarians declare that the rising generation—*you*—makes far more use of libraries than the present adult generation, and more intelligent use too—with, of course, room for improvement.

In the design of libraries, too, there have been vast strides. It used to be the done thing to have the inside of a library planned with the bookcases running from a central desk like the spokes of a wheel—the Radial Plan, it was called. The reason for this was that the idea of open shelves from which the readers could help themselves was fairly new, and it was feared that thefts and hooliganism would result unless all parts of the library could be properly supervised. But it was found that library readers are a law-abiding lot on the whole, and now the emphasis is on box-type planning, where recesses of bookcases round the walls disperse the people, making browsing more comfortable, and allow room for more books.

The architecture of new libraries is often striking. There is—
or was—a very fine modern library, designed by the famous architect
Aalto, in Viborg, in that part of Finland which the Finns had to
cede to Russia. In Stockholm there is a much-discussed library
shaped like a top-hat, which—however controversial its design—is
undeniably beautifully placed, with a hill above it upon which

Stockholm City Library

bronze statues stand outlined against the sky, and below it a children's paddling pool and a restaurant where little tables with gay
umbrellas flank the water. An even more bizarre library is that of
an American college, which is designed like a church, with the
librarians seated in the " confession boxes ", while, to add a finishing
touch of incongruity, the books are carried on conveyor belts.

In this country there are many fine libraries, each carefully
fitted to its purpose. Manchester Central Library, which was
designed by E. Vincent Harris, is a notable example of a large public
library. There have been several new university libraries built
comparatively recently. The one at Leeds—the Brotherton Library—

is particularly admired, while the University Library in London and the Cambridge University Library are both housed in conspicuous tower buildings, the one in white Portland stone, the other in brick.

To turn to a smaller library, the specialized library of the Royal Institute of British Architects is—appropriately enough—a model of its kind. And a good example of a branch library is the building which houses the library at Norris Green, Liverpool.

As a matter of fact, building restrictions have brought what used to be a rural expedience to the towns—the mobile or travelling library, by which many counties and towns now serve their outlying readers, especially in new suburbs.

The problems are always changing. Last century the problem was to get libraries established at all. Would people use them? Wouldn't education give them dangerous ideas? The kind of book was not much considered (if it were innocuous), and correlation of knowledge was left to the individual.

During this century librarians have concentrated on trying to find out just what books are available and where, and how to get them to the people who want to read them. In the old days it was possible to spend hours searching a general library for information (which it didn't have) that was " on tap " just round the corner in a special library.

Sometimes local arrangements were made to lend unusual or expensive books to other libraries, but it was only in the early 'twenties that the problem of inter-availability of library books was really tackled. This was with the formation of the Central Library for Students, which received much help from the Carnegie Trust. More and more libraries joined this " mutual aid " scheme until, in 1930, the Treasury acknowledged its national, and even international, importance with a grant, and its name was changed to the National Central Library. Now, together with its nine Regional Bureaux, the Yorkshire Regional System, and the Scottish Central Library, the National Central Library, in its quiet backwater at Malet Place, within sight of the tall tower of the London University Library and the massive British Museum, has access to 40,000,000 books—not counting the almost countless periodicals.

If the National Central Library is the blood-stream of the British library system, then the centre of the whole nervous system is the Library Association. The Library Association is housed in the fine modern building, Chaucer House, adjacent to the National Central Library in Malet Place. Both were built in the 'thirties as a result of the generosity of the Carnegie United Kingdom Trust.

It is the Library Association which knits together the librarians, examines them, stabilizes their position, acts as their mouthpiece to the Government, institutes research into the problems (material and spiritual) of library and librarian, and altogether is the foundation on which the profession stands. Its annual conference is regularly attended by over 1000 members, while its duly qualified Fellows and Associates—who have the right to describe themselves as chartered librarians—now number about 3000.

The Library Association was formed in 1877 at the first International Conference of Librarians in London, and it had a great deal to do with the all-important Library Acts which were passed towards the end of last century.

In the examination curriculum, too, there have been recent and important changes, brought about by the ever-increasing importance of the special library, in which everything relates to some special or technical subject. Subject approach to English Literature used to be a "must" for the Library Association final examination, but this tended to discriminate against the special in favour of the general librarian. Now this part of the Final allows candidates to sit in any of ten subjects, ranging from History and Archæology through the Sciences and Fine Arts, to Philosophy and Religion, and also Medicine.

The vast treasures of recorded human knowledge are making the old gag, that " the specialist is one who knows more and more about less and less ", ever more true, and led to the foundation, in 1924, of the Association of Special Libraries and Information Bureaux (now officially known as " Aslib "), which acts as a clearing-house for all kinds of specialized information.

Now in their new premises at 3 Belgrave Square, London, S.W.1, Aslib deals with such problems as:

(For a film company.) " What books are there on ' The Queen of Sheba ' ? " (A list provided.)

(From New York.) " What Public Schools include Agriculture in the curriculum ? " (Referred to the " Public and Preparatory Schools Year Book ", which gives curricula, and for further information to the Secretary of the Headmasters' Conference.)

A query about Norwegian wood turning was referred to the Timber Development Association; another on the maintenance and repair of surgical instruments was referred to the library of the Royal College of Surgeons and to the Information Service of the British Medical Association. In answer to another request, a list of books on power sewing machines was supplied. But during the war, Aslib's efforts to answer a public library's query on radio-controlled model aircraft brought Scotland Yard about its ears.

Of course, the information officers at Aslib make no attempt to *answer* these very complex riddles off their own bat, but their specialized knowledge of where all information is kept saves incalculable time and trouble to its members. Aslib answers only those questions put to it by its members, who include universities and learned societies, technical associations and industrial concerns, newspapers, and even individual enterprising journalists, nor are members by any means confined to this country.

The sheer volume of published information is now so enormous that handling and storing it, and finding each item when it is wanted, involves big problems. To investigate these problems, and find solutions to them, Aslib has now set up a Research Department.

In 1957 Aslib published the two-volume *Aslib Directory: a guide to sources of information in Great Britain and Ireland*, giving information on more than 3300 libraries, their aims, special collections, services and other details.

For this work, an even more detailed classification is necessary than the Dewey decimal system in use in the general libraries, and it is found in the U.D.C. modification of the Dewey system. This is specially suitable when there are many books on the same subject, and incidentally, in special libraries, articles in periodicals, giving the very latest developments, are often of even more importance than the books. Here is the Dewey classification for " gold and silver ": 669·2. That is, 669 for metallurgy, and ·2 to define one of the only nine subdivisions given to the subject. But in the modified U.D.C. decimal system as many as five decimal places may be used. For instance, metallurgy is broken into columns of subdivisions, extending to five decimal places. " Gold and silver—further treatment of precipitated metal " in this system becomes 669·213·68!

Unusual types of library services include the research departments of industrial firms and the libraries maintained by newspaper offices (where, of course, the right answer must be obtainable in a matter of minutes, often at an hour when usual sources of information are closed for the night), hospital services (as ordinary libraries are not allowed, for obvious reasons, to supply, for instance, sanatoria), and services designed for the blind.

One interesting recent development in the hospital services is the Projected Books for use by paralysed patients. The Order of St. John and British Red Cross Society now has 81 of these book projectors, 21 of them presents from sympathizers in the United States, the other 60 British-made. In these projected books, the text is reproduced on microfilm, and projected on to the ceiling. The paralysed patient works with his chin an electric switch which turns the pages. More than 800 books have been microfilmed, ranging from Beatrix Potter to *The Bible Designed to be Read as Literature*. Eight microfilmed copies of each of their monthly issues are given to the Order of St. John and British Red Cross Hospital Library Department by *The Reader's Digest*—a wonderful gift whose value to handicapped patients is inestimable.

Another splendid device is the electric page-turner, for which any book can be quickly and easily prepared by threading the pages.

Another library which is " special " in every sense of the word, is the special library of the National Institute of the Blind. This library caters for the student whose individual needs are not satisfied by the large general library of books in braille. Here are the fat quarto volumes bound in brown for history, red for biographies and travel, green for foreign languages, blue for the " heavies " of religion, science and philosophy, with their eighteen-line, thick-papered cream-coloured pages with those queer patterns of raised dots, which are the gateways to mental liberty for the blind intellectual. There are three and a half miles of shelves of books in the vaults below the N.I.B. building in Great Portland Street in London, extending down into the bed of an ancient river.

These books are prepared " in manuscript "—that is to say, on a small hand-braille machine about the size of a portable typewriter—largely by a team of about 250 volunteers, working in their homes.

Let us follow one of these books on its passage from print into the hands of its first student. Here is *Growing Up in New Guinea* by Margaret Mead, an " easy " book to braille. It is needed for a girl who has specialized in Psychology at the university and is now starting a nursery school of her own. Here, too, is *A Companion to*

Latin Studies, required by Worcester College, the boys' public school for the blind. It will be done in a limited edition of forty, for classroom use. Also under way is Topham's *Principles of Company Law* for a law student.

First author and publisher are asked for permission to braille. This is almost invariably freely granted. Then the books are issued with instructions as to the number of volumes, depth of margins, and so on, to voluntary workers for brailling.

It takes about six weeks to two months for an intelligent volunteer to learn the work. The idea appeals to many of us, but only a few have the painstaking determination necessary. Retired men accustomed to using their brains are conspicuously successful—senior officers of the Royal Engineers and Royal Artillery are specially commended. It was a Senior Wrangler who turned out perhaps the library's most difficult task—*The Handbook of Wireless Telegraphy*. In addition to the frighteningly complicated text, the book had eighty plates in each of its eighteen braille volumes, and, in addition, 350 diagrams. It took eight to nine months to complete, and is now a textbook at Worcester College.

Speed in brailling? A rush job had just been completed when I was there. A St. Dunstaner had been given a part in a play, and the whole play was brailled for him (two volumes) inside a week.

Braille, of course, those magic six raised dots in their sixty-four positions, takes much more space than print. For example, Trevelyan's *History of England* is one fairly large volume in print, but takes fourteen much larger volumes in Braille.

All this special library's work is pretty difficult, much of it in foreign languages. Books have been transcribed in French, German, Latin, Greek, Hebrew, Spanish, and even Afrikaans. One of the few assignments they could not carry out completely was a request for the Koran from an Eastern potentate. It had to be supplied in translation. Books on phonetics are almost the only kind of book which stick these indomitable experts, for in them those peculiar signs, evolved to indicate movements of the mouth, are too involved for reproduction.

When the volume has been brailled, it comes back to headquarters for proof-reading. This is carried out, page and page about, by a sighted reader reading from print, and a blind reader reading from braille. It is an inspiring experience to hear the blind proof-reader's even voice reading aloud at exactly the same pace as a sighted reader, while the sensitive fingers rustle smoothly from left to right along the patterned braille page.

Then comes binding, and the books are ready for issue to their eager students. All must go by post—they are too heavy for "changing at the library". Out of a roll of about 500 students, some two to three hundred are active and regular borrowers from this library. The general libraries serve ordinary reading tastes. Law is a particularly popular subject, and changes in the university syllabus make corresponding fresh runs on the library.

Perhaps libraries interest you so much that you would like to work in one? I asked one of the officials of the Library Association what he considered the essentials for a librarian. Firstly, he said, a desire to discover knowledge of all kinds from recorded material, ranging from books to gramophone records. Then precision and strict accuracy in work, for a slip from a librarian can have the most far-reaching consequences. Lastly, for the higher posts, administrative qualities.

Do you think that this is the career for you? If so, you must be prepared to qualify, for in librarianship, as in most other professions, advancement comes only to those who are qualified. The qualifications are given by the Library Association, who keep a register of Chartered Librarians divided into two groups: those with the general qualification who are called Associates (A.L.A.) and those with the advanced qualification who are called Fellows (F.L.A.). The latter qualification is sought by those who wish to get the senior and chief posts.

If you are a graduate, with a good degree, you have a choice of two ways of qualifying: to take a full-time course at the London University School of Librarianship and Archives, at University College, London, or to take a course at one of the schools in Technical and Commercial Colleges, and to sit for the Registration Examination held by the Library Association. Either way you can become a Chartered Librarian following success in your examinations.

If you are not a graduate, you must take the First Professional Examination of the Library Association before you will be admitted to the Registration Examination. The minimum educational qualification required for entry to the First Professional Examination is a General Certificate of Education with five passes at ordinary level, one being English language, or five lowers in the Scottish Leaving Certificate, one being English.

The subjects a librarian studies are Bibliography, Classification and Cataloguing, Assistance to Readers, Organization and Administration of Libraries, and the literature of a special subject. After passing the Registration Examination, the student-librarian may register as a Chartered Librarian in the category of Associate provided (1) he is aged 23, (2) he has completed the minimum of three years' approved library service, and (3) he has a General Certificate of Education in at least one other language besides English. If he goes on to pass the Final Examination, he can seek election as a Fellow when he is aged 25 years and has completed 5 years approved service.

The methods of study for the Library Association Examinations are four: by full-time attendance at a school of librarianship (one year each for the Registration and Final Examinations), by part-time study at day or evening classes (probably three to four years for each examination), by correspondence courses for those out of reach of oral tuition, and by unguided private study (not recommended to any but the most brilliant). The full-time schools of librarianship are to be found in Birmingham, Brighton, Ealing, Glasgow, Leeds, London, Loughborough, Manchester and Newcastle-upon-Tyne. Part time courses are usually to be found at the technical or commercial college in any large town.

Of course, additional qualifications are all to the good. In National and University libraries a good honours degree is an essential foundation. In special libraries a degree can be a great recommendation, and knowledge of languages an asset. There is a strong current demand for librarians in special libraries, particularly for those who have qualifications in technology and science.

LISTENING TO MUSIC

Perhaps you are one of those who feel that, just because they are unable to play an instrument, they are not musical, and are condemned to miss one of the most satisfying pleasures that life can offer.

If this is so, you are forgetting two important things: first, that before you can play, say, the piano, you must learn to read music and then practise; second, that the fact that you can't play a musical instrument does *not* mean that you're not musical. You see, being musical really means being able to appreciate and enjoy music, and that is something we all can do, provided we are willing to make the effort. Unfortunately, many people fail to realize this, and the reason, oddly enough, seems to be that nowadays music is everywhere. Thanks to the radio and the gramophone, we can hear music whenever and wherever we like. We can't listen all the time, and sometimes, instead of switching off the radio, we allow the music from it to become a background to what we are doing. Perhaps if I tell you this true story you will see just what I mean.

Not so very long ago, I was chatting with a lad who told me how much he regretted that he had not taken piano lessons. In an effort to cheer him up I said: " Never mind—you can still have a great deal of enjoyment in listening to music."

He snorted indignantly. " Listening to music? Huh! Anybody can do *that*!"

" Oh," said I, taken aback, " so you listen a good deal?"

" Sure; I have the wireless on every night while I'm doing my homework!"

Well—I could have suggested that he should *listen* to the music instead of using it as an accompaniment to his homework, but I didn't want to appear unkind. However, I did tell him some of the things I'm going to pass on to you in a moment.

I was sorry for Jackie. He'd got hold of the wrong end of the stick, and it wasn't entirely his own fault. You see, whether you play an instrument or not, music is a great adventure—an adventure which lasts all your life, and in which you are always discovering new pleasures and learning new things. But because of the fact that there is so much music to be heard nowadays, the adventure can go wrong. Unless you are willing to think, to listen, and to do something for yourself, you will become bewildered and lost, and finally all music will come alike to you. That is what happened to Jackie, and it happens to a great many people.

Perhaps you are asking, " What's this about music being an adventure? How should I start? What do you mean by ' making an effort '? What is there to do?" Well, let's get down to some thinking and planning.

First of all, let's do a bit of scouting. Is the path going to be smooth or will there be heavy going—or even danger? Well, I don't think the going will be heavy—exactly the opposite, if we take the right way with the right spirit. Dangers? Yes, I think there might be. The first big danger is that we confuse listening and hearing. I know I've hinted at this before, so perhaps we'd better have a clear idea of the difference between listening and hearing before we go on.

Imagine that you are alone in the house on a stormy night. While the wind is howling outside, you are sitting by the fire, deep in a book. You *hear* the wind, of course—you just can't help hearing its noisy gusts—but the book is an exciting one, and it has all your attention. And then suddenly from somewhere comes a strange sound. It is a sound you haven't heard before. You don't know what it is, and so you forget your book and cock your ears for it. Was it a board creaking? Has something worked loose in the gale? Is it, perhaps, an everyday sound which you may be able to recognize if you listen carefully? Yes, that's it—you must listen carefully, and now your book is shut and you *are* listening! Well, when we are listening to music, we must listen just as carefully as that, so that we may hear what the composer of the music has to say to us.

If you've got the difference between listening and hearing clear in your mind, let's take a look at another sticky patch, and it's this: *all* music is not worth listening to in this way. That sounds rather dreadful, but it's true. In fact, a great deal of the music which is broadcast is not meant to demand all our attention. For instance, there are the " Music while you work " programmes—half an hour of cheery tunes to help you to work better. And then, of course, there are programmes of what is called " light music "—generally pleasant, tuneful music that makes a pleasant accompaniment to five o'clock tea. The programmes of dance music, too, don't require us to sit down and concentrate—we may dance to them, or do some odd job in the house. Music of this kind is not bad music; it is good of its kind, and there's no harm in having a pleasant background of music—provided we realize that there *is* music which does demand all our attention. If we forget this, then the great music is allowed to slip into the background too, and all music comes alike to us. That is a danger we must avoid at all costs. If we don't, our adventure will come to a sticky end.

This may seem a little bewildering, but it simply means that you will have to try to make up your own mind on what kind of music deserves your attention. I don't think you'll have much difficulty. Good music generally holds your attention almost without your realizing it, and holds it so completely that you cannot bear an interruption of any kind.

I am not going to give you a list of pieces to which you should listen, but I will give you one or two hints as to what music you are likely to enjoy. Descriptive music, like Mendelssohn's overture *Fingal's Cave* (or *The Hebrides*) is always exciting listening, and a story told in music, like Dukas' *The Sorcerer's Apprentice*, also provides much enjoyment. Lively, tuneful music is to be found in music for ballets—*The Swan Lake* (Tchaikovsky) and *Coppelia* (Delibes) are well worth your attention. Before listening to ballet music, however, it is often worth while finding out the story of the ballet.

I could go on for a long time, hinting at the many exciting things in store for you—beautiful melodies, pictures in music, stories (there is even Sindbad in *The Arabian Nights*; the name of the piece, a long one, is *Scheherazade*), soothing music, music which is fierce and exciting, music to suit your moods, music which will make you feel that something wonderful has happened to you—but I have still much to tell you, and I shall have to pass on. Before we leave the subject of listening, however, there are two things worth remembering. The first is that you should never force yourself to listen, or listen because you feel you ought; listen because you want to listen. Secondly, you may come upon music which you find too difficult to understand. If this happens, don't lose heart and don't blame the music. Make up your mind to give it another trial later in your adventure when you have gained more listening experience and gathered more knowledge.

Now I think you'll see that our adventure is taking shape, and some of the things you can do for yourself are taking shape as well. One thing you can do is to find out something about the music you have heard and the music you intend to hear. It is very exciting to come upon a new piece of music unexpectedly—to find pleasure and excitement without planning for it. But it is a good scheme, too, to plan some listening in advance. If you're going to a concert, try to find out what the programme is going to be. Then choose one piece of music which you think you may particularly enjoy, and try to find out something about it or its composer. If you aren't able to attend concerts, have a look through the *Radio Times*, pick out one or two pieces you intend to hear during the week, and then do your detective work. If there is a library handy, there may be books there to help you; if not, ask your music teacher or some other musical friend to assist you.

Often interesting articles about composers and music appear in the *Radio Times* or in some of the illustrated weeklies. It is quite a good idea to cut such articles out and paste them in a scrapbook. Your " musical scrapbook " might also contain photographs of orchestras, conductors, singers, pianists, ballet dancers—in fact, any picture of interest musically. Such a scrapbook not only affords you plenty of fun, but is also something of lasting value.

There is one other big job that you should tackle—getting to know the orchestra. All the pieces I mentioned a few moments ago are orchestral pieces, and by far the greater part of the music you are likely to hear will be provided by the orchestra. If you know something about the instruments of the orchestra and what they sound like, you will add considerably to your enjoyment of music. So now, to round off this start to our adventure in music, shall we meet the orchestra?

Many people regard an orchestra as just a great number of persons playing different musical instruments. If you think for a moment, however, you will recognize that the orchestra is really one great musical instrument through which composers express their thoughts or feelings. Just as an organist in church can produce a great variety of sounds, and suit the tone of the organ to the mood of a hymn, so the orchestra can express the mood of a composer, and produce a range of sounds which no organ can equal. Believe me, there are few moments so thrilling as those spent in listening to a fine orchestra playing great music.

Now that we have chosen our instrument, let's take it to pieces and examine it. Big orchestras may number anything from fifty to over a hundred instruments, but each instrument belongs to one of four families. The names of the families are: strings, woodwind, brass and percussion, and I think you might find it interesting to meet the members of each family.

First, meet the four members of the string family—violin, viola, violoncello, and double bass. All these instruments have four strings, so you can see why we call them the string family. The thickness of the strings varies with the instruments. The strings of the double bass, for instance, are very much thicker than those of the violin. On all four instruments the strings are slackened or tightened by means of pegs. I expect you will have seen a violinist " tuning up "—that is, tightening or slackening the strings by turning the pegs.

The violin is the smallest instrument of this family, and the most important. Not only is it an ideal instrument for singing a melody, but it can produce many wonderful effects. By using his bow in a certain way, the violinist can produce two sounds at once. This is called " double-stopping ". Sometimes the music asks that the violinist pluck the strings with his finger. This kind of playing is called *pizzicato*.

No doubt you have heard the sweet singing tones of the violin, but you may not have heard the more wistful tones of the viola. The viola is about $3\frac{1}{2}$ inches longer than the violin and can produce deeper tones.

The 'cello, of course, is much bigger than the viola and the violin, and has a rich, mellow singing tone. The 'cellist sits when playing, and uses his thumb as well as his fingers for fingering the strings. Although the 'cello cannot produce the high notes of which the violin is capable, it can produce, in its deep rich tones, all the effects and tricks of the violin.

The largest instrument in the string family is the double bass. It is usually six feet in length, and is sometimes taller than the man who plays it! Its strings are so thick and heavy that cogwheels are fitted so that the tuning-pegs may be turned more easily. The double bass can produce very low notes, and its job is more or less to lay the foundations on which the other three members of the family build. Sometimes it does have a solo, however, and then we hear its deep, awe-inspiring voice. The double bass is also used in the rhythm section of a dance band, where it is always played *pizzicato*. Many musicians refer to this largest of the stringed instruments as " the doghouse "—a very undignified name for a very dignified instrument.

Next we meet the woodwind family, so called because the instruments are made of wood and are played by blowing. Have you ever tried to play the tin whistle, or to make a reed pipe? Well, the woodwind instruments are made on the same lines as the humble

'CELLO DOUBLE BASS

tin whistle, and are played in much the same way, except that they have metal keys for your fingers as well as holes. As in the string family, the smallest instruments produce the highest notes, while the largest instruments produce the lowest ones.

The smallest instrument in the woodwind family is the piccolo, but beyond adding some frills in a very high voice, it does little in the orchestra. More important is the flute which, like the piccolo, is held sideways. The flute has a lovely clear tone, and often has very quick and lively tunes to play. Although it is a woodwind instrument it is, in fact, often made of silver.

After the flute comes the clarinet, which is also used in military

bands and dance bands. You will have some idea of what the clarinet
can do when I tell you that it has been called the " violin of the
military band ". On its lowest notes it has a rich, round tone, and
on the high notes a clear, singing tone. The clarinettist in an
orchestra is kept busy, for he has often important tunes to play.
The clarinet itself is made of wood or ebonite, although there have
recently been experiments with all-metal clarinets, and has a cane
reed fitted in the mouthpiece.

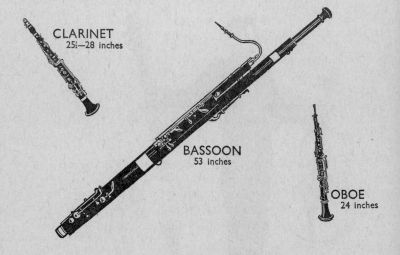

CLARINET
25½—28 inches

BASSOON
53 inches

OBOE
24 inches

Another very fine instrument in the woodwind section is the
oboe. It is a difficult instrument to play, for it has a double reed.
Oboes are generally made of rosewood or ebony.

If you practise listening for individual instruments—an excellent
habit to acquire—you will soon be able to recognize the oboe, for
it has a more biting tone than the clarinet. It, too, has often important melodies to play, and its tone adds a bite and a flavour to
the tone of the woodwinds. It has a big brother called the cor
anglais, or English horn. (Nobody knows why it was given this
name, as it isn't English and it isn't a horn.) The cor anglais is
bigger than the oboe, and has a heavier, sadder tone.

Lastly we come to the bassoon, a rather queer-looking instrument
resembling two thick pipes stuck together. The bassoon's job,
like that of the 'cello and double bass, is to supply the foundation

for the others by playing the low notes, although it is often given a tune to play. Somehow, most people find the bassoon amusing, and it has been called " the clown of the orchestra ". Certainly it can produce some amusing effects, and it is sometimes treated humorously by composers, but it may also be used in grave or sad passages.

The third of the orchestral families is the brass family, and its members are the horn, trumpet, trombone and tuba. These

HORN

TUBA

instruments are really brass tubes of different lengths with slides or valves for producing the different notes. The position of a player's lips and the amount of air which is allowed to pass through the tube of the instrument are also important in producing notes.

The horn is the most difficult of the four to play, and indeed is one of the most difficult of all orchestral instruments. It has a lovely mellow tone and sometimes the effect it produces is almost magical. Mendelssohn asks the horns to imitate the horns of fairy-land in his overture to *A Midsummer-Night's Dream*. On occasion, however, the horn can be almost frightening. When the Russian composer Prokofiev wrote his music for the story of Peter and the

Wolf, he chose the horns to represent the Wolf, and they certainly play the part well.

The trumpet and the trombone you will know already, I expect, for we also find these instruments in military bands and dance bands. The trumpet can be easily recognized by its brilliant, ringing tone, and much of the music the trumpets of the orchestra are given to play is of a stirring and heroic character.

The trombone has not such a brilliant tone as the trumpet, and has a deeper voice. The word " trombone " in Italian means " big trumpet ", so perhaps we might call the trombone the big brother of the trumpet, although they don't look like brothers. Unlike the trumpet, the trombone has no valves. Instead, it has a movable slide, which enables the player to alter the length of the brass tube, and thus produce the required notes. The trombones form the backbone of the brass section, and can produce a tremendous volume of sound, although as a rule there are only three of them. The tone they produce may be harsh and threatening or soft and velvety, as the occasion demands.

The largest instrument of the brass family, and the one which plays the lowest notes, is the tuba. The tuba looks a very complicated affair with its large brass bell and its mass of tubes and valves. It is really the double bass of the brass section, for it very rarely plays a tune.

Lastly we come to the percussion family—the " bangers "—known to orchestral players as the " kitchen department ". Many of the instruments in this family you will know already—the big bass drum, the side drum (with its snares of catgut stretched across the under-skin to help the rattle), the tambourine, triangle and cymbals. You may have heard the xylophone (often used in " variety turns ") and the castanets—wooden clappers worked by the fingers. You will also have heard the " tympani ", although you might not recognize them if you saw them. In appearance they are very like witches' cauldrons, and that, no doubt, had something to do with their being called " kettledrums ", that being their common name. A kettledrum is the only drum which can be tuned to produce different notes, and if you go to a concert you will see the drummer tuning his drum by turning screws round the rim, thus slackening or tightening the skin.

Three other percussion instruments which may be new to you are the tubular bells, glockenspiel and celesta. The tubular bells, as their name suggests, are metal tubes of different lengths which, when struck, produce what sounds like a peal of bells. The glockenspiel is very like the xylophone in appearance—a series of bars of varying length mounted on a kind of table—but, whereas the xylophone's bars are made of hardwood, the bars of the glockenspiel are made of metal. When the bars of the glockenspiel are struck with mallets, a sound like the tinkling of little bells is produced. The celesta, which looks like a very small piano, complete with keyboard, makes a magical kind of sound—a mixture of piano and little bell tone. If you want to hear what delicate and delightful music the celesta can produce, listen to *The Dance of the Sugar Plum Fairy* by Tchaikovsky. This was the first important piece of music to be written for the celesta, which was invented in 1886.

Last of all comes the harp—an instrument with a very long history. The harp which is used in the orchestra is very different from the harps we see in old pictures and drawings of ancient times. The modern harp is a large instrument and has forty-six strings. It also has seven pedals, by means of which it can be set in any key. Many brilliant and sparkling effects can be obtained from the harp, and modern composers often use it with great effect. As a rule, however, the harpist has not nearly so much to do as the other members of the orchestra.

Now that you have met the instruments of the orchestra, you may be wondering just how many of each instrument there are. Well, this table will give you some idea of the make-up of a big orchestra:

Strings: Violins, 30; violas, 10; 'cellos, 10; double basses, 8.

Woodwind: Piccolo, 1; flutes, 2; oboes, 2; cor anglais, 1; clarinets, 2; bassoons, 2. (Sometimes an extra oboe or clarinet is added if the music demands it.)

Brass: Trumpets, 2; horns, 4; trombones, 3; tuba, 1. (Sometimes extra trumpets or horns are added.)

Percussion: The number of percussion instruments depends on the requirements of the music, but we usually find the kettledrums, bass drum, side-drum, cymbals, gong, triangle, tambourine, castanets and xylophone.

The others you know, and they can be added if need be.

A little arithmetic will show that our orchestra numbers just above eighty players, and that by far the largest part of the orchestra

—more than half, in fact—is the string section. So large is the string section that the violins are divided into first and second violins, and each group has its own part to play. (This is rather like what happens in school when a class sings a two-part song. The boys and girls who sing the melody are like the first violins, while those who sing the descant or the second part are like the second violins.) Beside the large string section the other sections of the orchestra seem very small, but in fact the whole orchestra is nicely balanced, and no section is too powerful for the others. You can just imagine what would happen if an orchestra had a brass section of fifty and a string section of ten. It would indeed lift the audience right out of their seats!

Although we have so far talked only of instruments, I hope you are not forgetting the players themselves. Most of us regard playing an instrument as a pleasure. So do all good musicians, but please remember that although it is a pleasure, it is also, for the orchestral player, a job which demands a very high standard of musicianship and great powers of concentration. Nor is it all just " good fun ". Before a programme of music can be presented to an audience, it must be rehearsed, and rehearsing is often a very exhausting business. The players must, for three hours on end, think of nothing but the music and how they are going to play it. They must be able to do everything that is asked of them, and to obey their conductor's instructions. Very often six hours a day are spent in rehearsal, and in a busy season the orchestra may have to spend the morning rehearsing and then play at a concert in the evening. Just think of what the London Promenade Concert Season, with six concerts per week, means in terms of work to the orchestras taking part. The men and women of the orchestra are indeed worthy of our respect, not only for their skill, but also for their untiring efforts to bring to us the music we love.

There is one very important person about whom we have not yet spoken, and that is the conductor. How fascinating and thrilling his job must be, for he is in complete command of the orchestra. With an expressive movement of his hands he can draw from the orchestra a fury of sound, or, with a simple gesture, reduce the orchestra's voice to a mere whisper. Small wonder a young friend of mine came home from a school-children's concert and announced that he was not going to be an engine-driver after all, but the conductor of an orchestra! Most of us feel that way after our first concert, but few realize just what a conductor's work entails, and what makes a good conductor.

First of all, the conductor must himself be a fine and experienced musician, with a thorough knowledge of the instruments of the orchestra. In fact, many famous conductors have, at some time or another, been orchestral players themselves. Sir John Barbirolli, conductor of Manchester's Hallé Orchestra, was once a 'cellist. The conductor must, however, have more than a knowledge of instruments—he must have the qualities of leadership. He must be on good terms with his players, and be able to lead and inspire them as a good captain inspires a football team. This is something that cannot be taught, although it may be learnt by experience. A good conductor has this gift of inspiring his players to give of their best and do all that is asked of them without question or grumble.

The use of the hands is of very great importance in conducting, and part of a conductor's training is learning to use his hands to transmit his wishes to the orchestra. The movement of the baton, which is held in the right hand, must be precise, for it is the baton which controls the orchestra and gives the beat. All movements of the hands should be graceful, and their meaning clear to the orchestra. If a conductor has an elaborate system of signs, he will muddle the orchestra and be ugly to watch.

The conductor has his own music to follow, and it is called the "orchestral score". As the orchestral score contains parts for every kind of instrument in the orchestra, you can just imagine how complicated it looks. Most people, when they are learning the piano, find it difficult enough to read two lines of music at once. How would you like to have to read sometimes as many as twenty lines together? Yet many great conductors conduct from memory, so well have they studied the score.

In studying a score, the conductor must take several decisions which will affect the performance of the music. In the first place, he must decide at what pace the piece is to be taken. There are no hard-and-fast rules about how quickly or how slowly a certain piece of music must be performed. Composers generally indicate by Italian words the approximate speed at which they wish the music to be played. Thus *allegro ma non troppo* means, roughly, "fairly lively", but two conductors may have vastly different ideas as to just how fast "fairly lively" should be. The conductor is also responsible for how much or how little sound is drawn from the orchestra. Here again, composers use Italian words to indicate the volume of sound—*piano*, for instance, means "softly". The conductor must therefore make up his mind just how softly he wishes the music to be played.

Another important point conductors must consider is phrasing. You know yourself what a lot depends on how you say a phrase. "I like that!" looks simple enough on paper, but could mean either that the speaker was pleased or peeved, the correct meaning depending on how the phrase was spoken. In music, much the same thing happens. Phrase follows phrase, and what each phrase means to the listener depends on how the orchestra says it. This, in turn, depends on how the conductor thinks the orchestra should say it.

From what I have told you, you will realize that no two performances of the same piece of music will be exactly alike, for each conductor has his own idea of how the music should be played. But, although performances differ, the aim of all good conductors is the same—to carry out, as far as is humanly possible, the intentions and instructions of the composer.

Now that you have met the instruments, the players, and the conductor, I hope you will go ahead on your own and get to know the orchestra really well. The radio and the gramophone should provide you with opportunities of getting to know the instruments, and your music teacher at school will be glad to help you if you ask him.

If you have a gramophone at home, try to get hold of the records of *Peter and the Wolf*. This is a story in which all the characters, human and animal, are represented by various instruments of the orchestra. Peter himself, for instance, is represented by a string quartet, while the Wolf is represented by the horns. The person who tells the story introduces you first of all to the characters and the instruments which represent them, and this gives you a grand opportunity of learning to recognize the sounds of the various instruments. I think you could find *Peter and the Wolf* grand fun, but if you don't like the idea of a story told to music, then there are other records of the instruments of the orchestra—with no story attached—which you should try to hear.

And now, I think, the "briefing" for our adventure is over. The rest is up to you. But, before you set out, just one or two last words. First, a reminder that a great deal of enjoyment can be had from talking and arguing about music. Don't, therefore, keep all your discoveries to yourself—share them with other people. Another " don't "—don't be afraid to ask for help and advice, but don't simply swallow other people's opinions. Think for yourself, make up your own mind and stick to your guns! A last and important " don't "—don't laugh at the other fellow's kind of music. Music should bring you many new friends, but it won't bring you any if you set yourself up as a superior person beside whom others who know less or have less musical tastes are lowbrow or beneath contempt. But then, I don't think I needed to tell you that—you're not that kind of person, and I know you'll go into this adventure in the proper way. And as every really fine musician will tell you, that way is not only in an adventurous spirit, but in a humble one.

Off you go, then, and the very best of luck in your great adventure!

SOME ATTRACTIVE PETS

GOLDFISH AND AQUARIUMS

I should like to begin by telling you the story of George, because this fascinating fish lived longer in my home than any other one I have ever kept. George was probably born in a commercial breeding place in England where goldfish were bred. Or perhaps he came from Italy, for that country did a big export trade in goldfish before the war. He was about an inch and a half in length when I got him, a shimmering graceful figure with a large fantail and bright, golden body, unbroken by any marks. As he moved grandly through the water his flowing fins would flutter like a bride's veil.

Now George had a tank all to himself, a decorative affair which adorned my sideboard. There were about four gallons of water in the tank, which meant that handsome George was in splendid comfort. There is a general rule in the keeping of goldfish which you must observe. This is that you should provide a gallon of water for each inch of fish—and when you are calculating the length of a fish you do not count the tail.

But you require to be very particular about the shape of a goldfish tank. An oblong one, with the maximum amount of water surface, is infinitely better than any other kind. I mention this for, with the shortage of suitable glass, large tanks are sold with a very limited water surface. You know the kind I mean, the ones used in electrical equipment. George's room was facing south, an excellent outlook for him because the room was always bright. That did not mean that my finny friend was exposed to the bright glare of the sun for hours on end. George would have been a most unhappy fish had that been so. At no time of the day did the direct glare of the sun reach him.

And that is a most important thing to remember, by the way, with any pets. All animals require bright light at times, but the ideal situation is where they can retreat to shade if they wish, and their home does not become stifling with heat.

The tank which contained George seldom required to be taken into the kitchen, or bathroom, to have the water changed. In fact, in the five years I had him, I can hardly remember having to do this.

You will therefore be wondering what I did. Here is the secret. An aquarium, properly balanced, does not require to have the water changed. That is the theory, although, in practice, you must do something some time. But first of all I must explain balance. You know that a healthy pond outside, which contains life, never goes stagnant. Well, in your home you must create a healthy pond in miniature. That means that you must provide plants which give off oxygen, for fish require this in order to live happily.

I could have introduced my plants in two ways: (*a*) by covering the bottom with sand, and (*b*) by placing little dishes in the tank and planting the vegetation in them. I chose the latter way because I thought it looked nicer, and, moreover, the tank was easier managed. The little dishes had holes in them, and they were about one inch in depth.

One must be particular about the sand to use. I preferred the kind one buys for cage birds, but you must not use it just as it comes out of the packet. Wash it several times till all the particles are shining.

Plants are purchased from pet shops which specialize in such things. There are a host of them, all with impressive Latin names. Three very good ones are Myriophyllum, Sagittaria and Vallisneria. Apart from their value in making the fish healthy, plants in a balanced aquarium look very pretty indeed, particularly the first one I have named.

Now, although George was the only fish I kept in this particular aquarium, he was not altogether lonely. He had snails as companions. No, not the creepy, crawly ones we are all familiar with, but special snails which rejoice in the imposing name of *Planorbis corneus*. And you will get them also from pet dealers, or aquarists if you know any. Snails have a practical value and they are not in the aquarium entirely for the social atmosphere. They are scavengers.

I am being very honest when I tell you that there is a tendency to overestimate their utility so far as tidying up is concerned, but they will serve a limited purpose and provide a maximum of interest. Anyway, it is good fun going out in the morning and coming back at lunch-time to guess how far, and how fast, Johnny snail has travelled.

The snail is supposed to keep that green scum, known as algæ, under control. A tank in a bright situation will certainly have algæ sooner or later. Now, this greenish stuff is not really unhealthy as it is a vegetable, but it is unsightly. You can remove it by using a pad of wash leather, or by using a thin stick and rubbing the glass.

There are times, of course, when it becomes essential to change the water. I do not advise carrying the heavy tank—a four-gallon tank of water is very heavy—through the house to change the water. Do it this way. Buy a rubber tube, about two feet or so in length, and siphon. In case you have never done this, here is what you do. Place a tub below the level of the aquarium. First of all put the tube into the aquarium, and suck through the other end, with your

Veiltail Goldfish and Aquarium Plants
Myriophyllum   Sagittaria   Vallisneria

head below the level of the aquarium. But immediately you suck be sure to pull the end of the tube from your mouth. If you do not then you will get a most unpleasant mouthful of unpalatable water! The water should run freely, and keep it running till there is just enough water left in the tank to keep the fish covered. Never mind about removing that last quantity of water.

Then, take out the plants and cut away any dead shoots. Some care should be exercised in giving fresh water. If it is very cold, allow it to lie a bit till it gets heated by the temperature of the room. It is wrong to splash it in as this will surely disturb the fish. I used to give George his new tub easily by using an ordinary large milk jug. Instead of splashing in, I directed the spout against the side of the tank so that it was refilled with the minimum of fuss. I poured in water till it was about an inch from the top of the aquarium.

George used to dash about when he got lovely crystal-clear water, but not until everything had settled down did I replace the plants. My reason for this was that if the little dishes with the plants in them had been put in first, there was a good chance of disturbing the gravel and possibly uprooting plants.

Many people believe in covering the top of a tank as it keeps the water clean. I believe in that and I had a sheet of glass which all but covered the surface. A tiny slit here and there is all that is required to keep the tank healthy. And if you are handy you can make small rubber cushions for the covering glass to lie on. This allows the air to circulate at the surface. You know how dust gathers in a room, particularly in a room where there is a coal fire. Well, that is bound to settle on the water surface unless it is protected.

Now food. Well, that is, obviously, a most important matter. When I was a little boy we were told that there was nothing better than ants' eggs. And so we used to pile them generously into the tank. Occasionally we saw a fish come up and try to swallow one, but, so far as I can recollect, I never have seen a tiny goldfish tackle an ant's egg easily. In these more enlightened times there are excellent pet fish foods which you give strictly according to the instructions, and if the instructions are not clear then err on the side of giving too little. There is nothing which sours a tank more than an excess of food. As a tonic you can give the fish a touch of salt every two or three weeks. Enough to cover a threepenny—a silver one—should be given. But take care that you do not drop the salt on a snail. If you do, then you will likely see the snail fizzle out of its shell and die a horrible death. And even snails have feelings!

And dear old George was so tame. He used to eat from my hand. This is how I taught him. Every time I went to feed I tapped the tank. I always fed him at the same corner of the tank and very soon he learned that tap-tap meant food, and away he raced to the corner and sucked the powdery food from between my forefinger and thumb. Never once did he bite!

And now what about garden ponds? Well, that all depends on what facilities you have. In a general way the outside garden pond requires the same management as a tank. But there are naturally certain snags to be overcome. First of all take situation in the garden. If you place the pond under a tree which sheds its foliage in the autumn, the surface of the pond is going to be very dirty and untidy. Yet shade you must have and you should not put it where it will be in the full glare of a summer sun for hours in the day. The ideal garden pond is certainly the concrete one, with water from a depth of a few inches at the side, grading down to two feet. Or you can even go deeper. There are the elaborate affairs with shelves for the various plants—marginal ones, oxygenating ones and lilies at the deepest part. The pond should be situated so that it harmonizes with the other garden amenities, and not just stuck anywhere. But it must be recognized that a well-built concrete or cement pond is quite a builder's job. Yet, because many of us are not builders, or have no flair for it—and I definitely have not—that does not mean that we are to be deprived of the pleasure of a small pond in the garden.

As a matter of fact I built one very cheaply and quite easily. I merely sank a large, oblong tub in the garden, and round the side there was a marginal cement pad. Then plants were introduced round the side, and there was nothing wrong with this affair. I had my fish in a garden " pond "! And that was that. Naturally, they were small goldfish, yet they lived for several years. In the winter it used to freeze hard, but my fish survived, for there was a good depth of water.

However, no matter what you do, be careful that the pond is clean before the fish are introduced. And I should add, the plants too. If the bath, tub, vat, or whatever you use, has been used for oil or such like, then you can expect trouble. Fish and plants would be killed if they were put into such a pond without it being cleaned first. On the other hand, with such a pond, if it really is clean, you have a big start on the fellow with a concrete or cement pond.

It may take a matter of six months before the pond can be made safe, and you would require to have it hosed and cleaned out often during that period. There is a patent preparation which can be used immediately after constructing a concrete pond which is claimed to make it fit for use within a few weeks. But if one has gone to the expense and trouble of building a stout pond, it is well worth while doing a lot of scrubbing to rid the erection of the surface alkalinity. A good hard scrubbing brush and elbow grease is the method. There is no easy way. Then the patent preparation can be applied according to the maker's strict instructions.

The golden rule with a garden pond, as with a tank, is: not too many fish and not too much food.

When you are buying fish you want to be very careful in your choice. A healthy fish has an erect dorsal fin—the one on its back—and its scales are unbroken and the colour shiny and vivid. It is often necessary to handle a fish, and when it is do not use the hands. Which is something of an Irishism. " Handle " fish with a net only, for by holding carelessly in your hand you can injure or kill it. It is easy to tell when your fish are ill. They spend most of their time at the surface and their fins are droopy. When you see them like that it is not food they want. Something has gone wrong and the tank has been knocked off its balance.

And, lastly, fish are very soothing to the nerves. It is so restful to lie back on an easy-chair, or lounge in a camp-chair by the pond, and watch them moving about so happily. Everything is so leisured, and life, for them, just seems to stop still all the time.

GOLDEN HAMSTERS

I think it is safe to say that the golden hamster has ousted the guinea pig, white rat, and white mouse from the collections of many pet keepers. Hamsters are delightful little creatures, and at the moment we have them breeding happily in Glasgow Zoo, at Calderpark. I can strongly recommend them to boys and girls; the latter will not have the natural fear of them that they have for rats and mice. Before I tell you something about the keeping of them in the home, or garden hut, I must give you a sketchy note of their history, for they are extremely interesting little creatures and hold, in their own way, a most important place in science. They are quite new animals so far as we are concerned.

The hamster is a rodent and of restricted geographical distribution in the wild state. There was considerable uncertainty about its record up till the year 1930 when, in the neighbourhood of Aleppo, it was found in the desert by a zoologist from the Department of Zoology, Hebrew University, Jerusalem. The original specimens, an adult female and twelve young, were obtained by digging up a burrow which was eight feet in depth. The first litter to be born in captivity appeared about four months later. The following year two pairs were brought to this country, and I had the very good fortune to see them at Glasgow University. From this pair the tens of thousands of golden hamsters in this country were bred.

You frequently see them described as rat-cum-guinea pig, while some have even claimed that they are hybrids from familiar rodents. That is nonsense. They are a very distinct species. A full-grown golden hamster barely touches seven inches in length. It has a deep golden-brown coat, but towards the roots the hair is grey. Eyes are large and black and the tail is short and stumpy. They have well-developed cheek pouches in which they can pack an amazing quantity of food.

In captivity they become delightfully tame, although at times you might get a nip. But it cannot be claimed that they are very

Golden Hamsters

sociable. They have frequent quarrels if kept in a group, and even a pair will be rather distant at times. They have a very strong tendency to store food, and this instinct is present at a very young age.

Now, in keeping them you cannot do so with a wooden cage. Metal is most essential, and a suitable one is as follows: A galvanized-iron tray, 20 in. by 15 in. by 6 in., can be covered by an iron wire top, about 6 in. in height. The wire mesh will require to be as close as $\frac{1}{4}$ in. Food can be oats, raw carrot, bread, barley, puppy biscuits, and such like. It is extremely easy to breed them, and they are so prolific that, theoretically, one pair of golden hamsters could be responsible for the amazing number of 296,866 in two years. If you have young ones do not, on any account, disturb them. If you do, then there is every possibility that their mother will destroy them. Baby hamsters grow very quickly, and they can, in turn, be parents when a little over two months old.

You, or more likely your parents, will worry about their getting away, and thus giving all of us a worry like the mouse and rat problem. Well, if they escape they will not multiply, but would most probably die. If they didn't, well, hamster traps would be sold in all the shops!

GUINEA PIGS

These are attractive pets and easy to keep. One boar and several sows will live contentedly. A simple hutch can easily be made.

Long and Short-haired Guinea Pigs

You can make it with several pens, and the whole arrangement does not require to be more than 1 ft. in height. The front can be covered with ½-in. mesh wire. Feed and keep them in much the same way as you keep rabbits. Food should be provided about twice daily—oats, barley, hay, grass, cabbage, lettuce, bread, carrots and swedes. The floor of the hutch can be covered with sawdust or peat moss. Water, of course, should be at hand, and the secret of keeping them —and all pet livestock, for that matter—is cleanliness and regularity in attention.

TORTOISES

Tortoises are now coming back to the pet market, and it is good fun keeping them. Many people find that they seldom eat, and live long with no " visible means of support ". But that does not mean that we should treat them as pets which cannot eat. Give them lettuce, cabbage, bread, and even milk. If you are lucky enough you might have one which will eat from your hand, but, more often, when you extend your hand to your pet, it will with-

Grecian Tortoises

draw shyly into its shell. In the summer allow the tortoise on the lawn, but, although it moves so slowly, it might get lost if you don't keep your eyes on it.

CAGE BIRDS

In the minds of most people budgerigars and canaries have the monopoly of the cage-bird world. That is not so. Although I have kept and bred both canaries and cage birds, some of the happiest little pets in feathers come from Africa and Australia. They used to give me a great deal of happiness, and it is greatly to be regretted that we cannot buy them very easily to-day owing to certain restrictions on their importation. From Australia we get the gorgeous Gouldian finch, long-tailed grass finch, and Bicheno's finch, to mention a few, while the better-known African ones include the cordon bleu, fire-finches, amadavats, cut-throats, and so on.

An ordinary box cage with close wire will do for them, while a pair can easily be kept in a fancy cage, provided the wires are close enough as the birds I have mentioned are smaller than canaries, with one or two exceptions. They are all seed-eaters, those charming " wee foreigners " as we used to call them. They do splendidly on millet and canary seed, and it is fun seeing them climb and pick at millet spray.

One thing to watch in the keeping of them is draught. In fact, all pets must have draught-proof accommodation. It is also better to keep them in the room in your house where there is the least fluctuation of temperature. The usual type of box cage has a sliding bottom so that you can take it out easily to clean. Cover the bottom of the cage with gritty sand—the kind usually sold for cage birds. This should be changed once every week at least. You can provide

Three Australian Finches
Bicheno's finch.   Long-tailed grass finch.   Gouldian finch

a bath for those happy little creatures, but do not give it icy cold. Another thing about the bird bath—do not give it in the evening as some silly little birds will go and have a bath before going to sleep, and then they spend the night with damp plumage. And that is not good.

It may be, at times, the bird needs its claws cut. Be careful about this, and if you know someone who is experienced then leave it to him. The correct way is to hold the bird in your left hand, with its back to the palm of your hand. Do not squeeze the bird on any account. Hold the claw which is to be cut, between the forefinger and thumb, and hold it up to the light. You will see a shadow in the claw. Do not cut to this or the bird will bleed. There will be a clear bit of the claw near the point, and that is where you cut. The secret is to take very little off at a time. If you bleed the claw then apply iodine or Friar's balsam. But do try and avoid bleeding. Owing to something in a bird's blood it bleeds very freely and suffers much more from bleeding than a four-footed pet.

Some of our British birds make attractive pets in a cage, but I do not advise this unless they have been bred in captivity. The seeds and insects of our countryside will keep them well, and, of course, you can buy prepared foods in pet shops.

Then there is that grand old bird, the parrot. Polly needs special attention. In fact, if you ignore him he will either screech or go in the dumps, and when a parrot becomes bored it is liable to get sick and pull out its feathers. Once again the pet-store man has the seed for it, but Polly will also want more colour to his rations than he can get from what comes out of a packet. Give him fruit in season, and for a treat buy some maize, and boil it. Allow to cool off, of course, before serving. Being a big bird the parrot requires more attention than the smaller cage birds do. His cage should be cleaned regularly, and the tray covered at the bottom with a good layer of sand. This makes cleaning much easier.

It is not practical to give the parrot a bath, but you can buy a spray quite reasonably, and give him a regular shower. He will learn to love this. It is a good plan to give Parrish's chemical food to a parrot. Just a drop or two once each week—enough to discolour the water. In fact, nearly every pet I have mentioned will be the better for this valuable tonic now and again.

Teaching Polly to talk is fun. Keep repeating one word till it is mastered, then go on to a short sentence. It is well known that some people believe that to slit a parrot's tongue is the best way of making it talk. Such utter nonsense! It is terribly cruel, and to do this is to cause almost certain death. How it is done I have not the faintest idea, but I can assure you that any parrot I know—and we have quite a number at the zoo—would probably bite very severely if you attempted such an outrageous thing.

The best talkers in the parrot family are African greys. Those are the beautiful silvery grey birds with red tails. Next best are the Amazon parrots. Amazons probably talk more freely than any others but they have not the deep masculine voice of the greys. There is one thing to remember about all parrots, however. They are deceitful, and at any time might suddenly bite the hand that feeds them. They also take violent dislikes. Some do not like ladies, while others are most aggressive to children. That is generalizing, of course, because I have known individuals which have been pals with their owners for many years.

BREEDING AND RACING PIGEONS

There can be no more fascinating hobby for boys than that of pigeon keeping. Evidence of this is shown by the fact that its devotees are to be found in all classes of society. Rich and poor alike devote their leisure to it. It affords unlimited opportunity for the display of skill and initiative, and in it a young fancier, by his own enthusiasm and intelligence, may compete on equal terms with his seniors for the splendid awards which the sport offers.

There are many different kinds of pigeons, but lack of space forbids my giving details of them all. I will confine myself to a brief description of the most popular present-day fancy breeds and then proceed to enlarge on the racing pigeon.

The Pouter.—This is a most attractive bird. It has been called the king of pigeons. It has an erect, graceful body and abnormal size of crop which, when inflated, causes its owner to stand out conspicuously when congregated with other varieties. The Pouter's chief show points are slenderness of body, length and shapeliness of limb, and legs and feet closely covered with feathers; the standard colours being yellow, red, black, blue and pure white, in addition to many off colours.

Tumblers.—The Tumbler is one of the most popular breeds. It includes numerous varieties, such as long-faced, short-faced, baldheads, beards, &c. It derives its name from its inherent propensity of turning somersaults when in flight. House tumblers are so called because they tumble when flying across a room.

Owl, Turbit, Satinette and Blondinette.—Under this heading are included all the frilled and crested varieties, and they are among the most beautiful and graceful of domestic pigeon breeds. They all have a breast frill and some of them, such as the Turbit and Blondinette, have a crest at the back of the head. One of the finest sights of the feathered world is to behold an aviary full of these beautiful, strikingly coloured, shapely birds with their new feathers after the moult.

Fantails.—The Fantail is one of the commonest breeds of pigeons, not only in Britain but throughout the world. White is the principal colour, but blues, blacks and many off colours are quite common at the leading shows. The tail is the chief glory of the Fantail, and without a good tail no bird can be regarded as a superior specimen.

Jacobins.—The peculiarity of the Jacobin is the extensive feathery hood and mane which almost entirely covers the head and neck. To breed a good " Jack " is an honour and calls for the greatest skill on the part of the breeder.

Magpies.—No doubt the Magpie derives its name from the wild Magpie, the original colours being black and white. They are now bred in all colours, blue, yellow, red, &c. The Magpie is a very attractive bird with a long swan-like neck, neat thin body and prominent breast, tapering gracefully to the tail, legs clean and long, giving the bird a slim appearance.

Show Homers.—The Show Homer has been bred down from the Flying Homer, the external points having preference, and flying qualities neglected, with the result that this bird is now included among the fancy varieties, and is quite useless for racing purposes.

There are numerous other fancy varieties, such as Carriers, Dragons, Barbs, Nuns and Tipplers, but I have not the space to describe them here.

There is one serious objection to a boy taking up the breeding of some of the short-faced, fancy varieties, and that is that they are incapable of properly feeding their own youngsters, and foster-parents, such as Homers or Common Pigeons, have to be kept for this purpose.

Racing Homers.—Without a doubt, the racing pigeon is the most popular of all the various breeds. The sport of pigeon racing is indulged in by both king and commoner, and is popular in all civilized countries throughout the world. In Britain alone there must be well over 100,000 homing fanciers, almost every small village having its Homing Club. The marvellous work performed, and the lives saved in the Great War, and in the 1939–45 War, by these brave little birds has greatly popularized them in the eyes of the general public, and many people have joined the Fancy through this. The two principal racing clubs in this country are the National Flying Club in England and the Scottish National Flying Club. The membership of each of these clubs runs well into four figures; races of 600 and 700 miles are organized yearly, and prizes of over £5000 are offered for competition by each of these organizations. The sport is controlled in England by the National Homing Union, and in Scotland by the Scottish Homing Union. These unions issue rules for the proper conduct of the sport and guidance of the members, prosecute offenders for shooting, trapping or stealing Homing Pigeons, and look after all matters pertaining to the sport in general.

The English racing pigeon was originally imported from Belgium, where the sport is a national one. Owing to the severity of our climate, and the difficult routes over which our birds have to home, including the English Channel and mountains, the breed has been greatly developed and improved, and the English Homer is now considered second to none in the world, and is keenly sought after in America and other countries as a cross to give stamina and otherwise improve their own strains.

My advice to the boy intending to take up the sport of pigeon racing is to get into touch with some successful local fancier, who will advise him, and very often (if he sees the boy is keenly interested) will also present him with a pair or two of late breds to start. Another method is to procure a few pairs of common pigeons, get them mated and sitting on eggs, then purchase one or two pairs of eggs from good racing stock (which are often advertised in the Fancy journals) and put these below the common pigeons. This is a much cheaper method if the boy's purse will not allow of purchasing the pigeons. It is necessary to make sure that the eggs are changed within a day or two of the common pigeons laying.

In designing a loft, the important question is the number of birds it is intended to keep, as one of the most dangerous mistakes is overcrowding. It is impossible to keep birds in health and vigour if overcrowded. Make up your mind before starting. A loft 6 ft. square and 7 ft. high at the front, with a lean-to roof sloping towards the back, should accommodate about five pairs of birds. The front should be partly covered with wire netting or preferably with dowels. This will allow for plenty of ventilation and light. It is advisable to have two lofts of this size, one for the breeding pairs, and another for the young birds after they are weaned. Young birds develop better if kept by themselves. The loft should preferably be raised 18 in. to 24 in. above the ground. In this way it is kept much drier and is not a harbour for vermin below the floor. For fancy varieties, which, as a rule, are not allowed their liberties, the loft should have an aviary attached to the front. This will allow the birds to peck about the ground and get plenty of sunlight. The aviary should be made of wire netting, the same width and height as the loft, and 20 ft. to 30 ft. long. If the loft is for racing pigeons, an aviary is unnecessary, as they must have their liberty. Instead, a cage or trap is fixed to the front, through which the birds can leave and re-enter the loft after exercise. A nest box for each pair should be provided. Tate's sugar boxes are very suitable for this purpose. The front of the box should be covered with dowels, leaving a hole about 6 in. square as an entrance. Perches should be

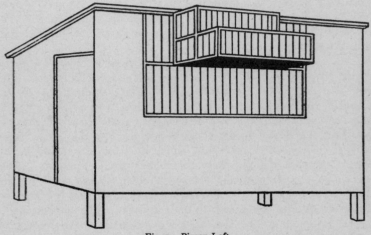

Fig. 1.—Pigeon Loft

fixed to the back wall. These should be preferably of box pattern made from 4 in. wooden battens, each perching box being about 10 in. square inside. Figs. 1 and 2, views respectively from the front and in sectional elevation, show a loft with nest boxes and box perches suitable for 5 to 6 pairs.

During the winter season (that is, from the beginning of September to the end of February) the sexes should be separated. When the breeding season begins, the pairs selected to be mated together should be shut in their respective nest boxes, but care must be taken to see that the male bird does not attack his intended wife (they can be very brutal if not watched) before they are properly mated. This can generally be avoided by placing an ordinary brick on end inside the box. The hen bird soon discovers that on the top of this she is safe from his attacks. In an hour or two the birds generally become quite reconciled to each other, when the brick can be removed and the newly mated pair allowed the run of the loft. Some hens are very stubborn and may take a day or two to mate. The first egg will be laid about the seventh to the tenth day after mating and the second egg about forty hours later. The time of incubation is eighteen days after the laying of the second egg. When the hen is nearing the laying stage, the cock bird commences

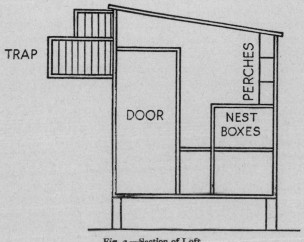

TRAP

PERCHES

DOOR

NEST BOXES

Fig. 2.—Section of Loft

to drive her all round the loft till he gets her into the nest. Many a novice gets alarmed when he sees this for the first time, but there is nothing to be concerned about; it is quite a natural procedure and stops when the eggs are laid.

The youngsters, if they are racing pigeons, must be rung. This is compulsory under the rules of the Homing Unions. The rings are issued by the unions and are placed on the young pigeon's leg when it is about seven days old. It is then on permanently and cannot be taken off.

When the youngsters are from twenty-five to thirty days old, they should be weaned from the parents and put into a loft with other youngsters, where they will develop much better free from molesting by the old birds in the breeding loft. If racers, they should be put in a cage on top of the loft for a day or two and then allowed their liberty before the wings become too strong. Don't force them to fly. Let them strut about to their hearts' content. In a few days they will take to the wing and be flying round and diving through the air full of life and vigour.

The staple food of pigeons is grain, but, as has been discovered during the two great wars, when grain was unobtainable, they can be taught to live healthily on almost anything within reason, such as toasted breadcrumbs, oatmeal and Indian meal made in a dry mash, broken-up acorns, &c. The chief grains for feeding are maple peas, Indian corn, tares, tic beans, dari, wheat, barley, lentils, small seeds such as hemp, Canary rape, and all seeds fed to cage birds. Green food should be given regularly. Cabbage leaves, lettuce and all other vegetable leaves are suitable: the best way to feed green food is to chop it small, dip into salted water and scatter on a clean part of the floor, or tie up a lettuce or cabbage high enough for the birds to peck at it. Whatever grain is fed to the birds should be sound and clean, free from dust and fungus. The best method of storing the grain is in wooden drawers or boxes with perforated zinc bottoms. By this method the air gets through and keeps it sweet and fresh. Some fanciers who are from home from morning till night feed by hopper. They fill up the hopper in the morning with sufficient grain to last the birds all day. Others again generally feed three times a day during the breeding season and once or twice a day in the winter. The grain is thrown on the floor for the birds to peck. The floor, however, must be perfectly clean. A better plan is to feed it in trays. Clean grit should always be before the birds, also a lump of rock salt. The last, but most important point of all, is fresh clean water in clean drinking vessels. These vessels should have a cover over them to keep the birds from fouling the water. More birds are put out of condition by shortage of water, or dirty water, than anything else I know of. A bath is another necessity, and should be given at least once a week summer and winter. An ordinary household bath about 4 in. to 6 in. deep is very suitable for this.

If it is intended to go in for racing, the first thing is to join a Homing Club, which automatically includes membership of the Homing Union. In the ordinary village club, the annual subscription is usually round about 10s. per annum, with a small entrance fee. There are two series of races flown on Saturday afternoons, one for old birds or birds over one year old, and the other for young birds bred during the year of the races. The old bird races start about the beginning of May and continue weekly till the middle of July, and those for young birds start in the middle of July and continue till the end of August. The first race is usually about 50 to 60 miles, with the distance gradually increasing till 400 to 500 miles is reached, the young bird races generally finishing at 150 miles. The birds are taken to the Club House the night before the race, where a rubber ring (on which is a secret number) is placed on the leg. They are then put into sealed baskets—15 to 20 birds to a basket—and taken by a convoyer by train to the starting-point, and liberated at the appointed time. The fancier, who has generally an idea when to expect them home, is awaiting their arrival. Immediately the racer enters the loft it is caught, and the rubber ring inserted in a special timing clock which prints the exact time the ring was inserted. The liberation-time being known, and the clock time, the secretary can tell the time the bird took to fly the distance. The distances are measured by the Great Circle system, and the distance from the race point to the fancier's loft can be calculated to within a few yards; the total flying distance divided by the time taken by the bird gives the average velocity in yards per minute, and the bird with the highest velocity wins the race.

Training the birds for racing starts when they are eight to ten weeks old, and have been flying well round home. If in the country, for their first toss they can be taken about half a mile and liberated together; if in a city or congested area, I would advise only 400 to 500 yards for the initial toss. They should be taken for training every other day, and the distance gradually increased till 30 to 40 miles is reached. They will then be ready for the first race. Always choose a clear day for training, and see that they are liberated clear of telegraph wires and other obstacles.

What a day of excitement it is to the novice on his first race, and what a thrill when he sees his pigeon diving from the skies on to the loft, possibly a winner!

During the War some marvellous feats were accomplished by homing pigeons. A young R.A.F. service pigeon, only a few months old, was sent to one of the Air Force lofts at Gibraltar, and it escaped and returned to England, a distance of about 1100 miles over strange country which it had never previously seen. This bird was afterwards sold by auction for the remarkable figure of £360. Many an airman " ditched " in the sea or forced down on enemy territory owes his life to the homing pigeon he carried with him in his plane. " Royal Blue ", one of the King's pigeons, was the first bird to bring home news of a forced landing by an air crew in enemy-occupied country. Eleven members of a flying-boat crew were rescued from the sea many miles from land, when a pigeon they carried with them, called " White Vision ", arrived at the base with the following message: " Aircraft ditched safely. Heavy swell on." Many more instances could be quoted of the valuable rescue work performed by the aid of these brave little birds.

A final word: Don't take up the hobby of pigeon keeping unless you intend to give the birds proper attention. Nothing is more abhorrent to a real fancier when visiting a pigeon loft than to find water vessels empty, the loft dirty, and the birds starving. It is cruel to keep pigeons under such conditions, for, being imprisoned, they cannot get out to fend for themselves.

PLAYWRITING AND ACTING

Writing a play is not very difficult once you have understood its shape and the way to set about it. The actions and speeches seem very lifelike to the public who see the finished play on the stage, but a good deal of hard work has gone into the production, and the author must know something about acting and the theatre. You too must remember the stage when you are writing a play.

Let us begin by studying a script. The " script " is the name given by actors to the copy or book of the play from which they read their parts. In a new play this may be typewritten. On the first page is the title of the play and the author's name. On the second page we see the list of characters or cast. In most modern plays there is just the heading, *The Characters*, with the name of each character in a separate line underneath, followed by a short description of their relationship to other members of the cast, or of their trade or profession. The names are usually put down in the order in which they appear on the stage, the first being at the top, then the second to appear, then the third, &c. If there are three or four characters on the stage when the curtain rises, the first one to speak is given first place, then the second one, &c. This order should be carefully kept, as it is a good guide to the audience.

On the next page of the script you will see the list of the acts or scenes, the description of each act being given in a separate line. The place and the time is given and how much time has passed between Act 1 and Act 2, also between different scenes. You will now see the beginning of the first act, which is on a new page, usually page 3 or 4 of the script. Short plays and sketches follow the same method.

The scene begins with a description of the setting—that is, the scenery on the stage, which looks like a room, a garden, a castle, or whatever is the place of the action. These descriptions are called " stage directions " and are not spoken by any of the actors; they are useful to the actor or actress and to the stage workers who have to provide the correct scenery and lighting for the play.

After the description of the setting you will see the beginning

of the dialogue—the speaking. The lines the actors say are called
"speeches". The word "dialogue" really means two persons
speaking, but is now used for any kind of scene with two or more
persons speaking. It refers to the words actually spoken aloud on
the stage. You can now see that the play is in two parts, roughly
speaking: the dialogue and the stage directions.

I will deal first with stage directions. These are printed in
italics (*like this*), and usually in brackets to separate them from the
spoken lines. If you have a friend with a typewriter who can type
your play, it is usual to underline these directions in the script.
I showed you how the first stage directions gave the description
of the scene. This is very important, and great care must be taken
that it is correct in every detail. If you are describing a room, say
exactly where the doors, windows and fireplace are; you must
remember that the stage room has only three walls—the sides and
the back of the stage—and that the *left* and *right* are usually given
from the actor's position as he faces the audience. If you think of
him reading his script for the first time and "moving through" his
part in the early rehearsals, you can easily understand why it is
better to have the directions like this. If there is a window in your
room describe the view outside too, and say whether it is a street,
a country scene, or a garden. You must describe the furniture in
the room and say whether it is modern, old-fashioned, new or shabby;
and add details about the pictures, curtains, flowers, books or ornaments which will tell the audience something about the house or
family. And don't forget the lighting. Is it early morning of a
summer's day? Then the electrician can put a spot or floodlight
outside the window to suggest sunshine. Or perhaps it is evening;
then he will put an orange gelatine in the floodlight to look like
sunset. If it is night, he will use a blue to suggest the moonlight.
Is there a fire burning in the grate? Then the electrician will add
a light to look like a fire.

If it is an outdoor setting, give a short description. Remember,
however, that a scene on the stage is built up with a backcloth and
wings. So try to make your setting fit in with this method of building
stage scenery.

As well as things *seen* on the stage, everything that is *heard*
should be mentioned too—that is, all sounds which are not spoken
words or voices of the actors and actresses. Natural sounds like
rain, thunder, howling wind, storm and breakers can be imitated

and used with effect; animal noises too can give the right atmosphere to country scenes: horses galloping, cows, pigs, ducks, hens, barking dogs. You may use mechanical sounds; a clock striking is a very good way to tell the audience the time at the beginning of a scene; the sound of a motor horn can suggest a car waiting outside.

These are examples of stage directions which help the producer

Natural sounds can easily be imitated ...

and stage manager to give the correct picture. The other stage directions help the actor and are mixed up with his lines.

The first stage direction for the actor is the one which tells him when he is to make his entrance. It is usually printed in a separate line of the script with the name in capital letters like this:

(*Enter* JOHN *from the hall door*.)

The line which is spoken just before his entrance is called his "cue". The "cue" for anything being done on the stage is the line spoken just before; thus you may have a cue for a movement, for going out, coming in. Then follows a short description of the actor:

(*He is a tall, well-built boy of fifteen, dressed in grey flannels*

> *and a sports jacket. He carries a tennis racquet, and comes in eagerly, smiling at the others.*)

Here is another example:

> (MARY *comes in quickly from the garden. She is a pretty girl of twelve in a light summer dress. She carries a book in her hand and appears to be rather cross about something.*)

Notice in these descriptions:

1. That the exact place of the entrance is shown.
2. The person is described, dress, appearance, age. But not too many details are given. It is best not to say that someone is " dark " or " fair " nor to mention the exact colour of hair or eyes. These things may be difficult or impossible to match with the actors and actresses taking part. It is also unwise to make your story rely on these details, unless you have some person in mind to play a certain part.
3. The way the entrance is made. This helps the actor or actress to get the feel of the part and to prepare for the scene which follows.

As you go on writing the dialogue you must put in from time to time more directions to help the actor. You need not describe all the movements, only the chief ones such as sitting: (JOHN *sits in the chair by the fireplace*); or rising: (MARY *rises from the table, flinging down her book*); or any other actions which are important for the story. Here are a few examples:

> (MRS. JARVIS *crosses to the window and looks out.*)
> (JIM *takes out the wallet and opens it, showing the notes.*)

You had better say something too about the positions of the persons on the stage. The chief characters had better be kept somewhere near the centre, and take care that they do not all sit on one side of the scene. You can avoid this by keeping a plan of the scene beside you as you write. Another good rule is to have two persons who carry on a fairly long conversation not too far apart. If you have them one each side of the room, following their conversation will be like watching a tennis match.

When the time comes for the actor or actress to go out, say this clearly in the stage direction:

> DICK. I'll never agree to that. (*He goes to the door.*) Not if you offered me ten times the money. (*He goes out in a temper.*)

Notice here that he moves to the door, then has a short line to say. This gives the actor time to cross the stage. This is his " exit ", and his line the " exit line ", which can be a very strong or dramatic speech. The person can run, walk, stumble, stagger, crawl or creep. Use the description which best suits your story.

At the end of the scene or act, you must say that the curtain is brought down. You may write just

CURTAIN

or you may describe the way in which the curtain is brought down. If a group of characters on the stage make a pleasant picture, they can keep their positions and you say:

(*They stand looking out as the* CURTAIN *slowly falls.*)

A comic scene might end with a (QUICK CURTAIN).

As well as for movements you may use stage directions to help the actors with their lines. This is essential if otherwise the meaning of the line is not very clear. The direction is then given at the beginning of the speech; for example:

DAVID (*in surprise*). What? You told him?

And especially if your characters say " Oh " or "Ah "—you must put in a direction to say exactly what this means:

MARY (*giving a scream of fear*). Oh!

DORIS (*with delight*). Oh! How lovely!

FRANK (*suspiciously*). Ah!

WILLIAM (*with a gasp of pain*). Oh!

You may also give directions in the middle of the speeches:

JOHN (*gruffly*). Come here at once. (*He takes the book.*) What is this? This is not the one I wanted. (*Angrily.*) Take it back and bring me the right one. (*Flings the book on the table.*)

Now to say something about the dialogue in your play. First you must notice that the character's name is printed on the left, and is usually kept clear of the spoken lines and stage directions. In some plays the character's name is put in the centre of the page and the speech underneath.

In writing dialogue the main thing to remember is that it is heard *only once* by your audience. So keep the sentences fairly simple and avoid long, flowery descriptions; there is no need for too many details about thoughts and feelings; your actors can show these by their movements and expressions. Remember, too, that stage dialogue is not just a piece of conversation. It must have some kind of plan; it must be to the point and should carry on the story or plot of your play. It is best to keep the speeches fairly short, and especially if the characters are in a very exciting scene. They may not even use complete sentences:

MARY: Help! Help! Fire!

DORIS: We're trapped! Oh!

JEAN. The flames—look—the flames!

Another good rule is to try to make the characters speak in a slightly different way. The more educated people might use longer words, quote proverbs, pieces out of books or plays or phrases of French or Latin. Working-class people, farmers, labourers, might use simpler language with country sayings. Tradesmen or professional people might say a few words about their particular calling; while foreign characters might use a few words of their own language. You have no doubt noticed too that people in different parts of Great Britain have their own ways of speaking; there are some words and phrases only used by Yorkshire people; others are used in Wales, Scotland, Somerset, Lancashire, &c. If you have any particular knowledge of these then you can use them, but do not try to introduce a Yorkshireman or a Welshman if you have no experience of your own of these characters.

Now comes the question of writing your play. How is your story to be given in the form of a script? Well, first of all choose a story which can be fairly easily changed into a play. Look for these points:

1. Can the story all take place in one or two scenes? Or can you rearrange the scenes to suit this plan?
2. Can the story be told by five or six characters? (You may use sounds, scenery, and lighting too.)
3. Can the story be made into a scene or scenes which are dramatic and will lead to a climax? Dramatic interest means some kind of struggle or fight between the characters, and the climax is the final " tug-of-war " when they get together.

If you think the story can be treated in this way then go on with your play. First write a rough plan of the action and draw up a list of characters. Then choose the scene of your story. It is best to choose a scene where you can bring all your characters on with the least improbability. For example, if there are two or three people of the same family in the story, you may set the scene in their house and find some excuse for bringing on the others. Here are a few ways: a family party, a celebration, calling for a friend, to ask for help, to borrow something or to look for someone. If you are writing a short play it is best to keep it all in one scene, and remember that a page of writing takes less than a minute to act. So watch the " timing " of your play. For example, if Mary goes out to change her dress on page 2, do not bring her back all changed on page 3. Poor Mary will have had less than a minute to do it!

The first few pages of your play should contain the list of characters, description of the acts, and the setting, as shown above. Then you must tell the audience something about your characters, who they are, what is their relation to one another, their work and interests. This information must be given to the audience in the dialogue. A very useful trick is to have two people coming on at the beginning and talking about the others in such a way that the audience will be interested; one way of making them interested is to make them wonder what the persons will do; suggest some kind of argument or fight. For example, here is the first page of a short play dealing with MARY and JOHN, a boy and girl who decide to run away from school because they have quarrelled with the English mistress. The action takes place in Mary's home, early one summer afternoon. Mary's mother and the servant, Dorothy, are tidying the room when the curtain rises:

MOTHER. I wish Mary would not be so untidy. She couldn't find her books this morning.

DOROTHY. Here's one—under the cushion. (*Picks up a book.*)

MOTHER (*taking it*). Oh, dear. That's her English book. She wants it to-day. She'll be put in detention again by Miss Throstle—that's the English mistress.

DOROTHY. Nobody likes her. Master John says that she never gives him more than four out of ten.

MOTHER. John is almost as bad. (*Picks up exercise book.*) Oh, dear, here's his essay book. And he sat up till eleven last night getting it finished. He *will* get into trouble.

DOROTHY. They'll both be kept in. Pity, and them going on the yacht with their uncle.

MOTHER. Their Uncle Henry spoils them. He should not have made a promise like that. They're so excited about it they can't think of anything else.

DOROTHY. There's the front gate. I wonder who it is?

MOTHER (*looking out of window*). It's Mary.

DOROTHY (*looking out*). And there's MASTER JOHN running up the lane after her.

MOTHER. But it's only three o'clock. School's not over for another hour.

DOROTHY. Perhaps they've come home for their books.

MOTHER. They wouldn't both come. I don't like this at all. It looks to me as if they're up to something.
(MARY *runs in, carrying a satchel, which she flings down.*)
Mary! Why are you home so early?

MARY (*sulkily*). I'm never going back to that horrid school again! Never!

DOROTHY. You don't look well. I'll get you a nice glass of lemonade. (*Goes out to kitchen.*)

MOTHER. You're running away?

MARY. I hate school. I hate the teachers. I'm never going back there!

MOTHER. I'll write a note to the headmistress to say you are not well. Everything will be all right in the morning.

(JOHN *comes in sheepishly.*)

JOHN. I don't feel very well either. I've had the most dreadful headache all the afternoon.

MOTHER (*severely*). You're only pretending. You'll both go to bed at once. You've been too lazy to do your work and now you're too cowardly to face the consequences.

MARY. Oh, Mother—Uncle Henry said——

JOHN. We're going on his yacht this afternoon.

MOTHER. You're both going to bed. (*Goes out.*)

The play now goes on to show Mary and John making up their plot to run away. The story develops to a climax in the appearance of Uncle Henry and Miss Throstle, who is an old friend of Uncle Henry's. She forgives Mary and John, who promise to try harder in

Having written your first rough sketch, go through it again

future. You might try writing the end of this little play yourselves.

Now, having written your first rough sketch, go through it again and look out for the following snags:

1. Do the characters all talk in the same way? If they do, try to alter one or two by making the speeches shorter or longer, or by giving the less bright ones incomplete sentences.

2. Have you remembered to give *every* character something to say when he or she is on the scene? If not, then put in a line or two here and there, saying " Yes " or " No, no ", agreeing or disagreeing with the others. You know how tiresome it is to sit still and watch the others having all the fun.

3. Did you give a complete list of the furniture and all the things used in the play at the beginning? If not, put them in now. The books must be under the cushions or on the floor in the above sketch.

4. Have you forgotten somebody's entrance? Try to bring on a character at the best time, when his entrance is most dramatic, that is, when it is a surprise or will make the audience excited about what will happen next.

5. Have you forgotten somebody's exit? You may have left out the stage direction that says MARY goes out. Again, try to make her EXIT a good one by careful timing.

6. Have you given away too much of your story at the beginning? If so, the audience will guess the ending and the play will be flat. Leave your audience guessing a little, so that they will wonder what is going to happen next. For example, I do not mention the friendship of Uncle Henry and Miss Throstle, or the audience would guess that he might be able to smooth things out.

7. Does your play go on too long after the struggle or drama is over? In a short play it is best to bring down the curtain quite soon after the climax has been reached.

Now you have finished your little play you might like to get it produced. Perhaps you will take part yourself. When you act, the first thing to remember is that your audience is some distance away. Whether you are in a classroom or in a real theatre, the people listening are a few yards away. This means that you have to overdo everything just a little in order to " get across ". This saying is used by theatre people and by artists and means that your appearance, voice, actions and expressions must look right to the audience.

Think of a poster. As you look at it across the street its bright colours appear quite pretty and gay. You read its message quickly and understand it. It " gets across " to you. If you go up to the poster and examine it closely, you may think it bright and gaudy and rather simple. From a distance it looks just right.

That is the best way to describe scenes on the stage. A play is like a poster. Everything must be made a little larger than life. You must use a louder voice; speak more clearly, use more emphasis; just as the scene painter uses colours which are very much brighter and sharper in tone than they are in nature. Your producer will tell you which words or phrases need special attention in this way. Or you might pick them out for yourself with a little practice; words which are important to the plot or in describing someone or some part of your own character which has a bearing on the story. Emphasis can be placed on these words by saying them more slowly, by pausing just before and after, or by altering your tone.

Another rule about speaking is this: comic scenes are usually played fast and sad scenes slowly. The speed is kept up by saying the speeches quickly, one after the other, so you have to learn your " cues " very thoroughly!

What about moving on the stage? The main rule is that you must be definite about it. If you have nothing to do *keep still*. If you move or fidget during another person's speech you are making the audience look at you instead of at the speaker. And that, apart from being selfish, spoils the effect of the scene. In moving on the stage, remember the poster again; all actions must be big and broad to look good from a distance.

Remember that you are one of a team and acting is like a game. If you don't do exactly what is needed and no more, you are letting your side down; while, if you learn your words, do the correct movements at the correct time, you will be proud and happy to know that you, whether your part be large or small, have helped to put the play across and given pleasure to the audience.

REFERENCE BOOKS ON PLAYWRITING

Writing for the Stage. George Taylor. (Vawser & Wiles.)
Craft in Playwriting. A. J. Talbot. (Frederick Muller.)
Writing for the Theatre. Ronald Jeans. (Arnold.)

BOOKS ON PRODUCTION AND ACTING

Dramatic Work with Children. Mrs. E. M. Langdon. (Dennis Dobson, Ltd.)
Teach Yourself Amateur Acting. John Bourne. (English Universities Press.)
Magic and Make-believe. Robert Newton. (Dobson.)

SEASIDE DAYS

A holiday in the country has its attractions, but, in my opinion, the finest holidays of all are those spent at the seaside. There are so many things to do and enjoy, such a variety of ploys and occupations that the fine summer days just seem to fly past and even the very longest of seaside holidays goes by in a flash.

Dunellan—which isn't its real name—is an ideal spot for holidays, and having gone there for many, many summers I am going to use it as my own particular example in writing about the seaside. I may describe pastimes and occupations that are not familiar or some that you have not sampled, but I'm pretty certain that if you have not done or seen the things I talk about, you will be able to adapt them to suit yourselves or, at least, to enjoy them in your imagination.

Dunellan is not a big place, but it has a little harbour where the fishing-boats lie, as well as a big pier where the river steamers make one call on week-days and two on Saturdays. On either side of the harbour and the pier the shore is rock and shingle, but between the two lies a fine stretch of sandy beach. There are not many houses—most of them are small with whitewashed walls and bright green doors—but there are four hotels in the place, so there are generally quite a lot of holiday-makers. Then the Dunellan people themselves are very hospitable and always seem to be having their friends down to stay with them.

I generally stay in The Benbecula—the hotel just above the big pier—and although it is very comfortable the thing about it that I like best is Poll Parrot, who swings in a cage outside the bedroom window above the front door. He's a cheeky parrot if ever there was one. He clicks his tongue whenever he sees a boy or girl going past sucking a stick of Dunellan rock, and then he cries, "Polly likes a lick!" at the pitch of his voice. Best of all, whenever the captain of the river steamer blows the boat's whistle Poll, in exactly the same voice as the guard on an American train, cries, "All aba-oo-ard!" and you see the late-comers go dashing down the pier as if they had been stung by a wasp.

The days in Dunellan are far too short. You can go down the

little harbour to watch the fishermen mending their nets and, before you know it, three or four hours have gone. It is fascinating to watch just how nimble the big heavy hands of a fisherman can be. His fingers seem to play over the nets like those of a musician on the strings of a harp. He knots broken meshes together again or he weaves new netting line into the huge rents and works the new line so that the whole fishing net is so skilfully mended that it would be difficult to find out where the tear had occurred.

Besides the fascination of watching their busy fingers you soon get to know the fishermen, and they will yarn away to you and tell you all about their job. Sitting on an empty herring-box during the fine days of summer a fisherman can soon make you feel wet and chilly, and maybe even a bit seasick, as he talks about his fishing exploits during the wild days of winter. He can make you feel the cold blast of an east wind driving the rain into your face until it feels as though it was being massaged by a carrot grater and, despite your oilskins and long rubber thigh boots, the rain and the sea-water have seeped in and soaked right through to your very skin. You can see the white horses riding the waves until they mount at the gallop and go charging over the deck of the fishing-boat, making things so uncomfortable that you don't care if there's another fish in the whole wide sea—all you want is to be snug and safe in harbour again.

Of course, he will tell you of going fishing in the fine nights of summer with the sea like a mill pond and the warm night air as smooth and soft on your face as a piece of new velvet. He will paint you a word picture of the fishing-boats strung round in a wide circle, their lights casting a soft radiance over the calm water, and glinting back from the green glass floats of the nets. Gradually the circle will narrow, the fishermen will start pulling and hauling on the nets and the harvest of the sea—a full hold of silver fish all glowing with phosphorescence—will send the fishing-boats speeding for harbour and a market for their fine cargo.

It is the tales of fishing during the wild weather that make the most exciting ones to listen to, but if you take my advice, you will make sure that the weather is " Set Fair " before you ask any of the fishermen to take you out with them. During the stormy weather the fishermen are far too busy looking after the safety of themselves and of their boat to take very much interest in a guest. In fine weather, however, they will take a delight in showing you around

their boat, give you a practical demonstration showing just how all
their gear works and permit you to give them a hand as they haul in
their nets. After the nets have been pulled in, the decks hosed, and
the hatches closed they will perhaps have time to get themselves a
meal, and, down in the little cubby-hole of a forecastle, you will
drink strong sweet tea out of big coarse mugs and sink your teeth
into thick bacon sandwiches.

The fine summer nights are the times to enjoy going out in the
big fishing-boats, and then, when you know your way about and
the fishermen think you can look after yourself, you can pick out a
night that looks like being a bit rough and see if they will have you
with them. It will be an adventure and, whether you like it or not,
it will give you some idea of the hazards of fishing in winter-time,
and show you the skill and bravery that must so often be shown
before we can stick our forks into the fish that sizzle in our frying-
pans of a morning.

Talking about going out with the fishermen suggests fishing from
a small boat, and, to do that, you need to get hold of some bait. In
Dunellan there are two methods of gathering bait—you can go digging for sandworms when the tide goes out, or you can go down
under the big pier, clamber among the rafters and collect the mussels
off the huge wooden piles that are the supports of the pier. Gathering
mussels means that you have the extra labour of shelling them, but,
as far as I am concerned, the extra work is rewarded by the oddity
of the new surroundings in which you find yourself.

To go under the big pier at Dunellan on a fine summer day is
to enter an entirely new world. The glare, the warmth of the sun,
and the normal everyday things are completely forgotten. As you
chip the biggest and fattest mussels off the piles of the pier and
into your container, it seems as though you were working in a magic
cavern. A modern magic cavern made by the hands of man, but
still with that unfamiliar, dream-like quality that is similar to the
one you share when you look at some beautifully contrived thing
such as the Aladdin's cave that is created on the stage for a Christmas
pantomime.

Under the big pier everything is cool and green and dim. Outside, between the piles, you can see the sun shining on the beach
and watch the flash and movement of the brightly coloured clothes
of other people disporting themselves. Under the big pier it is
very quiet indeed. In the distance you can here the faint cries of

your friends on the beach, but where you are there is only the little sound of the water lapping against the piles and the chip-chip as you pry some more mussels loose. Looking down the water is clear and emerald green, broken only by the black supports of the pier and you find yourself under a spell, a spell that is suddenly broken by the sound of a paddle steamer. Over your head there is the sound of footsteps as other holiday-makers come down the pier to meet their friends and, under your feet, there is a churning of the waters as the paddle steamer comes alongside, and when you look down the

Fig. 1.—A Long Line

smooth green water is veined and rippled with white like a mantelpiece of green marble, so you gather up your bait tin—which was nearly full, anyway—and clamber up the steps to the pier to see if anyone you know has arrived on the steamer.

Perhaps you will use the shelled mussels to go fishing in the evening along with your father and might like to make some experiments in setting lines. If you have a fair amount of fishing tackle at your command and the patience to bait lots of hooks you could try a Long Line or a Float Trot.

This is the Long Line—showing too the fish you will catch— and as you will see from the illustration (fig. 1) it consists of a length of line with two weights attached and a number of short lines with hooks bent to the main line with clove hitches. The Long Line is dropped over the stern of the dinghy at weight A and paid out until weights A and B are lying on the bottom. From weight B a line is led to a float of some kind—say, an old petrol tin—and you can go off and do a bit of hand-line fishing while leaving your Long Line to look after itself.

The Float Trot is rather a crafty bit of work to look at (fig. 2), but it is really only the Long Line carrying a cork float every fathom or so with a weight below each float. As you see, the line can be set at any depth but, usually, the Float Trot is set fairly near the surface of the water.

Using either of these methods you will catch a variety of fish

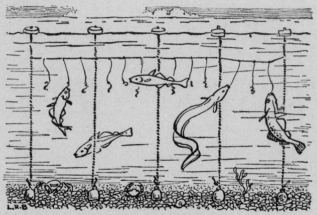

Fig. 2.—A Float Trot

at the same time, and I have seen mackerel, cod, haddock, flounders, saithe, and even a conger eel being hauled up on a twenty-fathom Long Line. Certainly you may be sure of one thing, and that is that you will seldom come home empty-handed as you might do with an ordinary hand line.

During the day, as you know, the fish don't bite anything like as well they do at night, and for quite a lot of our holidays we are all quite happy to go " messing about in boats ", as Water Rat says in *The Wind in the Willows*. Sailing dinghies, rowing dinghies, rubber dinghies—Dunellan has them all, and the stretch of water between the harbour and the big pier makes an ideal sailing ground. If you are lucky enough to have a sailing dinghy you can dodge about endlessly, making use of every puff of wind—tacking, gybing, luffing, and gradually perfecting yourself in the art of handling a sailing boat until you are ready to enter the sailing dinghy races run by the Dunellan Sailing Club, and you go home from your holiday bearing a silver cup won at the regatta.

A sailing dinghy is, of course, beyond the means of most of us at Dunellan, and we count ourselves lucky to get a spot of rowing on most days. The bay makes a fine place for pitting one rowing dinghy against another, but perhaps the most exciting ploy of all is to play follow-my-leader in a rowing dinghy. Under the pier, between the piles and keeping your head down to save it getting banged on the cross supports makes a good start for the game; then a quick pull across the bay, going twice round the buoy and into the little harbour where we dodge and follow among the fishing-boats, sailing dinghies, motor boats, and all kinds of craft that are snug at their moorings or moving about.

Perhaps the best fun of all can be had with a rubber dinghy or a raft. Every summer some of us make a big raft out of the driftwood planks that come ashore among the rocks on either side of the harbour and the pier. The planks are bound together with rope, string, bits of wire hawser, and anything else we can lay our hands on. At the four corners of the raft we lash on four oil drums—also picked up on the shore—and we use a length of mast or an old clothes-pole for punting the thing around in the water.

Naturally, the rubber dinghies and the rafts don't go far out into the bay, and, just as naturally, they are not intended for deep-sea mariners with all their clothes on. Bathing-suits or trunks are the only permissible wear for the sailing fraternity aboard rubber dinghies and rafts, and that, of course, is where all the fun lies. You don't have to worry about falling into the water if you're already wearing a bathing-suit, and a raft makes a first-class " base " to practise diving and new swimming strokes, as it is never far away when you get into the least bit of trouble, and can easily be punted towards you. The raft, too, makes the very best type of craft for voyages of ex-ploration or pirating excursions as, when your victims have to walk the plank, they're in good shallow water and already dressed for the occasion.

No matter how carefully you handle a rubber dinghy the water always gets over the side and into the cockpit. That's why trunks or a bathing-suit are a necessity for these craft, but they are good fun and, with their long paddles, it is amazing how swiftly they can be paddled around. With someone over the stern acting as a human propeller and kicking his feet we hold novelty races with the rubber dinghies, and they are so buoyant that they give you confidence in the water and improve your swimming. You can always scramble over the side and into the cockpit when feeling the least bit out of breath, and, on a really warm day, it's a wonderful sensation to go paddling around in a rubber dinghy with the sun beating down, doing its best to roast you while the water in the cockpit is up to your waist and keeping you delightfully cool.

The little harbour at Dunellan has an endless variety of attractions. Besides watching the fishermen mending their nets or painting their boats, it's the simplest thing in the world to spend a whole afternoon, just lying on your stomach, fishing for crabs from the end of the stone jetty. Armed with a herring head, or some other fishy tit-bit, tied to the end of a string, you devote the first half-hour or so to the earnest pursuit of coaxing the wily crab up from the depth and into the can by your side. After the first half-hour your eyes become accustomed to looking down into the deep water and, with the sun warm on your back, you realize that you have a front seat at a very interesting show.

It's difficult to believe, for instance, that those muddled dollops that you saw lying on the beach this morning are related to the beautiful animals floating around beneath your eyes, for the common jelly-fish really is a beautiful animal, with his gorgeous array of golden tentacles and a bluey-brown body that gleams in the sun. The tentacles, of course, consist of nothing but stinging cells, and one of the most unpleasant things in the world is to go swimming into their poisonous touch. However, as you look down into the water you will find that those same tentacles have their uses, for—hanging down from the body of the jelly-fish—they form a fearsome barrier, and inside this barrier very young fish, as well as tiny crabs, seek refuge from their many enemies.

Still looking down, you may see a codfish swim along and swallow the little crab that was just reaching for the bait on the end of your length of string. This may come as a bit of a surprise to you, for you might consider that the hard limy shell and the vicious nipper of the crab would make a very poor meal for any fish. Not a bit of it. The codfish will swallow half a dozen crabs as easily as you would deal with a bar of chocolate. The shell is dissolved in the fish's stomach by acid juices and there is very little substance wasted.

As you dangle your tasty bite for Mr. Crab you are not by any means the only enemy that he has, for even the sea anemone is fond of a little bit of crab meat for its supper. To look at the anemone you would never think of speaking a harsh word about it, for with its daintily tinted tentacles spread out like the petals of a dahlia or a chrysanthemum, it looks just as harmless as either of those flowers. Actually the anemones, without exception, are flesh eaters, and the next time you come across one on the beach try placing your finger within the innocent-looking array of tentacles. As soon as you touch the anemone the tentacles will curve around your finger and, with amazing strength, they will pull your finger towards its mouth. Don't leave it there for any length of time. Were it not for the tough outer skin that covers the human hand I shouldn't advise you even to touch an anemone, for it stuns its prey by means of thousands of poison darts that it throws out from special cells. These darts of poison are not powerful enough to affect humans, but they do not take long to render a fish or a crab completely helpless.

The poor old crab has lots of enemies—even his fellow crabs— and you will often see two of them fighting over a limpet which one of the crabs has turned over on its back to keep it from renewing its grip on the rocks. Perhaps the most dangerous time in every crab's life comes once a year when he is moulting or changing his shell. This is a marvellous operation, for the whole shell, right to the tips of the legs, is cast off practically in one piece. To do this the crab retires into a rocky crevice well out of the way, for, of course, at this time the smallest animal in the sea, without a tooth in its mouth, could take a sample of the naked crab's body. When the old shell is completely discarded the crab begins to grow very quickly, and as soon as sufficient growth has taken place his skin begins to harden and gradually the new hard shell is formed, similar in every respect to the old one, but just a trifle larger. Not exactly identical perhaps, for if, before his moult began, the crab had lost a leg or even a big claw his new shell will have a full and complete set of limbs and claws. Of course, there are many sea-shore animals that have the power of replacing limbs that they have lost either in battle or by accident. The starfish, for instance, may lose every one of its five arms and be none the worse for its adventure, for new ones grow very quickly.

A cousin of the starfish—the brittle-star—will deliberately cast

18 (G 487)

off one of its limbs when attacked. The part of the animal thus detached wriggles and kicks in such a fashion that it attracts the enemy's attention while the brittle-star makes off as fast as it can; this type of ruse is reminiscent of the curlew, which, to lead would-be pilferers from its nest, pretends that it has broken a wing and runs along the ground as though flight was impossible.

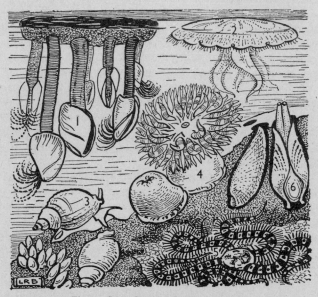

Fig. 3.—Some Common Seashore Animals

1. Goose Barnacle.
2. Jellyfish.
3. Dog-whelk and eggs.
4. Anemone (open and shut).
5. Brittle Star.
6. Rock-tunnelling Shellfish.

Before you know it the whole afternoon has gone and you are late for tea again. The sun goes down behind the hills in a lazy, leisurely kind of fashion, and the blue waters grow purple, then deep claret, and, finally, a deep dark indigo blue, and the soft blanket of the summer night spreads over Dunellan. Soon there is not a sound to be heard in the whole place, and even The Benbecula's Poll Parrot is snuggled down with a black cloth over his cage.

It is no hardship to get up early in the mornings at Dunellan. The morning air has a fine fresh tangy smell about it—just as though it has been washed in sea-water during the night. The sun sparkles and shines on the water, making sunbeams like newly minted pennies and the hills in the distance have the glowing green of summer. With the tide far out, the early morning is a grand time to go gathering driftwood or to go beachcombing along the sands and over the rocks. The receding tide leaves the sand firm and smooth for walking, and, as you walk, if you keep your eyes open you will see the morning's happenings illustrated on the sand.

Here are the footprints of the gull who got the early worm. Actually it was a sand eel stranded by the tide and, if you look closely, you will see the footprints of a second gull who arrived just a little too late for the titbit, but started an argument, for there are the footprints of the two birds weaving and bobbing around just like a pair of light-weight boxers sparring for the opening that will lead to a well-timed punch.

Scattered among the shells on the shore you may see an occasional limpet shell with a hole drilled neatly through the top and, naturally, no limpet. I wondered about this for a long time myself, and it was only recently that I discovered that these empty limpet shells were the work of the dog-whelk, a sort of second cousin to the ordinary periwinkle. The dog-whelk has a powerful file-like tongue, against which the shells of limpets, mussels, and even oysters are no protection, for the dog-whelk rasps away with its tongue till it makes an opening; then, hey presto! the soft interior is quickly eaten away and the dog-whelk moves in search of its next victim.

Perhaps, as you scramble over the rocks and inspect the pools left by the tide you may be lucky enough to come across a fairly deep crevice in the rocks that makes a water-filled stable for a pair of sea-horses. As you look at them you are not the least bit surprised at their name, for the sea-horse really has a wonderful resemblance to his four-footed and far-off relation. The sea-horse resembles another land animal, namely, the kangaroo. This resemblance comes about because the male sea-horse carries and hatches out the eggs of future sea-horses in a tiny pouch in front of its body, just as Mrs. Kangaroo carries around her family.

You may come across rocks lying around that look very similar to a sponge that has been turned to stone. The little holes and tunnels in these rocks are made by shell-fish which may be found if the rock is broken by a heavy hammer. To look at, these shell-fish resemble the cockle, and if you place one in clean water you will discover that it possesses a long double tube or siphon, by means of which a current of water is perpetually drawn past the animal's gills and provides it with air and food.

Another sea animal which looks like the cockle is the barnacle, although it actually belongs to the crab family. In its early days the barnacle is a roaming, fancy-free animal that goes floating around aimlessly like a cockle shell hanging on to the end of a leathery length of sea-weed. In time, however, it grows weary of roaming and fixes itself to the bottom of a ship, becoming a quiet, stay-at-home kind of chap. He does not bore his way into the ship's side or anything like that, but, gradually, he and his cousins accumulate to such an extent that they slow up the speed of a ship, and after a long voyage the vessel has to go into dry dock to have the bottom of her hull scraped. Scraping the barnacles off the hull of a ship isn't the most pleasant job in the world—particularly in the summer-time. There are literally tons of barnacles on a ship's bottom when she comes into dry dock, and as they are scraped off and fall into the dock the summer sun beats down on them, and they commence to become more than somewhat smelly, and the men working on the job talk about getting hold of gas masks so that they can take a deep breath for a change.

After climbing the rocks and investigating the pools it is pleasant to come up from the shore and go up the sandy road to Beach Farm for the morning milk. On the way to the farm we keep our eyes open while passing the pastures, as there are clumps of mushrooms to be found, and they make a very tasty addition to the breakfast bacon.

When there are no mushrooms to be found, and we know that the bacon ration is running low, we collect the milk and cut round the top of Dunellan to arrive at the top of the stone jetty, where the fishing-boats will have congregated again after their night's work. Here we buy fish for breakfast. Big, fat herring perhaps, reaching up to your elbow, stiff and fresh from the sea, to make a feast for the Gods.

One of the beauties of seaside holidays, of places like Dunellan, is that there is always something else to do, and, at times, the same thing to start all over again. There is the constant coming and going of the boats, the daily arrival of the river steamer with old friends to greet, or with new people who will arrive and be added to your circle of acquaintances. The movements of the little boats are a diversion in themselves. Sometimes a fussy little lighter will edge its way up to the harbour, and there will be a little bit of a stir as the cargo of coal is unloaded and wheeled up to the coal depots. There is excitement in watching the sailing-dinghy races or in watching the big six- and eight-metre yachts try out their paces against each other.

There are the picnic excursions to places like Lighthouse Point, where the lighthouse keeper will show you over his trim outbuildings and up the twisting stairs of the tall, white-painted, light tower, where he will explain the intricacies of the whirling prismatic lenses that cast their warning gleams far over the wide waters.

On every seaside holiday it's just as though one expedition goes dovetailing into another. Watching the fishermen mend their nets often means an invitation to a night's fishing. An early-morning stroll brings an investigation of the rock pools, and the discoveries made there send you to your Natural History books in search of more knowledge. A picnic may be the key that opens the door of a lighthouse, and picking up stray bits of shell can lead to a new hobby of collecting shells and using them to decorate all manner of things for presents.

That is why a seaside holidays flies past so very quickly and why it leaves you with so many pleasant memories. On a winter's night, as you go over your collection of sea-shells, or perhaps when you are helping to clean out a cupboard and you come across an old pair of sand-shoes from which a little trickle of sand forms a miniature castle on the carpet, you suddenly smell the " ozone " or find yourself looking down into the green water at the end of the stone jetty, with the sun on your neck and a crab at the end of your line. That's when you wish it was summer-time once more and you were making for the boat or train that will whisk you off to the finest holidays of all—Days at the Seaside.

INGENUITY ON DISAPPOINTMENT

On the 17th February 1908 the fine four-masted barque *Dundonald*, 2115 net register tons, owned by Messrs. Kerr, Newton & Calder of Glasgow, left Sydney, N.S.W., for Falmouth for orders with a full cargo of wheat. Four months passed during which nothing was heard of her; relatives and friends of the crew scanned the pages of *The Shipping Gazette* daily in the hope that she had been spoken; hopes and fears alternated. Soon after the fears were confirmed, for she was posted " Overdue at Lloyd's ". Still relatives hoped; for overdue ships have often turned up, while reinsurers gambled and underwriters hedged, trying to minimize the amount of their impending losses. The weeks passed; the premiums for reinsurance mounted; hopes were fading during that period when her fate seemed to tremble in the balance. On the 2nd October there came finality, for the *Dundonald* was posted missing. Fears were confirmed, and the underwriters had to calculate their losses.

Her loss was not regarded as a mystery; far too many sailing ships went missing for that, and there were so many ways in which they could be lost. Seamen who knew her naturally speculated; but, except by those who mourned, she was soon forgotten. On the 30th November, however, one of the mourners—a clerk in a London office—received this message by cable:

Bluff, New Zealand.

" Rescued—Charlie."

Mr. Eyre, the clerk, had a brother, Charles, who was an able seaman in the *Dundonald*, and when the terms of the brief cablegram were made known the keenest interest was aroused in shipping circles, and particularly at Lloyd's. One effect was that the vessel could not now be officially regarded as missing. Lost she probably was, since Charles Eyre had to be rescued, but not missing, since it must be presumed that Charles Eyre knew where she was. The following day Lloyd's agent at Bluff confirmed, by cable, that part of the crew had been saved.

Here, constructed from statements made by various members of the crew, is the story which explains the nine and a half months' silence of the survivors from the *Dundonald*.

I

During late summer the winds in the Tasman Sea are usually northerly, so when Captain Thorburn left Sydney he had every reason to expect a quick run down to Campbell Island, south of New Zealand, from whence he would take his departure for the six-thousand-mile dash across the South Pacific towards Cape Horn. From the first, however, everything went against him. He had little but calms and head-winds, and when she was a week out the *Dundonald* had only made three hundred miles—very poor sailing for a fast ship that had just made a record passage of forty-five days from Callao to Sydney. A week later she was only abreast of Cook Strait, with the whole length of the South Island still to be covered and a sea like glass. A light breeze sprang up; she got moving again, and about nine o'clock the mast-head and side-lights of a steamer making for Cook Strait were sighted. The steamer passed under the stern, and that was the last time the *Dundonald* was seen by anyone but her own crew.

Tuesday, the 5th March, opened with a northerly wind and torrential rain. No observations of celestial bodies were possible, but the noon position by dead reckoning was latitude 45° 40' south, longitude 168° east. That put her roughly one hundred and fifty miles due south of Stewart Island, which lies close to the southern tip of the South Island of New Zealand. The weather remained thick, but, the wind being fair at last, the great four-master, with every stitch of canvas set, was driving to the southward. At noon on Wednesday, again by dead reckoning, the latitude was 50° 25' south, and course was altered to the eastward to clear Campbell Island, the last remaining outpost, which was still a day's sail ahead. With gathering darkness the wind increased, and sail had to be shortened.

High seas were running, breaking over the weather rail and sweeping the main-deck. Overhead the clouds seemed to be racing just above the mast-heads; rain was lashing the dark and sodden canvas and running off the straining spars; every rope was dripping.

The ship was running blindfolded—but what did that matter? There was nothing to get in her way in those lonely waters. Eight bells were struck for midnight, and the look-out on the forecastle-head chanted " All's well ". The captain, on the weather side of the poop, was happily content and was thinking of going to his bunk.

" She's well clear of the Auckland Islands now, and we've really started to run the easting down at last," he remarked. " If we'd had this wind all the way we would have been half-way to the Horn by now."

He went below, leaving the mate—fifty-seven-year-old Mr. Peters—in charge of the deck. At half-past twelve one bell was struck, and the look-out again made the report " All's well " from forward. A few minutes later the weather cleared a little, though there was still a heavy drizzle. Well pleased with the change, the mate settled down more comfortably into the deep collar of his long black oilskin coat.

" Land on the lee bow!"

The mate saw the land almost at the moment that he heard the excited shout. Staring through his night-glasses he saw a grim pile of rocks standing out of a great cloud of spray.

" Lee forebrace! all hands on deck!" he roared.

He ran below and called the captain. On his return to the poop he ordered the helmsman to luff a point, thus bringing the land broader on the bow. The captain reached the poop, rubbed his eyes, and looked to leeward.

" It's land right enough, Mr. Peters," he said quietly, " but she'll clear it as she stands."

" Breakers on the weather bow!" came in another hoarse but stunning shout from forward.

A minute later the rocks to windward had joined those to lee-ward. The *Dundonald* was heading straight for a solid wall, a cul-de-sac, and those on board her could hear the thundering of surf and the crying of hundreds of seabirds. The sky was obscured by something very close, something black and white—black, beetling cliffs that towered two hundred feet; white, churning surf.

" There's no room to tack; we'll try to wear her short round," the captain cried. " Back the foreyards."

Crash! The *Dundonald* struck forward, rebounded, and struck again. With her fore-foot pounding heavily, but partially held, her stern swung away from the wind. It swung slowly at first, then so swiftly as to make men giddy. As it swung a great wave rushed at her broadside, adding its weight to the bewildering uproar that raged around her. Its crest toppled over her, surged far up the cliff, then receded into the boiling cauldron that tormented her. Sea-birds whirled madly through the spray between the masts as if resenting invasion, but now their cries were drowned by the thunderous roaring of the surf and the furious slatting of sails. With another crash her stern stopped swinging, and came to an uneasy rest under cliffs that rose high above her jigger truck.

II

It was the suddenness of it all that appalled. Less than ten minutes before the *Dundonald* had been a free thing, exulting in her strength and speed, eager to get on with her wild dash across the Pacific; now she was a prisoner—held for ever, for no human agency could restore her liberty. Orders rose to the captain's lips—orders to let go the topsail halliards and clear away the boats—but they were never issued; indeed if they had been they could neither have been heard in the uproar nor carried out. To launch the boats would have been quite impossible, because on the port side the ship was hard up against the cliffs, and on the starboard side there was a reef over which the great vessel had been flung. At times she was afloat; for she would heave upward nearly ten feet, scraping hard on the cliffs as she rose, then drop back on the reef with a soul-disturbing, body-dislodging thud.

All hands felt as if they were being shaken to death. Rain lashed them, and whirling spray lashed them. When they licked their lips the moisture was sometimes fresh, sometimes salt. A small group, which included the three mates, had reached the poop, and it seemed to them, as they glanced fearfully aloft, that the overhanging cliff must fall on them. For a moment they were almost panic-stricken by the threat, though in reality it was the cross-jack yards banging heavily on the rocks that constituted the real danger. The helmsman, a Swede, had stuck to the wheel, though several times the backwash had almost licked him away. He managed to attract the attention of the captain, who was hanging on to the starboard vang.

18*   (G 487)

" Can I leave the wheel, sir?" he asked.

" Yes—er—yes, certainly," the captain answered.

He spoke as if he had just come out of a reverie. A careful and competent navigator, he felt like a sculptor who with his *magnum opus* almost completed had suddenly and irretrievably spoiled it and was standing before it, appalled by the ruin, yet wholly unable to account for it.

" Mr. Peters!" he shouted into the darkness.

" Yes, sir."

" Serve out the lifebelts, then get all hands for'a'd. Maybe we'll find a way to get ashore when daylight comes in," the captain said.

Accompanied by his son, a lad of sixteen, he got as far as the break of the poop, then paused to look round. The main-deck was like a half-tide rock: fully awash when the ship lay on the reef, partially visible when she surged upward, and on it were storm-battered men splashing their way forward.

" I shall make for the top of the for'a'd house, Mr. Peters," the captain said.

" Very good, sir; I'll join you when I've rounded all hands up," the mate answered.

As he splashed about looking for stragglers he bumped into an enormous man who combined the duties of steward and cook. He was a Cornishman named Smith, who stood six feet two inches, weighed twenty-three stone, and was reputed to be the heaviest man at sea.

" Come on, steward, it's safer for'a'd," the mate cried.

" What's the use, sir?" the steward replied.

" We'll hang on there till daylight, then we'll probably get ashore from one of the upper yards."

" No good to me, sir," the steward said with resignation. " I'd never get as high as the top; I would break every ratline I put my foot on. I'm going to my room."

He vanished into the gloom, and the mate joined the captain and others on top of the forward house. They could hardly keep on their feet because of the terrific pounding. Some of them hung on to the gunwales of the boats, which rested on skids on both sides of the house. Two of them were clinging to the galley stove-pipe. On the forecastle-head others were hanging on to the capstan and rails. They were tortured by the cold and the rain, especially the men of the watch below, who had leapt out of their warm bunks at the dread call of " All hands on deck " and had no time to dress; but it was the pounding on the rocks that worried them most. Would they ever see daylight? Could anything fabricated by man stand for long that terrific battering? They could only hang on, numbed and miserable, and wait.

The captain was gloomy and intensely agitated by turns—not from fear: he was a stranger to that, but from something akin to remorse and a craving for self-torture.

" How did she get here? How did I put her here?" he kept on repeating.

He was one of those who were scantily clad, but he seemed to be impervious to the cold. He did not move about, or stamp his feet to bring warmth into them, as the others did. With his arm round his son he stood staring straight ahead. Round about two o'clock he called the mate.

" Mr. Peters," he said, " she must be on one of the Auckland Group. It can't be Campbell Island; that's over two hundred miles to the south-east. God knows how she got here, for I was certain she was well clear. There must have been some magnetic disturbance or a hostile current."

" Something like that, sir; probably both. Something you had no control over, anyway," the kindly mate said.

" Something I had no control over," the captain repeated wistfully. " You really think that, Mr. Peters?"

" I do, sir; I was certain myself that you had given the islands a wide berth."

" I wish to God I had made it wider," the captain burst out passionately. " There's twelve hundred miles of clear water between here and the Ice Barrier."

" I expect we shall get ashore at daylight, sir," the mate said by way of changing the subject.

" If she doesn't break up before then. I was reading about the Auckland Group in the *New Zealand Pilot* the night before last. In case we don't all get ashore, tell the others that there is a Government depot with provisions and clothing."

Ten minutes later the heavy pounding ceased and was succeeded by a strange and terrifying motion. It was as if the ship was writhing, shuddering, and straining, trying to free herself. The captain grabbed the mate by the arm.

" She's sliding off the reef!" he yelled. " All hands to the rigging."

A moment later the *Dundonald* plunged bows first. The hands on the forecastle-head dived for the forestay; those on top of the house made for the rigging. They were too late; the ship had gone from under them. When the mate got his head above water he found himself close to the fore-top—a small platform to which the topmast rigging was set up. The forward end of the ship had dived sixty feet in a few seconds. He swam to the top and found himself being hauled on to it. When he had stopped gasping and choking and cleared the water from his eyes, he discovered the other two mates and six seamen in the top. Cries from drowning men came to them, but in the darkness they could do nothing.

The ship settled till the top was awash, so the nine men climbed higher. As the masts were listing over towards the cliffs they took to the starboard topmast rigging, where they stood on the ratlines and clung to the shrouds. They heard voices above them, and two men came down from the lower topgallant yard. The cries of the drowning men died away, and those in the rigging concluded that they were the only survivors of the twenty-eight all told who had officered and manned the *Dundonald*. Mr. Peters prayed to God to have mercy on them, for the strain on the rigging was tremendous; and he feared that at any moment the masts and yards might come down. About four o'clock several of them thought they heard voices ashore, and hailed loudly. The second mate believed he heard shouting in reply, but could not be sure.

The topmast rigging consisted of three thin wire shrouds, with ratlines stretched between them, and to those the men clung in tiers of two, which extended almost up to the cross-trees, while the sea snarled under the feet of the mate and second mate, who were lowest. Cramped and perished, afraid the ship would disintegrate under them, they hung on grimly and prayed for daylight. It came in slowly that wild autumn morning, but blackness gradually turned to greyness, and the man who was highest up the rigging, near the cross-trees, could distinguish the features of those beneath him and learn for the first time with certainty who they were; could see also that their lips were blue with cold, their eyes red-rimmed with fatigue, their faces encrusted with salt and coated with congealed blood. As for the ship: the four masts rose straight out of the frothing sea, the only part of the hull that was visible being the upper half of the wheel and the top of the wheel-box behind it. From right aft there the vessel sloped downward, so that her fore-foot must have been resting nearly a hundred feet deep. Clearly there could be nobody alive in her. Between her and the sheer base of the cliff was nothing but snarling foam and kelp.

Quickly the survivors realized that they were unlucky. They were up the wrong mast; for through the driving rain they could see that the jigger topmast and the mizzen topsail yards were rubbing against the cliffs, which aft there rose to a height of two hundred feet. Abreast of where they were the cliff was lower, so that the topgallant yards were above its level, but some twenty feet off it. They heard voices; then, bending low against the blast, men came along the cliffs. The mate hailed them.

" How many of you got off?" he asked.

" Six, sir; but one fell down the cliff and got killed. We three got ashore off the mizzen lower topsail yard-arm; the other three got off the jigger cross-trees, but one of 'em, Low, was the one that got killed."

" What about the captain and his son?" the mate asked.

" We ain't seen 'em, sir; they must have gone. The steward's gone, too; he wouldn't try to save himself."

" I thought he wouldn't," the mate said.

It was now evident that twelve out of the twenty-eight souls had perished; for the cliffs were in full view, and the two men crouching on the ledge farther aft were the only human beings visible.

" If you throw us a rope's end, sir, we'll make it fast round this bit of rock and you can come ashore down it, hand over hand," one of the men on the cliff shouted.

" That's right," the mate answered. " Mr. MacLaughlin, get a rope's end ashore and get all hands up on the upper t'gallant yard to haul it bar taut. Then throw another rope ashore so that we can haul those two fellows up the cliff."

" Ay, ay, sir," the second mate replied cheerfully.

With the wind blowing onshore there was no trouble getting the ends of the ropes across; indeed they flew over the heads of the waiting men, who gathered up one of them and made the end fast. All hands were now on the upper topgallant yard, where they hauled the rope tight and secured it. It seemed as if they were just in time, for the mast was swaying.

"All fast, sir," the second mate reported. "Will you lead the way?"

"Me!" the mate snorted indignantly. "I'm in command of this vessel now, and I shall be the last to leave her."

"Very good, sir," the second mate said. "Ellis, you get over."

Ellis, a young ordinary seaman, got off the yard on to the rope, and was safely ashore in a few seconds. The men on the cliff were waiting to help him, and the rest followed, leaving Mr. Peters to the last. Anxiously they watched him getting down gingerly on to the foot-rope and preparing to swing himself off.

"That's why I wanted him to go first, so that we could help him on to the rope," the second mate declared uneasily. "I don't suppose he's been aloft for years."

Mr. Peters sat on the foot-rope of the yard for about a minute, then swung himself clear and hung with his feet dangling over the sea. It was no slight ordeal for a man of his years to work his way twenty feet across a single rope, with certain death awaiting him if he let go, but he was a lightweight and he quickly joined the others.

"Get those fellows up off that ledge," he ordered.

They went along the cliff and lowered the second rope down to the two marooned men. They hauled them up, one after the other, very carefully; for they feared that the rope would be chafed through by the rocks, but eventually they got them safely to the top of the cliffs, making sixteen survivors in all. It was a sad muster: in one night they had lost their captain, his son, and ten good shipmates.

"We'll rest in that hollow for half an hour, then go and look for the depot," the mate said.

They huddled together in the comparative calm of a grassy hollow and, one after the other, dropped off to sleep. The mate was the first to waken, and he awoke into a fog so dense that they could not see five yards. To go exploring would have been madness; they had no sense of direction; they might easily have fallen over the cliffs, so the mate ordered them to stay where they were. The fog lasted all day and night, and, though almost perished with hunger and cold, they perforce remained in the hollow. The fog cleared just before the dawn and the sun came up out of a clear horizon. It was a beautiful calm day, and after stretching their limbs in the sunshine they went to the top of a hill. The island lay stretched out beneath them, but there seemed to be something wrong with it. It was too small—too small to have a food depot, anyhow. It was bare and desolate, with nothing on it but sea-birds, of which there were thousands; for it was a breeding-place for the albatross and the mollyhawk. The mate shook his head and pointed seaward.

" There's the main island," he said.

He was right. The main island, the one with the depot on it, was there, but six miles away across a glittering sea. Though they did not know it, the name of the island they were on was Disappointment. They could not have thought of a more appropriate one.

III

It was a silent, solemn, and dispirited party that made its way back to the hollow. They were on a desolate, windswept island—one of a group of uninhabited islands—and between them they possessed what they stood up in: four knives, half a box of matches which one of the men who had got ashore dry from the jigger mast had saved intact, and the rope with which they had hauled the men up the cliff. That, and a stub of lead pencil—nothing else, absolutely nothing. The starving men threw themselves on the tussocky grass and gave way to despair. Their officers could say nothing to cheer them—what was there to say?—but there was the usual humorist.

" I've always wanted to be cast ashore on a desert island," he said, " an island where I could lie back on the coral beach, wake up an' knock a coconut off a tree for food and drink, then go to sleep again. I've got my island all right, but instead of coconuts there's nothin' but ruddy seagulls, an' it's too perishin' cold to sleep."

Cold it certainly was, for a damp wind had sprung up again; and as for sea-birds—from the top of the cliffs there came a continual screaming and cackling and a flurry of wings. They heard footsteps coming over the tussocks and started up, but it was only a keen, clever, young Russian seaman named Michael Pul, who, unnoticed, had slipped away from them before they returned to their resting-place—only Michael Pul, but he had with him the material with which to sustain life. In his hand he carried a mollyhawk.

" I got her off the nest," he explained. " There's plenty more and they're easily caught; they won't leave their young."

The men were so ravenous that they would have torn the bird to pieces and eaten it raw, but Mr. Peters was there to see that though the ship was lost her discipline was not. It was a voluntary discipline. The loss of the ship had cancelled the articles of agreement, so that the men were under no obligation to obey a single order; even their pay ceased the moment they left her—but none of those things worried Mr. Peters. He still felt himself responsible for their lives, and he knew that without discipline he could not save them. They were of many races. The first and second mates were Scots; the third mate, Mr. Knudson, and one of the seamen were Norwegian. Among the others three were English, two Irish, and one Welsh; one Australian and one from New Zealand; there were also two Russians, a Chilean, and a German. Men from ten different nations lay in that hollow, but when Mr. Peters rose to his feet the others rose also.

" Pul, take three of the hands with you and bring more of those birds," he ordered. " Mr. MacLaughlin, take the rest and bring brushwood out of that ravine we passed. Mr. Knudson, get some stones and sods and help me to build a fireplace down here where it's sheltered."

Within half an hour Pul and his party were back with the birds, the second mate had got the firewood and a bundle of dry grass, and a fireplace had been constructed.

" Qeerfeld," the mate said to the German sailor, " hand over those matches I heard you talking about; I'll take charge of them. Once this fire is lit it must not be allowed to go out, night or day, while we are on this island. As soon as we have fed we'll make a shelter for it."

Soon smoke was rising from the improvised fireplace, and the air was acrid with the smell of burnt feathers. They were too hungry to wait till the birds were plucked; they roasted them whole, then tore them limb from limb. The flesh was oily and it tasted of fish. The birds were burnt outside and almost raw inside, but to the famished men they presented a veritable banquet. Their hunger appeased, they thought of shelter for the night, which was likely to be a cold one, and somebody suggested rigging up a screen of brushwood.

" If three men got off the jigger topmast on to the cliff, we should be able to get from the cliff on to the jigger topmast," the third mate said. " What about trying to get hold of the gaff topsail, sir?"

" A capital idea, Mr. Knudson, and we've got a rope to haul it up with," the mate agreed. " Come along to the ship."

They reached the top of the cliffs and peered down. As the hull was completely submerged it was obviously impossible to get any provisions out of the ship, but retrieving the gaff topsail presented little difficulty. One of the men who had a knife was lowered down the cliff on to the ledge, and managed to get from there into the jigger topmast rigging. He first bent the rope round the sail, then cut it adrift. It was pulled up. The end of the rope was lowered again, and the man was brought safely to the top of the cliff. They carried the sail to the hollow, formed four low walls with sods, and spread the canvas over them. They now had a tent that would keep them moderately warm for that night, anyhow. After supper, which tasted a good deal better, as they took time to pluck and disembowel the mollyhawks, they sat round and talked.

" If I had me ould dudeen and a plug of tobacco now it wouldn't be so bad," one of the Irishmen said.

They all had a craving for a smoke, but had neither a pipe nor a scrap of tobacco between them. One by one they crawled under the canvas and huddled together for warmth; completely exhausted, most of them slept like logs. In the morning two of them returned from an early stroll and reported a very much better place for a camp on the other side of the island. There was a stream with clear water; it was much more sheltered, and close to a ravine which contained lots of firewood. The position they were in not being satisfactory and the water supply poor, Mr. Peters decided to shift.

Pul and his friends brought in more mollyhawks, and all hands had breakfast. Then seven of them, under Mr. Knudson, started off for the other side, carrying the sail and two of the precious matches. The mate gave them orders to make the walls of the new shelter higher, and to cut grass for bedding, so that the others should have a comfortable night when they eventually went over. A party, under the mate, then went over to the wreck to see what could be done about salving some more gear. Two of the more active men went back hand over hand across the rope by which they had reached the shore. They had the end of the other rope with them, and with its aid the party got the fore upper topgallant sail on to the top of the cliff. They then tackled the job of getting the yard adrift, as the mate thought it might eventually come in handy. Without marline-spikes it seemed hopeless, but working with their precious knives and with stones they at last managed to get it clear of the mast. It was almost dark, however, before they dropped it into the sea, where they left it attached to the rocks by a rope.

The mate now saw that it would be difficult to get across to the new camp in the gathering darkness; then, just to make sure, a dense fog covered the island. They could do nothing but huddle together under the topgallant sail—but worse was to follow. When morning came both the mate and the second mate were ill. Mr. Peters had left the shelter of the sail and was discovered crawling back; he had lost the use of his legs. He was fully old to be knocking about the oceans as mate of windjammers, though he was a very smart officer, and his fifty-seven years were telling now. The third mate came across to see what had detained the party. They tried to carry the mate across the island, but the ground was very boggy and they could not manage it. They brought him some clear water from the other side in his sou'wester, for he was very thirsty, and some cooked mollyhawk. The second mate's condition was causing anxiety, but they managed to get him to the other camp. When Mr. Knudson returned in the evening with another sou'wester full of water he found the mate very low.

" I can't last much longer," he said. " When I'm dead just put a few sods on top of me so the birds can't get at me." He closed his eyes for a little while, then spoke again. " Give these matches to Mr. MacLaughlin and tell him to guard them as if they were jewels," he said.

Making the mate snug under the topgallant sail, and promising to return early next morning, the third mate went off. When the dawn came there was a full gale blowing from the west, but he managed to struggle over. When he raised the edge of the canvas he saw that the water in the sou'wester had not been touched. Mr. Peters was on his knees with his head on his arms, dead and stiff. All hands, except the second mate who was still ill, came over, and, by his orders, they stripped the mate to his underclothing, for they would need the rest. They cut a strip of canvas from the sail, laid it on the body, and covered it with sods. Bare-headed they stood in reverence round the storm-swept, lonely little grave. Mr. Knudson remembered a bit of a prayer, but the real epitaph was supplied by one of the men.

" He was a proper sailorman; he knowed his job," the seaman said.

IV

Being on that side they took the opportunity to have a look at the wreck, but there was no wreck to look at. Mountainous waves rolled over the place where the *Dundonald* had temporarily rested, and washed in foam half-way up the cliffs; but of the ship not a vestige remained. She had completely broken up, so completely that they had to make sure they were looking over the right cliff. The topgallant yard they had so laboriously removed was gone, leaving a chafed fathom of the rope that had secured it—and that was all they found. Taking their topgallant sail with them they went back to the other side of the island.

Young Mr. MacLaughlin now became the leader, and as soon as he recovered he showed that the discipline inaugurated by Mr. Peters was going to be maintained. Within a fortnight they settled down as if they had never known any other life. They hunted and explored, and the most important thing they found was an edible root. It resembled a potato, but was much larger than any potato they had ever seen, some of the roots being nearly three feet long. Half the root grew above ground, and they varied in taste according to the part of the island in which they were found. Some were sweet, others salt; some tasted like potatoes, and it was those they tried to get. They put them on the embers of the fire until they were soft, then peeled them, and they made a tremendous difference to the bill of fare.

Two fires were in use and were tended night and day. The men kept what they called an anchor-watch; there was always one of them on duty, and they did two hours at a spell. Besides watching the fires the man on watch kept a look-out for ships; for all the time they were hoping that the Government steamer which maintained the depot would come round. Mr. MacLaughlin had no uneasiness about the fires; any neglect of those would have brought the criminal up against something greater than authority—a parliament of his shipmates, a government within a government. Never, once during their stay on the island, in spite of howling gales and nights of rain, sleet or snow, was one of the fires allowed even to die down.

Brushwood shelters were erected round and above the fires, and those led to the discovery that smoked mollyhawk was good.

A sailor, returned from hunting one evening, threw a brace of dead birds on top of one of those cook-houses and forgot about them. Two days later he found that the smoke seeping up through the brushwood roof had cured them, making the meat more tender, more palatable, and less fishy. Some parts of the island were white with mollyhawks, and the young birds were getting fat. Some of the men became particular and selective. When one of them got to a nest—a flimsy structure shaped like a flowerpot—the young bird would spit at him. He would then keep its head down with a stick to prevent its pecking, while with the other hand he would lift it to try its weight. If it was too light it was restored to the nest with an admonition to grow a bit fatter; if it was heavy enough its neck was wrung. A new bird put in an appearance, a small bird something like a duck. These birds did not rise off the ground, but were amazingly active on it, and they were usually stalked on moonlight nights. They were very tasty and fat, and greatly prized by the epicures. The men thrived on the food. They became stronger; but the dread spectre of winter loomed up—and winter on a wind-swept island near the fiftieth parallel of south latitude was likely to be very severe.

There was a housing problem and a clothing problem, and the latter was a serious one. Some of the men had no boots, others no socks; and what clothes they had were becoming threadbare. What was worse, no one possessed a blanket. It was the cheery, indomitable Michael Pul who solved both the housing and the blanket problem with one scheme. He had been brought up on a farm in Russia. He knew a good deal about building mud cabins for pigs, and one evening he put his scheme before a house-planning committee, of which Mr. MacLaughlin was chairman. Veronica shrubs, about six feet high, grew in sheltered nooks, and although none of the branches, which were all crooked, exceeded three inches in diameter, the committee decided they would do for scantlings for the proposed houses. The trouble was, however, that any erection they put up would be blown down by the fierce winds that swept the island. Michael Pul's suggestion was that the houses be sunk several feet underground.

A sheltered site having been selected, a plot ten feet long and six feet broad was marked off, and digging in the peaty soil was begun. They did not dare to risk their precious knives, so they dug with their hands till one day Mr. Knudson, strolling by the sea, discovered a bit of wreckage. It was a large splinter from a topgallant mast—probably one of the *Dundonald's*—and measured four feet long by six inches broad; it made a useful shovel. They struck water almost at once, but, as the whole island was damp, it did not increase. When they had excavated to a depth of six feet and covered the bottom with stones they began on the roof, for which they used the longest sticks they could find. The wood was hard, and as they had no axe it had to be broken from the shrubs with stones. The scantlings having been worked up to a point, the roof was thatched with long grass, with large sods on top. They worked from the ground upward, the upper sods overlapping the lower ones to allow the rain to run off. They lined the underground walls with reeds secured by wooden pegs, and put about a foot of brushwood covered with grass on the floor. The entrance was just large enough to crawl through, and it had a canvas screen for a door. So comfortable was the house that six more were built: a group of five, which included a storehouse and a cook-house, was called the village, and two more a little way off called the suburbs. The housing problem having been solved before the real winter set in, the canvas which had been used for tents was cut up for blankets.

Having proved his capacity as an architect, Michael Pul went into the shoemaking and hosiery businesses. On the rocks below some almost perpendicular cliffs there was a small seal rookery, which, however, seemed to be inaccessible. One morning Pul went off alone, and returned two hours later to report that he had found a way down the cliffs and had killed two seals. A party went off to bring up the flesh and skins. The following day they had their first meal of seal meat and blubber, which was by no means as palatable as mollyhawk, but promised a reserve of food should the birds, when fully fledged, leave the island. The next day they constructed a framework for drying the skins, and Pul promised them a pair of shoes each. The needles used were made from the small bones of birds, in which holes had been laboriously bored by pieces of wire, and the thread was unravelled from the edges of the canvas. The slippers were those known as "farm slippers" in Russia. They were twelve inches long, seven inches broad at the toe, and six inches at the heel. They were sewn up at both ends, and holes were made for laces, which consisted of rope-yarn from the bolt-rope of the gaff topsail. Pul next turned the dried wings of albatrosses outside in for socks, and with the feathers inside they were very comfortable. Mollyhawks provided some toilet requisites. The men used the skins for both soap and towel; they rubbed their faces with the greasy sides, then dried them with the feathered ones. They felt they could now face the winter without undue apprehension once a good stock of provisions had been laid in.

They decided to fill the storehouse with roots and smoked mollyhawks, so built what they called a smokehouse, which differed from the other houses in having a mud roof to keep in the heat. The first time they used it they hung up thirty birds on a line, lit the fire, and sealed up the door to prevent the smoke from escaping. A little later it was discovered that the smokehouse was on fire. The fat from the birds had dropped on the smouldering fire and caused it to flare up; the fire burnt the line and the birds fell down; the rafters caught and the roof collapsed. They built another smokehouse, but instead of hanging the birds on a rope they used a strand of wire from the foot-rope of the topgallant sail. After that the villagers took their civic duties seriously; they formed a fire brigade, with sou'westers for buckets.

With the stub of pencil they kept a careful tally of the passing days on a small piece of canvas. By midwinter day, the 21st June, they had been one hundred and sixteen days on the island, with little hope of immediate rescue, for the depot steamer was unlikely to come round in winter. The days were short and stormy and the nights long. Having no watch or clock they had to judge the time by the sun when it was visible and guess when it wasn't. They had got the true north by erecting a stick and noting the bearing when the sun cast its shortest shadow. They became expert at guessing the time. For instance, the man on anchor-watch at night rarely exceeded his two hours before calling his relief; and although the snow had often to be cleared away from the entrance to the hut before the relief could crawl out, there was little grumbling. They ate all their meals during the short spells of daylight, then slept away the hours of darkness in the black interior of the huts.

What worried them most as the days dragged past was the thought that their relatives must be getting anxious. Even one hundred and sixteen days was a long passage from Sydney for a speedy vessel like the *Dundonald*, and by the middle of July they could not doubt that she would be marked down as long overdue. They were tortured by the thought that the depot steamer might come round in thick weather, when their smoke signals could not be seen.

" We'll have to build a boat and risk crossing to the main island,"
Mr. MacLaughlin declared one evening.

" But, sir, the wood that grows here won't float; we've tried it,"
one of the men said.

" We'll make a canvas boat with wooden framework."

" How would we get it along, sir?" another man asked.

" We'll have to make paddles."

" Yes, yes; I can make paddles," Michael Pul declared eagerly.

V

By that time sealskins were drying all over the place; for from
one beach seals were coming ashore to sleep in the grass. The first
seaman to discover them had a fierce battle, with unsatisfactory
results. When disturbed the seals tried to get away; then, when
headed off, they showed fight. They stood up on their flippers and
barked like dogs. The man reported this to Pul, who was working
at the roof of a hut.

" Hit him a smack on the snout with a stick," Pul advised.

After that it was easy; one shrewd blow knocked the seal out.
Every man got a sealskin sleeping-bag, and readily gave up his
blanket to provide canvas for the boat. Still seal meat did not appeal
as food. Seal soup, fried seal liver, even seal liver curry, have made
welcome additions to the menus of Antarctic explorers; but the
unfortunate castaways from the *Dundonald* did not have a single
utensil with which to cook, not even an old tin can.

The plans for the proposed boat were drawn, full size, on a
flat piece of ground, and never were blue prints of battleship or
ocean liner more closely examined and criticized. As Pul and a
Chilean seaman had drawn the privilege of making the first attempt
to cross to the main island, they were allowed to carry out the plans
and build the boat, though they had many willing assistants. The
framework—which is now in the Christchurch Museum, New
Zealand—was made from the stoutest pieces of veronica they could
find. The boat was to be nine feet long by three feet in beam and
three feet in depth. The keel was in two parts, joined in the middle
by rope-yarn and strands of wire, the parts consisting of branches
which curved upward to form stem and stern-posts. The stern was

square. A branch three feet long was fastened at its middle to the head of the stern-post, and from its ends other branches were stretched to the head of the stem to form gunwales. These completed the longitudinal scantlings; and twelve ribs, six a side, from the gunwale to the keel formed transverse frames.

As the wood was too heavy to float, even in salt water, particular care had to be taken with the covering. The canvas was much harder than sealskin, so it was fortunate that they had a good supply of small bones, which they sharpened on stones. Some of the needles only lasted five minutes, and two men were constantly at work making them. The paddles were made of forked branches to which canvas had been wired. The boat completed, it was taken down to a sheltered beach for its trial trip. It floated; the craziest craft ever to put out on a winter sea floated; the two men who built it got in and paddled about close inshore; all that was now wanted was a calm day. It came after a spell of strong westerly winds, and at dawn on the 31st July Pul and his companion set out. All hands were down on the beach to see them off and wish them god-speed. Sitting in the bottom of the boat and paddling like natives in a dugout canoe they slowly made their way seaward. The boat had only a foot of freeboard, and before long all that could be seen from the beach were the tiny figures of the paddling men, apparently sitting in the sea, at times seeming to disappear under it. Presently distance swallowed them completely, and with anxious hearts the villagers returned to their huts.

Pul had been given a few of the precious matches and told to light two signal fires if they discovered the depot. All next day eyes were strained towards the main island, but no ascending smoke cheered them, and it was not even known if the intrepid voyagers had managed to land safely. Day after day passed and still no signals came. To alleviate the suspense of waiting Mr. MacLaughlin decided to build two more boats, and it was agreed to have a competition between officers and men to see which could produce the better one. The officers' boat was to be bigger than the one that had gone off, and was designed to carry four men.

One afternoon, while the others were preparing the supper, the look-out man was pottering about at one of the boats. From force of habit—they did it a hundred times a day—he looked across to the other island for smoke, then went on with his work. As he worked he sang a parody of the old chanty, "Whisky, Johnny":

> " Oh, mollyhawks are the life of man,
> Mollyhawks, Johnny.
> Oh, I'll eat mollyhawks while I can,
> Mollyhawks for my Johnny.
> Oh, mollyhawks tough and——"

A moment later he was hurrying towards the huts, stumbling over the rough and peaty ground and shouting at the pitch of his voice:

" A sail! a sail! a ship!"

Excited men left their huts and their fires and streamed towards the highest part of the island, where, against just such a contingency, dried grass, brushwood, and branches had been stored under cover. A large fire was quickly built, and one of the precious matches set it alight.

" Pile on plenty of grass," Mr. MacLaughlin said.   " That's the stuff to make smoke."

The strange vessel was a full-rigged ship, close-hauled on the port tack, and standing to the eastward. She was hull down, and it soon became obvious that it would be dark before she brought the island abeam.

" Will she see the fire, sir?" one of the men asked in trembling tones.

" She ought to," the second mate replied. " If there's anyone aloft overhauling buntlines they should see the smoke now. After dark they should see the glare of the fire from the deck, so pile on the wood."

Too anxious to return to their food, too excited to sleep, they hung round the fire all night, piling on the wood till the flames leapt twenty feet into the air. Dawn drew on very slowly, but broad daylight came in at last. There was no ship in sight. It was their most bitter moment since they lifted the canvas and found Mr. Peters dead, and even those indomitable men almost gave way to despair. Some slight compensation—which later turned to joy— came from the other island, from which there at last rose a column of smoke.

" Funny; they were going to light *two* fires," a sailor said.

" Yes; if they found the depot," the second mate answered.

" They've been trying to signal that ship, too," Mr. Knudson suggested.

" I expect that's it; anyhow, they're safe, thank God, even if they haven't found the depot," Mr. MacLaughlin said.

As a sort of last hope they tried to send off a message. They had noticed that the female albatross seemed to go a long way for food for her young. After leaving her nest she did not return for two days, so it was possible she went as far as New Zealand. They caught one after she had fed her young, tied a message written on canvas round her leg, and let her go. They watched her hopefully as she flew off to the north, but two days later she was back without the message.

"Perhaps it's been taken off her," one of the men suggested optimistically.

"I'm afraid it hasn't," the second mate said. "They would have to shoot her to get it; she must have pecked it off."

The following day the boat from the main island was seen returning, and all hands went to the beach to welcome it as it came ashore safely through the surf. Pul and his companion looked like skeletons, for they had been through a gruelling time. Thinking they would have no trouble in getting mollyhawks on the other island they had only taken two cooked ones with them; but, although they had seen pigs and seals, they had not seen a single bird. With considerable difficulty they had landed on the west side of the island, and had climbed a peak at once. They had seen no sign of a depot, but reported a series of bays on the eastern side. They tried to get across, but in places the stunted trees were so thick that they had to walk on top of them. At last they had to give it up, go back to their landing-place, and wait for a calm day. While they were waiting Pul built a small hut. He was obviously ashamed of his failure to find the depot. It was the size of the island that defeated him, he said; it looked like a small continent.

"There must be a depot on it, and, as the prevailing wind is westerly, it should be on the eastern side," Mr. MacLaughlin said. "Knudson, will you have a shot at it if our boat is anything like seaworthy?"

"Sure, I will," Mr. Knudson said.

VI

The sea provided the acid test for the two boats, and the sea gave a definite verdict. The boat built by the men capsized and sank; the other floated triumphantly. For companions Mr. Knud-

son picked Walters, a Norwegian like himself; Gretton, an Irish-
man; and the Londoner, Charles Eyre. They took with them
sufficient cooked seal meat for three days, and a fire. This they
carried on a large sod, in which they had cut a hole, resting on
stones in the bottom of the boat.

They had been exactly seven months on Disappointment Island
when they pushed off one calm morning, and as they had managed
to make bigger and more efficient paddles they made better progress.
As the boat crept across the sea with smoke rising from it, it reminded
those left behind of a Chinese family sampan. Following Pul's
directions they made for the same landing-place, but as they drew
near the wind and sea were rising and surf was breaking on the
beach.

" Well, we've got to land, so we'd better get at it before it gets
worse," Mr. Knudson said.

They turned the boat's head to seaward and backed her in, but
just as Eyre jumped out to drag her up on the beach a sea rushed at
her and bashed her on to the rocks. Half drowned, they managed to
scramble ashore, but the boat was smashed, the fire was out, and
most of the seal meat was lost. They managed to get the canvas off
the broken frame and drag it up to the hut that Pul had built. While
eating the small portion of meat they had saved they noticed a
seal coming down to the beach, and killed it. Thinking of next
morning's breakfast, they tried to kindle a fire by rubbing two sticks
together, but after half an hour of strenuous endeavour decided that
such a method might be all right with the dry tinder of the tropics,
but wasn't much use in 50° south.

The following day it blew so hard that they could do little but
huddle together in the hut, but during a lull they dragged the car-
cass of the seal they had killed to the hut and cut some of it up.
By noon they were so hungry that they had to eat it, and to make
it more palatable they garnished it with chopped grass. It rained all
the next day. The roof of the hut leaked badly, so they lay under
the canvas they had saved from the boat. They did not give way to
despair; they did not lament the lost fire that would have made
all the difference. Inspired by their splendid loyalty to their shipmates they waited patiently for the chance to explore the island and
find the depot. It came next day, which broke clear and cloudless.

Bundling up the rest of the seal meat and the canvas, they started
off. They climbed a hill, from which they got a good view and saw

the series of bays Pul had reported. One of them was long and sheltered by small islands, so they decided to make for it. The going was terrible; they climbed over steep, jagged rocks; they had to break their way through thickets. Footsore and almost exhausted, they reached the beach at last and turned to the east along it, hoping they were right. Before they had gone far they noticed that the grass seemed to have been trampled down. They rounded a bend, and there, standing out clear, was something that was neither scrub nor rock, nor anything that Nature had erected. They dropped everything and ran towards it. It was a signpost with a broad finger pointing along a rough path. On the finger they read:

To Food Depot

4 Miles

They cheered excitedly and were breaking into another run when Mr. Knudson stopped them.

" Bring the canvas; we've got to make a boat to get back," he said.

Having secured the canvas they hurried down the path which sometimes lay along the beach, at others through the woods. The sun was drawing down to the horizon, and they felt that they must get to this depot for shipwrecked mariners before dark.

" To-morrow we'll have to climb a high hill and make a smoke signal to our shipmates," Mr. Knudson panted.

They reached a clearing, and three houses loomed up through the twilight. They had reached the depot, which they hastened to look round before the light faded entirely. One house was evidently a sleeping-place, as there were bunks in it; another was full of stores; in another there was a *boat*—a real, seaworthy boat! By then it was too dark to find matches, but they found a tin of biscuits —the first thing in the nature of bread they had tasted since they left the *Dundonald*—and having eaten, unbelievably weary but supremely happy, they lay down on the floor, with the canvas for a blanket, and slept like logs.

They were up next morning as soon as they could see, and, eager as schoolboys, started to explore. Among their first finds was a mirror, and they saw themselves again. Of course, every man knew that his companions were tattered and filthy and had long matted beards and hair, but somehow he could hardly imagine that

he could be the same. The mirror told the ghastly truth, but close
at hand were the remedies—scissors, soap, shaving brushes, and
razors; and a stream that ran close to the depot. There were also
twelve suits of clothes; not enough to go round all hands, but in
the meantime they would have a suit each and make adjustments
later. They opened the first tin that came to hand and had a feed
of pressed beef and biscuits, after which Eyre and Walters, armed
with a box of matches, went up the highest hill to send a smoke
signal to their friends across the water.

" You'll be able to have a hot bath when you get back, boys,"
Mr. Knudson promised them.

He and Gretton continued to explore. Among the most welcome
finds was a large box full of books. There were also a gun and
cartridges, cooking utensils, packets of matches, an oil lamp, and
blankets. On a notice-board there was a message to say that the
New Zealand Government steamer *Hinemoa* had called at the depot
on the 10th February. Obviously she had not yet made her spring
call, so might be expected at any time. Before the other two returned
Mr. Knudson and Gretton had bathed, shaved and changed, and
it was not long before Eyre and Walters were wallowing in hot
baths. After that, all had a good meal, and the third mate decided
to call it a half holiday. Comfortable under a roof, feeling luxurious
in clean clothing, they loafed and read for the rest of the day; and,
perhaps greatest joy of all, they did not have to go to bed when it
got dark.

" Turn to, boys," Mr. Knudson said early next morning.

It was a long way to row a boat down the east coast, then across
to Disappointment; but to those experienced castaways the making
of a mast and sail was child's play.

" This is what is meant when they say the wheel has turned full
circle," Eyre said as he stitched at the canvas with a palm-needle
and twine from the depot. " This started off as a t'gallant sail,
then it was a tent, then a blanket, then the hull of a boat, and now
it's going to be a sail again."

On the 12th October, full of impatience to get back to their
shipmates, they launched the boat and started off. They had found
a chart of the Auckland Group and were able to pick out the other
islands. On the port hand as they sailed along parallel with the
coast of Auckland Island were Ross and Enderby Islands, and passing
close to them they noticed cows, which explained the gun and

cartridges at the depot. On another island there were goats. When they got to the open sea the wind blew fiercely from the south-west, which was right in their teeth, so they had to return.

They started off again at daylight next morning, sailed along the coast in smooth water, and reached the north-west end of it. Even from there they could see, looking like a Kaffir kraal, the little cluster of domed huts on Disappointment Island. Again the wind headed them, and they dropped the sail and took to their oars. When still two miles from the island they saw a column of smoke rising, as if another vessel were in sight. They thought it might be the rescue steamer, but could see nothing. They pulled on.

VII

On Disappointment Island the previous day one of the cook-houses caught fire, and the fire brigade, short of four men and their sou'westers, had been unable to put it out. As Mr. Knudson's men pulled towards the island those who were left on it were building another cook-house. Presently the look-out came rushing across the tussocks.

" Mr. MacLaughlin," he shouted, " there's a boat coming!"

" Mr. Knudson's boat?" the second mate asked.

" No, sir; a real boat! a ship's boat!"

" Light the fire signal," Mr. MacLaughlin ordered.

As they went down to the beach they speculated upon what the boat could be. There was no vessel in sight, but the rowers looked too well dressed to be shipwrecked mariners. The men on the island felt shy. After all those months they shrunk at the thought of meeting strangers.

" There's probably a sealing schooner anchored among the islands and they've sent a boat's crew across to see if there are seals on this one," Mr. MacLaughlin suggested.

The boat's keel grated up on the pebbly beach.

" Welcome to the island, gentlemen," Mr. MacLaughlin said courteously. " What ship are—good God! it's Knudson!"

" The very same," the third mate answered. " It's Knudson with a tin of biscuits for his friends on Disappointment Island."

At last Mr. MacLaughlin knew where he was. It was a great

reunion, and they talked long after dark, deciding to evacuate the island next day. Before leaving they filed bare-headed past the small cairn of stones that marked the remains of Mr. Peters. The fire that had been kept burning, night and day, for two hundred and thirty-one days was left to burn itself out. Two crossings were made. In the first, seven were landed at Pul's hut and given directions for crossing the island and finding the direction post; the remaining eight sailed right round to the depot. Shortly after the second party arrived the first was seen coming along the beach. By noon next day all hands were bathed, shaved and in their right minds, and for one thing they were thankful: they had kept entirely free of vermin the whole time.

" There's nothing like clean clothes for making a man feel *like* a man," Mr. MacLaughlin declared as he postured before the mirror. " I don't mind a spot of dirt, but, damn it, over seven and a half months without a wash—I ask you!"

After their experiences on Disappointment their stay on Auckland Island bordered on the idyllic. Several unsuccessful attempts to shoot a cow were made on Ross Island; then the gun was handed over to the ubiquitous Michael Pul, who returned with a fine young bull. One man declared that the smell of the roasting joint was worth all the hardships. Pul and the Chilean crossed to Ocean Island and came back with two nanny-goats, which were tethered beside the depot and supplied milk. On Ross and Enderby Islands there were sub-depots, and in one of them they found tea. Though there were still the heart-breaking thoughts that their relatives must have given them up for dead the time passed pleasantly, and there was always the knowledge that every day brought the rescue steamer nearer.

They were busy on every day except Sunday, when they loafed and read. Mr. MacLaughlin believed that hard work made contented minds, and discipline remained to the end. There were daily trips across to Ocean Island for grass to satisfy the enormous appetites of the goats; there were cows to be killed, and great competition to be among the beaters for Michael Pul when he went after the elusive pigs; and there was work around the depot. The flagstaff had been blown down and smashed, so they made and rigged a new one; then, with bunting, made a replica of the *Dundonald's* house-flag to hoist on it. When returning from a hunt they had to wade ashore with the carcasses, so to avoid wetting their feet they decided to build a jetty with trees, to which the boat could be moored. There were plenty of tools in the depot.

One day the two mates came across a small but trim graveyard containing four wooden crosses, and on the crosses were inscriptions that were eloquent of loneliness and of the privations that obtained before the depot had been established. The first grave they looked at was a tiny one, and on the small cross that surmounted it was the inscription: " Died 22nd Nov. 1850. Aged 8 months." The second inscription read: " Erected by the crew of the s.s. *Southland* over the remains of a man who had apparently died of starvation, and was buried by the crew of the *Flying Scud*, 3rd September 1865." The third inscription was: " Sacred to the memory of J. Mahony, Master Mariner, second mate of the *Inverauld*, wrecked on this island, 16th May 1864. Died from starvation." On the cross over the fourth grave was the one word " Unknown ".

While the officers stood bare-headed in that remote, lonely little cemetery they were thinking deeply, and their thoughts ran in the same groove.

" Mr. Peters must be buried here, where his grave can at least be tended twice a year," the second mate said.

" We'll see to it as soon as the steamer comes." Mr. Knudson agreed—and the remains of Mr. Peters lie there now.

The jetty was completed, and with the flagstaff, complete with signalling yard, erected, there seemed little left to do. Then the officers decided that the house-flag might give offence as being somewhat proprietary, so they made another flag out of white duck and sewed the word " Welcome " on it with blue bunting. On the morning of the 15th November it was blowing hard from the west and squally. Inside the sleeping-house men were stirring, for Pul was getting ready to go out after pig. A long blast from a steam-whistle echoed round the room, and all hands rushed to the door. Through the rain they could see the *Hinemoa* anchoring off the depot.

" Run up the flag!" Mr. MacLaughlin shouted.

Since the day when primitive man first launched his dug-out canoe into the waters of an estuary and inaugurated ocean navigation, mariners have been highly tried in peace and in war: tried by fire, gale, snow, fog, ice, and pounding seas; by gun, torpedo, bomb, and mine—yet seldom have seamen been more highly tried, or pulled through more gallantly, than the officers and men who saved themselves from the wreck of the *Dundonald*.